Corporate Environmental Management Information Systems:
Advancements and Trends

Frank Teuteberg
University of Osnabrück, Germany

Jorge Marx Gómez
University of Oldenburg, Germany

BUSINESS SCIENCE Reference

BUSINESS SCIENCE REFERENCE
Hershey · New York

Director of Editorial Content: Kristin Klinger
Director of Book Publications: Julia Mosemann
Acquisitions Editor: Lindsay Johnston
Development Editor: Joel Gamon
Publishing Assistant: Myla Harty
Typesetter: Keith Glazewski
Production Editor: Jamie Snavely
Cover Design: Lisa Tosheff
Printed at: Yurchak Printing Inc.

Published in the United States of America by
Business Science Reference (an imprint of IGI Global)
701 E. Chocolate Avenue
Hershey PA 17033
Tel: 717-533-8845
Fax: 717-533-8661
E-mail: cust@igi-global.com
Web site: http://www.igi-global.com

Library of Congress Cataloging-in-Publication Data

Corporate environmental management information systems : advancements and trends / Frank Teuteberg and Jorge Marx Gomez, editors.
p. cm.
Includes bibliographical references and index.
Summary: "This book summarizes the state of the art in the emergent field of Corporate Environmental Management Information Systems, showing researchers, managers, engineers and information technology specialists how to develop and implement effective CEMIS"--Provided by publisher. ISBN 978-1-61520-981-1 (hardcover) -- ISBN 978-1-61520-982-8 (ebook) 1. Environmental protection--Citizen participation. 2. Environmental protection- -Information services. I. Teuteberg, Frank, 1970- II. Gomez, Jorge Marx. III. Title.

TD170.C67 2010
658.4'083--dc22

2010000044

British Cataloguing in Publication Data
A Cataloguing in Publication record for this book is available from the British Library.

Editorial Advisory Board

Table of Contents

Detailed Table of Contents

Recently, there has been increasing recognition that computer-based information systems should better support corporate sustainability management. New administrative approaches, e.g. in the field of emission trading, and recommendations, for instance regarding carbon footprints of products, require a new type of information systems in companies. These new components can be called corporate environmental management information systems (CEMIS). What is the purpose of these systems? They should provide the required information for environmental or sustainability management. But what is the idea behind? What is the guiding principle of these systems? This chapter discusses efficiency as a guiding principle of CEMIS. It helps to understand better basic methodologies like life cycle assessment, and it provides presuppositional knowledge for the challenge of introducing these information instruments.

Businesses today must not only be concerned with their day-to-day operations and the making of profit, but also with a set of challenges related to the public perception, the environment, and the costs of energy consumption. The image of the company from the perspective of customers and the public in general must be carefully monitored as it relates to the environment and the use of natural resources and energy. The demonstration of effective strategies that allow for "greener" and more ecological awareness, will gain the respect of customers, businesses, stockholders, and other concerned groups. The protection of our environment is also a major agenda of firms today. This chapter discusses how "Green IT" along with the concepts of "Virtualization" can provide for better organizational, operational, and environmental outcomes.

The aim of this chapter is to discuss the deficits of the mainstream innovation theory in the context of sustainability in addition to the role and significance of innovation in environmental engineering. This especially includes the opportunities and limitations of eco-innovation with respect to the current environmental policies for sustainable economic growth. A future challenge for research from a business perspective is to align eco-innovation as an integral component of an environmental management information system (CEMIS). In this context, eco-innovation can make a major contribution to environmental protection. However, within the scope of this chapter, the focus is primarily on the rationale for sustainable innovation, in particular, eco-innovation.

The growth of micro-enterprises is a key driver of economic development. The ability of micro-enterprises to adopt IT can potentially increase their growth by 3.4% according to a World Bank expert. However these gains do not always take place as the challenges are many. Current theoretical models on IT adoption focus on the intent to adopt IT in large organizations where employees' attitudes and perceptions are measured in terms of their objectives within the structures of accountability. Micro-enterprises are unique in that the intention to adopt is an individual decision made by the micro-entrepreneur. It is often the innovative ways in which IT is used that enable the gains to be realized by micro-entrepreneurs. This chapter describes a process that can be used to enable micro-entrepreneurs faced with limited resources to adopt IT to grow their businesses. This process of IT therapy involves diagnosis, interventions and an assessment of IT for development outcomes. Examples and guidelines are provided to enable this process to be used by practitioners. This chapter concludes with alternatives for sustainable development and guidelines for achieving these improvements in micro-enterprises.

Evidences show that investments made in IT (Information Technology) area have a positive effect on the organizational performance, even if these benefits are difficult to measure and associate with the real intention of those investments. IT presents itself as a tool and not as a guarantee of success, as this determining factor depends on how it is used and directed towards the strategic alignment. This chapter seeks to evaluate how much IT governance positively interferes in the achievement of strategic goals, based on the control of investments and its correct management. The results show that the organizations which adopt IT governance have their performance highly improved in relation to other companies, especially concerning profitability. Besides, the use of enterprise architecture in IT governance shows a positive correlation with corporative governance elements, inciting the use of more efficient management mechanisms to promote a sustainable IT.

The evaluation of an organization's environmental performance is an integral part of a corporate environmental management information system. This chapter considers an organization's environmental impact assessment with respect to a water resource. It investigates formal approaches to the development of temporal monitoring designs for producing data sufficient to perform the assessment. In this study, simple random sampling, stratified random sampling, and designs obtained using greedy search have been investigated with respect to their compatibility with a corporate environmental management information system. All three approaches determine temporal monitoring designs with minimal costs and supply data sufficient for estimation of water quality indicators for a given level of uncertainty. It is shown that monitoring designs obtained using the greedy search approach will outperform other designs when the level of uncertainty in the estimate must be low. If high levels of uncertainty are tolerable, simple random designs become preferable due to their simplicity and effectiveness. The proposed approaches lead to automated procedures which can be easily integrated into a corporate environmental management information system.

sustainability reporting guidelines (G3). While developing the document structure, an existing XBRL FRTA (Financial Reporting Taxonomies Architecture) - common for business financial reporting- was used. Such a unifying document structure is a key for advanced reporting systems, particularly for current ICT applications like (web) content management systems. Using the reference architecture offers an impressive array of benefits, e.g. it helps: to facilitate data exchange between reporters and report users, to improve a company's information management, to support its reporting workflow, and to refine communication with its target groups in a meaningful way.

From an environmental, economic, social, and technical perspective, this chapter focuses on a sustainability assessment of concepts for the energetic use of biomass in order to provide decision support for different options of biomass use. In rural areas, bioenergy concepts are of particular interest in this context. These can for example be biogas plants which are operated by electric service providers, or a biogas plant owned by one farmer, or bioenergy villages. The topic relates to the development of suitable criteria and to the adaption of existing indicator systems to the special requirements of sustainable biomass use for energy. The results of this sustainability assessment consider the different biomass concepts' advantages and disadvantages, which are illustrated by multi-criteria valuation methods. Furthermore, the sustainability assessment of bioenergy concepts has specific requirements with regard to an information system in terms of data and information's demand and supply side.

In Germany, public environmental data are in the responsibility of several different public organisations and institutions. The German Environmental Information Portal PortalU® (www.portalu.de) is a web service operated by the environmental administrations to make digital environmental information easier accessible, usable and exploitable for both citizens and environmental experts. The fruitful long-time co-operation between the environmental administrations is an example for a well working organisational structure within a federal state. In this chapter the PortalU technology and the content of the portal are presented. Due to the current discussion referring to INSPIRE, a special focus is set on publishing INSPIRE conform metadata.

Part of manufacturers' responsibility when bringing out new products is to consider their environmental footprint. The legal supply chain combines hardware/software delivery, granting on-duty conformance to use preservation, and end-of-life take-back, with compulsory recovery targets. These entrepreneurial competencies appear externally, in respect to old manufacturing practices, which were internal. Networking options provide fundamental technological aids. This chapter analyses some technologically-driven solutions which stand out for the exploitation of net concerns at these three integration levels: business project co-operation, through spot-wise agreements; the factually united organisation or virtual corporation; joint and several liability, or extended corporation.

Compared to the DIN EN ISO Standard 14001 every organization has to create – in respect to environmental aspects and environmental system – processes so that internal communications between different organization levels and function, or proper questions and answer coming from outer site could be guaranteed. One of the possibilities to realize these requirements is the introduction of an organization wide GRI-guideline, created by the idea of the Global Reporting Initiative (GRI), which can easily be published in the Internet. But normally not all environmental information is necessary for everybody, resulting in an information flood. Following the idea to represent special information to special interest groups, the authors present an idea of how to convert these sustainability reports into a Topic Maps by using eXtensible Business Reporting Language (XBRL).

This chapter examines contemporary discussions on the current state of sustainable supply-chain management and green logistics. It presents a case study from the Fujitsu Corporation in Japan and explores models of information systems and RFID use in green logistics. Combining insights from the case and existing models the chapter explores an example of how a combined model can be used to explore the potential of a specific emerging technology (RFIDs) in 'greening' supply chains.

The history, current situation, policy system and three typical cases for eco-industrial parks in China have been described and analyzed systematically. On the basis of this, application of CEMIS to EIPs has been discussed. A CEMIS framework for EIPs has been proposed according to the Chinese policy system. Furthermore, a schematic control diagram for EIPs has been suggested using box model.

This chapter investigates how corporate sustainable practices can be supported by information management models and information and communication technology (ICT) applications. The empirical work is based on a single case study, a Brazilian company that is applying the concept of a sustainability balanced scorecard (SBSC) to put forward a triple bottom-line strategy. The results suggest that (a) implementation and use of the SBSC, (b) integration of the triple-bottom line concept within the SBSC, and (c) the place occupied by the eco-efficiency indicator at the heart of the strategic map represented three key factors that helped to enhance sustainability management. Moreover, the development of a sustainability-oriented culture and the strong business intelligence (BI) platform put in place enabled successful implementation of the SBSC in this particular company.

Foreword

Lately, the debate on Green IT and the – very successful – practical measures associated with this concept have given reason to also give some thought to "IT for Green" – i.e., the discipline of environmental informatics and the corporate application systems it provides, also known as Corporate Environmental Management Information Systems (CEMIS). The strong general interest in Green IT was motivated by the insight that IT contributes substantially to the Carbon Footprint of the economy and, as a result, to global climate change. The demand for resource efficiency, particularly energy efficiency, is closely linked to the claim for Green IT. Therefore, reducing ecological damage caused by IT and increasing its environmental and economic efficiency are important issues.

The appeal for Green IT has quite considerable effects on practice. As yet, however, "IT for Green" does not seem to have gained a similarly strong impact. This is surprising if one considers that the impact of the "IT for Green"-approach on environment and economy is generally anticipated to be much stronger than effects caused by Green IT, because Green IT in its narrow sense is restricted to the realm of information processing (at a company level), whereas "IT for Green" applies to the entirety of a company's business processes.

A closer look at companies' management practices reveals that, on the one hand, information systems developed by environmental informatics were created in response to environmental legislation demands. On the other hand, many of these IT systems supplement (standardized) environmental management systems. Unlike Green IT, they serve exclusively as an instrument of corporate environmental protection. This comparatively narrow focus may explain why CEMIS are of such little relevance to practice. As a general rule, most companies delegate environmental management and measures of environmental protection to environment departments or commissioners. In this way, these issues are no longer dealt with at strategic management level. Instead, they become subtasks of an operative management that usually lacks the (financial) means and strategic committment necessary to procure or develop integrated and comprehensive information systems.

Basically, "IT for Green" stems from the same root as Green IT. Despite its shadow existence, "IT for Green" is however potentially more effective and efficient than Green IT due to its larger scope of application.

In view of this situation, the discipline of environmental informatics is challenged to enlarge its focus from environmental issues to the broader concept of sustainability. It could then contribute to a paradigm shift which leads, for example, to the development and establishment of *strategic environmental information management*. This new paradigm would demand for integrated information systems that support the strategic goal of sustainability.

To conclude, the discipline of environmental informatics, viewed from a corporate perspective, needs to be modernized and expanded based on the outcomes of the sustainability debate. This volume is dedicated to these tasks, which are largely covered by the included chapters. It demonstrates impressively how the potential of CEMIS can be used for viable applications. The volume provides a means of orientation in a new world of CEMIS ("CEMIS 2.0"), which – for the reasons given above – are hoped to have a broad impact in the near future. May this volume encourage companies to make use of modern information and communication technology in order to contribute to the long-term goal of sustainable development.

We hope that a large community of readers will draw inspirations for their own work from this collection of promising ideas and well-founded studies.

Lorenz Hilty
St. Gallen

Horst Junker
Berlin

December 2009

Preface

TOWARDS THE NEXT GENERATION OF CORPORATE ENVIRONMENTAL MANAGEMENT INFORMATION SYSTEMS: WHAT IS THERE AND WHAT IS MISSING?

Today, environmental issues are frequently dealt with at corporate management level. The roots of this relatively new development can be traced back to the late 1980s. At that time, companies felt increasing pressure from international politics to internalize their impacts on the environment, drawing on the increasingly popular idea of sustainability which encompassed ecological, social, and economic aspects. The emergence of systems for voluntary eco-management, as e.g. EMAS or ISO 14001, further shifted the focus of environmental responsibility towards the companies, whereas the increasing number of environmental considerations that they had to face generally originated from company-external sources. In order to comply with environmental goals, a special category of information systems (IS) was created which is generally known as Corporate Environmental Management Information Systems (CEMIS). These systems were originally developed to meet a fairly restricted number of external environmental requirements. Nowadays, a large variety of highly specific, heterogeneous solutions for different environmental issues exists on the market. In spite of that, no truly integrative approach to the topic has been taken to date. In almost all cases where CEMIS contribute to the solution of large-scale problems, this happens at an operational level only.

Although there are external factors that can make the introduction of environmental management financially beneficial (e.g. marketing, reduction of resource consumption), it is questionable whether individual CEMIS that exist only at operational level are able to meet complex environmental goals. Additionally, such isolated solutions usually come with all the problems that business informatics experts try to prevent by constructing integrated systems, as e.g. data redundancy, heterogeneous user interfaces, inefficient communication etc. Bearing this in mind, it is even more surprising to see that the mistakes of the early 1960s and 1970s are still being repeated, leaving companies with the high costs of integrating separate, outdated legacy systems.

Considering the increasing public debate about a sustainable society, there is a growing demand on companies to go beyond a strict adherence to legal requirements. Instead of a mere response to external legislative demands, there is a clear call for companies to embrace active environmental protection. This does not only involve reducing unnecessary waste, but also improving the general efficiency of production processes in terms of production-integrated environmental protection, while at the same time satisfying the various stakeholders' needs. To achieve this, a more holistic approach to CEMIS needs to be developed in order to support the production chain as a whole.

First steps have been taken towards the integration of corporate environmental protection into the goals of business practice. Also, there is a growing insight that emission and waste reduction holds some economic advantages, too. Based on frameworks set by relevant environmental laws, companies can reduce resource consumption and improve risk assessment.

Environmental management has to become an integral part of the companies' long-term strategic goals to be effectively beneficial. Therefore, only roughly defined goals will not be sufficient. Ecological goals need to be specific and, where possible, quantifiable in order to set up means of evaluation and clear criteria for success or failure.

In the past, corporate environmental protection was regarded by many as causing nothing but costs. Since this image has been refuted, future research should highlight the cost-cutting aspects of CEMIS by demonstrating the synergies between economic and ecological goals. Researchers should strive for an integrated approach that supports both dimensions of sustainability in the form of a single information system.

In the light of the ongoing sustainability debate and the research results of the last years, the traditional definition of CEMIS has become largely obsolete. Former systems mainly supported operational goals, providing individual solutions for different, isolated problems without showing any integrative features. Nevertheless, the same is true for the majority of CEMIS that companies are working with today, i.e. CEMIS are still struggling with problems already known from the seventies and eighties.

The concepts and methods of EAI (Enterprise Application Integration) and information management should be applied to the field of CEMIS as well in order to provide an integrated view of environmental and economic problems, leaving behind the exclusive focus on operative management.

Based on the insights mentioned above, the following new definition of CEMIS can be suggested: CEMIS 2.0 are information systems that support the idea of sustainable development in a company and take a holistic and strategic approach towards material and energy efficiency, emission and waste reduction, recycling, stakeholder engagement, and legal compliance.

This volume includes contributions by researchers from Canada, China, Poland, Germany, Italy, Australia, Sweden, Denmark, Brazil, Switzerland, New Zealand, and the USA.

Section One of this book provides an introduction to fundamental aspects in the research area of CEMIS. It presents the new requirements and demands on CEMIS and discusses the goals that need to be addressed by CEMIS in the context of the sustainability debate. In his contribution, *Möller* outlines the guiding principles of CEMIS systems and basic methods, as, for example, life cycle assessment.

Section Two encompasses 9 contributions that are concerned with theoretical and empirical approaches to the topic of CEMIS. The article by *Chen* explains how Green IT – along with the concepts of virtualization – can improve organizational, operational, and environmental results. V*on Hauff and Jörg* discuss from a business perspective how to establish eco-innovation as an integral component of environmental management information systems, and hence as a major contribution to environmental protection.In the next chapter, *Kamal et al.* describe a process enabling micro-entrepreneurs with limited resources to enlarge their business by means of IT. This so-called IT therapy involves diagnosis, interventions and an assessment of IT for development outcomes. Based on the example of food industry companies, *Antoni-Komar et al.* examine how CEMIS could be enhanced to tackle the impacts of climate change. The following contribution by *Rapp and Bremer* explores the possibilities of existing approaches, including a detailed description of an advanced biomass procurement system. The chapter by *Golinska* addresses issues related to materials management for closed-loop manufacturing, based on the integration of material flows management systems with production planning and control systems (PPC) or business systems (like ERP) which are applicable in a remanufacturing environment. Subsequently, the contribution by *Ramos et al.* shows in how far IT governance positively influences the achievement of strategic goals, especially in view of the controlling and correct management of investments. *Erechtchoukova et al.* describe the assessment of an organization's environmental impact, exemplified by the impact on a water resource. The authors also examine formal approaches to the development of temporal monitoring designs that serve to produce sufficient data to perform the assessment. Finally, the chapter by *Gadatsch* introduces the reader to the field of Green IT and presents an IT management and controlling concept which has been modified on the basis of current survey results.

The six chapters of **Section Three** are dedicated to frameworks, reference models and methodologies for CEMIS. The section starts with the contribution by *Minke and Lessing,* who describe an implementation concept based on mobile sensors and its evaluation within a pilot scheme. Subsequently, the article by *Carlson* provides an introduction to the structure of a well-functioning environmental information system. The contribution by *Shakir* introduces a framework for eco-efficiency implementation suitable for a particular eco-efficiency strategy. The purpose of the chapter by *Akkaya et al.* is to outline fundamentals of environmental reporting based on a comprehensive literature review and a recent project in Germany. The contribution by *Bevilacqua et al.* proposes a multi-agent approach supporting the inter-municipal infrastructure in order to achieve an optimal management of the waste collection service. Finally, the research of *Erek et al.* applies the concept of sustainability to the field of IS management, using practical concepts such as the procedural model, the balanced scorecard and a maturity model.

Section Four consists of six contributions dealing with the area of CEMIS applications. Firstly, *Grünwald* illustrates the integration of environmental information into a tool for planning production processes, aiming at including environmental considerations into the detailed planning of techniques and processes. In the next chapter, *Isenmann* proposes a standardized reference architecture for sustainability reports based on the eXtensible Business Reporting Language (XBRL), followed by a discussion of the resulting benefits. The contribution by *Schmehl et al.* focuses on the sustainability assessment of concepts of energetic biomass use. In this way, the authors provide decision support with regard to the different existing options of biomass use. *Konstantinidis et al.* describe the technology of the German Environmental Information Portal "PortalU" and present the content of the portal. In the following chapter, *Michelini and Razzoli* analyze some technologically-driven solutions for companies within networks which can be divided into three different levels of integration. Part Four closes with the chapter by *Arndt and Graubitz* who, by following the idea of providing special information to special interest groups, present a possible way of converting sustainability reports into topic maps by means of the eXtensible Business Reporting Language (XBRL).

Section Five rounds off this volume with three articles on case studies and pilot projects. *Dukovska-Popovska et al.* analyze current debates on the state of the art of sustainable supply chain management and green logistics. They present a case study from the Fujitsu Corporation in Japan and explore models of information systems and RFID use in green logistics in order to develop a combined model. *Juan Wen and Xueqiang Lu* describe eco-industrial parks (EIP) in China and the application of CEMIS for EIPs in accordance with the Chinese legal system. Finally, *Pozzebon et al.* investigate how corporate sustainable practices can be supported by information management models as well as information and communication technology applications. Their article is based on a case study in a Brazilian company that implemented a sustainability balanced scorecard (SBSC).

Frank Teuteberg & Jorge Marx Gómez
Osnabrück, Oldenburg

Acknowledgment

First and foremost, the editors wish to thank all authors for their excellent contributions to this volume and for shouldering the bulk of the efforts it took to realize this project. The high quality of all papers included here was assured by a double blind review process (each submitted chapter was reviewed at least twice). All articles are part of the rapid progress that we are currently witnessing in scientific research on Corporate Environmental Management Informations Systems (CEMIS).

Furthermore, we would like to thank IGI Publishers, especially Elizabeth Ardner, Assistant Director of Marketing, and Joel A. Gamon, Assistant Book Development Editor, who have both supported this project at all phases of development in a constructive, professional, dedicated, friendly and open manner.

This book could not have been completed without professional preparation and organization. Therefore, we would particularly like to thank Ms. Anja Grube for her assistance in coordination and communication, as well as for proofreading and translating services.

We hope that this book will receive widespread recognition both from practitioners and the scientific community.

As for the contents of this volume, the editors are always open to any suggestions for improvement and are looking forward to the readers' comments and fruitful discussions.

Frank Teuteberg & Jorge Marx Gómez
Osnabrück, Oldenburg

Section 1
Introduction

Chapter 1
Efficiency: A Guiding Principle of Corporate Environmental Management Information Systems

Andreas Möller
Leuphana University Lüneburg, Germany

ABSTRACT

Recently, there has been increasing recognition that computer-based information systems should better support corporate sustainability management. New administrative approaches, e.g. in the field of emission trading, and recommendations, for instance regarding carbon footprints of products, require a new type of information systems in companies. These new components can be called corporate environmental management information systems (CEMIS). What is the purpose of these systems? They should provide the required information for environmental or sustainability management. But what is the idea behind? What is the guiding principle of these systems? This chapter discusses efficiency as a guiding principle of CEMIS. It helps to understand better basic methodologies like life cycle assessment, and it provides presuppositional knowledge for the challenge of introducing these information instruments.

INTRODUCTION

Taylor described in his book "The Principles of Scientific Management" the introduction of so-called scientific management at the Bethlehem Steel Company and especially pig-iron handling (Taylor, 1911, p. 24). His observations for a loading process showed that a pig-iron handler loads 12 ½ per day. Further analyses of the process discovered that 47 or 48 tons per day were possible. To achieve that outcome Taylor established task work as a new type of organization and combined it with an optimized workflow. Instead of \$1.15 per day, the pig-iron handlers earn \$1.85 per day if they load 47 tons based on Taylor's specifications. Obviously it was not possible to increase the output without increasing the expenses but it was possible to optimize the ratio: 47 / 1.85 = 25.4 instead of 12.5 / 1.15 = 10.86. With other words, Taylor optimized the labor efficiency of pig-iron handling.

DOI: 10.4018/978-1-61520-981-1.ch001

BACKGROUND

The introduction of scientific management at Bethlehem Steel Company stands for Taylor's philosophy: Main purpose of scientific management, and therefore of appropriate management information systems, is to increase efficiency. Taylor cited in the introduction of his book the former US president Roosevelt: "The conservation of our national resources is only preliminary to the larger question of national efficiency" (Taylor, 1911, p. 7). Today, Taylor is regarded as one of the most important representatives of the so-called efficiency movement in the early 1900s.

As in the pig-iron handling example, efficiency can be defined as a relationship between positive outcomes and required effort. A typical form of efficiency is a ratio. Coelli et al. call the ratio "productivity" (Coelli et al., 2005, p. 3). The enumerator represents the outcomes, e.g. in terms of revenues for sold products, the denominator the effort. The effort can be quantified by costs. With regard to environmental protection and sustainability other indicators come into consideration, e.g. contributions to climate change or cumulative energy demand. Other variants of eco-efficiency could be environmental intensity of production, environmental improvement cost and environmental cost-effectiveness (Huppes & Ishikawa, 2005c, p. 45). Schaltegger et al. consider eco-efficiency as a basic strategy in sustainability management. They compare efficiency with other basic strategies: sufficiency: "When an individual has enough of something then demand ceases and unnecessary use of resources is curtailed" (Schaltegger et al., 2003, p. 25), and consistency: "a composition of matter streams and energy forms which is able to exist permanently in an industrial ecology" (Huber, 1998, p. 27, cited and translated by Schaltegger et al., 2003, p. 26).

In case of pig-iron handling the information system was fairly simple. Taylor's insights were based on investigations and experiments (Taylor, 1911, p. 31), performed in company with a "young college graduate" and a stop-watch as an information instrument. Nowadays companies use more complex information systems and simulation tools. Nevertheless, these software systems have mainly the same purpose: they should help to discover inefficiency.

Taylor's two pillars of information – investigations and experiments – are supported by different types of information systems. Nowadays, investigations in larger organizations are based on enterprise resource planning systems (ERP systems). The ERP systems provide routinely generated information, whereas experiments can be performed using software tools, for example simulation tools. The purpose of experiments is to find and to enforce standards like Taylor's adaption of task work for pig-iron handling at Bethlehem Steel Company. The specification of processes, work flows and economic incentives should establish an adaptive control system. Ideally, such a system does not require further investigations and control at regular intervals.

Today's companies optimize not only labor efficiency but as well environmental performance: resource, energy and eco efficiency (Busch et al., 2006; Huppes & Ishikawa, 2005a, p. 2; Kuosmanen, 2005, p. 15). These new types of efficiency reference to global environmental problems (Huppes & Ishikawa, 2005b, p. 34) and damage categories, in particular human health, ecosystem quality, climate change and scarcity of resources (Jolliet et al., 2003, p. 324). Damage in the different categories can be result of different environmental interventions of human activity. For example, scarcity of resources is a problem of consumption of non-renewable energy or extraction of scarce minerals (Goessling-Reisemann, 2008, p. 10). Indictors closing the gap between human activity and damage categories are called midpoint indictors. One important damage category has only one midpoint indicator: climate change. The midpoint indictor is called global warming and expressed in carbon dioxide equivalents. As mentioned, scarcity of resource has two midpoint indicators, human health and ecosystem quality have at least five (Jolliet et al., 2003, p. 324). The following table shows how to determine the denominator of important resource, energy and eco efficiency indicators. The impacts are expressed in kg equivalents of the reference substance. E.g. in case of the midpoint category global warming all emissions, associated with a product or service, are expressed in carbon dioxide equivalents. In some industry sectors special indicators are required (Saling et al., 2002, p. 203; Landsiedel, Saling, 2002, p. 261; Bunke et al., 2003, p. 6).

Unfortunately, it is not possible to use Taylor's simple stop-watch to determine resource consumption, energy demand or environmental impacts. Based on the data of the stop-watch, it is fairly easy to calculate labor costs. Resource and energy consumption as well as environmental impacts increase the intricacy of investigations and experiments because they are long-range effects. Special modeling techniques are required to estimate these long-range effects. One important instrument is life-cycle assessment (LCA).

ECO-EFFICIENCY ANALYSIS & LIFE CYCLE ASSESSMENT

Environmental protection was considered in the past as a constraint of production and profit maximization: forbidden toxic substance, handling of hazardous materials, transport of hazardous goods etc. But since the early 1970s and particularly since 1990 scarcity of fossil energy and some raw materials as well as global environmental changes like climate change have become more and more important. Porter and van der Linde propose the concept of resource productivity as a guiding principle. They emphasize that "we are now in a transition phase of industrial history in which companies are still inexperienced in handling environmental issues creatively" (Porter & van der Linde, 1995, p. 127). The idea is to utilize the natural environment in an efficient and innovative way that makes a sustainable development possible. We can consider this as a new (eco) efficiency movement.

Based on a first definition in 1989 (Schaltegger & Sturm, 1989) Schaltegger and Burritt define eco-efficiency as "the ratio between value added and environmental impact added" (Schaltegger & Burritt, 2000, p. 358). As in Taylor's pig-iron handling example, enhancement of eco-efficiency can be achieved by increasing the positive outcome or by reducing the environmental impacts – or by a combination of both: For example the production of organic food normally allows higher prices and results in lower environmental impacts.

Schaltegger and Burritt emphasize that the ratio requires economic information as well as environmental information derived from ecological accounting. Whereas conventional ERP systems provide required economic information (e.g. revenues), corporate environmental management information systems (CEMIS) have to compute the denominator of the ratio, the environmental impact. In this regard, the CEMIS is an ecological accounting system. As a possible concept of such an ecological accounting system, life cycle assessment (LCA) comes into play (Brattlebø, 2005, p. 9).

ISO 14040 defines LCA as a "compilation and evaluation of the inputs, outputs and potential environmental impacts of a products system throughout its life cycle" (ISO 14040; Guinée, 2002, p. 5). LCA does not comprise all flows of a material and energy flow system, e.g. a company or supply chain, all flows must be related to a product or service (Consoli et al., 1993, p. 7; Berlin & Uhlin, 2004, p. 190; Frankl & Rubik, 2000, p. 2). This clarifies the intended application context of life cycle assessment: It is designed as a decision support instrument: "A decision-maker uses LCA for generating information on the environmental implications of products. For this purpose a model is set up covering the material and energy flows attributed to a product and their evaluation in view of their environmental impact" (Werner, 2005, p. 5).

However, LCA is not focused on a special damage category (e.g. climate change). "The environmental burden covers all types of impacts upon the environment, including extraction of different types of resources, emission of hazardous substances and different types of land use" (Guinée, 2002, p. 6). The different resource, energy and eco efficiency indictors, mentioned above (table 1), measure only single dimensions of possible environmental impacts. On the other side, LCA serves as information instrument for all types of ecological efficiency analysis.

The LCA approach provides two different steps to estimate negative environmental impacts (Figure 1). The first step is life-cycle inventory (LCI) analysis and the second life-cycle impact assessment. In the first step the anthropogenic material and energy flows, connected to the functional unit (the enumerator in the eco-efficiency equation), are quantified. The second estimates the impacts in the natural environment, like climate change or depletion of natural resources.

The definition of LCA points to the underlying philosophy of the concept. As mentioned above, efficiency is a relationship between means and end. The nominator of the efficiency equation is often quantified by the revenues. The challenge is mainly to quantify the denominator: to quantify the environmental impacts related to the positive outcomes. This is the same situation as in cost accounting: revenues and costs (Riebel, 1994, p. 520).

The cost accounting expert Riebel discusses three different interpretations of cause and effect chains: the causal interpretation, the means-end relationship (Riebel calls it the final interpretation), and the identity principle (Riebel, 1990). In the causal interpretation a causal relationship between two objects A and B exists if and only if (1) A exists before B, (2) A is essential precondition of B and (3) if A is on hand, B must occur without exception (Riebel, 1990, p. 70).

Riebel emphasizes that causal relationship cannot describe the relationship between products and impacts. We start with products, or more common with positive outcomes, and estimate the economic impacts (costs) or the impacts on the natural environment. We consider the positive outcome as cause A and the impacts as the resulting effects B. But this is contradictory to rule (1): Products do not exist before their raw materials. Another interpretation of the principle of cause and effect is the starting point for efficiency analyses: We want to quantify means-end relationships and in particular environmental impacts.

The modeling of anthropogenic material and energy flows in the first step of life cycle assessment (life cycle inventory analysis) is based on Riebel's first interpretation of cause and effect chains: causality. Causality is fundamental in physics and chemistry, for example chemical conversions are expressed by reaction equations. In material and energy flow models chemical conversions serve as nodes in the graphs or networks.

However, the challenge of life cycle inventory analysis and underlying concepts is to bring together the two different interpretations of cause and effect chains. Therefore, life cycle assessment as a means-end analysis requires a special type of material and energy flow modeling and several modeling constraints: (1) LCA-oriented material and energy flow models consist of linear process

Table 1. Important resource, energy and eco indicators

Damage Category	Midpoint Category	Midpoint Reference Substance
Resources	Non-Renewable Energy	kg-eq. crude oil
Resources	Mineral Extraction	Kg-eq. iron
Climate Change	Global Warming	kg-eq. carbon dioxide

Figure 1. Two step of life cycle assessment

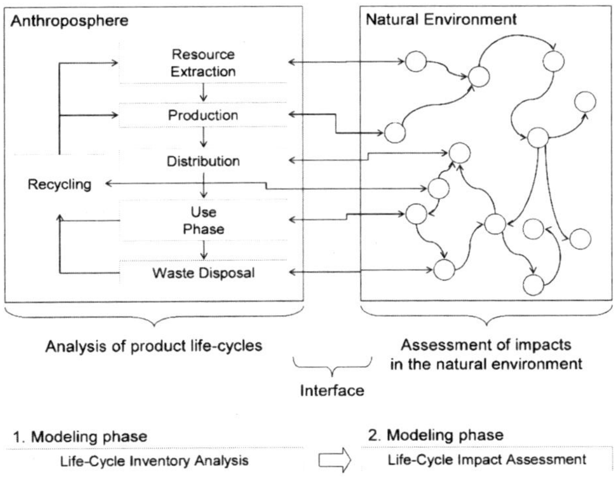

specifications and links between them. (2) Joint productions have to be disjointed into single-product processes. In case of joint production processes, so-called allocation rules have to be applied. (3) Even though stocks play an important role in environmental protection and sustainability, they are not allowed in the models.

Figure 2 shows a fictive example. The product system consists of three processes: final assembly, pre-product assembly and water supply. Each process is specified by a set of production coefficients (linear specification). The process specification result from e.g. measurements and/or reaction equations for chemical conversions. The example reveals how the processes and flows are scaled to a reference flow: It is a means-end analysis. In case of loops in the flow chart matrix methods have be applied: The flow chart represents nothing else than a set of linear equations (Hejungs, 1994; Heijungs & Suh, 2002). The solutions of these equations are process levels: contributions of the processes. The process levels allow calculating the inventory table, the exchange of material and energy flows with the natural environment (table 2).

However, the flow graph in Figure 2 does not contain loops and the sequential method can be applied. In our example it is assumed that the reference flow is product 1 kg. The step-by step calculation starts with this flow. It is the product of process "final assembly" so that we have to scale the input and output coefficients to 1 kg. We can calculate input and output flows like crude oil 1 kg, oxygen 2.4 kg or carbon dioxide 0.4 kg. Important flows are the internal flows water 0.5 kg and the intermediate product 0.8 kg. Because we want to calculate the material and energy flows caused by the final product, we have to scale process "pre-product" to 0.8 kg. Again, we can calculate input and output flows like crude oil 0.5 kg or methane 0.2 kg. Important is water input 1 kg. Now, we can scale the process "water supply" to 1.5 kg water output. Because there are no more internal flows, we can stop the calculation procedure and summarize the inputs and outputs. The inventory table 2, based on the flow chart of Figure 2, contains the material and energy exchanges with the natural environmental. The life-cycle inventory table becomes an "interface" to life-cycle impact assessment.

The second modeling step of life cycle assessment, life cycle impact assessment (LCIA), is not based on detailed analyses of substance flows in the natural environment; the compu-

Figure 2. Sequential calculation of a life cycle inventory

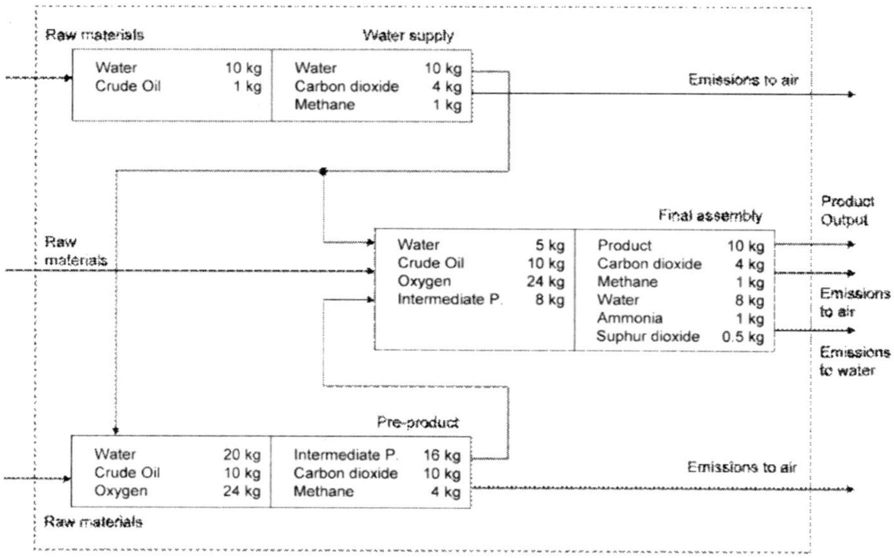

tational procedures of LCIA can be treated as a variant of aggregated performance measurement systems. LCIA "is the phase in which the set of results of the inventory analysis – mainly the inventory table – is further processed and interpreted in terms of environmental impacts and societal preferences. To this end, a list of impact categories is defined, and models for relating the environmental interventions to suitable category indicators for these impact categories are selected" (Guinée, 2002, p. 63). So, in the efficiency perspective, LCIA is the link between inventory analysis and the indicators, mentioned above (table 1). Reference substance is carbon dioxide (CO2). Time horizon is 100 years (GWP100) (Guinée, 2002, p. 75).

We use the predefined characterization methods for each damage or midpoint category. The methods are quite simple because they abstract from the interdependency of substances and the concentration of substances in a substance mix. In that way, it is possible to express the impact of a specific amount of each substance in the inventory table regarding the impact category equivalent the impact of a reference substance by a characterization factor. Table 3 shows a few

Table 2. Inventory table (the table does not include the reference flow 1 kg)

Input	Quantity	Unit	Output	Quantity	Unit
Water	1.5	kg	Carbon dioxide (0.6 + 0.4 + 0.5)	1.5	kg
Crude Oil (0.15 + 2.4 + 1.2)	3.75	kg	Ammonia	0.1	kg
Oxygen (2.4 + 0.5)	2.9	kg	Methane (0.15 + 0.1 + 0.2)	0.45	kg
			Water	0.8	kg
			Sulfur dioxide	0.05	kg

Table 3.Characterzation factors global warming / climate change (source: Guinée 2002, p. 185)

Substance	Input / Output	Characterization Factor	Unit
Carbon Dioxide	Output	1	kg-eq. CO2/kg
Methane	Output	21	kg-eq. CO2/kg
Dinitrogen oxide	Output	310	kg-eq. CO2/kg
CFC-11	Output	4000	kg-eq. CO2/kg
HCFC-11	Output	93	kg-eq. CO2/kg
Sulphur hexafluoride	Output	23900	kg-eq. CO2/kg
...	Output	...	kg-eq. CO2/kg

characterization factors regarding global warming or climate change.

To determine the denominator of the global warming eco efficiency indicator (the entry in row 3 of table 1) of a product or service, we have to multiply the output entries of the inventory table with the characterization factors in table 3 (the most entries of the inventory table will have a characterization factor 0). Thereafter, we have to add all the results, so that the impact is expressed in carbon dioxide equivalents. In the example of table 2, we can identify carbon dioxide (1.50 kg) and methane (0.45 kg). These are the classified entries in the inventory table. The global warming indictor is 1.5 * 1 + 0.45 * 21 = 10.95 kg-eq. CO2. This value is called the carbon footprint of the product (Weidema et al., 2008, p. 3).

CORPORATE ENVIRONMENTAL MANAGEMENT ACCOUNTING

If companies or associations apply eco-efficiency analysis and life cycle assessment they normally select a single product or service: Let us test the new methodologies using the example of product X. In a learning and transition phase such an approach is reasonable. But if the methodologies should serve as an underlying concept of computer-based information systems the assumption of a single product or service must be reconsidered. Most companies produce multiple products linked through jointness of production (Beattie & Taylor, 1985, p. 179; Möller & Prox, 2008). The same applies to supply chains. The question arise how it is possible to represent the material and energy flows and stocks within a company or supply chain in one model and evaluate such a material and energy flow model in such a way that we can perform life cycle assessments and eco-efficiency analyses.

The material flow networks are such an approach (Schmidt et al., 1997; Möller, 2000). Based on the concept of Petri Nets (Reisig, 1985; Jensen, 1992) material flow networks consist of three different types of elements: The nodes in the network may be either transitions (visualized as squares) or places (represented by circles). Between these nodes there are arrows as linking elements. Transitions are those locations in a material flow network, where material and energy transformation processes occur. Each transition can, on the one hand, be connected to places from which it is supplied with materials and energy (input), and on the other hand be connected to places to which it delivers materials (output). Places represent storages in which time conversions take place (Figure 3).

The objective of material flow networks is to trace the material and energy flows and stocks within a company or between different companies within a supply chain. The difference to conventional Petri nets is that this approach does not serve as an underlying methodology for discrete

Figure 3. Material flow network of a de-inking process in a paper mill

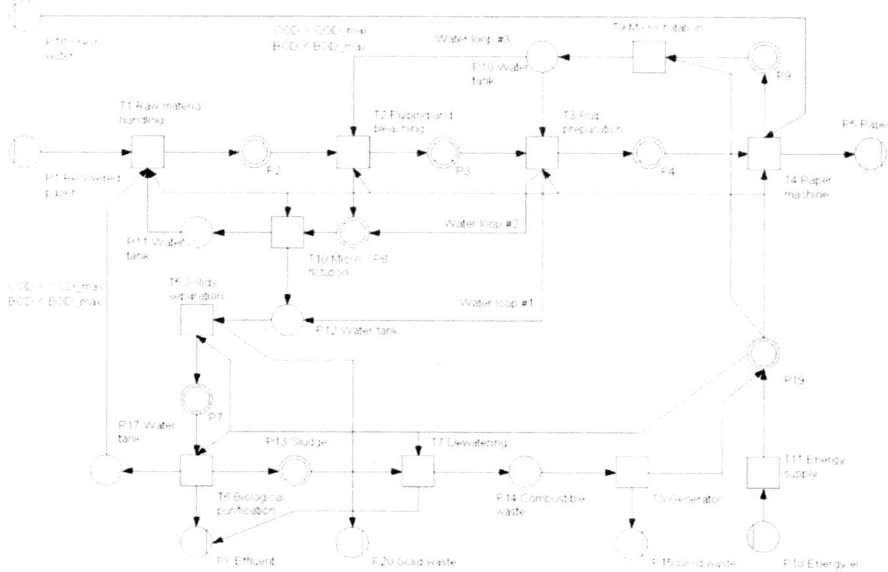

event simulation models. Rather, material flow networks can be interpreted as a new accounting system. Here, material and energy flows instead of financial flows are considered. This new type of accounting system is period oriented. It provides information on what material and energy flows have occurred in a period under review (fiscal year) and how the opening inventory has changed after this period (stocks).

Here, Riebel's first interpretation of the principle of cause and effect takes place. Note that such a modeling approach does not require categories like products, waste or raw materials. The identification of products or intermediate products in these models is a mental accomplishment beyond the model. However, this is required to perform life cycle assessments and eco-efficiency analyses based on period-oriented material and energy flow models: For all materials in these models must be specified whether they are desired or not. E.g. products are desired whereas waste is not. What we need is a conceptual link between the object level and the means-end-level. Here, the fundamentals of modern production theory can be applied (Dyckhoff, 1994; Schmidt, 2005; Laurin et al., 2006): We ask for the desirability or market price of all material and energy flows in the system. A material can have a positive, negative, or no market price at all. We call desired objects or objects with a positive market price "goods," undesired or with a negative market price "bads", and objects with no markets "neutrals." Thus, copper as a raw material is "good". In later stages copper can become a "bad," for instance within a wastewater stream.

If we then apply the good/bad classification to material flow networks, we switch over to means-end analyses: What are the positive outcomes of the system? What are the costs and environmental impacts? These questions are answered using the data provided by material flow networks. On the detail level, we know all input and output flows of the processes. Based on the good/bad classification, we can identify the revenues and expenses of each process: What are the bads that go into the process and what are goods that result from it? The goods on the output side and the bads on the input side together constitute the revenues of a process. If we identify more then one revenue, we have identified a joint production. The allocation of costs and environmental burden to revenues require the application of allocation rules. The application of allocation rules results in "single-revenue-processes." Using these virtual processes, it is possible to calculate the costs and environmental impacts of all system outcomes. As mentioned above, in simple cases without loops it is possible to use sequential methods (Figure 2), otherwise matrix methods are applied.

With regard to corporate environmental management information systems period-oriented environmental accounting concepts provide several advantages in comparison to direct life cycle assessment: (1) It is possible to perform consistent and comparable corporate efficiency analyses on the basis of only one consistent material and energy flow model (Möller, 2000). (2) Because period-oriented material and energy flow models do not force the application of allocation rules, optimization methods can be applied; in particular flexible joint processes often provide important decision variables (Schmidt et al., 2007). (3) Period-oriented material and energy flow models can be treated as a log of discrete event simulations or continuous simulations. The period-oriented material and energy flow model becomes an interface between process simulations and efficiency analyses (Möller, 2005).

In particular the third advantage is important because material flow networks provide important interfaces to already existing information instruments in companies, e.g. production planning and control systems (Rautenstrauch, 1994) and simulation tools, as they are used in chemical engineering. So, the main challenge is that some kind of consistency and integration is required to bring together the different instruments. Udo de Haes et al. (2004) call such a modeling strategy hybrid analysis. Hybrid analyses are facilitated by appropriate modeling frameworks. A modeling framework consists of different modeling components and interfaces between them. The interfaces and consistency checks should ensure consistent over-all models.

Each of the modeling components in such a framework has to accomplish two different functions. The first is to support the associated perspective; the other is to serve as a data provider for other model components in the framework. For example, process simulation tools provide information about waiting times, dwell times, bottlenecks and so on. But process simulation can also serve as a data provider for material and

Figure 4. Material networks (model #3) as a database and as an interface between different modeling tools

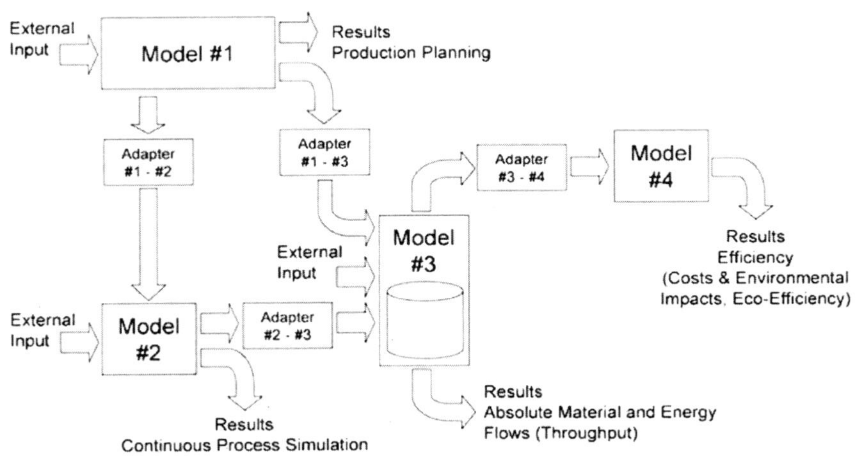

energy flow analyses and life cycle assessment (Wohlgemuth, 2005).

Ideally the output of one model can serve directly as data input of another. Unfortunately, in most cases some kind of mapping between the involved models is required. Following the adapter design pattern in software engineering, conceptual adapters are normally required between the different models and perspectives. One example is the already described combination of period-oriented material flow analysis and life cycle assessment. Period-oriented material flow analysis results can serve as data input for life cycle assessment, but not directly. Some adaptations are required, for example the application of allocation rules in case of joint productions.

Several network architectures are possible. The term "tool chain" describes one of them. The tool chain as a design pattern stands for a chain of different models or instruments, one model serves as a data provider for the subsequent. A generalization of the tool chain is the central database (Möller & Viere, 2005). One of the concepts has to provide a central database. On the one side, tools are used to insert data into the database (e.g. chemical engineering tools like Aspen Plus®); on the other side, tools evaluate the database under different perspectives (economic efficiency, carbon footprint, eco efficiency). This makes the central database more flexible than the tool chain. It is possible to add new components: data providers (for instance to represent production systems using discrete event simulation) and evaluation tools (for instance substance-flow-oriented Sankey diagrams).

DIMENSIONS OF EFFICIENCY

Diamond developed in his analysis about the viability and collapse of historic and modern societies a five-point framework of possible contribution factors: (1) "damage that people inadvertently inflict on their environment" (Diamond, 2005, p. 11), including fragility or resilience of the environment; (2) climate change, e.g. the "little ice age" from the early 1400s until the 1800s, (3) attacks by hostile neighbors; (4) decreased support by friendly neighbors; (5) the abilities of a society to response to its problems. Diamond presents for all these factors examples, including the last one: "A society's responses depend on its political, economic, and social institutions and on its cultural values" (Diamond, 2005, p. 15).

One keyword is not mentioned as a factor: efficiency. Of course, the first factor includes efficiency. Societies can reduce their impact on the natural environment by increasing resource, energy and eco efficiency. But the relationship between efficiency and viability is not as unambiguous as it seems. Diamond shows this with the end of the Greenland Norse colony in the 1200s (Diamond, 2005, p. 242). The impact on the environment was too high; the Norse did not use scarce resources in a sustainable way. Interestingly, they use relevant capabilities like ships for hunting walruses and polar bears far away from their villages instead of transporting lumber from "Markland" (Labrador or Newfoundland, the wood helps to reduce cutting trees and stripping turf in Greenland) because the coats allowed them to merchandise with Europe. Furthermore, the revenues were not used to close the sustainability gap. With regard to Diamond's criteria, the Norse acted inefficient but it was the only way for them to make money and profit whereas the shipping of wood from Markland has not direct positive outcomes.

So, we have two slightly different interpretations (or dimensions) of efficiency: On the one hand efficiency of a sustainable society that tries to avoid inadvertently damages on its natural environment and on the other hand an interpretation of efficiency which has its origins in the rules of economic system. Efficiency in the second interpretation is a generalized value in modern industrial societies.

The question is how to bring together the different interpretations or dimensions. This question brings the development of the Balanced Scorecard (BSC) and Strategy Maps to mind. With Kaplan and Norton, viability and operational value creation can be treated as different objectives of a company. But these objectives are not completely independent. There exist cause relationships between the two objectives: Viability is a precondition of operational value creation. Here, the strategy maps come into play. The strategy map is "a visual representation of the cause-and-effect relationships among the components of an organization's strategy" (Kaplan & Norton, 2004, p. 9). So, the strategy maps bring together different dimensions of a strategy, and the strategy has to balance the different dimensions: "Investing in intangible assets for long-term revenue growth usually conflicts with cutting costs for short-term financial performance" (Kaplan & Norton, 2004, p. 10). This describes exactly the relationship between the long-term objects of viability and the short-term objective of value creation. Kaplan's and Norton's conclusion is that "the starting point in describing a strategy is to balance and articulate the short-term financial objective for cost reduction and productivity improvements with the long-term objective for profitable revenue growth" (Kaplan & Norton, 2004, p. 11) – and with regard to sustainable development: viability.

Referring to Diamod's five-point framework it is possible to distinguish possible contribution factors to the viability of production plants and companies: (1) Direct feed-back of global environmental problems: extreme weather events, depletion of abiotic resources etc., (2) stakeholder perspective, (3) environmental regulations in order to initiate sustainable development and (4) according to Diamond's fifth factor the corporation's answer to its problems (Diamond, 2005, p. 14). Many companies are not confronted with direct feed-back of global environmental changes. E.g. climate change has no effect on the production of automobiles; nevertheless climate change is a serious challenge in automotive industry. More important for these companies are factors two and three. In particular future environmental regulations could compromise long-term value creation. For instance "the national strategic plan for establishing a recycling-based society in Japan shows individual recycling ratio targets for containers and packages, construction materials, food products, home appliances, and end-of-life vehicles" (Morioka et al, 2005, p. 206). Another example is the discussion about the "global sociometabolic transition" and an "industrial sociometabolic regime" (Krausmann et al., 2008, p. 637). International agreements, e.g. regarding

Figure 5. Different interpretations of efficiency within a strategy map

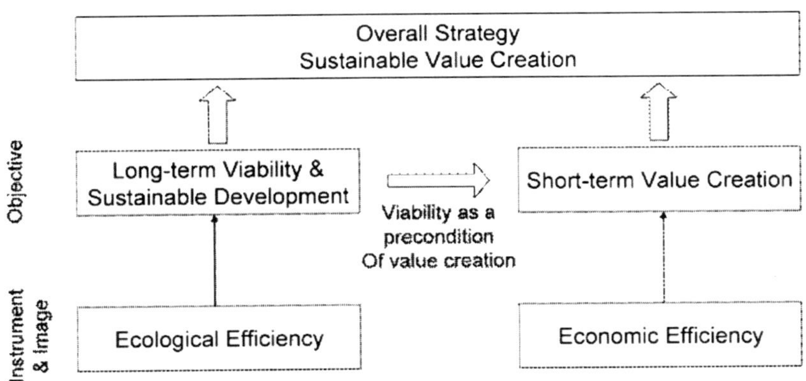

the mitigation of climate change, are first steps. Administrations are going to translate these agreements to regulatory frameworks.

Today's companies have to address several internal and external constraints and regulations – and they have to document that they comply with these constraints which requires ambitious reporting concepts. The challenges of global sustainable development will introduce further regulatory frameworks to institute corporate sustainable developments. Porter and van der Linde point out that environmental regulations "can and should promote resource productivity" (Porter & van der Linde, 1995, p. 129). They have efficiency and viability of a sustainable society in mind: The regulations and standards should ensure the viability of the society. Unsustainable processes should be transformed step by step into problems of the involved companies. But the regulations should not stipulate the way of solving the problems. They emphasize a critical principle of good environmental regulation: "Create maximum opportunity for innovation by letting industries discover how to solve their own problems". So Porter and van der Linde advocate the adoption of new forms of regulation within the framework of sustainable development. Today, several administrative approaches like the strategic plan for establishing a recycling-based society in Japan stand for such a new form of regulation. Because of the challenges of sustainable development it is likely that more and more of these standards will impose a heavy burden on companies. Corporate environmental management information systems have to deal with these developments.

Nowadays special software components support compliance management. With regard to environmental protection, appropriate software components are often called EH&S ("Environmental, Health and Safety"). These software components support the handling of processes which are subject of several restrictions and regulations, for instance transport and storage of hazardous goods. Another type of software components is focused on documentation and reporting. In the future, software components have to support more and more corporate sustainable development and corporate viability. Since several years life cycle assessment and eco-efficiency stand for organizational image which help to implement corporate sustainable development in companies. Life cycle assessment is discussed not only as an information instrument. Life cycle assessment is treated as a basic approach of a new kind of management philosophy: Life cycle management (Remmen et al., 2007). Strategies have to balance this objective as well as short-term value creation.

CORPORATE SUSTAINABILITY COMMUNICATION

Even though life cycle assessment and eco-efficiency produced successful new scientific communities, the success of these approaches in practice is quite restricted. Many companies apply the concepts but in comparison cost accounting, cost cutting and labor efficiency are much more important in everyday management in companies. Life cycle assessment and eco-efficiency analyses are welcome if they help to increase economic efficiency. Companies want to identify so-called win/win situations. Contrary to expectations of life cycle management (Remmen et al., 2007), life cycle assessment and eco-efficiency analyses have rather a helping function. The question is why?

This question is associated with Diamond's fifth factor: "the ubiquitous question of the society's responses to its problems" (Diamond, 2005, p. 14). So, it is not a technical question, it is rather a question of organizational culture and culture change. Schuhmacher distinguish two dimensions of culture change: Number of members and number of domains changing. If culture change affects only a few members and the number of domains is low, he characterizes this type of change a "drift". If the number of members and domains changing is high, it is a "transition" (Schuhmacher, 1997,

p. 114). "Transition is described here as change in many significant domains for a majority of the members of the culture. The magnitude here is so great that the identity of the culture is at least questioned, perhaps redefined" (Schuhmacher, 1997, p. 115). As shown above, life cycle assessment and eco-efficiency are not only information instruments. They are as well "Trojan horses" of new organizational images and metaphors: carbon-neutral companies, sustainable corporations, sustainable supply chains etc. (Winograd, 1986, p. 210). Many members of companies are affected and the changes are significant. So in fact, the instruments aim at a transition of societies and of corporations (Fischer-Kowalski et al., 2007). The subsequent question is how societies and corporations organize socio-economic transitions.

Habermas' concept of society (Habermas, 1985) distinguishes lifeworld and subsystems like the society's economy. In his concept, efficiency is a generalized action orientation in the subsystem economy. It is the result of a "social evolution as a second-order process of differentiation: system and lifeworld are differentiated in the sense that the complexity of the one and the rationality of the other grow" (Habermas, 1985, p. 153). The process is triggered by communicative action: "Action oriented to mutual understanding gains more and more independent from normative contexts. At the same time, even greater demands are made upon this basic medium of everyday language; it gets overloaded in the end and replaced by delinguistified media" (Habermas, 1985, p. 155). That's the paradox of communication: It is a co-evolutionary process and "modern societies attain a level of system differentiation at which increasingly autonomous organizations are connected with one another via delinguistified media of communication: these systemic mechanisms – for example, money – steer a social intercourse that has been largely disconnected from norms and values, above all in those subsystems of purposive rational economic and administrative action that, on Weber's diagnosis, have become independent of their moral-political foundations" (Habermas, 1985, p. 154). This concept allows understanding Taylor's citation of the former US president Roosevelt: economic efficiency as a generalized action orientation.

And Habermas' concept of society helps to understand why resource and eco efficiency are still not relevant in companies. (1) Resource and eco efficiency are not generalized action orientations in the economic system today. They are ignored as long as they are not compatible with the conventional interpretation of efficiency. The constellations of compatibility are called win/win situations. (2) Because resource and eco efficiency are regarded as irrelevant, appropriate (computer-based) information systems are not widely used. It is not surprising that these forms of efficiency are still not supported by ERP systems.

How could corporate sustainability become a generalized action orientation in organizations? In Habermas' concept the answer is communicative action. And nowadays computers can play a prominent role as a powerful medium of everyday communication: computers as a medium. Some of the web 2.0 experiments and implementations improve this new medium. Admittedly, the computer's role as an information system, a delinguistified medium of communication, cannot be replaced by Twitter or a chat. But there are interesting links between the two forms of application of computers: problematic systemic mechanisms and orientations can trigger communicative action. In that case, information systems provide data for good arguments; the data must be presented in a form that fits to the communication process.

First important steps are already done. Key words in this regard are sustainability / environmental reporting and corporate social responsibility (CSR). Environmental and sustainability reporting can be treated as a corporate communication instrument (Ebinger et al., 2006, p. 511; Isenmann et al., 2007, p. 63) and not only as an information instrument: not mono-directional stakeholder information or correspondence (Winograd & Flores,

1986, p. 17) but interactive stakeholder dialogue (Isenmann & Kim, 2006, p. 533).

If software systems or tools should support the transition process, they have to support environmental and sustainability reporting – in an effective way. In the transition phase, instruments like material and energy flow analysis, life cycle assessment and eco-efficiency analysis provide not only data for decision-making, the instruments become an important data source of environmental reporting (Marx-Gómez, 2004, p. 65).

But computer tools are not only data providers of environmental reporting. The tools make problems visible; they help to understand better the problems and possible solutions. In fact, many companies and associations establish life cycle assessment projects and test life cycle assessment tools. They gain new insights, try to anticipate stricter regulatory standards and hope for new competitive opportunities. LCA tools are designed to support these experiments. Computer support in the transition phase has completely different purposes than in phases with stable action orientations. Computers are used as a "tool" enhancing the capabilities of the users (Möller et al., 2006, p. 612). They provide information on an ad-hoc basis rather than routinely generated data (Burritt et al. 2002). Furthermore, we have seen that communication is required to change metaphors and images. This can be supported by another form of computer support: computers as a medium of internal sustainability communication. The software instruments serve as a new "language" in the transformation phase; they are containers of new forms of thinking (e.g. life-cycle thinking) and establish new forms of argumentation (e.g. in case of life cycle assessment new typical diagrams and flow charts).

As mentioned above (Habermas, 1985, p. 154), the main problem of communicative action is that it increases complexity. Ideally, all action should be based on communication and discourse: consensus-based action. This is not possible. So, successful corporate communication is not concerned with operational decisions. The focus is on new rules and new generalized action orientation. Images like "carbon-free company" play a prominent role in such a process, and Sankey diagrams or bar charts, as a result of life cycle assessment or eco-efficiency analysis, are good arguments in such a process. So, one important purpose of corporate sustainability communication is to replace it by other form of social integration: new systemic mechanisms. In other words, the vision of sustainability communication is a corporate environmental management information system which represents the new generalized action orientations and allows delinguistified social interaction and coordination (Figure 6). Today's software tools (LCA tools, Eco-Efficiency tools) do not support this purpose of corporate sustainability communication, even if they play an important role in the communication processes. At least, process databases like EcoInvent can be regarded as an important step in this direction (Frischknecht, 2004).

IMAGES OF CORPORATE ENVIRONMENTAL MANAGEMENT INFORMATION SYSTEMS

Page and Rautenstrauch defined Environmental Management Information Systems (EMIS) as "organizational-technical systems for systematically obtaining, processing and making environmentally relevant information available in companies" (Page & Rautenstrauch, 2001, p. 5). They agree with Taylor that efficiency is the most import purpose of these systems: "Above all, these systems aid in determining the environmental damage caused by companies and designing support measures to avoid and reduce it" (Page & Rautenstrauch, 2001, p. 5). As a consequence, Page and Rautenstrauch regard EMIS as information instruments in the Eco-Controlling concepts (Page & Rautenstrauch, 2001, p. 6). The Eco-Controlling cycle allows combining the prevention of inef-

Figure 6. Transition to sustainable corporations, appropriate computer support

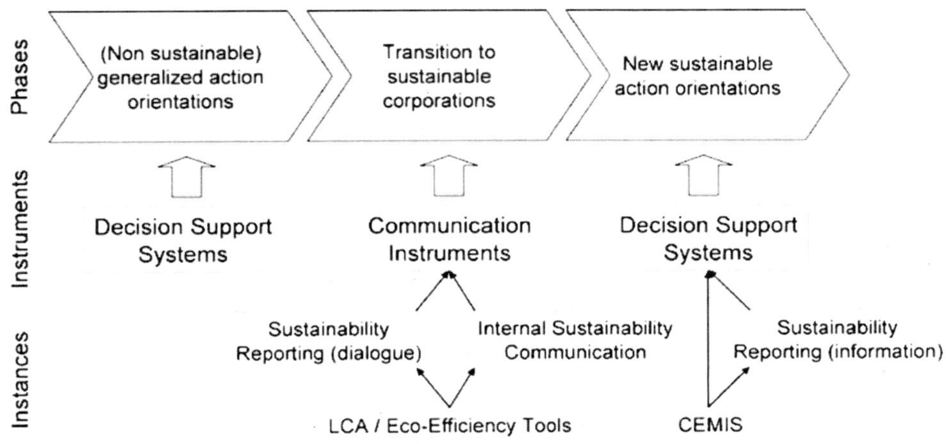

ficiency and compliance: External demands and internal guidelines.

Most work on EMIS or CEMIS respectively has been done in the context of ERP system integration. The idea is quite simple. A fully integrated EMIS component would guaranty that information which is required for modern environmental management can be collected "by the way". CEMIS components would profit from a general principle of ERP systems: It represents all relevant activities within a company (Möller et al., 2006, p. 608). How can an ERP system achieve this? – By a powerful business process management component. Additional data fields in the databases, which allow identifying for instance substances and energy, are maintained in the accounting records. CEMIS can be treated as evaluation components. They use the additional datasets and data fields to compile the data input for the CEMIS instruments: in particular for period-oriented material and energy flow analysis, life cycle assessment and eco-efficiency analysis.

A complementary step in this direction is done in the Eco-Integral project in the late 1990s (Kreeb et al., 1997). The Eco-Integral project was focused on future business processes in environmental management: life cycle assessment, material and energy flow oriented cost accounting etc. Appropriate business processes are developed and proposed. The idea: Eco controlling as a routine job in management.

Another important challenge is development and implementation of interface to existing ERP systems. Research on this field is technology driven. In the beginning, it was a technological challenge. Today, based on modern techniques and standards like web services interfacing ERP systems is – from a technical standpoint – not really a central issue (PAS 1025, 2003; Funk et al., 2009; Wohlgemuth et al., 2009).

Unfortunately, while technical problems are more or less solved, there are still methodological challenges. The intention of ERP systems is not fully compatible with the information demands of environmental management. Whereas from a theoretical point of view material and energy flow analysis should form basic components in ERP systems, CEMIS components or databases respectively are designed as add-ons to existing ERP system modules. The consequence is that CEMIS not only use existing databases and components, they inherit the underlying modeling concepts and models too. Even if ERP is an acronym of "enterprise resource planning" it is still not easy to implement resource efficiency and other sustainability-oriented methods as an add-on of ERP systems. The situation is comparable with the discussion about CIM ("Computer Integrated Manufacturing") concepts in the 1980s and early 1990s. The organizational image of CIM was in particular the "Y model" presented by Scheer (Scheer, 1988). This visualization points out that it is necessary to bring together an economic and a technical perspective (the upper two forks of the model). Methods on the left fork are derived from the production planning and control approach (PPC), models on the right side from computer aided design (CAD). In chemical industry chemical engineering tools like Aspen Plus® are used instead.

With sustainable development another perspective comes into play. Again, companies are confronted with a new kind of thinking ("life cycle thinking"), new languages (LCA, Eco-Efficiency, Impact Assessment etc.) and software tools (LCA tools, carbon footprint tools). And again, successful ERP system integration requires a redesign of ERP system components. CIM is a possible overall approach that could be enhanced. Other conceptual frameworks are Product Lifecycle Management (Eisert et al. 2001) or Supply Chain Management. Möller & Rolf have discussed the extension of PLM: Eco Product Lifecycle Management (Möller & Rolf, 2001). Life cycle assessment and eco-efficiency concepts are used in three phases of PLM: Product design, process design and life cycle design (Möller & Rolf, 2001, p. 741).

Several existing concepts are already enhanced with regard to corporate sustainability, for instance enhanced production planning and control systems (Rautenstrauch, 1999, p. 57) or cost accounting systems (Möller, 2000, p. 169; Schaltegger & Wagner, 2006). From an eco-efficiency and life cycle assessment perspective, material and energy flow analysis should be a core component of such a system; material and energy flow models should form the central database (cf. Scheer, 1988, p. 13). This joint effort is a serious challenge for software companies, consultancies and companies, but all methodological problems can be solved. The question is why should they do it? Porter and van der Linde say "managers must start to recognize environmental improvements as an economic and competitive opportunity" (Porter & van der Line, 1995, p. 130). And "better information and evaluation methods will help managers reduce environmental impact while improving resource productivity" (Porter & van der Linde, 1995, p. 132).

CONCLUSION

Today, efficiency is a guiding principle in designing corporate environmental management information systems – but with a slightly different interpretation: Efficiency does not serve directly profit maximization. Rather, efficiency as an overall concept of CEMIS contributes to viability of companies, supply chains and societies. So, the ideas behind CEMIS are not really far away from Taylor's "scientific management". The main reason for the limited success of these approaches until now is that it does not serve directly profit maximization. Porter's and van der Linde's link to profit maximization is that the principles facilitate innovations: "environmental improvements as an economic and competitive opportunity" (Porter & van der Linde, 1995, p. 130). In other words: Viability and increased eco-efficiency as a precondition of future economic success. Eco-efficiency is closely connected with life cycle assessment. Life cycle assessment can be seen as an instrument to determine the denominator of the eco-efficiency equation. But life cycle assessment is more: It is the paradigm in that field (Heiskanen, 2001, P. 31).

But viability and sustainability are new generalized action orientations and the organizational culture of many companies today does not comprise these orientations. Viability and sustainability imply serious cultural change: from "old thinking" to "new thinking". Such a transition requires communication. So, the corporate environmental management information system stands for a vision: Corporate sustainability is an important action orientation. Before, corporations have to pass through a transition phase, and computer support has to meet the demands in this phase: sustainability reporting, internal sustainability communication.

However, efficiency is not the all-embracing solution. Diamond's framework of possible contribution factors for the collapse of societies makes clear that efficiency is only an indirect factor. It can be criticized that the concepts are another example of thinking in the use-and-throw-away society. Key words are input/output, supply chain or life-cycle. Closed-loop material flow management should be the prime meta-strategy of the sustainability management of companies. This requires completely different images of organization. In this regard, "industrial metabolism" (Fischer-Kowalski & Hüttler, 1999) and "industrial ecosystem" (Korhonen, 2001) are prominent metaphors. Maybe, eco-efficiency and resource productivity are metaphors in a transition phase in the years. And maybe later so-called metabolism core indicators will complement and partly replace the efficiency indicators. At least, the efficiency approach is compatible with current images of organization. The concept does not require completely new images of organization. Hopefully, the efficiency concept contributes to a shift in thinking about value creation. It is possible to support this way by enhancing the CEMIS by additional metabolism core indicators: absolute material and energy flows, dynamics of stocks over time, Entropy.

REFERENCES

Beattie, B., & Taylor, R. (1985). *The Economics of Production*. New York: John Wiley & Sons.

Berlin, D., & Uhlin, H.-E. (2004). Opportunity cost principles for life cycle assessment: toward strategic decision making in agriculture. *Progress in Industrial Ecology, 1*(1/2/3), 187-202.

Brattlebø, H. (2005). Towards a Methods Framework for Eco-Efficiency Analysis? *Journal of Industrial Ecology*, *9*(4), 9–11. doi:10.1162/108819805775247837

Bunke, D., Gensch, C. O., Möller, M., Rüdenauer, I., Ebinger, F., & Graulich, K. (2003). Assessment of Toxicological Risks due to Hazardous Substances: Scoring of Risk Phrases. *International Journal of Life Cycle Assessment*, *8*(1), 6–7.

Burritt, R., Hahn, T., & Schaltegger, S. (2002). Towards a Comprehensive Framework for Environmental Management Accounting. *Australian Accounting Review*, *12*(2), 39–50. doi:10.1111/j.1835-2561.2002.tb00202.x

Busch, T., Liedtke, C., & Beucker, S. (2006). The Concept of Corporate Resource Efficiency Accounting. In Schaltegger, S., Bennett, M., & Burritt, R. (Eds.), *Sustainability Accounting and Reporting*. Dordrecht: Springer. doi:10.1007/978-1-4020-4974-3_5

Coelli, T. J., Rao, D. S. P., O'Donnell, C. J., & Battese, G. E. (2005). *An Introduction to Efficiency and Productivity Analysis* (2nd ed.). New York: Springer.

Consoli, F., Allen, D., Boustead, I., Fava, J. A., Franklin, W. E., Jensen, A. A., et al. (1993). Guidelines for Life-Cycle Assessment: A Code of Practice. Brussels, Washington, DC: Society of Environmental Toxicology and Chemistry (SETAC).

Diamond, J. (2005). *Collapse – How Societies Choose to Fall or Succeed*. New York: Penguin.

Dyckhoff, H. (1994). *Betriebliche Produktion. Theoretische Grundlagen einer umweltorientierten Produktionswirtschaft*. Berlin, Heidelberg: Springer. (in German)

Ebinger, F., Cahyandito, M. F., von Detten, R., & Schlüter, A. (2006). Just a Paper Tiger? Exploration of Sustainability Reporting as a Corporate Communication Instrument. In Schaltegger, S., Bennett, M., & Burritt, R. (Eds.), *Sustainability Accounting and Reporting*. Dordrecht: Springer. doi:10.1007/978-1-4020-4974-3_23

Eisert, U., Geiger, K., Hartmann, G., Ruf, H., Schindewolf, S., & Schmidt, U. (2001). mySAP Product Lifecycle Management. Bonn: Galileo Press (in German).

Fischer-Kowalski, M., & Haberl, H. (Eds.). (2007). *Socioecological Transitions And Global Change – Trajectories of Social Metabolism and Land Use*. Cheltenham: Edward Elgar Publishing.

Fischer-Kowalski, M., & Hüttler, W. (1999). Society's Metabolism – The Intellectual History of Material Flow Analysis, Part II, *1970 – 1998. Journal of Industrial Ecology*, *2*(4), 61–78.

Frankl, P., & Rubik, F. (2000). *Life Cycle Assessment in Industry and Business – Adoption Patterns, Applications and Implications*. Berlin, Heidelberg: Springer.

Frischknecht, R. (2004). Ecoinvent Database: Quality Control and User Interfaces for a Web-based Life Cycle Assessment Database. In Hilty, L. M., Seifert, E. K., & Treibert, R. (Eds.), *Information Systems for Sustainable Development*. Hershey, PA: Idea Group Publishing.

Funk, B., Möller, A., & Niemeyer, P. (2009). Integration of Environmental Management Information Systems and ERP Systems using Integration Platforms. In Athanasiadis, I. N., Mitkes, P. A., Rizzoli, A. E., & Marx Gomez, J. (Eds.), *Information Technologies in Environmental Engineering*. Berlin, Heidelberg: Springer. doi:10.1007/978-3-540-88351-7_4

Goessling-Reisemann, S. (2008). What Is Resource Consumption and How Can it Be Measured? *Journal of Industrial Ecology*, *12*(1), 10–25. doi:10.1111/j.1530-9290.2008.00012.x

Guinée, J. B. (final editor) (2002). Handbook on Life Cycle Assessment – Operational Guide to the ISO Standards. Boston: Kluwer Academic Publishers.

Habermas, J. (1985). The Theory of Communicative Action: *Vol. 2. Lifeworld and System: A Critique of Functionalist Reason* (3rd ed.). Boston, MA: Beacon Press.

Heijungs, R. (1994). A generic method for the identification of options for cleaner products. *Ecological Economics*, *10*, 69–81. doi:10.1016/0921-8009(94)90038-8

Heijungs, R., & Suh, S. (2002). The computational structure of life cycle assessment. Dordrecht, NL: Kluwer Academic Publishers.

Heiskanen, E. (2001). Institutionalization of Life-Cycle Thinking in the Everyday Discourse of Market Actors. *Journal of Industrial Ecology*, *4*(4), 31–46. doi:10.1162/10881980052541936

Huber, M. (1998). PVC im Kreuzfeuer der Kritik. Die publizistische Auseinandersetzung über den Werkstoff PVC nach dem Brand am Rhein-Ruhr-Flughafen. In Bentele, G., & Rolke, L. (Eds.), *Konflikte, Krisen and Kommunikationschancen in der Mediengesellschaft*. Berlin: Vistas. (in German)

Huppes, G., & Ishikawa, M. (2005a). Why Eco-Efficiency? *Journal of Industrial Ecology*, *9*(4), 2–5. doi:10.1162/108819805775248052

Huppes, G., & Ishikawa, M. (2005b). A Framework for Quantified Eco-Efficiency Analysis. *Journal of Industrial Ecology*, *9*(4), 25–42. doi:10.1162/108819805775247882

Huppes, G., & Ishikawa, M. (2005c). Eco-Efficiency and Its Terminology. *Journal of Industrial Ecology*, *9*(4), 43–46. doi:10.1162/108819805775247891

International Standardisation Organisation. (1996). Environemental Management – Life Cycle Assessment – Principles and Framework – ISO 14040, Paris.

Isenmann, R., Arndt, H.-K., Brosowski, J., Marx-Gómez, J., & Schappert, M. (2007). Using Internet Technologies and Services for Sustainability Reporting: Research Initiative, Agenda, Early Results. In Hryniewicz, O., Studzinski, J., & Romaniuk, M. (Eds.), *EnviroInfo 2007 – Environmental Informatics and Systems Research* (*Vol. 1*). Aachen: Shaker.

Isenmann, R., & Kim, K. (2006). Interactive Sustainability Reporting. Developing Clear Target Group Tailoring and Stimulating Stakeholder Dialogue. In Schaltegger, S., Bennett, M., & Burritt, R. (Eds.), *Sustainability Accounting and Reporting*. Dordrecht: Springer. doi:10.1007/978-1-4020-4974-3_24

Jensen, K. (1992). *Coloured Petri Nets – Basic Concepts, Analysis Methods and Practical Use* (*Vol. 1*). Berlin, Heidelberg: Springer.

Jouliet, O., Margni, M., Charles, R., Humbert, S., Payet, J., Rebitzer, G., & Rosenbaum, R. (2003). IMPACT 2002+: A New Life Cycle Assessment Methodology. *International Journal of Life Cycle Assessment*, *8*(6), 324–330. doi:10.1007/BF02978505

Kaplan, R. S., & Norton, D. P. (2004). *Strategy Maps – Converting Intangible Assets into Tangible Outcomes*. Boston, MA: Harvard Business School Press.

Korhonen, J. (2001). Some Suggestions for Regional Industrial Ecosystems – Extended Industrial Ecology. *Eco-Management and Auditing*, *8*, 57–69. doi:10.1002/ema.146

Krausmann, F., Fischer-Kowalski, M., Schandl, H., & Eisenmenger, N. (2008). The Global Sociometabolic Transition: Past and Present Metabolic Profiles and Their Future Trajectories. *Journal of Industrial Ecology*, *12*(5/6), 637–656. doi:10.1111/j.1530-9290.2008.00065.x

Kreeb, M., Dold, G., Enzler, St., Fischer, H., Hoffmann, A., Krcmar, H., Oettinger, M., Scheide, W., Seifert, E.K., Strobel, M., & Wagner, B. (1997). Fortschritt durch Eco-Intergral. *Ökologisches Wirtschaften*, 5, 16-18 (in German).

Kuosmanen, T. (2005). Measurement and Analysis of Eco-Efficiency. *Journal of Industrial Ecology*, *9*(4), 15–18. doi:10.1162/108819805775248025

Landsiedel, R., & Saling, P. (2002). Assessment of Toxicological Risks for Life Cycle Assessment and Eco-Efficiency Analysis. *International Journal of Life Cycle Assessment*, *7*(5), 261–268. doi:10.1007/BF02978885

Laurin, L., Möller, A., Prox, M., & Schmidt, M. (2006). How Production-theory can Support the Analysis of Recycling Systems in the Electronic Waste Sector. In *Proceedings of the 2006 IEEE International Symposium on Electronics & the Environment*. San Francsisco, CA.

Marx-Gómez, J. (2004). Automated Generation of Environmental Reports – a Case Study. *International Journal of Environment and Sustainable Development*, *3*(1), 65–75. doi:10.1504/IJESD.2004.004689

Möller, A. (2000). *Grundlagen stoffstrombasierter Betrieblicher Umweltinformationssysteme*. Bochum: Projekt Verlag. (in German)

Möller, A. (2005). Dynamic Material Flow Analysis in the Life Cycle Assessment Tool Chain. In Geldermann, J., Treitz, M., Schollenberger, H., & Rentz, O. (Eds.), *Challanges for Industrial Production*. Karlsruhe, Germany: Universitätsverlag.

Möller, A., & Prox, M. (2008). Efficiency Engineering - Requirements for Tools from Industrial Practice. In *Proceedings of the 2008 China Life Cycle Management Conference (CLCM 2008)*. Chengdu, China.

Möller, A., Prox, M., & Viere, T. (2006). Computer Support for Environmental Management Accounting. In Schaltegger, S., Bennett, M., & Burritt, R. (Eds.), *Sustainability Accounting and Reporting*. Dordrecht: Springer. doi:10.1007/978-1-4020-4974-3_27

Möller, A., & Rolf, A. (2001). Eco Product Lifecycle Management. In *Proceedings of the EcoDesign 2001: Second International Symposium on Environmentally Conscious Design and Inverse Manufacturing*. Tokyo, Japan.

Möller, A., & Viere, T. (2005). Material Flow Analysis between Dynamic Modeling and Life Cycle Assessment. In L. Filho, J. Marx-Goméz, & C. Rautenstrauch (Eds.), *Proceedings of the 2nd International ICSC Symposium on Information Technologies in Environmental Engineering (ITEE 2005)*. Aachen, Germany: Shaker.

Morioka, T., Tsunemi, K., Yamamotu, Y., Vabar, H., & Yoshida, N. (2005). Eco-Efficiency of Advanced Loop-closing Systems for Vehicles and Household Appliances in Hyogo Eco-Town. *Journal of Industrial Ecology*, *9*(4), 205–222. doi:10.1162/1088198057752479O9

Page, B., & Rautenstrauch, C. (2001). Environmental Informatics – Methods, Tools and Applications in Environmental Information Processing. In Rautenstrauch, C., & Patig, S. (Eds.), *Environmental Information Systems in Industry and Public Administration*. Hershey, PA: Idea Group Publishing.

PAS 1025 (2003). *Austausch umweltrelevanter Daten zwischen ERP-Systemen und betrieblichen Umweltinformationssystemen*. Berlin: Beuth-Verlag (in German).

Porter, M., & van der Linde, C. (1995). Green and Competitive – Ending the Stalemate. *Harvard Business Review*, *73*, 120–134.

Rautenstrauch, C. (1994). Concepts for Integrated Production and Recycling Planning and Scheduling Systems. In K. Feldmannn (Ed.), *Proceedings of the 2. International Seminar on Life Cycle Engineering RECY'94*. Bamberg, Germany.

Rautenstrauch, C. (1999). *Betriebliche Umweltinformationssysteme – Grundlagen, Konzepte und Systeme*. Berlin, Heidelberg: Springer. (in German)

Reisig, W. (1985). *Petri nets: an introduction*. Berlin, Heidelberg: Springer.

Remmen, A., Jensen, A. A., & Frydendal, J. (2007). *Life Cycle Management – A Business Guide to Sustainability*. Paris: UNEP/SETAC Life Cycle Initiative Publications.

Riebel, P. (1990). *Einzelkosten- und Deckungsbeitragsrechnung* (6th ed.). Wiesbaden: Gabler. (in German)

Riebel, P. (1994). Core features of the 'Einzelkosten- und Deckungsbeitragsrechnung'. *European Accounting Review*, *3*(3), 515–546. doi:10.1080/09638189400000034

Saling, P., Kicherer, A., Dittrich-Krämer, B., Wittlinger, R., Zombik, W., & Schmidt, I. (2002). Eco-Efficiency Analysis by BASF: The Method. *International Journal of Life Cycle Assessment*, *7*(4), 203–218. doi:10.1007/BF02978875

Schaltegger, S., & Burritt, R. (2000). *Contemporary Environmental Accounting – Issues, Concepts and Practice*. Sheffield, UK: Greenleaf Publishing.

Schaltegger, S., Burritt, R., & Petersen, H. (2003). *An Introduction to Corporate Environmental Management – Striving for Sustainability*. Sheffield, UK: Greenleaf Publishing.

Schaltegger, S., & Sturm, A. (1989). *Ökologie-induzierte Entscheidungsprobleme des Managements. Ansatzpunkte zur Umgestaltung von Instrumenten*. WWZ-Discussion Paper No. 8914. Basel: WWZ (in German).

Schaltegger, S., & Wagner, M. (2006). Managing Sustainability Performance Measurement and Reporting in an Integrated Manner. Sustainability Accounting as the Link between the Sustainability Balanced Scorecard and Sustainability Reporting. In Schaltegger, S., Bennett, M., & Burritt, R. (Eds.), *Sustainability Accounting and Reporting*. Dordrecht: Springer. doi:10.1007/978-1-4020-4974-3_30

Scheer, A.-W. (1988). *CIM Computer Integrated Manufacturing – Computer Steered Industry*. Berlin, Heidelberg: Springer.

Schmidt, M. (2005). A production-theory-based framework for analysing recycling systems in the e-waste sector. *Environmental Impact Assessment Review*, *25*(5), 505–524. doi:10.1016/j.eiar.2005.04.008

Schmidt, M., Lambrecht, H., & Möller, A. (2007). Optimisation Approaches in Material Flow Models for Manufacturing Systems. In Hryniewicz, O., Studzinski, J., & Romaniuk, M. (Eds.), *Environmental Informatics & Systems Research* (*Vol. 1*). Aachen: Shaker.

Schmidt, M., Möller, A., Hedemann, J., & Müller-Beilschmidt, P. (1997). Environmental Material Flow Analysis by Network Approach. In Geiger, W. (Eds.), *Environmental Informatics '97* (*Vol. 2*). Marburg, Germany: Metropolis.

Schuhmacher, T. (1997). West Coast Camelot. The Rise and Fall od an Organizational Culture. In Sackmann, S. A. (Ed.), *Cultural Complexity in Organizations. Inherent Contrasts and Contradictions*. Thousand Oaks, CA: Sage Publications.

Taylor, F. W. (1911). *The Principles of Scientific Management*. New York: Harper & Brothers Publications.

Udo de Haes, H. A., Hejungs, R., Suh, S., & Huppes, G. (2004). Three Strategies to Overcome the Limitations of Life-Cycle Assessment. *Journal of Industrial Ecology*, *8*(3), 19–32. doi:10.1162/1088198042442351

Weidema, B., Thrane, M., Christensen, P., Schmidt, J., & Loekke, S. (2008). Carbon Footprint – A Catalyst for Life Cycle Assessment? *Journal of Industrial Ecology*, *12*(1), 3–6. doi:10.1111/j.1530-9290.2008.00005.x

Werner, F. (2005). *Ambiguities in Decision-oriented Life Cycle Inventories*. Berlin, Heidelberg: Springer.

Winograd, T. (1986). A language/action perspective on the design of cooperative work. In *Proceedings of the 1986 ACM conference on Computer-supported cooperative work*. Austin, Texas.

Winograd, T., & Flores, F. (1986). *Understanding Computers and Cognition*. Reading, MA: Addison-Wesley Publishing.

Wohlgemuth, V. (2005). *Komponentenbasierte Unterstützung von Methoden der Modellbildung und Simulation im Einsatzkontext des betrieblichen Umweltschutzes*. Aachen, Germany: Shaker. (in German)

Wohlgemuth, V., Schnackenbeck, T., Mäusbacher, M., & Panic, D. (2009). Conceptual Design and Implementation of a Toolkit Plattform for the development of EMIS based on the Open Source Plugin-Framework Empinia. In Wohlgemuth, V., Page, B., & Voigt, K. (Eds.), *Environmental Informatics and Industrial Environmental Protection: Concepts, Methods and Tools*. Aachen: Shaker.

Section 2
Theoretical and Empirical Approaches

Chapter 2
Green Information Technology and Virtualization in Corporate Environmental Management Information Systems

Edward T. Chen
University of Massachusetts Lowell, USA

ABSTRACT

Businesses today must not only be concerned with their day-to-day operations and the making of profit, but also with a set of challenges related to the public perception, the environment, and the costs of energy consumption. The image of the company from the perspective of customers and the public in general must be carefully monitored as it relates to the environment and the use of natural resources and energy. The demonstration of effective strategies that allow for "greener" and more ecological awareness, will gain the respect of customers, businesses, stockholders, and other concerned groups. The protection of our environment is also a major agenda of firms today. This paper discusses how "Green IT" along with the concepts of "Virtualization" can provide for better organizational, operational, and environmental outcomes.

INTRODUCTION

The large number of personal computers that are present in businesses and the high quantity of servers that are available twenty-four hours and seven days use tremendous amounts of energy and space. Strategic and tactical solutions can be put in place that can effectively reduce costs for organizations and allow for "greener" overall results (Boursas, Hegering & Hommel, 2009; Lee, Eom, Kim & Katerattanakul, 2007). Additionally, by using various Virtualization techniques for hardware, software, and systems, many daily operations can be made more efficient. Incorporation of various strategies can lead to new ways of conducting business such that higher cost savings and less environmental impact can be realized (Casazza, Greenfield & Shi, 2006; Ho, Au & Newton, 2003; Kroeker, 2009; Overby, 2008).

Organizations must always attempt to resolve financial, logistical and environmental issues in order to remain competitive and to be perceived

DOI: 10.4018/978-1-61520-981-1.ch002

superior in the industry and in the public eye. In order to be viable as an organization in this century, concerns for the environment must be considered (Raufflet, 2006). Failures to recognize or act upon these looming challenges will ultimately destroy companies and economies (Schäfer, 2005; Vandermerwe & Oliff, 1990). Creative tactics must be taken into account to strengthen the corporation as well as the world around it (Alexander, 1991; Beaumont, 1992; Brown, Dillard & Marshall, 2005). While organizations are exploring creative alternatives to save billions of dollars, they need to make our environment healthier and more stable (Collison, Lorraine & Power, 2003; Jain, 1984; Lewis, 2004; Pun, Hui, Lau, Law & Lewis, 2002; Walker, Pitt & Thakur, 2007).

WHAT IS GREEN IT

There has been much discussion over the past several years about our environment and the effects of global warming. Organizations such as Greenpeace and influential people such as Nobel-prize winner Al Gore and his documentary, "An Inconvenient Truth", have certainly put much focus on these topics (Alleven, 2008). Perhaps it is this awareness that has made each of us more conscious of the potential outcomes that may ensue if we continue to ignore our environment. This knowledge has moved from our own consciousness to the organizations in which we work. Green Information Technology (IT) is the term used to capture this awareness and to study the potential ways to solve the problems with pollution and consumption of vast amounts of energy in the computing world (Dignan & Perlow, 2007; Sliwa, 2008).

The concerns for economic viability, social responsibility and the effect on the environment are all encapsulated in this concept of Green IT. The outcome of developing solutions that can be more friendly to the environment and at the same time more economical for the corporation has led many to believe that the ultimate goals of an organization are simply to take advantage of the concept by exploiting and touting the concept of being "green" for marketing purposes and for the potential profit gains that could be realized. Although this argument may contain some truth, one should ask the following question. Is it not better that companies be concerned for the environment, whether it be for legitimate reasons or selfish reasons, so that the ultimate goals of society can be realized? A corporation has an obligation to both its shareholders and to the economic viability of society in general (Tiemstra, 2003). If the outcome of being "green" allows a company to be more profitable either by means of better efficiency or by better public relations, then so be it, as long as the ultimate worldly consequences are reduced (Brown, Dillard & Marshall, 2005; Collison, Lorraine & Power, 2003).

WHAT IS VIRTUALIZATION

The term "Virtualization" has multiple meanings depending on the context of the discussion, but it can be summarized as the creation of logical pools of IT resources not linked to physical devices (Scheier, 2007). When used in the context of servers, virtualization refers to the use of special software which allows systems administrators to install multiple operating systems on the same physical piece of hardware. When used in the context of desktops, it refers to the hosting of individual user sessions or desktop operating systems at a central location. When used in the context of storage, virtualization refers to the dissemination of data over a wide range of physical locations in an attempt to achieve optimized access across a large geographical area.

Virtualization, in a broad sense, is the simulation of a real physical entity. In the information technology field, this term is used to describe a means of hiding the physical characteristics and technical details of a system from the user (Casazza, Greenfield & Shi, 2006; Ho, Au & Newton, 2003; Kroeker, 2009). For example, virtual servers are computer systems that can provide multiple users with a perception that they are being used exclusively, but in fact, the same computer system may be serving the needs of several users. The system has the power to serve the needs of many applications but physically consists of one set of hardware. This allows a better utilization of equipment such that idle time of a computer is minimized. The result of this Virtualization is better utilization of hardware and thereby an ultimate reduction in the use of energy to run the systems (Casazza, Greenfield & Shi, 2006). Costs are reduced not only by the reduction in necessary hardware and infrastructure but also in costs to power the systems and the surrounding infrastructure (Kendler, 2007).

POWER CONSUMPTIONS

The amount of power that is used by IT equipment is increasing at an enormous rate. With the cost of fuel and the impact on the environment, recent efforts as well as older initiatives have been an issue among IT professionals as well as among government and regulatory agencies. Back in 1992, the US Environmental Protection Agency (EPA) began the Energy Star program as an attempt to ask computer manufactures to develop systems that are more energy efficient. Initially this program got off to a slow start and then became a big focus of some manufactures attempting to capitalize on the marketing capabilities that this type of public relations advertising could potentially stimulate. Eventually, the energy compliance became more of a standard and was expected by the public. Thus, it is diminishing the marketing agenda (Sanchez et al., 2008).

In May and June 2007, IBM, Google, and Intel launched initiatives in an attempt to address the issues of power consumption. IBM launched a one billion dollar program entitled, "Project Big Green", which was structured to design and promote energy in all of their corporate data centers (McLaughlin, Liu, DeGroff & Fleck, 2008). Similarly, Google and Intel launched a program entitled, "Climate Savers Computing", to reduce the consumption of PC power (Kempf, 2008). It is evident that many of the big players in the computing industry recognize the importance of these initiatives and are taking major steps in attempting to help with the issues at hand. Although the reasons for these major efforts are not just for the environment, the response and example being set by these corporations is extremely important. From a selfish point of view, these initiatives are critical to the corporations as well. Power consumption and costs are having a major impact on the businesses of today. It is important for the viability of these corporations that action is taken.

The amount of power that is consumed by a single PC or server has been increased rapidly over the past several years due to the need for increased performance and smaller packaging. Computer servers used in data centers need to constantly be upgraded and replaced with higher performing systems. Due to a lack of physical space, these servers have also been reduced in size. The result is a server that is smaller, more powerful, and unfortunately more power consuming. This results in an increase in the overall density per square foot of real estate. For example, in the past decade, the increase in power density per square foot has increased by more than ten-fold. An average power density of 300 watts ten years ago is now at 4000 watts (Wang, 2007). This trend is still apparent today and is still growing at similar rate or higher.

A large amount of energy is needed in these systems to power hardware that is not always needed or used one-hundred percent of the time. A typical power supply that converts the line voltages from the power company's alternating current grid to a direct current power for a computer system is not efficient. There is an inherent loss in power in the form of heat that occurs during this conversion. Having power supplies in each of these systems therefore wastes a considerable amount of energy. In the near future, efforts must be made to lower the power consumption of peripheral devices, such as display monitors, by using lower power technology. More efficient power supplies need to be produced that convert power without expending as much waste in the form of heat. Shifting systems into a low power mode when peak performance is not needed can also be scheduled. Each and every small effort that is made to reduce power consumption and the dissipation of heat should be put into action. The law of diminishing returns may prevent what is really needed in this industry. Virtualization will become more and more prevalent to reduce our current energy consumption rates. Eventually, however, the demand for additional performance and quantity of servers will reduce the effectiveness of Virtualization as well. More innovative technology, better forms of reusable energy and creative thought must be given to this continuing problem.

HELPING THE ENVIRONMENT

We need to find ways to lower our power consumption and reduce the amounts of heat and other pollutants into the atmosphere. Additionally, the amount of hardware that is used and is then discarded, due to newer technology or better performance, must be reused or recycled. It is estimated that carbon dioxide emissions from servers and other computing components account for 0.75% of all annual amounts of emissions. Contributing to this amount, other IT and telecommunications equipment constitutes at least two percent to this output (Fuchs, 2008). Additionally, alone the United States uses twenty-five percent of the entire world's electricity of which one and one-half to three percent is absorbed by data centers alone. This amount of energy has doubled in the past five years and is expected to more than double again in the next five year period (Anonymous, 2009).

In order to combat these frightening numbers, Green IT initiatives must be developed and deployed. Utilization of more efficient cooling systems and the use of better insulation techniques will aid towards the reduction of data center power usage and production of excess waste (Kavanagh, 2009). Applications of Virtualization to reduce the quantity of servers in data centers thereby reducing the amount of energy consumption for power and cooling of servers will also be better for the environment (Overby, 2007; Wang, Du, Chen & Li, 2008).

Marketing Perspective

Marketing executives are banking on the "Green" concept to develop plans that will allow them to demonstrate to the public and to their customers that they are concerned for the well being of the world. Through the corporation's product offerings and demonstration of green tactics, the organization can not only benefit from the publicity of the concept but can also benefit from potential cost savings in the production of their products. This "do-good-and-win scenario, image and the substance behind it – is everything" concept is what marketers feel, is an opportunity ready for the "picking" (Kilbourne & Marshall, 2005).

In recent surveys of American consumers, it was found that ninety percent would choose products that are produced from environmentally conscious companies as long as the costs were comparable (Marketing News, 2008). Because of information like this, marketers believe that it is essential for corporations to take action in ensuring that their image is viewed in a positive manner from a customer's "green" expectations perspective. It is important that consumers understand the commitment to both their needs as well as the needs of the environment. Demonstrations and leadership in the Green initiative can provide both short and long term benefits to the firm (Xu & Roland, 1995).

In order for firms to benefit from this new and potentially explosive opportunity, it is important that they understand the level of commitment and resource that will be necessary to undertake such a change in operations and tactics. It should also be realized that this opportunity to differentiate the firm from others is short in time. Consumers really care about these topics today and will continue to care about them in the future; however, the opportunity to be viewed as a pioneer will not last forever. Eventually, the actions of being green will be expected and customers will not reward companies for their involvement in what is considered routine and required. In comparison to a historical episode that occurred in the 1980's, quality systems such as six-sigma were initially used by marketing professionals to tout the advantages their firms had in developing better and more cost effective products (Marketing News, 2008). This advertising proved to be very beneficial to the leaders that developed and utilized this process. However, many competitors quickly invest in the same processes. It eventually causes many of the marketing benefits to diminish. One should note that these programs, even though expected, still provide much benefit to organizations. Although the marketing benefits may be reduced, the concepts and the benefits of better quality systems and better cost savings are still tangible assets to an organization. On a larger scale, being Green is better for the world, and that principle should not be undervalued (Beaumont, 1992; Kilbourne & Marshall, 2005; Koch, 2000).

Corporation Benefits

Going Green is not only good for the environment and the world in general but is also good for business. Employing the various concepts of Green IT can strengthen a corporation and provide side benefits that are not obvious upon immediate evaluation. In the past decade, the emphasis has been on buying more and more computer power with higher and higher processing capabilities. It was assumed that the necessary infrastructure, including power, cooling, and building space was readily available and affordable. This is not the case today. Infrastructure is the predominant concern and limiting factor for most businesses today. As businesses attempt to grow they are challenged by the excessive costs of energy, lack of space, government regulations, and pressure from society (Kavanagh, 2009; Wildangier & Jensen, 2006).

As businesses have grown, their reliance on computer systems and data has grown as well. Google, for example has close to a half million servers in its network. Their continued expansion is requiring more powerful and faster computing power in addition to more storage capacity for their data (Wang, 2007). This ultimately results in higher energy costs and more facilities to house the equipment. Unfortunately, many of the existing facilities that exist today are not equipped to handle the massive amounts of power required or the cooling capabilities necessary to keep the facilities at appropriate temperatures. The heat generated by all of this equipment must be removed properly in order to insure proper reliability. It is estimated that reliability of hardware decreases by fifty percent for every eighteen degrees above seventy-eight degrees Fahrenheit (Wang, 2007). These levels of poor reliability would be devastating to organizations, especially those that rely on data warehousing as a primary operation for their business. The reality of the situation is that it is now costing a substantial amount of operating budgets to power and cool equipment. These costs are overshadowing the costs of actual equipment. It is interesting to note that the problems with facilities and the ability to power and cool equipment is at critical stages for almost 50% of businesses in operation today (Kavanagh, 2009). These limitations cause businesses to have limited growth potential even though the need for their services and products is in high demand. In today's competitive and global environment, issues like this are a thorn in a firm's operations.

In addition to the operational obstacles that hinder business growth, governments are raising concern for the environment and are putting pressure on IT organizations to identify and develop solutions to the power consumption and environmental issues that their businesses are contributing to. One way or another, corporate officers, customers or governments will eventually demand that all businesses deal with the issues that are confronting our society (Tiemstra, 2003). The cost of doing business will certainly need to anticipate these changes. Establishing a plan for the infrastructure needs to deal with these issues is of upmost importance. Ensuring that this plan meets the rapidly expanding demands of the future is a business practice that will have long lasting benefits (Walker, Pitt & Thakur, 2007; Videras & Alberini, 2000).

Cost Effectiveness

Corporations are learning new ways to cut costs by experimenting with various conditions and measuring the overall benefit. It is important that companies share this information so as to provide others with similar benefits. Many of these cost optimization techniques potentially bring firms to a competitive edge. Corporations may hold those cost reduction practices as confidential and proprietary properties. On the other hand, there is sometimes a contradiction in doing the most admirable thing for a business versus doing the right thing for society. Other times, there is somewhat of an overlap and both entities benefit from the outcome (Kavanagh, 2009; Overby, 2007).

Reduction of costs can be accomplished in a variety of manners. There are quite a few obvious approaches that have been touched upon in preceding sections of this document. Other approaches are a little more creative but equally provide high potential outcomes. A few approaches are listed below for the reader to consider and ponder upon.

It has been determined from a study performed by a consortium of companies that are dedicated to maximize the efficiency of data centers, that at least sixty percent of the power required to cool IT equipment is wasted due to inefficient infrastructure (Overby, 2007). Costs saving can be enhanced by simply controlling the costs of power and cooling by methods previously described and by making certain that the way in which facilities are cooled and insulated meets appropriate standards. Efforts should be made to improve the facilities layout and thermal infrastructure. For example, taking the hot air produced from equipment and moving it to other areas that require heat to maximize and utilize a by-product of the IT equipment in an effective manner. Moving a facility to another part of the world where alternative energy can be used rather than fossil fuel based energy is both a cost effective tactic as well as an environmentally conscious activity (Kavanagh, 2009; Overby, 2007).

It has also been estimated that most servers and desktop computers are only used eight to fifteen percent of the time. Unfortunately, when computers are idle, their power draw is not. The hardware itself, whether idle or active, consumes sixty to ninety percent of typical workload power requirements (Kavanagh, 2009; VMWare, 2008). A simple way to address these issues and to cut costs is to make certain that systems purchased have a low power mode of operation such that when not on active duty, they consume less energy. Automatically powering down servers during periods of low demand can decrease energy costs by as much as eighty percent (Kavanagh, 2009; VMWare, 2008).

Finally, Virtualization is one of the most important and perhaps the most common method of cutting costs by effectively reducing the number of servers required to perform the work in demand. Even though it may be relatively easy to determine the costs of power and cooling for IT servers and equipment, it is not always easy to justify a large scale restructuring in terms of return on investment. Reduction in servers by using Virtualization techniques can save on the cost of utilities. But, there is also a cost associated with replacing the lower performance servers and a cost associated with buying the Virtualization software and supporting infrastructure. These costs are not insignificant and will be scrutinized by management. A solid business case must be developed to demonstrate the benefits both in terms of the bottom line and in terms of the long term strategic viability and benefits (Casazza, Greenfield & Shi, 2006).

MOTIVATION AND CHALLENGES FOR VIRTUALIZATION

In the early days of computing, the mainframe was considered to be the most powerful and useful computing machine of the twentieth century. The advent of the personal computer then became the next major innovation to take over the high technology sector. A shift from centralized to distributed computing appeared to be the most efficient means of supporting the demand for industry. Now a shift to virtualized computing has taken on a new set of issues. In a way, some of the concepts of the mainframe are coming back into play (Brookshire, 2001).

Mainframe computers which house a significant amount of resource capabilities can be used in similar ways that high performance servers can be used. The efficiency of a single mainframe that can be structured to handle multiple operations and applications simultaneously is a strong contender for managing enterprise level applications. Depending on the processing load, one could argue that a high performance and large scale mainframe might be more effective than a cluster of individualized servers. Depending on the design of the system, mainframe computer systems may come back as a viable platform to support multiple applications and concurrent operations (McLaughlin, Liu, DeGroff & Fleck, 2008). Needless to say, Virtualization may have a place in the mainframe platform as well. Perhaps mainframes will be used in conjunction with a variety of other systems. In fact, it should not be of concern to the application developed or to the end user if the true intent of Virtualization is to be honored.

It should be noted that Virtualization will, by definition, bring about the benefits of efficiency and flexibility. The true test, however, is in the way that it will be able to deal with the issues of security, reliability, maintenance, and overall performance (Aiken, Boroumand & Wolff, 2004; Fisher, 2005). In current traditional server based architectures, there is a close knit association between the specific application and a dedicated server. Although this is effective from a programming and maintenance perspective, it does not facilitate the easy distribution of services to balance workload requirements.

Virtualization, on the other hand, does provide all of the necessary functionality to allow highly decoupled hardware and software integration. This ultimately allows applications to be deployed to the most appropriate and available server (capability and size) at any instant in time. More or less servers can be commissioned either manually or automatically based on demand needs or other criteria. There are some challenges that must be addressed with Virtualization. First, it will be important to demonstrate that virtual systems are robust, fault tolerant, secure, predictable in performance and cost effective. The ability to demonstrate these attributes will determine how successful an IT manager is in convincing management for the endeavor. Additionally, hardware costs are typically about ten percent of the IT budget whereas administrative and maintenance activities constitute approximately seventy percent of the budget. The suggestion to replace large quantities of servers with virtualized systems helps with hardware costs but may increase costs of overhead. This makes the approach less attractive to management (Fisher, 2005). An approach that outlines the overall long term benefits in terms of cost and in terms of environmental impacts must be stressed on multiple dimensions. Finally, on a very specific note, software licenses distributed by vendors typically are issued to a fixed quantity of servers. If Virtualization is to be employed, an appropriate licensing scheme or new business model must be developed since it is rather difficult to track the effective use of a particular application submitted to a virtual environment.

CORPORATE SHIFT TO SERVICE-BASED IT

It is always interesting to look back into the past and to compare the current state of affairs with those of a period a long time ago. In the world that we live in today, it seems unlikely that events of another century would have any applicability to the present, however, this is not the case. Take for example the case of electric power generation at the turn of the twentieth century. For years, each industrial organization developed the necessary power to supply its plant by using natural resources such as waterfalls to generate electricity or steam engines to drive electric generators. In years to follow a shift from self supplied energy to utility supplied grid energy occurred (Carr, 2005).

At first, the economic and logistical benefits were not very obvious. Today most would agree that the business of producing energy should be left to the utility companies (Bryden & McCorkle, 2005). It is far easier to purchase the necessary power than to actually generate it. It seems highly likely that in the years to come, IT infrastructure could shift to follow a similar utility type model. This type of revolutionary change will change the entire IT landscape for corporations. As discussed above, the issues of power consumption, cooling and infrastructure in general could be shifted to a utility company. The net effect is that a business can re-focus on its business and not have to be concerned with the burdens introduced by IT complexities. "IT is shifting from being an asset companies own to a service they purchase." (Bia & Kalika, 2007; Carr, 2005).

In most scenarios, the cost to purchase services from utility companies is too economically feasible to ignore. The reality is that, a transition to this model will take time. There is evidence, however, that a shift may lie in the horizon. The current atmosphere suggests that the time is coming when utility based capabilities will be available. Shifting to centralized supply tends to be more attractive when overcapacity is coupled with redundant functionality. This is currently the case with most large scale IT firms. If a system were to be put in place, it seems likely that a shift would occur. Obviously, this shift would take time and effort to fully accomplish (Bia & Kalika, 2007; Carr, 2005; Kraut, Steinfield, Chan, Butler & Hoag, 1999).

Once a move to utility based computing occurs, the need for personal computers and other standalone devices will potentially diminish. The concept of providing devices that allow connection to a service based utility for computing will take the place of PC's. This will allow a centralized infrastructure to be put in place and thereby eliminate the massive number of systems deployed in businesses that are essentially sitting idle on desks the majority of the time. Cost savings, power savings, and environmental savings will be enhanced astronomically (Waters, 2005).

INFORMATION STRATEGY TRIANGLE: IMPLICATIONS

According to the Information Systems Strategy Triangle, links between business strategy, organizational strategy and information strategy must always be kept in balance. If they are not, corporate crisis can potentially result. It is important that the cart follow the horse. That is to say, the following rules should apply when discussing the IS Strategy Triangle (Pearlson & Saunders, 2006):

- Business strategy must drive both organizational and information strategy
- Organizational strategy must complement business strategy
- Information strategy must complement business strategy
- Organizational strategy and information strategy must complement each other

When deciding the level of changes to make to the IT segment of the business, it is important that a clear definition of the business strategy be formulated. Regarding this context, it should be noted that before decisions to launch a "Green" initiative are made, the business strategy must first be laid out (Tinsley, 2002). If it is not in the interest of the firm to spend additional capital and resources on investigating and implementing a green strategy, then the program should be immediately dismissed. If the business strategy supports the efforts to move in the direction of the green initiative, then, both the organizational and IT strategy must be planned and reviewed. Organizationally, a plan must be put in place to define, coordinate and control all of the necessary processes that will be needed to achieve success with the business plan outlined. IS-wise, a determination of the necessary corporate capabilities and the architecture to achieve the desired goals must be put in place.

Let us take an example that illustrates the effects of altering one side of the IS Strategy Triangle. This example (Williams & Curtis, 2008), modified slightly, is a clear example of the cause and effect relationships that are created when one aspect is dynamically altered. When a company decides to allow employees to telecommute in an effort to save on office space and to help the environment at the same time, the effect is that more IT infrastructure is needed to support the effort. The business decision to take on this venture causes organizational changes as well as IT changes. Additional computer systems are required and a virtual private network (VPN) needs to be established. This in turn affects the organization because more employees will be needed in the IT department to handle the maintenance and setup of the VPN and surrounding infrastructure. Simultaneously, the fact that employees are no longer working under the same roof has caused communication and coordination problems amongst the staff.

In order to resolve these issues of energy consumption, video conferencing has been determined to be the solution. This in turn puts further burdens upon the IT team. Meanwhile, the interaction with the customer base has been affected because of the lack of coordination between sales and service personnel. Was the decision to move employees to home offices a good one? From the perspective of the operating costs and environment, it might be. From the perspective of the business and customers it may not have been. The point is, detailed planning and coordination across the whole organization is essential to the successful implementation of a companywide strategic change (Cowherd & Luchs, 1988; Ferguson, 1996; Koch, 2000).

When making decisions about the implementation of a Green approach, all departments and organizational entities need to carefully evaluate whether or not a change in one area will have positive effects in another area. If programs are simply put in place for the sake of being green only to upset the balance of the organization, the net success will not benefit the corporation. It is important that the positive outcomes of going green also benefit the organization, employees, and customers such that ideally a win-win situation prevails. There is no perfect solution that will satisfy the needs of all organizations or corporate strategies.

Cost savings in one area will most likely produce higher costs in another area. There will always be different perspectives from the various segments of the firm. Some will see the changes in a more positive light than others. The important thing to focus on is whether or not the outcome meets the business objectives established. If the outcome creates more work or higher levels of planning in one part of the organization but produces higher profits for the company for the business strategy plan, the plan can be considered as successful (Green & Ryan, 2005; Lee, Eom, Kim & Katerattanakul, 2007). The following set of lists (table 1) demonstrates the interactions of technology areas, potential impact areas and the metrics that may be used to measure success (Williams & Curtis, 2008).

Each of the technology areas are potential areas where changes can and will be made. The effects of these changes will impact various areas within the organization. The measurement of success is dictated by the metrics that are established based on the goals and objectives that were initially intended.

DOES IT PAY TO BE GREEN?

Many argue that the additional costs of attempting to be "Greener" counteract any potential business benefit that a firm may realize. So, the real question is why a firm would want to invest in being green if it cannot justify it from a cost basis. Research has shown that greener organizations tend to exhibit better economical performance than less green organizations but there is no supporting evidence that it is a result of their level of greenness (Telle, 2006; Liu, Sia & Wei, 2008).

It may not be cost justified to become green for the sole and selfish reason of the bottom line, but it may be justified based on ethics and a general overall concern for the environment. Providing benefits to society may not be tangible assets for a company to possess but the good-will that is demonstrated will certainly provide priceless satisfaction and credibility to the organization. This demonstration of concern will solicit customer loyalty and will ultimately reward the firm in ways that may not be easily traceable. In summary, it seems quite obvious that ultimately it pays to be green for the sole purpose of demonstrating good-will and showing concern for society.

Obviously there are many challenges for a company to overcome to become Green. The important parts are related to the success of the business and the overall benefit to the environment. Decisions and tactics should be put in place to maximize the benefit of both these objectives. One must also be aware that there is no perfect solution that will satisfy the needs of all. In fact a positive outcome in one area is probably offset by a negative outcome in another area. Establishing business objectives that advance the firm's best interests and allow a firm to play an important part in society should be the ultimate objective. The rest will follow by a course of natural events.

CONCLUSION

Over the next few decades it will be interesting to see the overall ambition of corporations in response to the environmental challenges that our world is

Table 1. Interactions of technology areas

Technology Areas	Impact Areas	Metric Areas
Client Platform	Customer Experience	Business
Business Execution Platform	Employee Experience	Regulatory
Operating Execution Platform	Partner Experience	Carbon Footprint
Management Platform	Public Experience	Power Consumption
Communications Platform	IT Operations	Pollution Amount
Facilities Platform	Business Operations	

being exposed to. This coupled with the fact that costs of doing business are accelerating at rapid rates makes it interesting to forecast the future business landscape. Corporations and individuals bear the challenge and respond with wise decisions regarding the use of vital resources and the production of environmental toxins. We can find a happy medium where profits can be made at little or no expense to the surrounding world. Our technical advancements and desires will make the world a better place for this generation as well as our great grand children's generation. Now is the time to respond to the challenges. As executives and managers in the businesses that we work in, it is our responsibility to force change that can minimize our footprint on the world. It is also our responsibility to facilitate the profitability of the firms in ways that ensure success but do not compromise our surroundings. Both agendas are achievable.

Though there is a lack of a comprehensive research literature for the specific topic of Green IT and Virtualization, this paper draws on research results and insights from a broad array of disciplines. Much of the information of Green IT and Virtualization was provided in the sources found as listed in the references. Several of the topics researched in this paper gave the readers a better comprehension what server Virtualization is all about and how changes in the IT landscape provide substantial benefits to organizations and at the same time to help our challenges on earth.

Future research should analyze the viability of moving to a service based IT infrastructure in the United States. Following the model of electricity at the turn of the twentieth century, it would be an interesting exercise to dive into the details of making a twenty-first century mapping of an "IT Computing Grid". Looking at all of the similarities to electric power but recognizing all of the subtle and difficult scenarios that exist, it would be interesting to research, experiment and perhaps prototype a working model of this structure.

REFERENCES

Aiken, R. J., Boroumand, J., & Wolff, S. (2004). Network and computing research infrastructure: Back to the future. *Communications of the ACM*, *47*(1), 93–98. doi:10.1145/962081.962086

Alexander, J. A. (1991). Adaptive Change in Corporate Control Practices. *Academy of Management Journal*, *34*(1), 162–193. doi:10.2307/256306

Alleven, M. (2008, April 2). Going Green. *Wireless Week*, 14-15.

Anonymous,. (2009). Green remediation information available on the Web. *Hazardous Waste Consultant*, *27*(2), 1–5.

Beaumont, J. R. (1992). Managing the environment: Business opportunity and responsibility. *Futures*, *24*(3), 187–205. doi:10.1016/0016-3287(92)90030-J

Bia, M., & Kalika, M. (2007). Adopting an ICT code of conduct: An empirical study of organizational factors. *Journal of Enterprise Information Management*, *20*(4), 432–446. doi:10.1108/17410390710772704

Boursas, L., Hegering, H., & Hommel, W. (2009). Standards and new technology for systems and virtualization management: A report on SVM'08. *Journal of Network and Systems Management*, *17*(1-2), 99–104. doi:10.1007/s10922-009-9117-5

Brookshire, R. G. (2001). Letter from the editor: Large scale computing and the technology curriculum. Information Technology, 24(2), i-iii.

Brown, D. L., Dillard, J. F., & Marshall, R. S. (2005). Strategically informed, environmentally conscious information requirements for accounting information systems. *Journal of Information Systems*, *19*(2), 79–103. doi:10.2308/jis.2005.19.2.79

Bryden, M., & McCorkle, D. (2005). Virtual engineering: in powerful new workspaces, the next-generation power plant is only the beginning. *Mechanical Engineering-CIME*, *127*(11), 38–41.

Carr, N. G. (2005). The End of Corporate Computing. *MIT Sloan Management Review*, *46*(3), 67–73.

Casazza, J. P., Greenfield, M., & Shi, K. (2006). Redefining server performance characterization for virtualization benchmarking. *Intel Technology Journal*, *10*(3), 243–251. doi:10.1535/itj.1003.07

Collison, D., Lorraine, N., & Power, D. (2003). An exploration of corporate attitudes to the significance of environmental information for stakeholders. *Corporate Social Responsibility and Environmental Management*, *10*(4), 199–212. doi:10.1002/csr.45

Cowherd, D. M., & Luchs, R. H. (1988). Linking Organization Structures and Processes to Business Strategy. *Long Range Planning*, *21*(5), 47–55. doi:10.1016/0024-6301(88)90104-5

Dignan, L., & Perlow, J. (2007). Green IT: Why it matters? *ZDNet*. Retrieved April 26, 2007 from http://blogs.zdnet.com/BTL/?p=4929

Ferguson, G. T. (1996). Strategy in the digital age. *The Journal of Business Strategy*, *17*(6), 28–31.

Fisher, M. A. (2005). Virtualised computing infrastructure. *BT Technology Journal*, *23*(3), 52–58. doi:10.1007/s10550-005-0030-5

Fuchs, C. (2008). The implications of new information and communication technologies for sustainability. *Environment, Development and Sustainability*, *10*(3), 291–319. doi:10.1007/s10668-006-9065-0

Green, A., & Ryan, J. J. (2005). A framework of intangible valuation areas (FIVA): Aligning business strategy and intangible assets. *Journal of Intellectual Capital*, *6*(1), 43–52. doi:10.1108/14691930510574654

Jain, S. C. (1984). Environmental scanning in U.S. corporations. *Long Range Planning*, *17*(2), 117–128. doi:10.1016/0024-6301(84)90143-2

Kavanagh, R. (2009). IT virtualization helps to go green; businesses can use their green IT effort to enhance their public image, increase their agility and cut their operating costs. *Information & Management*, *19*(2), 20–27.

Kempf, P. (2008). Green, Greener, Greenest: the New Technology Horizon. *Canadian Electronics*, *23*(2), 6–11.

Kendler, P. B. (2007, August 1). Virtualization Reality: by optimizing computing resources, virtualization can lower infrastructure operating costs while improving business agility and speed to market. *Insurance & Technology*, 42.

Kilbourne, W. E., & Marshall, K. P. (2005). The transfer of for-profit marketing technology to the not-for-profit domain: Precautions from the theory of technology. *Journal of Marketing Theory and Practice*, *13*(1), 14–25.

Koch, C. (2000). Building coalitions in an era of technological change: Virtual manufacturing and the role of unions, employees and management. *Journal of Organizational Change Management*, *13*(3), 275–289. doi:10.1108/09534810010330922

Kraut, R., Steinfield, C., Chan, A. P., Butler, B., & Hoag, A. (1999). Coordination and virtualization: the role of electronic networks and personal relationships. *Organization Science*, *10*(6), 722–741. doi:10.1287/orsc.10.6.722

Kroeker, K. (2009). The Evolution of virtualization. *Communications of the ACM*, *52*(3), 18–20. doi:10.1145/1467247.1467253

Lee, J., Eom, M., Kim, B. O., & Katerattanakul, P. (2007). Virtual Organization: Resource-Based View. *International Journal of E-Business Research*, *3*(1), 1–16.

Lewis, G. J. (2004). Uncertainty and equivocality in the commercial and natural environments: the implications for organizational design. *Corporate Social Responsibility and Environmental Management, 11*(3), 167–177. doi:10.1002/csr.64

Liu, C., Sia, C., & Wei, K. (2008). Adopting organizational virtualization in B2B firms: An empirical study in Singapore. *Information & Management, 45*(7), 429–437. doi:10.1016/j.im.2008.06.005

Marketing News (2008, February 1). Going Green. *Marketing News*, 15-18.

McLaughlin, G. T., Liu, L. Y., DeGroff, D. J., & Fleck, K. W. (2008). IBM Power Systems platform: Advancements in the state of the art in IT availability. *IBM Systems Journal, 47*(4), 519–533. doi:10.1147/SJ.2008.5386517

Overby, E. (2008). Process Virtualization Theory and the Impact of Information Technology. *Organization Science, 19*(2), 277–292. doi:10.1287/orsc.1070.0316

Overby, S. (2007, March 26). How Green Data Centers Save Money. *CIO*, 1-5.

Pearlson, K. E., & Saunders, C. S. (2006). *Managing & Using Information Systems – A Strategic Approach* (3rd ed.). Hoboken, NJ: John Wiley & Sons.

Pun, K. F., Hui, I. K., Lau, H. C. W., Law, H. W., & Lewis, W. G. (2002). Development of an EMS planning framework for environmental management practices. *International Journal of Quality & Reliability Management, 19*(6/7), 688–709. doi:10.1108/02656710210429573

Raufflet, E. (2006). Re-mapping corporate environment management paradigms. *International Studies of Management & Organization, 36*(2), 54–73. doi:10.2753/IMO0020-8825360203

Sanchez, M. C., Brown, R. E., Webber, C., & Homan, G. K. (2008). Savings estimates for the United States Environmental Protection Agency's ENERGY STAR voluntary product labeling program. *Energy Policy, 36*(6), 2098–2108. doi:10.1016/j.enpol.2008.02.021

Schäfer, H. (2005). International corporate social responsibility rating systems: Conceptual outline and empirical results. *Journal of Corporate Citizenship, 20*, 107–120.

Scheier, R. L. (2007). Virtualization 101. *Computerworld*, (October): 15, 54–56.

Sliwa, C. (2008). Green IT: Buzzword or strategy? *Tech Targets*. Retrieved February 27, 2008 from http://searchcio.techtarget.com/tip/0,289483,sid182_gci1302716,00.html?track=NL-983&ad=626565&asrc=EM_NLT_3154136&uid=2470905The

Telle, K. (2006). It Pays to be green – A premature conclusion? *Environmental and Resource Economics, 35*(10), 195–220. doi:10.1007/s10640-006-9013-3

Tiemstra, J. P. (2003). Environmental policy for business and government. *Business and Society Review, 108*(1), 61–69. doi:10.1111/1467-8594.00009

Tinsley, S. (2002). EMS models for business strategy development. *Business Strategy and the Environment, 11*(6), 376–390. doi:10.1002/bse.340

Vandermerwe, S., & Oliff, M. D. (1990). Customers Drive Corporations Green. *Long Range Planning, 23*(6), 10–16. doi:10.1016/0024-6301(90)90096-M

Videras, J., & Alberini, A. (2000). The appeal of voluntary environmental programs: Which firms participate and why? *Contemporary Economic Policy, 18*(4), 449–461. doi:10.1111/j.1465-7287.2000.tb00041.x

VMWare. (2008). Green IT - reduces energy costs and goes green with VMWare virtualization. *VMWare*. Retrieved April 12, 2008 from http://www.vmware.com/

Walker, D., Pitt, M., & Thakur, U. J. (2007). Environmental management systems: Information management and corporate responsibility. *Journal of Facilities Management*, *5*(1), 49–61. doi:10.1108/14725960710726346

Wang, D. (2007). Meeting Green Computing Challenges. *IEEE*, 1244-1253.

Wang, X., Du, Z., Chen, Y., & Li, S. (2008). Virtualization-based autonomic resource management for multi-tier Web applications in shared data center. *Journal of Systems and Software*, *81*(9), 1591–1608. doi:10.1016/j.jss.2007.11.719

Waters, B. (2005). Software as a service: A look at the customer benefits. *Journal of Digital Asset Management*, *1*(1), 32–39. doi:10.1057/palgrave.dam.3640007

Wildangier, A., & Jensen, J. (2006). Virtual infrastructures in GXP regulated industry. *Journal of GXP Compliance*, *11*(1), 48–53.

Williams, J., & Curtis, L. (2008). Green: The New Computing Coat of Arms. IEEE, 12-16.

Xu, X., & Roland, K. G. (1995). Building market intelligence systems for environment scanning. *Logistics Information Management*, *8*(2), 22–29. doi:10.1108/09576059510084975

Chapter 3
Innovation and Sustainable Development:
From Mainstream Innovation Theory to Sustainable Innovation Research

Michael von Hauff
University of Kaiserslautern, Germany

Andrea Jörg
University of Kaiserslautern, Germany

ABSTRACT

Many economic roundtables have proclaimed innovation as the key to economic growth. The theoretical basis for this view is amply demonstrated by today's modern innovation theory. However, the fact that innovation also carries ecologic risk was, until recently, largely ignored. The potential for ecologic risk occurs when technologies are developed that threaten environmental damage that perhaps, does not become significant until well into the future. Risk may also occur indirectly when new technologies generate higher productivity but are also responsible for an additional burden on the environment. In principle, within the context of the sustainable development paradigm, innovation must be compatible with the three dimensions: Ecology, Economy and Society. The aim of this paper is to discuss the deficits of the mainstream innovation theory in the context of sustainability in addition to the role and significance of innovation in environmental engineering. This especially includes the opportunities and limitations of eco-innovation with respect to the current environmental policies for sustainable economic growth. A future challenge for research from a business perspective is to align eco-innovation as an integral component of an environmental management information system (CEMIS). In this context, eco-innovation can make a major contribution to environmental protection. However, within the scope of this paper, the focus is primarily on the rationale for sustainable innovation, in particular, eco-innovation.

DOI: 10.4018/978-1-61520-981-1.ch003

INTRODUCTION

Innovation is desirable from both an economic mainstream perspective as well as in the interests of sustainable growth. Nevertheless, each of these perspectives stresses the importance of innovation for vastly different reasons. Innovation per se is good from the economic perspective as long as it fulfills the following condition: if an invention brings success in the market, the innovation is deemed positive. However, from the perspective of sustainable development the positive effects accrue only if all three dimensions, i.e., ecologic, economic, and social are considered in the development of the innovation. Consequently, the manner in which innovation in the economy has been discussed and classified until now is the subject of further review in this paper. However, within the scope of this paper only a few important justifications for innovation research can be adequately discussed. A comprehensive overview of the study of innovation is provided by Welsch (2005) and Corsten (2006).

Innovation has a special significance in economics. It is often viewed as the result of technological progress. Technological progress, in turn, is seen as the motor of economic growth. This implies that the competition to be innovative in a market economy is a major determinant in the dynamics of growth. In a narrow sense, innovation is described as any technical advance that improves the production output. However, a fact that frequently goes unnoticed from the perspective of sustainable growth is that the innovation can also have a negative effect, for example, on the environment or on the health of the population.

In the study of innovation, the examination or analysis of an individual innovation is increasingly seen as insufficient because the situation during the early development and realization of the innovation is not considered. The modern study of innovation, which had its origins in 1980s, has attempted to point out that to fully understand an individual innovation and its development, it is necessary to consider it as part of an innovation system. Although there is still question as to whether innovation systems in the context of sustainable development can be more easily judged as negative or positive based on their impact.

The paradigm of sustainable development presents specific requirements, which naturally apply also to innovation. Innovation has to be integrated in the triad of ecological, economic, and social considerations. However, in a review of past sustainable innovation studies, it must be noted that the focus has been on the ecological sustainability. The chief concern has been on the progress in environmental engineering or eco-innovation. An Environmental Management Information System can be of major importance for the strategic promotion of eco-innovation: CEMIS, as a special kind of information system, promotes strategic goals which seek to integrate economy and ecology. The optimization potential is to a large extent related to the system boundaries.

In contrast to the focus on the relationships between ecology and economy, it appears that the conceptual linking of all three dimensions in the study of sustainable innovation is at a very early stage. The general challenges for sustainable innovation are presented in the next section along with a discussion of the distinctions between the two theoretical approaches to sustainable innovation and a review of the contrasting positions. The conclusion is concerned with the resolution of this controversy. A summary of the major findings is presented in the concluding section.

INNOVATION AND SUSTAINABILITY

Sustainable innovation is a new paradigm in the study of innovation. Consequently, we first look at the mainstream economic research concerning innovation and then list the specific requirements for sustainable innovation.

Differentiating Innovation

The characterization of innovation usually starts with the distinction between process and product innovation. This is generally understood as the objective, initial introduction of a new production process or a new product to the market. New production processes are associated with an improvement that allows the same level of output to be achieved with less input (OECD – Eurostat, 1997). In the case of a product innovation, for many years new goods were focused on material goods, whereas, this has been expanded more recently by the inclusion of new services. An important aspect here is to specify the degree of innovation. Basic innovations, i.e., production processes or products that capture previously unknown application areas and markets are often differentiated from larger process and product modifications. Basic innovation is discussed in terms of the Kondratieff cycle. The Kondratieff cycle is based on the work conducted in 1920s by the Russian scientist Kondratieff, and includes a period of 40 to 60 years (Kondratieff, 1926).

The exhaustion of economic growth potential through basic innovation extends over several decades and leads to a long term growth dynamic. The process and product modifications are more or less a matter of comprehensive change applied to an existing process or product. The degree of innovation is what matters. Basically, the term innovation from an economic perspective includes an assessment of the market success of the invention. A successful market introduction of a new invention generates a monopolistic profit for the company. Limiting our understanding of innovation to technical engineering is increasingly subject to criticism. It was noted fairly early on that innovation goes beyond process and product innovation and includes new management and organizational processes (Konrad & Nill, 2001). For this reason, the term is used to a growing extent for non-technical improvements such as changes in company structure or project design. This is why current empirical research includes, in addition to process and product innovation, also organizational innovation (Rennings, 2005). Organizational innovation is further broken down into the optimization of business structures and processes and new management concepts like environmental management.

If we were to move away from the assessment criterion "inventions per se are good if they are commercially successful" and introduce as the assessment criterion the principle of sustainable development, it could lead to conflict in evaluating those innovations that do not satisfy the requirements for sustainable development. An innovation can be assessed as successful under the market economy criteria without any consideration given to the external effects, which may compare negatively according to the principle of sustainable development if the innovation is linked, for example, to health problems.

Schumpeter is widely acknowledged as the first economist to have analyzed the importance of technological innovation to the economic development process in depth (Schumpeter, 1964). According to Schumpeter, the development of market systems is characterized by uncertainty, interaction, and change. Economic growth, according to Schumpeter, is therefore a "process of creative destruction". Consequently, those products or processes must be abandoned when pushed out by new innovations. In economic innovation research, Schumpeter's differentiation of the innovation process as a linear sequence of phases has asserted itself as the dominant model. Here, inventions are generated and subsequently developed in the invention phase, especially by the professional research departments of large corporations, and then introduced to the market. For many years, innovation remained on the periphery of economic theory (Welsch, 2005). The growth theories discussed the supply of new technologies as the engine for growth, which subsequently lead to the technology-push hypothesis.

In contrast to the technology-push hypothesis, Schmookler proposed the need-pull (demand-lead) hypothesis, whereby innovation arises from a perceived market need (Schmookler, 1966). The ensuing debate lasted for many years with no clear outcome. Today however, there is a broad consensus, that both supply factors and demand factors play an important role in the innovation process (Hemmelskamp, 1999).

Innovation Systems

This brief discussion of the theoretical approaches demonstrates the complexities underlying the innovation processes. A major reorientation in the study of innovation is emerging with the introduction and explanation of technological progress as an endogenous process in growth theory. Technological innovation is subject to greater control under this view. As a result, the linear models of the innovation process have been rejected. Recent approaches focus more on the interaction among the actors and the overall framework conditions. This serves as the basis for the reorientation on national and regional innovation systems, which tend to take evolutionary and institutional economic aspects more into account.

Lundvall's general description of an innovation system consists of interactive elements and relationships in the production, diffusion and use of new and economically useful knowledge (Lundvall, 1992). Freemann goes further to relate the innovation system to a network model, in which he defines the innovation system as a network of institutions in the private and public sectors whose activities and interactions create, import, modify or distribute new technologies (Freemann, 1987). In this respect, several authors have pointed out what is essential for innovation in the context of sustainable development, i.e., the optimal conditions or the best basis for interactive innovation cannot be created by the market alone or by the hierarchies (Welsch, 2005). Therefore, networks appear to be highly suitable. It can be assumed that they support the key factor, i.e., the social capital needed to generate and develop the innovation process.

In terms of the difference between national and regional innovation systems, it can be said that the national systems are characterized by features strongly influenced by the respective national economic and social system. The regional differentiation today, since the dissolution of the planned economies of the socialist system, focuses on differences in the western industrial nations between the Anglo-Saxon market economies and the types of social economy found in continental Europe. Analog to this are the different national innovation systems.

The national innovation systems are differentiated still further. In terms of the subdivisions listed above, national innovation systems are considered in both a narrow and in a broader sense. In the narrow sense, national innovation systems are noted above all for their private sector research and development facilities, universities, and research institutes. In a broader sense, the production sector, the market system, and the financial system are considered as subsystems of the innovation system. Hübner and Nill distinguish between the knowledge sector, i.e., the actors, organizations, and rules applicable to the production of knowledge, and, the productivity sector, i.e., the actors that decide the choice between alternative technologies and manner of employment of these technologies (Hübner & Nill, 2001).

In this context, special attention is given to the institutional landscape, for example, under the framework of institutional economics as discussed by North (North, 1990). Modern innovation systems are thus integrated to a large extent within the institutional structures of the government and the large companies. In order to classify national innovation systems, the factors that influence the innovation process have to be analyzed. In this respect, methods have been developed that permit the quantification of inputs and outputs of a national innovation system by the use of indicators (Patel

& Pavitt, 1994). The individual indicators, which include subcategories like education, science and research, innovation funding, and the production of high tech goods, are grouped to form composite indicators which are then used to measure the efficiency of the national innovation systems. In the case of Germany, four important fields of action are indentified that have a strong relationship to the principle of sustainable development: promote investment in education, support participation by a broad sector of the population in the innovation processes, strengthen incentives to innovation, and insure diversity in national innovation systems (Belitz & Schrooten, 2008).

The regional innovation systems are defined differently than the national innovation systems. Interest in these systems is increasing, with terms like clusters or innovative milieus entering the vocabulary (Braczyk et al., 1998). They are most often clearly characterized by the geographic boundaries that limit the spillover of knowledge. It is still important in the context of the subsystems of an innovation system to consider the impact of innovation on social, economic, and cultural conditions in a country or region as well as how those systems can influence innovation.

To this extent, it may be said that there is an interdependent process, in which the innovation system is not only affected by institutional arrangements but that it also affects them as well. Unruh introduces the idea of the "techno–institutional complex" (Unruh, 2000). Established and stabilized by a techno–institutional system, the system is highly resistant to change. A typical example, cited by Unruh is the energy market and the production of electrical power. Structural change in this sector is very difficult because of extremely high resistance by the electricity generating plants. Without massive government intervention, new or renewable sources of energy have only a small chance of being implemented (Foxon et al., 2005). In summary, it is clear that both national and regional innovation systems can provide a solid basis for meeting the challenges of sustainable development.

Nevertheless, such expansion is sometimes met with ambivalent opinions. From the sustainable development perspective, there is an advantage in overcoming the fixation on technology-based innovation. On the other hand, expanding the scope of the definition of innovation too far may result in the inclusion of all kinds of change processes or inventions and the term loses its effect. This also applies to sustainable innovation, where the objective is not a listing of all sustainability potential; rather it is about identifying requirements for specific sustainable innovation.

Technological innovation exhibits a clear dominance while, in contrast, the study of social innovation is relatively recent. The relationships between reforms, social innovation, and social change are being constructed in the process. Gillwald defines reform as government action and intervention into the societal regulatory and institutional structures. In this respect, reforms can be viewed as a subset of social innovation (Gillwald, 2000). Against this, Gillwald assigns social innovation as a subset of social change. The commonality between technological and social innovation is that both are the result of human design. In terms of the emergence of new processes and products or elements, innovation in a social context is possible and not only in the technical engineering sense.

Requirements for Sustainable Innovation

Summarizing the overall economic discussion to date about innovation, we find the major success factor is economic success: an invention becomes a successful innovation when it succeeds in the market. However, from today's sustainability perspective, additional dimensions have to be taken into account, like the social and ecologic dimensions. The issue is not exclusively about the direction of the innovation, but rather about the range of social and ecological change brought about from the innovation. An understanding of sustainability as a three dimensional model requires appropriate identification as well as an integrative assessment of the three dimensions (Fichter, 2005).

Another problem in the assessment of sustainable innovation arises from the fact that, ex ante, it occurs more or less under conditions of uncertainty. This has to be considered in the selection of criteria as well as the evaluation methods. Scenario techniques as well as the Delphi method are particularly useful here, for example, in answering the question of what technologies are to be classified as a risk technology. A potential conflict – as mentioned above – can arise when the sustainability oriented technologies do not possess the same impact as risk technologies. A solution is to subsidize research activities in the sustainability oriented technologies to increase its impact to a point where it can compete with the risk technology. This requires a path correction. In other words, in the context of sustainable innovation research it is necessary in addition to process and product innovation, to consider institutional, organizational, and even behavioral change to a much greater extent.

In the following discussion, it must be acknowledged that the ecological dimension has made a stronger contribution in scientific research than the social dimension. For this reason, the focus of the next section on ecological sustainability is about innovation. The conceptual linking of ecological, economic, and social dimensions is still in the early stages of sustainable innovation research.

Innovation in Ecological Sustainability

Since the mid-1990s, ecological innovation (or eco-innovation) has been the subject of increasing attention. In the process, eco-innovation has come to include all measures taken by the actors (corporations, government agencies, associations, churches, private households) to develop, introduce, or apply new ideas and behaviors, products, and production processes that help to preserve the environment or contribute to ecologic sustainability (FIU, 1997).

The application of eco-innovation provides the certainty that a specific level of output can be attained with lower inputs of non-renewable resources and less consumption of renewable resources, i.e., these innovations increase resource efficiency and reduce the negative effects on the environment (Ewringmann & Koch, 2006). According to Porter and van der Linde – as seen in an idealistic way by the innovator – ecological innovations enable economic gains and relief for environmental stress (Porter & van der Linde, 1995). In this context, a market for environmental protection technologies has developed that returns above average growth rates. In this respect, two problems are worthy of brief mention here (Hübner & Nill, 2001):

- Ecological innovation is linked to a large extent with positive external effects, which has a tendency to lead to an undersupply of innovation. Positive external effects occur outside of the markets. In principle, this can benefit everyone.
- Ecological innovation meets with resistance. The reason for this is the path dependency of existing development models. From a sustainability perspective, this poses the risk of suboptimal innovation paths being selected.

For ecological sustainability, it is important that the eco-innovations include the economic and social dimensions required for the implementation of the innovation. Again, it is emphasized that innovations for ecological sustainability feature a broad, tangible content and a specific direction of progress. It is all about new or modified processes, technologies, systems, or products to avoid or reduce environmental damage. This rather broad definition is developed by Hemmelskamp and others, as they classify every type of innovation as an eco-innovation that contributes to an improvement in the quality of the environment, independent of whether it is technological, organizational, economic, legal, or behavioral and regardless of the motivation that leads to the eco-innovation (Hemmelskamp et al., 2000). Technological innovation is the main focus of the following sections because it lends itself to better formal presentation, for example, in the endogenous growth theories.

According to the Oslo Manual of the OECD (1992), technological innovation is differentiated – as described above – between two types: process innovation and product innovation. In addition, a distinction is made between precautionary and aftercare measures. These measures are further differentiated between integrated and downstream measures (the so called, additive or end-of-pipe technologies). However, the integrated technologies have the major role when it comes to sustainable development (UBA, 1997; BMBF, 1997).

INNOVATION IN THE CONTEXT OF NEOCLASSICAL AND ECOLOGICAL ECONOMICS

A controversy arises concerning the reasons for eco-innovation in discussions about mainstream ecological economics. It is necessary to first review eco-innovation in the context of neoclassical economics and ecological economics to better illustrate this controversy between the two opposing positions. The concept of "balanced sustainability" has been proposed as a possible solution to this issue. Eco-innovations have the tendency to aim for economic and ecologic sustainability, while often neglecting the social dimension. Nevertheless, here we will examine eco-innovation in the broad sense and attempt to integrate the social dimension into the discussion.

Innovation in Neoclassical Economics

The eco-innovation mentioned above is different from other innovation in that it possesses a double externality. This double externality is explained as follows: every type of innovation generates a positive external effect (spillover effect) from the basic R&D efforts. The spillover results from the fact that the newly generated knowledge is not just available to the innovator but also to the general public. The special character of the eco-innovation emerges in parallel to this. New products and processes are invented, which have an external benefit in and of themselves (e.g., lower costs), but also provide a benefit the general public. In a perfect market this external effect is internalized and the problem of double externality is averted. In this way, eco-innovations can be treated as normal innovations (Rennings, 2005).

This is why in neoclassic economics, coordination of environmental and innovation policy is only necessary during a transition phase that allows for the internalization of all "externalities" into the budgets. Environmental and innovation policy can be seen as partially complementary. A sound innovation policy makes it possible to reduce the development costs of eco-innovation, especially in the invention and market introduction phases (Rennings, 2005). Innovation policy can further contribute to the maturation of the innovation in the diffusion phase. However, in an imperfect market, coordination of innovation policy and environmental policy is necessary to resolve the second externality.

Left uncoordinated the double externality tends to create a shortage of eco-innovation which forces another peculiarity – a regulatory conditionality. The underlying determinants of eco-innovation are the rate of technological progress (technology push) and the market influences (market pull). Pavitt has shown that both of these determinants are relevant (Pavitt, 1984). The technology push factors include for example, better eco-efficient technologies, whereas preferences for environmentally friendly products or corporate image aspects are listed among the market pull factors. Technological push and market pull factors alone are not adequate to insure the success of eco-innovation and special regulatory supports are required. In this context, there must be a differentiation of integrated and additive environmental technologies.

The major motivation for the introduction of integrated environmental protection technologies is cost savings, whereas this is not relevant for additive technologies. In contrast, strict environmental control statutes have a positive effect on both types of innovation (Frondel et al., 2004). Product innovations are more influenced than process innovations by market factors while the latter is more driven by regulation (Cleff & Rennings, 1999). In neoclassic eco-economics, tools such as taxes or tradable credits are viewed as the policy tools with the greatest dynamic efficiency. Dynamic efficiency means that the measures provide a long term incentive for a cost efficient decline in pollution. Following this discussion of innovation in neoclassic economics, the next section explores innovation in ecological economics.

Innovation in Ecological Economics

In contrast to neoclassical theory, which proceeds from the concept of limitless substitution of natural capital by man-made capital, the ecological economists understand the limited availability of nature. This poses a major problem for sustainable development, which also has substantial relevance for growth policy. When sustainable development is the goal, innovation is necessary in order to decouple economic growth from the negative effects on nature. It clearly highlights the requirement to limit expansion and the need for an absolute reduction in the depletion of natural resources, especially the non-renewable resources (Costanza et al., 2001). There are three types of growth in terms of the sustainability dimensions –ecologic, economic, and social (Luks, 2005): economic expansion (measured by the indicator GNP), growth in resource consumption (for example, measured by the indicator energy flow rates), and advances in the quality of life (for example, measured by the indicator water quality).

This calls into question the possibility of a sustainable economic expansion within a limited environment and the related question, what role does innovation have in this situation. Sustainable expansion is only possible when there is a decoupling of the material and energy flows. This decoupling in turn is dependent on innovation. In an economic expansion, an absolute reduction in natural resource consumption or a positive change in macroeconomic resource efficiency are only possible if there is ecological change that affects the economy.

Several of the arguments expressed pose problems. First, production "out of thin air" brings us no closer to the goal and, secondly, the decoupling always measures only a periodic change in the flows from one period to the next. There are no findings reached about the "cumulative inventory" of ecological damage – to include already existing environmental pollution. If the carrying capacity of the ecosystem is overburdened, the goals must be set short of this capacity limit. This is not necessarily guaranteed by decoupling. Furthermore, there is always a risk that the growth rate of the gross national product will overcompensate for the efficiency gains that enable decoupling. This is the fundamental problem in the innovation, expansion, and sustainability relationship.

Ecological economics requires an economy without growth for sustainability (Costanza, 2001). This implies from an ecological economic standpoint that a physical, quantitative, steady-state expansion at the macroeconomic level is not possible. However, growth is possible, in the shape of a qualitative change. The crucial problem involves the relationship between physical expansion and qualitative development. Here, innovation plays a decisive role as it is the major factor in the process of decoupling between scale and gross national product (Luks, 2005).

Innovation reflects two assumptions from an economic-ecological view. One is that economic growth (i.e., without decoupling from resource depletion) is directly associated with ecological disadvantages. The other is that innovation always leads to ecological opportunities, i.e., a relative lowering of the depletion of natural resources. In other words, it can lead to a decoupling of growth and the environment. Proponents of ecological economics recognize the risk in overestimating the contribution that innovation can make to sustainable development. The divergent positions of neoclassic and ecological economics relative to innovation have been presented, which serves to explain the current controversy.

Controversy between Neoclassical and Ecological Economics

The proponents of neoclassic environmental economics tend to think that natural capital can be substituted with man-made capital and propose the paradigm of weak sustainability. The preservation of nature is not of primary importance, rather the safeguarding of the common welfare. Growth is the key to sustainability for the supporters of weak sustainability. In 1974 a concept was formulated at the Symposium on the Economics of Exhaustible Resources that proposed a non-declining optimal consumption per capita over time. This would permanently preserve the average social welfare of man.

The key axiom here is the interpretation assigned to the rule of capital preservation. The aggregate capital stock is the abstracted total of man-made capital and the state of the environment expressed in the form of natural capital. The environmental economists, in terms of the capital preservation rule, have the goal of preserving the aggregate capital for the long term. The safeguarding of a non-declining capital per capita leads to intergenerational fairness. By holding capital stock at a constant level, the average value also remains constant. This begs the question of how to assess the future costs of ruining nature today.

For innovation theory, this means environmental oriented innovation is to be preferred only when it is cheaper than non-environmental oriented innovation. Furthermore, in the neoclassic approaches, incomplete information about the technological options, the unforeseeable, and the high transaction costs is further neglected. Beyond this, the approaches in environmental economics follow a simple stimulus-response model of regulation and neglect the fact that there is a complex bundling of determinants that influence innovation decisions at the company level as well (Rennings, 2005).

Ecological economics on the other hand is concerned with the unsolved problems of environmental economics and arrives at the paradigm of strong sustainability. Many proponents of ecological economics take a very critical attitude about quantitative economic growth. Correspondingly, the economic subsystem ceases any further expansion and perhaps, in the industrialized countries, it should even shrink. Man-made capital is not a substitute for natural capital. For this reason, the core principle of weak sustainability is rejected. Strong sustainability stands in opposition to the discounting approach and the possible compensation of future generations (weak sustainability). Apart from repudiating the concept of unlimited substitution of the two kinds of capital, supporters of strong sustainability assume that future generations do not prefer to be compensated for the loss of nature with man-made capital.

As a consequence of continuing destruction of the natural environment, natural capital may become a limiting factor of production, which according to economic logic will require investment to replace. The depletion of non-renewable resources must be reduced and replaced with an increased use of renewable resources, although not through the use of other forms of capital. The relevance of innovation is not yet appreciated in the process. Ecological economics has not adequately embraced the phenomenon of "innovation" and the more recent insights of modern innovation theory. Physical, quantitative growth is not possible in ecological economics, but development i.e., qualitative change is possible. Another problem is that growth limits cannot be determined on the basis of scientific perceptions. This is why in terms of growth and the role of innovation, the main challenge for sustainability policy rests in communicating the finiteness of the environment (Luks, 2005).

A Resolution to the Controversy

The so called "balanced sustainability" is an attempt to combine the strengths of each concept and avoid the "too strong" or "too weak" assumptions. In contrast to strong sustainability which considers the slowdown or stop of expansion as an imperative, weak sustainability aspires to more growth as the key to sustainability. It claims that a general rejection of growth fails to take into account the positive effects that may be produced by a controlled expansion. According to the Brundtland Report, the best way to combat poverty is through growth in the industrial and developing countries. Even environmental protection for motivational, structural and financial reasons is facilitated by growth. Both factors, growth and environmental quality, must be decoupled from one another, which appears possible through increased efficiency, conservation, recycling, structural improvement, and the greater use of renewable resources.

Balanced sustainability considers the slowdown or stop of expansion solely as a potential result of an ecological restructuring of the society (Steurer, 2001). It strives for the harmonization of growth and environmental quality. Balanced sustainability also makes the assumption that not only must aggregate capital be preserved but, because of the limited substitutability of natural capital, at least the most essential elements of natural capital (climatic equilibrium, global material cycles, forests, wetlands, ozone layer, etc.) must be kept constant. Natural capital and man-made capital are neither totally complementary, nor completely interchangeable (Ott & Döring, 2004). Therefore, a minimum reserve for the less critical elements is advocated (Pearce & Turner, 1990).

In the next section, we introduce a model for growth that conforms to the concept of balanced sustainability by taking innovation in the form of environmental technologies into account. In the model, the ecological dimension is represented by the environmental quality and the state of the environment, the economic dimension by economic growth and the social dimension by the benefits that accrue to the individual from a cleaner environment.

INNOVATION, GROWTH AND SUSTAINABILITY

In the concept of balanced sustainability innovation is essential in order to generate sustainable growth. Here, both additive and integrated environmental technologies are of special interest. With respect to the inputs, environmental technologies involve the substitution of environmentally harmful substances and the use of secondary raw materials in place of primary ones. Changes in the production processes permit the integration of new process components (e.g., heat recovery) and the substitution of single process components and, in some cases, even the substitution of an entire production process. Integrated measures can further reduce residues and emissions or even eliminate them entirely.

When the innovation helps to implement a preemptive environmental technology – especially an integrated protective measure – it is possible that this sustainable innovation will generate sustainable growth, while at the same time providing for the ecological sustainability dimension. Concurrent with the lower consumption of natural capital, an ecological improvement may result.

The mid- to long term advantages of the integrated technologies compared to the additive technologies with regard to ecological and economic efficiency leads to the assumption that integrated technologies will be of increasing micro- as well as macroeconomic importance. Additionally, in view of international competition it is quite reasonable to promote environmental technology and realize the full potential at an integrated level. Of course, it is important to acknowledge that even in the future additive engineering will not be entirely replaced by the unbounded use of integrated technologies. Only an appropriate combination of additive and integrated technologies will ease the burden on the environment in the future. Thus, even the increased use of integrated technologies cannot prevent every harmful emission.

Sustainable innovation must also consider the economic and social dimensions in addition to the ecological dimension. This approach is the only way to realize the comprehensive goals of sustainable development. The ecologic dimension describes how the environment is impacted by economic variables and feedback mechanisms. The economic dimension, identified with the manufacturing function, describes how economic goods are produced from man-made and natural inputs. The social dimension is characterized by the utility function, which includes the utility of both natural and man-made goods.

The Ecological Dimension

$$\dot{N} = \frac{dN}{dt} = E(N, R)$$

Economic activities draw upon the resources of nature and for every emission level R, there will be a constant level of environmental quality N.

$N = Nb - U$ with $U = Z + R = (> 0$ if $U < Reg$; ≤ 0 if $U \leq Reg)$

The state of the ecology is calculated as the beginning stock N_b, less the environmental pollution U generated in production processes. Here, the environmental pollution is considered as the sum of resource consumption Z and the associated pollution R. The environmental burden (U) takes on a positive value when the pollution generated in production is greater than nature's capacity for regeneration (Reg). In other words, if the regeneration rate of nature was greater than the burden (a negative U), the result would be a better state than at the start.

In contrast, when the increase in the level of pollutants is greater than nature's regenerative ability, which can also be expressed as the increase in the rate of return on renewable resources, the regeneration and absorption capacity of the environment is reduced. When the environmental quality is at a highly sound level, nature is able to absorb contaminants or emissions and the pollution is relatively less damaging to regenerative capacity as is the case with an initially poor environmental quality. On the other hand, higher levels of pollution do in fact increase the stress on nature. The best environmental quality is defined as a world in which pollution does not exist. However, nature can no longer reach a state where there is no pollution nor can it continue to absorb additional pollutants, because the regenerative capacity is limited. The capacity of the environment to accept stress as a waste dump is limited.

$R = G (Ra, Ri, Rz)$

This reflects a breakdown of the pollutants R into Ra, Ri, and Rz:

- **Ra:** Pollutants from additive technologies
- **Ri:** Pollutants from integrated technologies
- **Rz:** Pollutants from the combined use of additive and integrated technologies
- **G(.):** Function for determining aggregate emissions

It is irrelevant how the emissions are produced; there is always an increase to the aggregate emissions. Therefore, it is important to examine how the expected change in the type of emission impacts the aggregate pollution.

The level of emissions is higher with the use of additive environmental engineering compared to integrated technologies due to the fact the former technology is added at a later stage and does not solve the actual problems (harmful substances) that are generated during the production processes. Although problem substances are removed downstream by filter units, some pollutants still reach the environment in spite of these units. Likewise, the subsequent necessity of emptying the filters creates a further problem for the environment when used as a waste dump. Integrated technologies are introduced earlier in the production process and, in this way, preclude the occurrence of the environmental pollutants. Therefore, the ensuing environmental problems are fewer with integrated technologies than with additive engineering and there is less overall strain on the environment.

The assumption is that the introduction of integrated technologies can decrease the amount of pollution generated in the production processes and in turn, reduce the aggregate level of emissions. An increased use of integrated technologies implies less reliance on the additive technologies. By reducing the aggregate level of emissions there is less pollution and a declining demand to use the environment as a waste dump.

The substitution of additive with integrated technologies means more natural capital is preserved because there is less environmental pollution i.e., there is a reduction in both pollution and resource consumption. In this way, the result is a decline in the consumption of natural capital over time.

The Economic Dimension

The economic dimension is divided into two sectors. The first sector is for man-made goods manufactured either for purposes of consumption or investment. This sector is called the capital manufacturing sector. The second sector is called the knowledge or environmental sciences R&D sector. In this sector, investment in human capital is made to generate an accumulation of knowledge about environmental protection technologies.

The model recognizes three types of capital: natural capital (N), "physical" capital (K), and environmental engineering knowledge (human capital h).

$$Y = F(N, K_Y, U_Y, A)$$

The production yield Y is to large extent a function of the production factors: natural capital N, capital employed in production K_Y, environmental strain U_Y and the environmental protection expense A. Increasing the use of natural capital N places a limit on production as the continued depletion of resources and the emissions must be reversed. The situation can be improved through the introduction of integrated eco-technologies that reduce both the demand for resources and the emissions and simultaneously, the burden on the environment. The result is an increase in production yield (Y) with the same input level of natural capital.

The production yield can also be increased by raising the level of employed capital, although the input of K is, as shown above, a rival capital. The additional capital can either be employed to raise the production yield or be invested in the R&D sector of the environmental protection technologies. In order to result in an improvement in natural capital, the additional capital must be employed in the R&D sector of the environmental protection technologies to support the development of new integrated technologies that in turn improve environmental quality. More capital must flow to the manufacturing sector to insure an increase in the production yield and economic growth. However, this would then be at the expense of R&D in the environmental engineering sector.

Production yield can also be raised by increasing the strain on the environment. However, this corresponds to greater depletion of natural capital. The key to the integrated technologies is that the same production yield can be attained with declining resource input or, with the same resource input the yield can be increased. Therefore, economic growth is possible at a constant level of resource input. However, any severe decline in a resource input would result in declining economic growth, a situation which is precluded in this model.

Increasing the expenditures for environmental protection lowers the production yield. The conversion of production facilities to integrated technologies initially generates higher environmental protection expense for the company although these amortize or even overcompensate over time. The environmental protection expense, in the form of pollution taxes, certificates and other obligations, decline with the use of integrated technologies because fewer emissions and waste products are being generated.

The environmental engineering knowledge is dependent on the employed capital in the environmental engineering R&D sector. A gain in environmental engineering knowledge has a direct affect on the continuing development of integrated engineering technologies. A decline in the employed capital would result in a stagnation of knowledge. Clearly for this reason, investment is required.

In summary, it can be observed that capital can be employed either to invest in the R&D sector or to increase production. As an investment in the environmental engineering R&D sector, the capital input has the effect of lowering production, as this capital does not lead directly to a higher output. However, because of such an investment there is a rise in the environmental control standards through integrated technology. This, in turn, lowers the demand for natural capital, reduces the damage to the environment and lowers the pollution tax expense. In the longer term, it does produce an increase in productivity.

If capital is directly employed towards production, there is a rise in output. However, this also places a higher demand on the environment, an immediate depletion of the natural capital and to higher environmental protection expenses. As a result, the actual production yield declines. The question is which of these production yields is valued as the most desirable.

The Social Dimension

The social dimension shows that individuals benefit, both from consumer goods C, as well as the environmental quality N where ϑ represents the subjective time preference. The removal of pollutants improves environmental quality and there is an improvement seen in the social dimension in the form of utility gains because of the better quality of the environment, for example, in better health and the quality of life. This is the corresponding outcome of the transition from additive to integrated environmental technologies, along with a greater overall benefit to the individual.

$$W = \int_0^\infty U(C, N) \cdot \exp(-\vartheta t)\, dt$$

Conditions for a Balanced Growth

An increase in the production yield or, economic growth, can be achieved in several different ways. Even with the lower consumption of natural resources and reduced levels of harmful pollutants being generated, higher outputs are possible with less damage to the environment simultaneously just through the substitution of additive engineering by integrated technologies. The assumption in the model is that the introduction of integrated technologies will decrease the amount of pollution generated in the production processes and in turn, reduce the aggregate level of pollution. Likewise, through integrated engineering, resource depletion is lowered. Consequently, the individual derives a greater benefit from an improved environment. The input of capital to the R&D sector leads to an increase in environmental engineering knowledge and to the constant advanced development of integrated environmental engineering. In this way, natural capital is preserved as fewer emissions are generated and the demand for resources is reduced. This creates less stress on the environment and again lowers pollution tax expense. The production yields are higher and there is economic growth.

The input of capital solely to the manufacturing sector also leads directly to an increase in production. Therefore, for an optimal increase in output and economic growth, capital should be employed in both the manufacturing sector and the knowledge sector.

Critical Analysis and Outlook

The findings based on the model illustrate that the shift from additive technologies towards integrated engineering systems can ease the burden on the environment while simultaneously advancing economic growth and improving utility for the individual. In this way, innovation generates sustainable growth. The explanation for this is found in the lower demand for resource input and in the production of fewer harmful emissions. Nevertheless, even with integrated environmental technologies, resource depletion can also occur over and above the regenerative capacity of nature. Furthermore, emissions may be generated that could permanently damage the eco-systems and the volume of pollutants may be higher than the natural assimilation limits of the environment as a waste dump. This also depends on the time period involved in making the shift to the integrated technologies and how large the percentage of affected additive engineering is. It is also further dependent on the rate of technological progress.

Some factors remain outside the scope of the model, i.e., the initial state of the environmental quality is a critical determinant. For this reason, the quality must be defined right at the beginning of the observation period so that the optimal resource consumption and the optimal volume of emissions can be determined. In this respect, considering the ever-changing events (e.g., ecological disasters like forest fires) environmental quality is not assumed to be fixed. The environmental quality is subject to continuous change, which of course, may also be positive (e.g., establishment of new protection zones or forest areas). This requires constant adjustment for the changing situation, something which is very difficult to model. Nevertheless, it has been demonstrated that under certain conditions, higher growth rates are possible in conjunction with environmental conservation.

Empirical Findings

Considering the progress in environmental engineering over time, especially in terms of the differentiation in additive and integrated technologies, different development trends become evident. One of the first empirical studies of the manufacturing trades is supported by environmental protection investment data collected by the German Federal Office of Statistics (v. Hauff & Solbach, 1999). Data is available for the period from 1975 to 1994. The data categorizes total investment in environmental protection in the production process according to purpose, i.e., as expenditures for additive, integrated, or product related investments.

The study revealed that integrated environmental protection during this period, in contrast to expectations, played a less significant role. On average, only 18 percent of the total investment in environmental protection was contributed by integrated engineering. The greatest share, at 76.6 percent of investment was represented by the additive protection measures. Only 5.3 percent was invested in product related environmental protection measures. Noticeable also was the fact that all sectors of the manufacturing industry had a similar investment structure. Over the entire period, investments in additive environmental protection rose, whereas product related declined. The portion of integrated environmental protection meanwhile remained nearly constant. This means that additive environmental protection even extended its dominant position compared to integrated engineering over time.

More recent empirical studies have concluded that integrated environmental engineering has made substantial gains (Frondel et al., 2004). A comparative country study of seven OECD nations for the year 2003, found that on average 76.8 percent of investment was in the integrated environmental technologies and only 23.2 percent went towards the additive environmental technologies. However, there was also a great difference between the countries: Germany, with a share of 57.5 percent in integrated environmental technologies was in last place, while Japan with 86.5 percent was the group leader. These findings have also been confirmed by other studies (Rehfeld et al., 2004).

Contrary to this was the pattern concerning the relative percentages for environmentally friendly product innovation. Of the surveyed companies, only 15.6 percent have decided to focus on environmentally friendly product innovation. However, the facts discussed below concentrate on environmentally friendly process innovation. In comparing the empirical findings from the mid-1990s with those from 2003, it must be noted that the survey from 2003 was distributed only to companies with more than 50 employees. Therefore, the findings from this survey do not include observations from the category of small sized companies.

Nevertheless, it may be assumed here that as the size of the company grows smaller, both the environmentally oriented process as well as product innovation has a tendency to decline. This is how a study of the topic "Raising the competitiveness of small businesses through eco-efficiency" determined that many small companies ignore the subject of eco-efficiency, i.e., in both process and product innovation (Hauff et al., 2005). If a representative study of all business were to be conducted, the findings would show that in Germany at least, but in many other OECD countries as well, the percentage of end-of-pipe technologies is the highest.

These findings lead to the following conclusion: the shifting of investment from additive towards integrated environmental engineering has a positive impact on the environment. This improvement is evidenced by the lower consumption of natural resources and fewer pollutants in the production process. Nevertheless, the question remains open as to what extent the companies will implement these environmental solutions with investments in the necessary technology. Any enforcement requires a deliberate eco-policy political instrument.

SUMMARY

This paper examined various aspects of innovation. In particular, eco-innovation was analyzed in the context of sustainable growth. The analysis differentiated neoclassical environmental economics from the more recent ecological economics. This was followed by a review of the characteristics of "strong" and "weak" sustainability. The concept of "balanced" sustainability was proposed as a possible solution to the controversy that ensued from these contrary positions and represents an attempt to form a bridge between them. In addition, a new economic growth model of the endogenous growth theory was presented. The model satisfies the requirements of balanced sustainability and was used to illustrate the possibility of generating balanced growth through the use of innovation, especially, the use of integrated environmental technologies. Consequently, it is necessary to substitute additive engineering with integrated technologies to a much greater extent. Despite fewer harmful substances being produced and the lower demand for natural resources, the result is an increase in productivity with a simultaneous decline in environmental stress. In this way, sustainable growth becomes a real possibility. Sustainable growth is substantiated by relieving some of the strain on the ecological systems (ecologic dimension), a higher rate of economic growth (economic dimension), and an improvement in the individual utility (social dimension). From a business perspective, strategic support for eco-innovation within the framework of an environmental management information system is quite possible. Nevertheless, continued research is required to determine the specific details for a CEMIS.

REFERENCES

Belitz, H., & Schrooten, M. (2008). Innovationssystem – Motor der Wirtschaft. *Vierteljahreshefte zur Wirtschaftsforschung*, *77*, 5–10. doi:10.3790/vjh.77.2.5

BMBF. (1997). *Bundesministerium für Bildung, Wissenschaft, Forschung und Technologie*. Bonn: Forschung für die Umwelt – Programm der Bundesregierung.

Braczyk, H. J., Cooke, P., & Heidenreich, M. (1998). *Regional innovation systems – the role of governances in a globalized world*. London: UCL Press.

Cleff, T., & Rennings, K. (1999). Determinants of Environmental Product and Process Innovation – Evidence from the Mannheim Innovation Panel and a Follow-Up Telephone Survey. *European Environment, Special issue on Integrated Product Policy, 9*(5), 191-201.

Corsten, H., Gössinger, R., & Schneider, H. (2006). *Grundlagen des Innovationsmanagements*. München: Verlag Vahlen.

Costanza, R., Cumberland, J., Daly, H., Goodland, R., & Norgaard, R. (2001). *Einführung in die Ökologische Ökonomik*. Stuttgart: Lucius & Lucius UTB.

Ewringmann, D., & Koch, L. (2006). Einleitung in die Problemstellung: Chemische Industrie, Nachhaltigkeit und Innovationen. In Koch, L., & Monßen, M. (Eds.), *Kooperative Umweltpolitik und nachhaltige Innovationen* (pp. 2–26). Heidelberg: Physica. doi:10.1007/3-7908-1661-2_1

Fichter, K. (2005). *Interpreneurship – Nachhaltigkeitsinnovationen in interaktiven Perspektiven eines vernetzten Unternehmertums*. Marburg: Metropolis.

FIU (Forschungsverbund innovative Wirkungen umweltpolitischer Instrumente) (1997). *Letter in September.* Essen.

Foxon, T. J., Gross, R., Chase, A., Howes, J., Arnall, A., & Anderson, D. (2005). The UK innovation systems for new and renewable energy technologies. *Energy Policy*, *33*(16), 2123–2137. doi:10.1016/j.enpol.2004.04.011

Freeman, C. (1987). *Technology Policy and Economic Reformance. Lessons from Japan*. London: Pinter Pub.

Frondel, M., Horbach, J., & Rennings, K. (2004). End-of-Pipe or Cleaner Production? An Empirical Comparison of Environmental Innovation Decisions Across OECD Countries. *ZEW Discussion Paper*, 04-82.

Frondel, M., Horbach, J., Rennings, K., & Requate, T. (2004). Environmental Policy Tools and Firm-Level Management Practices: Empirical Evidence for Germany. *RWI Mitteilungen Quarterly*, *54/55*(2), 87–111.

Gillwald, K. (2000). *Konzepte sozialer Innovation.* Paper P00-519 der Querschnittsgruppe Arbeit und Ökologie des Wissenschaftszentrums Berlin.

vHauff, M., Kleine, A., & Jörg, A. (2005). *Förderung der Wettbewerbsfähigkeit in Kleinunternehmen durch Ökoeffizienz*. Sternenfels: Verlag Wissenschaft und Praxis.

vHauff, M., & Solbach, D. (1999). Perspektiven integrierter Umweltschutztechnologie in der Bundesrepublik Deutschland. *Zeitschrift für Umweltpolitik & Umweltrecht*, *1*, 67–86.

Hemmelskamp, J. (1999). *Umweltpolitik und technischer Fortschritt*. Heidelberg: Physica.

Hemmelskamp, J., Rennings, K., & Leone, F. (2000). *Innovation-Oriented Environmental Regulation – Theoretical Approaches and Empirical Analysis*. Heidelberg: Physica.

Hübner, K., & Nill, J. (2001). *Nachhaltigkeit als Innovationsmotor. Herausforderungen für das deutsche Innovationssystem*. Berlin: Edition Sigma.

Kondratieff, N. D. (1926). Die langen Wellen der Konjunktur. *Archiv für Sozialwissenschaft und Sozialpolitik*, *56*, 573–609.

Konrad, W., & Nill, J. (2001). Innovationen für Nachhaltigkeit. *Schriftenreihe des IÖW*, 157.

Luks, F. (2005). Innovationen, Wachstum und Nachhaltigkeit: Eine ökologisch-ökonomische Betrachtung. In F. Beckenbach, U. Hampicke, C. Leipert, G. Meran, J. Minsch, H. G. Nutzinger, R. Pfriem, J. Weimann, F. Wirl & U. Witt (Eds.), Jahrbuch Ökologische Ökonomik, Band 4: Innovationen und Nachhaltigkeit (pp. 41-62). Marburg: Metropolis.

Lundvall, B. A. (Ed.). (1992). *National Systems of Innovation: Towards a Theory of Innovation and Interactive Learning*. London: Pinter Pub.

North, D. C. (1992). *Institutionen, institutioneller Wandel und Wirtschaftsleistung*. Tübingen: Mohr Siebeck.

OECD. (1992). *Technology and the Economy: The Key Relationships*. Paris: OECD.

OECD. (1997). *Eurostat Oslo Manual. Proposed Guidelines for Collecting and Interpreting Technological Innovation Data*. Paris: OECD.

Ott, K., & Döring, R. (2004). *Theorie und Praxis starker Nachhaltigkeit*. Marburg: Metropolis.

Patel, P., & Pavitt, K. (1994). The continuing, widespread (and neglected) importance of improvements in mechanical technologies. *Research Policy*, *23*, 533–546. doi:10.1016/0048-7333(94)01004-8

Pavitt, K. (1984). Sectoral Patterns of Technical Change: Towards a Taxonomy and a Theory. *Research Policy*, *13*, 343–373. doi:10.1016/0048-7333(84)90018-0

Pearce, D. W., & Turner, R. K. (1990). *Economics of Natural Resources and the Environment*. Baltimore: John Hopkins University Press.

Porter, M. E., & van der Linde, C. (1995). Toward a new conception of the environment competitiveness relationship. *The Journal of Economic Perspectives*, *9*(4), 97–118.

Rehfeld, K. M., Rennings, K., & Ziegler, A. (2004). *Integrated Product Policy and Environmental Product Innovations: An Empirical Analysis*. ZEW Discussion Paper, 04-71.

Rennings, K. (2005). Innovationen aus Sicht der neoklassischen Umweltökonomie. In F. Beckenbach, U. Hampicke, C. Leipert, G. Meran, J. Minsch, H. G. Nutzinger, R. Pfriem, J. Weimann, F. Wirl & U. Witt (Eds.), Jahrbuch Ökologische Ökonomik, Band 4: Innovationen und Nachhaltigkeit (pp. 15-40). Marburg: Metropolis.

Schmookler, J. (1966). *Invention and Economic Growth*. Cambridge: Harvard University Press.

Schumpeter, J. (1964). *Theorie der wirtschaftlichen Entwicklung*. Göttingen: Duncker & Humblot.

Steurer, R. (2001). Paradigmen der Nachhaltigkeit. *Zeitschrift für Umweltpolitik und Umweltrecht*, *4*, 537–566.

UBA. (1997). *Nachhaltiges Deutschland – Wege zu einer dauerhaft-umweltgerechten Entwicklung*. Berlin: Erich Schmidt Verlag.

Unruh, G. C. (2000). Understanding carbon lock-in. *Energy Policy*, *28*(12), 817–830. doi:10.1016/S0301-4215(00)00070-7

Welsch, J. (2005). *Innovationspolitik – eine problemorientierte Einführung*. Wiesbaden: Gabler.

Chapter 4
How can Information Technology be Adopted by Micro-Enterprises:
Guidelines for Sustainable Development

Mehruz Kamal
The College at Brockport, State University of New York, USA

Sajda Qureshi
University of Nebraska at Omaha, USA

Peter Wolcott
University of Nebraska at Omaha, USA

ABSTRACT

The growth of micro-enterprises is a key driver of economic development. The ability of micro-enterprises to adopt IT can potentially increase their growth by 3.4% according to a World Bank expert. However these gains do not always take place as the challenges are many. Current theoretical models on IT adoption focus on the intent to adopt IT in large organizations where employees' attitudes and perceptions are measured in terms of their objectives within the structures of accountability. Micro-enterprises are unique in that the intention to adopt is an individual decision made by the micro-entrepreneur. It is often the innovative ways in which IT is used that enable the gains to be realized by micro-entrepreneurs. This chapter describes a process that can be used to enable micro-entrepreneurs faced with limited resources to adopt IT to grow their businesses. This process of IT therapy involves diagnosis, interventions and an assessment of IT for development outcomes. Examples and guidelines are provided to enable this process to be used by practitioners. This chapter concludes with alternatives for sustainable development and guidelines for achieving these improvements in micro-enterprises.

DOI: 10.4018/978-1-61520-981-1.ch004

INTRODUCTION

Micro-enterprises are the predominant form of business in developing communities – especially in areas where infrastructure and resources are limited. At the same time growth of micro-enterprises is essential to the development of these communities. The survival of these businesses remains a challenge because they are led by the one micro-entrepreneur who trades skills and/or products to earn a living. Adoption of ICT is difficult because the resources to purchase equipment are limited and training is often unavailable or inadequate. However when micro-entrepreneurs do adopt IT, their businesses may grow by 3.4% according to one study (Qiang et al., 2003). Research over a period of time has shown that ICTs can contribute to poverty reduction when applied in a manner that is appropriate to the context (Avgerou, 1998; Kenny, 2000; Cecchini & Christopher, 2003; Akpan, 2003; Krishna & Walsham, 2005). It has also been demonstrated that ICTs contribute to growth (Baliamoune-Lutz, 2003; Kauffman & Kumar, 2008). This suggests that there are opportunities that need to be addressed when applying ICTs to enable development.

While little has been done to research the adoption of ICTs in micro-enterprises, examples include the use of mobile technologies by fishermen to access markets and increase efficiencies and lead to improved economic growth (Abraham, 2007; Waverman, Meschi & Fuss, 2005). Raymond et al. (2005) observed a 4% increase in sales as well as 5% increase in export performance in SMEs in the manufacturing sector in Canada when they adopted e-business techniques. By using technologies such as websites, email and telephones to communicate with customers, SMEs can provide better customer service and expand their customer base to help reach out to both local as well as international consumers for their products. Increased utilization in IT is not always evident through increased revenue of businesses. As a study by Southwood (2004) shows, IT investments by SMEs in South Africa resulted in profitability gains from cost savings rather than from an increase in sales.

While these efforts may appear to be very successful, they do not address the sustainability and growth of these businesses or of the communities and regions within which they reside. This is because the adoption of IT by micro-enterprises is not straightforward. It requires assistance on a number of levels. First an assessment of their needs has to be made in order to find out how they can be assisted. Every micro-entrepreneur has very unique needs and aspirations. They are also part of communities that determine what the micro-entrepreneur considers important. Hence a needs assessment not only should consider the micro-enterprise by itself but also the community. Second, the technology itself is often not the solution; it is the innovative ways in which the technology is used that enable the micro-entrepreneur to grow their business using IT. Third, the implementation requires a combination of training, technology and most importantly education on resources available to the business. Finally the sustainability of these initiatives needs to be considered in the light of economic, social and human considerations.

This chapter addresses the above four needs through a process called IT Therapy (Wolcott, Qureshi & Kamal, 2007; Wolcott, Kamal & Qureshi, 2008; Qureshi, Kamal & Wolcott, 2008). It reports on the success of current initiatives using IT therapy with micro-enterprises in an underserved community in Omaha, Nebraska. Following the IT therapy interventions, it was possible to bring about economic, social and human development over a period of time. Insights from the results obtained from the IT therapy initiatives are used to formulate guidelines for informing practitioners working with micro-enterprises to help foster development in underserved communities. Recommendations for sustaining such efforts are also suggested.

BACKGROUND

While many problems faced by micro-enterprises are not fundamentally related to technology, selective use of technology can be beneficial. In her model of information technology for development, Qureshi notes that ICTs can help businesses gain better access to information and expertise, reach new markets and customers (or more generally, stakeholders), administer the business more efficiently and effectively, and grow in the knowledge and skills needed to run the businesses better (Qureshi, 2005). Levy et al. (2001) formulated an analytical framework (focus-dominance model) to examine the potential for SMEs to realize value from IS capabilities. The framework shows where SMEs would fit in terms of the trend they show in IT investments and market strategies. The framework may be viewed as providing four different approaches to ICT adoption. The efficiency quadrant may comprise SMEs that exploit simple systems such as word processing and trivial accounting processes (Naylor & Williams, 1994). The co-ordination quadrant is composed of those SMEs that have a need to increase market share and their customer base. The collaboration segment then attracts SMEs that attempt to incorporate emerging technologies to manage relationships with the businesses' major customers. And finally the innovation quadrant comprises of those SMEs that actively seek to adopt new information and communication technologies to help achieve competitive advantage. In a follow-up study, Levy et al. (2002) investigated 43 SMEs to observe their positions in the focus-dominance model. The results revealed that most of the 43 SMEs make only one move, from efficiency to co-ordination, or from efficiency to collaboration. SMEs taking either one these routes tend to avoid losing control and so opt to stay within their current markets. It was also seen that only 17 of the 43 SMEs wanted to move to the innovation quadrant possibly due to an environment scan whereby they become aware of "best practices" and strategies that would assist them to manage business growth. While the Levy et al. (2002) shed light on trends in growth of SMEs, it fails to highlight the barriers or drivers that would enable the business growth to take place by moving it from one quadrant to another within the focus-dominance model. In a longitudinal study investigated the implementation of ICT into a management college in Tanzania over a span of 10 years, Furuholt & Ørvik (2006) found very limited impact and change. They identified that the main reasons for the limited development of IT usage and implementation were:

- **Lack of top management engagement:** The common theme in most of the interviews conducted was that there was a lack in sufficient support and enthusiasm for the top level management which resulted in resistance in the implementation of IT.
- **Knowledge barriers and staff resistance:** Younger faculty members were more inclined to using technology than older faculty members. Older faculty members were too old to learn and they had no incentive to attend IT training sessions that did not offer any form of compensation for them to attend and learn the new technology. Additionally, there was a lack of pressure from the environment i.e. the staff members didn't have to use the technology. They could get away without it.
- **Lack of Utilitarian value and other personal incentives:** In this context it was seen that the demand and pressure for IT was coming from others and the benefits going to others (e.g. students learning computers to get better jobs) than those who would have to put in considerable effort to upgrade their skills to train the students. And so there was little incentive to put in the considerable effort needed when it came to the use of IT tools and technology.
- **The Symbolic value of Information Technology:** This was an interesting find-

ing in the sense that most of the top level management within the institution had personal computers but never used them. And so it points maybe toward more of a cultural aspect where the prestige value is realized in having the technology rather than actually utilizing it.

- **Poor Organization:** The computer center had no dedicated IT personnel to look over computer related hardware and software issues. Existing staff member of the institutions who were given the responsibility of handling the computer center did not take the responsibility seriously. They viewed the IT job to be of less value or prestige as compared with their teaching job.
- **Poor infrastructure:** The institution did not have sufficient IT facilities or trained staff.
- **Other contextual and culture-based reasons:** The concept of time is very different in Africa than in developed countries. The value of the present is much larger and the future is much smaller. This difference perspective indicates that long-term planning and thinking ahead might not be prevalent in the African culture.

Another problem for SMEs is the fact that these forms of businesses have an inclination to miscalculate and underestimate the amount of time and effort that might need to be spent in implementing information technology solutions (Yap, 1989). It is often the case with small businesses that they are subjected to external pressures from large suppliers, vendors and other competitors to adopt certain technologies to enable them to conduct business with their larger counterparts (Thong et al., 1996). When situations like that arise, the smaller businesses fall prey to implementing the technologies – but they tend to take a short-range view of the IT implementation and not investigate how the technology may be efficiently used to their benefit. Duncombe & Heeks (2002) as well as Moyi (2003) highlight a number of challenges for rural micro enterprises in their ability to adopt and use information and communication technologies. The challenges relate to issues of remote locations, lack of education and literacy on the part of the business owner, poor business skills, poverty and lack of affordability, and lack of transportation. Other literature in this area also provides ample support of the above and additional issues surrounding the adoption and use of IT within micro enterprises. Mansell & Wehn (1998) and Hazan (2002) investigated the problems surrounding the affordability of information and communication technologies for poor under-privileged populations.

A study by Owen & Darkwa (1999) looked at the issue of awareness about IT and how not being aware of the potential transformational power of IT may serve to inhibit people and small businesses from growing and flourishing. An important issue of operational consideration of ICTs was investigated by Baark & Heeks (1998). That study looked at the success of technology transfer to organizations and highlighted some of the reasons behind technology transfer being successful as well as unsuccessful. One of the basic requirements for any form of IT implementation is to have a basic infrastructure in place that will support the new form of technology that is being introduced into that environment. Lack of such infrastructure will be a major barrier to the adoption and use of IT. A number of studies have looked into the issue of poor infrastructure (Latchem & Walker, 2001; O'Farrell, Norrish &Scott, 1999; Barton & Bear, 1999). The private sector of an economy coupled with government policies that regulate information and communication technologies also play an important role in either facilitating or inhibiting the development of IT infrastructures to promote increased IT adoption and use (Lefebvre & Lefebvre, 1996). The study by Lefebvre and Lefebvre (1996) also looked at management's capacity to incorporate IT into small business environments.

Warschauer (2003) provides a rather different perspective in helping to understand why ICT adoption and implementation efforts may fail in one setting yet succeed in another. He says that the key issue revolves around "not unequal access to computers (IS/ICT) but rather the unequal ways that computers (IS/ICT) are used." Warschauer (2003) also highlights an important point whereby he states that "Technology does not exist as an external variable to be injected from the outside to bring about certain results. It is woven into social systems and processes...the goal of bringing technology to marginalized groups is not merely to overcome a technological divide but instead to further a process of social inclusion." Warschauer's statement has strong policy implications that should be kept in mind in going forward with any IS adoption and implementation. In a study of a set of eleven micro-enterprises in an underserved community, Wolcott et al. (2008) investigated the numerous challenges that micro-enterprises face when it comes to adopting ICTs. Figure 1 summarizes the various challenges identified. As can be seen from the figure, the challenges are clustered under categories such as capabilities, resources, access, attitude, context, and operations.

The findings from that study showed that in terms of attitudinal changes, there were variations in the level of motivation and engagement of the micro-entrepreneurs with the ICT adoption and implementation phase. They also differed on their knowledge of technical skills and became frustrated easily when they were not able to control the technology for their purposes. The set of micro-enterprises in the study all portrayed the common feeling that technology could potentially help their business. The issue was that, they just did not know how - resulting in a lack of awareness and lack of confidence. In terms of operational challenges, almost all the micro-enterprises have little to no ICT support to turn to for assistance. Limited budgets restrict them from being able to hire IT consultants or having a dedicated IT staff for their business. To add to the mix, the small business owners have poor troubleshooting skills resulting in increased discouragement and frustrations towards ICTs. In terms of resources, lack of money, time and information play a major role in hindering micro-entrepreneurs to adopt ICTs. Most micro-enterprises also have poor IT infrastructures that prevent them from conducting their daily business efficiently.

Despite the numerous challenges faced by small firms, there is a sense that they hold the promise of growing incrementally on existing capabilities, and providing a seedbed for the emergence of dynamic and efficient larger national firms (Levy, 2001; Mathews, 2007; Servon & Doshna, 2000). In their study of 1000 small business enterprises in the US, Riemenschneider

Figure 1. Challenges to ICT adoption by micro-enterprises

et al. (2003) found that businesses were prepared to overcome obstacles to IT adoption to achieve web presence. This is because pressures to keep with the competition and promote services to customers are greater than the obstacles to setting up websites. It also appears that the promise of eBusiness adoption by micro-enterprises can potentially provide these businesses with the ability to access new markets and reduce costs through administrative efficiencies (Brown & Lockett, 2004; Pateli & Giaglis, 2004).

However, the use of ICT by Small and medium Sized Enterprises (SMEs) remains a challenge in both developed as well as developing countries (Schreiner & Woller, 2003; Sanders, 2002; Lichtenstein & Lyons, 2001; Hyman & Dearden, 1998; Honig, 1998; Piscitello & Sgobbi, 2004). In particular the opportunities opened up by the internet are limited in SMEs especially due to the challenges faced by globalization (Piscitello & Sgobbi, 2004). Past studies have shown that the use of ICT can play an important role on the growth of small businesses (Matthews, 2007; Sullivan, 1985; Qiang et al., 2006; Raymond et al., 2005). Cragg & King (1993) have shown that there is a gradual increase in the number of small firms that either adopt various new technologies or take steps to upgrade what they currently possess. The studies suggest that IT can be employed to bring about increased competitiveness if it enables businesses to create new jobs, increase productivity and sales through access to new markets and administrative efficiencies (Qureshi, 2005; Matthews, 2007).

It then appears that in order to help micro-enterprises overcome the many challenges that they face – particularly paying attention to their constraints of tight limited budgets and time – there is a need to arm them with ICTs to help them reap the many benefits that technology has to offer. This can be achieved through a process of IT therapy (Wolcott et al., 2007; Wolcott et al., 2008; Qureshi et al., 2008). This chapter assesses current IT therapy initiatives in terms of their sustainability of micro-enterprises and their communities for human, social and economic development. The following sections delineate the process of IT therapy and discuss outcomes from current IT therapy initiatives. Analysis of the IT therapy initiatives gives way to guidelines that can be used by practitioners as well as recommendations to foster and bring about sustainable development in this context.

METHODOLOGY

The research methodology followed for this study is that of Action Research. Action research involves the application of tools and methods from the social and behavioral sciences to practical problems with the intention both of improving the practice and of contributing to theory and knowledge in the area studied. Action researchers participate directly or intervene in a situation or phenomenon in order to apply a theory and evaluate the value and usefulness of that theory (Checkland, 1981, 1991; Galliers, 1991). Action research is a change oriented research methodology that seeks to introduce changes with positive social values, the key focus being on a problem and its solution (Elden & Chisholm, 1993). Action research is typically carried out as part of an attempt to solve problems by allowing the researcher to become a participant in the action, the process of change itself becoming the subject of research (Checkland, 1981).

In action research, the researcher has a remit for action (Checkland, 1981). This means that the organization in which he or she is doing research has given him/her the go ahead to solve their particular problem or help manage change processes. Action research is best seen as an iterative cycle in which the researcher begins with a plan of how to carry out the activity, then act to intervene to solve the immediate problem, observe the results of the intervention and reflect on the impact and next steps (Zuber-Skerrit, 1991; Avison et al., 1999).

Carried out as part of an academic service-learning course, the action research was supplemented by the absorbing of knowledge through classroom lectures and discussion. The cycle continued to action or intervention, to solve the problem or manage the change process; this is where the researcher collects data. On location at the micro-businesses, researchers worked with business owners to understand the business and existing technology, implement technology-based projects, and train business owners as appropriate. This process was referred to as "IT therapy" in which assistance was given to the micro-business owner to solve their immediate IT needs. Additional data on the situation or phenomenon being studied were gathered through observation while implementing the IT therapy. The following reflection entailed interpretation of the data, and consequences of action that then fed into the planning stage to modify the methodology or model that then determine what action would be taken in the next cycle. Further cycles of activities continued until a desired end-state is achieved (Zuber-Skerrit, 1991; Avison et al., 1999, p.96). The following section describes the IT therapy process and illustrates how the action research process was carried out.

THE IT THERAPY PROCESS

The IT therapy process can best be described as a very context-sensitive IT assistance process that involves applying innovative IT interventions to help micro-enterprises grow. It is important to note that IT assistance comprises the gamut of not only IT implementations, but also training, educating, and creating awareness by providing information on the potential power of IT and how it can be tailored to fit each business. The IT therapy process entails a number of steps. The first step is to meet with the micro-entrepreneur to get an understanding of the micro-entrepreneur's goals and aspirations for his/her business. To obtain such an understanding, the researchers ask the micro-entrepreneur questions relating to their current business conditions, and what is currently obstructing them from reaching their business goals. The researcher also asks the owner as to how he/she feels towards technology and what if any form of technology they have used in their business. The second step of the IT therapy process is for the researcher to formulate an action plan comprising of specific IT interventions that may be beneficial for the business and move it one step forward towards achieving the micro-entrepreneur's business goals. The designs of the IT interventions are based on the unique needs of each micro-enterprise. As an example, an IT intervention for a micro-enterprise could be as simple as providing the owner with information about a certain commercial software package. The third step in the IT therapy process involves the researcher developing what he/she thinks are the appropriate IT interventions for the specific micro-enterprise. The next step then entails the researcher explaining to the micro-entrepreneur, the chosen IT intervention and why and how it would help the micro-enterprise.

Once a shared understanding has been reached on the mode of action, the IT intervention is then applied. A point to highlight here is that the process of getting a shared understanding between the researcher and the micro-enterprise is not always an easy or a one-shot process as highlighted by Wolcott et al. (2008). To achieve shared understanding, developing and fostering a sense of trust is crucial. The researchers need to build a relationship of trust with the micro-entrepreneur so that he/she has confidence in the process being carried out. The IT therapy was carried out within an action research cycle as illustrated below:

The action research cycle shown in Figure 2 was used in the studies by Wolcott et al. (2007) and Qureshi et al. (2008) as a research approach that utilized students - taking a service learning course – paired with micro-enterprises to help the small businesses with their IT needs. The actual IT implementations or interventions that were applied to each micro-business occurred in the 'Act' phase of the action research cycle. It is important to emphasize that the process of IT therapy is a cyclical process. In other words, after an intervention is applied to a micro-enterprise, researchers observe whether the intervention fixed the needs expressed by the micro entrepreneur. If not, then modifications are made to the interventions and they are re-applied. This is represented by the connection between the 'Act' phase and the 'Observe/Inquire' phase in Figure 2.

Some examples of IT interventions or IT therapy tasks that were conducted in prior IT therapy initiatives (Wolcott et al., 2008; Qureshi et al., 2008) are: fixing one micro-entrepreneur's Internet connection which was very unreliable; setting up an Excel spreadsheet for another owner to enable him to provide better statistics to stakeholders; teaching another owner how to create PowerPoint presentations of her products to show to potential clients; setting up a central data repository for customer information so that it was no longer scattered in many different places; synchronizing accounting systems so that the owner did not have to maintain duplicate accounting systems for work and for home; updating and teaching a micro-entrepreneur how to make changes to the business website; upgrading software and installing virus protection for another micro-entrepreneur; training a micro-entrepreneur to make backups of data. In summary, the IT therapy tasks can be grouped into a number of categories. These are shown in Table 1 below.

IT Therapy Outcomes

In her model of IT for development, Qureshi (2005) shows how through the implementation, adoption and use of ICTs within a society might give rise to effects in the form of (i) better access to information, knowledge, and expertise, (ii) improved competitiveness and access to markets, (iii) administrative efficiencies, (iv) learning and increased labor productivity, and finally (v) poverty reduction. Table 2 below classifies the IT therapy interventions performed by researchers in prior IT therapy initiatives (Wolcott et al. 2007; Wolcott et al. 2008; Qureshi et al., 2008) in the major categories of IT effects on development as mentioned in Qureshi (2005).

It is evident from Table 2 that, most of the micro-enterprises faced immediate needs in the areas of administrative efficiencies and, to a lesser extent, access to markets. Access to information, knowledge, and expertise was a less pressing concern; the entrepreneurs understood their businesses quite well and in most cases had sufficient information and expertise to run them. Using technology to connect with, for example, other entrepreneurs or business development resources certainly offers great potential, but likely future benefit. The learning and increased labor productivity category focuses on the use of technology

Figure 2. Applying the action research methodology

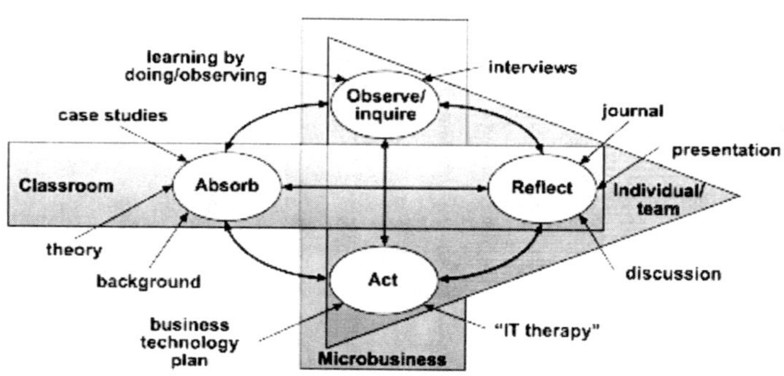

Table 1. Categories of IT interventions

Category	Interventions	Example
1	• Hardware/Software installation • Training	• Internet connectivity • Connection various computer peripherals to work in synch
2	Use of simple office software packages to enable administrative efficiencies	• Word Procressing software • Excel Spreadsheets
3	• Website development • Basic e-commerce functionality	Developing a website to sell the business's products/services
4	• Maintaining own website • Training	Being able to update one's own website by adding or deleting products/services.

Table 2. Outcomes from the IT therapy interventions

Effect of IT implementation on development (Qureshi 2005)	Number of IT Therapy tasks
Access to information, knowledge, and expertise	2
Competitiveness and access to markets	8
Administrative efficiencies	14
Learning and increased labor productivity	0
Contribution to poverty reduction (e.g. job creation)	1

(Wolcott et al., 2007; Wolcott et al., 2008; Qureshi et al., 2008)

to provide training and education. The example of job creation observed during a span of 4 months was of a micro-enterprise that was a halfway house in which a guest residing there was able to find a job by using the new Internet connection that was set up as part of an IT intervention applied to that micro-enterprise to post his resume on the web.

Social development took place as the micro-entrepreneurs acquired skills and access to information and expertise to grow their businesses. Economic development took place when the micro-entrepreneurs were able to generate income, reduce costs and employ additional people and resources to grow their businesses. The combined benefits enabled the micro-entrepreneurs to become empowered in their own abilities to take control of their businesses. Together there is the effect of increasing the ability of the communities in which the micro-entrepreneurs work to grow. While detailed case studies have been published in Qureshi et al. (2009) that depict how the micro-enterprises were able to adopt technology to grow their businesses, this chapter focuses on providing guidelines that can enable similar outcomes to be achieved. These are illustrated in the following section.

GUIDELINES FOR SUPPORTING MICRO-ENTERPRISES WITH IT

These guidelines are based upon the research described in this chapter and practical experiences of the authors as they worked with the micro-entrepreneurs to help them adopt IT to grow their businesses.

1. **Diagnosis:** This involves understanding the needs faced by the micro-entrepreneur. Given that each micro-entrepreneur is unique as are the challenges faced by them, a questionnaire is administered to understand the key challenges and opportunities. The history, aims, social and economic background is also ascertained at this point.
2. **Planning:** Once the needs have been ascertained, then a decision needs to be taken as to whether the micro-entrepreneur is a candidate for IT Therapy. Criteria for selection

include, size, income, motivation, potential for growth, training and access to technology.

3. **Intervention:** Both technology and training interventions to solve pressing problems get the micro-entrepreneur working with the technology. Such interventions include but are not limited to hardware or software installation, quick fixes and showing how to use a certain program.
4. **Observation:** After each intervention it is important to observe and record the progress made by the micro-entrepreneur. These observations need to be shared with other IT therapists in case there is a larger problem or project to be addressed with an IT solution.

Subsequent interventions lead to progress in the micro-entrepreneurs ability to adopt IT. The effects of these interventions in enabling the micro-entrepreneur to grow their business should be recorded and shared at various intervals.

SUSTAINABILITY OF IT THERAPY FOR MICRO-ENTERPRISE DEVELOPMENT

Although the IT therapy process described in this chapter has proven to bring about substantial improvements to micro-enterprises in underserved regions, steps need to be taken to foster and bring about sustainable development through such innovative efforts. The concept of sustainable development according to the World Bank entails the simultaneous achievement of economic (growth, equity and efficiency), social (empowerment, participation, social mobility, social cohesion, cultural identity and institutional development) and ecological objectives (ecosystem integrity, carrying capacity, biodiversity and protection of global commons). This definition has also been cited by Vargas (2000) who uses this definition to assess the sustainability of projects in underserved communities. The World Bank's definition of sustainable definition is a comprehensive and an umbrella concept which may not be fully applicable to all contexts. It appears that for the micro-enterprise context, community development efforts to support micro-enterprise growth can enable sustained improvements to be achieved (Vargas, 2000; Steinberg, 2003; Southwood, 2004; Warschauer, 2003). A sustainable development strategy will therefore have to support the community in which the micro-enterprises operate. In tailoring the World Bank's definition of sustainable development for the micro-enterprise context, we offer the following framework for achieving sustainability of IT therapy efforts on micro-enterprise growth:

Economic Objectives

Sustained improvements in micro-enterprises can be achieved by stimulating growth, equitable distribution of resources and increasing the efficiency of factors of production through the IT therapy training and technology interventions. In order to sustain these improvements the following need to be in place for the micro-enterprises:

1. Micro-loans or financing that can be easily paid back.
2. Credit availability in remote areas through mobile technologies.
3. Follow-up and evaluation of micro-enterprise growth through time. Provide financial incentives for successful management.
4. Partnerships with IT company foundations such as eBay and Microsoft to ensure targeted technology support.

These economic objectives can only be achieved through coordinated actions to improve the social and human conditions of the micro-entrepreneurs. In particular, their ability to grow their businesses can only be sustained through improvements in their living conditions, healthcare and education. These are addressed in the following section.

Social Objectives

Sustained improvements in micro-enterprises can be achieved by empowering owners through participation in social and cultural activities that reinforce their identity. Institutional development for supporting micro-enterprise owners need to include the following:

1. Provide training on IT applications and business plan development – which can be achieved through various Business development institutions and NGOs.
2. Developing a cybercafé within the community with facilities for business development and technical assistance. This would also provide a social space in which micro-enterprises owners could come to share ideas and their experiences and help one another.
3. Connect the cybercafé to local university infrastructures for remote technical assistance and maintenance to micro-enterprises.
4. Local universities need to develop IT therapy skill sets for graduates going into the workforce to enable them to stimulate growth in micro-enterprises.

The above objectives are part of a socio-economic framework for sustainable development of micro-enterprises. It is a framework because it provides possible courses of action to sustainable micro-enterprise development.

CONCLUSION

Micro-enterprises are the back-bone of most economies in the World today. It is seen that these tiny businesses are the main form of business in both developed as well as in developing countries. Despite their majority, they are hindered from growing to their potential due to their lack of use of IT. This chapter has described a process of IT therapy that can be used to enable micro-entrepreneurs faced with limited resources to adopt IT to grow their businesses. This process of IT therapy involves diagnosis, interventions and an assessment of IT for development outcomes. This chapter reports on earlier efforts taken to apply the IT therapy process and its outcomes. Examples and guidelines have been provided to enable this process to be used by practitioners. This chapter concludes with a discussion and suggested recommendations for attaining sustainable development of micro-enterprises.

The discussion presented in this chapter has the potential to form the foundation for future research in multiple directions. A natural path is to observe a set of micro-enterprises over an additional extended period of time to investigate the long-term effects of the IT interventions and validate the guidelines for sustainable development. Doing so will also provide an indication as to how the relationships between the various IT for Development effects as outlined in Qureshi's IT for development model (2005) play out. Another direction of future research that may be fueled by the discussion from this chapter is based on the issue that the exact same IT intervention may produce differing outcomes – subsequently also leading to differing levels of attaining sustainable development. One micro-entrepreneur may be able to take control of their business through IT as opposed to another micro-entrepreneur who may have received the same intervention. Such findings may open the door to additional research that is needed to understand why the same intervention may produce very drastically different results. Speculations as to the cause may be along the lines of differences in motivation, business task priority issues, time restrictions, etc. Future research will shed insight into understanding the factors behind the same interventions producing different outcomes.

Another very interesting and promising direction of future research is the moving away from the individual view of a micro-enterprise to the community view of micro-enterprises. There is some preliminary evidence to support community development and strong social networks to help micro-enterprises improve their survival (Vargas, 2000). Vargas (2000) notes that communally oriented microenterprises become more attractive to investors by virtue of their enhanced stability, size, and cohesion. In addition, targeting technology to facilitating community and social networks has implications for economic growth (Hoff, 1998). The above studies provide initial support for potential ways in which micro-enterprises may sustain their operations through IT.

The IT therapy steps described in this chapter have strong implications for development practitioners that work to assist micro-enterprises to adopt and use technological innovations in underserved regions to further the overall development goals of that region. The IT therapy steps of *diagnosis*, *planning*, *intervention*, and *observation* are based upon the research and practical experiences of the researchers as they worked with the micro-entrepreneurs to help them use IT to grow their businesses. The findings described in this chapter have shown that through a very context sensitive diagnosis of issues and application of IT, interventions as outlined in the IT therapy steps brought about improvement in terms of administrative efficiencies, access to new markets, and other IT for development outcomes in the micro-enterprise cases. As a result, evidence from this research suggests that practitioners need to focus on working very closely with micro-entrepreneurs to teach them – not in a classroom environment but at the micro-enterprise location itself - how they can use IT to accomplish their business tasks. This research also suggests that carrying out such context sensitive interventions has the potential to empower the micro-entrepreneurs to take small steps to be in control of their business through the use of IT. Therefore, practitioners need to focus on using empowering interventions which will help people, organizations, and communities become more self-reliant and self-governing and less controlled by external forces – which is the ultimate goal to achieving sustainable development.

REFERENCES

Abraham, R. (2007).Mobile Phones and Economic Development: Evidence from the Fishing Industry in India. *Information and Technologies and International Development, 4*(1).

Adam, L. (1996). Electronic communications technology and development of Internet connectivity in Africa. *Information Technology for Development, 7*(3), 133–145.

Akpan, P. I. (2003). Basic-needs to globalization: Are ICTs the missing link? *Information Technology for Development, 10*, 261–274. doi:10.1002/itdj.1590100405

Avgerou, C. (1998). How can IT Enable Economic Growth in developing Countries? *Information Technology for Development, 8*(1).

Avison, D. E., Lau, F., Myers, M., & Nielsen, P. A. (1999). Action Research. *Communications of the ACM, 42*(1), 94–97. doi:10.1145/291469.291479

Baark, E., & Heeks, R. (1998). *Evaluation of Donor-Funded Information Technology Transfer Projects in China: A Life-Cycle Approach.* Retrieved August 12, 2009, from http://idpm.man.ac.uk/wp/di/di_wp01.htm

Baliamoune-Lutz, M. (2003). An analysis of the determinants and effects of ICT diffusion in developing countries. *Information Technology for Development, 10*(3), 151–170. doi:10.1002/itdj.1590100303

Barton, C., & Bear, M. (1999). Information and Communications Technologies: Are they the Key to Viable Business Development Services for Micro and Small Enterprises? *Report for USAID as part of the Microenterprise Best Practices Project.* Retrieved December 12, 2007, from http://www.mip.org/PUBS/MBP/ict.htm

Brown, D. H., & Lockett, N. (2004). Potential of critical e-applications for engaging SMEs in e-business: a provider perspective. *European Journal of Information Systems*, *13*(2), 21–34. doi:10.1057/palgrave.ejis.3000480

Cecchini, S., & Scott, C. (2003). Can information and communications technology applications contribute to poverty reduction? Lessons from rural India. *Information Technology for Development*, *10*, 73–84. doi:10.1002/itdj.1590100203

Checkland, P. (1981). *Systems Thinking, Systems Practice*. New York: John Wiley & Sons.

Checkland, P. (1991). From Framework through Experience to Learning: The Essential Nature of Action Research. In H.-E. Nissen, H. Klein & R. Hirschheim (Eds.), Information Systems Research: Contemporary Approaches and Emergent Traditions (pp. 397-403). North Holland: Elsevier Publishers.

Cragg, P. B., & King, M. (1993). Small-Firm Computing: Motivators and Inhibitors. *Management Information Systems Quarterly*, *17*(1), 47–60. doi:10.2307/249509

Duncombe, R., & Heeks, R. (2003). An information systems perspective on ethical trade and self-regulation. *Information Technology for Development*, *10*(2), 123–139. doi:10.1002/itdj.1590100206

Elden, M., & Chisholm, R. F. (1993). Emerging Varieties of Action Research: Introduction to the Special Issue. *Human Relations*, *46*(2), 121–142. doi:10.1177/001872679304600201

Furuholt, B., & Ørvik, T. U. (2006). Implementation of Information Technology in Africa: Understanding and Explaining the Results of Ten Years of Implementation Effort in a Tanzanian Organization. *Information Technology for Development*, *12*(1), 45–62. doi:10.1002/itdj.20030

Galliers, R. D. (1992). Choosing Information Systems Research Approaches. In R.D. Galliers (Ed.), Information Systems Research: Issues, Methods and Practical Guidelines (pp. 144-162). Henley-on-Thames: Alfred Waller.

Grosh, B., & Somolekae, G. (1996). Mighty oaks from little acorns: Can micro-enterprise serve as the seedbed of industrialization? *World Development*, *24*(12), 1879–1890. doi:10.1016/S0305-750X(96)00082-4

Hazan, M. (2002). Virtual South: E-Commerce for unprivileged artisans. Retrieved December 12, 2008, from http://www.iicd.org/stories/

Honig, B. (1998). What determines success? Examining the human, financial, and social capital of Jamaican microentrepreneurs. *Journal of Business Venturing*, *13*(5), 371–394. doi:10.1016/S0883-9026(97)00036-0

Hyman, E. L., & Dearden, K. (1998). Comprehensive impact assessment systems for NGO Microenterprise Development Programs. *World Development*, *26*(2), 261–276. doi:10.1016/S0305-750X(97)10022-5

Kauffman, R. J., & Kumar, A. (2008). Mapping the multi-tiered impacts on the growth of IT industries in India: A combined scale-and-scope externalities perspective. *Information Technology for Development*, *14*(3), 225–252. doi:10.1002/itdj.20094

Kenny, C. J. (2000). Expanding Internet access to the rural poor in Africa. *Information Technology for Development*, *9*(1), 25–32.

Krishna, S., & Walsham, G. (2005). Implementing Public Information Systems in Developing Countries: Learning from a Success Story. *Journal of Information Technology for Development*, *11*(2).

Latchem. C. & Walker, D. (2001). *Telecentres: Case Studies and Key Issues*. Vancouver: The Commonwealth of Learning.

Lefebvre, L., & Lefebvre, L. A. (1996). *Information and Telecommunication Technologies: The Impact of their Adoption on Small and Medium-sized Enterprises*. Retrieved December 12, 2007, from http://web.idrc.ca/en/ev-9303-201-1-DO_TOPIC.html

Levy, M., Powell, P., & Yetton, P. (2001). SMEs: Aligning IS and the Strategic Context. *Journal of Information Technology*, *16*(3), 133–144. doi:10.1080/02683960110063672

Levy, M., Powell, P., & Yetton, P. (2002). The Dynamics of SME Information Systems. *Small Business Economics*, *19*, 341–354. doi:10.1023/A:1019654030019

Lichtenstein, G. A., & Lyons, T. S. (2001). The entrepreneurial development system: Transforming business talent and community economies. *Economic Development Quarterly*, *15*(1), 3–20. doi:10.1177/089124240101500101

Mansell, R., & Wehn, U. (1998). *Knowledge Societies: Information Technology for Sustainable Development*. Oxford: Oxford University Press.

Matthews, P. (2007). ICT Assimilation and SME Expansion. *Journal of International Development*, *19*, 817–827. doi:10.1002/jid.1401

Moyi, E. D. (2003). Networks, information and small enterprises: New Technologies and the ambiguity of empowerment. *Information Technology for Development*, *10*, 221–232. doi:10.1002/itdj.1590100402

Naylor, J., & Williams, J. (1994). Successful Use of IT in SMEs. *European Journal of IS*, *3*(1), 48–56.

O'Farrell, C., Norrish, P., & Scott, A. (1999). *Information and Communication Technologies (ICTs) for Sustainable Livelihoods*. Burton Hall: Intermediate Technology Development Group.

Owen, W., & Darkwa, O. (1999). Role of Multipurpose Community Telecentres in Accelerating National Development in Ghana. *First Monday*, *5*(1), 1–23.

Pateli, A. G., & Giaglis, G. M. (2004). A research framework for analyzing eBusiness models. *European Journal of Information Systems*, *13*, 302–314. doi:10.1057/palgrave.ejis.3000513

Piscitello, L., & Sgobbi, F. (2004). Globalisation, E-Business and SMEs: Evidence from the Italian District of Prato. *Small Business Economics*, *22*(5), 333. doi:10.1023/B:SBEJ.0000022208.34741.55

Qiang, C. Z., Clarke, G. R., & Halewood, N. (2006). The Role of ICT. In *Doing Business Information and Communications for Development – Global Trends and Policies*. Washington, DC: World Bank.

Qureshi, S. (2005). How does Information technology effect Development? Integrating Theory and Practice into a Process Model. In *Proceedings of the 11th Americas Conference on Information Systems (AMCIS), Omaha, NE.*

Qureshi, S., Kamal, M., & Wolcott, P. (2009). Information Technology Therapy for Competitiveness in Micro-Enterprises. *International Journal of E-Business Research*, *5*(1).

Raymond, L., Bergeron, F. O., & Blili, S. (2005). The Assimilation of E-business in Manufacturing SMEs: Determinants and Effects on Growth and Internationalization. *Electronic Markets*, *15*(2), 106–118. doi:10.1080/10196780500083761

Riemenschneider, C., Harrison, D., & Mykytyn, P. (2003). Understanding IT Adoption Decisions in Small Business: Integrating Current Theories. *Information & Management*, 40.

Sanders, C. K. (2002). The impact of microenterprise assistance programs: A comparative study of program participants, nonparticipants, and other low-wage workers. *The Social Service Review*, *76*(2), 321–340. doi:10.1086/339664

Schreiner, M., & Woller, G. (2003). Microenterprise Development Programs in the United States and in the Developing World. *World Development*, *31*(9), 1567–1580. doi:10.1016/S0305-750X(03)00112-8

Servon, L. J. (1998). Credit and social capital: The community development potential of US microenterprise programs. *Housing Policy Debate*, *9*(1), 115–149.

Southwood, R. (2004). ICTs and Small Enterprise: A Motor of Economic Development in Africa. IICD Research Briefs 9. The Hague.

Steinberg, J. (2003). Information Technology and Development Beyond Either/Or. *The Brookings Review*, *21*(2), 45–48.

Sullivan, B. C. (1985). Economics of Information Technology. *International Journal of Social Economics*, *12*(1), 37. doi:10.1108/eb013983

Vargas, C. M. (2000). Community development and microenterprises: fostering sustainable development. *Sustainable Development*, *8*(1), 11. doi:10.1002/(SICI)1099-1719(200002)8:1<11::AID-SD119>3.0.CO;2-7

Warschauer, M. (2003). Demystifying the Digital Divide. *Scientific American*, *289*(2), 42–48. doi:10.1038/scientificamerican0803-42

Waverman, L., Meschi, M., & Fuss, M. (2005). The impact of telecoms on economic growth in developing countries. *The Vodafone Policy Paper, Series 2.*

Wolcott, P., Kamal, M., & Qureshi, S. (2008). Meeting the Challenges of ICT Adoption by Micro-enterprises. *Journal of Enterprise Information Management*, *21*(6). doi:10.1108/17410390810911212

Wolcott, P., Qureshi, S., & Kamal, M. (2007). Information Technology Therapy Approach to Microenterprise Adoption of ICTs. In *Proceedings of the 13th Americas Conference on Information Systems (AMCIS), Keystone, Colorado.*

Zuber-Skerrit, O. (1991). *Action Research for Change and Development.* Aldershot: Gower Publishing.

Chapter 5
Additional Challenges for CEMIS Due to Impacts Caused by Climate Change

Irene Antoni-Komar
Carl von Ossietzky University Oldenburg, Germany

Marina Beermann
Carl von Ossietzky University Oldenburg, Germany

Hedda Schattke
Carl von Ossietzky University Oldenburg, Germany

ABSTRACT

The aim of this paper is to evaluate how CEMIS could be enhanced to cope with impacts caused by climate change. In our time, firms have to deal with the resulting challenges such as increasing complexity and dynamics of the environment. By developing cultural competences, firms will be empowered to handle these new challenges appropriately. CEMIS itself as a managerial tool has an excellent potential to increase organizational resilience against vulnerabilities due to impacts caused by climate change. CEMIS could provide climate change scenarios for different impacts in global and regional dimensions. Scenarios as alternative images of how the future might unfold are an appropriate tool to analyze how driving forces may influence future emission outcomes and to assess the associated uncertainties and risks. They assist in climate change analysis, including climate modeling and the assessment of impacts, adaptation and mitigation. Theoretical enlargements of the CEMIS concept will be discussed by resilience thinking, which is promising for CEMIS because of its turning away from the equilibrium assumption, its widespread comprehension of the environment and its influences, its assumption of flexibility and adaptiveness through the adaptive capacity. The discussion will be exemplified by firms from the food industry, which are highly vulnerable towards direct and also indirect impacts caused by climate change along certain supply chains. Changing qualities and quantities of resources, temporary shortage of resources or conflicts between energy and food can all have drastic effects on firms in the food industry. Supported by CEMIS as a critical information system, emerging conflicts due to changing societal and cultural processes can be recognized sensitively, reflected critically, and reconfigured creatively to the aim of sustainable strategic management. Based on the theory of social practice and

DOI: 10.4018/978-1-61520-981-1.ch005

the competence theory of the firm, the development of cultural competences, as an integral part of the practical intelligibility of firms and as a learning concept for adaptive capacity, enables firms to handle these new challenges in times of expanding uncertainty and risk appropriately.

INTRODUCTION

The idea of a Corporate Environmental Management Information System (CEMIS) stands for the ecological goal of reducing environmental impacts to ensure the viability of the firm (cf. Lang, 2007; Marx Gómez et al., 2007). Due to the need for encompassing information along the supply chain, environmental management systems in general track different steps: the identification of impacts or risks, the process of assessment, supervision and controlling. During all these steps, similar problems have to be considered. On the one hand, detailed and encompassing information is required. On the other hand, this involves increasing complexity and the need for evaluating information concerning its importance and correctness. Furthermore, diverse spatial and time scales have to be considered. Consequently, CEMIS relies on a continuous exchange and comparison of information concerning environmental and societal changes in order to supply the firm with sufficiently updated and relevant information.

Climate change and its potential environmental, social and cultural impacts highlight a new and additional challenge for individuals and organizations. The increasing complexity and dynamics of the environmental system have to be considered for further conceptual and theoretical development of CEMIS. CEMIS as a *managerial tool* and *critical information system* has the potential to support firms in the learning process of building adaptive capacity concerning new challenges caused by climate change (cf. Berkhout, 2006).

Climate change caused challenges appear above all as societal and cultural challenges, because on the one hand climate change influences societal and cultural processes, and on the other hand climate change is intensified by societal and cultural processes. The cultural dimension implies that actual and future tasks have to be considered at an early stage. For this purpose, cultural processes and path dependencies in society and the reactions to the market have to be considered in strategic management. Impacts caused by climate change can reinforce the need for an interactional and recursive view of firms, concerning the importance of building capacities for adaptation and mitigation while catching up with cultural processes like technological formations of society, specialization of production, and social acceleration.

In this context, the idea of resilience is a fitting and promising concept. By developing *cultural competences* as an element of strategic management, firms will be empowered to handle these new challenges appropriately and to become resilient to both varied and complex vulnerabilities.

THE IDEA OF RESILIENCE

The resilience concept originates from ecosystem science. The ecologists Eugene P. Odum (cf. Odum, 1971) and C.S. Holling described how ecosystems by means of homeostatic mechanisms organize themselves in order to reach an ecological balance. Holling (1973) developed a model that was designed to interpret the dynamics and resilience of complex ecosystems, which are thought to go through phases of an "adaptive cycle". The model is based on two dimensions, connectedness and accumulated capital, which determine the growth, conservation, release and reorganization phases of ecosystems.

It can be assumed that complex ecosystems move from rapid growth to a mature phase designated conservation. While developing this phase, an ecosystem would become more rigid, thereby making the system more vulnerable. Eventually, a disturbance would cause sudden collapse, which would be followed by reorganization. Depending on the specific circumstances, the system would then restart the adaptive cycle or move into a new configuration. In this context, the system's resilience refers to the amount of change a system can undergo while maintaining its function and structure (cf. Holling, 1973). On the one hand, the concept of resilience clarifies that change is taken as something that has to be handled and on the other hand it points out the vulnerabilities of systems. For business management the concept of resilience is promising due to

- its turning away from the equilibrium assumption,
- its widespread comprehension of the environment and its influences,
- its assumption of flexibility and adaptiveness through the adaptive capacity,
- its focus on the preservation of essential system functions and structures,
- its potential for widening sustainability concepts.

Consequently, the resilience concept is not about the search for an optimal state. Furthermore, resilience is understood to have a buffering capacity, which allows fluctuations but the scale and amount of fluctuation is dependent on the context and on value-laden aspects.

Within business management literature, there are the first approaches for a resilience management of firms (Günther et al., 2007; Starr et al., 2003; Resilient Organizations, 2007). Analyzing these, one realizes that current resilience management approaches mainly contain a lack of practical information. Existing concepts are based on different theoretical assumptions and therefore no common resilience definition within business management literature exists to this point. In addition to the resilience definition of the Resilient Organizations (2007, p. 1), the authors understand resilience as "a function of an organization's

- situation awareness,
- management of keystone vulnerabilities, and
- adaptive capacity in a complex, dynamic and interconnected environment".

Against the background of increasing climate change and the resulting uncertainties and risks, the resilience concept tends towards a change of perspective: Resilience implies that the future changes too rapidly for an immediate response. Perrings (2006, p. 424), for example, states that "the most resilient systems in the long term are not necessarily the most productive in the short-term". Whereas risk management approaches give operation guidelines after a disturbance has taken place, considering the resilience idea implicates that the system's design has to be pro-actively changed in advance. Criteria for this can be building redundancies, flexible structures, diversity, modularity and buffering capacities.

Amongst international discussions, the concept of resilience becomes increasingly important, especially in the context of adaptation measures to climate change, its potential impacts as well as for sustainability concepts. The sustainability concept is characterized by diverse principles (e.g. precautionary principle) and originated from a structure based on the triple-bottom-line, which defines sustainability as a balanced mix between economic, social and ecological goals (Brundtland Report, 1987). Today, sustainability is understood in a dynamic way in terms of regulative ideas (Pfriem, 2006) and different strategic types and focuses on corporate environmental management systems (Sroufe & Sarkis, 2007). According to this dynamic perspective of sustainability, the resilience concept is also characterized by a turning away from the equilibrium assumption. Levin et al. (1998) argues that the concept of resilience offers ways of thinking about sustainability of economic-environmental systems. According to that, Perrings (1998, p. 503) deals with the concern that "desirable states or processes may not be sustainable [...and] that individuals and society may get locked-in into undesirable states or processes." He further concludes that "resilience switches the attention away from long-run-equilibria, and towards the system's capacity to respond to short-run shocks and stresses in a constructive and creative way" (Perrings, 1998, p. 517). Concerning a special issue regarding resilience and sustainable development, published in 2006, Perrings concludes that "a development strategy is not sustainable if it is not resilient: i.e. if it involves a significant risk that the economy can be flipped from a desirable state (path) into an undesirable state (path), and if that change is either irreversible or only slowly reversible" (2006, p. 418).

Amongst business management literature there still exists no common understanding about the relationship between sustainability and resilience (Beermann, 2009). Enhancing CEMIS as managerial tool with resilience thinking might bring new stimuli for research in this direction.

The authors therefore suggest perceiving the idea of resilience as a guiding principle to cope with impacts caused by climate change. Aside from the importance of theoretical implications for firms and their strategic coping with climate change caused impacts (see paragraph 3 and 4), additional challenges according to the application of a Corporate Environmental Management Information System (CEMIS) have to be considered for further conceptual and theoretical development. Figure 1 shows which theoretical and conceptual improvements can potentially be achieved by transferring the resilience idea to strategic management needs.

The resilience idea has to be integrated within the structure of CEMIS. Criteria for designing a system's structure can be building redundancies,

Figure 1. Table of resilience as a guiding principle for a system's design – challenges for CEMIS due to impacts caused by climate change

Direct Impacts	Fish Sector	Meat/Poultry Sector	Vegetable/Fruit Sector
Rise in Temperature	0	+	++
Rise in Average Rainfall	0	+	++
More Extreme Weather Events	0	+	++
Rise of Sea-Level	+	0	0
Rise of Sea Temperature	++	0	0
Indirect Impacts			
Change of Transport Conditions	+	+	+
Risks for Supply Chain Management	+	+	+
Rise of Production Insecurities	++	+	++
Changes in Demand	++	++	+

Degree of vulnerability	0	+	++

flexible structures, diversity, modularity and buffering capacities. Consequently, resilience can be understood as an encompassing guiding principle of the ability (of a system) to absorb disturbances and to retain basic function and structure. The abilities and capacities of a system play an important role in keeping the system in a dynamic balance and in sustaining its structure and function.

For Corporate Environmental Management Information Systems, resilience can bring new stimuli to handle these new challenges. The following paragraph will provide examples to demonstrate the need for resilient structures and processes within different sectors of the food industry. Against this background, the fourth paragraph will demonstrate that management systems have to broaden their theoretical as well as strategic focus towards possible climate change and consequential societal and cultural changes.

IMPACTS CAUSED BY CLIMATE CHANGE AND THE NEED FOR RESILIENT PROCESSES

First of all, impacts caused by climate change are complex, dynamic and due to the adaptive capacity of firms in general, difficult to handle. Depending on the country and region, a firm operates in supply chains and depending on their complexities, impacts caused by climate change have to be identified. Therefore, the food industry is a good example to understand how climate change can have different impacts on sectors and firms within the food industry. The food industry is characterized by its supply chain encompassing variety. Especially in the meat sector, a supply chain-wide perspective and exchange of operational environmental information systems is necessary (Keßeler, 2000). Aside from agricultural primary production, different production and processing sectors exist, e.g. the fish, vegetable/fruit and meat/poultry sector. They are all characterized by certain conditions and degrees of climate change vulnerabilities. Figure 2 shows examples of some direct and indirect vulnerabilities within the food industry in North Western Germany due to impacts caused by climate change. They are the results of an entrepreneur workshop held in May 2009 in the research project nw2050. Even though it is not always possible to identify certain limits of a sector's specific vulnerabilities, this simplified scheme is able to clarify several important insights:

- Besides direct impacts, indirect impacts caused by climate change also have to be considered.
- Climate change is a worldwide process which affects firms in various ways, e.g. in the context of supply chain management, production planning, marketing strategies, etc.
- Unexpected discontinuities can be relevant for certain processes even if they are not directly coupled with climate change. Even more difficult to handle are outcomes of indirect climate change caused impacts.

The coloured boxes show the expected relevance for certain sectors:

Figure 2 shows that all three sectors in the food industry (fish, vegetable/fruit, meat/poultry) are more vulnerable through *indirect* than direct impacts. Due to that, firms have to consider that challenges caused by climate change can be highly complex and that the outcomes can be more uncertain than expected. While direct impacts are

Figure 2. Table of vulnerabilities within three sectors of the food industry caused by climate change

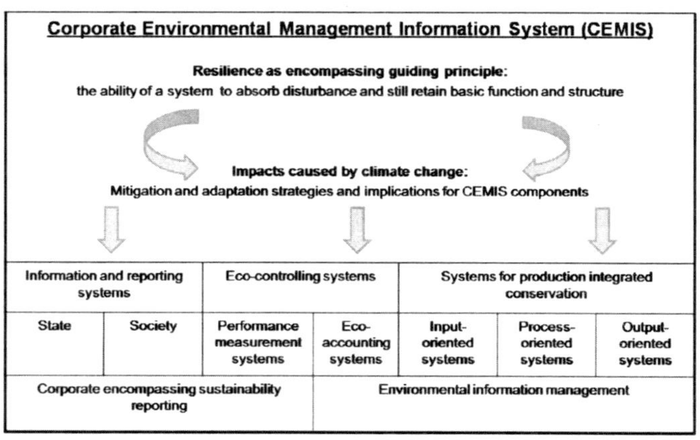

the perceived natural weather conditions such as temperature and rainfall, indirect impacts implicate a high factor of uncertainty for firms because of potential variations in production or disturbances along the supply chain. Furthermore, figure 2 illustrates specific differences between the sectors in detail. Problematically for the fish sector is the rise in sea temperature, because some species cannot grow or survive under warmer conditions. In general, effects on the supply chain could be changes in offer and demand (changing eating habits) and insecurities concerning production processes. In contrast to the meat sector, the vegetable and fruit sector is more vulnerable through direct impacts and the rapidly changing weather conditions that can lead to crop failure or extreme variability. For the meat and poultry sector, however, the indirect impacts are more afflicted with risk, for example the global development of prices for animal feed and changes in consumer demand towards Mediterranean eating habits in times of rising outdoor temperatures. Furthermore, direct impacts of rising temperature can also affect the supply chain, because hygiene problems in stables can lead to inefficiency and epidemic disease. The results show the different degrees of indirect and direct impacts of climate change and their variation according to certain sectors in the food industry. Therefore, a specific strategic handling of these challenges is necessary for firms.

Regarding these insights, the need for robust and resilient structures and processes becomes clear. In the case of the food industry, firms have to realize and be sensitive to the meaning of direct and indirect impacts caused by climate change. They have to inform themselves as to ways in which the firm might be vulnerable towards discontinuities (cf. Beermann, 2009) and integrate concepts of adaptation in their strategic management practice. It is important to realize that firms operate in a highly networked and globalized environment so that structures can also be affected by changes due to climate change occurring in other countries. Therefore changes become not only apparent in varying prices and availabilities but also in the changing quality of resources, consumer demands or technical challenges as a consequence of the described impacts of figure 2. Even if many paths for innovations in the context of climate change for the firms in the food industry exist, first of all, the challenges have to be recognized as chances for change and not only as risks (cf. Beermann & Schattke, 2009). These chances and choices of adaptation and/or mitigation strategies as a reaction to climate change challenges can be answered through the resilience concept which in this context can be seen as an encompassing guiding principle, also for CEMIS. The encompassing guiding principle is necessary because CEMIS itself reacts to the environmental information in general. The information due to climate change is complex, multidimensional and is interpretable as to whether the direct or indirect impacts are more dangerous or more influential for the system state. Therefore, CEMIS as managerial tool could provide a system component that includes a consideration of the decision, the striking course and their following consequences which can help the firm to deal with climate change.

To operationalize the resilience concept as a guiding principle and capacity of adaptation and mitigation in times of uncertainty and risk, firms have to develop cultural competences as a learning concept in strategic management. CEMIS can be a highly helpful *managerial tool* to support and to develop this difficult process of learning, and to enlarge the capabilities of firms' agents for corporate foresight and for participation in the future quality of society.

The following paragraph will give theoretical insight into which preconditions have to be considered by the strategic management of firms in order to successfully handle impacts caused by climate change.

THE RELEVANCE OF CULTURAL COMPETENCES IN STRATEGIC MANAGEMENT: THE "NEW" ROLE OF FIRMS

The Idea of Interactional Economics

In addition to the importance of corporate foresight within strategic management, the role of firms in modern society nowadays has to be reflected upon. The role of firms therefore is not only characterized by offering organizations and demanding consumers but also by interactional and recursive processes between economical, societal and cultural relationships and challenges (cf. Giddens, 1984; FUGO, 2004). This approach defines firms as social agents and raises the question: How can firms evolve themselves to a capacity in order to be able to interact appropriately and successfully with the recursiveness between supply and demand, and societal and cultural processes?

In order to understand interactional relationships between society and entrepreneurial development (cf. Sachs, 2000) as a form of responsibility, it is necessary for firms to build strategies that take the societal mind and consciousness into account. This concept of an interactional and recursive strategic management identifies firms as creative and pro-active agents with the capacity to change or develop the future quality of society. Thus, it is necessary to recognize that economic activity does not solely rely on timeless regularities of mechanics and self-interest but is merged into societal and cultural processes. This theoretical conception implies that social and cultural phenomena are not objectively given – but rather to be always interactively produced. Kenneth Boulding considered in his essay „Toward the Development of a Cultural Economics", published in 1972, the fact that a recuperation of the reflection of the cultural context could help economics to overcome the mechanistic abstract thinking as it resonates in the rationality paradigm of the *homo oeconomicus* and in numerous mathematical models. He supports focusing on learning processes: „The emphasis on learning is perhaps the crucial difference between mechanistic economics and cultural economics. Mechanistic economics tends to take preferences and even skills and techniques for granted, as the data or ultimate determinants of the economic process. Cultural economics must look upon both preferences, skills, and techniques as essentially learned in the great processes of cultural transmission. (…) Social learning, indeed, is the central concept of culture." (Boulding, 1972, p. 273)

Analyzing the meat sector clarifies that firms in the food industry, in general, hold a special role as societal agents due to their society influencing corporate, economical, societal and cultural developments. Considering this, the need for interactional and recursive strategic management is obviously which focuses on the importance of specific capacities in strategic management of firms. The German meat industry illustrates this context. Especially the method of industrialized technical production in industrial livestock farming and the high degradation of automation in slaughterhouses lead to a new situation for producing firms, which is mainly a consequence of societal and cultural processes like acceleration, subjectivism and technical formations. These developments lead to estrangement effects of society from the meat sector and the methods of producing this natural food. The consequences are an isolated, unknown and non-transparent sector with huge problems with public relations, advertising and publicity, which in the end leads to a bad reputation for the whole meat sector (cf. Schattke, 2008; Albersmeier & Spiller, 2009). Against this background, a promising approach is seen in a culturally based corporate communication strategy (cf. Pfriem, Schattke & Uphoff, 2009) which can only be successful if strategic management processes are understood interactionally and recursively between firms and customers on the one hand, and societal and cultural processes on the other hand. Climate change caused impacts can reinforce the need for a recursive and interactional view of the society's consciousness concerning the importance of being resilient and building adaptive capacities (cf. Beermann & Schattke, 2009). In order to cope with increasing complexity and dynamics due to impacts caused by climate change, firms have to develop *cultural competences*, which enable them to handle new challenges appropriately. Climate change caused challenges appear above all as cultural challenges because they influence the cultural processes and they are also intensified by these.

The next paragraph will evaluate how the question of development and realignment of strategic management due to impacts caused by climate change is linked to the theory of social practice and the competence theory of the firm.

WITH PRACTICE BASED STUDIES TO STRATEGIC COMPETENCE MANAGEMENT

In order to comprehend and to cope with the complexity and the dynamics of the described challenges due to climate change, the development of specific competences in firms is necessary. In this paragraph, the theoretical approach to *cultural competences* as an essential element of strategic management of firms will be outlined. Above all, the term competence includes a program which covers the need for self-organization of actions due to increasing economical, social and cultural complexity and dynamics (cf. Weinert, 2001; Schmidt, 2005). Below, the term is linked to the theory of social practice and to the competence based theory of the firm.

While former theories of action privilege the intentionality of agents, from which derives meaningful action (in the tradition of Weber and Parsons), the theory of social practice locates the source of significant patterns in how conduct is enacted, performed or produced in interaction and recursively (in the tradition of Dewey, Mead, Garfinkel and Giddens). In general, Practice Based Studies (PBS) define a 'practice' as a routinized type of behavior consisting of several elements, interconnected to one another: forms of bodily activities, forms of mental activities, 'things' and their use, a background knowledge in the form of understanding, know-how, states of emotion and motivational knowledge (Reckwitz, 2002, p. 249). For Schatzki knowledge is "*practical intelligibility*" (Schatzki, 1996, p. 75). Practical intelligibility combines both the incorporation of routines (*culturally based knowledge*) and the performance of a competent doing or saying (*doing knowledge)* (cf. Reckwitz, 2004, p. 45; Hörning & Reuter, 2004).

The concept of social practice, developed by Hörning (2004), originates from Cultural Studies, which emphasize the important role of the creative competence of agents in constructing everyday culture (cf. Hebdige, 1979; Willis, 1990). Social practice therefore has a three-part structure of action and quality of knowledge:

1. *Unconscious actions* as coordinated procedures of action over-subjectively embedded in routines of social interaction processes (education practices, practices of private lifestyle, time practices, communication practices, practices of negotiation, work practices, practices of political debate).
2. *Collective repertoires of knowledge*, which find their implicit expression as collective meaning and action knowledge. Collective repertoires of knowledge form the condition of homogenous action forms.
3. *Creative competence of agents* (cf. Hörning & Reuter, 2004).

Apart from routines and/or unconscious actions as procedures of reproduction, there exists a high relevance of a creative and innovative potential in the *competence of agents*. This implicit double-sidedness of social practice as a form of *reproduction* and *innovation* justifies the strength of the practical turn in action theory, which is also highlighted by Alan Warde: „The principal implication of a theory of practice is that the sources of changed behaviour lie in the development of practices themselves. The concept of practice inherently combines a capacity to account for both reproduction und innovation." (Warde, 2005, p. 140).

These described approaches, in order to outline the term competence in the theory of social practice, are elaborated for individual agents, but not especially for organizations. Gherardi contextualizes the theory of social practice with a critical discussion of knowledge and competence in managerial and organizational studies. She points out the knowledge-based and interactional quality of practices: "Knowing is something that people do together, and it is done in every mundane activity, in organizations when people work together, and also in academic fields. To know is to be able to participate with the requisite competence in the complex web of relationships among people, material artefacts and activities" (Gherardi, 2009, p. 118). Thus, knowing in organizations means *to be competent in a network of connections-in-action*.

The prominent position of competence in the social practices of firms as an interactional networking concept marks the link between the theory of practice and the competence theory of the firm. In competence theory, a firm is characterized as an open system of asset stocks and flows including tangible assets like production equipment and intangible assets like capabilities and cognitions. The firm as a managed open system pursues a set of organizational strategic goals that collectively motivate the strategic actions of the firm (cf. Sanchez & Heene, 1997, p. 306; Sanchez, 2001). Sanchez et al. (1996, p. 6) also observed competences as an instrument for "competitive interactions between firms": "... analyzing competition as a dynamic contest between competences seems to strike a useful balance between a need to encompass the complexity and dynamism of real-world competition, on the one hand, and the need for sense making by humans with limited cognitive capabilities form understanding dynamic complexity, on the other. Taking competences as the unit of analysis in strategy research and theory-building appears to cast the right size conceptual net into the sea of competitive interactions between firms." Thus, competence theory intends to provide a conceptual framework for linking the dynamics of firms' internal processes and their external competitive interactions.

Maria Joutsenvirta and Liisa Uusitalo suggest that certain *cultural* competences should be considered as the key factor for the success, innovativeness and legitimacy of business organizations which operate in an ever more globally interlinked, culturally diverse and socially concerned world (cf. Joutsenvirta & Uusitalo, 2009). In earlier Practice Based Studies, cultural competences have been studied especially as individual characteristics of citizens and consumers who try to improve their position in a social hierarchy within a specific field (cf. Bourdieu, 1984). Joutsenvirta and Uusitalo outline cultural competence of firms as an organizational capacity to interact between firms and customers considering societal and cultural processes: *"Cultural competence refers to the sensitivity of the firm toward the surrounding societal and cultural changes, especially changes in customer values and behavior, and the ability to transfer this knowledge into meaningful business practices"* (Joutsenvirta & Uusitalo, 2009, p. 2). An organization's capacity to create a sense of community and trust in its relationships with customers, personnel, and commercial partners is also a part of cultural competence. Furthermore, cultural competence is expressed in a pro-active approach to marketing and consumers, i.e. searching and developing markets for new innovations and seeing the customer as a co-producer and partner. In addition to Joutsenvirta & Uusitalo, *cultural competences can be seen as the practical intelligibility of firms and as a learning concept for adaptive capacity. In order to cope with increasing complexity and dynamics due to impacts caused by climate change, cultural competences enable firms to handle these new challenges appropriately. In times of expanding uncertainty and risk, cultural competences help to increase the resilience of the firm against vulnerabilities, by recognizing sensitively, reflecting critically, and reconfiguring creatively emerging conflicts due to changing societal and cultural processes to the aim of sustainable strategic management.*

Especially by the paraphrased example of the food industry, the changing societal and cultural processes, added to the direct and indirect impacts caused by climate change, demonstrate the necessity of cultural competences for firms to develop resilient system structures for the future. Supported by CEMIS as a critical information system, emerging conflicts due to changing societal and cultural processes can be handled at an early stage in order to develop sustainable management strategies. Besides this background of competence in theory of practice and competence theory of the firm, we propose to consider the societal and cultural context of practices, because challenges caused by climate change appear above all as societal and cultural challenges.

The extension of the Practice Based Studies to an interactional and recursive strategic management therefore implies three process steps (cf. Antoni-Komar, Lautermann & Pfriem, 2010):

1. The *recognition* of cultural processes as ambivalent temporal pathways,
2. The *critical reflection* of the embarrassment by cultural processes, of their action-structuring function and socio-political dimension,
3. The *reconfiguration* of social challenges with the aim of sustainable development.

Due to this strategic change in *recognizing* the multiple and ambivalent cultural processes as an important part of economic practice, the critical *reflection* and after all the productive *reconfiguration,* the black box of firms as social agents can be opened. Figure 3 illustrates against the background of a practice-theoretical understanding of economic actions, how firms can strive for strategic competence management. Firms are constructing societal and *cultural processes* by

Figure 3. The firm as a social agent: cultural competences as an element of strategic management

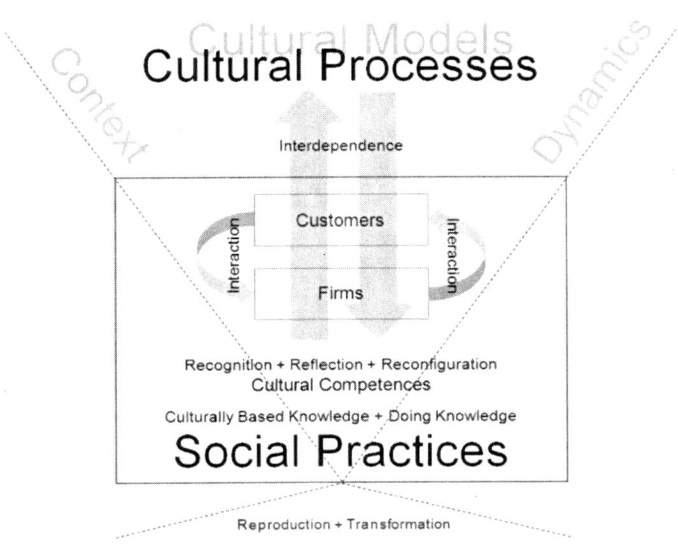

social practices as a combination of *culturally based knowledge* and *doing knowledge*. Strategic competence management is an *interactional* networking between *firms and customers* as agents and an *interdependent* one between *agents and societal and cultural processes*. *Cultural competences* are an essential element of strategic management and help to successfully manage the resulting challenges of *contextual* and *dynamic* complexity. Against the background of *cultural models* as guiding principles, both *reproducing* and *transforming* of societal and cultural processes are possible.

The question of the development of specific strategic management competences is therefore coupled with the problem of cultural competences as *practical intelligibility* and context-referred knowledge of firms. With this pro-active concept of a cultural approach in economic theory, the authors focus on the adaptive capacity of firms. Therefore, firms should notice, react promptly and sensitively as well as assimilate market-referred cultural processes in society, which are utilized in their own current and possible future business activities. Due to current challenges of climate change and sustainability (e.g. climate protection and climate adaptation), available strategic approaches are to this point not sufficient. This means to recognize the critical reflection of multiple historical and intensified reciprocal processes (e.g. technological formations of society, social acceleration (hastening), subjectivism, scientification, medialization), because these can counteract the sustainable development of society (cf. Antoni-Komar, 2009; Antoni-Komar & Pfriem, 2009).

Thus corporate responsibility is not an exogenous demand to the firm, but is rather mobilized as self-organized cultural competences, that unpredictable problems are solved in unpredictable contexts (cf. Schmidt, 2005, p. 21) – a difference thus between heteronomy and self-determination. As a result, cultural competences enable firms to participate in the future quality of society and to develop trust in its relationships with customers, personnel, and commercial partners (cf. Joutsenvirta & Uusitalo, 2009). However, only in the performance of the firm, the production and distribution of goods and services and their market-referred strategies, the cultural competences can be observed and ascribed to the firm itself by customers. That means conversely that firms not only reflect social practices and competences in the firms' internal processes itself, but also the social practices and competences of the consumers as co-producers and partners, including their socio-cultural dimension and their climate impacts. The special relevance of the development of cultural competences indicates: the cultural competences of firms get their legitimation not only by handling contingency, but also by the reflection of interactional and recursive structures.

CONCLUSION

Besides the importance of theoretical implications for firms and their strategic coping with impacts caused by climate change, this paper also presents the additional challenges due to the application of a Corporate Environmental Management Information System (CEMIS) which should be considered for further conceptual and theoretical development. First of all, the use of the system-theoretic terminology and the resilience concept leads to the possibility of rethinking and reconfiguring future strategic management of a certain sector and its corporate environmental information systems. The new challenges caused by climate change have to be integrated in planning, configuration and implementation of CEMIS, in reference to the emerging challenges in societal and cultural processes. The question of the adaptive capacity or resilience of the firm (or the system) can be answered through their underlying cultural competences. So CEMIS itself as a *managerial tool* has an excellent potential to increase organizational resilience against vulnerabilities due to impacts caused by climate change by considering the interactional and recursive structures of strategic management (Figure 4).

Firms have to cope with additional challenges due to impacts caused by climate change, which increase the existence of dynamic and complex uncertainty and risk. Against the background of the food industry, this paper illustrates in which way climate change can cause direct and indirect impacts that lead to the need to identify corporate specific resources like *cultural competences*. In this difficult and manifold learning process, CEMIS has the potential to become a relevant and helpful *mediator of knowledge* for the adaptive capacity of firms against multidimensional vulnerabilities. For example CEMIS could provide quantitative and qualitative climate change scenarios for different impacts in global and regional dimensions. Scenarios as alternative images of how the future might unfold are an appropriate tool with which to analyze how driving forces may influence future emission outcomes and to assess the associated uncertainties and risks. They assist in climate change analysis, including climate modeling and the assessment of impacts, adaptation and mitigation. While handling the new challenges for firms by recognizing and integrating the described circumstances, a methodical widening of CEMIS needs to be fostered due to the fact that besides quantitative data, also qualitative data can contain important key information.

Using the food industry as an example, this paper illustrates, that impacts caused by climate change require new methods of corporate coping. CEMIS as managerial tool helps to support firms, that have to take impacts by climate change into account, with appropriate information. A precondition for this is the building of specific competences which enables firms to use the information given by CEMIS in an appropriate, i.e. reflective way. That implies considering not only internal processes of the firm but also external, i.e. societal and cultural developments. Resilient structures and processes therefore depend on certain capabilities of social agents and on the adaptive capacity of the firm. The adaptive capacity encompasses learning processes that contain the resilience idea.

The paper demonstrates, against the background of the food industry, the need for an enhancement of CEMIS. Next research steps need to analyze how this conceptual approach can be transferred to other sectors, e.g. information and

Figure 4. New challenges for CEMIS and firms due to impacts caused by climate change – resilient structures against vulnerabilities through cultural competences

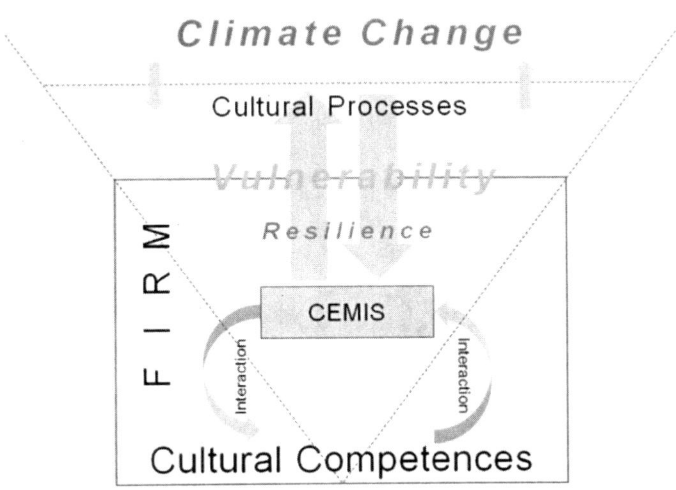

communication technology or the energy sector. Furthermore, future research concerning CEMIS has to strengthen the inter- and transdisciplinary approach, which becomes even more important against the background of impacts caused by climate change. The link between a more technical implementation of CEMIS and an interactional strategic management-orientated focus needs further cooperation between firms and customers, between technological science, natural science, social and cultural sciences for the successful handling of new challenges within corporate environmental management information systems.

REFERENCES

Albersmeier, F., & Spiller, A. (2009). Das Ansehen der Fleischwirtschaft: Zur Bedeutung einer stufenübergreifenden Perspektive. In J. Böhm, F. Albersmeier, & A. Spiller (Eds.), Die Ernährungswirtschaft im Scheinwerferlicht der Öffentlichkeit (pp. 213-250). Lohmar, Köln: EUL Verlag.

Antoni-Komar, I. (2009). Die Neudefinition von Lebensqualität: Kulturelle Implikationen ökonomischer Praxis. In I. Antoni-Komar, M. Beermann, C. Lautermann, J. Müller, N. Paech, H. Schattke, U. Schneidewind, & R. Schulz (Eds.), Neue Konzepte der Ökonomik. Unternehmen zwischen Nachhaltigkeit, Kultur und Ethik (pp. 329-347). Marburg: Metropolis Verlag.

Antoni-Komar, I., Lautermann, C., & Pfriem, R. (2010). Kulturelle Kompetenzen. Interaktionsökonomische Erweiterungsperspektiven für den Competence-based View des Strategischen Managements. In M. Stephan, W. Kerber, T. Kessler, & M. Lingenfelder (Eds.), 25 Jahre ressourcen- und kompetenzorientierte Forschung. Der kompetenzbasierte Ansatz auf dem Weg zum Schlüsselparadigma in der Managementforschung (pp. 465-489). Wiesbaden: Gabler Verlag, (forthcoming)

Antoni-Komar, I., & Pfriem, R. (2009). Kulturalistische Ökonomik. Vom Nutzen einer Neuorientierung wirtschaftswissenschaftlicher Untersuchungen. WENKE2-Diskussionspapier 06/09. Oldenburg.

Beermann, M. (2009). *Enterprise resilience: a concept for coping with climate change challenges. Theoretical considerations.* Conference contribution from 15th Annual International Sustainable Development Research Conference. Utrecht/Netherlands.

Beermann, M., & Schattke, H. (2009). Innovationspotenziale für die Ernährungswirtschaft: Das Resilience-Konzept als Perspektivwechsel. In I. Antoni-Komar, M. Beermann, C. Lautermann, J. Müller, N. Paech, H. Schattke, U. Schneidewind, & R. Schulz (Eds.), Neue Konzepte der Ökonomik. Unternehmen zwischen Nachhaltigkeit, Kultur und Ethik (pp.119-141). Marburg: Metropolis Verlag.

Berkhout, F., Hertin, J., & Gann, D. M. (2006). Learning to Adapt: Organisational Adaptation to Climate Change Impacts. *Climatic Change*, *78*(1), 135–156. doi:10.1007/s10584-006-9089-3

Boulding, K. E. (1972). Toward the Development of a Cultural Economics. *Social Science Quarterly*, *53*(2), 267–284.

Bourdieu, P. (1984). *Distinction: A social critique of judgement of taste*. London: Routledge and Kegan Paul.

Forschungsgruppe Unternehmen und gesellschaftliche Organisation (FUGO) (Ed.). (2004). *Perspektiven einer kulturwissenschaftlichen Theorie der Unternehmung*. Marburg: Metropolis Verlag.

Gherardi, S. (2009). Introduction: The Critical Power of the 'Practice Lens'. *Management Learning*, *40*, 115–128..doi:10.1177/1350507608101225

Giddens, A. (1984). *The Constitution of Society: Outline of the Theory of Structuration*. Cambridge: Polity Press.

Günther, E., Kirchgeorg, M., & Winn, M. (2007). Resilience Management: Konzeptentwurf zum Umgang mit Auswirkungen des Klimawandels. *UmweltWirtschaftsForum*, *15*, 175–182.

Hebdige, D. (1979). *Subculture: The Meaning of Style*. London: Taylor & Francis. doi:10.4324/9780203139943

Holling, C. S. (1973). Resilience and Stability of Ecological Systems. *Annual Review of Ecology and Systematics*, *4*, 1–23. doi:10.1146/annurev.es.04.110173.000245

Hörning, K. H. (2004). Kultur als Praxis. In F. Jäger, & B. Liebsch (Eds.), Handbuch der Kulturwissenschaften (pp. 139-151). Stuttgart, Weimar: Akademie Verlag.

Hörning, K. H., & Reuter, J. (2004). Doing Culture: Neue Positionen zum Verhältnis von Kultur und sozialer Praxis. Bielefeld: transcript-Verlag.

Joutsenvirta, M., & Uusitalo, L. (2009). Cultural Competences: An Important Resource in the Industry–NGO Dialog. *Journal of Business Ethics*. doi:.doi:10.1007/s10551-009-0089-x

Keßeler, T. (2000). Kettenübergreifender Austausch von einzelbetrieblichen Umweltinformationen in Unternehmen der Land- und Ernährungswirtschaft. In L.M. Hilty, D. Schulthess, & T.F. Ruddy (Eds.), Strategische und betriebsübergreifende Anwendungen betrieblicher Umweltinformationssysteme (pp. 125-142). Marburg: Metropolis Verlag.

Lang, C. V. (2007). Modeling of a Corporate Environmental Management Information System (CEMIS) for Production Processes. In Marx Gómez, J. C., Sonnenschein, M., Müller, M., & Welsch, H. (Eds.), *Information Technologies in Environmental Engineering* (pp. 231–240). Berlin, Heidelberg: Springer Verlag. doi:10.1007/978-3-540-71335-7_24

Levin, S. A., Barrett, S., Aniyar, S., Baumol, W., Bliss, C., & Bolin, B. (1998). Resilience in natural and socioeconomic systems. *Environment and Development Economics*, *3*(2), 222–234. doi:10.1017/S1355770X98240125

Marx Gómez, J. C., Sonnenschein, M., Müller, M., & Welsch, H. (Eds.). (2007). *Information Technologies in Environmental Engineering: ITEE 2007 – Third International ICSC Symposium*. Carl-von-Ossietzky-Universität Oldenburg. Berlin, Heidelberg: Springer Verlag.

Odum, E. P. (1971). *Fundamentals of ecology* (3rd ed.). Philadelphia: Brooks Cole.

Organisations, R. (2007). Resilience Management: A Framework for Assessing and Improving the Resilience of Organisations, Research Report 01/2007. Retrieved October 29, 2009, from http://www.resorgs.org.nz/pubs/Resilience%20Management%20Research%20Report%20ResOrgs%2007-01.pdf

Perrings, C. (1998). Resilience in the Dynamics of Economy-Environment Systems. *Environmental and Resource Economics*, *11*(3-4), 503–520. doi:10.1023/A:1008255614276

Perrings, C. (2006). Resilience and sustainable development. *Environment and Development Economics*, *11*, 417–427. doi:10.1017/S1355770X06003020

Pfriem, R. (2006). *Unternehmensstrategien: Ein kulturalistischer Zugang zum Strategischen Management.* Marburg: Metropolis Verlag.

Pfriem, R., Schattke, H., & Uphoff, K. (2009). Nachhaltigkeit als kommunikationspolitische Herausforderung der niedersächsischen Fleischwirtschaft. In J. Böhm, F. Albersmeier, & A. Spiller (Eds.), Die Ernährungswirtschaft im Scheinwerferlicht der Öffentlichkeit (pp. 251-271). Lohmar, Köln: EUL Verlag.

Rautenstrauch, C. (1999). *Betriebliche Umweltinformationssysteme: Grundlagen, Konzepte und Systeme*. Berlin, Heidelberg: Springer Verlag.

Reckwitz, A. (2002). Toward a theory of social practices: A development in culturalist theorizing. *European Journal of Social Theory*, *5*, 243–263. doi:10.1177/13684310222225432

Reckwitz, A. (2004). Die Reproduktion und die Subversion sozialer Praktiken: Zugleich ein Kommentar zu Pierre Bourdieu und Judith Butler. In K.H. Hörning, & J. Reuter (Eds.), Doing culture: Neue Positionen zum Verhältnis von Kultur und soziale Praxis (pp 40-54). Bielefeld: transcript-Verlag.

Report, B. (1987). *Report of the world commission of environment.* Retrieved October 29, 2009, from http://www.bne-portal.de/coremedia/generator/unesco/de/Downloads/Hintergrundmaterial_international/Brundtlandbericht.pdf.

Sachs, S. (2000). *Die Rolle der Unternehmung in ihrer Interaktion mit der Gesellschaft*. Bern: Paul Haupt Verlag.

Sanchez, R. (2001). Resources, dynamic capabilities, and competences: Building blocks of integrative strategy theory. In Elfring, T., & Volberda, H. (Eds.), *Rethinking strategy* (pp. 143–157). Thousand Oaks, CA: Sage Publications.

Sanchez, R., & Heene, A. (Eds.). (1996). *Strategic Learning and Knowledge Management*. Chichester: John Wiley & Sons.

Sanchez, R., & Heene, A. (1997). Reinventing Strategic Management: New Theory and Practice for Competence-based Competition. *European Management Journal*, *15*(3), 303–317. doi:10.1016/S0263-2373(97)00010-8

Schattke, H. (2008). Nachhaltigkeit und Qualitätskommunikation in der niedersächsischen Fleischwirtschaft: Eine empirische Annäherung. Schriftenreihe des Lehrstuhls für Allgemeine Betriebswirtschaftslehre, Unternehmensführung und Betriebliche Umweltpolitik, 47, Oldenburg.

Schatzki, T. R. (1996). *Social Practices. A Wittgensteinian Approach to Human Activity and the Social*. Cambridge: Cambridge University Press. doi:10.1017/CBO9780511527470

Schmidt, S. J. (2005). *Lernen, Wissen, Kompetenz, Kultur: Vorschläge zur Bestimmung von vier Unbekannten*. Heidelberg: Carl-Auer Verlag.

Sroufe, R., & Sarkis, J. (2007). *Strategic Sustainability: The state of the art in corporate environmental management systems*. Sheffield: Greenleaf.

Starr, R., Newfrock, J., & Delurey, M. (2003). *Enterprise Resilience: Managing Risk in the Networked Economy*. Retrieved October 15, 2009, from http://www.boozallen.com/media/file/139766.pdf

Warde, A. (2005). Consumption and Theories of Practice. *Journal of Consumer Culture*, *5*, 131–153. doi:10.1177/1469540505053090

Weinert, F. E. (2001). A concept of competence: A conceptual clarification. In Rychen, D. S., & Salganik, L. H. (Eds.), *Defining and selecting key competencies* (pp. 45–65). Seattle: Hogrefe.

Willis, P. (1990). Common Culture: Symbolic work at play in the everyday cultures of the young. Milton Keynes: Open University Press.

Chapter 6
Paving the Way towards Virtual Biorefineries

Barbara Rapp
Carl von Ossietzky University Oldenburg, Germany

Jörg Bremer
Carl von Ossietzky University Oldenburg, Germany

ABSTRACT

Biomass nowadays gets an ever increasing importance as a substitute for fossil fuels and as a source of energy as well as of materials for chemical products. In comparison with other raw materials, biomass has distinguishing and additional production or rather clearing characteristics that have to be taken into account for sustainable and successful biomass supply chains. This chapter explores the drawbacks and opportunities of existing approaches to biomass logistics and continues with a detailed description of an advanced procurement system, which has been developed as a proof-of-concept by the authors. Procurement driven by meta-data based data acquisition will be discussed as a starting point for a variety of missing features in today's environmental information system's support for forming inter-business linkages in regional biomass networks. These ideas are further developed into a concept for a virtual biorefinery as an advanced system for an appropriate treatment of biomass concerning economical, ecological and sociological sustainability issues at the same time.

INTRODUCTION

The current age of fossil oil will come to an end. As yet, it might still be unclear when and moreover why this will happen, but if we are on the verge of the age of biomass, it is worth thinking about design considerations in time. Sheik Ahmed Zaki Yamani, former Minister of Oil and Mineral Resources of Saudi Arabia, has put it this way already in the 70s:

"The Stone Age came to an end not for a lack of stone, and the oil age will end, but not for a lack of oil."

The use of biomass gets an ever increasing importance: as a substitute for fossil fuels as well as a source of energy and materials for chemical

DOI: 10.4018/978-1-61520-981-1.ch006

products. This increased demand for non-food applications competes with the maintenance of crops as the most important feedstock for food and feed. Biomass is basically stored solar energy collected by plants. Captured CO_2 is converted to plant material during photosynthesis. Therefore, biomass covers recently produced organic materials from plants including materials from animals that have fed on plants. Biomass ranges from crop, foresting or wood processing residues, animal wastes (incl. human sewage), municipal solid waste (excl. non-organic components), food processing wastes, cultivated energy crops to short rotation forests (International Energy Agency, 2007) as well as marine crops, e.g. algae. However, biomass is not inexhaustible, as a scarce commodity it has to be exploited in a way that different basic needs are fulfilled while the full potential is completely taped. Thus, intelligent management strategies are required for linking producers and consumers with intermediate preprocessing actors so that superior sustainability objectives are achieved. At this point, a need for information technology support arises since complex cross company concerns have to be managed, linked and optimized.

This chapter will explore the possibilities of existing approaches and continue with a detailed description of an advanced biomass procurement system, which has been developed as a proof-of-concept by the authors. These ideas are further developed into a concept for an advanced system including economical, ecological and sociological sustainability issues; reflecting visions of a virtual biorefinery from the University of Oldenburg and CUTEC-Institut GmbH.

BIOMASS CHARACTERISTICS

Biomass is a very flexible and multiply usable resource. Biomass is an utmost needed and essential source of food as it has always been. The same holds true for biomass as a source of feed not only for cattle but also for the whole wildlife. However, biomass - especially wood - is also a famous building material as it has always been. Relatively new is the use of biomass as a raw material for chemical products. Biomass also has always been an important source of energy as it still is in large proportions of the world (cf. Agbontalor, 2007). But, firewood for personal cooking and heating is not the only option for using biomass as an energy resource. Apart from producing electricity by directly firing biomass, today it is handled as a promising resource for fuel production – although not undisputed if not exploited carefully (cf. e.g. Zah et al., 2007, Davis, Anderson-Teixeira & DeLucia, 2008), as it is as a substitute for chemicals made of crude oil. Applications of biomass for energy are especially important, because it is a storable form of energy and therefore capable of providing base and peak energy. Research is still at an early stage, but there are already a lot of possibilities for new bio-based products, too.

It is the universalism in applicability that often breeds criticism and competing applications. Biomass is a scarce resource, but overall it is a symbol for life. Corn, crop, cereals are often seen as synonyms for food security, quality of life and social responsibility. Using biomass for energy conversion might be sensed as destruction or wastage of food. Energy conversion of biomass is often blamed for boosting food prices. According to the advisory board for renewable primary products (Beirat für nachwachsende Rohstoffe, 2005) of Lower Saxony, Germany, it is justifiable to convert biomass to energy (and other non-food products) if the requirements for food are met. It is in the responsibility of the biomass producers to show respectful consideration of today's generation needs before arguing with preservation of resources for future generations. Thus, it would be of an enormous advantage if biomass producers had a means to demonstrate that their mix of land use does no harm when partly producing for energy conversion.

The concept of using biomass for multiple purposes is not a new one, it is the natural one. But the human concept of usage is often completely alien to natural ecosystems (Agbontalor, 2007), as ecosystems have to completely recycle their matter (Patzek, 2004) and to be flexible enough to adapt continuously to changes in order to survive.

As has quite often been seen in history, the human race tends to overshoot exploitation of resources and then is 'intelligent' enough to go on and adapt to other resources or if that is not applicable to other regions. As a paragon for human induced ecological catastrophes Rap Nui (also known as Easter Island) is frequently adduced, although newer results suggest that at least a sequence of several circumstances has to be blamed (Hunt, 2007). The ancient islanders are said to have overstrained their wood consumption (partially for the lugging of statues) till nothing was left. Because no regard was paid to ecological interrelations, due to erosion effects the remaining soil finally did not yield enough crops anymore.

A better way was to adapt attitude and consumption to the possibilities of a resource - or if that is not applicable, adapt the way of exploiting this resource. Thus, the upcoming age of biomass should become the age of intelligent and sustainable exploitation of natural resources. The idea of businesses forming a symbiosis to cycle and recycle residues and wastes as well as by-products, in order to create added value by forming interlinkages within regional networks, is not new as well, as show books on this topic from the early nineteenth century as pointed out by Desrochers (2000).

Biomass Supply Chains

In comparison with other raw materials, biomass as a resource has distinguishing and some additional production or rather clearing characteristics that have to be taken into account for sustainable and successful biomass supply chains. Biomass supply chains therefore show some discriminating characteristics. A biomass supply chain consists of several stages of handling across different and maybe changing parties at each echelon (cf. e.g. Vlachos, Iakovou, Karagiannidis & Toka, 2008; Sambra, Sørensen & Kristensen, 2008). Activities include for example harvesting or collecting, pretreatment (e.g. drying, baling), storage, (short-distance) transport, (long-distance) transshipment and utilization - not necessarily in this order and not necessarily in a constant sequence.

Figure 1 depicts the supply chains for three applications (circles with diagonal stripes). The

Figure 1. Interlinked biomass supply chains

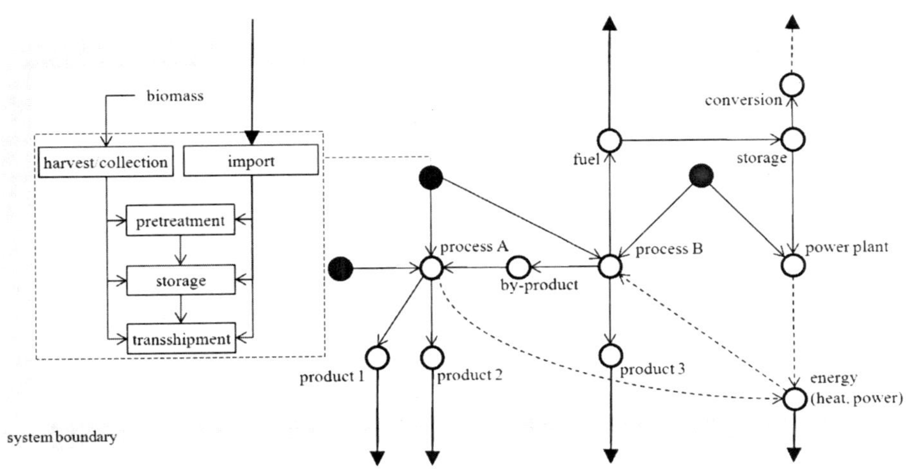

inter-woven structure shows that the chains form a network rather than distinct chains, if they are organized in an optimal way. The network contains three initial sources (filled circle), each representing a specific sub-net, like the one enclosed in the dashed box. The box input could be either on-site cultivated or imported biomass. In the first case harvest or collection is typically the first step and hence the first activity within a biomass supply chain. Even for one and the same type of crop, different procedures of harvest may apply, resulting in different treatment for storage and transport. Another crucial point is the best point in time for harvest, which is greatly influenced by the weather and may result in ad hoc decisions. Then, quick communications and coordination with other players within the supply chain may become necessary. As depicted, the next steps could be a mixture or a determined sequence of pretreatment (or preprocessing or conditioning), storage and transshipment. Each arrow can be regarded as transport. Transport costs are often assessed monetary, without taking into account the reduced net energy yield of the transported biomass. Thus, for a sustainable exploitation of energy content at least economic and ecologic issues have to be taken into account. As shown in figure 1, each source can be regarded as an input for several applications. Energy can be extracted from biomass both by explicit conversion and indirect as a by-product. The network illustrates just an instance of inter-linked material (solid arrows) and energy flows (densely dashed arrows). A more detailed description of different inter-woven technical procedures can for example be found in Kamm & Kamm (2004) or van Ree & Annevelink (2007).

Logistics of Biomass Supply Chains

Sambra et al. (2008) pointed out the following main characteristics as having a major impact on the logistics efficiency of a biomass supply chain: distributed production over larger geographical areas, limited availability windows due to seasonal issues and voluminous materials that have to be handled.

Talking about distribution, two types of biomass resource have to be distinguished: biomass especially grown for use as energy crop and biomass taken from forestry residues or waste. Especially in Germany, crops are usually grown on rather small patches. Thus, in order to have a sufficient amount, the yields of several distributed patches have to be combined. Medium size and large scale exploitation demands for an amount of input that can only be satisfied by several (independent) suppliers. Therefore, the supply is often gathered from large geographical areas.

Another option is importing biomass from abroad. That often imposes outsourcing nearly the whole supply chain to less developed countries. So the consequences of changing land use (higher emissions of greenhouse gases, reduction or damage of the role as sinks, limited working ecosystems or expulsion of ecosystems) are also sourced out and less developed countries have to face problems that are still unsolved. So, the responsibility is shifted to somebody else. Palm-oil may serve as a prime example (cf. Koh & Wilcove, 2008).

Biomass from residues and waste, on the other hand, usually comes from even more scattered sources. Typically, residues are scarcely and unevenly distributed over larger geographical areas. Two examples may serve for illustration. One example promising quite a large amount of wood material for firing or as a source for a portfolio of ligno cellulosic-based products (cf. van Ree & Annevelink, 2007) is the exploitation of beetle infested trees. As for instance in Canada, the so called mountain pine beetle killed approximately 500 million cubic meters of wood from trees distributed over almost half of British Columbia within a period of only three years (cf. Stennes & McBeath, 2006). It is expected that almost half of this material would remain unsalvaged if no new uses are found. Additionally, it has to be kept in mind that this is an example for a temporal supply stream that has to be substituted from (possibly far-off) regions in time, in order to keep prizes stable and customers in business. The second example is the collection of food or gardening waste which is to be collected from a large number of widespread points. Each point alone usually yields scarcely enough for worthwhile exploitation.

Sometimes, sources have to be considered for both cases at the same time: as cultivated energy (or food) crop and as a residue for additional exploitation. Rapeseed is such an example. The main product is the seed. In the first place it is used for producing oil either for food industry or for conversation to bio-based fuel with the latter one gaining an ever increasing importance today and even more in the future. The same holds true for other oil seeds. However, after harvesting the seeds, the straw remains as a residue. In order to give an added value to the rapeseed the straw could be used for firing in a power plant. This gives an example for two geographically coupled (and timely constrained but not coupled) starting points for supply chains. Perhaps, the residue is delivered along with the biomass fraction to the same site, e.g. for combustion for process heat. In this way, biomass is given an added value and made more competitive (International Energy Agency, 2007). Maybe, disposal costs are avoided, too.

Material flows of biomass are affected by several uncertain seasonal fluctuations. The variations of the seasonality span into at least two dimensions: time and amount. Crops usually do have one or maybe few availability windows - at least without taking into account transshipment from around the world. The availability as well as the availability window is mainly influenced by the weather. Weather determines the time for proper harvest as the weather history has mainly an impact on the yield. Thus, biomass supply has uncertainties in time as well as in quantity. And there is another source of seasonality on longer terms, too, that in addition has an effect on temporal variation of geographical distribution: Land is usually farmed by using crop rotation techniques in order not to overstrain the soil. However, in addition to these variations, there is another one: variation in quality. Weather has a major impact on the quality of cultivated biomass as well as it has considerable impact on the quality of biomass from residues and waste. On the other hand, biomass from waste mostly varies in composition, because it is collected from various small sources.

As has been seen, biomass exhibits some characteristics that induce the need for special treatment for design and management of supply chains. Considering organization and management of biomass logistics, we agree with Sambra et al. (2008). All the different activities along the biomass supply chain have to be planned from a perspective with the whole chain in view. For example, a harvesting activity that is planned individually by one player due to cost and efficiency may have expensive impacts on storage and transport for the next one.

Biomass logistics has to fulfill the task of satisfying the needs of a great number of participants in a global optimal way, i.e. for the benefit of all players. The term player here involves more than just the participants of one single chain. Regarding the multiple applicability of biomass, players from competing chains have to be taken into account. A scarce resource needs for an intelligent control of the material flows from a global point of view. Additionally, players like the environment or the community have to be taken into account, too, in order to avoid damage and especially to gain acceptance.

Information is the key factor for a successful and sustainable biomass supply chain. Communication and information exchange is essential for coordination and integration of all involved parties. Decision makers at different stages need information and proper decision support in order to make decisions that benefit all. Parties who are not a constant factor within a supply chain because they serve different paths in different chains, need access to all relevant information about the current status of the chain at all times; as do parties who have to keep production processes continuously running by ensuring a steady supply. Companies depending to a high degree on a series of others have a strong need for near real-time information. Information can make the difference between success and failure, and it is crucial that it is pre-processed (prepared) information that is accessed and not raw data, information that has been derived from a global point of view. To this end, it is a common knowledge base that is needed.

For external or new suppliers the problem of finding appropriate trading counterparts arises. Which processes and chains fit best to my biomass supply? Which alternative biomass could or should I take into account for optimally using my land. What are the time dependencies considering longer terms and different crop rotation needs? How can I best take part? The same holds true for companies depending on biomass supply of a certain quality. Does the new offer meet my quality standards? A reliable and standardized communication is essential for avoiding misunderstandings. Therefore, an appropriate IT-support should be the basis for successful biomass markets that benefit all participants. At the same time, such a system could serve to keep track of all environmental issues, helping to ensure the acceptance of large scale biomass use.

COMPUTERIZING THE SEARCH FOR CREDIBLE COUNTERPARTS

The main question that has to be answered within a biomass supply network is the question for an appropriate trading counterpart. Depending on the degree of dynamics within the network, it has to be answered multiple times. In order to answer the question for credible counterparts, issues of material quality, timing, volumes and transporting capacities have to be taken into account.

Bridging the gaps between biomass supply and demand technically calls for a means of communication and advertising. However, a proper means, with regard to contents, not only offers the opportunity for choice but also assistance in choosing.

Corporately accessible means (with or without IT support) already have undergone an evolution for quite a while. Starting out from advertisements in print media (in more or less specialized frequently appearing journals, newspapers, etc.) which have a long tradition, a first improvement was made by web-based notice boards. On the one hand, such boards ease searching the data pool in contrast to printed advertisements. Free text descriptions lead to unsatisfactory search results, on the other. In case of biomass, such an advertisement might contain all or - more likely - an arbitrary subset of the following information: type and subtype (not necessarily according to a standardized taxonomy), amount, cargo, transport, location. What about quality (moisture content, grain, contamination, etc.) or applicability? Moreover, free text leads to typing mistakes (mg vs. Mg), synonyms (timber vs. wood) and ambiguity induced by homonyms (cf. Brehm, Mahmoud, Marx Gómez & Memari, 2008). Due to the unstructured description of biomass, the search for suitable trading counterparts can only be done manually by text-based searching. Hence, complex queries, which involve more qualified conditions, can not be formulated and the search returns only a subset of the suitable items.

Therefore these boards are mostly suitable for short term intermittent trade and one-to-one relations. Due to a lack of computer processable information, a higher-level management of material flows or at least an automated procurement of materials is not feasible.

Regional recycling networks may serve as an example for many-to-many linkage between businesses. Sterr and Ott (2004), for example, proposed an IT-solution for material-flow-management incorporating all participants in a decentralized control system of several interacting software components. These networks were organized as contractual consortium for stable long term collaboration. Waste data (partially structured) together with processing and transport related information was captured individually on-site and send to an central analyzing server, where experts were to analyze possible flows with the help of specialized software. Due to demanded nondisclosure agreements it was impractical to tap the full potential of identified room for improvement, because the major part of data was not open to other firms. Nevertheless, the captured data was helpful for generating environmental reports. In case of biomass supply networks, nondisclosure would probably be not the major problem as long as no corporate secret for processing description is involved. However, an obligatory standard for description of quality and applicability of biomass is still missing. Recently, electronic biomass exchanges have become available on the internet. However, their functionality for bridging the gap between supply and demand usually goes not far beyond notice boards and hence they are not treated separately here.

Compared to other biomass research sectors, few models have been developed in order to optimize flows for biomass logistics (e.g. Vlachos et al., 2008; de Mol, Jogems, van Beek & Gigler, 1997) or to find and dimension optimal sites (cf. Velazquez-Marti & Annevelink, 2008). Some models just estimate the potential of biomass and/or cost of transport and conversion routes (e.g. Suurs, 2002). In general, the majority of research in the rapidly growing field of biomass for energy production focuses either on mere technological or on ecological issues. The field of biomass supply chain management and biomass logistics is still rather scarcely scrutinized (Vlachos et al., 2008).

Optimization of biomass flows and network structures is currently mostly reduced to a linear programming problem which can easily be solved using a readily available software package. On the other hand, such a treatment of the problem is only suited for rather static and simplified scenarios. An optimal supply chain is determined in advance. Such an approach might serve well for strategic decisions for investors of large scale biomass sites. Environmental considerations seldom play a significant role in such models. Optimizing biomass networks is a task that has to consider multiple objectives at the same time: Every player along the chain wants to have his fair share of benefit (a Pareto optimal situation in itself). Diekema, de Mol, Annevelink & Elbersen (2005) list six different goals for maximizing the overall profit. In case of energy production the net yield of energy in relation to the used land has to be maximized. The scarce resource land has to be shared and fairly split up between competing use cases. Environmental and socio-economic issues have to be assessed and added to the cost functions. Focusing on static network structures is a major drawback, because such a network is not flexible enough to continuously adapt to changes in conditions or circumstances without having to determine a completely new and different supply network from scratch. Flexibility is a major prerequisite for a robust operation of the network. New and unforeseen upcoming events (including new demands or offers) should be capable of being integrated into existing networks, pushing them towards the new situation in an optimal way. An active biomass network is a dynamic structure. So, optimality must be defined over time and include considerations about (seasonal as well as strategic and durable) change of structure and flows (quantity, quality and directions). This leads to a far more complicated optimization problem for which new solutions are to be developed. Sokhansanj, Kumar & Turhollow (2006) proposed a model containing time considerations as calculated delays of availability due to changing processing conditions at every stage. However, this model aims at simulation, not optimization. A software agent-based model for exploring the sustainability of different development pathways of local bioenergy networks and for simulation of governmental incentives is given by Kempener (2008). Viewing networks as complex adaptive systems, possible stimulations for improving industrial networks behavior towards social and environmental sustainability are compared in value.

Research in the field of biomass supply management and logistics is mainly done by agricultural or biomass experts using general software tools. At the same time computing science develops new methods for automatic formation of optimal ad hoc networks (e.g. de Morais Cordeiro & Agrawal, 2006), semantic services, knowledge discovery and representation, new web-based communication and integration services (e.g. Süpke, Marx Gómez & Isenmann, 2009), intelligent soft optimization techniques for hard problems (e.g. Michalewicz & Fogel, 2000) and many more solutions that would be highly suitable for building up new integrated management systems for intelligent and sustainable biomass networks. The remaining sections will focus on the computing science point of view for interlinked biomass networks.

META-DATA DRIVEN ACQUISITION, SEARCH AND PROCUREMENT OF BIOMASS WITHIN A WEB-BASED MARKETPLACE

This section will focus on the related problem of formation of recycling networks and discuss approaches revealed there for the case of biomass networks. Apart from desired products many manufacturing processes result in unwanted by-products. A recirculation of those undesired products, using them as input for other processes often works for companies producing a sufficiently large range of goods but rarely for small and medium-sized businesses. Thereby, the disposal of by-products as waste is usually chosen, whereas converting by-products to secondary material would result in relieving dumping grounds and achieving a reduction of limited raw material. As has already been said, exchanges are suitable for short-term intermittent trade. Building up regular material flows, as a better alternative, demands the formation of a recycling network characterized by purposive collaboration of different business with complementary input-output-dependencies which usually appear as many-to-many relations. To tap the full potential of recycling networks, information about material flows is required. As a result of two Bachelor's theses (Bremer, 2005; Rapp, 2005) an electronic market has been developed as proof-of-concept implementation on which by-products can be offered and secondary materials can be requested. The underlying application is able to procure between offers and requests in order to provide a means for closed materials cycle.

Obvious weaknesses of existing web-based materials and/or waste exchanges had been scrutinized to develop an improved ansatz for a better business support easing the task of finding appropriate trading counterparts. Although the focus had not been especially on biomass, this prototype can be seen as a step forward to automated formation of network structured trade relations with the objective of achieving sustainable overall benefits.

If one wants to build-up networks rather than one-to-one trade relations, there is an urgent need for unambiguous descriptions of the materials to ensure that one has the right material and that it is of an appropriate quality. There is also a need for geographical and transport related information in order to keep transport costs as low as possible. Additionally, information about timing is needed to ensure that every material is in the right place at the right time. So, the objective of these projects was the design of a web-based system which allows for an overall optimal allocation of offered residues to suitable request. To fulfill this task, different descriptions for different types of residues are important for a proper identification. In addition, all collected advertisements were supposed to respect given schema descriptions in order to allow for automated processing for procurement and other algorithms.

The system was implemented as component-based J2EE web-application as a prototype mainly as an easily extensible testbed for ideas, algorithms and software components (Bremer, Rapp, Vogel & Sonnenschein, 2007). Of essential importance for the whole concept is the meta-data component. Grouped around this central component are the other components, of which the residue administration component is the most important, because it constitutes the main user interface for interaction with the underlying information system. It provides assistance for capturing, editing and managing a user's residue related data stock. It provides repository functionality and ensures in tight interaction with the meta-description component an adequate and correct data capture by guiding the advertiser through the capturing process with the help of automatically generated wizards. Thus, the user is guided through the process in a sequence of self-contained steps where at each stage all data is verified (syntactically) and analyzed (semantically) in order to ensure correctness and to decide on the appropriate next step.

The following sections will describe the most important components, which are essential for an understanding of the underlying philosophy, in greater detail. Technology related issues that go beyond the scope of this chapter, are not discussed.

Meta-Descriptions of Residues

Meta-data already was of major importance for this prototype since it was supposed to support an adequate description of different classes of residues on the one hand as well as automatic post processing on the other. In order to describe each residue properly we have used an XML-based meta-description system. In future, in order to adapt properly to biomass procurement, an ontology-based technique would yield some added advantages. The meta-data itself was coded using XML Schema, allowing for an adequate definition of structure as well as of arbitrary complex data types. As it was important to have an object oriented approach for data storage and processing, XML Schema gave the competitive edge of automatically generated data objects and validation of entered data. In this way, e.g. an easy automated generation of user-input forms as well as an automated validation of the user's input became possible. Both helped to ensure the homogeneity of related residue descriptions and hence enable automatic processing.

In addition to the residue management component, a separated repository component is offered by the system. This component receives a residue's meta-description from the meta-data component by request. It takes the meta-description as input, generates suitable input forms for the specific residue at hand and ensures a persistent storage in the repository. A taxonomy for residues provided by the system's catalog component supports a hierarchal structure of the stored residues. The residue administration has been designed in tight interaction with the meta-description component. This means that attributes needed for residue administration are solely and exclusively provided by the residue component and all attributes required for meta-description are sourced out to the meta-description component. This separation of concerns poses several advantages: On the one hand, efficient database queries such as obtaining all offers by advertiser or similar become possible at low computational cost. On the other hand, it offers the possibility for flexible meta-descriptions that are extensible and exchangeable and allows for easy integration of such descriptions into the system. A residue administration that is designed this way, guarantees an adequate and correct data capture by guiding the advertiser through the whole capturing process and making sure that all registered advertisements are compliant with the corresponding meta-description. This ensures local as well as global homogeneity of residue descriptions.

Each type of residue is described by its own set of meta-data. The set of all meta-descriptions is administered with the help of a specialized component. This meta-data administration component offers a series of characteristics that are qualified for the description of each residue. In general, each residue traded within the system is completely described by three separately treated sets of attributes: administrative attributes, general descriptive attribute and specific descriptive attributes.

The same subdivision would apply to non-residual materials as for instance for energy crops. Contrary to administrative residue attributes, descriptive residue attributes are divided into two classes: those that are exclusively adapted for describing residues from one special residue class, and those that are more comprehensive and qualified for describing residues from each residue class. The following example may serve as an illustration for the biomass case: Attributes like moisture content or options for further processing are common to all types of biomass since all biomass is from organic material and sought after as input for special purposes. On the contrary, oil content does not apply to straw but is of importance for oilseeds. Options for further processing, at the same time doubles as an example for a complex, composed attribute.

A suitable data structure that meets the requirements for distinct residue classes, each with attributes in arbitrary number and nuances, is the extensible markup language (XML) in conjunction with XML Schema. Both are semi-structured, support data self-labeling and provide the required flexibility. The implemented component provides different schemata of which exactly one schema covers the universal attributes that can be used for describing all residue classes. Alongside that schema, many residue class specific schemata exist that are appropriate for exactly one residue class. Every schema allows for a dynamic validation of the entered parameter values towards the expected parameter values defined by the schema itself. Each schema also contains information about how to execute a mapping or matching. By means of this information, it is possible to decide what attributes have to be compared in order to ascertain the identity, similarity or an existing includes relationship between one or more residues. Included information for visualization, e.g. for an HTML representation, allows for generating the desired input forms (e.g. wizard-style) for dynamical data capturing at runtime. All input forms generated at runtime are tailored for a specific residue class, because the information needed for displaying the input form is extracted from the specific residue class schema.

In order to ensure extensibility, the implementation of the meta-data administration allows for an upload of new residue meta-descriptions at runtime followed by automated translation and compiling. Such a modus operandi provides an opportunity for adding new residue descriptions to the system at runtime and using them directly without having to restart. At the same time, the performance advantage of using compiled classes instead of interpreted code is preserved. In the course of such an upload process, the new description is added to the taxonomy of the catalog component simultaneously. This allows for extending the system easily.

Browsing and Searching for Residues

In a market with different categories of goods and, moreover, distinct descriptions of these goods, it is important to have some discriminating means in appropriate support of searching. Finding appropriate input for bio-fuel production for example requires different search criteria than querying for combustion material. The description of different materials differs not only in some different naming of attributes or minor differences in, for example, describing the same quality slightly different: liter for volume instead of cubic meter. Description here may vary in range and number of attributes as well as it is possible that the same attribute has discriminative meanings for different types of residues. Therefore, it is essential to have a search facility that treats different types of residue in a discriminative way.

A data independent search which is specific to each class of residues was realized by an XML-based description scheme for defining such search modules. Such an approach allows for an on-the-fly integration of new search modules for new residue classes as well as for new components.

We have denoted this component-based concept with separated meta-descriptions for specific search modules as search-mandate principle. This means that a so-called mandator defines a search. The mandator can be an arbitrary software component that wants to integrate some search functionality into its own portfolio. Thus, it can make use of readily available functionality by merely defining a description of its own requirements for searching. Afterwards it has not to take care of any stage of a query cycle. The input of search parameters, the execution of the query and the presentation of the search results are delegated to the search component. In this way, the search functionality needs to be implemented only once, and the user can always work in a homogeneous and consistent way. The search mandate principle works in an object-oriented way. To this end, the mandate description provides information about the mandator itself and its data objects. Information about these objects includes information about which attributes define the search criteria and how to display them when the user is prompted for search criteria. The same applies to the result that is presented to the user. An object instance which is used for holding the entered search parameter values indirectly provides information about data format and constraints regarding acceptable values using the underlying meta-data. From the information contained in a search-mandate, proper input forms are automatically generated.

For faster execution, a search index is automatically and continuously maintained by the search component whereby the consistency between index and data stock is guaranteed by means of aspect oriented programming (Elrad, Filman & Bader, 2001), i.e. data access calls are delegated 'through the back door' to the search component following the so called cuckoo's egg design pattern. The mandator's compiled data access object class is instrumented (appropriate modification of the Java bytecode) after compilation in a way that redirects method calls. Calls to the data access tier therefore are made by the search on behalf of the mandator while the index is appropriately updated simultaneously. This is an automated process. Thus, a developer of new components has not to take care about this process.

In order to support queries with geographical restrictions, i.e. limiting the resulting set to one's own vicinity or to a given region, each address entered into the system is associated with a geographical reference using the zip code. The restriction to zip code coded geographical description is due to time this prototype has been developed. Nowadays (although scarcely 4 years later) much more sophisticated (and open source) services for a geographical enrichment of web-based systems are readily available. However, a geographical representation here serves as an additional orientation for the user while browsing through the advertisements. The catalogue component presents the information from residue meta-descriptions and shows its spatial position in a GIS map. In addition, the catalogues taxonomy forces the existence of an appropriate meta-description in order to assure a consistent data capture and data representation by the catalogue. Such integrated geographical support would become especially important in case of an adaptation of the system to biomass markets.

Automatic Procurement of Supply and Demand

Manually exploring an information system of supply and demand advertisements does not guarantee a distinct identification of dependencies (especially not for many-to-many trade relations) and thus no optimal matching between supply and demand, neither with respect to single advertisements nor for the formation of a recycling network. Moreover, manual search is a tedious and error prone work. An information system for the management of biomass supply chains should afford support even for ad hoc decisions of players along the chain, e.g. when weather conditions urge for quick harvest. Meta-descriptions also contain annotations for an automated mapping between corresponding supply and demand. These annotations allow for an autonomous procurement, which associates suitable advertisements with each other and returns groups of suitable goods.

The major concern of the procurement component is to pay attention to different and sometimes opposed interests. This means that procurements can be achieved according to multiple economical and ecological criteria. For example, on the one hand, the total transportation effort has to be minimized to serve public interests, i.e. less CO_2 or noise emission. On the other hand, salesmen tend to maximize their profits. Such a Pareto optimal allocation of supply to demand is achieved by a procurement process consisting of three steps:

1. Advertisements are divided into sets of substitutable goods. This process leads to a so called standard transportation problem.
2. Each problem is solved according to different objective functions, what leads to a set of solutions for each single problem.
3. Finally, a compromise solution is determined for each single problem, whereby different conflicting (economy, ecology) optimization objectives are solved.

First, the set of all advertisements from all residue classes is divided into a set of sets of suitable advertisements. The decision which residues are suitable to go into the same group is made according to assigned meta-data. During this clustering, sets which exclusively consist of offers or requests and hence are not placeable are rejected for the following procurement.

As a result of the previous step, the problem of procuring one set of distinct items from different residue classes has been broken up into a set of smaller, classical transportation problems which can be solved by means of well known algorithms. Here we made use of Vogel's approximation (Reinfeld & Vogel, 1958) which does not guarantee an optimal solution, but often obtains one for small to medium sized problems, which were to be expected here. For further improvement on the solution's accuracy, it can easily be taken as an initial solution for exact algorithms for refinement. For each transportation problem, the procedure is rerun with a particular objective function to address various environmental and economical interests.

The second step leads to a specific set of approximate solutions for each transportation problem representing the minimal costs of each optimized objective, each one leading to another distribution according to the respective objective. To achieve a sustainable compromise for all involved parties, a game theory approach has been chosen to find a feasible overall solution.

In order to illustrate the advantage of automatic procurement over manual search, some simulations have been done. Figure 2 depicts the results of a simplified toy example with one cost function for minimizing the overall transport effort. For this purpose several players (offers as well as requests) have been randomly generated. Two scenarios are considered: Within scenario A the participants are equally distributed over an area of 12154 km^2. The offered or requested amount varies from 0.2 to 5 tons of the same type of biomass. In scenario B the locations are not equally distributed over the whole area, but grouped into three clusters in order to emulate interacting regions. Manual search has been simulated by choosing randomly the first offers of sufficient amount. The results (figure 2) are based on 5000 simulation runs each. The improvement in necessary transport performance varies from approx. 40 to 85 percent depending mainly on

Figure 2. Simulation results for automated procurement and manual search

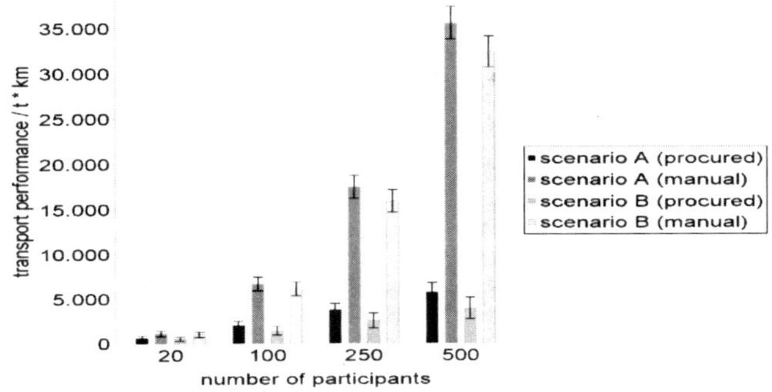

the number of participants. The improvements in scenario B are slightly better because the procurement algorithm prefers intra-cluster over inter-cluster matching.

The aim of this prototype was to evaluate and solve (software-) technical issues related to the requirements for a web-based support of recycling networks. Thus, the procurement procedure was provisionally designed to be offered to the users as a special service. Every advertisement that is registered with this service takes part in this procedure that periodically results in a submission of proposed co-operations between users by email, personal message board or downloadable spread sheets. In this way, voluntarily attending parties came to enjoy an additional service, but it was finally their own responsibility to make a personal profit out of it. Of course, such an approach does not at all guaranty an overall (Pareto) optimal solution. Quite the contrary, if some participants act according to the made suggestions but some do not and act after their own findings by manual search for trading counterparts, the overall cost might change for the worse. Therefore, more sophisticated algorithms as well as an appropriate policy for the participation in such automatically generated network structures have still to be developed.

ADDING SUSTAINABILITY BY VIRTUAL BIOREFINERIES

Having described the first prototype for the evaluation of information technique issues, this section will now focus on current and future research directions. In this sense, this section introduces ongoing work.

A recently discussed approach is the idea of biorefineries. Van Ree and Annevelink (2007) condensed a wide range of definitions to: "Biorefinery is the sustainable processing of biomass into a spectrum of marketable products and energy". However, biorefineries are mostly regarded as centralized and static sites. Kromus et al. (2004) additionally discusses decentralized and semi-decentralized biorefineries, but again with a predefined, rather fixed structure. The key to sustainable biorefineries is the management of various supply chain stages, product portfolio as well as an adjustment of distributed technical potential. To achieve this objective, a linkage of life science, chemistry as well as energy and process engineering is necessary (cf. de Jong & van Ree, 2006). In our opinion at least computing science has to be added. We will here force the idea in the light of corporate environmental information systems.

The technical aspects of biomass exploitation on the one hand and biomass production on the other are currently put forward trough research and development projects, whereas cascades of use increasingly gain in importance. A so far undiscussed issue is adequate dynamic structures for optimal regional networks. Taking into account, that various forms of biomass (particularly including residue) have different sustainability for different usage opportunities and furthermore are available temporal and spatial distributed, the dynamic problem of finding the global optimal matching between limited resources and consuming processes arises. Since systematic cultivation of renewables could be achieved by various options of land use, the number of possible network inter-linkage and design options increases significantly. A decentralized pretreatment can also be advantageous if, for example, organic residues are (partly) scheduled for return to land. If grass is pressed on harvest side in order to yield the nutrient green liquor, only the much more compact liquid needs to be transported; transport of the residues back to field is reduced to a minimum.

The current practice of manually searching for trading partners neither allows for analyzing existing trade relations nor identifying alternative network inter-linkage and design options, because the focus is not on the communities vantage but on sole participants. Currently, most existing IT-solutions merely allow for advertisements without structured annotation of the data entered, resulting in the problems mentioned before. The same holds for requests, where the quality of suitable offers depends on the intended purpose, especially on the production process.

The objective of establishing sustainable inter-connected networks for biomass flows can not be achieved by using such tools. However, combining the following interdisciplinary skills will facilitate in achieving the objective: For identifying and defining adequate classifying attributes for various biomass types, an in-depth knowledge of material's traits and processing options is mandatory. Also, competent knowledge and experience of renewable resources, the utilization of residue, biomass and process traits and of sustainability assessment is necessary. Moreover, it is mandatory to have expertise in the fields of semantic engineering, business and inter-business environmental information systems, material-flow-management systems, mathematical modeling and heuristic optimization to be able to map the expert knowledge onto an information system.

The Concept of a Virtual Biorefinery

At this point, we would like to introduce the concept for a virtual biorefinery. With the term virtual, we refer to a loose coupling of decentralized biomass players (from all over the chains) in contrast to centralized biorefineries, doing all processing in one large site.

As stated by Pierre Desrochers (2000) for the case of Eco-Industrial Parks, "Planning localized waste flows as if they were not subject to change simply does not accord with historical evidence and the logic of market processes". This thought must be kept in mind when considering networks for biorefineries, too. Economic as well as technological development has always been in a flux and will continue to be. Products and/or markets emerge and disappear. New products might creatively use what today is called waste; innovative substitutes might emit different residues. Thus, inter-firm-linkage will also be in a steady flux.

The crucial key is, to have an appropriate common IT-system for the management of the dynamics of varying linkages. The discussed virtual biorefinery aims at establishing a web-based knowledge management and information system for building up regional biomass networks and their prosperous and sustainable management in order to combine existing resources and processing options in an intelligent manner.

The concept is based on the presence of a standardized, standard compliant capture of specific biomass and process characteristics that in turn are based on adequate meta-descriptions. Initially a technically oriented trait definition of different biomass types has to be prepared, whereas technical requirements of high-value material and energetic utilization have to be spotlighted. Similarly preprocessing, pretreatment and conditioning on various points within the supply chain have to be considered. By mapping process characteristics on meta-descriptions, new exploitation chains can be defined by linking different exploitation processes and their sustainability assessment can be achieved by reusing existing knowledge.

Such a capturing and persisting of relevant characteristics, applicability and assessment criteria as meta-descriptions allows for vast possibilities of knowledge discovery and therefore semantic linkage. First of all, matching offers and requests are mapped automatically for an efficiently linked network design. The automated matching of offers and requests uses e.g. material traits, temporal conditions, transportation costs and other available economic, ecologic and social aspects as basis of decision-making. The discussed matching strengthens the cooperation between participating stakeholders.

As a second step this local matching has to be extended by a global optimization approach, which allows for having a look at energy efficiency, ecological rucksack and other higher-level optimization objectives. The available entities (biomass, by-products and processes) will be linked on different paths, identifying optimal cascades of usage while taking into account possible options of land use, as will be seen. This helps to attenuate competing aims and to put sustainable regional added value networks (inter-woven supply chains) into action. Figure 1 therefore can also be seen as a virtual biorefinery (depicted as system boundary) if enriched by proper IT-support. It may require imported biomass as input but outputs products and energy (depicted as arrows with a thick tip).

The discussed concept aims at sustainable usage of the scarce commodity biomass, decentralized energy supply based on renewables as well as utilization, but without constraining conventional use cases like food production. Based on captured and semantically linked data the system can provide knowledge and information about biomass flows and consequently about the capability of an examined region.

Building Blocks

What are the building blocks needed for the setup of a virtual biorefinery? On a high level of abstraction there are only two major ingredients:

First, biomass players those are willing to submit selfish benefit to public benefit in order to strengthen their own region. In this context, Hanson & Edwards (2002) complained (for the Canadian case, but the same should hold for arbitrary countries) that benefit is captured somewhere else and "...not on the farm" if there is no broad availability of research tools for farmers. Factories using biomass material must be located in the country in order to add value and protect environment coevally. If this could be managed, rural regions will continue to be places worth living in. Jacobson et al. (2009) pointed out, that providing producers or landowners with access to different markets will result in the development of sustainable cropping systems and the preservation of the agricultural landscape.

Secondly, access to common knowledge and data about the past, current and anticipated state of the whole network for proper personal planning, decision making and optimal operation. Demonstrable sustainability arises from this knowledge as added value for the participants.

As research is just starting out, it seems appropriate to organize a supporting software system in a component-based manner. In this way, single components may easily be adapted or replaced as soon as new research results and developments become available. For a loose coupling of these components we suggest a service oriented exposure of the components' interfaces. Such an approach would have some favorable effects, e.g.:

- Easing integration of existing systems like (regional) web-based biomass exchanges.
- Easing extension and replacement of functionality in the case of new circumstances.
- Semantic web-services allow for an automated identification of appropriate services.

For setting up a base system for semantically managed biomass flows within a virtual biorefinery, the following components are indispensable: an ontology in conjunction with an inference system, a meta-descriptions component as knowledge base, search assistance, a matching component, assessment of costs and sustainability, a data management and the provision of GUI components.

Even in cases where total categorization of materials is used, integration requires a common understanding among all diverse players. A thesaurus of biomass terminology is the minimum requirement in order to unify all used terms. For a better matching precision, an ontology of biomass is advised as an extended thesaurus. Such ontology will at least define the terms for biomass descriptions (traits), processing options and sustainability issues. Each offer and request will be positioned as an instance of a leave of the ontology in terms of offered or requested material, offered or requested usage process and their ecological footprint. As a result it will get its full and standardized description as a semantic aim.

The task of the inference system is the automated derivation of further knowledge about the biomass network, the participants, the available feedstock and demanding processes in tight coupling with the ontology component. Whereas the ontology describes the structure (and relationships) of the network entities, the inference system allows for automated reasoning and therefore generates new options for possible inter-linkages beyond the ones manually entered by the users.

A meta-description component will store the description of the current state of each entity (traits, environmental impacts, geographical information, etc.) and of the whole system and thus exposes the knowledge for further processing. At the same time, interfaces for registration, modification and deletion of entities are provided. Data management substitutionally stands for further data base related tasks as for instance for authorization (user) management or the offers and request data management.

A system like the one considered here calls for an improved component for querying. In addition to the mentioned prototype search component, in this improved version, knowledge must be searchable, too. The task of the matching component will be to find appropriate offers for given requests and vice versa. Using the ontology and given descriptions, the allocation will be able to take into account traits of biomass and processes as well as environmental interests for a specific order of precedence. A procurement algorithm will try to allocate the entirety of offers and requests for an optimal distribution of the biomass resources, taking into account all the different interests. Thus, such an algorithm will go for a Pareto optimal compromise solution. An advanced procurement component would additionally be able to work with the hypothetical option derived from the inference system in order to act out alternative scenarios for a recommendation of even better inter-linkage. The procurement procedure can run either in a centralized manner, refreshing periodically (or ideally after any change) or in a decentralized manner by representing each offer or request by a software agent with customizable objectives, beliefs, ranges and tolerances.

The sustainability and cost assessment component will be responsible for an assessment of costs for a given link between offer and request incorporating environmental considerations. Reports about the own environmental behavior resulting from the registered trade linkages will be easily available.

It is suggested to expose all these services as web-services with no integrated user interface. In this way, the functionality will easily integrate with a variety of existing software systems including existing web-based biomass exchanges, business environmental information systems, production planning and control systems etc. Hence, some specialized rich client GUI elements have to be provided for individually generated input forms, search forms etc. Harnessing e.g. advanced scripting web-technologies, an (at least partly) client-side preprocessing of the data becomes possible.

Sustainability Objectives

If biomass data (supply and processing) is captured in a semantically enriched way, it becomes open to algorithmic processing. If alternative use is captured as well or - much the better - automatically derived, regional biomass flows in conjunction with their ecological, economical, sociological, spatial and temporal inter-dependencies become processable for intelligent software systems. Due to the qualified specification of each entity within a regional biomass network, complex interactive structures are revealed that are hardly detectable by manual search. This provides a knowledge basis for decision-making and gives way to alternative action strategies.

Thus, if a global optimization approach is realized, a comprehensive survey of energy efficiency, green house gas reduction and further global objectives can be incorporated into the network formation. Equally, considerations of social sustainability (price trends, food supply, etc.) might be taken into account. Forming regional biomass networks in this way no longer discounts global sustainability interests. However, adding reasoning about temporal change to a concurrent optimization leads to a dynamic adjustment of biomass flows with the objective of steadily minimizing the deviation from real sustainability.

Businesses usually analyze the environmental impacts of their activities and material flows in production and logistics by means of isolated systems. By integrating sustainability issues from different isolated systems into a holistic CEMIS (e.g. the proposed virtual biorefinery) the impacts can be analyzed from a global point of view. The holistic knowledge is more than the sum of its parts. In return, participating companies get enriched information e.g. for sustainability reporting, eco-efficiency or marketing.

COMPARISON OF THE DISCUSSED APPROACHES

Before concluding this chapter, we will give a short comparison in order to pass in review the different discussed approaches and their respective contribution to a sustainable as well as fair distribution of the scarce commodity biomass. We will not submit a rating, because every approach naturally inherits the capability of improvement and contributes features for future integrated approaches.

Table 1 lists the major features of the four discussed approaches. The feature of semi-automated procurement for the approaches three and four is substituted by a fully automated procurement. The second approach implements it manually with the help of different and independent software tools. Sustainability issues taken into account for optimization are minimizing both transport cost and waste dumping in the context of approach two (Sterr & Ott, 2004).

CONCLUSION

We have drawn a picture for sustainable, regional biomass networks. Starting out from the complexity of biomass supply, comprising fluctuating temporal and spatial distribution, uncertainty, competing flows, unclear socio-economic and environmental assessment and so forth, the need for proper IT-support became obvious. We have traced the evolution of solutions including drawbacks. The search for credible counterparts has already grown from digit search to digital

Table 1. Comparison of the discussed approaches: the used symbols denote: supported (+), not supported (-), partly supported (o) and manually (*)

		notice boards & exchanges	**regional recycling network**	**proof-of-concept**	**virtual biorefinery**
access	fee	some	contract	none	none
	runtime environment	browser	software	browser	arbitrary
search	free text	+	-	+	+
	semantic	-	-	+	+
procurement	semi-automated	-	+*	(-)	(-)
	fully automated	-	-	+	+
material flow management		-	o*	-	+
trade relations		1-to-1	n-to-n	n-to-n	n-to-n
optimization	multi-criteria	-	o*	+	+
	sustainability issues	-	o	-	+
	temporal variation	-	-	-	+
sustainability reporting		-	+	+	+

search. The next step must be the relief of manual search as a (regional) biomass network is a highly dynamic system if organized in a sustainable, cooperative way.

Sustainable growth is an oxymoron (Fougère & Solitander, 2009). If a biorefinery is the structure that combines the different pathways for new biomass applications for energy and chemicals, than it should be integrated into the ever since existing network of competitors for the finite resource biomass. Connecting the existing (decentralized) and the new (possibly decentralized) biomass players, leads to the need for intelligently and flexibly controlled flows. The flows are varying due to their natural uncertainty and they will concurrently adapt to new technologies, markets and circumstances. In order to maintain a continuously sustainable and working network, a continuous optimization has to be performed that can not be managed from isolated and partial points of view. Therefore, we proposed an IT solution that tries to ensure sustainability by looking at the whole picture and hence generates durable benefits for all participants and extraneous stakeholders.

Berndes, Hoogwijk & van den Broek (2003) have reviewed 17 studies on the contribution of biomass in future global energy supply. Although largely varying in achievable amount, the potential for a steady growth to a considerable proportion is commonly foreseen. However, as a major flaw of most such studies they pointed out a neglect of an interlinked dynamic between the growth of the bioenergy sector and other land uses. They mostly ensure a conflict free physical achievability of the stated contributions by modeling the food and materials sector (if any) exogenously. In this way, the bioenergy sector is defined as not affecting food, feed and chemical needs. Such models do not reveal much insight in possible socio-economic consequences. Therefore, the attractiveness of using biomass as a substitute for fossil oil has been often degraded in the past. A holistic perspective is important for a holistic assessment of biomass usage. But, it has to be an integrated view as well. Hence, we proposed a corporately managed network between all actors involved in harnessing biomass for future supply of food, feed, chemical materials and energy in synergy. Because the term sustainability applies to a part only if the whole is sustainable.

REFERENCES

Agbontalor, E. A. (2007). Overview of Various Biomass Energy Conversion Routes. *American-Eurasian Journal of Agricultural & Environmental Sciences*, *2*(6), 662–671.

Beirat für nachwachsende Rohstoffe (2005). *Erklärung Bioenergie und Ethik* (Statement). Hannover, Germany: Niedersächsisches Ministerium für Ernährung, Landwirtschaft, Verbraucherschutz und Landesentwicklung.

Berndes, G., Hoogwijk, M., & van den Broek, R. (2003). The contribution of biomass in the future global energy supply: a review of 17 studies. *Biomass and Bioenergy*, *25*(1), 1–28. doi:10.1016/S0961-9534(02)00185-X

Brehm, N., Mahmoud, T., Marx Gómez, J., & Memari, A. (2008). Towards Intelligent Discovery of Enterprise Architecture Services (IDEAS). *Journal of Enterprise Architecture*, *4*(3), 26–37.

Bremer, J. (2005). *Modellierung und protoypische Realisierung von Komponenten für die Datenexploration und Reststoffvermittlung bei der kooperativen Konzeption eines Sekundärrohstoff-Marktplatzes*. Unpublished Bachelor's Thesis, University of Oldenburg, Germany.

Bremer, J., Rapp, B., Vogel, U., & Sonnenschein, M. (2007). Metadata Driven Acquisition, Search and Procurement of Secondary Materials within an Internet-based Marketplace. In L. M. Hilty, X. Edelmann und A. Ruf (Eds.), *Proceedings of the 8th World Congress on Integrated Resources Management*. St. Gallen, Switzerland: Empa.

Davis, S. C., Anderson-Teixeira, K. J., & DeLucia, E. H. (2008). Life-cycle analysis and the ecology of biofuels. *Trends in Plant Science*, *14*(3), 140–146. doi:10.1016/j.tplants.2008.12.006

de Jong, E., & van Ree, R. (2006). Biorefineries Co-production of Fuels, Chemicals, Power and Materials from Biomass (New Task Proposal). Retrieved July 15, 2009, from http://www.biorefinery.nl/iea-task-42/proposal/

de Mol, R. M., Jogems, M. A. H., van Beek, P., & Gigler, J. K. (1997). Simulation and optimization of the logistics of biomass fuel collection. *Netherlands Journal of Agricultural Science*, *45*, 219–228.

de Morais Cordeiro, C., & Agrawal, D. P. (2006). *Ad hoc & sensor networks: theory and applications*. Singapore: World Scientific Publishing.

Desrochers, P. (2000). *Eco-Industrial Parks and the Rediscovery of Inter-Firm Recycling Linkages* (Working Paper). Retrieved July 13, 2009, from http://mises.org/journals/scholar/Eco6a.PDF

Diekema, W. H., de Mol, R. M., Annevelink, E., & Elbersen, H. W. (2005, October). *Combining goals in the logistics bio-energy chains*. Paper presented at the 14th European Biomass Conference, Paris, France.

Elrad, T., Filman, R. E., & Bader, A. (2001). Aspect-Oriented Programming. *Communications of the ACM*, *44*(10), 29–32. doi:10.1145/383845.383853

Fougère, M., & Solitander, N. (2009). Against corporate responsibility: critical reflections on thinking, practice, content and consequences. *Corporate Social Responsibility and Environmental Management*, *16*(4), 217–227. doi:10.1002/csr.204

Hanson, J., & Edwards, S. (2002). *Towards a Biobased Economy: Issues and Challenges Paper*. Retrieved July 27, 2009, from http://www.pollutionprobe.org/Reports/biobased.pdf

Hunt, T. L. (2007). Rethinking Easter Island's ecological catastrophe. *Journal of Archaeological Science*, *34*, 485–502. doi:10.1016/j.jas.2006.10.003

International Energy Agency. (2007). *Bioenergy Project Development & Biomass Supply - Good Practice Guidelines*. Paris, France: Author.

Jacobson, J. J., Searcy, E., Muth, D., Wilkerson, E., Sokhansanj, S., Jenkins, B., et al. (2009). Sustainable Biomass Supply Systems. In *Proceedings of the 2009 AIChE Spring National Meeting.*

Kamm, B., & Kamm, M. (2004). Principles of biorefineries. *Applied Microbiology and Biotechnology*, *64*(2), 137–145. doi:10.1007/s00253-003-1537-7

Kempener, R. T. M. (2008). *From Organisational Behaviour to Industrial Network Evolutions: Stimulating Sustainable Development of Bioenergy Networks in Emerging Economies*. Unpublished doctoral dissertation, University of Sydney, Australia.

Koh, L. P., & Wilcove, D. S. (2008). Is oil palm agriculture really destroying tropical biodiversity? *Conservation Letters*, *1*(2), 60–64. doi:10.1111/j.1755-263X.2008.00011.x

Kromus, S., Wachter, B., Koschuh, W., Mandl, M., Krotscheck, C., & Narodoslawsky, M. (2004). The Green Biorefinery Austria – Development of an Integrated System for Green Biomass Utilization. *Chemical and Biochemical Engineering Quarterly*, *18*(1), 7–12.

Michalewicz, Z., & Fogel, D. B. (2000). *How to solve it: modern heuristics*. Berlin: Springer-Verlag.

Patzek, T. W. (2004). Thermodynamics of the Corn-Ethanol Biofuel Cycle. *Critical Reviews in Plant Sciences*, *23*(6), 519–567. doi:10.1080/07352680490886905

Rapp, B. (2005). *Modellierung und protoypische Realisierung von Komponenten zur Interaktion zwischen Unternehmen und Marktplatz bei der kooperativen Konzeption eines Sekundärrohstoff-Marktplatzes*. Unpublished Bachelor's Thesis, University of Oldenburg, Germany.

Reinfeld, N. V., & Vogel, W. R. (1958). *Mathematical Progamming*. Englewood Cliffs: Prentice-Hall.

Sambra, A., Sørensen, G., & Kristensen, E. F. (2008). Optimized harvest and logistics for biomass supply chain. In *Proceedings of the 16th European Biomass Conference and Exhibition*. (pp. 84-91). Valencia, Spain.

Sokhansanj, S., Kumar, A., & Turhollow, F. (2006). Development and implementation of integrated biomass supply analysis and logistics model (IBSAL). *Biomass and Bioenergy*, *30*(10), 838–847. doi:10.1016/j.biombioe.2006.04.004

Stennes, B., & McBeath, A. (2006). *Bioenergy options for woody feedstock: are trees killed by mountain pine beetle in British Columbia a viable bioenergy resource?* (Information Report BC-X-405). Ottawa, Canada: Canadian Forest Service.

Sterr, T., & Ott, T. (2004). The industrial region as a promising unit for eco-industrial development - reflections, practical experience and establishment of innovative instruments to support industrial ecology. *Journal of Cleaner Production*, *12*(8-10), 947–965. doi:10.1016/j.jclepro.2004.02.029

Süpke, D., Marx Gómez, J., & Isenmann, R. (2009). Web 2.0 for sustainability reporting: Approach to refining communication on sustainability. In Wohlgemuth, V., Page, B., & Voigt, K. (Eds.), *EnviroInfo 2009 - Environmental Informatics and Industrial Environmental Protection: Concepts* (pp. 219–229). Berlin, Germany: Methods and Tools.

Suurs, R. A. A. (2002). Long Distance Bioenergy Logistics: An assessment of costs and energy consumption for various biomass transport chains (Report NWS, Vol. E-2002-01). Utrecht, The Netherlands: Utrecht University, Copernicus Institute.

van Ree, R., & Annevelink, B. (2007). *Status Report Biorefinery 2007 (Report 847)*. Wageningen, The Netherlands: Wageningen University and Research Centre, Agrotechnology and Food Sciences Group.

Velazquez-Marti, B., & Annevelink, E. (2008, June). *Mathematical algorithm to transform digital biomass distribution maps into linear programming networks in order to optimize bioenergy delivery chains*. Paper presented at the International Conference on Agricultural Engineering. Hersonissos, Greece.

Vlachos, D., Iakovou, E., Karagiannidis, A., & Toka, A. (2008). A strategic supply chain management model for waste biomass networks. In K. D. Bouzakis (Ed.), *3rd International Conference on Manufacturing Engineering* (pp. 797-804).

Zah, R., Böni, H., Gauch, M., Hischier, R., Lehmann, M., & Wäger, P. (2007). *Ökobilanz von Energieprodukten: Ökologische Bewertung von Biotreibstoffen (Final Report)*. St. Gallen, Switzerland: EMPA.

Chapter 7
From Traditional Non-Sustainable Production to Closed Loop Manufacturing:
Challenges for Materials Management Based on PPC and EMIS Integration

Paulina Golinska
Poznan University of Technology, Poland

ABSTRACT

The scope of this chapter addresses the issues related to materials management for closed loop manufacturing based on the integration of material flows management systems with production planning and control systems (PPC) or business systems (like ERP) applicable to remanufacturing environments. It aims to identify and discuss the main issues and further research steps needed in order to improve materials management, as well as assessment of the environmental impact of remanufactured products. The main problems that appear in the area of materials management by shifting from non-sustainable production to closed loop manufacturing have been identified and discussed. The integrated materials management approach has been presented.

INTRODUCTION: ON THE WAY TO SUSTAINABILITY

For almost two decades companies have made an effort to meet the goal of sustainability of their operations. The Burndtland Commission defined sustainability development, as "development that meets the needs of the present without compromising the ability of future generations to meet their own needs" (WCED, 1987). In order to be competitive in the market, companies have to enter two new elements in their strategy beside Profitability; namely People and Planet (the 3Ps). The circular economy concept introduced by D. Pearce (1990) is opposite to the open-ended approach. It introduces thinking about the economy as a closed system. It highlights four economic functions of the environment (Andersen, 2007):

DOI: 10.4018/978-1-61520-981-1.ch007

1. amenity values
2. a resource base for the economy
3. a sink of residual flows
4. a life-support system

From a materials management perspective; it is essential to not only minimize waste streams (sink function) but minimize the usage of both renewable and non-renewable raw materials (resource based function). The circular economy concept is now very strongly promoted in China where its main goal is the promotion of resources usage minimization and the introduction of cleaner production technologies. In a number of countries a big effort is made in the framework of circular economy, in order to reduce material throughput and introduce friendlier eco- designs of products.

Growing concerns of sustainability exert huge pressure on companies to measure their impact on the environment and engage in environmental reporting to account for the energy and other resources they consume and the resulting footprint they leave behind (Kleindorfer et al., 2005). Primary activities that contribute to their footprint are manufacturing operations and logistics operations, as transportation and storage. The secondary activities that contribute to the footprint are connected to remanufacturing, recycling and reuse operations. The closed loop supply chain model, which is described in detail in next section, provides a suitable framework to integrate and to follow all the material and information flows. Companies are likely to improve their operations under pressure from strict legislative regulations. However, companies don't need to make trade-offs between sustainability and profitability.

Porter (1991, pp. 96) argued that "properly constructed regulatory standards which aim at outcomes and not methods, will encourage companies to re-engineer their technology. The result, in many cases, is a process that not only pollutes less but also lowers costs and improves quality". Companies very often face the question of how to commit to strict environmental health and safety regulations in the most cost- effective manner. The sustainable 3Ps operations model should be treated as a new business opportunity to improve the competitiveness of a company. The closed loop supply chain refers well to this shift in business approach. The closed loop supply chain provides the integration of traditional 'forward' supply chain processes and 'reverse' supply chain processes (Guide & Wassenhove, 2003). The ideal closed loop supply chain (CLSC) can be defined as a zero-waste supply chain that completely reuses, recycles or composts all materials (Golinska et al., 2007). The main factors influencing the sustainable "closing the loop" approach in a manufacturing company are presented in Figure 1.

Legislative regulations provide an impetus to change from non-sustainable to more environmentally friendly operations, but their influence

Figure 1. Factors influencing on the process of closing the supply chain loop

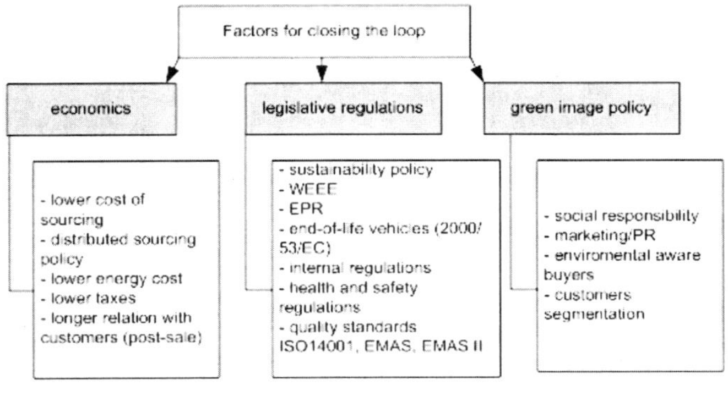

should be not overestimated. The industry practice (especially in the automotive or consumer electronics sectors) shows that closing the loop can be an answer to problems that companies face, namely:

- the increasing cost of energy,
- the increasing cost of raw materials,
- the increasing cost of waste disposal.

This approach also helps to prolong the relationship with customers after the sale by the application of the used products collection program, "give old-get cheaper new" actions or refund policy. It also helps to improve the procurement policy by the distribution of sourcing across traditional suppliers and recyclers. In times of crisis, efficient reverse materials management (re-supply) can be perceived as a new opportunity to lower the raw materials acquisition. In order to gain the advantages of "two-way" economy, efficient information management is needed to balance both economic and ecological impacts.

CLOSED LOOP SUPPLY CHAIN

In Figure 2, the framework for sustainable extended supply chain management in manufacturing organizations is presented. The continuous arrows present the direction of flow of materials. The forward supply chain processes include activities connected to purchasing, transportation and storing of the raw materials and new components that are input to the manufacturing system, as well as all value adding processes that transform the raw materials and components into final products according to customers' actual demand or demand forecasts. The final stage of the forward material stage is distribution, which refers to all activities needed to provide the customers with ordered/demanded products. Distribution usually consists of transportation, storage and sales services. In the case of closed loop supply chains the distribution processes might include the optional collection of end-of-life products from customers. The closed loop approach highlights the importance of efficient reverse flows management in order to reduce the size of waste being disposed. It helps to maximize the reuse, recycling and remanufacturing of products, as well as allows the minimization of the overall environmental impact of products and technology. Reverse processes start with all activities rendering used products available and physically moving them to the place of further treatment (collection). The inspection/separation denotes all operations determining whether a given product is in fact re-usable and in which way.

Figure 2. Extended sustainable supply chain (closed loop approach)

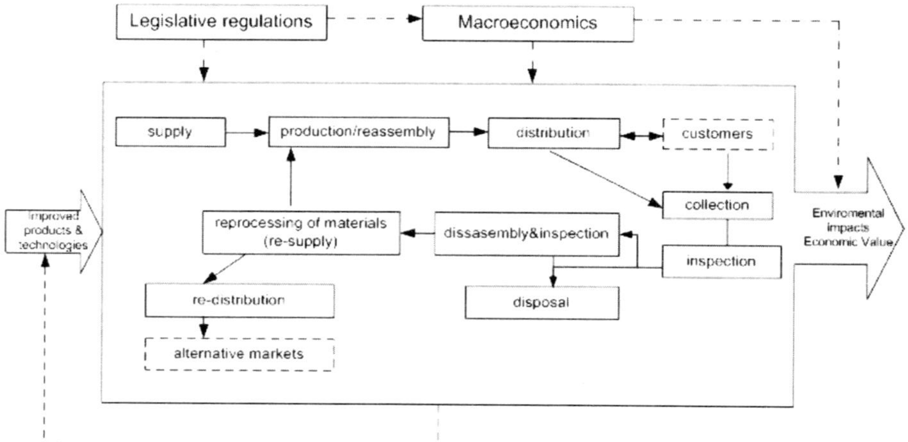

It results in splitting the flow of used products according to distinct re-use and disposal options (Dekker et al., 2003). Reprocessing may take different forms including recycling, repair and remanufacturing. In addition, activities such as cleaning, replacement and re-assembly may be involved. Re-distribution includes all activities needed to direct delivery of re-usable products to a potential market. In this chapter the emphasis is put on planning and coordination of the materials management in the CLSC, so issues related to re-distribution are not included. Sustainable supply chain management requires a continuous course of actions in order to decrease the environmental impact of products and technology used by a manufacturer and its pre-chain (suppliers) and post-chain (collection, inspection and reprocessing activities).

Application of environmental management systems helps to measure and manage the impact of products, operations and technology. "In practice, the success of environmental management systems depends upon their integration with enterprise source planning systems"(Funk et al., 2009, pp.54). In the following sections the author will discuss how corporate environmental management and the accompanying integration of information management is applied in detail in the materials management area.

CEMIS APPROACH: RELATED WORKS

In corporate environmental management, the main focus is on the continuous reduction or avoidance of environmental burdens for all processes in connection with product manufactures (Rautenstrauch, 1999).

"A long-range integration and extensive variation of the procurement, the production, the distribution and the disposal can only be realized by means of an integrated and complex environmental management information system" (Lang, 2007, pp. 233). The holistic CEMIS approach creates a possibility to reduce and optimize the internal company material flows and to assess the economic advantages of cost saving with reduction of environmental impacts. The aim of corporate environmental management in the area of materials management is to:

- optimize resource consumption of both raw materials and energy,
- minimize emissions that appear by material value adding processes within production system,
- reduce environmental risk, such as usage of hazardous materials or production systems failures.

To reach these aims, careful planning and control of material and energy flows is essential. A holistic CEMIS approach results from the integration of tasks and objectives from the economic optimization functions of business information systems (BIS, e.g. ERP, PPC) and the environmental impact assessments of environmental management information systems (EMIS). Its application can be realized by the integration of information systems/data sources dispersed across the company and it's whole supply chain in two ways:

- linking the isolated systems by modifying system structure by interface,
- replacement of the isolated systems by integrated solutions (Hassis et al., 1995).

It was expected that the integration of functionality of Environmental Management Systems (EMIS) into Business Systems (e.g. PPC) would become a standard (Rautenstrauch, 2007). In industry, environmental management systems are loosely coupled with ERP or PPC systems. Previous studies have shown (e.g. Rautenstrauch 2007; Funk et al., 2009; Lang et al., 2004; Lang-Koetz &Heubach, 2007) that the integration concept is based mainly on a full lifecycle assessment (LCA). The LCA assessment accounts for all emissions in cradle-to-grave products (Funk et al., 2009). Most of these studies have not passed the prototypical stage of development.

The ERP systems allow making the assessment of material flows in production systems, but a large manual effort is required to enter material relations and the environmental impacts of materials from data owned by the other supply chain participants. The closed loop approach also includes post sale materials flow, the so-called reverse flow that makes the whole problem even more complex. From an operations management perspective the most important area for integration is material flow management with production planning and control (Rautenstrauch, 2007). In the area of material flows integration there are a number of problems, such as:

- different granularity of data in ERP and EMIS systems (Marx Gómez et al., 2004),
- semantic gap in LCA approach based systems (Funk et al., 2009),
- availability of data/dispersion of data among external and internal databases.

The common approach of integration uses material flow networks, bill of materials (BOM), work plans and production orders (Rautenstrauch, 2007). There is a research gap regarding the examination of the integration potential of disassembly bill of material structure (DBOM), as described in Ferrer &Whybark (2001).

From a materials management perspective, the integration of information systems (the so-called information layer) should be preceded by the introduction of the closed loop concept in manufacturing operations and supply chain. The main problems with materials management based on the holistic CEMIS approach will be discussed in the next section.

SUSTAINABLE MATERIALS MANAGEMENT: MAIN PROBLEMS

Sustainable materials management is fully encompassed by the closed loop supply chain concept. In traditional non-sustainable manufacturing, the optimization of materials management activities is regarded as the minimization of the product delivery cost to customer, including the total cost of manufacturing, distribution and sale. The costs of product repairs and disposal are not usually taken into consideration by business decision making. The main goal of closed loop chain materials management is to provide the continuity of remanufacturing activities and to simultaneously minimize the amount of waste being generated in the whole supply chain. Materials management for closed loop manufacturing is more complex than in traditional manufacturing. The main reason is uncertainty inherent in:

- timing of re-delivery (reverse lead time),
- quality of returns and material recovery rate,
- quantity of returns.

In a situation where returns are not appropriate for reuse, they have to be substituted with raw materials. A number of companies face difficulties with materials management due to the fact that reverse flows have different characteristics to raw material flows. Moreover, the crossing of forward and reverse materials streams in manufacturing systems cause problems with materials flow management due to traceability issues.

Sustainable materials management requires:

- selection of materials that are able to be recycled, remanufactured and reused,
- modularity of products for remanufacturing,
- cooperation with suppliers in area of recycling,
- minimization of waste and remains.

The lack of reliable data on products and inventory levels causes inefficiencies for manufacturers who would like to shift from a traditional mode (very often non-sustainable) to closed loop manufacturing. Due to the problems in forecasting of reverse flows and variable materials reuse rate, remanufacturers face problems to use standard PPC systems. Closing the supply loop deals not only with synchronization of material flows but also with an integration of information flows regarding materials and products that are dispersed among different entities involved in recovery network. The product's life cycle management provides a suitable framework for the better understanding of information flow characteristics in such an environment. Product life cycle can be divided into three phases (SETAC 1993): beginning of life (BOL), middle of life (MOL) and end of life (EOL). Figure 3 presents the model of the closed loop manufacturing concept that reflects particular product life cycle phases.

Between the BOL and MOL phases of the product life cycle the information flow is quite complete and supported by a number of IT systems: mainly very large business applications (VLBA) e.g. MRP/ERP. The information flow is less efficient as a product moves from the manufacturer up to the customer. The feedback of data, information and knowledge from MOL maintenance and EOL recovery processes to the BOL producers is interrupted after a product's sale (Zheng et al., 2007). Lack of appropriate data and information makes the decision-making process during the EOL phase very difficult. Decisions about the optimization of sustainable materials management are based on incomplete information from BOL systems. Very often, decisions are based on the rule-of-thumb experience. There is a need for IT solutions that will synchronize information flow among parties involved in the closed loop supply chain, in order to reach better information exchange in the area of supplies and re-supplies.

REMANUFACTURING: THE MOST SUSTAINABLE FORM OF MATERIALS REPROCESSING

Industry Insights

Remanufacturing is an industrial process in which a new product is reassembled from an old one and, where necessary, new parts are used to produce fully equivalent and sometimes superior, in performance and expected lifetime, to the original new product (Lund, 1983). Remanufacturing is distinctly different from repair operations, since products are disassembled completely and all parts are returned to a like-new condition, which may include cosmetic operations (Guide, 2000).

Remanufacturing fulfills the corporate environmental management goals regarding optimization of resources and minimization of emissions

Figure 3. System life cycle phases in closed loop manufacturing

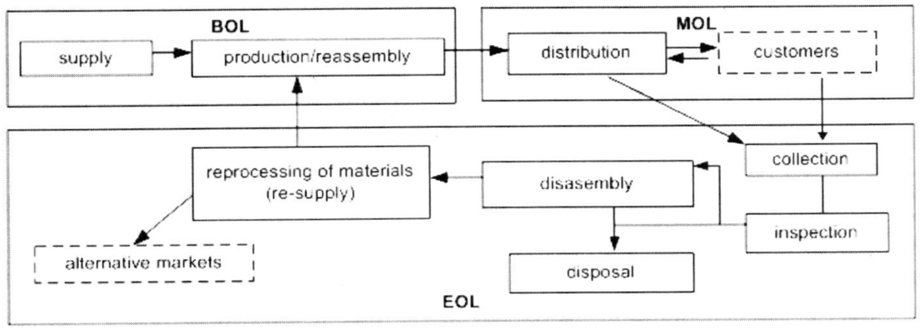

better than the other closed loop solutions like recycling. Recycling is putting used materials back into the manufacturing chain at a very basic level. The output of the recycling process could be the same products, when the quality is good enough (e.g. steel, automotive plastics), or new ones in cases where used materials are not meeting the quality standards.

Recycling of products has a large potential for conserving natural resources. Recycling processes, giving up the energy that has been embodied in the initial products, need a lot of additional energy to arrive at the next products (Steinhilper, 1998). However, their energy requirements are in most cases still below those of manufacturing new products from only raw materials. Some material recycling processes, nevertheless, need even more energy to close the loop than processes which start from ore (Steinhilper, 1998). Sometimes the recycling process is connected with emissions that accompany materials recycling.

Remanufactured products conserve not only the raw material contents, but also much of the value added during processes required to manufacture new products (Seliger, 2006). Remanufacturing allows companies to capture the residual value-added in forms of materials, energy and labor. Remanufacturing conserves the energy embodied in a product with very minimal additional energy consumption compared to recycling or traditional manufacturing. Lund (1998) has identified seven criteria for profitable remanufacturability:

- the product is a durable good,
- the product fails functionally,
- the product is standardized and the parts are interchangeable,
- the remaining value-added is high,
- the cost to obtain product is low compared to the remaining value,
- the product technology is stable,
- the costumer is aware that remanufactured goods are available.

In cases when the remaining value is not high enough for remanufacturing, or the cost to obtain a product is high compared to the remaining value, then reuse is an option. Reuse can be divided into:

- straight reuse by other user with lower quality expectations (less developed markets),
- refurbishment – cleaning, lubricating or other improvement,
- repair/rebuilt,
- redeployment &cannibalization – using working parts elsewhere.

Reuse has the potential for raw materials and energy savings, due to the fact that it allows, in many cases, the replacement of single use products with reusable products and also reduces the number of manufacturing operations. Moreover, it allows a reduction in the disposal of waste. From the perspective of corporate environmental management goals regarding optimization of resources and minimization of emission, reuse is only the option for very simple products and packing materials. In cases of high-tech products, reuse can be hazardous or less energy efficient. Remanufacturing aims to bring the product to a "like new condition", when in cases of reuse only limited maintenance takes place. Transfer of products to be reused in the less developed economies, where they are used in fact for many years after their initial end-of-life phase, can place a higher cost burden to the environment as a whole. Moreover, reusable products need to have longer durability than single use products and very often require more material per item.

Nowadays environmental regulations regarding the post sale treatment for technical products focus on recycling ratios and prohibition of toxic materials (e.g. WEEE, End of Life Vehicle ELV Directive 2000/53/EC, directive on type approval of vehicles for reusability, recyclability, and recoverability RRR 2005/64/EC), but experts forecast that regulations in the future will be developed into sustainable manufacturing, namely remanufacturing.

Differences in Materials Management in Manufacturing vs. Remanufacturing

The purpose of materials management for remanufacturing is determined by the closed loop supply chain type. The motivation of particular manufacturers to collect the returns defines the design of the reverse network. Manufacturers do not make much effort to optimize reverse logistics operations when they do not perceive the reverse flow to be an area with economical profits potential.

The studies conducted in the US market (for example: Lund, 1998) have showed that a large number of US manufacturers are involved in remanufacturing in order to lower the material acquisitions costs. They apply a market-driven product-acquisition approach to returns. They make an effort to optimize the commercial returns and warranty return flows in order to catch as much added-value from it as possible. In Europe most of the manufactures are closing the supply loop due to legislative requirements. European firms seem to rely on the waste stream for acquiring recoverable products (Guide, 2003). However in some industries, for example automotive, the manufactures have started to apply a less passive approach. The following closed loop supply chain types can be defined depending on the returns characteristics (Kirkke et al., 2004):

- control,
- responsive,
- efficient.

The control supply chain deals mainly with negative externalities when collection is obligatory by laws or regulations. It reflects the EU policy for Extended Producer Responsibility (EPR) (Leifsit & Lombardi, 1997). The responsive supply chain operates with returns that have value-added capture potential, however the timing of their collection as well as quality is uncertain. The efficient closed loop supply chain is dealing with returns, like scrap and plastic packing with predictable quality, quantity and time of delivery/collection. Table 1 presents the returns types that appear in particular closed loop supply chain type.

The responsive supply chain seems to have the biggest potential for improvement of material management for remanufacturing purpose. In order to point the requirements for efficient materials management for the purpose of remanufacturing, there is a need to identify the differences between traditional manufacturing and remanufacturing.

There are a number of dimensions that can characterize the conditions of materials management in a particular company. The most important are: production volume, production standardization, inventory level, inventory cycle (understood as a period of time during which particular inventories are kept on average), storage conditions, replenishment strategy, lead time, sources of supplies and deliveries' stability.

Table 1. The characteristics of returns in particular CLSC models, modified after Kirkke et al., 2004

	Control	Responsive	Efficient
End-of-life returns	X	X	
Commercial returns		X	
Warranty returns		X	
Production scrap and by-products			X
Reusable packaging material			X

Table 2 presents the comparison of a traditional manufacturing process (line production) versus a remanufacturing process, taking into consideration the above mentioned criteria. Due to the fact that remanufacturing of automotive parts equals to 2/3 of all remanufacturing operations, the organizational conditions that appear in the automotive industry are taken as an example. The automotive industry has applied a circular economy approach as one of the major focus. This approach is highlighted in the fulfillment of following goals:

- steady improvement in vehicle recovery rates,
- increased use of renewable resources and recycled materials,
- increased utilization of used parts,
- reduction of hazardous substances like lead, mercury, cadmium, and hexavalent chromium,
- reduction of CO2 emission.

The minimization of raw materials usage, energy saving and eco-design is a benchmark for all companies in the sector. The development of automotive parts remanufacturing is one of the pillars of this sustainable policy. Automotive product remanufacturing is a 53 billion dollar industry in the USA alone and at least 100 billion dollar industry throughout the world. Almost 10% of all cars and trucks require an engine replacement during their life. About €120 million worth of remanufactured products were sold in 2005 worldwide (Kim et al., 2008). Starters and alternators are the most typical products to be remanufactured, due to the fact that most cars require two of each throughout their lives, and these two components are mass produced and remanufactured by thousands of companies. Alternator and starter motors are ideal candidates for profitable remanufacturing as these components have very high production volumes and low un-manufacturability (Severengiz et al., 2008). About 300 starter motor and alternator remanufacturers are active worldwide, 50% of the companies are US producers; another 30% of the companies are located in Europe.

Production volume is low due to technical innovations and variable demand. Product standardization is low and size of batches is small because not many products are designed for remanufacturability. Model explosion in customized mass production of new products seriously influences the possibility of batch optimization in the remanufacturing area. Inventory level is high because of uncertainties of delivery timings and their quality. Remanufacturing companies carry much higher level of inventories than in traditional manufacturing in order to buffer

Table 2. Manufacturing vs. remanufacturing in automotive industry

	Manufacturing	**Remanufacturing**
Production volume	High	Low
Product Standardization	High	Low
Inventory level	Low Just- in-Time	High in order to buffer the uncertainty
Inventory cycle	Short	Long
Storage conditions	Reduced storage size	Place consuming
Replenishment strategy	Standardized procedures	Variable, ad hoc
Lead time	Standard	Variable
Source of supplies	Concentrate	Very distributed
Deliveries' stability	High	Low

against uncertainty. Also, product differentiation influences the inventory levels at remanufactures. Moreover, due to a less predictable material recovery rate MRR (Guide, 2000), a higher level of work-in-progress inventory is kept. MRR defines the frequency that a material recovered from a disassembled unit is remanufacturable. Due to a variable MRR for the returned products or raw materials to substitute, non-remanufacturable elements are stored longer than in traditional manufacturing (inventory cycle). The need for having high stock levels causes storage problems. Returned products are stored at different reprocessing phases. The size of a single unit of the complete product waiting for disassembly and a partly disassembled part is bigger than the size of the raw material unit stored by traditional manufacturers. Moreover, some of the returns include residual liquids that have to be stored under prescribed conditions. On average, for remanufacturing, there are a larger number of models work-on than in traditional manufacturing. This situation causes significant problems with traceability and access to particular variants of element/returned products from stock when needed. There is a need to provide and gather information that is required for assessment of environmental impact of such inventory and its footprint.

Remanufacturers face problems to use standardized approaches in inventory replenishment when a lack of particular parts/product types appears due to changes in demand, problematic forecasting of reverse material flows or variable MRR. The remanufacturing lead time differs significantly and it depends on reprocessing activities needed in order to disassemble and recover the used parts. Moreover, the reprocessing might include different operations for the same type of returns depending on their condition. Some operations/tasks are known with certainty but appearance of the others might be probabilistic. There is the problem of stochastic routings of materials for remanufacturing operations and highly variable processing times. It makes setting accurate lead times for remanufacturing very difficult.

Collection of returns depends on the stage of the product life cycle. Commercial returns are collected from distributors or retailers but end-of-life (EOL) products are gathered from a large number of customers. The environmental impact of all the temporary storage at the collection side, as well as the transportation process should be appropriately measured. The stability of deliveries is low due to the fact that the quantity and timing of returns is difficult to forecast. Nowadays companies have started to make an effort to manage the acquisition/collection of returns, but still a number of problems have to be solved in order to match the demand with supply (Guide, 2003) and reach a higher stability of supply and its profitability.

Most of the above mentioned problems result from lack of appropriate information on material flows. The traditional business information systems are not able to provide all needed information for efficient materials management according to corporate environmental management requirements.

INTEGRATED APPROACH IN MATERIALS MANAGEMENT

The scope of data available in the manufacturer's production planning and control systems (PPC) or resource management system (ERP) is not sufficient to reach the goals of the circular economy (CE). CE requires symbiosis and synergy between separate entities and very different processes within the supply chain. Production planning and control systems are focused mainly on shopfloor control based on different business architecture models. More developed ERP systems beside manufacturing oriented modules are more and more often equipped with environmental components (e.g. SAP PLM), but they do not provide the whole scope of information required by fulfillment of corporate management goals.

Closed loop manufacturing requires information that is generated and stored in the databases and information systems that are dispersed amongst the whole supply chain. The integration of all data stored in the supply chain regarding production processes, technologies, life cycle assessment of products and the environmental impact of logistics processes is needed. The technical issues related to the design of the integration platform/interface are not covered by the scope of this chapter. The aim here is only to present the scope of information needed by the planning of efficient and environmental friendly materials management (holistic CEMIS approach) activities in closed loop manufacturing environments. These are as follows:

- **Supplier Information Systems:** should provide information regarding Life Cycle Inventory, raw materials/components environmental impact, environmental impacts of supply processes (like preprocessing, storage and delivery),
- **Manufacturer ERP/PPC:** provides data on procurement, production and sales, especially information about bill of materials (BOM), production orders, production capacities, disassembly BOM (if applicable, DBOM could be also obtained from external data sources),
- **Distribution Systems:** provide data regarding product distribution, detailed location of sale points and amounts of sales (needed for returns flows forecast and the design of recovery network), as well as should provide assessment of environmental impact of distribution activities,
- **Recycling Institutions information systems/data bases:** provide data on returns collection, products' returns structure, capacities of recovery network, as well as data on returns forecast,
- **External Life Cycle Assessment databases (LCA DB):** provide the estimates on product life cycle assessment based on products classification,
- **Manufacturer EMIS:** provides material flow networks and energy flows, company environmental data regarding resource consumption and environmental impact of the production process. It addition, the environmental impact assessment of the whole company that cannot be allocated to a particular production process should also be taken into consideration.

Figure 4 presents the process layer and information layer of sustainable (closed loop) manufacturing phases (grey area). As mentioned before, between the BOL and MOL phases of product life cycle the information flow is quite complete and supported by PPC and MRP/ERP systems. The integration of dispersed data sources between supply chain participants is crucial in order to bridge the information gap between the middle-of–life phase and EOL recovery and remanufacturing processes. The proposed approach simplifies the decision making process and helps with optimizing the materials management in a sustainable manner, based on complete information from post-sale phases. The goal of better information exchanges in the area of supplies and re-supplies can be reached.

The integration of the above mentioned data sources allow the goal of reduction of resource allocation and emissions by maximization of returns and minimization of raw materials and new components usage to be reached. The mechanism for the materials requirement calculation in a sustainable manner is presented in the next section.

Integration Logic: The Mechanism for Materials Requirement Calculation in the Sustainable Manner

Rahman & Schroer (1998) addressed the choice between MRP, just-in-time (JIT) systems and optimum production technique (OPT) to determine the conditions that would lead to the preference of

Figure 4. Closed loop manufacturing- process and information layer

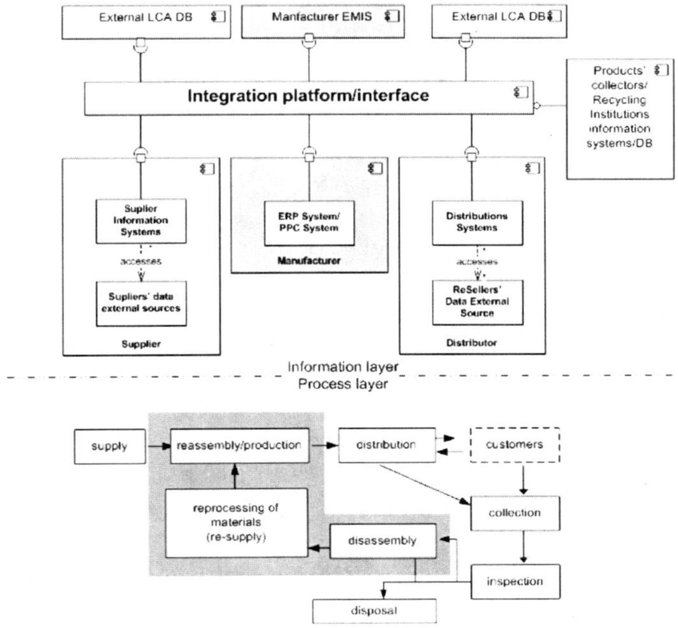

one planning approach over the other. The MRP logic is preferred in highly variable processes using batch production. MRP has the added advantage of providing a structure for treating the commonality of parts in different products. All these conditions (variability, batches, and commonality) are present in a remanufacturing facility, so this approach utilizes MRP logic and records.

The modification of MRP logic to closed loop manufacturing conditions is presented in Figure 5. The idea of the approach is to minimize the lifecycle inventory of products as well as their footprints. As mentioned before, remanufacturing in high-tech industries (e.g. electronics equipment, automotive industry) has the biggest potential for materials and energy savings, so the remanufactured elements should have the priority over new parts. Moreover, the net requirement should be calculated in a sustainable manner meaning:

- taking into consideration the overall environmental impact of the process,
- with minimization of raw materials usage and maximization of returns,
- with minimization of energy.

Implementation of the above mentioned planning logic requires the integration of the dispersed data sources, as mentioned in the previous section. The calculation of the external cores inventory (products to be remanufactured) is based on the data from External Life Cycle Assessment databases, Recycling Institutions information systems/databases and Distribution Systems. The Supplier Information Systems, as well as manufacturer's PPC system, and the External Life Cycle Assessment databases are used for the calculation of the Master Production Schedule.

CONCLUSION

The shift from traditional manufacturing to sustainable closed loop manufacturing is still a mainly theoretical concept. However the number of com-

Figure 5. Materials requirements planning for remanufacturing purpose

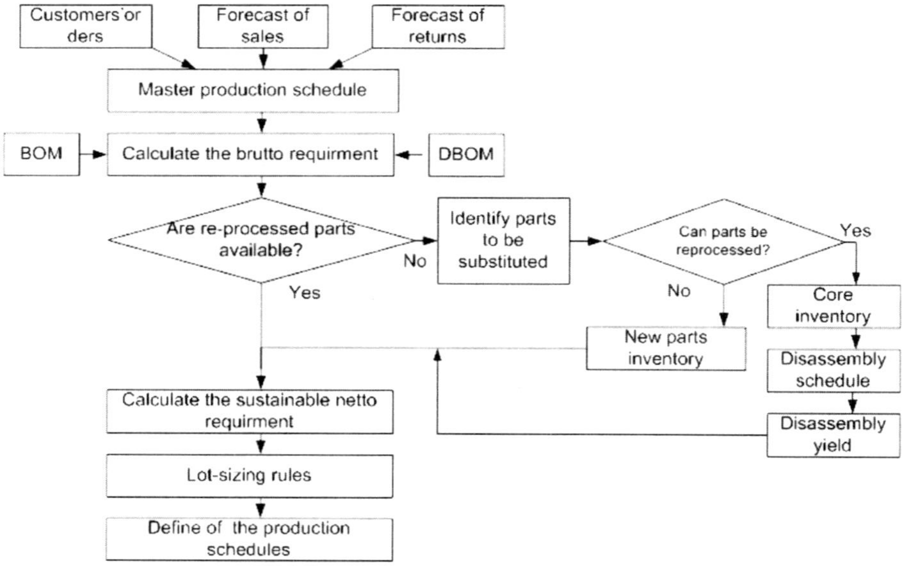

panies that are involved in remanufacturing operations is growing. This chapter presents the areas that are crucial for improvement of the materials management for the purpose of remanufacturing in the closed loop supply chain. An overview of the BIS (or PPC) and EMIS integration problems was presented.

The main challenge that requires additional research is still the problem of collection and utilization of dispersed data sources. As pointed out in the text, materials management in the corporate environmental management approach needs very complex data originating from systems of different structure. It still can be observed in industry practice that post sale parts of the supply chain act as black holes for manufactures' planning activities. An integrated information flow regarding the nature, quantity and quality of returns flows is a must. The proposed approach of integration identified the scope of information that is crucial for efficient material management between product life cycle phases. The information gap was identified.

The main limitation of the proposed approach is the lack of existing cost-efficient integration platforms that can synchronize the information exchange between the parties that are involved in a closed loop supply chain. Further studies should focus on the identification of the integration platform technical requirements. The issue related to increasing trust and safety for information exchange between entities involved in supply chains should be examined. The corporate environmental management systems are highly dependent on national legislative regulations. So their impact on information demand for decision making should be measured in the transnational closed loop supply chains.

REFERENCES

Andersen, M. S. (2007). An introduction note on the environmental economics of the circular economy. *Sustainability Science*, *2*, 133–140. doi:10.1007/s11625-006-0013-6

Dekker, R., Fleischmann, M., Inderfurth, K., & Van Wassenhove, L. N. (Eds.). (2003). *Reverse Logistics: Quantitative Models for Closed-Loop Supply Chains*. Berlin: Springer.

Ferrer, G., & Whybark, D. C. (2001). Material Planning for a Remanufacturing Facility. *Production and Operations Management*, *10*(2), 112–124.

Funk, B., Moeller, A., & Niemeyer, P. (2009). Integration of Environmental Management Information Systems an ERP systems using Integration Platform. In I. N. Athanasiadis, P. A. Mitkas, A. E. Rizzoli, & J. Marx Gómez (Eds.), *Information Technologies in Environmental Engineering. Proceedings of the 4th International ICSC Symposium Thessaloniki, Greece, May 28-29, 2009* (pp. 64-77). Berlin, Heidelberg: Springer.

Golinska, P., Fertsch, M., Marx Gómez, J., & Oleskow, J. (2007). The concept of Closed-loop Supply Chain Integration Through Agent-based System. In J. Marx Gómez, M. Sonnenschein, M. Müller, H. Welsch, & C. Rautenstrauch (Eds.), *Information Technologies in Environmental Engineering, ITEE 2007, Third International ICSC Symposium* (pp. 189-202). Berlin, Heidelberg: Springer.

Guide, V. D. R. Jr. (2000). Production planning and control for remanufacturing. *Journal of Operations Management*, *18*, 467–483. doi:10.1016/S0272-6963(00)00034-6

Guide Jr., V. D. R. (2003). Matching Demand and Supply to Maximize Profits from Remanufacturing. *Manufacturing and Service operations Management*, *5*(4), 303-316.

Guide, V. D. R. Jr, & Van Wassenhove, L. N. (Eds.). (2003). *Business Aspects of Closed-Loop Supply Chains*. Pittsburgh, PA: Carnegie Mellon University Press.

Hassis, H. D., Hilty, L. M., Hundscheind, J., Kuerzl, H., & Ratenstrauch, C. (1995). *Umweltinformatik in der Production*. Marburg: Metropolis.

Kim, H. J., Severengiz, S., Skerlos, J., & Seliger, G. (2008). Economic and Environmental Assessment of Remanufacturing in the Automotive Industry. In *Proceedings of the LCE 2008: 15th CIRP International Conference on Life Cycle Engineering, Sydney, Australia* (pp. 195-200).

Kleindorfer, P. R., Singhal, K., & van Wassenhove, L. N. (2005). Sustainable operations management. *Production and Operations Management*, *14*(4), 482–492.

Krikke, H., le Blanc, I., & van de Velde, S. (2004). Product modularity and the design of closed-loop supply chains. *California Management Review*, *46*(2), 23–39.

Lang, C., Steinfeld, M., Loew, T., Beucker, S., Heubach, D., & Keil, K. (2004). *Konzepte zur Einfuehrung und Anwendung von Umweltcontrollinginstrumenten in Unternehmen*. Endbericht des Forschungsprojekts INTUS.

Lang, C. V. (2007). Modeling of a Corporate Environmental Management Information System. In J. Marx Gómez, M. Sonnenschein, M. Müller, H. Welsch, & C. Rautenstrauch (Eds.), *Information Technologies in Environmental Engineering, ITEE 2007, Third International ICSC Symposium* (pp. 231-240). Berlin, Heidelberg: Springer.

Lang-Koetz, C., & Heubach, D. (2007). *Umweltcontrolling Umsetzen – Erstellung von Kennzahlen für Stoff-Energieströme und deren Integration in die betriebliche IT*. Stuttgart: Frauenhoffer IRB Verlag.

Leifsit, R., & Lombardi, D. R. (1997). Who should pay and why? Some thoughts on the conceptual foundations for the assignment of extended producer responsibility. In *Proceedings of the International Workshop on Extended Producer Responsibility, OECD, Ottawa.*

Lund, R. (1983). *Remanufacturing: United States Experience for Developing Nations*. Washington, DC: The World Bank.

Lund, R. (1998). Remanufacturing: An American resource. In *Proceedings of the 5th International Congress on Environmentally Conscious Design and Manufacturing*. Rochester, NY: Rochester Institute of Technology.

Marx Gómez, J., Prötzsch, S., & Rautenstrauch, C. (2004). Data Defects in Material Flow Networks – Classification and Approaches; Cybernetics and Systems. *Cybernetics and Systems, 35*(5-6), 549–558. doi:10.1080/01969720490451931

Pearce, D., & Turner, R. K. (1990). *Economics of natural resources and the environment*. London: Harvester Wheatsheaf.

Porter, M. (1991). America's green strategy. *Scientific American, 264*(4).

Rahman, M. M., & Schroer, B. J. (1998). Optimum Production Conditions for JIT, MRP, OPT. In *29th Annual Meeting of the Decision Sciences Institute* (pp. 1158-1162). Las Vegas, NV: Decision Science Institute.

Rautenstrauch, C. (1999). *Betriebliche Umweltinformationssysteme- Grundlagen, Konzepte und Systeme*. Berlin, Heidelberg: Springer.

Rautenstrauch, C. (2007). Integration of MRP II and Material Flow Management Systems. In J. Marx Gómez, M. Sonnenschein, M. Müller, H. Welsch, & C. Rautenstrauch (Eds.), *Information Technologies in Environmental Engineering, ITEE 2007, Third International ICSC Symposium* (pp. 261-269). Berlin, Heidelberg: Springer.

Seitz, M., & Peattie, K. (2004). Meeting the Closed-Loop Challenge: The Case of Remanufacturing. *California Management Review, 46*(2), 74–89.

Seliger, G. (Ed.). (2006). *Sustainability in Manufacturing: Recovery of Resources in Product and Material Cycles*. Heidelberg, Berlin: Springer.

SETAC. (1993). *Guidelines for Life Cycle Assessment: A 'Code of Practice'. Proceedings of a Workshop in Sesimbra, Portugal*. Brussels: Society of Environmental Toxicology and Chemistry (SETAC).

Severengiz, S., Sezgin, C., & Yonk, N. K. (2008). *Automotive Remanufacturing in Europe: Survey Results*. TU Berlin.

Steinhilper, R. (1998). *Remanufacturing the ultimate form of recycling*. Stuttgart: Frauenhoffer IRB Verlag.

World Commission on Environment and Development. (WCED, 1987). Our common future. New York: Oxford University Press.

Zheng, L., Hui, C., Folan, P., Potter, D., & Browne, J. (2007). RFID-based Information Management in the Automotive Plastic Recycling Industry. In J. Marx Gómez, M. Sonnenschein, M. Müller, H. Welsch, & C. Rautenstrauch (Eds.), *Information Technologies in Environmental Engineering, ITEE 2007, Third International ICSC Symposium* (pp. 397-408). Berlin, Heidelberg: Springer.

Chapter 8
Enterprise Architecture Applied Towards Sustainable IT Governance

Karoll Haussler Carneiro Ramos
Universidade de Brasília, Brazil

Luis Fernando Ramos Molinaro
Universidade de Brasília, Brazil

Adson Silva Rocha
Universidade de Brasília, Brazil

Paulo Henrique Portela
Universidade de Brasília, Brazil

Ana Carolina Kalume Maranhão
Universidade de Brasília, Brazil

Flávio Elias de Deus
Universidade de Brasília, Brazil

ABSTRACT

Evidence shows that investments made in the IT (Information Technology) area have a positive effect on organizational performance, even if these benefits are difficult to measure and associated with the real intention of those investments. IT presents itself as a tool and not as a guarantee of success, as this determining factor depends on how it is used and directed towards strategic alignment. This chapter sought to evaluate how much IT governance positively interferes in the achievement of strategic goals, based on the control of investments and its correct management. The results show that the organizations which adopt IT governance have their performance highly improved in relation to other companies, especially concerning profitability. Besides, the use of enterprise architecture in IT governance shows a positive correlation with corporative governance elements, encouraging the use of more efficient management mechanisms to promote sustainable IT.

DOI: 10.4018/978-1-61520-981-1.ch008

INTRODUCTION

Since the first systems were developed, executives and scholars have been facing constant challenges related mainly with the efficiency of IT investment measurement, IT management effectiveness and IT alignment with the organizations' strategic goals (Matlin, 1979; Weill & Oslon, 1989; Bacon, 1992; Fitzgerald, 1998; Dehning, Dow & Stratopoulos, 2004). The importance of such challenges and their reach contributed to the increase of exploratory research into IT management, mainly on the efficiency of IT investments in organizational performance (Luftman & Mclean, 2004; Dehning, Richardson & Zmud, 2007).

Recent research is conducted into the correlation of types of IT investments and into its impacts on organizational performance. Statistical techniques and methods have been used in an attempt to measure costs and benefits from investments (Gunasekaran, Ngai & McGaughey, 2006).

Other studies suggest that IT investments either do not bring competitive advantages to organizations (Brynjolfsson, 1993; Strassman, 1997), or just avoid competitive disadvantages (Carr, 2003; Tiernan & Peppard, 2004). However, there is contrary data which asserts that investments in IT assure competitive advantage to the organizations (Hitt & Brynjolfsson, 1996; Stratopoulos & Dehning, 2000; Dehning, Richardson & Zmud, 2003; Becker, Lunardi & Maçada, 2003; Maçada, Becker & Lunardi, 2005).

Many IT projects with high initial investments ended up not presenting the expected earnings nor did they meet the clients' expectations. In the worst cases, the projects were not even completed (Peterson, 2004a; Turban, Mclean & Wetherbe, 2004). This fact makes the correlation between the amount of IT investments and organizational performance harder due to some conflicting results (Strassman, 1997; Dehning & Richardson, 2002).

A common error among IT executives lies in the thought that IT investments are a guarantee of profits for the organization (Marchand, 2005). An expressive number of studies take into account the quantitative aspect of IT investments, but disregard the way those investments are allocated and consequently disqualify the qualitative aspects (Smith & Mckeen, 1993; Devaraj & Kohli, 2003; Peterson, 2004). However, it is a complex task to determine how the investments should be set aside. This task is the goal of many researchers. (Schwarz & Hirschheim & 2003).

Besides this, there are other factors that may influence the organization's performance, for example, the field of performance, sector of competitiveness, type of business, etc. This aspect does not depend on the good application of IT investments (Porter & Millar, 1985; Dedrick, Gurbaxani & Kraemer, 2003; Melville, Kraemer & Gurbaxani, 2004). Thus, it is necessary that IT managers know the main aspects that currently guide the organizations.

Indeed, the leading purpose of this chapter is to orient IT managers on the better use of IT resources considering the main aspects which guide the organization's business through enterprise architecture.

The implementation of enterprise architecture aligned with the concept of IT sustainable governance may generate a competitive differential once the resultant solution provides a better exploration of the attributes of interoperability, flexibility cost effectiveness and innovation power.

This chapter will review the current situation regarding IT management and governance. Additionally an approach will be presented that aims at IT development from a sustainable point of view.

THEORETICAL REFERENCE

The theoretical reference presents the main knowledge base that underpinned the proposed model. The concepts of corporative governance to be addressed in the theoretical reference are IT governance, IT strategic alignment and business, IT governance as a competitive differential and enterprise architecture.

CORPORATIVE GOVERNANCE

The disagreement between enterprise managers and stockholders has generated many conflicts with an unfavorable impact on the organizations' performance throughout the years. These conflicts' intensity favored the definition of agency relations. According to Jense & Meckling (1976), an agency relation can be interpreted as a contract in which job relations are defined between the contracting and contracted parties.

Agency relations establish incentives to managers and via monitoring, also define the boundaries of their activities. This use of monitoring implies necessary costs (agency costs) to align the managers' interests with the stockholders' or the owner's (Jensen & Meckling, 1976).

The practices of agency relations are within the Agency Theory. This theory proposes a collection of activities focused on management in the regulation and control of relations among the organization's stockholders. They aim at the efficiency and efficacy of allocated resources, besides the reduction of agency costs (Fama & Jensen, 1983). Thus, the collection of internal and external mechanisms of incentive and control for reducing agency costs is defined as corporative governance (Barros, Fama & Silveira, 2003).

Corporative governance is a system through which societies are guided and monitored. The governance system allows that the mission, the vision and the strategy be transformed, considering goals and desired results.

However, only in the mid 90's did the term "governance" become more prominent through the Cadbury Report which is regarded as the first code of good practices in corporative governance (IBGC, 2009). The referred to document was in answer to the scandals in England's corporative and financial market at the end of the 1980's. This document ended up influencing the publication of codes in many countries.

In 2000, the World Bank and Mckinsey concluded in a study that investors would pay between 18% and 28% more for companies using corporative governance, proving that controlled and oriented management positively reflect on the value added to the organization's brand name (IBGC, 2009).

The increase in stockholders' confidence is due to the expressive amount of information provided by the organizations using corporative governance (Pelanda, 2006).

In conclusion, organizations depend on information tools and governance matters cannot be solved without an intensive use of IT. Therefore, concern about access to information demands more nimbleness in processes which contribute to disseminating information and help in decision-making as well as in the strengthening of IT.

IT GOVERNANCE

IT governance appears as an attempt to certify that investments in technology are adding value to the organization's business (De Haes & Van Grembergen, 2005).

According to the IT Governance Institute (2001), IT governance is a responsibility of the Board of Directors and an essential part of corporative governance. IT governance manages organizational structures and processes that assure the sustainability and improvement of an organization's strategy and objectives.

Grembergen (2004) defines IT governance as an organizational capability practiced by high level administration, plus the executives and IT management controlling IT strategy formulation and implementation, so as to assure IT alignment with the organization.

According to Weil & Ross (2004), IT governance serves the practices defined by corporative governance and aims to answer the following questions:

1. Which IT capabilities improve your company's competitiveness?
2. Are all company managers aware of their responsibilities regarding IT management and its effective use or do they assume this is only an IT area problem?
3. Which IT investments aim to reach the strategic goals – or does your company waste resources and investments just to comply with tactic initiatives and operational needs?

Although IT governance is evident, many of its concepts and definitions remain undefined resulting in misunderstandings and misuses (Peterson, 2004; Mclane, 2003). In a simplistic view, IT governance is a variation of corporative governance but is centered on IT strategic management, focusing on the value of IT governance for the business and the control as well as reducing risks (Peterson, 2004; ITGI, 2003 ; Hardy, 2006).

While most of the published papers about governance discuss its definition (Korac-Kakabadse & Kakabadse,2001), structure (Sambamurthy & Zmud, 1999; Weill & Woodham, 2002; Weill, 2004; Willcocks, Feeny & Olson, 2006; Verhoef, 2007), practices (Rau, 2004; Ridley, Young & Carroll, 2004; Hardy, 2006; Peterson, 2004a; Perteson, 2004b), relation to the Sarbanes-Oxley law (Chan, 2004; Kaarst-Brown & Kelly, 2005; Haworth & Pietron, 2006) and its potentials (Sujitparapitaya, Janz & Gillenson, 2003; Chin, Brown & Hu, 2004; De Haes & Van Grembergen, 2006; De Haes & Van Grembergen, 2005), very little emphasis is given to the analysis of the existing relationship between IT governance and the organizations' performance.

According to Sambamurthy & Zmud (1999), governance is seen as a component of organizational structure and as a part of IT management architecture. Schwarz & Jirschheim (2003) defend that governance is related to the IT role in the organization as a reflection of IT management's decision-making responsibilities. For Keyes-Pearce (2002) governance acts as an internal auditing tool for IT, emphasizing control of the organization's financial monitoring.

Considering IT governance as a coordination tool, Peterson (2004a), De Haes & Van Grembergen (2005) argue that control would work as an integrating mechanism. Weill & Woodham (2002) exemplified this thought, pointing out the importance of different governance mechanisms to assure the efficiency of IT alignment with the business. For Sambamurthy & Zmud (2000), more important than managing IT tasks, it is indispensable to develop the main capabilities of IT in the organization. Vitale (2001) believes IT governance must be a pattern applied to decision-making, in which the processes orient actions and monitor their performance.

As Brancheau (1994) and Farrell (2003) assert, alignment is an important management tool to mitigate frustrations from the misuse of IT investments and consequently to obtain competitive advantages. It fortifies cohesion among the IT, the functional and the business areas (Texeira Júnior, 2003), providing cost reductions, income generation and improvement in the ability to reachorganizational goals (Synnot, 1987; Farrell, 2003; Texeira Júnior, 2003).

Brodbeck & Hoppen (2000) assert that alignment cannot be static. It should be seen inside strategic planning, within a 5-year cycle.

The question is how to promote and keep this alignment. Some authors argue that management instruments are able to do that, as they can measure and stimulate the learning process, which will nurture alignment improvement (Brodbeck, 2000), for instance, the Balanced Business Scorecard (Zee & Jong, 1999). Nevertheless, it is believed that alignment really happens when all involved are aware of and committed to the companies' objectives, goals and plans (Reich & Benbasat, 2000).

Lunardi, Dolci, Becker & Maçada (2008) conducted research to identify the IT governance mechanisms most common among Brazilian companies, in addition to their main benefits to IT management. ITIL, COBIT and SOX were the most common mechanisms in the 110 companies analyzed between 2002 and 2007.

In the research, the main benefits derived from these best practices were gathered in seven categories: processes, IT area, security, projects, services, infrastructure and IT involvement with other areas. The 110 companies were organized into three big economic sectors, and listed by the year those companies started their IT governance process. This movement is very recent among Brazilian companies.

It is worth mentioning that some methods of performance measurement are linked to all of the best practices listed before. And the main critic on these best practices regards the excess of provisions for the performance monitoring.

Performance measurement refers to any systematic and integrated approach that promotes operational performance in an efficient, effective and economic way i.e., whatever contributes to accomplishing the organization's strategy, mission and vision (Salem, 2003).

According to Attadia & Martins (2003), the performance measurement considers that decisions and actions be taken based on information, as they quantify the actions' efficiency and efficacy through collection, examination, labeling, analyses, interpretation and dissemination of suitable data.

Performance measurements can be dealt with in an individual or systematic way. The former deals with the measure in its isolated form, as a basic element of performance measurement. The latter deals with the collection of logical measures, which form a system of performance measurements (Attadia & Martins, 2003).

Measuring an organization's performance through indicators has been accepted and used by organizations throughout the world for decades. The historical course of performance management and measurement is marked by two distinct moments. The first moment, from 1880 to the beginning of 1989, was characterized by the dominance of a system of financial indicators.

The historical context of this period takes into consideration the cycle of the exploration, the industrial and the retailing revolutions as well as the world wars. In this perspective, financial indicators represented the most reliable way to assess an organization. However, the emphasis on financial indicators became outdated at the end of the 20th century, once financial indicators were neither able to assess nor manage intangible and intellectual assets (Kaplan & Norton, 1997).

The second moment of performance measurement started in 1980 and is currently in use, with emphasis given to an offset of financial and non-financial indicator systems. This moment can still be subdivided into two generations: the "measurement myopia" and "crazy measurement" (Neely & Austin, 2000).

The "measurement myopia" happened when it was detected that the new system of indicators was not suitable. The "crazy measurement", which currently refers to companies' obsession for measuring - everything must be measured regardless of knowing why and what for (Attadia & Martins, 2003).

IT GOVERNANCE AS A COMPETITIVE DIFFERENTIAL

Several case studies have been conducted to better assess IT governance's real impacts on organizations. Heier, Borgman & Mileos (2009) analyzed governance's software impact on supporting IT in current information technology governance processes and on supporting the true business value generated by the application of IT.

Te & King (1997) researched about the evolution of integration between business planning and information systems planning. The research confirmed the existence of an evolution pattern which was classified into four types and range from administrative integration to full integration. The study found that few companies reached full integration.

The Information Technology Process Institute (ITPI[1]), Carnegie Melon University, Florida State University and Triwiew Inc examined 1.000 companies labeled as high-performance by Fortune magazine. This research was aimed at analyzing the common aspects of IT management in each company.

Six specific subjects were analyzed in the research: access, change, resolution, configuration, release and service-level management. It was verified that the Pareto principle is suitable for the controls of these subjects, which even when reduced to 20% would have the same impact as the total set of controls (IT audit, 2007). Actually, the controls identified are those mainly responsible for IT efficient and effective management.

The results showed that it is possible to apply some parts of the best practices collection, as this action promotes a reduction of IT costs and bureaucracy. A proposed suggestion is to rethink the indiscriminate use of the best practices that support IT governance, making good use of what is really necessary to each organization.

SUSTAINABLE IT GOVERNANCE

Based on what was presented before, there is still a concern about IT as an instrument in the sustainable development of organizations.

Tachizawa (2001) considers the protection of the environment and improvement of its quality with the help of patterns based on performance and on the sensible use of economic instruments as one of the biggest market challenges of this millennium. This market should cater to its clients who will demand ethical organizations, a good institutional image in the market, responsible environmental performance and sustainable development.

For Jacob (apud Oliveira, 2004), sustainable development is made up of the following dimensions: economic efficiency; social justice; and ecologic prudence. These definitions are supported by means of economic calculations, biophysical aspects and social-political behavior.

So, a management method is necessary that makes good and responsible use of resources, avoiding irreversible impacts. This concern has stimulated the development of Green IT with clean technologies, decreases in waste and sustainable management (Oliveira, 2004).

Mello (2002) points out that one of the organization's concerns is how to improve its image in society. In view of this, information appears as a means of communication between organizations and stakeholders.

According to Albertin & Sanchez (2008), a sustainable governance model assumes a consistent strategy and a detailed work plan that organizes and prioritizes activities according to an organization's strategy.

Considering this aspect, Albertin & Sanchez (2008) list some aspects that give credit to the acceptance of the IT area. They are:

- Technological solutions that assure maximum adherence to business demands with an effective added value;
- Focus on innovation and simplification of business processes;
- Updated and reliable information and data for supporting decision-making;
- Efficient Project management, assuring the identification of needs and an effective control of costs and activities;
- Clear roles and responsibilities for IT organization and for the business areas involved in the main projects and technological solutions;
- Formalized service levels in relation to corporative users, with the previously established indicators;
- Trained, certified and recycled users for an efficient use of IT resources, with suitable support and documentation;

- High standardization and maximization of IT resources, solutions and services;
- Contingencies available for technological and system infrastructure as a business continuity plan for critical processes;
- Development and qualification of IT people in business processes;
- Constant assessment of IT performance and level of user satisfaction.

An adjustment to these aspects could possibly provide better knowledge and control of all processes and procedures in IT management. Besides, the use of efficiency and security performance indicators that aggregate value to IT may serve as parameters for the sustainable growth of organizations.

ENTERPRISE ARCHITECTURE

A concept that aims to meet these demands for sustainable IT is enterprise architecture.

Enterprise architecture seeks to communicate the essential elements that explain the organization's operation, allowing its managers to have a clear idea about which points should be tackled to reach the desired goals. Therefore, it represents the whole organization, expressing and aligning targets, visions, strategies, governance principles, operational processes, organizational structures and automation aspects, like information systems and technological infrastructure.

According to Dragstra (2005), enterprise architecture represents a coherent set of principles, methods and models that are used in the organization's structural project and its execution, in business processes, in information systems and in technical infrastructure.

To Prahalad & Krisshnan (2008) enterprise architecture can be divided into technical and social architecture, both being connected through business processes.

The focus of technical architecture is to structure the database, the system, the application and the analytical functions. In organizations, the most used technical architecture is IT and Communication Architecture, formed by an organized collection of blocks, such as suppliers and partners, clients, investors, property and analytical patterns, IT applications, software engineering, software platforms, public architecture and telecommunication engineering.

To Prahalad & Krisshnan (2008, p.148), social architecture "is the sum of systems, processes, beliefs and value that determine behaviors, perspectives and individual abilities in the organization". The influence of behavior and mentalities on the managerial processes reinforces the creation of rules and patterns that guide the decisions related to opportunities, competitiveness, clients and the organization's performance.

Enterprise architecture's ability of representation allows IT to be continuously refined, without spoiling the alignment with the organization's business, thus promoting permanent knowledge retention that eases the decision-making process.

In August 2009, IBM published a report analyzing some frameworks that support architecture. They are:

- ArchiMate framework;
- Business Architectures Working Group;
- Business Motivation Model;
- Business Process Modeling Notation (BPMN);
- Business Concepts;
- Enterprise Business Architecture;
- Event-Driven Process Chain;
- Enterprise Business Motivation Model;
- TOGAF Business Architecture;
- Component Business Model.

The results of this study revealed that enterprise architecture frameworks are different in target, maturity and the level of practical methodology that aggregate value to the organization's transformation (IBM, 2009).

This research presented the following facts: i) divergence in the main aspects that distinguish an enterprise architecture; ii) the framework focus on enterprise architecture's paradigms, as a centered view in IT, processes and governance (Dragstra, 2005).

The first and second conclusion may have an impact on the transformation of business initiatives based on enterprise architecture. This fact is justified because the knowledge is restricted to some knowledge domains, making the organization search for new complementary models.

The researched frameworks have an expressive penetration in the market and they end by distorting the broad meaning of enterprise architecture. So a structure that leads to the organization's comprehension as a whole is necessary. To this end, a review will be made of Rummler & Brache's classic model (1994). Rummler & Brache (1994) present an organizational integration model through performance levels.

SUSTAINABLE ORGANIZATIONAL PERFORMANCE

Rummler & Brache (1994) organizational integration model contributed to refining knowledge about business process management. Currently, this model helps the development of organizational architectures and of models that seek organizational alignment.

, This model finds support nowadays, given that the classic management theories have not been developed to act in complex and unstable environments. Those classic theories worked (and still work) based on a strong hierarchical and specialized structure called vertical vision.

Rummler & Brache (1994) consider that an organization's vertical vision prevents managers from contemplating the business. Vertical vision limits understanding of the company in regards to its organizational chart, which neither shows the clients, the products nor the services of the organization.

One risk of this vision is when considering that the strategic objectives of an organization do not depend on the organizational dynamic. In other words, it means ignoring the organization as a system where all variable are related. This vision helps in forming an organizational "silo" (high and thick structures without windows). In a "silo" organization, a department, area or division is only concerned about its own internal performance, ignoring the rest of the organization.

In place of the vertical vision, a model of horizontal vision was developed. This vision includes in the decision-making an analysis of the client as well as the product and workflow, which allows checking how the work is actually done. The horizontal vision has process management as its basic element, which permeates through functional borders. These processes show the internal relationships between client-supplier, through which products and services are produced (Rummler & Brache, 1994).

To complete the understanding of the horizontal vision, Rummler & Brache (1994) propose a model based on three performance levels: organization, processes and work/executor.

The organizational level takes into consideration and assesses strategies, governance, structure, organizational architecture and employment of resources, in addition to the instruments that help in comprehending the clients', suppliers' and human resources' view in order to improve the organization's business.

According to Rummler & Brache (1994, p.25), "in the organizational level it is examined the business nature and direction, in addition to the way it is established and managed [...] and the objectives which are part of the business strategy."

Alignment of the organizational level with other levels is done through strategy, as it allows us "to be sure we are keeping our resources in a suitable form, manage our critical business processes and reward the correct performance" (Rummler & Brache, 1994, p.97).

Rummler & Brache (1994, p.22) consider that at the process level "we can see the workflow – how it is done, [...] where the outputs are produced - through countless inter-functional work processes." In order to fulfill their mission, the processes must be managed by a collection of techniques that assure the monitoring and improvement of processes essential to the business.

The main technique used in this plan is the cross-functional model. According to Damelio (1996), the cross-functional model illustrates how the work should be done in organizations, highlighting its inputs and outputs, the sequences (activities flow), people, functions and business rules.

The cross-functional model shows how all functions are involved when an order is processed. This mapping format allows the team: to see all critical interfaces; to meet the deadline; to complete all subprocesses of the map; and to identify the "disconnected wires" (non logical, strange or missing stages).

To Rummler & Brache (1994), the desired performance of each process must be defined from the current measured situation and the errors identified. The identification of these errors must be followed by the implementation of solutions which includes a review of employee competences.

In the work/executor level, "the jobs and people who perform works regardless of the hierarchy" are followed up on, in order to "put capable people in an environment that supports the accomplishment of work objectives" and "includes hiring and promotion, responsibilities and job standard, feedback, rewards and training" (Rummler & Brache, 1994, p.79).

To Rummler & Brache (1994) the organization's efficiency and efficacy is only noticeable when all organizational levels are in the same direction. To this end, a measurement network is necessary that retains the indicators, the strategies and the processes.

Performance Pyramid

BPTrends[2] is an evolution of the Rummler and Brache Performance Level Model. In this version, after adopting IT, the work/executor level started to be called the Implementation Level. The Rummler & Brache (1994) Performance Level Model

Figure 1. Performance pyramid

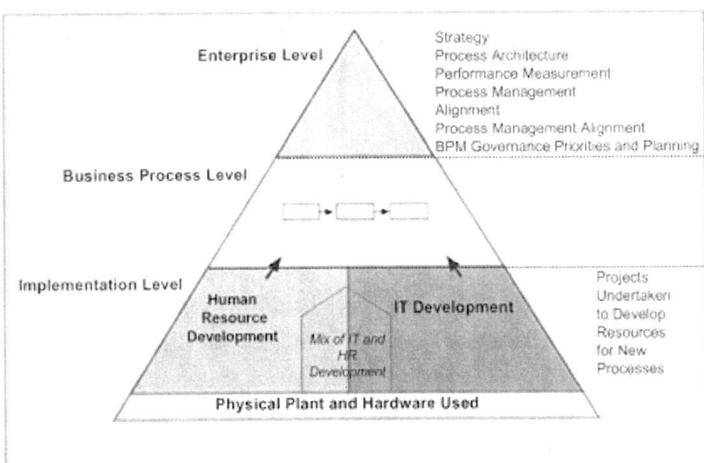

received a pyramid form, thus being called the Performance Pyramid (Figure 1).

As one passes through these performance levels, an accumulation of knowledge in the organization takes place, resulting in the important point of creating and maintaining a knowledge base that allows the positive influence of the learning and growing processes inside an organization.

Management and Governance Sustainable Cycle (MGSC)

After considering the performance levels of an organization, the next step is the development of the enterprise architecture. Therefore, enterprise architecture development must consider two points: the strategic architecture and business architecture. Strategic architecture is responsible for the component's transformation procedures, which includes changing the current situation into a desired situation. Business architecture is responsible for the structure used in offering and consuming daily services.

Strategic and business architectures are composed of social architecture, business process and technical architecture, according to Prahalad & Krisshnan's (2008) approach.

Such architectures are functions of enterprise architecture. So, when enterprise architecture is used to change the current situation into a desired situation, it is defined as strategic architecture. When enterprise architecture is used to describe the component's daily operation, it is defined as business architecture.

After the enterprise architecture is developed, the company must define what will be its governance and management processes. The Management and Governance Sustainable Cycle is proposed at this moment, which supports the management and governance dimension of each IT functionality and works as a link to the business.

The cycle represents the governance and management aspects that involve assessment of business results, strategy clarity and business model improvement through decision-making. This cycle must consider corporative governance needs, business processes and information technologies.

The cycle was developed to highlight that IT management and governance should work together on the strategic architecture and the business architecture.

In order to implement the cycle, the main stages that explain how it works are pointed out (Figure 2). They are:

- **Stage 1:** Strategy;
- **Stage 2:** Guides and Management Best Practices and Environmental Management;
- **Stage 3:** Enterprise Architecture As Is (Control and Monitoring);
- **Stage 4:** Diagnosis;
- **Stage 5:** Enterprise Architecture To Be;
- **Stage 6:** Migration Project;
- **Stage 7:** Project Implantation;
- **Stage 8:** Enterprise Architecture As Is (Execution).

In Stage1, the strategy is formulated on an enterprise level, where the context is analyzed so as to find new opportunities, trends or a suitable solution for a particular situation. In this phase strategic planning and strategy management are created, which involve the assessment of business results, strategy classification and business model improvement through decision-making. This stage corresponds to the MGSC Strategy and Decision-Making.

Stage 2 considers the guidelines and collections of best practices (BSC, COBIT, ITIL, CMMI, ISO 27002, PMBOK, etc.) that may help with the strategy. It is important to state that the guidelines have rules, laws, principles, frameworks, models, methods, and even best practices that support sustainable environmental management. This stage also corresponds to the MGSC Strategy and Decision-Making.

Figure 2. MGSC main stages

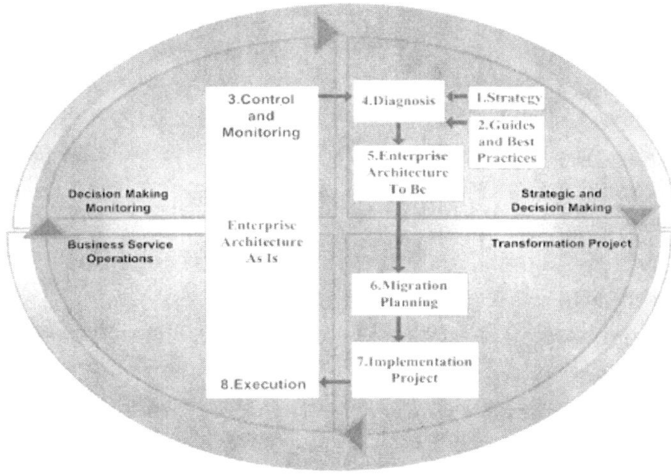

In Stage 3, how the enterprise architecture is working is assessed. The analysis is based on enterprise architecture monitoring of results, which include performance, processes, people and technological indicators. This evaluation must occur on the enterprise, processes and implementation levels. Stage 3 is inside the Decision-Making Monitoring and MGSC Business Service Operation.

In Stage 4, based on best practices strategies, guides and collections and on the Enterprise Architecture As Is assessed, a diagnosis is proposed to define the gaps in the enterprise architecture. This analysis observes how organizational alignment is affected. This stage corresponds to the MGSC, Strategy and Decision-Making.

In Stage 5, the gap report of Stage 4 will work as input for improving proposals that will define the Enterprise Architecture To Be. This stage corresponds to MGSC Strategy and Decision-Making, once the action plan target has been defined. All performance levels are involved in the future architecture elaboration activity.

In Stage 6, the new enterprise architecture construction project is created. Here will be defined the project team and aspects of the management changes. In the MGSC, this stage is the Transformation Project. This activity involves all performance levels; however depending on the kind of transformation one performance level may be more requested.

In Stage 7, the project is implemented. The creation of a prototype is suggested before product implementation in the organization (Sordi, 2003; Presman, 2006; INSADI, 2005).

In Stage 8, the new enterprise architecture starts operating, corresponding to MGSC Business Services and Operation. The enterprise architecture is monitored and controlled constantly. Thus, as the organization's environment is dynamic and evolves all the time, a new Governance and Management Sustainable Cycle begins.

FUTURE RESEARCH DIRECTIONS

IT Best practices do not aggregate performance indicators and control objectives that take environmental issues into consideration, which is an opportunity for improvement and adjustments.

Most researched frameworks are not very familiar with Corporate Environmental Management Information Systems. It may be stated that there are opportunities that lead to one or more frameworks of specialization, in such a way that construction of IT environments that unite environmental issues becomes easy.

The present chapter proposes improvements through a descriptive inquiry about the best practices of IT governance based on public and private organizations. The goal is to analyze and observe organizational performance.

Within the results, the chapter constructs a relationship between IT governance and enterprise architecture, with sights on establishing Green enterprise architecture that aligns initiatives of Green IT with sustainable IT governance.

CONCLUSION

This chapter concludes that, through the analysis of several authors' reports, IT governance acts in a positive way inside the organizational performance structure. It has been reinforced by the fact that the use of formal mechanisms of IT governance reflect on the financial results of the organization. These improvements may be strongly pronounced by a reduction in costs and better use of companies' assets. Another aspect highlighted in the chapter was the presence of a "lag" effect in the impact of the IT governance mechanisms on the performance of the organizations. This issue involving IT's maturity time has been identified as an important factor in the relationship between IT and organizational performance.

Also, the existence of a strong relationship between management performance and IT's efficient use (as the use of IT assets, its cost-benefit relationships, company's financial growth and the flexibility of business) has been noticed. There is a direct link between the organization's performance and its organizational architecture. The better the organizational performance is in different IT governance focus areas, the more efficient will be the use of IT in the organization. This contributes to constructing an optimized organizational architecture performance.

Particularly, this chapter proposes a Management and Governance Sustainable Cycle in order to be applied together with some of the enterprise architecture frameworks. This point of view contributes to promoting the rational and sustainable management of information systems.

REFERENCES

Albertin, A. L., & Sanchez, O. P. (2008). *Outsourcing de TI: impactos, dilemas, discussões e casos reais*. Rio de Janeiro, Rio de Janeiro: FGV.

Attadia, L. C. L., & Martins, R. A. (2003). Medição de desempenho como base para evolução da melhoria contínua. *Revista Produção, 13*(2).

Bacon, C. (1992). The use of decision criteria in selecting information systems/technology investments. *Management Information Systems Quarterly, 16*(3), 335–353. doi:10.2307/249532

Becker, J., Lunardi, G., & Maçada, A. (2003). Análise de eficiência dos bancos brasileiros: um enfoque nos investimentos realizados em tecnologia de informação (TI). *Revista Produção, 13*(2), 70–81.

Bharadwaj, A. (2000). A resource-based perspective on information technology capability and firm performance: an empirical investigation. *Management Information Systems Quarterly, 24*(1), 169–196. doi:10.2307/3250983

Bharadwaj, A., Bharadwaj, S., & Konsynski, B. (1999). Information technology effects on firm performance as measures by Tobin's q. *Management Science, 45*(6), 1008–1024. doi:10.1287/mnsc.45.7.1008

Brancheau, J. C., & Wetherbe, J. C. (1994). Key issues in information Systems. *MIS Quaterly Executive, 10*(2), 225–242.

Brodbeck, A. F., & Hoppen, N. (2000, September). *Modelo de alinhamento estratégico para implementação dos planos de negócio e de tecnologia de informação.* Paper presented at the Xxiv Encontro Nacional da ANPAD. São Paulo.

Brown, A., & Grant, G. (2005). Framing the frameworks: a review of IT governance research. *Communications of the Association for Information Systems, 15*, 696–712.

Brynjolfsson, E. (1993). The productivity paradox of information technology: review and assessment. *Communications of the ACM, 36*(12), 66–77. doi:10.1145/163298.163309

Carr, N. (2003). IT doesn't matter. *Harvard Business Review, 81*(5), 41–49.

Chan, S. (2004). Sarbanes-Oxley: the IT dimension. The Internal Auditor, *61*(1).

Chin, P., Brown, G., & Hu, Q. (2004). The impact of mergers & acquisitions on IT governance structures: a case study. *Journal of Global Information Management, 12*(4), 50–74.

Damelio, R. (1996). *The basics of process mapping.* New York, New York: Productivity Press.

De Haes, S., & Van Grembergen, W. (2005). IT governance structures, processes and relational mechanisms: achieving IT/business alignment in a major Belgian financial group, *Hawaii International Conference on System Sciences.* Proceedings of the 38th Hawaii International Conference on System Sciences (pp.237b). Hawaii.

De Haes, S., & Van Grembergen, W. (2006). Information technology governance best practices in Belgian organizations, *Hawaii International Conference on System Sciences.* Proceedings of the 39th Hawaii International Conference on System Sciences (pp.195b). Hawaii.

de Mello, R. F. L. (1999). *Em busca da sustentabilidade da organização antropossocial através da reciclagem e do conceito de auto-eco-organização.* Curitiba, Paraná: UFPR.

Dedrick, J., Gurbaxani, V., & Kraemer, K. (2003). Information technology and economic performance: a critical review of the empirical evidence. *ACM Computing Surveys, 35*(1), 1–28. doi:10.1145/641865.641866

Dehning, B., & Dow, K. E., & Stratopoulos. (2004). T. Information technology and organizational slack. *International Journal of Accounting Information Systems, 5*(1), 51–63. doi:10.1016/j.accinf.2004.02.003

Dehning, B., & Richardson, V. (2002). Returns on investments in information technology: a research synthesis. *Journal of Information Systems, 16*(1). doi:10.2308/jis.2002.16.1.7

Dehning, B., Richardson, V., & Zmud, R. (2003). The value relevance of announcements of transformational information technology investments. *Management Information Systems Quarterly, 27*(4).

Dehning, B., Richardson, V., & Zmud, R. (2007). The financial performance effects of ITbased supply chain management systems in manufacturing firms. *Journal of Operations Management, 25*(4), 806–824. doi:10.1016/j.jom.2006.09.001

Devaraj, S., & Kohli, R. (2003). Performance impacts of information technology: Is actual usage the missing link? *Management Science, 49*(3), 273–289. doi:10.1287/mnsc.49.3.273.12736

Dragstra, P. (2005). *Enterprise architecture: the select process of an Enterprise Architecture Toolset to support understanding and the governing enterprise.* Unpublished master dissertation, Technische Universiteit Eindhoven, Netherlands.

Fama, E., & Jensen, M. (1983). Separation of ownership and control. *The Journal of Law & Economics*, *26*, 301–327. doi:10.1086/467037

Farrell, I. J. (2003). *Alignin IT to corporate objectives: organizational factores*. Unpublished doctoral dissertation, Macquarie University, Sydney.

Fitzgerald, G. (1998). Evaluating information systems projects: a multidimensional approach. *Journal of Information Technology*, *13*(1), 15–27. doi:10.1080/026839698344936

Grembergen, W. V. (2004). *Strategies for information technology governance*. Hershey, PA: Idea Group Publishing.

Gunasekaran, A., & Ngai, E., & McGaughey. (2006). Information technology and systems justification: A review for research and applications. *European Journal of Operational Research*, *173*(3), 957–983. doi:10.1016/j.ejor.2005.06.002

Hardy, G. (2006). Using IT governance and COBIT to deliver value with IT and respond to legal, regulatory and compliance challenges. *Information Security Technical Report*, 55–61. doi:10.1016/j.istr.2005.12.004

Haworth, D., & Pietron, L. (2006). Sarbanes-Oxley: achieving compliance by starting with ISO17799. *Information Systems Management*, *23*(1), 73–87. doi:10.1201/1078.10580530/45769.23.1.20061201/91775.9

Heier, H. Borgman, Hans P., & Mileos, C. (2009). Examining the Relationship between IT Governance Software, Processes, and Business Value: A Quantitative Research Approach, Hawaii International Conference on System Sciences. In *Proceedings of the 42nd Hawaii International Conference on System Sciences* (pp. 1-11). Hawaii.

Hitt, L., & Brynjolfsson, E. (1996). Productivity, business profitability, and consumer surplus: three different measures of information technology value. *Management Information Systems Quarterly*, *20*(2), 121–142. doi:10.2307/249475

Hu, Q., & Plant, R. (2001). An empirical study of the casual relationship between IT investment and firm performance. *Information Resources Management Journal*, *14*(3), 15–26.

IBGC. (2009). *Linha do Tempo*. Retrieved November 09, 2009, from http://www.ibgc.org.br/LinhaTempo.aspx.

IBM. (2009). *A Comparative Review of Business Architecture*. IBM Research Report. Retrieved November 01, 2009, from http://domino.research.ibm.com/library/cyberdig.nsf/papers/E3E920683AB1AEF6852576250052CD22/$File/rj10451.pdf

INSADI. (2005). *Apostila do Curso de Formação de Gestores de Processos*. São Paulo, São Paulo: Insadi.

IT Governance Institute. (2005). *Cobit 4.0: control objectives, management guidelines, maturity models*. Rolling Meadows, Illinois: IT Governance Institute.

Itaudit. (2007). Reaching Compliance through Foundational IT Controls. *Institure of Internal Auditors, 10*.

ITGI. (2003). Board briefing on IT governance. *IT Governance Institute*. Retrieved October 20, 2009, from www.itgi.org.

Jensen, M. C., & Meckling, W. H. (1976). Theory of the firm: managerial behavior, agency costs and ownership structure. *Journal of Financial Economics*, *3*(4). doi:10.1016/0304-405X(76)90026-X

Kaarst-Brown, M., & Kelly, S. (2005). IT governance and Sarbanes-Oxley: the latest pitch or real challenges for the IT function? *Hawaii International Conference on System Sciences. Proceedings of the 38th Hawaii International Conference on System Sciences* (pp.236a). Hawaii.

Kaplan, R. S., & Norton, D. P. (1997). *A Estratégia em Ação: balanced scorecard*. Rio de Janeiro, Rio de Janeiro: Campus.

Keyes-Pearce, S. (2002). Rethinking IT governance in the eWorld. *Pacific Asia Conference. Proceedings of the 6th Pacific Asia Conference* (pp. 062). Tóquio.

Korac-Kakabadse, N., & Kakabadse, A. (2001). IS/IT governance: need for an integrated model. *Corporate Governance, 1*(4), 9–11. doi:10.1108/EUM0000000005974

Kudyba, S., & Vitaliano, D. (2003). Information technology and corporate profitability: a focus on operating efficiency. *Information Resources Management Journal, 16*(1), 1–13.

Li, M., & Ye, L. (1999). Information technology and firm performance: linking with environment, strategic and managerial contexts. *Information & Management, 35*(1), 43–51. doi:10.1016/S0378-7206(98)00075-5

Luftman, J., & McLean, E. (2004). Key issues for IT executives. *MIS Quarterly Executive, 3*(2), 89–104.

Lunardi, G. L., Dolci, P. C., Becker, J. L., & Maçada, A. C. G. (2008, October). *Governança de TI no Brasil: uma análise dos mecanismos mais difundidos entre as empresas nacionais*. Paper presented at the SEGeT – Simpósio de Excelência em Gestão e Tecnologia, Rio de Janeiro.

Maçada, A., Becker, J., & Lunardi, G. (2005). Efetividade de Conversão dos Investimentos em TI na Eficiência dos Bancos Brasileiros. *Revista Contemporânea de Administração, 9*(1), 9–33.

Marchand, D. (2005). *Reaping the business value of IT*. Business & Economic Review.

Matlin, G. (1979). What is the value of investment in information systems? *Management Information Systems Quarterly, 3*(3), 5–34. doi:10.2307/248786

McLane, G. (2003). *IT governance and its impact on IT management (a literature review)*. Unpublished master dissertation, University of Technology Sydney, Sydney.

Melville, N., Kraemer, K., & Gurbaxani, V. (2004). Review: information technology and organizational performance: an integrative model of IT business value. *Management Information Systems Quarterly, 28*(2), 283–322.

Molinaro, L. F. R., et al. (2009, October). *Governance and Management of Information Technology: Decomposing the Enterprise in Modular Building Blocks Based on Enterprise Architecture and Business Oriented Services*. Paper presented at the CENTERIS-Conference Enterprise Information System.

Neely, A., & Adams, C. (2000). Perspectives on performance: the performance prism. *Centre for Business Performance*. Retrieved January 10, 2006, from http://www.exinfm.com/pdffiles/prismarticle.pdf

Oliveira Filho, J. (2004). Gestão Ambiental e Sustentabilidade: um novo paradigma eco-econômico para as organizações modernas. *Domus On Line*: Ver. Teor. Pol., soc. *Cidad. Salvador, 1*(1), 92–113.

Pelanda, M. L. (2006). *Modelos de governança de tecnologia da informação adotados no Brasil: um estudo de casos múltiplos* Unpublished master dissertation, Universidade Metodista de São Paulo, São Bernardo do Campo.

Peterson, R. (2004a). Integration strategies and tactics for information technology governance. In Van Grembergen, W. (Ed.), *Strategies for information technology governance* (pp. 37–80). Hershey: Idea Group Publishing.

Peterson, R. (2004b). Crafting information technology governance. *Information Systems Management, 21*(4), 7–22. doi:10.1201/1078/44705.21.4.20040901/84183.2

Phahalad, C. K., & Krishnan, M. S. (2008). *The new age of innovation: driving co-created value through global networks*. New York: McGraw Hill.

Porter, M., & Millar, V. (1985). How information gives you competitive advantage. *Harvard Business Review, 63*(4), 149–160.

Pressman. (2006). *Software Engineering: a practitioner's approach*. New York: McGraw Hill.

Rau, K. (2004). Effective governance of IT: design objectives, roles and relationships. *Information Systems Management, 21*(4), 35–42. doi:10.1201/1078/44705.21.4.20040901/84185.4

Reich, B. H., & Benbasat, I. (2000). Factors that influence the social dimension of alignment between business and information tecnology objectives. *MIS Quarterly Executive, 24*(1), 81–113.

Rezende, D. A. (2002). *Tecnologia da informação integrada à inteligência empresarial: alinhamento estratégico e análise da prática nas organizações*. São Paulo, São Paulo: Atlas.

Ridley, G., Young, J., & Carroll. (2004). P. COBIT and its utilization: a framework from the literature. *Hawaii International Conference on System Sciences. Proceedings of the 37th Hawaii International Conference on System Sciences* (pp. 80233). Hawaii.

Rummler, G., & Brache, A. P. (1994). *Melhores desempenhos das empresas*. São Paulo, São Paulo: Makron Books.

Salem, H. (2003). Organizational Performance Management and Measurement: The Lebanese Experience, Beirut. *Economic and Social Council*. Retrieved October 04, 2009, from http://unpan1.un.org/intradoc/groups/public/documents/un-escwa/unpan010860.pdf

Sambamurthy, V., & Zmud, R. (1999). Arrangements for information technology governance: a theory of multiple contingencies. *Management Information Systems Quarterly, 23*(2), 261–290. doi:10.2307/249754

Sambamurthy, V., & Zmud, R. (2000). Research Commentary: the organizing logic for na enterprise's IT activities in the Digital Era – a prognosis of practice and a call for research. *Information Systems Research, 11*(2), 105–114. doi:10.1287/isre.11.2.105.11780

Schwarz, A., & Hirschheim, R. (2003). An extended platform logic perspective of IT governance: managing perceptions and activities of IT. *The Journal of Strategic Information Systems, 12*(2), 129–166. doi:10.1016/S0963-8687(03)00021-0

Smith, H., & McKeen, J. (1993). How does Information Technology affect Business value? A reassessment and research propositions. *Canadian Journal of Administrative Sciences, 10*(3), 229–240.

Sordi, J. O. (2003). *Tecnologia da informação aplicada aos negócios*. São Paulo, São Paulo: Atlas.

Strassman, P. (1997). *The squandered computer: evaluating the business alignment of information technology*. New Canaan, Connecticut: The Information Economics Press.

Stratopoulos, P., & Dehning, B. (2000). Does successful investment in information technology solve the productivity paradox? *Information & Management, 38*(2), 103–117. doi:10.1016/S0378-7206(00)00058-6

Sujitparapitaya, S., Janz, B., & Gillenson, M. (2003). The contribution of IT governance solutions to the implementation of data warehouse practice. *Journal of Database Management*, *14*(2), 52–69.

Synnot, W. R. (1987). Information Weapons. *Information Strategy*, *4*(1), 12.

Tachizawa, T., Andrade, R. O. B., & Carvalho, A. B. (2002). *Gestão ambiental: enfoque estratégico aplicado ao desenvolvimento sustentável*. São Paulo: Pearson Education do Brasil.

Teixeira Júnior, F., & Ponte, V. M. R. (2003). Alinhamento estratégico: estudo comparativo das percepções dos executivos de negócios e TI. *Revista Eletrônica de Administração*, *7*(5).

Teo, T. S. H., & King, W. R. (1997). Integration between business planning and information systems planning: An evolutionary-contingency perspective. *Journal of Management Information Systems*, *14*(1), 185–214.

Tiernan, C., & Peppard. (2004). J. Information technology: of value or a vulture? *European Management Journal*, *22*(6), 609–623. doi:10.1016/j.emj.2004.09.025

Turban, E., Mclean, E., & Wetherbe, J. (2004). *Tecnologia da informação para gestão*. Porto Alegre, Rio Grande do Sul: Bookman.

Verhoef, C. (2007). Quantifying the effects of IT-governance rules. *Science of Computer Programming*, *67*(2-3), 247–277. doi:10.1016/j.scico.2007.01.010

Vitale. (2001, October). *The dot.com legacy: governing IT on internet time*. Paper presented at the Information Systems Research Call, Baurer College of Business, Houston.

Weil, P., & Ross, J. W. (2004). *It Governance: How Top Performers Manage It Decision Rights For Superior Results*. Boston, Massachusetts: Harvard Business School Press.

Weill, P. (2004). Don't just lead govern: how top-performing firms govern IT. *MIS Quarterly Executive*, *3*(1), 1–17.

Weill, P., & Olson, M. (1989). Managing investment in information technology: mini case examples and implications. *Management Information Systems Quarterly*, *13*(1), 3–17. doi:10.2307/248694

Weill, P., & Woodham, R. (2002). Don't just lead, govern: implementing effective IT governance. *Center for Information Systems Research*. Working paper n. 326. Retrieved August 10, 2009, from http://biblioteca.universia.net/ficha.do?id=21878

Willcocks, L., Feeny, D., & Olson, N. (2006). Implementing core IS capabilities: Feeny- Willcocks IT governance and management framework revisited. *European Management Journal*, *24*(1), 28–37. doi:10.1016/j.emj.2005.12.005

Zee, J.T.M, & Van Der; Jong, B. D. (1999). Alignment is nor enough: integrating business and information technology management with the balanced business scorecard. *Journal of Management Information Systems*, *16*(2), 137–156.

ENDNOTES

1. ITPI and SEI both have studied the characteristics of organizations with high performance seeking to investigate, identify and define the performance indicators, control objectives and common processes.
2. BPTrends is a renowned organization that works as an information source about best practices in Business Process Management (BPM) (www.bptrends.com).

Chapter 9
Investigation of Environmental Monitoring Designs for Corporate Management Information Systems

Marina G. Erechtchoukova
York University, Canada

Stephen Y. Chen
York University, Canada

Peter A. Khaiter
York University, Canada

ABSTRACT

The evaluation of an organization's environmental performance is an integral part of a corporate environmental management information system. This chapter considers an organization's environmental impact assessment with respect to a water resource. It investigates formal approaches to the development of temporal monitoring designs for producing data sufficient to perform the assessment. In this study, simple random sampling, stratified random sampling, and designs obtained using greedy search have been investigated with respect to their compatibility with a corporate environmental management information system. All three approaches determine temporal monitoring designs with minimal costs and supply data sufficient for estimation of water quality indicators for a given level of uncertainty. It is shown that monitoring designs obtained using the greedy search approach will outperform other designs when the level of uncertainty in the estimate must be low. If high levels of uncertainty are tolerable, simple random designs become preferable due to their simplicity and effectiveness. The proposed approaches lead to automated procedures which can be easily integrated into a corporate environmental management information system.

DOI: 10.4018/978-1-61520-981-1.ch009

INTRODUCTION

There is an increasing awareness that the health and socio-economic well-being of our society are inherently tied to the quality of the environment. Systematic methods to address the adverse environmental impact of business activities on the environment are needed. One such approach has been formulated as a set of protocols underlying environmental management systems. The environmental management systems verify and reduce the impact of an organization's activities on the environment. These systems also help organizations to formulate environmental goals and to evaluate how well they have been achieved through sustainable management. An organization's environmental performance evaluation can be done by measuring 'the interactions between the business activity and the environment' (Bennett & James, 1999). According to ISO 14031 standard, the evaluation of an organization's environmental performance has to be done by using two general categories of indicators which describe the management and operation performance and the environmental condition indicators that reveal the organization's impact on the environment.

The challenge with sustainable management of an environmental resource is to assess the current status, predict future states of the resource under an organization's impact, and determine direct and indirect consequences of the impact on natural systems. The assessment of an environmental resource state and the quantification of an organization's impact on the resource are performed using observations and measurements of environmental parameters that provide information about changes in environmental conditions. Following a systems approach to monitoring and evaluation, the assessment must take into account all major aspects of the resource. Monitoring and assessment are interrelated steps since the first supplies the data for the second, and the assessment step dictates what needs to be measured and/or observed, how it should be implemented, where it needs to be measured and/or observed, and when (i.e., how often) observations and measurements have to be performed.

This chapter considers environmental impact assessment with respect to a water resource, and it investigates formal approaches for temporal monitoring design subject to producing sufficient data for the assessment of an organization's impact on an aquatic environment.

BACKGROUND

An organization's environmental performance evaluation is a multi-step process. There are several frameworks for an environmental management system. European Union's Eco-Management and Audit Scheme (EC, 2001) and EPA's Performance Track and the Code of Environmental Management Principles (US EPA, 1997) are among them. One of the most popular frameworks for an environmental management system was described in ISO 14001 standard (ISO, 2004). This framework requires the development of an environmental policy and the assessment of its fulfillment through four steps: (1) planning, (2) implementation and operation, (3) checking and corrective actions, and (4) management reviews. Monitoring and measurements are critical steps of the process since they supply decision makers with data and information on all steps of the performance evaluation (Stapleton et al., 2001).

Environmental Performance Evaluation

The ISO 14001 standard provides generic recommendations to organizations on how to incorporate environmental management into their operations and governance, but it leaves the details of a particular implementation outside of the document. The details of various implementations have been investigated for case studies (e.g., Lopez-Fernandes & Serrano-Bedia, 2007; Christini et al., 2007). The conclusions drawn from these case studies consistently recommend modifications to the existing information systems or the introduction of new systems to include information technology support for environmental management into enterprise-wide management information systems (Oktem et al., 2007).

In response to business needs, software tools incorporating environmental considerations into decision making and risk management activities that are compliant with ISO 14000 standards have been developed, e.g., Intelex Environmental Management Systems or Environmental Management Information Systems created by US EPA. Features of these systems facilitate automated data and information processing of real-time and routine monitoring data, acceleration of information flows, knowledge sharing through real-time reporting, and/or support of simulation models.

There are several critical aspects in the implementation of environmental management information systems. The complexity of data collection, data compatibility, and difficulties in integrating environmental, financial, and economic data with qualitative characteristics are among them (Cagno et al., 2007). Effective evaluation of an organization's environmental performance must be based on a set of indicators reflecting operational activities including consumption of an environmental resource and the resulting waste. The latter is required for evaluation of the organization's impact on the environment. For this purpose, environmental performance indicators must be complemented by the environmental condition indicators in order to assess current and future impacts and to identify improvements or deterioration. The environmental condition indicators reflect a cumulative effect on the environment resulting from all of an organization's activities (Azzone et al., 1996). These indicators can be used for regulatory purposes demonstrating that the organization conforms with existing regulations or to determine cause-and-effect relationships between operational indicators and the environmental impact.

In order to assess an organization's environmental performance – to identify problems, their causes, and the required mitigating actions; the systematic collection of data on selected indicators is necessary. These data are usually supplied by a monitoring system which operates under a specified program. Monitoring and measurements require clear understanding and development of the procedures for sampling key characteristics of an environmental resource and organizational activities which generate significant environmental impact on this resource, for tracking performance, and for data collection and processing. Traditionally, values of environmental indicators are compared against existing standards to demonstrate whether or not the organization meets the requirements. Since monitoring is always subject to logistics and budgetary constraints, it is important to select indicators which help to quantify and track significant impacts of the organization on the environmental resources.

Measuring Organization's Impact on Aquatic Environment

Verfaillie & Bidwell (2000) recommend measuring an organization's environmental performance via the concept of eco-efficiency. This measurement framework is based on an estimation of the influence imposed on the environment during product creation. The five indicators of influence are specified as: (1) energy consumption; (2) material consumption; (3) water consumption; (4) greenhouse gas emissions; and (5) ozone depleting substance emission. With respect to an aquatic environment, the interaction of a business activity and the habitat results not only in the water uptakes, but also in using the natural water body as places to deposit wastewaters. Thus, the list of indicators must be extended to include indicators reflecting quality and quantity of pollution discharges into aquatic systems. The ISO 14031 standard also suggests to consider contaminant concentrations in surface waters for environmental performance evaluation.

Water quality in a water body is described by a set of physical, chemical, and biological properties reflected in the values of concentrations of water chemical constituents and other parameters. These parameters characterize the resulting state of an aquatic environment under anthropogenic impact. Commonly used objectives for water quality are formulated in terms of maximum allowable concentrations of water constituents, and an assessment consists of a comparison of the observed concentrations of pollutants in a water column with these objectives.

The US EPA Clean Water Act introduced another approach to tracking an organization's impact on an aquatic environment – Total Maximum Daily Load (TMDL) process. This process determines the amount of a pollutant that can be tolerated by an investigated water body without violating water quality standards. The evaluation of TMDL takes into account pollution loads from point sources including industrial and municipal water treatment facilities and non-point sources such as runoffs from urban, forested and/or agricultural areas. Chemical loads represent the total amount of water constituents that pass through a cross section over a certain period of time. They are usually calculated using the values for water discharges and the corresponding values of concentrations of an investigated parameter in the discharged water. Evaluation of both indicators requires systematic measurements at a given site where wastewaters are released into a water body.

A list of water constituents which must be monitored depends on the composition of wastewaters. Although automated samplers which can generate detailed series of water quality parameters are preferable, not all parameters can be measured in this way. For such water constituents, their concentrations are derived from water samples collected manually with subsequent analytical processing in a laboratory. When observations and measurements are implemented manually, a monitoring design prescribing frequency of sample collection in time and space is required.

Monitoring Designs

Data for environmental performance evaluation must be collected from one or more observation sites. In order to generate compatible data sets, samples are collected periodically at the same sites according to temporal monitoring designs. In many cases, monitoring designs are developed using expert knowledge, intuition, and subjective judgment. Since monitoring systems operate in a changing environment and are subject to budgetary constraints, the evaluation of the design efficiency and possible improvements in data collection are urgent. These issues of water quality monitoring and design have received due attention in modern literature. Optimization of a monitoring system is a complex multidisciplinary problem. There are several frameworks for monitoring system development. Thus, Groot & Schilperoort (1983) proposed a framework for optimization of water quality monitoring networks based on cost-effectiveness analysis. Another water quality monitoring framework (WQTG, 2006) describes important activities for comprehensive assessment of water resources.

The effect of sampling frequencies on water quality assessment was investigated by Naddeo et al. (2007). Palmer & MacKenzie (1985) suggested an iterative procedure which maximizes the power of the monitoring network for a given budget or minimizes the cost of the network for a specified statistical power requirement. The interdisciplinary nature of a monitoring system dictates the necessity to consider different and sometimes contradicting aspects of the system during its optimization. Thus, the problem of monitoring optimization can be solved as a multi-objective mixed integer programming model with constraints (Ning & Chang, 2002), or as a constrained optimization problem using generic algorithms (Icaga, 2005; Cieniawski et al., 1995).

OPTIMIZATION OF MONITORING DESIGNS

Formal optimization techniques require quantification of the effectiveness of a monitoring design in order to weigh it versus the design cost. Since monitoring activities are always subject to financial and logistics limitations, constrained optimization techniques are deemed more suitable for this purpose. It is important to introduce criteria demonstrating to what extent one monitoring design outperforms another. Following (Bodo & Unny, 1983; Erechtchoukova & Tsirkunov, 1987; Erechtchoukova & Khaiter, 2008), the optimization problem has been formulated to determine a monitoring design with minimal cost that keeps the effectiveness of generated data at or above a specified threshold.

Problem Articulation in Terms of Mathematical Programming

Cost estimates are preferable from a managerial perspective since they allow for straightforward comparisons to the available budget and among various monitoring designs. The cost of a monitoring design includes such items as the cost of a water sample collection, conservation, delivery to the laboratory, analytical processing, etc. Although exact values of the costs are not available, the assumption that the cost of a monitoring design increases monotonically with the number of samples collected at each monitoring site and the number of sites seems valid. Focusing on the optimization of a temporal monitoring design at a given site, the current study uses the number of samples collected at a given site to measure the cost of a monitoring design.

To obtain a formal definition for the effectiveness of a monitoring design, a measure of the monitoring outcomes and their usefulness must be introduced. Since the main outcomes of a monitoring system are data sets and information derived from these data sets, the measure should reflect the compliance of data with the chosen monitoring objectives. The resultant measure describes the quality of data supplied by a certain monitoring design. The uncertainty in the information supplied by a monitoring system is one of the key design challenges. According to Quality Assurance Plan (US EPA, 2003), it is important to understand and quantify the uncertainty and to incorporate its estimates into environmental assessment. This issue has been investigated from different perspectives. Harmel et al. (2006) considered uncertainty of data obtained from monitoring systems. It is worth mentioning that data become valuable only after they are transformed into information by applying mathematical models and/or statistical formulae. The estimation of the resulting uncertainty of the information derived from the monitoring data is more important. Therefore, model uncertainty must be considered along with the uncertainty of values of water quality parameters (Erechtchoukova & Khaiter, 2008). Traditionally, monitoring data are analyzed statistically, which implies that the fewer the number of samples used for an estimate, the greater the uncertainty in the final result.

The uncertainty of estimates derived from data supplied by a monitoring design is used to measure design effectiveness. Under the assumption that the cost of a sampling program is a monotonically increasing function with the number of observations, an efficient monitoring design can be found as a solution of an optimization problem to minimize the cost of a monitoring design such that the design effectiveness is still at or above the acceptable threshold. This optimization problem can be rephrased as the problem of minimizing the total number of observations such that the resulting uncertainty still meets a desired level:

$$n \rightarrow \min \text{ subject to } D(I) \leq V, \qquad (1.1)$$

where n is the number of required observations, I is the selected estimator for the water quality indicator, $D(I)$ is the estimator uncertainty, and V is the acceptable level of uncertainty. The expression of D depends on an estimator I selected for a particular case study and a measure chosen to describe possible deviations of estimated values from the actual ones.

Uncertainty Measures

Estimates obtained from monitoring data contain uncertainty which can come from several sources such as data uncertainty and model uncertainty. Data uncertainty comprises observational artifact and uncertainty due to discretization. Observational artifact is caused by measurement tools and analytical methods used in the laboratories in order to obtain values of environmental indicators. Although some improvements in the results are possible, this type of error is always present in monitoring data. Monitoring data reproduce a discrete approximation of continuous fields of water quality parameters. The fields are described by aggregate values of characteristics over a certain neighbourhood of observation points in space and time. The larger the data set used, the smaller the uncertainty of data due to discretization. Model uncertainty is added at the stage of data processing. Traditionally, monitoring data are analyzed based on statistical estimators whose uncertainty is measured as a ratio of its variance. The latter depends on mathematical properties of the formula or model used and a data set available for the estimation (Erechtchoukova & Khaiter, 2008).

If an investigated water quality parameter is evaluated using simple statistics, the uncertainty can be described as the variance of the estimator. The acceptable level of uncertainty can be expressed as an allowable deviation d of the parameter value x calculated on available data from its actual value X. Under the assumption that x is normally distributed, the deviation d can also be expressed in terms of the variance of the estimator of X:

$$d = U_{1-\alpha}\sigma_X, \tag{1.2}$$

where σ_X^2 is the variance of x, α is the level of confidence, and $U_{1-\alpha}$ is the normal deviate corresponding to an allowable probability 1-α such that the error won't exceed the desired margin. The formula for the variance of the estimator depends on the statistical properties of x.

Monitoring data can be used to obtain estimates of indicators with different, sometimes even contradicting, properties. This makes it preferable to have a monitoring design that provides the best possible fit for a curve of concentrations of a pollutant. Values of observed concentrations can be used to reconstruct the dynamics of concentrations for a selected water constituent based on interpolation:

$$D(I) = \frac{|I_c - I_a|}{I_a}, \tag{1.3}$$

where I_c is the indicator estimate calculated using interpolation, I_a is the actual value of the selected indicator. Observation points are selected with the objective of keeping the sum of absolute deviations of the interpolated curve from the actual one below a certain level of uncertainty. This level of uncertainty can be determined as a fraction of an estimate of the selected indicator.

Developing Monitoring Designs

An efficient temporal monitoring design can be determined as a solution of the problem (1.1) with the uncertainty in the form of (1.2) or (1.3). In the former case, the total number of required observations is calculated from an analytical expression, under an assumption that the samples are randomly distributed over an investigated period. As a result, a simple random sampling design is derived.

Hydrological and hydrochemical regimes of many water bodies are characterized by distinct seasonal variations. Statistically, these variations are better described by stratified estimators. The replacement of a selected estimator by a stratified one results in stratified random designs which prescribe a certain number of randomly distributed observations for each stratum and these numbers vary between strata. For stratified estimates, the goal function of the optimization problem must be rewritten as:

$$n = \sum_{j=1}^{h} n_j, \tag{1.4}$$

where n_j is the number of observations per j-th stratum, and h is the number of strata.

Substitution of formula (1.3) into problem (1.1) gives another operations research model which has been solved using a greedy search technique (Erechtchoukova et al., 2009). Under the assumption that daily observations provide the most complete series of pollutant concentrations, the monitoring design is described as a vector of 365 binary coordinates in which 'ones' denote days when observations are conducted and 'zeros' represent the days when no sample is collected. In a greedy approach using the scheme 'one decision at a time without backtracking', a solution is obtained by eliminating the least informative observation date from a complete series of 365 daily observations of a selected water quality indicator. The algorithm stops when the closest approximation to the given level of uncertainty is obtained.

The resulting solution prescribes a set of particular calendar dates for observations which provide sufficiently good interpolation of a selected indicator over a given period of time. These dates are determined *a posteriori*. The selected dates depend on overall variability of the concentrations which is affected by the organization's wastewater releases and hydrological regime of the water body receiving the discharged waters. These factors can vary from year to year, so the developed monitoring design is suitable only for periods that have the same operational and environmental dynamics. To improve the robustness of the algorithm, the formula (1.3) has been modified by adding a "sliding window" with the size representing the largest deviation in the observation dates when the collected samples will still be able to provide measurements of the water quality indicators that meet the desired accuracy levels:

$$D(I) = \max_{sw}\left(\frac{\left|I_c - I_a\right|}{I_a}\right), \tag{1.5}$$

where sw is the size of the sliding window (i.e., the number of days) around a proposed date when a sample can be collected.

Testing Monitoring Designs

Investigation of different approaches to monitoring design has been conducted for two water quality indicators: the average concentration of a water constituent over an investigated period of time in a selected cross section of a water body and the total chemical load of the same water constituent over the same period of time. Since many organizations evaluate their performance on an annual basis, a period of one year was chosen for estimation of values of selected water quality indicators. Testing monitoring designs derived from different approaches requires very detailed data. While the average concentration can be calculated using values of observed concentrations only, water discharges must also be taken into account to calculate the total load of a water constituent. Usually, values of water discharges can be obtained with at least daily frequency and concentrations of water constituents are measured rarely. It was assumed that a series of daily values of a water quality parameter is sufficient to accurately estimate both selected water quality indicators.

It is worth noting that such detailed data are very difficult to obtain. Monitoring designs were developed for the cross section Vyatskiye Polyany, the Vyatka River, due to the availability of long series of concentrations of chloride ions at this site. The Vyatka River is a large Eastern-European river located in the Russian Federation. Its length is about 1,370 km and the watershed area is 129,000 km^2. The average water discharge is as high as 700 m^3/s. Observation data were selected for four years with different hydrological characteristics. Year 1 and Year 2 exhibited a unimodal type of hydrograph with large water discharges only in the late spring-early summer period. Year 3 and Year 4 had two periods of high flow events in spring-summer and in the late fall. Observed concentrations of chloride ions varied from 0.04 to more than 9.0 mg/L. Missing values of concentrations were restored by linear interpolation between two adjacent observations. The annual average concentration of chloride ions has been estimated between 3.83 and 4.83 mg/L with the annual load of this water constituent changing from 42,338 to 63,907 t.

Simple random sampling designs for the concentrations and the total load of chloride ions were developed by substituting the expressions for variance of the mean value and total value in formula (1.2). The numbers of observations required to achieve different levels of uncertainty of the estimates were calculated with the confidence interval of 95% (see Table 1).

The hydrological regime at the studied cross section is characterized by distinct seasonal variations with high flow events in spring and fall and lower water seasons in summer and winter. The series of concentrations and instantaneous loads of chloride ions also exhibit seasonal dynamics. At the same time, values of water discharges, concentrations, and instantaneous loads have different variability. The parameter with the largest variation was the water discharge with coefficients from 1.19 to 1.47 compared to the concentrations with coefficients from 0.34 to 0.51 and instantaneous loads of chloride ion with coefficients of variation from 0.40 to 0.85. Although water flow notably affects the dynamics of the constituent, this is not the only process contributing to the constituent levels in a water column. High data variability with distinct seasonal oscillations supports the use of stratified estimates.

In stratified estimates, an investigated population is divided into a finite number of strata which

Table 1. Simple random monitoring designs for estimation of the average concentration (C) and the total annual load (L) of chloride ions for specified levels of uncertainty

Period	Indicator	Uncertainty level, %			
		5	10	15	20
Year 1	*C*	120	40	19	11
	L	274	157	92	58
Year 2	*C*	183	73	37	22
	L	171	66	33	19
Year 3	*C*	192	79	40	24
	L	210	93	48	29
Year 4	*C*	169	65	32	19
	L	147	52	25	15

are determined with respect to a certain factor. The final estimate is obtained as a weighted total or average value. Temporal stratification can significantly reduce the total number of observations required for the estimates of the selected indicators with a given level of uncertainty if the variance of the selected estimator within strata is less than the variance among strata (Cochran, 1963). Although not all temporal stratifications result in more efficient estimates of the indicators, the current study's strata were defined rather subjectively leading to satisfying, but not optimal, stratification. The series of the water quality parameter can be split into subpopulations according to three different factors: values of daily concentrations, daily water discharges, and instantaneous loads.

For estimating the average annual concentration of chloride ions, stratified monitoring designs were developed for the given four strata which were constructed manually based on the series of concentrations of this water quality parameter (see Table 2). These four strata overlap with the main hydrological seasons observed at the investigated cross section. The temporal stratification for the total annual load estimates also contains four strata derived from the series of instantaneous loads.

As it is shown in Tables 1 and 2, temporal stratification may significantly reduce the total number of required observations in order to achieve an established level of uncertainty of the estimates. At the same time, application of stratified estimates results in monitoring designs with frequencies

Table 2. Stratified random monitoring designs for estimation of the average concentrations of the chloride ions (stratification is implemented based on the series of concentrations)

Period			Strata				Total number of observations
			I	II	III	IV	
Year 1	Duration, days		233	23	64	45	
	Uncer-tainty, %	5	23	4	30	22	79
		10	6	1	12	9	28
		15	3	1	6	4	14
		20	2	0	3	3	8
Year 2	Duration, days		129	113	70	53	
	Uncer-tainty, %	5	12	6	30	50	98
		10	3	2	11	42	58
		15	2	1	5	34	42
		20	1	0	3	26	30
Year 3	Duration, days		126	52	110	77	
	Uncer-tainty, %	5	21	19	34	51	108
		10	6	7	11	25	49
		15	3	3	5	14	25
		20	2	2	3	8	15
Year 4	Duration, days		72	165	69	59	
	Uncer-tainty, %	5	15	6	27	42	90
		10	4	1	10	22	37
		15	2	1	5	13	21
		20	1	0	3	8	12

of observations changing from one stratum to another. Consequently, it results in monitoring recommendations which are hard to follow. In all investigated years, stratification schemes differ significantly with year specific strata boundaries. Since the designs can be obtained for the given strata only, it is important to know strata boundaries *a priori* in order to provide correct sampling recommendations, whereas dates of typical hydrological and hydochemical events vary from year to year making the stratification scheme very inaccurate and corresponding recommendations hard to follow due to a human factor. A particular scheme is predetermined by the actual values of the selected water quality parameter which, in its turn, is affected by underlying processes, such as hydrological processes and an organization's activities. Thus, a stratification scheme unavoidably depends on a selected water constituent leading to different frequencies for water constituents where concentrations are determined from the same water sample. All these issues make stratified designs less preferable compared to simple random designs.

It is worth noting that the disparity in costs of stratified designs versus non-stratified ones is tangible only for the high levels of accuracy in the estimates. The difference in total numbers of observations in both types of the designs becomes negligible when the tolerable threshold of the uncertainty of the estimates goes up (see Figures 1 and 2). This effect is common for both selected indicators, but the absolute number of required observations and the level of uncertainty when simple random designs produce almost the same results vary among the years and indicators.

Another set of monitoring designs for estimation of the same water quality indicators has been developed by substitution of the uncertainty measure (1.5) into problem (1.1). The solutions were obtained using the greedy search approach previously described. The summary of the designs for the average concentration estimation is presented in Table 3. Similar to the simple random designs and stratified random designs, the total number of observations is affected by such factors as the variability of the selected water quality indicator, hydrological features of the investigated period, and the uncertainty level in the estimate. In addition to these factors which are common for all developed monitoring designs, a new factor – the size of the sliding window – has been introduced.

Figure 1. The difference between simple random designs and stratified random designs vs. the uncertainty of the estimates of the total chemical load of chloride ions in year 2

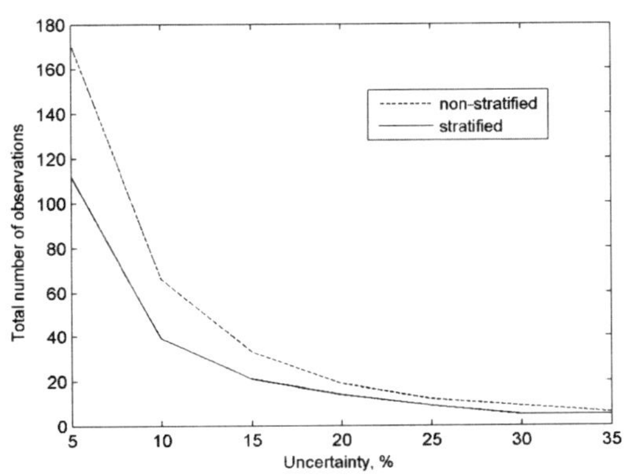

Figure 2. The difference between simple random designs and stratified random designs vs. the uncertainty of the estimates of the average concentration in year 2

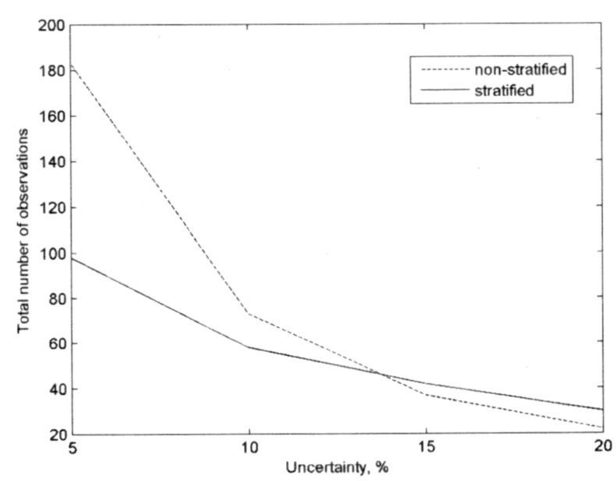

Table 3. Number of samples in monitoring designs developed by the greedy search algorithm for estimation of the average concentration of chloride ions vs. the size of the sliding window

Period	Uncertainty, %	Size of the sliding window, days							
		0	7	15	31	61	91	121	181
Year 1	5	14	17	20	22	22	24	23	24
	10	9	11	11	13	15	15	16	16
	15	6	8	7	8	10	11	11	11
	20	5	6	6	6	8	8	9	9
Year 2	5	13	18	22	25	26	29	29	30
	10	10	12	14	15	16	18	19	19
	15	7	8	11	11	13	14	13	15
	20	6	7	11	9	11	10	11	12
Year 3	5	14	9	20	22	22	23	23	24
	10	6	8	11	13	13	13	14	14
	15	4	4	6	6	7	8	9	9
	20	3	3	4	4	5	7	7	7
Year 4	5	10	12	14	16	17	17	18	19
	10	6	7	9	10	11	11	12	12
	15	5	5	6	8	8	8	9	9
	20	5	5	6	6	7	7	7	7

The total numbers of observations in the designs for the same indicator and with the same level of uncertainty vary up to two and a half times depending on the size of the sliding window.

The size of the sliding window is an important parameter which affects not only the total number of observations in a particular monitoring design, but also their distribution over an investigated period. A larger window size leads to a more robust sampling recommendation with respect to when observation dates can be. Thus, setting the value of the sliding window to zero means that the year to come is expected to have the exact same hydrological events occurring on the exact same calendar dates. Such an assumption is hardly valid, but even in the best case scenario, the drawback is obvious—missing the exact calendar dates for sample collection will result in the uncertainty of the estimates being higher than has been established. At the same time, using very large values of the sliding window (e.g., 91 days or more) leads to unnecessary oversampling. An interesting result is that with larger numbers of samples, they become more evenly distributed over the investigated period. Increasing the size of the sliding window shifts the goal of observation from measuring extreme values of the investigated water quality parameters to registering the main changes in the dynamics of the investigated water constituents. As the sliding window increases, single samples at local minima and maxima are replaced with multiple samples throughout the hydrological event (see Figure 3).

Identification of the sliding window parameter is an important task. Formal approaches to this task require further elaboration. However, the following aspect can be taken into account for formulating a heuristic rule. Every design has time intervals of variable length between days when samples have to be collected. The maximal interval shrinks with the increasing size of the sliding window since the total number of observations increases. When

Figure 3. Monitoring designs for estimation of the total annual load of chloride ions with 10% uncertainty developed for year 3 vs. the size of the sliding window

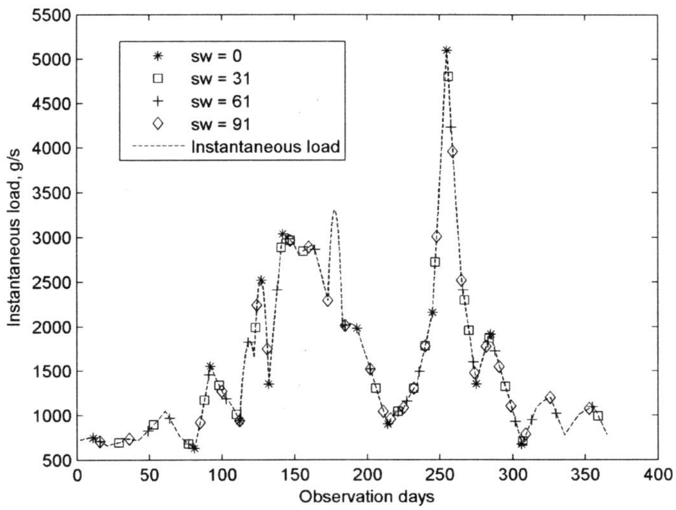

the size of the window becomes larger than the maximal interval between two consecutive observations, the overlap may result in oversampling. Thus, the size of the window which matches the maximal interval between two subsequent observations seems reasonable (see Table 4). For the investigated case study, the sliding window of 31 days (i.e., one month approximately) has been chosen as the most appropriate.

The designs developed using the greedy search approach require fewer observations, especially when the level of uncertainty of the estimates is low. For the high level of uncertainty, the recommended total number of observations from these designs remains small. However, due to the dramatic decrease in the total number of observations in simple random designs, the costs of both designs become comparable and the simple random designs can be preferable since they are easier to develop and to use.

The designs developed using the greedy search approach and recommended specific dates of observations imply sampling recommendations which are easier to follow compared to stratified random designs. Instead of exact dates for adjusting the frequency of observation, these designs provide the time interval (e.g., 31 days) within which required samples can be collected. The

Table 4. Comparison of monitoring designs for estimation of the total annual load of chloride ions with 5% uncertainty in year 3 with respect to the size of the sliding window

Characteristics	**Size of the sliding window**							
	0	11	21	31	41	61	91	181
Total number	22	34	38	41	43	45	47	51
Average Interval	15	10	9	9	9	8	7	7
Minimal Interval	5	3	3	3	4	3	4	3
Maximal Interval	31	22	20	25	23	18	20	16

sliding window adequately addresses the issue of varying dates for hydrological and hydrochemical events from year to year.

At the same time, the designs are constructed under the assumption that the main features of the dynamics of the investigated water quality parameters remain steady – an assumption which is not always valid. Thus, these designs are again site, indicator, and water constituent specific.

Implications for Corporate Environmental Management Information Systems

The overview of environmental management information systems (EMISs) presented in (Teuteberg & Straßenburg, 2009) demonstrates that EMISs can be very diverse. They are classified into information systems for external reporting, eco-controlling systems for internal operation research, life cycle assessment systems, key performance indicator based systems, early warning systems, etc. Although standard components of EMISs have yet to be determined, the majority of researchers agree that monitoring and audit must be included in such systems. The ISO 14031 standard, a well known source used by companies for evaluation of their environmental performance, suggests that indicators of environmental condition have to be taken into account for this purpose. Seamless integration of a monitoring component into EMISs can provide an organization's management with timely information on attainment of environmental goals, adequacy and effectiveness of undertaken measures, potentials for accidents, and emergency situations.

Integration of a monitoring system for environmental performance evaluation with an organization's information system calls for automated procedures to support data collection and processing. Approaches to the development of water quality monitoring designs investigated in this chapter require historic data on water quality parameters which are used for estimation of the selected indicators. For simple random sampling, an analytical solution of the problem (1.1) with the uncertainty measure in the form of (1.2) can be obtained with relative ease. This solution can be directly coded and embedded into a corresponding module of an organization's information system. For stratified random sampling, a solution of the problem (1.1) with the goal function in the form of (1.4) can be obtained using various techniques of mathematical programming (e.g., Lagrange multipliers method), assuming that an appropriate temporal stratification of an investigated period is provided. As it was discussed above, all temporal stratifications do not lead to an efficient estimate, and stratification of water quality data is affected by many factors. For these reasons, expert involvement is necessary in the process of monitoring design using stratified random sampling, so integration and automation become more challenging.

A greedy search approach to environmental monitoring design provides an algorithm suitable for automated procedure, but the size of the sliding window has to be set *a priori*. Although there is no formal approach to the selection of the size of the sliding window, the computational efficiency of the greedy search algorithm allows for multiple runs at various parameter settings to be used to identify an appropriate value. The overall, approach can thus lead to an automated procedure which can still be easily integrated into an organization's information system.

The investigated approaches have been developed for the assessment of an organization's impact on water resources. An obvious benefit of these approaches is that all models are evaluated using basic statistics on observed and linearly interpolated data. The *sw* parameter is site independent and does not require site specific parameterization. It makes the approaches suitable for water bodies of various size and watershed area. Although their application to measuring an organization's impacts on other components of natural environment (e.g., air or soil) is not straightforward and most likely will require some modification, the general framework will be the same since it generates efficient monitoring designs which supply not only data sufficient for reliable assessment, but also uncertainty estimates which are important for decision making.

FUTURE RESEARCH DIRECTIONS

Concentrations of several water constituents with different variability are usually determined from the same sample. Therefore, an efficient monitoring design should balance the designs for each water quality parameter. It can be done by allowing different levels of uncertainty in the estimates of water quality parameters with values derived from the same water sample (Erechtchoukova & Khaiter, 2007). Alternatively, the methods of multi-objective optimization can be employed. In this respect, the uncertainty measure expressed in formula (1.5) can be easily extended to cover a few water quality parameters. The statistical characteristics of this measure of uncertainty and designs constructed using a modified version of the objective in formula (1.5) are a subject for further investigation.

Stratified random sampling and greedy search approaches to the development of monitoring designs for evaluation of an organization's environmental performance use expert knowledge to various extents. Modifications and enhancements leading to automated procedures for monitoring design are important and will be considered in the near future. The greedy search approach still requires further improvement with respect to selection of an appropriate sliding window depending on the quality of waste and natural waters, the hydrological regime of a water body, and an organization's operations.

CONCLUSION

Measuring and evaluating an organization's impact on the aquatic environment is an important component of corporate environmental management information systems. The choice of eco-efficient production processes or their re-engineering depends on the overall organization's environmental impact which can be evaluated only based on a monitoring system generating data for the evaluation. In the current study, three approaches – simple random sampling, stratified random sampling, and designs with specified dates of observations obtained using greedy search algorithm – have been investigated with respect to their compatibility with a corporate environmental management information system. All three approaches determine temporal monitoring designs with minimal costs that supply data sufficient for estimation of water quality indicators with the given level of uncertainty.

Analysis of the monitoring designs showed that all designs are site and constituent specific. They are significantly affected by the processes contributing to the level of an investigated water constituent in the water column. Simple random sampling is the simplest approach in terms of their development and their implementation. This approach can also be integrated into an environmental management information system with relative ease. The obvious drawback of this approach is that the generated designs will require a high total number of observations when the level of uncertainty in the estimates must be low. Stratified random sampling leads to designs which in many cases outperform simple random sampling designs. However, this approach is not fully automated. It requires temporal stratification of data over an investigated period which is a rather subjective process. Moreover, such designs can involve sampling recommendations which are hard to follow. Integration of this approach with an environmental management system is possible, but a user's required involvement in the design development is higher. The designs with specified dates of observation developed using the greedy search algorithm are the most efficient with respect to the total number of observations. Sampling recommendations associated with these designs are flexible enough to collect the required data under various organizational and environmental conditions. A fully automated procedure for their development can be easily integrated with an information system.

Finally, the difference in the created designs based on these approaches is only notable for low levels of uncertainty in the estimates. When high levels of uncertainty (e.g., 20% and more) are tolerable, the difference in total numbers of observations become negligible. In such cases, simple random designs become preferable due to their simplicity and effectiveness.

REFERENCES

Azzone, G., Noci, G., Manzini, R., Welford, R., & Young, C. W. (1996). Defining environmental performance indicators: an integrated framework. *Business Strategy and the Environment*, *5*(2), 69–80. doi:10.1002/(SICI)1099-0836(199606)5:2<69::AID-BSE48>3.0.CO;2-W

Bennete, M., & James, P. (1999). ISO 14031 and the future of environmental performance evaluation. In Bennett, M., & James, P. (Eds.), *Sustainable measures: evaluation and reporting of environmental and social performance* (pp. 76–97). Sheffield, UK: Greenleaf Publisher.

Bodo, B., & Unny, T. E. (1983). Sampling strategies for mass-discharge estimation. *Journal of Environmental Engineering*, *109*(4), 812–829. doi:10.1061/(ASCE)0733-9372(1983)109:4(812)

Cagno, E., Tardini, L., & Trucco, P. (2007). EPIDesign: integrating corporate strategies into the development process of an environmental performance evaluation system. In Sroufe, R., & Sarkis, J. (Eds.), *Strategic sustainability. The state of the art in corporate environmental management systems* (pp. 20–42). Sheffield, UK: Greenleaf Publisher.

Christini, G., Harzam, M. W., Mattews, D. H., & Hendrickson, C. (2007). A comparison of environmental system components and practices. In Sroufe, R., & Sarkis, J. (Eds.), *Strategic sustainability. The state of the art in corporate environmental management systems* (pp. 43–55). Sheffield, UK: Greenleaf Publisher.

Cieniawski, S., Ehart, J., & Ranjithan, S. (1995). Using genetic algorithms to solve a multi-objective groundwater monitoring problem. *Water Resources Research*, *31*(2), 399–409. doi:10.1029/94WR02039

Cochran, W. G. (1963). *Sampling Techniques* (2nd ed.). New York: John Wiley.

Erechtchoukova, M. G., Chen, S. Y., & Khaiter, P. A. (2009). Application of optimization algorithms for the improvement of water quality monitoring systems. In I. N. Athanasiadis, P. A. Mitkas, A. E. Rizzoli, & J. Marx Gómez (Eds.), *Information Technologies in Environmental Engineering. Proceedings of the 4th International ICSC Symposium, Thessaloniki, Greece, May 28-29, 2009* (pp. 176-188). Berlin, Heidelberg: Springer.

Erechtchoukova, M. G., & Khaiter, P. A. (2007). Uncertainty reduction in modelling of chemical load in streams. In L. Oxley & D. Kulasiri (Eds.), *MODSIM2007 International Congress on Modelling and Simulation. Modelling and Simulation Society of Australia and New Zealand, December 2007* (pp. 2445- 2451).

Erechtchoukova, M. G., & Khaiter, P. A. (2008). Role of models for building an efficient monitoring design. In M. Sànchez-Marrè, J. Béjar, J. Comas, A. Rizzoli, & G. Guariso (Eds.), *iEMSs2008: International Congress on Environmental Modelling and Software. Integrating Sciences and Information Technology for Environmental Assessment and Decision Making, July 2008* (pp. 528-535).

Erechtchoukova, M. G., & Tsirkunov, V. V. (1989). Determination of sampling strategy for calculation of mass-discharge in streams with a given accuracy. In *Proc. of the Conf. Problems of Surface Hydrology, February, 1987* (pp. 171-189). Leningrad: Gidrometeoizdat.

European Commission (2001). *Regulation (EC) No 761/2001 of the European parliament and of the council of 19 March 2001 allowing voluntary participation by organizations in a Community eco-management and audit scheme (EMAS)*. L. 114, v. 44, 42 April 2001.

Groot, S., & Schilperoort, T. (1983). Optimization of water quality monitoring networks. *Water Science and Technology*, *16*, 275–287.

Harmel, R. D., Cooper, R. J., Slade, R. M., Haney, R., & Arnold, J. G. (2006). Cumulative uncertainty in measured streamflow and water quality data for small watersheds. *Transactions of the ASABE*, *49*(3), 689–701.

Icaga, Y. (2005). Genetic algorithm usage in water quality monitoring networks optimization in Gediz (Turkey) river basin. *Environmental Monitoring and Assessment*, *108*, 261–277. doi:10.1007/s10661-005-4328-z

International Organization for Standardization. (2004). *Environmental management systems – requirements with guidance for use (ISO 14001:2004)*. Jersey City, NJ: International Organization for Standardization.

Lopez-Fernandez, M. C., & Serrano-Bedia, A. M. (2007). Organizational consequences of implementing an ISO 14001 environmental management system. An empirical analysis. *Organization & Environment*, *20*(4), 440–459. doi:10.1177/1086026607309388

Naddeo, V., Zarra, T., & Belgiorno, V. (2007). Optimization of sampling frequency for river water quality assessment according to Italian implementation of the EU Water Framework Directive. *Environmental Science & Policy*, *10*, 243–249. doi:10.1016/j.envsci.2006.12.003

Ning, S. K., & Chang, N. B. (2002). Multi-objective, decision-based assessment of a water quality monitoring network in a river system. *Journal of Environmental Monitoring*, *4*, 121–126. doi:10.1039/b107041j

Oktem, U., Lewis, P., Donovan, D., Hagan, J. R., & Pace, T. (2007). EMS and sustainable development: a model and comparative studies of integration. In Sroufe, R., & Sarkis, J. (Eds.), *Strategic sustainability. The state of the art in corporate environmental management systems* (pp. 56–75). Sheffield, UK: Greenleaf Publisher.

Palmer, R. N., & MacKenzie, M. C. (1985). Optimization of water quality monitoring networks. *Journal of Water Resources Planning and Management*, *111*(4), 478–493. doi:10.1061/(ASCE)0733-9496(1985)111:4(478)

Stapleton, P. J., Glove, M. A., & Davis, S. P. (2001). *Environmental Management Systems: An Implementation Guide for Small and Medium-Sized Organizations*. NSF International.

Teuteberg, F., & Straßenburg, J. (2009). State of the art and future research in environmental management information systems – a systematic literature review. In I. N. Athanasiadis, P. A. Mitkas, A. E. Rizzoli, & J. Marx Gómez (Eds.), *Information Technologies in Environmental Engineering. Proceedings of the 4th International ICSC Symposium Thessaloniki, Greece, May 28-29, 2009* (pp. 64-77) Berlin, Heidelberg: Springer.

US Environmental Protection Agency (1997). *Implementation guide for the Code of Environmental Principles for Federal Agencies.* EPA-315-B-97-001.

US Environmental Protection Agency. (2003). *Elements of a state water monitoring and assessment program (EPA 841-B-03-003).* Retrieved June 19, 2009, from http://www.epa.gov/owow/monitoring/elements/index.html

Verfallie, H. A., & Bidwell, R. (2000). *Measuring eco-efficiency. A guide to reporting company performance.* Report produced for the World Business Council for Sustainable Development. Retrieved June 19, 2009, from: http://www.gdrc.org/sustbiz/wbcsd.html

Water Quality Task Group. (2006). *A Canada-wide framework for water quality monitoring.* PN 1369. Retrieved June 19, 2009, from: http://www.ccme.ca/assets/pdf/wqm_framework_1.0_e_web.pdf

Chapter 10
Corporate Environmental Management Information Systems Influence of Green IT on IT Management and IT Controlling

Andreas Gadatsch
Bonn-Rhine-Sieg University of Applied Sciences, Germany

ABSTRACT

Green IT (Green IS, Green ICT) is a concept of saving energy consumption to reduce IT costs. A current survey shows that only few companies in German speaking countries consider this aspect in their daily business. This is important facing the current situation of attempts of cost saving during the current economic crisis worldwide. This paper introduces into Green IT and presents an IT management and controlling concept. Then the main results of a currently presented survey are used to modify the concept. Finally an agenda for future research is given.

INTRODUCTION

It has been discussed that ecological thinking has positive effects on the economic performance (Telle, 2006). Sustainable risen energy prices have indicated thinking and rethinking in companies. Like the "bio wave" in the food market some years ago now we are faced by a "Green IT wave" among IT suppliers and their customers. The public opinion has been focused to the enormous amount of used energy for running IT servers of public known companies. Google for example runs 450.000 servers which needs more than 800 million kWh per year (Chou, 2008). This simple example underlines the importance of a need for action.

We can understand Green IT as the idea of saving energy when using IT resources. That includes investments in hardware, services and changing the business and IT strategy. However different industry studies show that there is no common understanding of green IT although it is an emerging trend (Chou, 2008). In a lot of cases the IT management does not know the energy cost

DOI: 10.4018/978-1-61520-981-1.ch010

of running their central IT systems (server in data centre and more) and decentralised workplace systems (desktop systems, laptops and other). A current survey among German speaking countries shows that one third of the companies don't know their energy costs of running their IT (Gadatsch & Juszczak, 2009). Furthermore the energy cost does not have a high impact on decisions about IT investments. At the same time analysts like the Gartner Group predict a strong increasing market for IT services around the buzz word "green IT" (Eriksdotter, 2009). In the past the efforts to save energy costs of central data centres were in the foreground. Now the efforts are expanding to the decentralized IT resources like workplace systems (desktop, laptops and more). The investigations of the Experton Group show that more than 60% of the IT driven energy costs were reasoned out of the central data centres in offices and other parts of the companies (n. a., 2008). This paper tries to figure out the impact of green IT on IT controlling in the future.

The IT controlling department is focused on effectiveness and efficiency in using ICT. The motivation of this paper is to address Green IT as a future challenge for IT controller. They should take a more active part in managing "Green IT" to save energy for environment and costs for companies.

GREEN IT

Technologies and Concepts

Green IT is not a new concept. Since the beginning of the nineties the "energy star" certification is known (EPA, 2009). It attests that IT hardware is compliant to energy saving criteria. Risen energy costs lead to a rethinking in using energy for IT. Like the "biologic wave" in the food industry years ago we currently feel a "green wave" in the IT industry. Enterprises which control innovative technologies and concepts for restructuring their business processes can improve their competitiveness by reducing their energy costs (Ryan, 2008).

Green IT definitions cover different point of views. The discussion is going on. Murugesan (2009) defines Green IT as "the study and practice of designing, manufacturing, using, and disposing of computers, servers, and associated subsystems ... efficiently and effectively with minimal or no impact on the environment". A short definition is that Green IT is using IT resources in an efficient way (Curley & Donnellan, 2008). Green IT can be defined as the usage of energy saving technologies (hardware, software, cooling), organisational concepts (job instructions) and technical rules (construction of buildings).

A common view is the changing focus of Green IT. The meaning is shifting from a pure technical view in information systems (Green in IT) to a business oriented view (Green with IT). In the future more strategic views are estimated (Green IT Strategy) by the consulting company Ernst & Young (cf. Figure 1).

Two technological sectors are relevant: energy saving hardware and software as well as technologies for cooling and buildings. Normally a companywide change of hardware is necessary to get enough effects. This is joined with new concepts of data centre organisation like server virtualisation. New concepts to create buildings and reuse of heating energy need changes in buildings or new buildings for data centres. In the hardware area often the concept of server virtualisation is used. That means several logical servers are served by one physical machine. At the end user side thin clients (desktop simulation on server) reduces the energy consumption. The potential of energy saving is enormous. A typical data centre reaches a utilization of only 20-30% (Bohrer et al., 2002). In the software area the delivery of energy saving software functions has a great importance. This includes automatic shut down, stand by, cooling technology, load balancing. The building services engineering support concepts for heat recovery, heat insulation and

Figure 1. From cost reduction to enabling business value (Ernst & Young, 2009, modified)

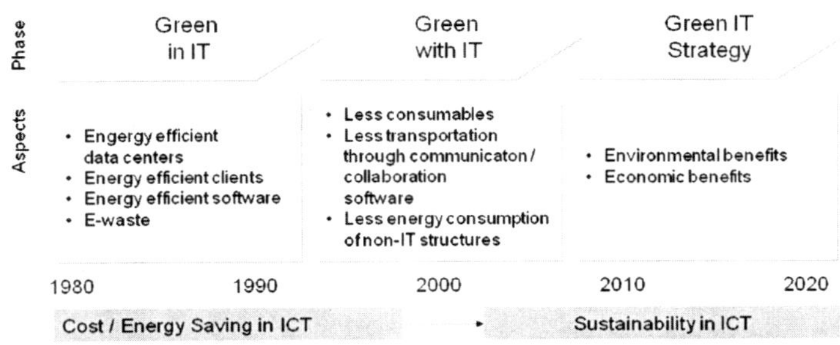

other technologies. At the moment single technical concepts are dominating. There is a lack in integrated approaches which start at the business and IT strategy and include staff information, business process design and more. There is a demand for independent certifications.

Research and Development

At the moment Green IT is mainly pushed by the hardware and software industry and IT vendors. The IT consumption companies are in the transition phase. The academic environment has produces only a few important works. It can be assumed that the activities in Green IT will increase in the future according to the high relevance. A high demand in research can be identified in the context of maturity models. Independent German technical consultants (e. g. the "Technischer Überwachungsverein Rheinland TÜV") offer first concepts to certify data centres.

Alternatives

Cloud computing uses IT resources on demand via internet from different vendors. Often cloud computing is suggested as an alternative to Green IT. It supports a solution to companies that need IT resources quickly or with a highly dynamic level of demand (Rings et al., 2009).

The demanding company needs no own IT infrastructure. It procures the IT services from different suppliers. A precondition is only access to the internet. This concept does not give any influence to the energy consumption because that's the supplier's responsibility.

IT MANAGEMENT AND CONTROLLING

IT Process Model

IT controlling is an expression which is mostly used in German speaking countries. IT controlling describes an interdisciplinary task between the area of conflict of the business information systems and the general company controlling. Narrow interpretations emphasise the function of information, measurement and evaluation (Schauer, 2006). Broader proposals provide the IT controlling with decision making power to ensure that the company can reach their targets (Gadatsch, 2009). Examples are decisions about the planned IT project portfolio or the amount or structure of the IT budget.

In Figure 2 a grossly IT process model depicts selected tasks of information management and the coverage of IT controlling. Strategic IT controlling is oriented without time horizon at companies' targets. It is used to increase the efficiency of the company. IT is known as a competitive relevance contribution to support the company targets. The transition to the operational IT controlling concept is floating. It increases the efficiency of the defined activities inside of a fixed time horizon. The success is measured by the profitability of the activities and other criteria.

During the first step an IT strategy is developed which takes care for the transformation and supervision of the activities to reach the targets of the company. The content of the IT strategy are principle decisions for procurement of standard application software or developing individual software, type and extension of outsourcing or the structure of cost and performance accounting. The development of an IT master plan is very important. This master plan specifies used and planned information systems. To avoid problems of integration and to decrease IT costs standards for hardware, software and security have to be defined. The IT portfolio planning identifies concrete projects and set priorities by criteria which were derived from the IT strategy.

The process step IT development supports the development and maintenance of individual software as well as the introduction and implementation of standard application software for typical company applications like enterprise resource planning or office software.

After the software implementation the IT operations follows. The tasks there are planning and building up of the IT infrastructure. The IT infrastructure (also called IT landscape) covers all information systems, hardware and other facilities of a company (e. g. Hess, 2006). Furthermore the information systems have to be operated and a IT compliant strategy and IT service (answering to enquiries, incident management and others) have to be ensured.

IT Controlling Tools

The IT controlling management uses strategic and operative tools to reach the challenges. Central tools are listed in Table 1.

By using of the strategic tools the IT controller supports the head of IT management by defining, transfer and monitoring of the IT strategy of the company. The IT strategy supports IT standards (operating systems, office software and other) which are mandatory for the user. The supervising of started arrangements is supported by the balanced scorecard method which is used more and more. The participation at the IT portfolio board for strategic IT projects is necessary to reach the IT controlling goals. The IT portfolio board prepares and decides about the prioritisation of IT projects.

The operative IT controlling tool box includes the classic cost and performance accounting modified for the needs of the IT. IT projects needs high external support by vendors and consultants. An established IT controlling service networks a

Figure 2. IT process model

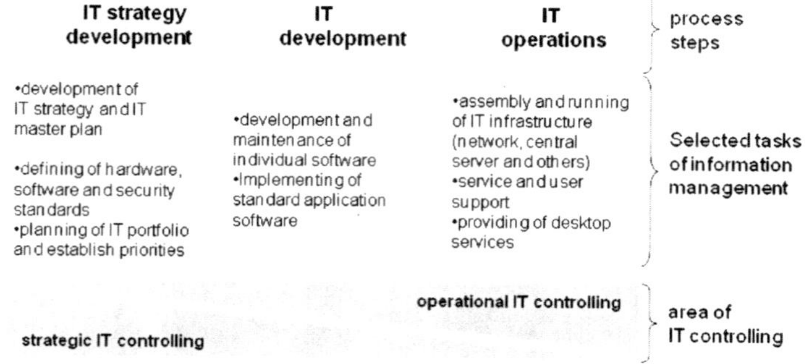

Table 1. Strategic and operative IT controlling tools

Level	Tool	Task
Strategic	IT strategy	Support of formulate and review of the effectiveness and transfer of the IT strategy
	Strategic benchmark	Analysis and repositioning of the IT-Strategy with integrated strategic benchmarking tools
	Balanced Scorecard	IT strategy monitoring, creating of IT performance indicators, analysis and monitoring of reaching targets
	Standardization	Support of the IT management by definition and enforcing of IT standards
	IT portfolio management	Measuring, selection and controlling of new development or maintenance projects
Operative	IT cost and performance accounting	Cost type, cost centre and cost unit accounting, break-even-analysis, IT invest planning, efficiency analysis, project calculations, analysis of depreciations
	Business partner management	Contract management, IT consultant management and benchmarking, management of service level agreements
	IT accounting and performance indicators	IT accounting, IT performance indicators, IT project status reports
	IT project controlling	Support of IT project team members as a project controller, planning techniques (critical path method), formal procedures for project acceptance, requirements specifications, reviews and audits, project benchmarking
	IT process management	IT process modelling, Process cost accounting, process benchmarking, IT supply process, IT asset management, IT outsourcing, IT offshoring, ITIL, CoBiT, IT-CMF

comprehensive contract and consulting management to benchmark the included business partner. Service level agreements ensure a high level of performance of business partners. This allows the IT controller to intervene at contract injuries by time. The concept includes a contract management to ensure the targets concerning content, time, organisation and finance which are connected with the IT contracts. On the technical side the contract controlling is added by special contract management tools to manage the high amount of IT contracts. A lot of IT contracts are not supervised after the conclusion of a contract. This is followed by not seeing of cancellation periods or fees for not used equipment. The IT reporting based on the data of accounting and special report. This delivers the IT controller indicators and project status report about planned, running and finished IT projects.

The active participation of the IT controller in IT project teams allows affecting IT projects in an early stage. The authorisation of IT projects will be standardized by formal procedures for project acceptance. This avoids to start risky and inefficient projects. Regularly hold reviews control running projects to correct weaknesses and erroneous trends early. The project benchmarking inside of companies guarantees a competition between several IT projects. Comparisons of planned and current data are easier to be done.

In a lot of companies business processes have to be modelled to get a documentation and basis for running process improvements. Core processes of the company like sales, production and more are preferred. Also IT processes like the development of individual software, the implementation of standard application software are to be included. The process cost accounting gives decision relevant data to analyse in detail the costs of processes at administration departments.

The cost for the IT supply process like supply, installation, run and disposal of IT workplaces have to be included in the process management. The IT asset management takes care for the inventory and administration of the IT resources in companies. The IT controller has access to the assets and analyses data to optimize quantities of IT resources. IT outsourcing is used for several years to simplify the IT processes and mainly to reduce the IT costs. The dislocation of IT services into low cost countries (IT offshore) is increasing (Mertens et al., 2005). These activities need a long term oriented analysis of efficiency and risks by an independent IT controller.

IMPACTS OF GREEN IT

Green IT in German Speaking Countries

The discussion about Green IT shows very different statements. It reaches from "old topic" to "current trend" (n. a., 2009). Some international oriented Green IT studies have been published during the last years. Examples are the surveys of the Business Performance Management Forum or Forrester Research (BPMF, 2009; Forrester Research, 2007). To boost the discussion the Bonn-Rhein-Sieg University of Applied Sciences has made a short survey among selected German IT experts and IT management staff in the German speaking area (Gadatsch & Juszczak, 2009).

The locations of business of the 132 companies which have answered (survey return rate = 13%) are mostly in Germany (figures in brackets = number of companies per country). Managing directors, IT controller, chief information officer and IT manager were selected as contact persons. Primarily the participants of the controlling conferences (2004-2008) at the Bonn-Rhein-Sieg University of Applied Science, Sankt Augustin, Germany and other personally known people were selected. Hence this study has the character of an expert questionnaire. The companies mostly can be allocated to the business sectors finance and insurance, capital goods business, trading and energy (cf. Figure 3: Participants grouped by business sectors).

The questions cover the actuality of Green IT, running and planned activities to save energy and the companies' targets. Finally the effects on several areas of the company have been asked for.

Green IT Targets

The main aims of Green IT among the asked companies are energy saving and cost reduction (cf. Figure 4: Green IT targets). But these targets have not been reached yet. Although they achieved a lot of success the companies want to increase their efforts. Over 80% of the companies mentioned that they want to meet those targets in the future as well. Targets in marketing and innovations do not play a higher role than now (15.2% and 24.2% respectively).

Relevance and Responsibility of Green IT

For 62.3% of the companies Green IT is a relevant current topic. It can be assumed that the importance will increase in the future. On the "CeBIT-PreView 2009", one of the biggest journalist events before starting the CeBIT faire, 300 specialised journalists voted about CeBIT trends in 2009. Green IT was voted by 29.3% as the most important topic of the trade. Interesting is that the importance has grown compared with the year before (n. a., 2009).

The energy costs for the IT operations are only partly known (45.5%) e. g. for the data centre, but not for devices like personal computers or laptops. Nearly 30% of the companies don't know any of their IT energy costs. Only 25% claim that they know their IT costs. A high potential for activities can be deduced from this fact because it is

Figure 3. Participants grouped by business sectors

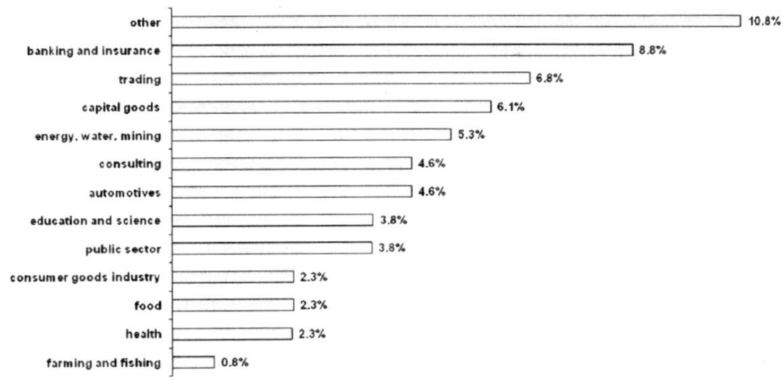

to assume that this situation mirrors the current situation but not the desired one.

For the majority of the company's energy costs are only one of several factors within the decision process for IT investments (71.8%). Only 1.7% of the companies state that the IT energy costs are crucial for their decisions. It is interesting that one quarter of the companies do not use the energy costs as a basis for their IT investment decisions.

The responsibility for the IT energy costs is established inconsistently (cf. Figure 5). A very high share places the responsibility to the IT management or the CIO (59.8%) or the business department (42.5%). IT controllers are seldom responsible for IT energy costs. This seems to be remarkable why they are responsible for reducing IT costs in total. They actually miss a chance to reduce the consumption of energy and the connected IT costs.

Activities for Energy Saving in IT

In the middle of the nineties of the last century Eder (1994) already described the properties of a "green computer". The foreground of the discussion was energy saving of hardware components which had to be proved by certificates or seals. The paper of Pernici et al. (2008) analysed how energy proportional systems can be designed. In de future we need integrated concepts with a central focus on energy saving as a core element for IT infrastructure, hardware and building services engineering.

Figure 4. Green IT targets

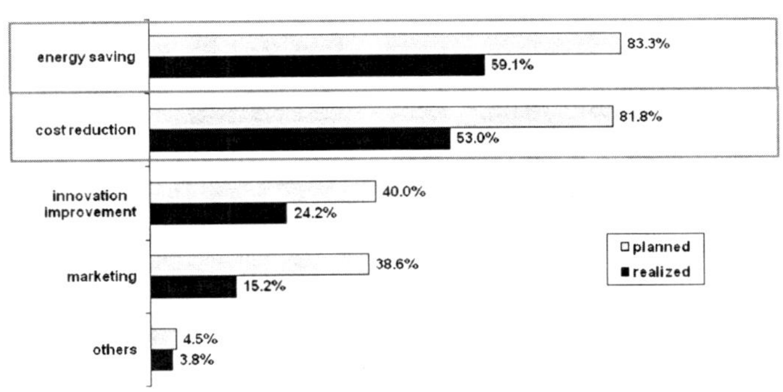

Figure 5. Responsibility for IT energy costs

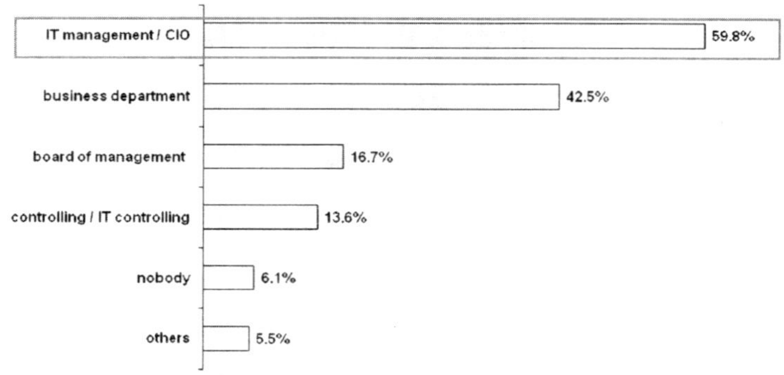

A lot of companies already have invested in energy saving projects or have concrete plans (cf. Figure 6). The top favourites are energy saving hardware or virtualized hardware (76%). The second place is taken by energy saving buildings or building services engineering. Standard activities are software modifications, e.g. standby options, or energy saving cooling systems. Further typical activities are assessments that were followed by an extensive catalogue of improvements. Examples are fuel cell technologies, block heating stations or heat recovery. It is interesting that a number of answers show that in some companies there have not been any activities yet.

Areas of Impacts of Green IT

The companies were asked about the impact on Green IT to several aspects (Figure 7). Although the high targets and complex activities the current impacts on staff qualification, software, IT processes are on a low level. Only the procurement departments expect greater changes. They have to identify more energy saving components and supplier. A further area of changing is the IT cost- and performances accounting which has to supply more detailed management information about energy consumption in the IT area.

At the moment the IT is caused by the high amount of energy consumption part of the "problem discussion" of our society. But IT services only supplies the business processes of the companies which are responsible for the energy consumption. In the future the IT has to be used as a tool for intelligent design and controlling of the business processes supplied with suitable technologies to avoid or reduce the energy consumption. So IT can be identified as a catalyst of solutions instead as a problem (Buhl et al., 2009, p. 58).

Figure 6. Planned or realized activities

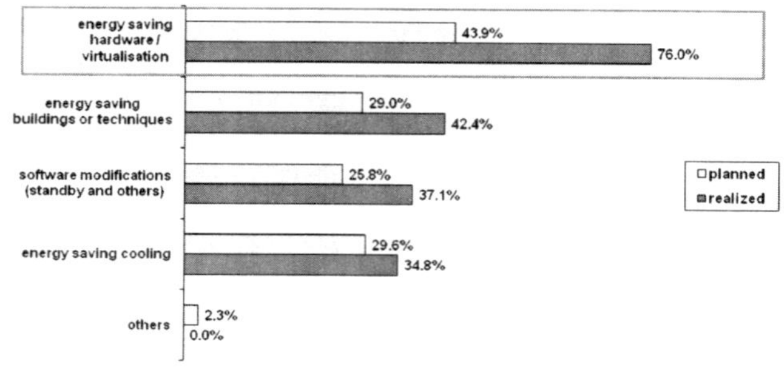

Figure 7. Green IT impacts

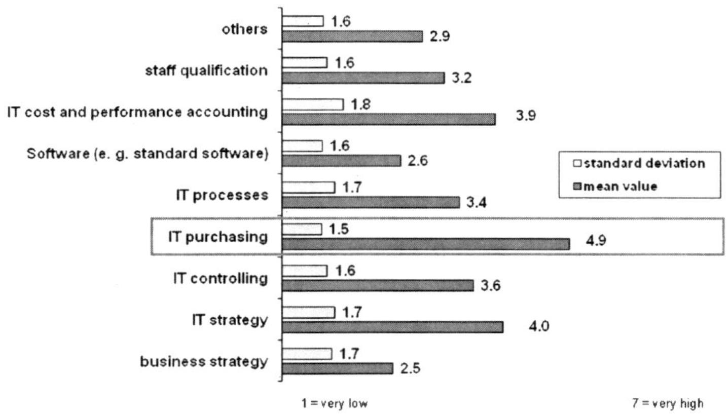

Organisation

From a viewpoint of a company it is necessary to increase the responsibility for Green IT more. An ideal solution might be a "chief Green IT officer" (CGO) or better a "chief sustainability officer (CSO)". The CSO is responsible for the company wide coordination of sustainability and Green IT as a specialised topic. He should be a member of the board of management to enforce all necessary tasks. The responsibility is not restricted at the IT area rather than to increase the chance of awareness all over the company. IT controlling as a specialised part of the organisation has to be meet this challenge and to modify their tools.

IMPLICATIONS FOR ACADEMIA AND PRACTICE

Monitoring Green IT targets

The Green IT targets have to be monitored by the management. The Balanced Scorecard (cf. Kaplan & Norton, 1992) was developed to support planning and supervising the business strategy. The method is established since years as an efficient tool for IT management to supervise the IT strategy. The method allows integrating individual views e.g. an ecological view (cf. Hahn & Wagner, 2001). Furthermore it is possible to integrate ecological targets into the already used views.

Table 2 shows some ecological (green) targets which can be integrated into a balanced scorecard system.

Adapting the Balanced Scorecard

Figure 8 shows an example of a simple balanced scorecard which integrates ecological (green) targets into the classic commercial views market and customer, IT processes, staff and finance.

Challenges of a Research Agenda

Green IT is established in companies and organisations as an important topic. But the activities are dominated by the aspect of energy and cost saving. The integration of Green IT into the corporate and IT strategy is an exception up to now. Controller and IT controller don't have identified Green IT as a task for their business. Certifications of the maturity level are an exception, too. So it can be assumed that Green IT as an important task of IT management and IT controlling is in a very early stage with chances for further developments.

Table 2. "Green targets" for IT management and controlling

Level	Tool	Targets concerning Green IT
Strategic	IT strategy	Reducing of energy consumption and CO2 emissions, Checking of alternatives (e. g. of data centres), using of innovative technologies (fuel cells), creating of "green" data centres
	Strategic benchmarking	Integrate efficiency targets into maturity models like IT-CMF
	Balanced scorecard	Considering of energy consumption and CO2 targets in activities and performance indicators
	Standardisation	Reducing of energy consumption by technical standards like server virtualisation, desktop virtualisation (thin client), video conferencing, sharing of office space and equipment (shared desk), energy save modus, remote shut down functions of equipment (avoiding overnight running of IT equipment), cooling systems, printer decentralisation
	IT portfolio management	Criteria enhancement to consider of Green IT relevant projects, increasing of cost and energy efficiency
Operational	IT cost and performance accounting	Calculation of energy costs and CO2 emissions
	Business partner management	audits at supplier, regularly surveys among IT customer and supplier to ensure the compliance of the Green IT strategy
	IT reporting and indicators	Creation and analysis of relevant reports, suggestion of counteractions concerning energy consumption and CO2 emission in relevant views (IT customer, systems, projects and other criteria)
	IT project controlling	Observance of energy consumption and CO2 targets by the IT projects, early information of project manager and originator
	IT process management	Internal marketing for Green IT targets, information and training of the staff, modifying of supply processes (privileging of energy saving products and supplier), changing of withdrawal processes for old equipment and consumable material (toner for printer, batteries), real time monitoring of energy consumption of IT equipment, automatic shut down by not using

Figure 8. Green IT balanced scorecard (sample)

Market / Customer			
Target	**Indicator**	**Target Value**	**Measures**
Improve ecology appearance	Turnover share with ecology customers	Improvement > 10%	Analyse customer requirements Ecology campaign Reduce energy consumtion of IT hardware
	Share of energy saving IT hardware	Share > 50%	

IT Processes			
Target	**Indicator**	**Target Value**	**Measures**
Reduce cost of running IT data centres Increase maturity in Green IT	Energy consumption je working hour	Kilowatt hours < xxx	Virtualisation Use energy saving certified devices Department printer Automatic shut down energy consumption supervision
	Energy consumption per computer hour	Kilowatt hours < xxx	

Staff			
Target	**Indicator**	**Target Value**	**Measures**
Establishing of a sustainable culture	Energy consumption by staff members	X kilowatt hours per year	Training Self committment Adapt payments Adapt Company suggestion plan
	Suggestions per staff member (awarded)	Number > 2	

Finance			
Target	**Indicator**	**Target Value**	**Measures**
Decrease energy consumption Increase profit with energy saving IT products	Energy costs per IT workplace or working hour	Energie costs < X EUR	Energy cost analysis Integrate energy cost registration in cost accounting system
	ROI	ROI > 10%	

A central task for the companies is the development of integrated environment management concepts which includes Green IT and more. The up to now used single activities don't reach because of a missing strategic target controlling. For this an enhancement of the business and IT strategy is necessary. Tool for strategic controlling like the balanced scorecard have to be enhanced by suitable attributes (targets, performance indicators, measurements and activities). The ecological awareness of the staff has to be sharpened.

A further aspect is the question of measurement of progress in the companies and from a whole economic perspective. The development of maturity models and concepts for certification stands at the first steps, too. Only few models have been published (Greuel, 2009, pp. 68-77). There is a considerable potential for research and chances for transfer. Companies should use now already available concepts of certification from independent suppliers. Researcher should create or develop concepts of certification and adjust them with established management instruments of economics.

REFERENCES

na. (2008). *Netzkomponenten, 60 Prozent des IT-Stromverbrauchs außerhalb des Rechenzentrums, Experton Group: Green Office kommt*. Retrieved December 15, 2008, from www.lanline.de

na. (2009). *Journalisten haben gewählt: Die CeBIT – Trends 2009*. Retrieved February 12, 2009, from http://www.ad-hoc-news.de/journalisten-haben-gewaehlt-die-cebit-trends-2009--/de/Wirtschaft-Boerse/Marktberichte/20037194

Bohrer, P., Elnozahy, E., Keller, T., Kistler, M., Lefurgy, C., McDowell, C., & Rajamony, R. (2002). The Case for Power Management in Web Servers. In Graybill, R., & Melhem, R. (Eds.), *Power Aware Computing* (pp. 261–289). New York: Kluwer Academic/Plenum Publishers.

BPMF. (2009). *The Business Performance Management Forum: IT Sustainability Imperatives in Internet and eCommerce Business*. Retrieved November, 12, 2009, from http://www.rackable.com/thinkecological/pdf/IT-Sustainability.pdf

Buhl, H. U., Laartz, J., Löffler, M., & Röglinger, M. (2009). Green IT reicht nicht aus. *Wirtschaftsinformatik & Management*, *1*(1), 54–58.

Eder, P. (1994). Grüne Computer. *Wirtschaftsinformatik*, *36*(6), 600–603.

Elkington, J. (2004). Enter the triple bottom line. In Henriques, A., & Richardson, J. (Eds.), *The Triple Bottom Line: Does It All Add up?* (pp. 1–16). London: Earthscan.

EPA. (2009). *EPA – United States Environmental Protection Agency. About Energy Star*. Retrieved November 19, 2009, from http://www.energystar.gov/index.cfm?c=about.ab_index

Ernst & Young. (2009). *Green IT in kleinen und mittleren Unternehmen (KMU): Ein Blick auf das Thema aus Sicht von IT-Verantwortlichen in KMU*. Retrieved November 12, 2009, from http://www.ey.com/publicationwwLUAssets/Green_TI/Green-IT in KMU.pdf

Forrester Research. (2007). *Umwelt ist ein wichtiger Faktor in der IT*. Retrieved May 3, 2009, from http://www.computerwoche.de/knowledge_center/green-it/592768/

Gadatsch, A. (2009). IT controlling – concepts and transformation in practice. *Business Information Systems and Engineering*, *1*(3), 254–262.. doi:10.1007/s12599-009-0043-6

Gadatsch, A., & Juszczak, J. (Eds.). (2009). Results of the short survey concerning the status of Green IT in German speaking countries (Green IT 2009). Schriftenreihe des Fachbereiches Wirtschaftswissenschaft Sankt Augustin, Hochschule Bonn-Rhein-Sieg, vol. 25. Sankt Augustin: Hochschule Bonn-Rhein-Sieg.

Gartner (Ed.) (2008). *Gartner identifies the Top 10 Strategic Technologies for 2009*. Retrieved November 18, 2009, from http://www.gartner.com/it/page.jsp?id=777212

Greuel, V. (2009). *Economic Benefits of Green IS*. Unpublished thesis, Bonn-Rhein-Sieg University of Applied Science, Sankt Augustin, Germany.

Hahn, T., & Wagner, M. (2001). *Sustainability Balanced Scorecard*. Lüneburg, Germany: Center for Sustainability Management.

IDC (Ed.). (2008). *IDC Predictions 2009: An Economic Pressure Cooker Will Accelerate the IT Industry Transformation*. Retrieved November 18, 2009, from http://www.idc.com/getdoc.jsp?containerId=215519

Kaplan, R. S., & Norton, D. P. (1992). The Balanced Scorecard – Measures that drive performance. *Harvard Business Review*, *70*(1), 71–79.

Mertens, P., Große-Wilde, J., & Wilkens, I. (2005). *Die (Aus-)Wanderung der Softwareproduktion – Eine Zwischenbilanz*. Arbeitsberichte des Instituts für Informatik, vol. 38, Nr. 3. Erlangen, Germany: Friedrich-Alexander-Universität Erlangen-Nürnberg.

Murugesan, S. (2008). Harnessing Green IT: Principles and Practices. *IT Professional*, *10*(1), 24–33. doi:10.1109/MITP.2008.10

Pernici, B., Ardagna, D., & Cappiello, C. (2008). Business Process Design: Towards Service-Based Green Information Systems. In P. Forbrig, F. Paternò, & A. M. Pejtersen (Eds.), *Human-Computer Interaction Symposium: Proceedings of the IFIP 20th World Computer Congress, Milano, Italy* (pp. 195–203). Berlin: Springer.

Pflueger, J. (2008). *Re-Defining the "green" data center. A dell technical white paper. Managing the data center by efficient use of IT resources*. Retrieved November 22, 2009 from http://www.dell.com/downloads/global/vectors/dec_2008_re-defining.pdf

Rings, T., Caryer, G., Gallop, J., Grabowski, J., Kovacikova, T., Schulz, S., & Stokes-Rees, I. (2009). Grid and Cloud Computing: Opportunities for Integration with the Next Generation Network. *Grid Computing*, *7*, 375–393. doi:10.1007/s10723-009-9132-5

Ryan, E. (2008). Building Sustainable IT. *Cutter IT Journal*, *21*(2), 6–12.

Schauer, H. (2006). Vergleichende Buchbesprechung IT-Controlling. *Wirtschaftsinformatik*, *48*(3), 212–218. doi:10.1007/s11576-006-0046-6

Telle, K. (2006). "It Pays to be Green" – A Premature Conclusion? *Environmental & Resource Economics, 35*, 195–220. DOI 10.1007/s10640-006-9013-3 The Green Grid (2009). *The Green Grid Data Centre Power Efficiency Metrics: PUE and DCiE*. Retrieved November 22, 2009 from http://www.thegreengrid.org/en/Global/Content/white-papers/The-Green-Grid-Data-Centre-Power-Efficiency-Metrics-PUE-and-DCiE

Section 3

Frameworks, Reference Models & Methodologies

Chapter 11
Environmental Monitoring, Data Mining, and Dynamic Analysis

Anneke Minke
University of Hildesheim, Germany

Helmut Lessing
University of Hildesheim, Germany

ABSTRACT

Online-monitoring systems as well as systems regarding environmental observation have evolved from classic analytic methods on the laboratory scale. Still, they are structured mainly medially and sectorally. At this point, the multi-sensorial array-technology opens up new possibilities. Today, the integration of these multi-sensorial chips into mobile units of the automotive domain or into cell phones and the transmission of empirical data to an integrated network are possible; there are no fundamental technological barriers. Nevertheless, the examination of this data collected by mobile sensors which are often in motion and the extraction of reliable, supra-regional information yield a new class of problems. In this chapter, an implementation concept will be described which will be evaluated within a pilot scheme.

INTRODUCTION

The dynamic observation of environmental changes – based on regions and countries – is a task that federal states as well as the federal German government and the other EU-members have to comply with, forced by EU-directives and their according laws at federal and state level. These legal requirements aim for an exact capture of changes in biotic and abiotic as well as in anthropogenic, urban, and technical systems – in general and in detail, too.

To achieve this goal, complex monitoring systems have been implemented in Europe over the past twenty years which continually monitor climate, oceans, lakes, rivers, ecosystems, soil and land use, and sealing and emissions in urban metropolises. By means of satellite and remote sensing, it is already possible to gather this kind of data cross-nationally and on a large scale (Landsat 30m*30m) (cf. Satpix, 2009). Using graphical data processing, the raw data is processed to a

DOI: 10.4018/978-1-61520-981-1.ch011

graphical representation which is intuitively comprehensible. This way, it is possible to precociously detect changes regarding the ozone shield or the glaciation of the polar caps which are relevant to the climate. Among the multitude of satellite systems available today, the ENVISAT carrier current system of transmission of the European Space Agency (ESA, 2009) has turned out to be particularly efficient.

Recently, in addition to remote sensing procedures, online-sensor systems have been able to prevail; they record different parameters at a certain position to a predefined point in time using specific sensors, and they transfer this data to a central unit. Particularly, the parameters in question are concerned with emissions in the lower atmospheric levels, such as the intensity of radiation, ozone formation, temperature, and precipitation. Thus, online-systems have been implemented in Germany which monitor all medial domains such as air quality, water, soil, or nuclear technological facilities; the German Federal Environmental Agency collects data of the different federal states and periodically reports the results (cf. Umweltbundesamt, 2008). Furthermore, the German Weather Service ("Deutscher Wetterdienst", DWD) possesses a comparatively close-meshed sensoring network of fixed measurement stations. Mathematical exploration and modelling methods enable the derivation of a laminar observation. Under these circumstances, accurate real-time information concerning local environmental parameters (temperature, ozone, radiation, humidity, and pollen count) only exists when a measurement station is available nearby. But investments for constructing and operating these monitoring systems are significant. Therefore, a sufficient "mesh network" of measurement stations is often lacking, with only a few stations being positioned at particularly representative or problematical locations.

This chapter focuses on the current state of environmental monitoring and innovative ideas in the area of monitoring systems as well as new, mainly theoretical aspects of sensor systems and how such a monitoring system can be implemented for collecting the data. In order to analyze the recorded data, different data mining techniques are essential. Hence, an overview of established data mining methods as well as research outcomes in the field of data mining and, in particular, fuzzy clustering will be given.

This chapter is organized as follows: In the next section, an overview of related work concerning the field of environmental monitoring will be given, followed by an overview of the sensor technology and the description of the general layout of the monitoring scenario. The mathematical considerations and algorithms used for analyzing the collected data will be introduced in the following section. The chapter concludes by giving an outlook to further research tasks.

BACKGROUND

Classic monitoring and environmental observation systems are structured sectorally and medially. This way, the "Luftmessnetz Niedersachsen" (LÜN; Niedersächsisches Ministerium für Umwelt und Klimaschutz, 2009) continuously measures different parameters concerning air quality such as carbon monoxide, particulate matter, ozone, nitrogen oxides, and sulfur dioxide as well as meteorological data like precipitation, wind direction and speed, air pressure, global radiation, temperature, and humidity at 29 selected positions employing technologically standardized containers. This data is immediately analyzed and aggregated to form an air quality-index. The index is shared with controlling institutions as well as the public over the internet. Furthermore, current measurements, temporal violations of limits concerning particulate matter, and measurement value progresses are provided.

On the one hand, these containers are positioned at places with critically high emission like, e.g., the intra-urban area of Hanover. On the other hand, there are containers which are allocated at rather noncritical locations such as the coast of the North Sea with a single air quality representative for an entire area. Nevertheless, the extrapolation of the area is hardly possible as strong emissions – in particular carbon monoxide, particulate matter, and hydrocarbon – often occur regionally and temporally limited and therefore remain undetected due to the loose data-acquisition grid. The technologies employed by LÜN have been developed for more than 15 years; manpower and expenses generate operating costs of more than 1.5 million Euros every year.

A similar monitoring meshwork is maintained by the hydrology administration of Lower Saxony ("Gewässerkundlicher Landesdienst", GLD). Within the context of water monitoring in Lower Saxony ("Gewässerüberwachungssystem Niedersachsen", GÜN), several monitoring meshworks are maintained at waters above ground (rivers and lakes) as well as at coastal waters which continuously gather parameters like water line, wind, undulations, temperature, pH-value, conductivity, and oxygen. Furthermore, aquifers are monitored by the GLD; this data is collected in order to be processed and provided to public authorities.

Similarly to the system installed in Lower Saxony, there are comparable systems implemented in all federal states. The air monitoring system and the data acquisition of the German Weather Service can stand representatively for these structures and form the technological basis of monitoring and environmental observation systems. Furthermore, production facilities – in particular the chemical industry, (nuclear) power plants, barrages fixes, disposals, and incineration plants – can be monitored continuously. The systems register abiotic parameters in air, water, and soil based on methods which have evolved from laboratory analytics. Today, even more complex hydrocarbons such as benzol and methane can be recorded by automated gas-phase chromatographs. These systems are fully automated and transmit the data online. The different monitoring systems support and complement each other. Based on these systems, the German Federal Environmental Agency periodically publishes results concerning the general state of the environment ("Daten zur Umwelt"). The operating costs for supporting these classic medial and state-specific segmented montoring systems in Germany are enormous. A comparison of internet-based environmental monitoring information systems of the 16 German federal states points out several deficiencies, although Berlin, Bremen, Saxony-Anhalt and Baden-Württemberg stand out rather positively (cf. Voigt, 2002). Of course, this effort is not completely avoidable, nevertheless it is possible to reduce it by installing a monitoring system based on mobile units (vehicles) and clustering methods (Figure 1).

MAIN FOCUS

Sensor Technology

The structural deficiency of existing monitoring systems can be compensated partiallly by installing mobile sensor systems using cabs, private automobiles or busses and analyzing the collected data with adequate mathematical methods. This system can be realized by installing a specially adapted antenna on the roofs of the vehicles. In order to record the data needed for analysis, vehicles which are present in the examined region transmit the data concerning the required environmental parameters directly online to a monitoring provider, independently of whether they are moving and if so, where they are. Additionally, they can be addressed actively by the monitoring provider. Most of the time, however, cars are standing and not moving. Nevertheless, if a vehicle is standing outside, its sensor data can be relevant and useful.

Employing a sufficiently large number of mobile units, cluster techniques can be applied to regional situations with respect to the environmental parameters in order to analyze differences

Figure 1. Structure of a mobile environmental monitoring and data mining system

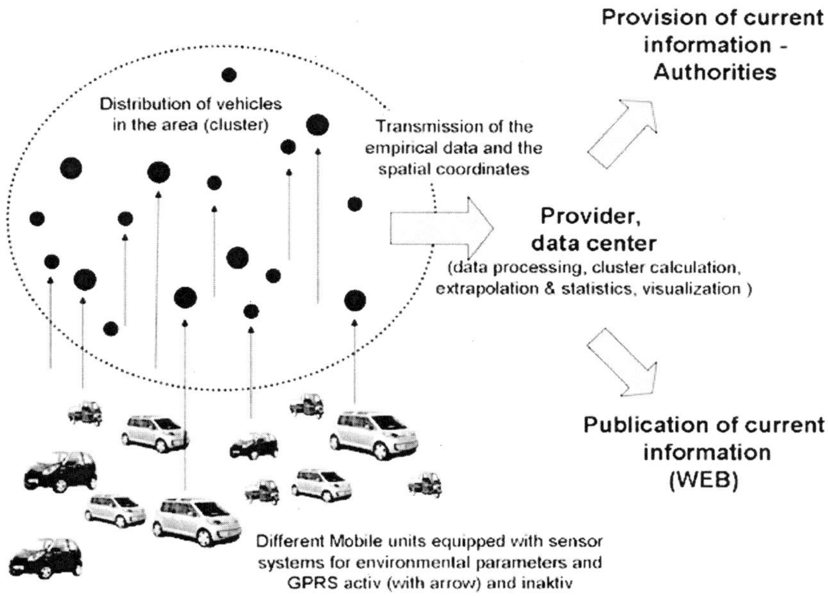

as well as inter-regional developments. In this, standing and moving cars can be distinguished.

This is a novel approach. The mobile units can be equipped with sensors that collect suitable environmental parameters along the way and transfer the data via mobile communication to the provider.

By means of mobile monitoring systems, an observation of formerly undetected areas would be possible, e.g. by sending mobile units in an area when required. Therefore, signs of ecological incidents could be verified. The data collected by mobile units would be analyzed and the results would be provided to the public authorities. In this context, clustering techniques could support the evaluation of supra-regional areas as well as of a local area, a novelty as a detailed, site-specific collection, and evaluation of environmental data would be impossible due to fixed sensor units and measurement stations. Up to now, there have been no commercial providers of such a technology (cf. umwelt-monitoring-systeme, 2009; ecoTech, 2009; Technidata AG, 2009).

The system would be market-oriented. The services could be offered to public authorities as well as other non-government organizations by a provider. Thus, there might be a chance to replace outdated, cost-intensive monitoring systems in some areas in an economic way, and it could bring relief to public finances.

Specific Sensor Technologies

ChipSensors Ltd. (2009), an Irish company, has been offering a sensor chip for a short time which can record temperature, humidity and further parameters simultaneously and with high precision. The 0.13μm chip has a 4x4mm body; it needs 1.8-3.6V direct current and only 400μA. It was developed for deployment in the automotive area, in industrial HVAC-systems, and for data-logging. ChipSensors Ltd. is also currently developing an ultra-low-power wireless version of this sensor which integrates all signal conditioning, microcontroller, memory, and RF transceiver functions.

Furthermore, Sensortechnics GmbH (Compamed, 2009), a company which specializes on the development of prototypes, provides complete solutions and assemblies of customer-specific sensors. Using state-of-the-art chip-on-board technology, individual sensor elements are attached to various bases and are contacted, allowing manifold possibilities of sensor design as well as a high degree of miniaturization and a large packing density. For its sensors and systems, Sensortechnics GmbH offers integrated analog and digital signal processing and individual sensor calibration and programming.

At the academy for engineering and economics in Karlsruhe (Hochschule Karlsruhe für Technik und Wirtschaft, 2009), a sensor chip for analyzing volatile hydrocarbons was developed. This micro-structured sensor chip is built on hybrid-technology (electrodes, heating in DC-sputter-technology, sensitive coating in serigraphy), realizing four different gas-sensitive ceramic coatings. The chip was built to identify present gas based on numeric analyses and to determine its concentration. Moreover, a survey is being executed which evaluates whether the multi-sensor chip can enable analysis of elementary compositions of volatile hydrocarbons.

Thereof independent, new highly-integrated sensor systems (arrays) were developed within the last decade, which are based on chip technology (cf. Mescheder et al., 2007; Krittwattanakhorn et al., 2006). These systems can integrate several sensors for different parameters on a miniaturized basis on a single chip. Throughout the world, more than 180 enterprises have specialized on development and marketing of these highly-integrated sensor chips, particularly concerning biosensors and abiotic sensors (compression, temperature, radiation as well as light, humidity, oxygen, ozone and the like). Several developments address highly-integrated arrays which can detect different parameters simultaneously. In particular, these latest developments can form the technological basis and are suited for the construction and the application of new monitoring systems.

This technology allows the integration of sensor chips into existing IT-systems as they are available in automobiles and cell phones. The transmission of the data does not constitute a problem either because it can be achieved using established communication technology. However, the examination of data collected by carrier systems which are moving and arbitrarily distributed is a not yet solved problem.

Data Collection

In the proposed environmental monitoring scenario, the data, i.e. parameters regarding air quality, is collected by mobile units, specifically vehicles used for public transportation, although it is imaginable to use private cars as well. These mobile units feature the sensors described above so they can measure the different environmental parameters. The data is obtained as follows: The equipped vehicles move in the pre-defined area of concern and measure the different parameter values in fixed time intervals. Subsequently, the data is transmitted online to a central database where it is permanently stored. In addition to the environmental data, the coordinates where it was taken and a binary value representing whether the vehicle was moving while recording have to be transmitted and stored as well in order to monitor the general situation and the development in the area. In case of public transportation vehicles used as mobile units, it is reasonable to save the specific vehicle which provided the data as well; this leads to a better maintenance of the sensors since faulty sensors can easily be identified and either be repaired or sorted out, and the erroneous data can be deleted.

Because of the fact that the vehicles are moving, the data is collected rather arbitrarily and not at stationary measurement units. In this context, it is important that vehicle sensor systems can produce a stream of relevant environmental data.

When the amount of collected data is sufficiently large, it can be analyzed employing certain data mining methods.

Mathematical Models

In order to analyze the collected data, data mining techniques are essential. First of all, the relevant data has to be extracted from the database because not all data points are of interest when it comes to monitoring the general development as well as the development of areas with an accumulation of certain environmental factors. As mentioned before, the focus of this work is on monitoring different environmental factors like e.g. ozone, solar radiation, CO_2 etc.

Extraction of Data

As the data is collected quite arbitrarily by vehicles touring in the area of concern, not all data points are relevant for the analysis. The main interest is in finding areas with higher pollution factors, i.e. finding clusters of data points with high parameter values. Nevertheless, simply applying standard clustering algorithms to the database suffers from two major problems concerning the geographical position of the data points.

First of all, clustering all data points regarding their geographical positions might yield results showing accumulation points of vehicles used for measuring different environmental parameters without regarding the actual degree of pollution since the spatial closeness of the objects highly influences the calculation of the similarity and might even outvote the measured similarity concerning environmental factors. Due to this problem, it seems suggestive to leave out geographical information or at least to decrease its weight when calculating the similarity of objects. However, this approach leads to the second problem that data points are clustered regardless of their closeness. This yields results with clusters of data points which are similar concerning their occurrence of the different factors, i.e. data points with a high ozone level are clustered in one cluster, those with high CO_2 occurrence are clustered etc., although the points within a cluster may be spatially distributed over the whole monitored area. In this context, a possible result might be that on the one hand, the German cities of Leipzig and Munich are clustered as they have a relatively high particular matter emission, and on the other hand, Bieberach and Wolfsburg are grouped because of having similar low values (cf. Umweltbundesamt, 2009). Therefore the main challenge is to extract the needed data and to cluster it bypassing both of these problems.

Clustering the geographical positions of different objects, i.e. different points of measurement, becomes reasonable if there is previous knowledge that all examined objects have some inherent similarity like the general degree of pollution. Hence, the data can be extracted from the database using different kinds of thresholds so that only those objects are extracted that exceed some given thresholds. E.g., when looking at Figure 2 regarding possible CO_2-values, clustering all data points would not yield anything relevant. However, clustering those objects that exceed the threshold of 100ppm – and therefore all but the objects represented by circles – yields the four clusters shown in Figure 3(a). A different result is obtained when clustering those objects that exceed the threshold of 200ppm. Obviously, the detected clusters do not necessarily have to overlap as the bottom left cluster in Figure 3(a) only includes data points with a CO_2-value smaller than 200ppm whereas there are two well-separated areas in the upper right cluster that exceed the threshold of 200ppm. Therefore, different thresholds can yield different results concerning the number of clusters and their centers.

The employed threshold is context-dependent. In areas with rather low pollution factors, lower thresholds are needed in order to identify the worst spots than, e.g., in large cities such as Munich or Berlin.

Figure 2. Geographical position of measurements regarding possible CO_2-values

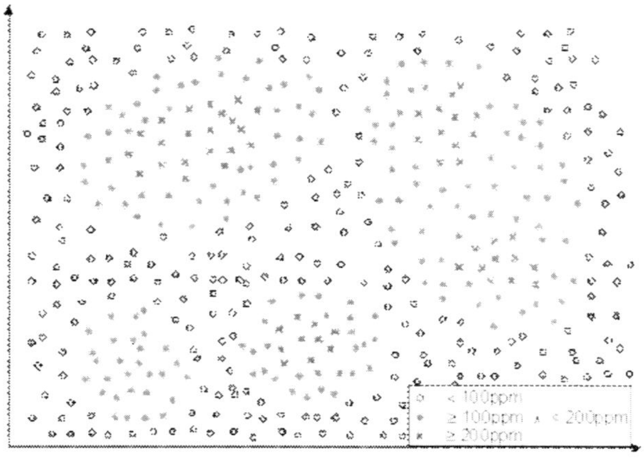

Figure 3. CO_2-values ≥ 100ppm (b). CO_2-values ≥ 200ppm

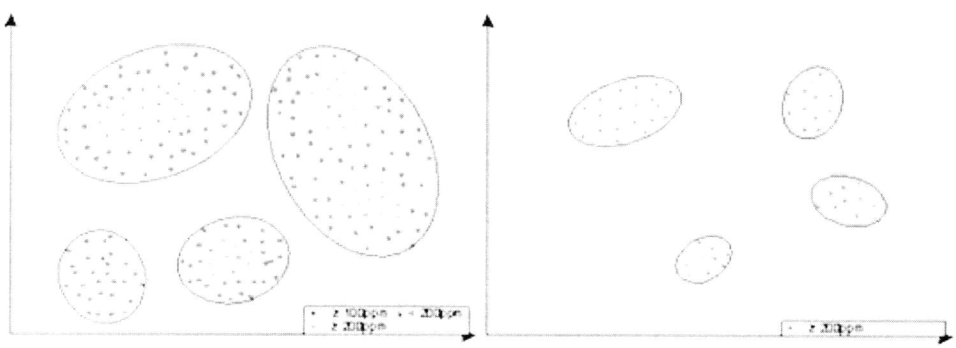

Cluster Analysis

Depending on the main purpose of the analysis, different cluster algorithms can be employed. If the main focus is on identifying clusters and their geographical position, simple hard cluster algorithms like hierarchical agglomorative clustering or *k*-means are sufficient (e.g. Cios et al., 2007, pp. 263 et seq.; Bramer, 2007, pp. 224 et seq.). However, if further analyses like the development of clusters over time are of interest, more complex methods are essential.

The usage of hard cluster algorithms which assign each object, i.e. each data point, to exactly one cluster, bears the advantage that they are quick and easily scalable. There are two different classes of hard cluster algorithms: hierarchical methods and partitioning methods. Hierarchical methods determine a sequence of partitions by successively merging or splitting existing clusters based on their dissimilarity. On the contrary, partitioning methods estimate a single partition, generally by minimizing an objective function regarding a given number of clusters. However, hard {0,1}-memberships bear the problem that all objects assigned to a cluster have the same influence on the position of the cluster center and therefore on the overall position of the cluster. Especially in context of the introduced approach of extracting data from the database, it seems suggestive to estimate continuous membership degrees in order to identify outliers as well as true cluster centers in addition to further advantages of continuous membership degrees. Hence, fuzzy clustering techniques as introduced in, e.g., Bezdek (1981) and Höppner et al. (1999) are needed. In general, fuzzy cluster algorithms are objective function-based algorithms. There are two main classes of fuzzy clustering algorithms, probabilistic algorithms and possibilistic algorithms. In case of the probabilistic algorithms, the assigned membership degrees represent the probability for an object that it belongs to a certain cluster. Therefore, the overall membership degree of a single object to all c clusters has to add up to one, incorporating the constraint given in Eq. (1) with u_{ij} being the membership degree of object j to cluster i.

$$\sum_{i=1}^{c} u_{ij} = 1 \qquad \forall j = 1, \ldots, n$$

In case of possibilistic fuzzy clustering, the membership degrees represent the typicality of an object compared with a cluster center rather than its probability of belonging to the cluster. Therefore, the constraint given in Eq. (1) is dropped. This bears the advantage that the estimated membership degree of an object is no longer influenced by its relative position to all the clusters but only by its distance to the cluster in question. In Figure 4, there are obviously two clusters which overlap at object x_3. When applying probabilistic fuzzy clustering techniques, x_1 might get a membership degree of 0.95 to the left and 0.05 to the right cluster, respectively; x_2 has opposite degrees. Intuitively, it seems quite straight-forward that object x_3 should have the same membership degree to the left cluster as x_1 since it is equally far from the center; the same holds for the right cluster when compared with x_2. However, because it is as distant to the right cluster center as to the left, it has equal membership degrees to both clusters, i.e. its membership degree is in each case 0.5. By dropping the constraint given in Eq. (1), possibilistic clustering would yield similarly high membership degrees to both clusters as x_1 and x_2, respectively. This bears the advantage that the alignment and shape of the clusters can actually be estimated.

A further advantage of continuous membership degrees representing the typicality of objects is that they enable the analyst to evaluate whether the chosen thresholds used for extracting the data were appropriate. By calculating the correlation between membership degrees and original parameter values used for extraction, it is possible to evaluate whether the estimated cluster centers are close to the true centers, i.e. the real peak of pollution. However, if there is no considerable correlation between membership degrees and parameter values, there must be several different peaks within the detected cluster and therefore, the threshold used for the extraction should be increased. Again, when looking at Figure 3(a), the membership degrees obtained for the upper left cluster correlate with the parameter values

Figure 4. Butterfly problem

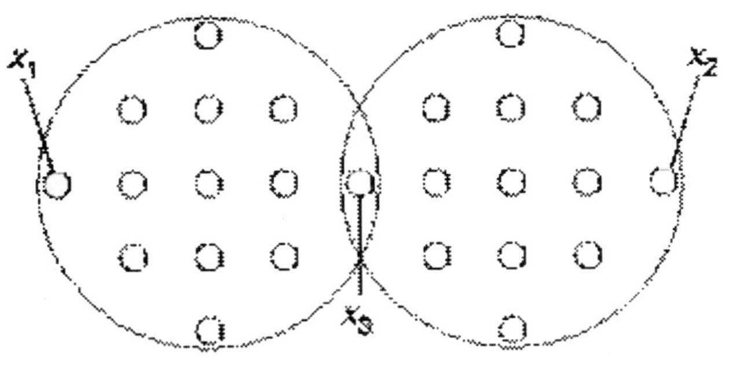

for the ozone level so one can reason that the chosen threshold is sufficient concerning this very cluster. Nevertheless, when looking at the upper right cluster in the same figure, there will be no considerable correlation between parameter values and membership degrees and hence, the chosen thresholds are not adequate in order to identify the peaks in this area.

Furthermore, in case of possibilistic fuzzy clustering, an object can be assigned to several clusters with a high membership degree as well as not be assigned to any clusters at all, identifying it as a true outlier. In context of the introduced monitoring approach, there are two possible reasons for outliers. First of all, there might only be a single data point, i.e. only one vehicle provided exploitable data in the area and therefore the monitoring procedure suffers from insufficient data. The alternative is that there are quite a few vehicles and therefore objects in the area that are not extracted as they fall below the given threshold. In this case, further analyses are required in order to explore the reason for the appearance of the outlier. Possible causes are that the outlier barely exceeds the threshold whereas other objects fall just below it, or that there are measuring faults, e.g. caused by a defective sensor or a sensor which is placed close to a pollution source, or the like. This kind of problem can be resolved, e.g., by comparing the parameter values of the outlier to those of surrounding objects and by adjusting the extraction threshold where required.

However, when employing fuzzy clustering techniques, there is always the problem of identifying the number of clusters in the data set. Especially in case of objective function-based algorithms as those employed in fuzzy clustering a pre-specified number of clusters is needed for initialization. For instance, the number can be obtained by executing a hierarchical analysis as pre-step.

Dynamic Analysis

When monitoring different environmental parameters, not just the current status is of interest but the general development within a certain area. There are two different kinds of developments that can be analyzed using the introduced monitoring approach.

First of all, the changes in the cluster structure during a single day can be revealed. It is possible to identify those areas which are particularly environmentally stressed during the off-peak hours with need for action. For this kind of analysis, it is usually sufficient to execute the cluster analysis repeatedly.

The second sort of development is the changing of the overall situation. E.g. there is a need to evaluate the efficiency of certain actions within a specific area like the implementation of the environmental badge and low emission zones in several German cities. In general, there are two major developments that need to be analyzed. On the one hand, there may be clusters which decrease in size and eventually disappear. On the other hand, new clusters may appear or grow in size, which would be a call for actions. In both cases, the reasons have to be identified; a readjustment of the threshold can give first hints of the development. However, especially in the second case, an early identification of the development is crucial in order to avoid further damage. When monitoring general developments, there is no need for a new analysis in each period, rather an analysis based on previous clustering results is required; possible changes can be identified during the clustering process. In literature, different aspects of the dynamization of fuzzy clustering are given (e.g. see Angstenberger, 2000; Neumann, 2008). Still, the employment of the possibilistic clustering may fail due to general problems of the possibilistic approach as stated by, e.g., Borgelt (2005, p. 53). These general problems include the problem of cluster attraction. If clusters highly differ in shape or density or if they are rather close to each other, the possibilistic approach tends to detect only one cluster instead of two (see Borgelt, 2005, p. 53; Timm, 2002, pp. 45 et seq.). Especially in the scenario of the rather arbitrary collection of data by a mobile sensor system, avoiding this problem becomes a major task as the density of the clusters may differ because of a differing number of vehicles in the area. Possible extensions to the original possibilistic approach as introduced by Krishnapuram et al. (1993) are given in Timm (2001) and Minke et al. (2009) which counteract this problem at the expense of additional computation time. The approach by Timm (2001) is based on the heterogeneity between clusters which is modeled by introducing a penalty term punishing clusters which are rather close, comprising some kind of cluster repulsion. However, this approach needs additional parameters which highly depend on the distance between clusters and their individual sizes, both criteria which vary over time; hence they have to be adjusted dynamically, depending on the collected data in each period. The second approach given by Minke et al. (2009) is based on modeling the homogeneity within clusters rather than the heterogeneity between them. This seems suggestive as clusters may be quite close to each other due to the fact that different peaks can be quite close as shown in Figure 3.

As mentioned before, for the analysis of the general development the results of previous periods are needed. But on what condition do previous periods, i.e. previous time frames when measurements where taken, qualify as being suitable? Assuming that a day is divided in several sections, each one containing, e.g., the data of two adjacent hours, the true preceding period will not be sufficient. Only comparable data will help to identify possible changes. Therefore, it seems more reasonable to use data of a similar period, e.g. the results of weekdays between 8 and 10 a.m. can be compared. Nevertheless, there is a further modification as it is not appropriate to compare daily data as overall changes do not occur on a day-to-day basis. Furthermore, the extended possibilistic algorithms are rather complex and therefore computationally quite expensive. Hence it seems reasonable to update the cluster structure on a longer basis like weeks or even months, taking into account the data of these time frames as a single period.

When analyzing the data of a new time frame, a pre-step is needed in order to determine whether any particular changes have occurred. This can be achieved by using the previous clustering results and assigning the new data points to the given clusters. If the correlation between parameter values and membership degrees of both time frames is still sufficient, there are no mentionable changes in the cluster structure, i.e. there are no new clusters and the cluster diameters remain unchanged. On the contrary, if there are dense spots of outliers, a new cluster has occurred; are these dense spots lacking, the cluster diameters may have changed as cluster sizes may vary. Additionally, a cluster may have vanished which can be detected as there are no new objects assigned to this cluster with a considerable membership degree. Only if any changes are detected, a new analysis has to be started based on former clustering results and the additional knowledge concerning the number of clusters and their approximate position.

Critical Review

A mobile monitoring system installed on the roof of a vehicle and equipped with flexibly addressable data transfer technology (GPRS and GPS) can transmit static environmental information of its location whenever it is standing, but it can also transmit data streams when moving.

The statistical reliability of the results concerning current environmental parameters of the selected areas depends on the number of available mobile sensor systems (vehicles) and on their distribution in the area of concern. In this context, it is important that the mobile units can be actively sent to the area in question and that they can create and transmit data streams covering the area.

This way, the empirical effort can be adapted to the desired level of statistical reliability.

The mobile environmental monitoring system described above consists of well-known and well-tried technical components and mathematical methods, but their composition is a novelty. Therefore, their combined deployment has to be evaluated empirically regarding the components separately as well as in combination. If these evaluations yield promising results, new services can be provided which will enable cost reduction of stationary monitoring systems.

CONCLUSION AND FUTURE RESEARCH DIRECTIONS

A new approach of monitoring environmental parameters regarding air quality and emissions within the lower atmospheric levels was introduced. It is based on providing a mesh-network of sensors by attaching them to mobile units, particularly to vehicles used for public transportation. For future work, extending the monitoring approach and the sensor network to other mobile units like mobile devices such as cell phones is thinkable. However, when using private devices, there are several questions concerning data privacy which have to be regarded, complicating the general monitoring framework.

The collected data is analyzed using clustering techniques, extracting the data from the database in consideration of pre-defined thresholds in terms of minimum emission levels in order to employ standard clustering techniques. A dynamic examination of the general development within an area can be obtained using fuzzy clustering techniques to identify possible changes and to evaluate the effectiveness of environmental actions like, e.g., the implementation of the emission badge in Germany.

A mobile environmental monitoring system based on mobile vehicles, mobile communications and multi-sensoral arrays does not yet exist. Such a system can help to reduce the high expenditures of existing monitoring and surveillance systems. Dynamic mathematical clustering methods are needed. Additionally, a new quality of monitoring and observation of the environment can be reached as the system can be repositioned any time to any region whenever necessary.

Nevertheless, the approach needs to be tested in a real-world application and the results have to be evaluated and compared to other monitoring techniques. This practical test application is planned for the near future. In 2010, the systematic approach will be empirically evaluated in the region of Hildesheim.

REFERENCES

Angstenberger, L. (2000). *Dynamic Fuzzy Pattern Recognition*. Doctoral dissertation, RWTH Aachen. Retrieved July 18, 2007, from http://darwin.bth.rwth-aachen.de/opus/volltexte/2001/167/pdf/ Angstenberger_Larisa.pdf

Bezdek, J. C. (1981). *Pattern Recognition with Fuzzy Objective Function Algorithms*. New York: Plenum.

Borgelt, C. (2005). *Prototype-based Classification and Clustering*. Professorial dissertation, Otto-von-Guericke-Universität Magdeburg. Retrieved March 07, 2008, from http://edoc.bibliothek.uni-halle.de/receive/HALCoRe_document_00005337?lang=de

Bramer, M. (2007). *Principles of Data Mining*. London: Springer.

ChipSensors™ (2009). Retrieved November 18, 2009, from www.chipsensors.de

Cios, K. J., Pedrycz, W., Swiniarski, R. W., & Kurgan, L. A. (2007). *Data Mining – A Knowledge Discovery Approach*. Berlin, Heidelberg, New York: Springer.

Compamed (2009). Retrieved November 18, 2009, from www.compamed.de ecoTech (2009). Umwelt-Monitoring: enviLog Maxi Datenlogger. Retrieved November 18, 2009, from www.echotech-bonn.de/de/produkte/monitordaten/envilogmaxi.html

European Space Agency (2009). *Earthnet Online*. Retrieved November 18, 2009, from envisat.esa.int

Hochschule Karlsruhe. (2009). Retrieved November 18, 2009, from www.hs-karlsruhe.de

Höppner, F., Klawonn, F., Kruse, R., & Runkler, T. (1999). *Fuzzy Cluster Analysis – Methods for Classification, Data Analysis and Image Recognition*. Chichester: Wiley.

Krishnapuram, R., & Keller, J. M. (1993). A Possibilistic Approach to Clustering. *IEEE Transactions on Fuzzy Systems*, *1*(2), 98–110. doi:10.1109/91.227387

Krittwattanakhorn, J., Bauersfeld, M. L., Kovacs, A., Mescheder, U., Müller, B., Rademacher, S., & Wöllenstein, J. (2006). Optimization of Platinum Adhesion in Electochemical Etching Process for Multisensor Systems. In Enoksson, P. (Ed.), *Proceedings of Eurosensors 20th Anniversary* (*Vol. II*, pp. 376–377). Göteborg, Sweden.

Mescheder, U., Kritwattanakhorn, J., Kovacs, A., Müller, B., Ament, C., & Peter, A. (2007). Sensorarray zur Luftqualitätsmessung. *Horizonte*, *30*, 3–8.

Minke, A., Ambrosi, K., & Hahne, F. (2009). Approach for Dynamic Problems in Clustering. In I. N. Athanasiadis (Ed.), *Proceedings of the 4th International ICSC Symposium on Information Technologies in Environmental Engineering* (pp. 373-386). Berlin: Springer.

Neumann, A. (2008). *Fuzzy Clustering in Dynamic Problems*. Unpublished technical report: Universität Hildesheim.

Niedersächsisches Ministerium für Umwelt und Klimaschutz. (2009). Luftmessnetz Niedersachsen (LÜN). Retrieved November 18, 2009, from http://www.umwelt.niedersachsen.de/master/C21884990_N41769409_L20_D0_I598.html

Satpix (2009). NOAA Satellitenbilder aus Tolk. Retrieved November 18, 2009, from www.satpix.de

Technidata, A. G. (2009). NMC Messzentrale für Umweltmonitoring. Retrieved November 18, 2009, from www.technidata.de/envinet/documents/ENVINET_NMC_D_000.pdf

Timm, H. (2002). *Fuzzy-Clusteranalyse: Methoden zur Exploration von Daten mit fehlenden Werten sowie klassifizierten Daten*. Doctoral dissertation, Otto-von-Guericke-Universität Magdeburg. Retrieved July 25, 2006, from http://iws.cs.uni-magdeburg.de/~htimm/data/dissertation.pdf

Timm, H., Borgelt, C., Döring, C., & Kruse, R. (2001). Fuzzy Cluster Analysis with Cluster Repulsion. In: *Proceedings of the European Symposium on Intelligent Technologies*. Aachen: Verlag Mainz, CD-ROM.

Umweltbundesamt (2008). Daten zur Umwelt 2008. Retrieved November 18, 2009 from www.umweltbundesamt-daten-zur-umwelt.de

Umweltbundesamt (2009). Luftdaten. Retrieved August 13, 2009, from www.env-it.de/ luftdaten/trsyear.fwd?comp=PM1&state=UB&year=2009&month=8&boxed=1&order=0 umwelt-monitoring-systeme (2009). Retrieved November 18, 2009, from www.ums-muc.de

Voigt, K., Welzl, G., Brüggemann, R., & Pudenz, S. (2002). *Bewertungsansatz von Umweltmonitoring-Informationssystemen in Ballungsräumen. Umweltwissenschaften und Schadstoff-Forschung*. Berlin, Heidelberg: Springer.

Chapter 12
Structuring Information for Industrial Environmental Management

Raul Carlson
Viktoria Institute, Sweden

ABSTRACT

Environmental management of an organization is to a large extent about management, interpretation and development of environmental information. Therefore, for any organization to have a functioning environmental management system a matching well-functioning environmental information system is needed. To develop such a well-functioning information system it is necessary to structure all the relevant dimensions, ranging from indicators, reporting paths, material management and process management. This chapter provides an introduction to the structuring of the environmental information system.

INTRODUCTION

This chapter gives an introduction for information systems developers to the specifics of structuring information systems elements for industrial environmental management. Structuring of the different parts of an information system is a natural part of planning and developing information systems. This is equally true if the system is built from scratch or whether it is the construction of new applications for existing information systems. This chapter gives a crucial briefing for the building of any environmental information system. It is crucial since the structuring of an information system is fundamental for

- the technical and logic functionality of the components of the whole system
- the applicability of the system in an organizational context and
- the usefulness of the information system for each intended user.

The structuring of information is also a major part of the system development projects, where much intellectual effort is focused during project

DOI: 10.4018/978-1-61520-981-1.ch012

phases when commissioners and end users have no tangible results to refer to or reflect upon. The information structuring parts of projects therefore suffer from a scarce access to competence and knowledge from end users and domain experts. This chapter intends to fill this knowledge gap by providing guidance to information systems developers when structuring key elements of industrial environmental management systems as well as when structuring entire environmental control systems for corporations.

In the following sections different information system structure issues are introduced and presented, ranging from environmental performance indicators, evaluation methods, material properties, processes, reporting models and architectural principles. The chapters summarizes with presenting a general framework for how to structure environmental information systems.

SCOPE OF THE ENVIRONMENTAL INFORMATION SYSTEM

There are several reasons why a company or other organization publishes environmental reports, keeps environmental records and acquires environmental information. Major reasons are (Taprantzi, 2001; Svending, 2003; Carlson, 2005; Erlandsson, 2006):

- Legislative compliance
- Management and control of production facilities
- Strategic business analyses of production, and of sales and supply markets
- Design of products and production facilities
- Recording of properties and contents of sold items and goods
- Procurement and purchase support and requirements

A specific organization can have one, several or all these reasons to handle environmental information. If it has only one or two of these reasons it may not be necessary to establish integrated and coordinated, compatible environmental information structures, but if the organization has several or all these reasons to handle environmental information it may have much to gain from by putting more emphasis on the information structuring. This text has the ambition to support those who structure complex environmental information systems, but it also gives good guidance when developing less complex systems.

ENVIRONMENTAL INFORMATION STRUCTURES

Industrial Environmental Information Systems in Practice

Five different and practical mini-scenarios from industry introduce this chapter on environmental information structures. These scenarios are picked from real industry projects and are chosen because they represent typical situations when the questions of a more advanced view of environmental information structuring needs to be introduced into the environmental management system in an organization.

Corporate Sustainability Report

Environmental coordinators acquire information from production to compile the corporate sustainability report. The report will eventually describe a number of sustainability performance parameters about the overall production capacity of the company. The production units are geographically distributed and due to technological differences and differences in nature the environmental issues at each different production unit are very different. Major problems associated with the task of compiling a corporate sustainability report therefore are:

- **Performance indicators**: To define the common sustainability performance parameters of the technologically and environmentally heterogeneous organization.
- **Data acquisition**: To acquire the necessary information from measurement equipment and logs at the different production units.
- **Reporting**: To compile the heterogeneous data into a common credible format.

Further details about this are described in (Carlson, 2004b; Taprantzi, 2001; Svending, 2003).

Product Design

A company seeks to design its products towards better environmental performance. Since products can impact the environment in many different ways the product design has many environmental improvement possibilities. Four examples of environmental perspectives on product design are:

- **Life cycle perspective**: To acquire the overall environmental knowledge about all materials and functions of the product, from raw material extraction to scrapping and waste management.
- **Production processes**: The environmental production perspective, which means to understand the environmental consequences on the production processes resulting from different design choices.
- **Material data and environmental risk**: Chemical risks and other environmentally related risks need to be handled with specific risk analytical approaches, such as by the help of detailed analysis of the material and chemical contents and study of how the product is produced, transported, handled and treated at end of life.
- **Material data and recyclability**: There are often environmental benefits from recycling materials or energy content of products. Some of the environmental benefits from this are reduction of waste and a reduced need to extract natural resources. By choosing recyclable material, by designing the product so that it can be recycled and by providing information about material content and recycling are important aspects of the product design process.

Further details about this are described in (Carlson, 2005), and experiences from developing prototype information systems for handling many different environmental management tasks with a single information source is described in (Carlson, 2006a; Carlson, 2006b).

Green Marketing

To regain green investment costs a company needs to tell its market about its environmental efforts and improvements. Such environmental statements can either be general green claims without facts to back them up, or they can be backed with environmental facts that the customers considers to be important, such as the carbon footprint of the company or its products, the recyclability of the product or its content of renewable material. There are also a number of eco labeling, eco categorization and eco performance systems that communicate some environmental properties of products. Facts that are communicated in these ways to the market needs to be prepared for different validity tests that may be performed by competitors, NGOs or authorities. Already at acquisition and through the compilation and reporting the underlying data need to be made available for review for a claim to be an effective statement to the market. Hence, major issues for fact-based green marketing are:

- **Environmental facts**: To understand and define the environmental facts that makes sense to customers.
- **Data acquisition**: To acquire, compile and report data that can be transparently reviewed.

Further details about this are described in (Carlson, 2001).

Environmental Evaluation

A company is set to evaluate how it products and processes relates to the environment, both in terms of how well it performs in relation to some goals and benchmarks as well as in terms of how the products and processes impacts the environment. In order to do so it needs to perform environmental evaluation. There are many different tools for evaluating the environmental performance or impact of production processes, product life cycles, products, businesses, materials and projects. Each of these different tools is basically related to the material environmental impact from resource use, waste generation, emissions and environmental risks of the business. Hence, there are needs not only for the databases with basic data, such as materials, emissions and energy efficiency data, but also data about the natural environment, such as ecologic sensitivity data, emissions dispersion data and data about how to prioritize between different environmental consequences. It is also necessary to have information about how to perform the different environmental evaluations, either in the form of for example manuals or standards or in the form of software that automatically performs much of the evaluation algorithms. In summary what is needed for environmental evaluation:

- **Material data**: Data about substances, processes or products that are to be environmentally evaluated.
- **Consequence/Dispersion data**: Data about how decisions inside the company may spread into physical changes to the eco systems, such as how a small change in the design may lead to increased or decreased resource extraction or how air or water emissions are dispersed throughout the local, regional or global environment.
- **Ecological data**: Data about how natural resources, eco systems or human health may be impacted as consequence from the business activities.
- **Value data:** Data about how different environmental impact may be prioritized, as for example natural severity, cultural value or economic value.
- **Knowledge base or procedural tools:** Guidelines, documents or software that describe how the evaluation is to be performed.

Further details about these examples are described in (Tivander, 2004a; Tivander, 2004b).

Mandates to Make a Difference

A company wishes to stimulate the natural environmental concern among their employees, in order to increase the general environmental performance of the company and to maintain the employee´s motivation. Any employee within an organization may identify environmental possibilities. Environmental coordinators, product designers, procurement specialists, machine operators and office clerks can carry or invent ideas about big or small potentials to improve the environmental performance of the company and of its products. But most such ideas will not lead to real environmental improvements unless employees have mandates to make a difference. For example

- **Environmental coordinators** may experience difficulties with arguing for the installation of waste water cleaning equipment unless the company director has clearly communicated the degree of priority for the company's environmental proactive profile.
- In the choice between different product features the **product design team** will

eventually decide on those features that are in line with the explicit company product strategies.

- The **procurement specialist** may lack the environmental procurement guidelines unless such guidelines have been developed during the product design or by the environmental management team.
- The **machine operator** may use an excess of lubrication oils, cleaning solvents and energy unless she is given the clear mandates to prioritize minimized use and energy efficient machine operation over production speed.
- The **office clerks** may prioritize energy efficient office lighting, Energy star computers, double side printers and a more efficient office temperature if these priorities are mandated from the management.

For these environmental possibilities to happen in reality it is not sufficient for the company board and directors to say that environment is a big thing for this company, but to make things happen it is as important to break down each environmental issue into target areas and responsibilities as it is to break down the budget into target areas and responsible persons. Else environmental intentions will not be fulfilled by anyone. Hence, the board and directors need to decide on which environmental issues to materialize and how success shall be measured, and to communicate responsibilities and mandates down through the organization, and to request feedback reports from each unit. This is the way to turn a decision into a physical difference, and it requires a well-designed information system.

Essentials Information Structures of Industrial Environmental Information Systems

The previous section, *Industrial environmental information systems in practice*, gave examples of the roles and functions of industrial environmental information systems in practical use. These examples provide the context to this subchapter, the essential structures of the industrial environmental information systems. The examples showed that it is crucial to be able to describe the environmental performance of products, material and processes, that it is essential to perform environmental evaluation in order to do so, and that this requires information handling, from data acquisition, through compilation, to reporting. These are the essential elements of any environmental information systems, and they will be further elaborated in this subchapter.

Five different information structures need to be taken into account to effectively manage the environmental performance of an organization and its business or service activities. These information structures are described in the following, and the examples refer to the previous section *Industrial environmental information systems in practice*:

- **Environmental performance**: The environmental performance of activities, projects, processes and products. In the previous section the practical aspects of deciding which environmental issues to deal with was exemplified, with regards to which issues to present in the corporate sustainability report, which criteria to address in the product design, what to express in the green marketing statements, and which environmental issues to prioritize and mandate throughout the organization. The importance of deciding how to measure the environmental performance cannot be underestimated. It is essential, and it sets the frame for the entire environmental information system.
- **Environmental evaluation**: The environmental impact assessment and the evaluation of its significance to the business. In the previous section the practical aspects of environmental evaluation was exemplified, particularly considering the un-

derstanding of the consequences of material use and dispersion of emissions, and how this leads to resource use, ecological impacts or health issues, as well as how to prioritize avoidance of different consequences. Environmental evaluation is important when choosing which environmental issues to prioritize, and it is important to the overall business strategies and to guide business decisions, such as product design choices and choices about production process improvements.

- **Products and material**: The products and the purchased material at a level of detail that is sufficient from the environmental viewpoint. In the previous section the practical aspects of the environmental significance of products and material are exemplified in several ways, regarding the product design, regarding green marketing, regarding environmental evaluation and regarding the mandates for product designers to make a difference. The examples show the many-faceted necessity to have information about the products and all materials and substances in a good structure.
- **Requests and reporting**: The information request and information reporting paths within the organization and its business responsibility domains. Environmental reporting needs to be made for many different reasons, towards many different target groups and about different aspects of a company. The previous section exemplifies by the external reporting needs from the corporate sustainability report and green marketing statements. The previous section also describes the necessity to communicate the environmental targets, responsibilities and mandates as well as the feedback from the different parts of the organization. An effective environmental management needs to succeed both with its external market communication and with its internal environmental reporting routines.
- **Processes**: The process monitoring and reporting, including production plants, transportation, supply chains and full life cycle overview. The previous section exemplifies with describing how corporate environmental reporting generally describes the environmental performance of production units. The subchapter also describes that life cycle assessment is performed to evaluate the total environmental performance of products, and that today the carbon footprint value is often requested. Hence, today it is important to keep a good structure of the environmental information about both the production units within the organization and the processes upstream throughout the supply chain, and often also downstream to waste management and recycling systems.

The coming five sections presents the most important information structures needed when establishing an industrial environmental information system. Section *Environmental performance* presents the information structures needed to describe the environmental performance of the organization and its activities, functions, products, production plants, supply chain and for its products in use and during end of life. Section *Environmental evaluation* presents the general structural elements necessary to evaluate and assess the impacts from the environmental loads invoked by the organization, such as emissions, resource depletion or a combination of such loads. Section *Products and material* presents the necessity to distinguish between two different ways to structure environmental data about materials and components, based on whether the properties may be considered stable under normal circumstances or whether the environmental properties are clearly based on situation. Section *Requests and reporting* presents the general structure for producing any piece of environmental information, regardless of whether it is a simple figure, an advanced corporate environmental report or a life cycle assessment report. Section *Processes* presents the structural elements of information to describe any type of processes for the purpose of environmental systems analyses.

Environmental Performance

Measurement of the environmental performance of an organization is based on a definition of what the *environment* means for the organization. The meaning of *environment* for an organization is defined by the identification and acknowledgement of its *environmental aspects*. Environmental aspects may be for example electricity consumption, use of non-renewable resources, waste generation, emissions or production of environmentally harmful products. Having identified and acknowledged which environmental aspects are most significant for the organization the next step is to define how to monitor these aspects. This is done by defining quantifiable indicators for each aspect. Some aspects have one indicator, while other aspects may need several indicators and in some cases several aspects can be handled by a combined indicator. By having defined the indicators the head and tail of the organization's environmental information system are defined; all information requests invokes the necessity to acquire data from some monitored indicator, and all data reporting results in the quantification of such an indicator.

Figure 1 gives a simplified view of five key functions in a business where different indicators can be used to measure the environmental performance of different parts and aspects of the organization. The five key functions are chosen from the authors experience from working together with many industrial companies. Experience have shown that successful companies tend to spend most their environmental focus on these five areas, or functions, and when they do they are successful at implementing real change in environmental performance and green business success.

The five key functions are the *Strategic board*, the *Product and business development*, the *Plant operation*, the *Sales and marketing* and the *Procurement*. Each of these functions can play a key role in the environmental performance of the entire business of the organization if they are individually monitored and controlled by the aid of well-designed indicators for their partial environmental performance. In the following a number of example indicators are presented. These

Figure 1. Examples of how the environmental performance of the strategic and operative functions of an organization may be measured by environmental performance indicators

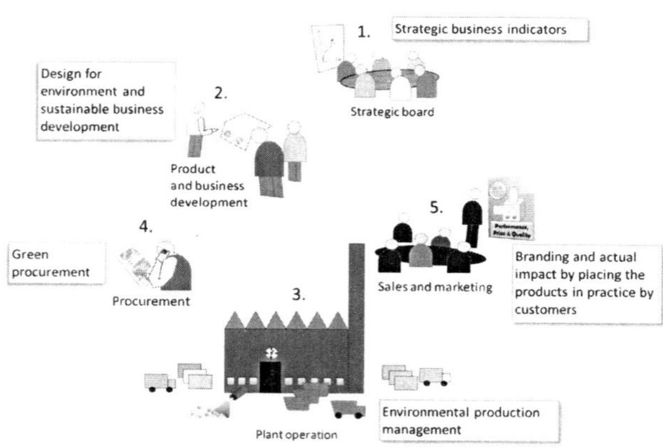

examples of indicators are chosen to represent a wide range of environmental responsibilities while also being both relevant and realistic in many industries. Not all these indicators can apply to one and the same company or business, but they are chosen to exemplify the generic idea of how board members, procurers, sales and marketing people, product and business developers and environmental production coordinators are given responsibilities and mandates within a generic and sound business. A specific company implements these responsibilities and mandates in different ways. These exemplified indicators are not intended to be meaningful or significant outside the company or even outside of the organizational function where they are used. They are therefore not intended to be compatible with for example the Global Reporting Initiative indicators (GRI, 2009), which are intended for external reporting. The example indicators do however sometimes match with the GRI indicators.

Each of these example indicators serves as a structural element of the environmental information system for an environmental management system. Each indicator implies a cascade of requirements on the information system that will have to be established in order to quantify its performance value.

1. Strategic board; Examples of strategic business environmental performance indicators are:
   - % reduction of carbon footprint / turnover
   - % reduction of environmental risk / turnover
   - % increase of eco-efficiency

2. Product and business development; Examples of environmental performance indicators for design of material products are:
   - % increase of energy efficiency of product
   - % increase of energy efficiency for production
   - % increase of energy efficiency for end of life
   - % increase of energy efficiency pre-production
   - % increase of renewable material/ton
   - % increase of recyclable material/ton

   Examples of environmental performance indicators for sustainable business development are:
   - % increase of energy efficiency compared with competing product
   - % reduction of carbon footprint compared with competing product
   - % reduction of carbon footprint /aftermarket value

3. Plant operation; Examples of environmental performance indicators for environmental production management are:
   - % reduction of energy consumption/ turnover
   - % reduction of waste/turnover
   - % reduction of emission X/turnover (where 'X' is a specific emission, such as nitrous dioxide or dust)

4. Sales and marketing; Examples of environmental performance indicators for the branding and by successfully placing environmentally better products in use are:
   - % increased share of estimated green market
   - % reduction of green products/total sales
   - % reduction of carbon footprint /total market

5. Procurement; Examples of environmental performance indicators for green procurement are:
   - % increase of recycled material/ton
   - % increase of suppliers with EMS

- % reduction of carbon footprint /ton received goods
- % reduction of carbon footprint / tonkm sales
- % reduction of carbon footprint /ton waste

To compile a quantitative environmental performance value for any of the example indicators it is necessary to have a good definition of which data is needed for each one, and how the compilation is done for each one. For example:

- Carbon footprint is calculated as a life cycle assessment with specific and well-defined system boundaries and only carbon dioxide and carbon dioxide equivalent emissions. See particularly section *Processes*.
- Corporate environmental risk may be calculated in different ways, such as by estimating the risks that environmental accidents occur at any production plant, that some newly bought facilities have hidden environmental problems, or that the products will turn up as environmental problems at the market or end of life treatment. Reduction of corporate environmental risk would mean to acquire better information about the environmental risk situation and to take measures against identified risks. See particularly sections *Environmental evaluation* and *Processes*.
- Eco-efficiency is a compound measure that describes the relationship between environmental and economic performance. The better the lesser environmental impact and the better the economic result, the higher the eco-efficiency. See particularly section *Environmental evaluation*.
- Increased energy efficiency for a specific system is calculated by defining the system and by measuring the energy needed to perform the function of the system. See particularly section *Processes*.
- Share of renewable material, recyclable material and recycled material may be measured either as average values of typical materials or by making specific assessments for the materials considered. See particularly section *Products and material*.
- Amounts of different emissions are calculated by monitoring the emissions in different ways, sometimes by a continuous measurement in furnaces and water outlets, and sometimes as calculation models based on other process parameters, such as fuel consumption and furnace temperature. See particularly section *Requests and reporting* and *Processes*.
- Share of estimated green market can be measured based on the combination of a definition of 'green market', the estimation of the size of this market and the actual market share within this market. See particularly section *Processes*.
- Share of green products sold in comparison to total sales is calculated by first defining 'green product' and to calculate a ratio between such products sold and the rest of the products sold. See particularly section *Requests and reporting*.
- Percentage of suppliers with an EMS (Environmental Management System) is calculated on basis of what the suppliers respond to the question as to whether they have an EMS or not. See particularly section *Requests and reporting*.

These examples show that for an organization to measure the environmental performance based on environmental performance indicators it is essential to have well-structured environmental information, including environmental measurement at production plants, definitions of green products, materials databases, life cycle databases for carbon footprint measurement and more, and to have this information in such form and order that the indicator values can be readily produced, normalized to different economic data, and presented and compared as necessary.

Case studies and methodologies concerning environmental performance indicators can be read in (Carlson, 2002; Carlson, 2004a; Carlson, 2004b; Carlson, 2009). The international standard ISO 14031 is also recommended (ISO, 1999), though this version of the standard is now old and is currently being updated in within the International Organization for Standardization, ISO, to be released around 2011.

Environmental Evaluation

The previous section describes ways to express and measure the environmental performance in different dimensions, exemplified as energy and material efficiency, emissions of different substances and share of green market. It is unusual that an organization needs to measure only one of these environmental aspects, and it is more common to monitor several aspects with different environmental significance and caused by different business activities. When the indicator is measured for regulatory purposes it is more common that there is threshold value for the individually monitored aspect that must not be exceeded. The value itself is not negotiable or open for tradeoff with other environmental loads. But for the needs of continuous improvement of an environmental management system it is necessary to be able to make tradeoffs between different environmental impacts. Environmental control and improvement through monitoring single indicators is only sufficient when no tradeoffs can be done between different aspects. An example of a tradeoff situation is when it may be necessary to increase the electricity consumption to decrease emissions (electric filtering). Tradeoff implies policy discussions and subjectivity. To which degree is it acceptable to increase one environmental impact to reduce another?

For evaluation of the significance of different environmental impacts to each other, it is necessary to have support tools for environmental evaluation. Depending on business and on the type of environmental impact such support tools can be very different, ranging from toxicological laboratories that produce decision support and risk management advice to simple rules of thumb. Regardless of the actual complexity of this evaluation support, it is intended to provide guidance on how to evaluate and prioritize between different important environmental aspects. The result of the decision support may be quantitative, intended to rate different indicators to each other, or it may be categorical which means that if for example a threshold value is met a certain raw material needs to replaced by a less harmful substance in the product design.

Environmental evaluation generally consists of a number of steps. The steps need not be made in exactly the same order as described here. The numbering is made only for easier referencing in the text. Some things need to go before others, but this is mainly obvious and the consecutive necessities are therefore not further stressed here. The evaluation is a systematic procedure starting with defining an entity to evaluate, traversing through steps of analysis and synthesis, and resulting in an informed evaluation. This is described in more detailed in the following.

1. Identify key environmental protection areas, such as climate change, ozone depletion, human health, biodiversity, clean water, resource depletion etc.
2. Identify the environmental aspects, i.e. which components and raw material, which energy demanding processes, which waste and which emissions, which products and business processes that contributes to the key environmental protection areas. Examples are energy use, air emission of nitrous oxides, generation of waste, an energy demanding product etc.
3. Assess how each different environmental aspect impacts the different environmental

protection areas. This is generally done in two steps:

a. Classify the contribution from each aspect, which means to identify which environmental protection area is impacted by which aspect. For example, energy use contributes both to resource depletion and to climate change, emission of nitrous oxide may contribute to impact on acidification, biodiversity, agricultural productivity and human health, generation of waste can contribute to increased waste landfill and an increase in resource depletion etc.
b. Measure the contribution from each aspect. The contribution onto the different environmental protection areas are measured in different ways, depending on aspect, protection area and other parameters. For example, emissions the impact from energy use on resource depletion depends on which natural resources that are used to produce the energy, and the contribution on impact on human health impact from emissions of nitrous oxide depends on where the nitrous oxide is emitted and under what circumstances, etc.
c. Estimate the environmental consequence on each relevant environmental protection area. This is a complex task, which means to combine information from step b with information about the environment. This will produce information that describes how the business actually impacts the environment.

4. Weight different impacts, which mean that different environmental impacts such as resource depletion, landfill, loss of biodiversity, climate change and human health are compared with each other and are given different relative importance. This weighting is generally not done within the organization, but is a matter for scientists, stakeholders and political groups.
5. Prioritize efforts within the organization. When having assessed the environmental significance of each environmental aspect, through steps 3 and 4 it is necessary for the management of the company to prioritize between the different environmental aspects and to place them in the regular business priorities, in order for the organization to move in coordination. It is necessary for the personnel in their daily operation to know how to prioritize between reduction of energy consumption and speed, between waste management and hygiene, between emission reduction and costs etc.

Each of these five steps of environmental evaluation is in itself an information entity in an

Figure 2. The five major information entities of environmental evaluation

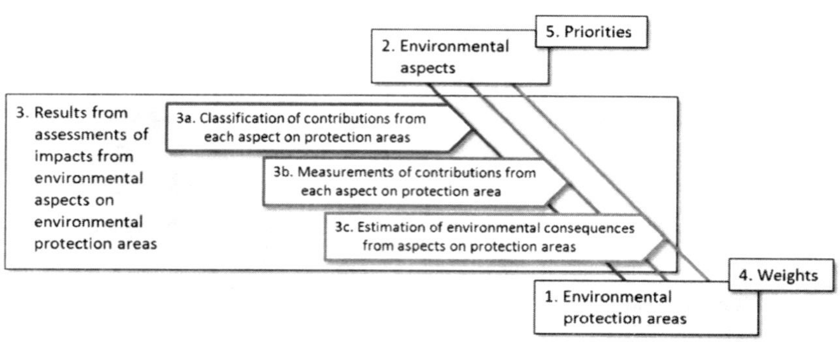

industrial environmental information system. Depending on actual situation a specific entity may be more or less detailed or more or less distinct from the other entities. A further detailed study of different evaluation methods would lead too far for an introductory text.

The international standard ISO 14044 gives guidance about how to structure information about environmental evaluation (ISO, 2006). Further reading about environmental evaluation from the viewpoint of information structuring can be read in (Carlson, 2002; Erixon, 2003; Tivander, 2004a; Tivander, 2004b).

Products and Material

A major part of the environmental impact from an organization originates from the product or service that the organization delivers and from the material and energy that the organization takes in for its production. In order to minimize this environmental impact it is necessary to know which impacts that are caused by the product and by its components and materials. This is particularly difficult for companies and organizations that produce or trade with complex products, materials or services. For this purpose it is necessary to establish databases of materials and their environmental significance and potential impacts, over the life cycle, from raw material extraction to waste management.

There are different ways to structure this information but generally it can be categorized into two types; *Stable properties of materials* and *Scenario based materials properties* (Dewulf, 2001).

Stable Properties of Materials

Environmental properties of materials should as far as possible be structured similarly as any other property of materials, such as mechanical properties, corrosive properties and density. This is possible for all relatively stable properties, such as toxic properties within the range of the use of the product, renewable, recyclable and some other relatively stable properties. This is relatively simple and straightforward, and the three main questions are 1) which properties to consider, 2) which format to use for the data, and 3) which data quality level to settle with.

Scenario Based Material Properties

Many environmental properties of material are not stable, but depend on situation and circumstance. Examples are transport distances, waste production, actual recycled material, etc. In some situations it may not be possible to find a justifiable typical or average value to denote as material property, it is instead necessary to deal with this in some other way. To build up information structures that enables data storage and/or modeling of different situations, i.e. the role and behavior of materials in different processes, scenarios and environments. Examples are life cycle models and scenarios for risk assessment. See also section *Processes*. Setting up these types of databases have several challenges, ranging from the system boundary of the different processes described in the process data, nomenclatures for different scenario types, and how to relate different material scenarios to different complex products.

An exhaustive and encompassing description of environmental data about products is given in (Carlson, 2005).

Requests and Reporting

Regardless of intentions and choices of performance indicators, an environmental management system is only as good as the infrastructure of its information requests and reporting paths. A defined architecture that links each information request with the full reporting paths all the way to the data and information sources is needed.

The structure of such information architecture establishes a channel that enables reporting between the physical reality and the reality of the environmental management. The architecture works well if it is open and compatible with general organizational functions for acquiring, preparing and using data, both within the organization and towards its suppliers, customers and other stakeholders while also ensuring transparency and data quality maintenance.

One structure that has these properties is the PHASES model (Carlson, 2000) which has six distinctly separate phases. These phases can be viewed either from the information-push or the information-pull-perspective. From the information-pull-perspective, the six consecutive phases may be presented as:

- **Concise request:** Environmental information is requested for a purpose, such as the monitoring of legislative conformance, reporting of environmental business performance or for the reporting of the result of a life cycle assessment or risk assessment.
- **Compilation of system report:** Compile and produce the environmental information report for example the plant or the product, the product life cycle or the risk scenarios associated with a specific substance.
- **Compilation of information elements:** Compile the necessary information items that are needed to reply to the request about for example the plant, the product, the product life cycle or the substance.
- **Perform statistics:** Prepare statistically meaningful information items from raw data, i.e. sort out irrelevant, unnecessary or spurious data, treat data gaps, produce ranges and statistical width etc.
- **Acquire raw data:** Acquire the data, which for example might mean to read data from measurements, calculate estimations, take notes from experts, haul in data from questionnaires or transcribe data from literature.
- **Define data items:** Describe the meaning of the data that is required, in terms of the definition of the measurement from where the data is taken or in terms of the intended meaning of an estimated, guessed or transcribed data value.

The structure can be regarded from either the pull (1-6, then 6-1) or the push (only 6-1) In general, the pull perspective is the more highly recommended for environmental management systems, but it is acknowledged that there may also be situations where environmental data needs to be pushed up through the organization.

Detailed descriptions about requesting and reporting environmental data within organizations are presented in (Carlson, 2000; Carlson, 2001).

Processes

The environmental impact from a business does not originate only from the processes owned by the business itself, but are the results from decisions taken within the business regarding for example suppliers, materials and components and regarding waste management routines. Such decisions imply choices of upstream and downstream processes and their environmental impacts. To which degree the business needs to take these aspects into account depends partly on the choice of responsibility accepted by the company, and partly on external drivers, such as customer interests, requirements from financiers and other important stakeholders. If the management of a company takes such responsibility they also need to handle information not only about the processes they own inside the organization, but also processes upstream and downstream from the business operations.

Monitoring of the environmental impact from the processes throughout the entire life cycle of the products and services of the organization can be structured so that the information can be interpreted and analyzed by the same tools regardless of whether the production facilities are localized at the same geographical place or not, whether the production is outsourced or not, and whether the production is made by other organizations upstream or downstream the supply chain. It shall also be possible to describe transports, waste management, use and service by the same compatible process data, in order for the organization to optimize the entire life cycle of its full business. One example is the so called 'carbon footprint', which is a method used to measure the aggregated carbon emissions from raw material extraction to final product by acquiring information about all processes involved in the life cycle.

The monitoring of the environmental impact from processes follows the same general structures as described in sections *Industrial environmental information systems in practice* and *Requests and reporting*. Point 3 in the list of indicators in the section *Environmental performance* exemplifies three environmental performance indicators for the operation of production plants. In order to calculate these performance indicators it is necessary to monitor, acquire, prepare and report the underlying data. In these cases the underlying data are:

- Sources of energy consumed by the production plant, including oil, electricity, coal, wood pellets etc.
- Waste generated by the production plant, probably including packaging waste and spill as well as hazardous waste, while possibly distinguishing between waste for landfill, waste for recycling and other types of end of life waste treatment.
- Emissions from the production plant. Which emissions that are actually monitored depend on types of processes, regulatory requirements and policy decisions. Toxic and acidifying air emissions, biologically and chemically active water emission and long lived soil emissions that may leak down to the ground water are among the common priorities. Examples are emissions from incineration of coal, wood and oil, emissions from different types of surface coatings, heavy metal emissions from mineral industries and oils and fuels from machinery and pump installations.

There may also be other environmental aspects to monitor about a process, such as the input of components and raw material, the production rate, the land area usage or quantifications of different environmental risks.

When storing information about a process in databases for the purpose of environmental analysis and assessments, the following items are crucial to take into consideration (Carlson, 1995; ISO, 2002; ELCD, 2009):

- A description of what the process produces, since this describes to which degree the process is needed at all.
- The system boundaries, in terms of sub systems that are inside and that are outside of the boundary.
- A justification for what is inside and what is left out from the system boundary.
- A description of the specifics about the process, such as certain technology, certain time validity or anomalies to regular conditions for this specific process.
- A list of all monitored inflows and outflows into and out from the process, together with quantitative data about each inflow or outflow. Each such quantity should be produced by the support of the structure presented in section *Requests and reporting*.

Section *Requests and reporting* describes the structure for producing each environmental data item and for compiling them into an environmental data report for a process. If to report about several processes, for a corporate report, for an LCA study or to compile some industrial average environmental profile, that structure can be used iteratively at consecutively higher levels so that the 6th phase is the definition of the system boundary of an entire process etc.

The report (Flemström, 2004) describes how process analysis, like LCA, can be integrated with risk analysis of inputs and products of the processes.

THE FRAMEWORK FOR STRUCTURING INFORMATION

The previous subchapters have presented the key elements of information structures of industrial environmental information systems. By getting these elements right during the build-up of such an information system, it is likely that the system will be both technically and scientifically functioning (with regards to how it describes the environmental impact and performance of the organization and its activities and products). This subchapter provides additional guidance about how to ensure that the information system also becomes effective and makes real environmental improvements. By following the principles presented in this subchapter the information system can also become understandable and meaningful to its intended users, it can relate to the economic business reality and to the physical reality of the environmental issues. It can also be based on a realistic quality maintenance principle, which can ensures that the data has a sufficient quality level at all times of the life time of the information system.

In theory environmental management of an organization needs only the information structures that have been described in the subchapter *Environmental Information Structures*. These are sufficient to establish strategic targets, control the material and the processes, to evaluate the environmental impact, to weight impacts and to prioritize aspects, to measure performance and to have a controlled way to acquire and report all information. But in reality it is always necessary to customize these information structures for the needs and requirements for any specific organization. To support the practical structuring of information for the environmental management of industrial systems a practical and pragmatic framework has been developed. The framework points out four fundamental principles to apply when structuring environmental information:

- **Ontology:** Establish a concrete reference to the physical reality. This means that information shall be structured so that there is a transparent path between the information item and the physical reality which the information item addresses. For example if a corporate environmental report states that the company has reduced its greenhouse gas emission by 20%, it shall be possible to trace all figures back to the different physical greenhouse gas emission sources, such as the actual electricity providers and the actual transport routes or even vehicles before and after the reduction.
- **Understandability and meaningfulness:** Ensure that the information is understood by its intended users. This means for example that if it is not evident that the intended information user understands what is meant by the term 'greenhouse gas' and why it is important, then this needs to be handled with in some way. It can be handled by educating the users or by changing the information so that it instead is presented as for example 'contribution to climate change', if the user understands this better, or to 'reduction of electricity use' if this is easier to understand and more relevant. The information may also be supplied with some comparative information, such as the contribution of greenhouse gas from a similar product.
- **Quality management:** Structure the information so that data and information items are open for quality maintenance and management. This means for example

that it shall be possible to supply core data items with metadata about deviations, data gaps, uncertainties, anomalies and subjective decisions and that aspects which are particularly sensitive to quality deviations are designed particularly carefully. The structuring can for example be made in accordance with the structure described in *Requests and reporting*, and at each of the six phases all significant information shall be made available to the next phase.

- **Economy:** It is difficult to provide only the necessary and the sufficient information structuring. Some information system designers tend to go too far into details, which results in an information system that expects too much information from the users. This may make the system too costly to use. Other information systems designers tend to simplify too far, so that there for example is no place for necessary metadata. Such oversimplified information structures can lead to that data quickly gets old and useless because its background, scope and limitations are soon forgotten since it could not be documented. A good information structure is simplified as far as the application allows, but not more than so.

These four principles are somewhat common sensual, but still too many corporate environmental information systems and environmental information tools are still designed with an obvious lack of one or more of these principles. Many environmental reports are based on pure desktop assessments, without clear references to the physical realities of the organization addressed. This is especially true for complex assessment methods such as life cycle assessment or risk assessment. But it is true also for environmental data systems used as product design support and even for the strategic discussions during business development. It is also still common that the environmental information systems in companies deliver information results that are not at all understood by its target audiences. Examples are technical terms like 'acidification potential', 'eco-toxicity' or 'damage costs'. Whether such terms are practically useful depends on whether they are correctly understood by the intended user or not. Many corporate environmental information systems have been designed on the fly by an environmental expert, often as an MS Excel sheet that has grown organically into a big and complex sheet of data as demands have increased. Too often the short perspectives win before the long term gains in the economic trade-off when designing environmental information systems. This is often true when designing solutions for maintaining data about supply chains and material databases. Such databases may have a high initial cost and to reduce these initial costs organizations often neglect to establish a good structuring of both the acquisition and reporting routines, and of the metadata documentation. Such neglect often results in that the initial investment is eventually found useless when the data shall be reused some years later.

A fuller presentation of the principles for structuring information for the purpose of industrial environmental management is presented in Carlson (2006a). In Carlson (2006b) an example information system prototype is described, and in Pålsson (1998) and Pålsson (2006) guidance about industrial environmental data quality maintenance are presented.

CONCLUSION

This chapter presents the most important information structures to manage the environmental performance of an organization. The structural elements of the indicator function as control metrics for the environmental management. The structure of the environmental evaluation relates business parameters and aspects to their environmental significance. At a day to day basis the environmental information management concerns processes and materials. Each data item need to be logically and transparently produced. The information structuring provides the matrix for the whole corporate environmental information system.

REFERENCES

Carlson, R. (2002). Environmental Performance Indicators. *Insight (American Society of Ophthalmic Registered Nurses)*, *5*(2), 22–23.

Carlson, R. (Ed.). (2005). Establishing common primary data for environmental overview of product life cycles, Users, perspectives, methods, data, and information systems, Swedish EPA-report, Utg 2005-12 Nr 91-620-5523-2. Stockholm, Sweden: Naturvårdsverket.

Carlson, R. (2006a). *Framework For Structuring Information For Environmental Management Of Industrial Systems*. Göteborg, Sweden: CPM, Chalmers University of Technology.

Carlson, R. (2009). Eco-Efficiency. – The conceptual model, the concept model and an operational data structure. [Göteborg, Sweden: CPM, Chalmers University of Technology.]. *CPM-report*, *2009*, 2.

Carlson, R., Erixon, M., Erlandsson, M., Flemström, K., Häggström, S., Pålsson, A. C., & Tivander, J. (2006b). Implementation of integrated environmental information systems [Göteborg, Sweden: CPM, Chalmers University of Technology.]. *CPM Report*, *2006*, 18.

Carlson, R., Erixon, M., Forsberg, P., & Pålsson, A. C. (2001). System for Integrated Business Environmental Information Management. *Advances in Environmental Research*, *5*(4), 369–375. doi:10.1016/S1093-0191(01)00088-0

Carlson, R., Häggström, S., & Pålsson, A. C. (2004a). Policy controlled environmental management work - Manual [Göteborg, Sweden: CPM, Chalmers University of Technology.]. *CPM-report*, *2004*, 11.

Carlson, R., Häggström, S., & Pålsson, A. C. (2004b). Policy controlled environmental management work - Final report [Göteborg, Sweden: CPM, Chalmers University of Technology.]. *CPM-report*, *2004*, 10.

Carlson, R., Löfgren, G., & Steen, B. (1995). *SPINE, A Relation Database Structure for Life Cycle Assessment, IVL-Report B 1227*. Göteborg, Sweden: Swedish Environmental Research Institute.

Carlson, R., & Pålsson, A. C. (2000). *PHASES Information models for industrial environmental control*. Göteborg, Sweden: CPM, Chalmers University of Technology.

Carlson, R., & Pålsson, A. C. (2001). Industrial environmental information management for technical systems. *Journal of Cleaner Production*, *9*, 429–435. doi:10.1016/S0959-6526(01)00002-6

Carlson, R., & Pålsson, A. C. (2002). *Documentation of environmental impact assessment, compatible with SPINE and ISO/TS 14048, IMI-report 2002:1* (2nd ed.). Göteborg, Sweden: Department of Computer Science and Engineering, Industrial Environmental Informatics, Chalmers University of Technology.

Dewulf, W., et al. (2001). *Integrating Eco-Efficiency in Rail Vehicle Design*. Leuven, Belgium: Leuven University Press. *ELCD, European Life Cycle Database*. Retrieved August 10, 2009, from http://lca.jrc.ec.europa.eu/lcainfohub/datasetArea.vm.

Erixon, M., Carlson, R., & Pålsson, A. C. (2003). *Measuring the environmental impact of products. CPM report 2003:1, Swedish Environmental Protection Agency Report 5349*. Stockholm, Sweden: Naturvårdsverket.

Erlandsson, J. (2006). *Company and Product Related Environmental Information Management – A pilot field study*. Göteborg, Sweden: Chalmers University of Technology.

Flemström, K., Carlson, R., & Erixon, M. (2004). *Relationships between Life Cycle Assessment and Risk Assessment – Potentials and Obstacles. Naturvårdsverket Rapport 5379*. Stockholm, Sweden: Naturvårdsverket.

GRI. (2009). *Global Reporting Initiative*. Retrieved November 04, 2009, from http://www.globalreporting.org.

ISO 14031:1999Environmental management – Environmental Performance Evaluation – Guidelines. International Organization for Standardization.

ISO 14044:2006, Environmental management – Life cycle assessment – Requirements and guidelines. International Organization for Standardization.

ISO/TS 14048:2002, Environmental management – Life cycle assessment – Data documentation format. International Organization for Standardization.

Pålsson, A. C., & Carlson, R. (1998). Maintaining Data Quality within Industrial Environmental Information Systems. In H. D. Haasis, K. C. Ranze (Eds.), *Proceedings of the 12th International Symposium 'Computer Science for Environmental Protection', Bremen: Vol. 1. Computer Science for Environmental Protection* (pp. 252-265). Marburg: Metropolis.

Pålsson, A. C., Enqvist, A., Karlsson, G., Loviken, G., Möller, Å., & Nilseng, A. B. (2005). Methodology for handling forest industry environmental data – Method report [Göteborg, Sweden: CPM, Chalmers University of Technology.]. *CPM-report, 2005*, 1.

Pålsson, A. C., Enqvist, A., Karlsson, G., Loviken, G., Möller, Å., & Nilseng, A. B. (2005). Methodology for handling forest industry environmental data – Manual [Göteborg, Sweden: CPM, Chalmers University of Technology.]. *CPM-report, 2005*, 2.

PAS 2050:2008– Specification for the assessment of the life cycle greenhouse gas emissions of goods and services. United Kingdom: British Standards Institute.

Svending, O. (2003). *Industrial Management of Environmental Data – Suggested procedures for internal allocation based on stakeholder needs*. Thesis to earn the degree of licentiate of engineering. Göteborg, Sweden: Chalmers University of Technology.

Taprantzi, A. (2001). *A Systematic Approach for Acquiring Industrial Data and Information for Environmental Applications. Procedures for modelling the communication of environmental inquiries within an organisational structure*. Falun, Sweden: Stora Enso Research, Falun Research Centre.

Tivander, J., Carlson, R., Erixon, M., & Pålsson, A. C. (2004a). OMNIITOX Concept Model Supports Characterisation Modelling for Life Cycle Impact Assessment. *Intl. Journal of LCA*, *9*(5), 289–294. doi:10.1007/BF02979418

Tivander, J., Carlson, R., Erixon, M., & Pålsson, A. C. (2006). IMPRESS integrated data format [Göteborg, Sweden: CPM, Chalmers University of Technology.]. *CPM Report, 2006*, 15.

Tivander, J., Carlson, R., Erlandsson, M., Erixon, M., & Geiron, K. (2004b). *Concept Model for the OMNIITOX Information System Including OMNIITOX Data Format Definition – OMNIITOX project report D20 and D26, 2004, EC contract G1RD-CT-2001-00501*. Göteborg, Sweden: IMI, Chalmers University of Technology.

Chapter 13
A Framework for the Implementation of Eco-Efficient Business Systems

Maha Shakir
Zayed University, UAE

ABSTRACT

Environmental sustainability is an important issue for many individuals, businesses, and governments nowadays. One of the road blocks to sustainable practice is cost, which is an important consideration, particularly for business. The eco-efficiency movement was initiated to address this concern. This chapter reviews the eco-efficiency concept and explains why it is becoming a current issue for many organizations today. The chapter further aims to understand eco-efficient implementation strategies and methods, and the important role that information systems play in creating the required organizational capabilities for these implementations. A framework of eco-efficiency implementation is developed through mapping eco-efficiency strategies to different implementation methods. The framework illustrates how each method is suitable for a particular eco-efficiency strategy. With the understanding that information systems form an integral part of most eco-efficiency implementations, the role of information systems in creating eco-efficiency capabilities is highlighted to enrich the framework.

INTRODUCTION

Environmental sustainability has come to the forefront of issues that are important to individuals, governments, and businesses during the last ten years (Montiel, 2008). There now exists a shared understanding that the earth's resources have been over used during the last one hundred years, that these resources are finite, and that unless current generations proactively address this issue, future generations will suffer (Sutton, 2004). Technological advances supporting mass production in areas such as agriculture, manufacturing, mining, and tourism have greatly contributed to the depletion of the earth's resources. In societies that have encouraged consumerization, technology has been mainly used to exploit resources with little or no consideration of negative

DOI: 10.4018/978-1-61520-981-1.ch013

environmental side effects (Nidumolu, Prahalad & Rangaswami, 2009). Development of technology has been geared to improving product quality, increasing efficiencies, and reducing production costs. This exploitation has become ingrained in common business practice. When environmental sustainability concerns have been raised, the costs of addressing these issues were often prohibitive, particularly in a competitive business environment. This has necessitated a fresh approach to looking at sustainability which is eco-efficiency. Eco-efficiency combines cost reductions with ecological friendliness as a key driver for sustainable development (Lehni, 2000). This presents a major mindset shift in business practice and hence presents key challenges that need to be well managed in order to attain the promised benefits.

Organizations develop different capabilities through the bundling and unbundling of different resources to carry out the tasks they were established to do. The resource based view of the firm posits that a resource is an asset which could be a strength or a weakness (Wernerfelt, 1984). These assets are physical, human, and organizational (Eisenhardt & Martin, 2000). Organizational capabilities cover areas such as human resources, financial, technology, processes, collaboration, etc. A mindset change to embrace eco-efficiency requires building organizational capabilities that support eco-efficient business practice. Information systems are one of the key capabilities to support these changes.

The objectives of this chapter are to:

- Understand the eco-efficiency concept and why eco-efficiency is now an issue for many organizations
- Outline and briefly review different eco-efficiency strategies
- Understand the key features of different types of corporate information systems (CIS)
- Outline and briefly review the different methods used to enact change in organizations
- Explore the role that CIS play in creating organizational capabilities for the implementation of eco-efficient business operations
- Develop a framework for eco-efficiency implementation by mapping eco-efficiency strategies to different implementation methods

The audience for this chapter is undergraduate students, practitioners, and academics. The expected area of study for undergraduate students would be in information systems (IS), information technology (IT), management information systems (MIS), or environmental sustainability. The practitioner audience is generic and is expected to be a mix of IT and non-IT professionals. For undergraduate students and practitioners, the chapter develops a foundation for understanding eco-efficiency and the role of different types of CIS in supporting eco-efficient business operations. For practitioners and academics, the chapter suggests a framework that relates different eco-efficiency strategies to organizational change management methods.

This chapter is structured as follows. The next section reviews the eco-efficiency concept, origins, and history. It also explains why eco-efficiency is an important issue for many organizations today and the roles of different stakeholders in promoting eco-efficient practices. The following section focuses on implementing eco-efficiency in businesses operations. It maps eco-efficiency strategies to different implementation methods, and describes the role that information systems play in creating the required organizational capabilities for eco-efficient business operations. Finally, challenges to the successful adoption of information systems are discussed along with some recommendations. The chapter ends with concluding remarks and a discussion of future research directions.

BACKGROUND

Eco-efficiency arises from combination of ecology and economics and describes a management approach which promotes environmentally friendly sustainable business practice that delivers cost benefits (Lehni, 2000). Its origins can be traced to the 3M's 1970's Pollution Prevention Pays (3P) program. In 1991, the eco-efficiency concept was launched worldwide by the Business Council for Sustainable Development (BCSD). Since then, eco-efficiency concepts have become widely prevalent in the business community. Despite the fact that many companies are lagging behind in practice, the business community is coming to understand that sustainable business practice is a key requirement for business growth and survival in the future (Speth, 2009).

Role of Stakeholders

Several stakeholders are driving the change towards sustainable business practice (Bortz, 2007; Gabrielli de Azevedo, 2009; MacLean, 2008; Roosevelt Iv & Llewellyn, 2007; Verfaillie & Bidwell, 2000). These include governments, regulators, suppliers, customers/consumers, investors/shareholders, competitors, environmental interest groups, local communities, creditors, insurers, standards bodies, analysts, boards of directors, management, and employees. Table 1 provides a list of these stakeholders and their roles in driving sustainable business practice. It is evident that the drive towards sustainability is taking place at many levels: individual, group, community, industry, national, regional, and global. This proves that all businesses need to deal with environmental sustainability issues now or in the near future.

Eco-Efficiency Strategies

One of the first articles discussing business sustainability to a business practitioner audience was by Hart (1997). The Harvard Business Review article suggested that companies need to consider three basic strategies to improve sustainability. These are: (1) Manage production; (2) Manage the product/service lifecycle; and (3) Innovate. It is important to note that the underlying assumption of these strategies is that problems and benefits are shared in our interconnected world (WBCSD, 2008). A piecemeal approach that resolves a problem for one business but creates more problems for others should be avoided.

The goal of the first strategy, *manage production*, is to cut down or eliminate pollution that is a result of production operations. A newspaper's printing facility, for example, needs to identify production pollutant products in order to minimize or eliminate them. The goal of the second strategy, *manage product/service lifecycle* (also known as product stewardship, choice influencing, choice editing, or linking production to consumption), is to eliminate or cut down on pollution that is a result of product movement and use in the extended supply chain. A newspaper publisher, for example, needs to identify pollutant side effects that result from delivering, reading, storing, and disposing of newspapers in order to minimize their harmful lifecycle effects. The goal of the third strategy, *innovate*, is to develop new products and/or services that have low or minimal levels of environmental pollution (clean technology). For the newspaper example, the industry needs to think of innovative ways to deliver news that minimizes or eliminates paper production and newspaper lifecycle waste. This could be achieved through the online production and delivery of news using the Internet.

Nidumolu, Prahalad and Rangaswami (2009) posit that organizations often follow these strategies in stages (i.e., sequentially). The first stage, manage production, is focused on examining one's own business operations to fix problems

Table 1. Stakeholders' role in driving sustainable business practice

Stakeholder	Role
Governments	Countries are coming together to address environmental sustainability through multiple channels. These include: agreements (UNFCCC, 2009); expert groups ("Intergovernmental Panel of Climate Change (IPCC)," 1988); conferences such as COP15 The UN Climate Conference in Copenhagen in December 2009 (Bülow, 2009); and regulations such as those that increased the proportion of renewable energy in both Denmark (Ministry of Climate and Energy of Denmark, 2009) and the UK (Carlisle, 2009).
Regulators	There is a growing demand on businesses to improve information transparency. Triggered by the fall of giant companies such as Enron and the recent financial crisis, this demand has been mainly addressed through improving the transparency of financial information. The future will see a widening of the transparency scope to include environmental sustainability as well. The European Union has taken a proactive role to improve the sharing of environmental information through the use of ICTs (Commission of the European Communities, 2008).
Suppliers/Supply Chain Partners	Every business is part of a larger supply chain. Even if direct supply chain partners are not pursuing some kind of sustainability compliance, distant partners are. This puts a pressure on all businesses to deal with these demands, if not now then in the near future.
Customers/ Consumers	Some end users of a product or service include sustainability criteria in their buy decisions. Products/ services which can document good eco-efficiency practice, will receive higher ratings.
Investors and shareholders	Capital is becoming more and more tied to demands from investors to ensure that non-financial factors, such as social responsibility and environmental sustainability, are addressed.
Competitors	Many businesses feel pressure to meet the same level of disclosure to that of their competitors.
Interest groups	Different local and global community groups are showing more and more interest in environmental issues. Such groups are becoming very active in promoting awareness which can trigger actions by different stakeholders.
Communities	The community where the business operates could exert pressure that challenges how the business operates. This is especially true where local regulations support strong community involvement.
Creditors	Creditors, lenders, and banking institutions are starting to use eco-efficiency indicators as a criterion in their lending decision.
Insurers	Insurance companies could use eco-efficiency indicators as one means for identifying and assessing potential risks.
Standards bodies	The business may seek accreditation or certification from these bodies. Compliance could then become a potential driver for eco-efficiency improvements.
Analysts	Research entities conducting environmental sustainability evaluations of companies, businesses, or industries could influence the public image a company holds.
Boards of directors, management, and employees	Each of these internal stakeholders influence the company's direction, strategy, and day-to-day operations.

and comply with regulations. The second stage, manage product/service lifecycle, is focused on fixing problems and creating opportunities across the supply chain. The third stage, innovate, is focused on innovation, which they classify as three types: designing sustainable products and service, developing new business models, and developing new platforms. By analyzing the examples Nidumolu et al. (2009) provide, we can identify the intensity of stakeholder influence for each stage (refer to Table *2*).

An examination of Table *2* shows that in the earliest stage, attention is on compliance with laws, rules, and regulations imposed by government, industry groups, standard bodies, investors, creditors, and insurers. During the second stage, suppliers and customers have more influence and will demand improvements across the whole sup-

Table 2. Stakeholders' influence in driving sustainable strategies

Stakeholder	Manage production	Manage product/service lifecycle	Innovate
Competitors		XX	XXX
Analysts	X	X	X
Boards of directors, management, and employees	X	X	XXX
Communities	X	XX	XXX
Suppliers/Supply Chain Partners	X	XXX	X
Customers/ Consumers	X	XXX	X
Governments	XXX	XX	
Regulators	XXX	XX	
Interest groups	XXX	XX	
Standards bodies	XXX	XX	
Investors and shareholders	XXX	XX	XX
Creditors	XXX	XX	XX
Insurers	XXX	XX	XX

ply chain. The third stage is a time for the business to capitalize on the knowledge and experience gained in the previous two stages to produce innovations. The influencing parties here are competitors, employees, and community groups.

Corporate Information Systems

Information systems plays an important role in creating the organizational capabilities required for improving eco-efficiency in business operations (European Commission, 2009). Corporate information systems are an integral part of business operations today. In order to understand the role CIS play in supporting business operations, we list different types of CIS and provide a brief review of their key features. Corporate information systems' characteristics have gradually evolved over the years. In the early days of computers, computer systems were standalone, specialized, and serviced a specific business function. The emergence of PCs in the1980s and then local area networks increased the number of users and enabled information sharing between business functions. With the surge in worldwide adoption of the Internet and enterprise system implementations (e.g., enterprise resource planning systems, supply chain management systems, and customer relationship management systems), information systems nowadays are more connected and integrated. This integration minimizes information redundancies and inconsistencies within the same enterprise, as well as across the supply chain. Corporate information systems play a key role in supporting, managing, controlling, and reporting about business operations.

The main categories of CIS (Laudon & Laudon, 2006), classified according to their main function, are: productivity systems, transaction processing systems (TPS), management information systems (MIS), business intelligence (BI) and data warehousing (DW) systems (formally known as decision support systems), collaborative systems, performance management systems (formally known as executive information systems), inter-organizational systems (such as supply chain management and customer relationship management), and specialized systems. This section provides a brief description of these systems and discusses their roles in developing the organizational capabilities required for instituting eco-efficient business systems.

Productivity systems, as the name implies, enable individuals carry out day-to-day operational tasks efficiently. While these applications are designed for the generic user, their advanced capabilities are geared towards the information worker. These systems improve productivity by making the user's job easier and less time consuming through: (1) built-in tools such as those that provide spell checking and formatting in a word-processing application or calculations in a spreadsheet application; (2) editing tools that facilitate revising a working document; (3) standardization tools, which can be customized if needed, such as templates and macros. Productivity systems can play a great role in improving environmental sustainability through minimizing resource waste. Productivity information systems, if effectively used, minimize the time required to complete tasks and improve quality. Compare the time and effort needed to prepare a hand written report that requires multiple revisions with the same report prepared using a word processor. This kind of waste reduction is taken for granted nowadays when the majority of employees use computers for administrative and reporting tasks. However, one major waste item resulting from the use of productivity systems is paper waste. Many users print hard copies of documents to review, edit, and process. Reductions in print copies in conjunction with print management minimize paper waste and improve the environmental sustainability of system use. Print management systems which control the number of printed copies or force two-sided printing alone are not enough. To control this source of paper waste, it is the development of eco-efficiency awareness among users that leads to huge waste reductions. Advancements in human computer interaction design could also positively reduce paper use when the user can view and manipulate the information electronically through a computer screen, mobile phone, or scanner. Figure 1 shows the relationship between productivity systems and other CIS. The diagram shows that the main inputs and outputs of productivity systems are to or from the user. Other productivity system outputs are inputs to other systems. For example, inputs to TPS (scanning a train ticket) or input to MIS (exporting a spreadsheet to prepare a budget report).

Transaction processing systems (TPS) are systems that capture the data generated by the hundreds, thousands, or millions of transactions that a business generates. The bulk of the data that these systems capture is required for accounting purposes. However, recent advancements in hardware, software, storage, and telecommunications technologies enables capturing much more data. This data can be exploited to provide value to other business stakeholders, both inside and outside of the organization. Transaction processing systems have become a key feeder for other CIS such as MIS, BI, DW, and performance management systems. For this reason, TPS play a key role in capturing, storing, and providing raw data on different aspects of environmental sustainability and eco-efficiency, particularly key performance indicators. With increasing worldwide demand for information transparency, TPS will be a gold mine for data that can be analyzed, tracked, graphed, and integrated into other CIS.

Management information systems (MIS) provide the tools required to summarize the data collected by TPS for management and control operations. Summary reports are used by supervisory staff for short and medium term business reporting and control. As the diversity and coverage of the data collected by TPS increases, the reports created by MIS become more specialized. Consequently, more opportunities arise for other CIS to utilize the data. With proper reporting, managers can exercise better controls to achieve higher levels of environmental sustainability, a practice they currently follow when managing production quality, deliveries, inventories, etc.

Figure 1. Relationships between different corporate information system categories

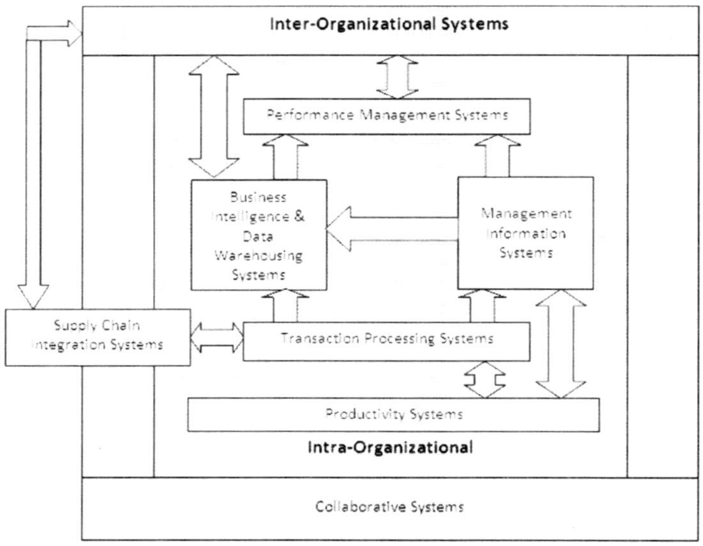

Note. The specialized information system category is not included in this figure as its relationship to other systems differs depending on industry, business operations, and company size.

Business intelligence (BI) and data warehousing (DW) systems are analytical systems that slice-and-dice aggregated data to make inferences about certain trends within the business. Their main source of data is TPS, however, the data analyzed by these systems is much older than that utilized by MIS. External data can also be imported into these systems if required. For this reason, the accuracy of the data may suffer as a result of the data cleansing process required to combine data from internal and external sources. While in the past these systems were used by specialized staff, the current trend is to deploy these systems to operational users to aid in on-the-job decisions. These systems serve environmental sustainability by identifying opportunities for controlling and minimizing negative environmental effects. This creates organizational capability for environmentally friendly business process delivery and innovation.

Collaborative systems are indispensible nowadays not only for corporate users but for anyone with a computer and access to the Internet. As the name implies, these systems encourage online collaboration between individuals and groups. Collaboration can be synchronous or asynchronous, one-to-one, one-to-many, or many-to-many, and within rich or thin contexts. Collaborative systems, if used effectively, can be a great medium for sharing and disseminating information on environmental sustainability goals, objectives, strategies, and practices. Some collaborative systems, such as email, intranet, portals, databases, and knowledge bases, are formally instituted within the organization. Others, such as blogs, wikis, discussion boards, mailing lists, and online social networking applications, are publically available. Organizational change towards an environmentally sustainable business practice requires an understanding of the local environment and the social, political, and economic issues that could be impacted by this change. Collaborative systems can then play a key role to promote awareness, participation, and engagement of key stakeholders, both within and outside the organization (Li & Bernoff, 2008).

Performance management systems are used to build organizational capability for tracking and reporting on important business goals. The process often starts by identifying a handful of key performance indicators (KPIs) for each goal. Performance management systems are used to track organizational progress on each KPI to ensure these goals are achieved. Inputs into these systems are both internal (from MIS and BI systems) and external. Environmental indicators can alert an organizational user to act quickly on environmental concerns. Environmental sustainability indicators vary depending what the business identifies as important and can include energy use, paper use, and waste production/reduction (Verfaillie & Bidwell, 2000).

Inter-organizational information systems are used to share information across the supply chain. In a global environment, it is usual for businesses to have relationships with other businesses on local, national and global levels. One way these relationships can be formalized is through an inter-organizational information system. On the supply side these systems are called supply chain management (SCM) systems, and on the customer side they are called customer relationship management (CRM) systems. Supply chain integration systems enable the sharing of transaction data between an organization and its external stakeholders. Hence these systems play an important role for building organizational capabilities for lifecycle product management.

Specialized information systems vary depending on the nature of the business. A specialized information system can be a design system for an engineering company, a logistics and scheduling system for a bus company, or a publishing system for a newspaper company. Different businesses have specialized information systems depending on the nature of the product/service they provide. Sometimes these systems are standalones (i.e., they are not integrated with other CIS). Others are integrated into other systems, such as TPS, MIS, etc. Since specialized information systems serve core business operations, they can play a key role in supporting business process innovation.

This section provided a review of different CIS and briefly discussed the role each can play in creating the organizational capability needed for eco-efficient business operations. Figure 1 illustrates the relationships between different CIS, and between CIS and inter-organizational systems. Table 3 lists the different categories of CIS with details of users, data input, data output, delivery strategies, and integration capabilities.

IMPLEMENTATION OF ECO-EFFICIENT BUSINESS OPERATIONS

In this section, we identify the different methods used for eco-efficiency implementations. We then create a framework of eco-efficiency implementations through mapping the three eco-efficiency strategies to five implementations methods. We support the framework with examples that demonstrate the role of CIS as a key organizational capability. Finally, we discuss challenges to the adoption of CIS to support eco-efficiency and provide practical recommendations for business managers.

Implementing Eco-Efficiency in Business Operations

As mentioned in the introduction, introducing eco-efficiency improvements in business operations requires change. Organizations can use one method or a combination of methods to enact change. This section provides a quick review of these methods and highlights the role CIS play in creating the required organizational capabilities for change to happen. Methods include: business process re-engineering (BPR), redesigning products and services, business process collaboration, finding new ways of meeting customer needs, and using proxy instruments. Table 4 lists these methods and provides examples.

Table 3. Corporate information system categories

IS type	User	Data captured from	Data output to	Delivery method	Integration	Example
Productivity systems	Generic users	Users	Users, other users, or collaborative systems	Mainly local through user's PC but online delivery methods are possible	Often not	Word processing, spread sheets, scheduling, and calendaring applications such as the MS Office suite, Open Office suite, Google Documents, and Adobe Acrobat reader
Transaction processing systems (TPS)	Function group users and other systems	Users and/or other systems	Users, other users, and/or other systems	Mainly online within the same enterprise	Within the same enterprise but inter-organizational integration is becoming popular	Enterprise systems (ES) applications such as ERP, CRM, SCM, etc. Examples of ERP applications are SAP and Oracle
Management information systems (MIS)	Function group users, cross-function users, and other systems	Mainly TPS	Function group users, cross-functional users, and other systems	Mainly online within the same enterprise	Within the same enterprise but inter-organizational integration is becoming popular	Report generation applications that are part of or are add-ons to ERP applications such as Cristal Reports
Business intelligence (BI) and data warehousing systems (DW)	Mainly specialized users and other systems but function group users and cross-function users are joining	Other systems	Mainly specialized users and other systems but function group users and cross-functional users are joining	Mainly online intra- and inter-organizational	Intra- and inter-organizational	Analysis and control applications that are often integrated into ERP or other ES application such as Cristal Reports.
Collaborative systems	Individual users and other systems	Users and other systems	Users and other systems	Always online	Inter-organizational	Email, conferencing, chat, wikis, blogs, networking systems
Performance management systems	Mainly specialized users but function group users and cross-function users are joining	Users and other systems	Mainly specialized users but function group users and cross-function users are joining	Mainly online intra- and inter-organizational	Inter-organizational	Analysis, scenario, and dashboard applications that are often integrated into BI, DW, ERP or other ES application such as Business Objects, Hyperion, and SAS.
Inter-organizational systems	Function group users, cross-function users, and other systems	Users and other systems	Users and other systems	Mainly online intra- and inter-organizational	Inter-organizational	Supply chain management (SCM) and customer relationship management (CRM) systems
Specialized systems	Function group users	Users and/or other systems	Users and/or other systems	Online or offline	Varies	Design, scheduling, newspaper, and publishing systems

Business process re-engineering or re-designing business processes is a key change management approach that is often used to streamline business operations. The re-design intensity varies between the two extremes of small incremental change and significant abrupt change. The start-

Table 4. A framework of eco-efficiency implementation of business operations

Eco-efficiency strategy	Example	Implementation method					Key CIS required
		Business process re-engineering	Redesigning products and services	Business process collaboration	Finding new ways of meeting customer needs	Using proxy instruments	
		1	2	3	4	5	
Manage production: Minimize waste in production operations	– ArcelorMittal (steel manufacturing) and Petrobras (Brazilian oil producer) embedded sustainability principles in their general contracts (ArcelorMittal, 2009; Gabrielli de Azevedo, 2009).	X	X	X			Performance management IS for documentation, control, and reporting
	– Lura Group (leading Croatian producer of dairy products) now purifies waste water for re-use in production. The remaining sludge is treated and sold as compost (Lehni, 2000).	X	X				Control IS to support production operations and performance management IS for quality management
Manage product/ service lifecycle: Minimize waste in the extended supply chain (customers, suppliers, and intermediaries)	– Xerox leased copiers recycling scheme (Kumar & Putnam, 2008; Meyer, 2000).		X	X	X		TPS to support lease operations and inter-organizational systems connecting Xerox with customers and connecting copiers with Xerox support
	– Nokia redesigned its mobile phone chargers to reduce the no-load consumption of batteries. The company was also the first to introduce alerts in its devices telling users when their phone batteries were fully charged so they could be unplugged. [i]		X				Specialized IS (design and production operations), collaborative IS (customer awareness and marketing), and inter-organizational systems (customer market research)
Innovate: Create new sustainable processes and products/ services	– Owners of clean energy power generation entities can claim renewable energy certificates (RECs). They can sell these RECs to companies that buy them to offset their own carbon emissions.		X	X		X	TPS to keep track of RECs and inter-organizational systems for connecting buyers, sellers, and regulating bodies
	– SBB in cooperation with Mobility combine train ticket sales with car sharing in Switzerland (Lehni, 2000).[ii]	X	X	X	X		Inter-organizational systems connecting SBB, Mobility, and customers

ing point for change can be a clean sheet of paper (i.e., a new design) or it can be constrained by the boundaries of existing organizational systems, processes, and structures. Both the academic and practice literature report the great level of interdependency between business change and the organizational capabilities needed to enable the change. Corporate information systems play a key role in developing the required capabilities for implementing eco-efficiency in business operations. A building management system that responds to occupancy variations and controls the temperature, ventilation, humidity, and lighting is an example of a BPR method that uses CIS as a key change enabler (Lockwood, 2006). The re-configuring of the company's servers to share resources is another BPR example that create eco-efficiency through improvements in IT operations (Bright, 2009).

While BPR is concerned with the re-organization of business operations, the *redesign of products and services* is concerned with the design of the end product. The objective for both, however, is improving eco-efficiency and minimizing harmful environmental impacts. This improved eco-efficiency has direct value to the customer (or consumer). While an information system may not be an essential component of an eco-efficient product, many innovations in eco-efficient business operations are information system enabled. Examples in Table 4 include the embedding of suitability principles in contract documents (ArcelorMittal and Petrobras) and leasing instead of selling copiers (Xerox). The first needs the support of a performance management system to track suppliers' efforts while the second needs the exchange of data between inter-organizational systems to facilitate lease management.

Business process collaboration is concerned with the re-organization or re-configuration of the extended supply chain. This often involves collaboration with suppliers and customers but could also include other groups (e.g., government, community groups, competitors, standard bodies). Examples in Table 4 include working with subcontractors to enforce minimum eco-efficiency standards (ArcelorMittal and Petrobras) and with customers by providing a business offering that is both cost effective and eco-friendly (Xerox).

Finding new eco-efficient ways of meeting customer needs involves developing innovative business methods, procedures, and processes, many of which are supported by information systems. Examples of these are the electronic books vs. paper books, electronic documents vs. paper documents, and video conferencing vs. face-to-face meetings. Examples in Table 4 include delivering a photocopying service instead of a photocopying machine to Xerox customers and combining train ticket sales with car sharing by SBB in Switzerland.

Using proxy instruments could be a quick approach for many companies to demonstrate a commitment to environmental sustainability. Examples of proxy instruments are renewable energy certificates (RECs) and sponsorship of green initiatives within the community. The business here makes a financial commitment that is expected to yield sustainability improvements in areas that the business has no control over. However, there is some negative stigma associated with the use of proxy instruments (Schendler, 2007). This is because this method is passive hence companies could be perceived to be doing it as green washing. Another key challenge for adopting this approach is the difficulty of measuring the quality of the different instruments that are on offer (Roosevelt Iv & Llewellyn, 2007). This could become a potential problem when demand exceeds supply. An information system is a key element to this approach as it is used to collect, control, evaluate, and report on environmentally sustainability indicators.

Implementing strategy requires that the business thinks about what method or method combination to apply and what supporting CIS are needed for successful implementations. The framework in Table 4 can be used to facilitate making these choices in relation to a particular eco-efficiency strategy. The framework also demonstrates the interdependencies between strategies, methods, and CIS. Therefore, it can be used to analyze cases of eco-efficient business practice (retrospective approach) or to develop a blueprint for new implementations (prescriptive approach).

Challenges to the Successful Application of CIS

Many information systems projects are implemented successfully meeting time, budget, and goal constraints but ultimately fail because the users avoid using them. These problem systems are ignored, discontinued, or replaced shortly after going live. There are different reasons why an information system fails the assimilation test (Caldeira & Ward, 2003; Fichman, 2000; Fink, 1998; Kalle & Daniel, 1999). Failure can be because of reasons related to the system's requirement definition meaning that the business needs were poorly defined. This often results in a system that does not add value and as a result is abandoned. Other causes for assimilation failure can be operational. Operational causes include one or a combination of financial, operational, and contextual constraints.

Financial constraints occur when the system's operational expenses exceeds its benefits. This can be true for many CIS supporting environmental sustainability because many such systems are considered in their early stages of maturity. A continuous revenue stream is needed to keep environmental CIS operational. These expenses need to be factored in early in the life of the project as part of the total-cost-of-ownership. If not, a financial drawback could very quickly signal an end to a successful implementation. One approach to deal with this problem is to commercialize the environmental CIS to create a future stream of revenue and possibly lower future costs when costs are shared among a large group of users (Dias & Brewer, 2009).

Operational constraints are related to running the information system post the go live date. Questions such as whether users have the appropriate skills, and if not, did they receive the required training and support need to be asked. Other issues that need to be raised are: Are there any incentives for users to continue using these systems? Do users see any value in using the systems? Does the effort users put in to utilize the system outweigh the rewards? These questions need to be answered and countermeasures need to be put in place to ameliorate identified operational constraints.

Contextual constraints are related to adapting the information system to the nature of the environment where it is implemented. This is especially important for software packages that are developed in one context but deployed in another. The initial implementation may be successful in satisfying business needs at the time of go live. However, no business is static and changes are a basic fact of life. Is the new information system agile enough to overcome these constraints?

Recommendations for Business Managers

It is wise to say that improving the environmental sustainability of business operations is not an easy task. However, it is possible by understanding the rationale, strategies, methods and capabilities required to create a sustainable business. As stated earlier, many different stakeholders are driving this eco-efficiency transformation. Therefore, it is important for business managers to understand the influence of each stakeholder and their role. Managers need to identify their organizational eco-efficiency targets and choose suitable strategies and methods for meeting these targets. Creating organizational capabilities, particularly through integrating different information systems, is a key step to ensure successful implementations.

FUTURE RESEARCH DIRECTIONS

This chapter developed a framework for the implementation of eco-efficient business operations.

The conceptual development of the framework was supported by examples from the practice literature. One possible research approach would be to validate the framework using case studies of eco-efficient business implementations. This could shed light on the implementation process by answering questions such as: Do eco-efficiency strategies follow the projected sequence? Do they overlap? Who are the influential stakeholders? How do they influence strategy? And when? What method or method combinations are used to realize strategy? Another research approach would be to identify the critical success/failure factors that are particular to each strategy and understand the level of influence these factors have.

CONCLUSION

Environmental sustainability compliance is becoming an issue of concern for many businesses. Compliance often involves changes in business operations, both internally and externally. Some of these changes are initiated by the business, while others are influenced by different stakeholders the business is involved with. This chapter advocated for eco-efficiency improvements in business operations as a corner stone to improving environmental sustainability. Different strategies for achieving eco-efficient business operations were presented and the role different stakeholders have in driving these strategies was noted. The role information systems play in creating eco-efficient organizational capability was highlighted. A framework that relates eco-efficiency strategies to implementation methods was developed to show the complementary relationship of the two with implementation examples that are supported by information systems. This chapter is of interest to students, academics and practitioners. It will benefit undergraduate students in both business and environmental disciplines as it integrates environmental issues with business concerns. It also emphasizes the role of information systems in creating the organizational capabilities required for environmental sustainability improvements to occur. For academics, it provides a succinct presentation of the current status, issues, and challenges of eco-efficiency implementations. Scholars could identify specialized areas of interest for further exploration and investigation. As for practitioners, the chapter not only provides a clear exposition of eco-efficiency definitions, issues, and strategies but includes suggestions of possible combination of change methods with suitable information systems for strategy implementation.

REFERENCES

ArcelorMittal. (2009). Building sustainable supply chains in Brazil. *World Business Council for Sustainable Development (WBCSD)*, 1-3. Retrieved July 2009, from http://www.wbcsd.org/includes/getTarget.asp?type=d&id=MzI5OTI

Bortz, C. (2007). Conversation: An interview with Alyson Slater. *Harvard Business Review*, *85*(10), 32–32.

Bright, M. (2009). Data center: The next generation. *Oracle Magazine*, 29-34. Retrieved 8 March, 2009, from http://www.oracle.com/oraclemagazine

Bülow, M. V. (2009). The essentials in Copenhagen. *COP15 Copenhagen 2009*. Retrieved July 2009, from http://en.cop15.dk/news/view+news?newsid=876

Caldeira, M. M., & Ward, J. M. (2003). Using resource-based theory to interpret the successful adoption and use of information systems and technology in manufacturing small and medium-sized enterprises. *European Journal of Information Systems*, *12*, 127–141. doi:10.1057/palgrave.ejis.3000454

Carlisle, T. (2009). UK lays out low-carbon blueprint. *The National, July 19*. Retrieved July 2009, from http://www.thenational.ae/apps/pbcs.dll/article?AID=/20090719/BUSINESS/707199988

Commission of the European Communities. (2008). *Addressing the challenge of energy efficiency through Information and Communication Technologies, Brussels, 13.5.2008*. Retrieved July 2009, from http://ec.europa.eu/information_society/activities/sustainable_growth/docs/com_2008_241_1_en.pdf

Dias, M. B., & Brewer, E. (2009). How computer science serves the developing world. *Communications of the ACM*, *52*(6), 74–80. doi:10.1145/1516046.1516064

Eisenhardt, K. M., & Martin, J. A. (2000). Dynamic capabilities: What are they? *Strategic Management Journal*, *21*(10/11), 1105–1121. doi:10.1002/1097-0266(200010/11)21:10/11<1105::AID-SMJ133>3.0.CO;2-E

European Commission. (2009). *Smarter use of energy*. Retrieved July 2009, from http://ec.europa.eu/information_society/activities/sustainable_growth/energy_efficiency/index_en.htm

Fichman, R. G. (2000). The diffusion and assimilation of information technology innovations. In Zmud, R. W. (Ed.), *Framing the Domains of IT Management: Projecting the Future...Through the Past* (pp. 105–128). Cincinnati, OH: Pinnaflex Educational Resources Inc.

Fink, D. (1998). Guidelines for the successful adoption of information technology in small and medium enterprises. *International Journal of Information Management*, *18*(4), 243–253. doi:10.1016/S0268-4012(98)00013-9

Gabrielli de Azevedo, J. S. (2009). The Greening of Petrobras. *Harvard Business Review*, *87*(3), 43–47.

Hart, S. L. (1997). Beyond greening: Strategies for a sustainable world. *Harvard Business Review*, *75*(1), 66–76.

Intergovernmental Panel of Climate Change (IPCC). (1988). *2009*. Retrieved July 2009, from http://www.ipcc.ch/organization/organization.htm

Kalle, L., & Daniel, R. (1999). Learning failure in information systems development. *Information Systems Journal*, *9*(2), 85–101. doi:10.1046/j.1365-2575.1999.00051.x

Kumar, S., & Putnam, V. (2008). Cradle to cradle: Reverse logistics strategies and opportunities across three industry sectors. *International Journal of Production Economics*, *115*(2), 305–315. doi:10.1016/j.ijpe.2007.11.015

Laudon, K. C., & Laudon, J. P. (2006). *Management Information Systems: Managing the Digital Firm* (9th ed.). New Jersey: Prentice Hall.

Lehni, M. (2000). Eco-Efficiency: Creating more value with less impact. *World Business Council for Sustainable Development (WBCSD)*, 1-33. Retrieved July 2009, from http://www.wbcsd.org/web/publications/eco_efficiency_creating_more_value.pdf

Li, C., & Bernoff, J. (2008). *Groundswell: Winning in a world transformed by social technologies*. Boston, Massachusetts: Harvard Business Press.

Lockwood, C. (2006). Building the green way. *Harvard Business Review*, *84*(6), 129–137.

MacLean, R. (2008). The green conversation. *Harvard Business Review*, *86*(9), 58–62.

Meyer, H. (2000). The greening of corporate America. *The Journal of Business Strategy*, *21*(1), 38–43. doi:10.1108/eb040058

Ministry of Climate and Energy of Denmark. (2009). *17 percent renewable energy – and on the way up. COP15 Copenhagen 2009*. Retrieved July 2009, from http://en.cop15.dk/climate+facts/research/17+per+cent+renewable+energy+%E2%80%93+and+on+the+way+up

Montiel, I. (2008). Common futures corporate social responsibility and corporate sustainability: separate pasts. *Organization & Environment, 21*(245), 245–269. doi:10.1177/1086026608321329

Nidumolu, R., Prahalad, C. K., & Rangaswami, M. R. (2009). Why sustainability is now the key driver of innovation. *Harvard Business Review, 87*(9), 56–64.

Roosevelt Iv, T., & Llewellyn, J. (2007). Investors hunger for clean energy. *Harvard Business Review, 85*(10), 38–40.

Schendler, A. (2007). When being green backfires. *Harvard Business Review, 85*(10), 35–38.

Speth, J. G. (2009). Doing business in a postgrowth society. *Harvard Business Review, 87*(9), 18–19.

Sutton, P. (2004). A Perspective on environmental sustainability? A paper for the Victorian Commissioner for Environmental Sustainability. *The State of Victoria, 12-April [Version 2.b]*. Retrieved July 2009, from http://www.green-innovations.asn.au/

UNFCCC. (2009). *Kyoto Protocol*. Retrieved July 2009, from http://unfccc.int/kyoto_protocol/items/2830.php.

Verfaillie, H. A., & Bidwell, R. (2000). Measuring eco-efficiency: A guide to reporting company performance. *World Business Council for Sustainable Development (WBCSD)*, 1-33. Retrieved July 2009, from http://www.wbcsd.org/web/publications/measuring_eco_efficiency.pdf

Wernerfelt, B. (1984). A resource-based view of the firm. *Strategic Management Journal, 5*(2), 171–180. doi:10.1002/smj.4250050207

World Business Council for Sustainable Development (WBCSD). (2008). *Sustainable Consumption: Facts and Trends from a Business Perspective*. Retrieved from.http://www.wbcsd.org/includes/getTarget.asp?type=d&id=MzI2ODM

ENDNOTES

i Research by the Finish communications company Nokia found that two-thirds of the power consumed by a mobile phone is wasted when its battery is full but its charger remains plugged in. This is referred to as a charger's "no load" energy consumption (WBCSD, 2008).

ii The Swiss Federal Railways (SBB) in cooperation with Mobility, a car-sharing company, offer car lease services to travelers. Registered customers can pick up the cars from predefined places for a pre-arranged period of time. The sharing concept allows customers to use a car that is suitable for their needs when they need one without having to own one.

Chapter 14
Efficient Information Provision for Environmental and Sustainability Reporting

Cigdem Akkaya
Technische Universität München, Germany

Petra Wolf
Technische Universität München, Germany

Helmut Krcmar
Technische Universität München, Germany

ABSTRACT

Environmental concerns have become a key issue for society as well as for individuals and businesses. To cope up with the pressure imposed by their various stakeholders increasingly demanding for "green" production, enterprises are constrained to balance their goals of economic growth, environmental protection and usage of natural resources. Environmental reporting provides a comprehensive and structured approach to inform the target groups about the proper environmental strategies and to present a transparent profile. Recent studies show that environmental reporting is spreading rapidly. To enable consistency and comparability, several organizations provide guidelines, standards and recommendations to guide organizations in their environmental management. Environmental reporting is mainly used by organizations as a medium to demonstrate compliance with applicable national and European level environmental regulations. In the last decades, they are also increasingly being used as a tool to communicate environmental matters to various stakeholders. The purpose of this chapter is to deliver fundamentals of environmental reporting based on a comprehensive literature review and a recent project in Germany. Moreover, the authors suggest two approaches to support data gathering and report generation processes for environmental reporting purposes of organizations.

DOI: 10.4018/978-1-61520-981-1.ch014

INTRODUCTION AND BACKGROUND

Economic growth and development are among the major aims of most countries. Along with their benefits for economic growth, they have also serious impacts on the environment such as air and water pollution, soil degradation and desertification. Environmental problems caused by enterprises have become a big concern for governments and the public. As a result public attention has been constantly increasing and various reporting measures on green production have been introduced, which forces enterprises to take appropriate measures. To satisfy their various stakeholders, they need to implement credible environmental strategies and strengthen environmental management practices to ensure a more efficient use of natural resources and protection of the environment.

According to a recent McKinsey & Company global survey of 7,751 consumers in Brazil, Canada, China, France, Germany, India, the UK, and the USA, 87 percent of consumers are concerned about the environmental and social impacts of the products they buy (Bonini, Hintz & Mendonca, 2008). In another study, 95 percent of consumers state that they would buy "green products" if they had the right information and satisfactory products (Deloitte & Touche LLP & Grocery Manufactures Association (GMA), Green Shopper Study, p. 13). The European Commission has taken concrete measures in order to raise awareness of organizations about Corporate Social Responsibility (CSR). The commission aims to raise awareness further and promote the exchange of best practices as CSR continues to evolve (Commission of the European Communities, 2007).

As various stakeholders demand greater environmental responsibility, organizations look for ways to minimize adverse environmental impacts of their products and processes and inform the stakeholders via different channels (Biloslavo & Trnavcevic, 2009). An increasing number of customers and suppliers require organizations to receive an external certification, which demonstrates the reliability and credibility of organizations' environmental policy. In order to be able to minimize the risks on environment, problems should be recognized very quickly. Tools such as the Life Cycle Assessment (LCA) are commonly used by organizations to track environmental impacts of products and services throughout their life cycle. However, the variety and complexity of environmental data in enterprises are quite high which necessitates more systematical approaches. To deal with various amount of data efficiently organizations set up environmental management systems (EMS) to incorporate environmental considerations into their business operations. In order to identify and manage significant environmental impacts however, more advanced systems of Corporate Environmental Management Information Systems (CEMIS) are being increasingly used. They enable enterprises to record, process and analyze the environmental relevant information systematically.

Environmental reporting is accepted as a generic term that covers various means by which companies disclose information about their operations and their impacts on the environment. More specifically two terms are commonly used in literature: Corporate Environmental Reports (CER) (Kolk, 1999) and more commonly Corporate Social Responsibility (CSR) (Bassen, Jastram, & Meyer, 2005) reports. Organizations utilize these reports to demonstrate how they align their operations with the needs and expectations of stakeholders— including environmental organizations, financial investors, shareholders, employees, auditors, suppliers, contractors, customers, local communities and the public.

Although there are a number of mandatory schemes to be delivered at the European level such as the Pollutant Release and Transfer Registers (PRTR) (The European Commission, 2008), most of the remaining reports are based on national regulations (European Commission; International Organization for Standardization). The differences among the national regulations cause difficulties especially for those multinational companies, who have to adjust the gathered data according to different local regulations. Without any structured framework, even the reports based on the same local regulation would lack comparability and consistency. To avoid this problem and increase standardization, more and more countries tend to support international efforts on global standards such as Global Reporting Initiative (GRI, 2006).

The main focus of the chapter consists of the following sections:

Section 1: includes a brief introduction to environmental management, gives a review of sustainable development and discusses the main environmental management standards.
Section 2: provides information regarding the content and structure of environmental reports introduces structured approach for sustainability reporting and delivers an overview of legal reporting duties of companies in Germany.
Section 3: introduces life cycle assessment as a comprehensive concept for environmental management and discusses its limitations.
Section 4: suggests two approaches for an efficient generation of environment-related data for organizational reporting.

MAIN FOCUS OF THE CHAPTER

Environmental Management

Environmental problems are a key area of concern in the 21st century. In a world of rapid global transformations, companies must account for the way they impact the communities and environments where they operate. CSR reporting is accepted as a valuable opportunity to build key relationships and communicate with stakeholders.

CSR reporting has become "a norm instead of an exception within the world's largest companies" (KPMG International, 2008, p. 2) globally – over 80 percent of Fortune 250 companies report on CSR according to an international survey carried out by KPMG (2008). The research demonstrates a remarkable increase compared to the figure of 50 percent in 2005. Yet, according to a research of KDPaine & Partners and Brad Rawlins of Brigham Young University (2008), Fortune 50 companies are using CSR "as a public relations tool to position companies favorably on environmental issues, rather than to hold companies accountable to stakeholders for environmental performance" (p. 1).

Among the global organizations, Europe issues more reports than any other region – in 2008 49 percent of GRI sustainability reports were issued by European organizations, the vast majority of which came from EU countries (2008). Strauss and Bird (2009) discuss the state of CSR reporting in Europe based on the recent report of European Commission (2009) as follows:

In **Austria**, *government and business have jointly developed guidelines for sustainable reporting, which are addressed to all enterprises in Austria.* **Belgium** *notes that environmental reporting is being mainstreamed among enterprises.* **Denmark** *has a long tradition for CSR reporting practices. In* **Finland**, *an annual competition on CSR reporting has been organized thirteen times.* **France** *was the first country to mandate triple bottom-line reporting for publicly-listed companies. In* **Germany**, *both CSR and sustainability reporting are voluntary. Government in* **The Netherlands** *encourages voluntary action on CSR reporting by the private sector, in close consultation with stakeholders. In* **Spain**, *since 2004, most of the companies quoted on the Stock Exchange have published information on their CSR policies, mainly based on the Global Reporting Initiative. In* **Sweden**, *since 1999 certain companies have been required to include in their annual financial accounts information on the environmental impact of their activities. (Strauss & Bird, 2009, pp. 1-5)*

The above analysis about the state of sustainability reporting in Europe shows that the incorporation of environmental issues into the framework of corporate social responsibility reporting systems has been encouraged in many European Union (EU) countries over the past decades. More remarkably still is the trend of many governmental organizations towards providing reporting guidelines to the companies. While sustainability reporting is in some of the EU Member States mandatory, a greater number encourage voluntary reporting.

Since more than 80 percent of the world's 250 largest companies report on corporate social responsibility, it seems nowadays merely a question of how to report on environmental issues, and no longer whether to report at all (Marshall & Brown, 2003). The increasing trend towards reporting brings the following consequence: The importance of clear corporate communication and reporting strategies involving and reflecting the operations of the company as well as the needs and demands of the stakeholders are nowadays more critical for companies than ever.

Sustainable Development

Sustainable development is about balancing the economic, social, and environmental issues over the short- and long-term. The Brundtland Report (United Nations World Commission on Environment and Development, 1987), which is known as the seminal environmental documents of the 20th century, has developed a definition for sustainable development over 20 years ago. It is broadly accepted today and defines sustainable development as development that "meets the needs of the present without compromising the ability of future generations to meet their own needs" (p. 43).

The concept of sustainable development can be broken down to three constituent parts: economic, social and environmental sustainability. The overlapping circles model is commonly used since it clearly demonstrates that the three dimensions need to be closely integrated (see Figure 1).

Figure 1. Scheme of sustainable development – at the confluence of three constituent parts (Adapted from Darabaris, 2008, p. 195)

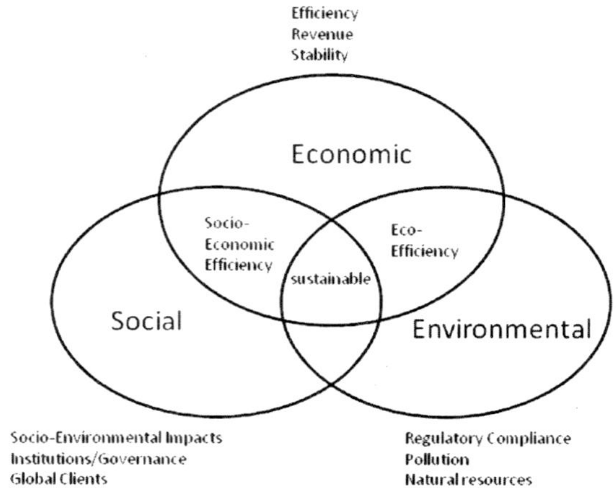

Economic sustainability: A sustainable system is one with sustainable income. Hicks (1946) defined income as "the maximum amount that a person or a nation could consume over some time period and still be as well off at the end of the period as they were at the beginning" (p. 172). Economic sustainability requires that, in some time period, economic benefits (revenues) received exceed or at least balance the costs spent.

Social sustainability: Social sustainability strives to take future generations into consideration, and to live with the awareness that our actions make an impact on the world at large, both today and in the future. Therefore, social sustainability takes a broader view into consideration in relation to number of people with jobs, the available opportunities for education and training, community, health, human rights and globalization.

Environmental sustainability: Natural capital is "an extension of the traditional economic notion of capital, which is generally defined as the manufactured (human-made) means of production" (Prugh, Costanza, & Cumberland, 1999, p.

49) to environmental goods and services. It consists of the land, air, water, minerals, living organisms and all formations of the Earth's biosphere that yields a flow of valuable ecosystem goods and services into the future. Environmental sustainability requires that natural capital is consumed at a rate at which it can be replenished naturally, so that it will be available also for future generations. If the renewable resources are used more than the nature's ability to replenish, then it will result in an environmental degradation which is not sustainable. Therefore, sustainability requires that human activity uses nature's resources only at a rate at which they can be replenished naturally.

Sustainable development is based on the assumption that there is a trade-off between continuous economic growth and sustainability of the environment. Thus societies need to manage three dimensions of sustainability, which may not be substitutable and their consumption might not be reversible. It is however possible to operate successfully with minimal emissions of pollutants and minimal use of non-renewable resources by following sustainable strategies and policies.

What is Environmental Management?

Environmental management strives for environmental sustainability in Figure 1. Environmental management helps to increase the transparency of the environmental activities. Weiß and Bentlage (2006, p. 19) define environmental management as "management of an organization's activities which have or may have an impact on the environment" (p. 19). Environmental management includes the management of interaction with the environment to ensure environmental friendly processes and products.

For an effective environmental management of organizations, environmental aspects and impacts of processes have to be analyzed. Environmental aspects and impacts are defined in ISO 14001 as follows:

An environmental aspect is a feature or characteristic of an activity, product or service that affects or can affect the environment. Environmental impact is a change to the environment. Such a change can be positive or negative. Environmental impacts are caused by environmental aspects (International Organization for Standardization).

The goal of corporate environmental management is the limitation of emissions and risks as well as the protection of resources (Lang, 2007). An increasing number of companies respond to the demands of the environmental concerns of their stakeholders by implementing active environmental management measures as one of the cornerstones of their corporate philosophies. The increasingly serious environmental problems of the world have increased the sensitivity of the subject and as a result force companies to reconsider their environmental damaging behaviors.

An Environmental Management System (EMS) provides a systematic approach to managing the environmental aspects of an organization in a comprehensive and documented manner. EMS is based on a continuous improvement process following a "Plan-Do-Check-Act" quality model introduced by Deming in the US in the 1950s (Deming, 1986, p. 131). This is an instrument to manage the environmental impacts of an organization, both current and future. An EMS integrates environmental management into the daily operations of an organization, as well as into its long term plans and other quality management systems. The potential environmental risks and their liabilities as well as the necessary measures to avoid them should be included in long term planning of the organization. An effective EMS is, therefore, built on Total Quality Management concepts (U.S. Environmental Protection Agency) and should address risk management.

Interest in the EMS reaches out beyond the organizations which implement them. Regulators are especially interested in their potential to contribute to effective environmental protection (Darnall, Jolley & Handfield, 2008).

Once an organization implements an EMS, it may decide to have it certified according to various EMS standards. This demonstrates that an organization is committed to environmental issues. There are two main EMS standards which are discussed in Section 1.3.

Environmental Management System Standards

Environmental standards help organizations to address their environmental issues by delivering a set of standards and guidance documents. There are various EMS standards available to facilitate organizations to implement environmental management systems. EMS standards describe specific requirements for setting up an effective EMS.

In the early 1990s several countries have developed their own EMS standards as a response to concern about environmental risks and damages. The first EMS standard was BS7750 which was introduced in 1992 (Wenk, 2005, p. 25). The early EMS standards were used as a model to develop the global standards. The most widely recognized ones are the European Eco-Management and Audit Scheme (EMAS) (European Commission) and the International Organization of Standards 14001 (ISO 14001) (International Organization for Standardization).

ISO 14001 was implemented in 1996 and updated in 2004 (International Organization for Standardization). EMAS has been available for participation by companies since 1995 and was originally restricted to companies in industrial sectors (European Commission). Since 2001, it became open to all economic sectors including public and private services. In July 2008, the European Commission proposed to revise EMAS to increase the participation of companies and reduce the administrative burden and costs, particularly for SMEs.

Eco-Management and Audit Scheme (EMAS)

The European Commission has introduced EMAS –known as EMAS I– in 1995 as an environmental policy tool in a step towards the Community's goal of sustainable development. Since 2001 EMAS –known as EMAS II– has been open to public and private organizations of all economic sectors operating in the European Union and the European Economic Area (EEA) – Iceland, Liechtenstein and Norway. Furthermore, EMAS II has allowed registration on the basis of the concept of organization, whereas EMAS I was a site-based registration system. An increasing number of candidate countries also implement EMAS in preparation for their accession to the EU.

Participation to EMAS is voluntary. The aim of EMAS is to recognize and reward organizations that continuously improve their environmental performances. To receive an EMAS registration, organizations need to conduct an environmental review, establish an EMS, carry out an audit and provide a statement of performance. The environmental review, EMS, audit procedure and the environmental statement must be approved by an accredited EMAS verifier. The validated statement must be sent to the EMAS Competent Body for registration and made publicly available before an organization can use the EMAS logo (European Commission).

International Organization of Standards

Outside of the EU, ISO 14001 is the primary EMS option, with relatively few alternatives (Wisconsin Department of Natural Resources). ISO 14000 is a series of international, voluntary environmental management standards and guidelines developed under ISO Technical Committee 207 (International Organization for Standardization). The ISO 14000 standards are voluntary instruments, reflecting input from a variety of interested parties worldwide, which are intended for use in countries at all stages of economic development, under a wide range of governmental systems.

The ISO 14000 family has two main standards specifying requirements and providing guidance on the implementation of an environmental management system: ISO 14001:2004 (ISO 14001) (Environmental management systems -- Requirements with guidance for use) and ISO 14004:2004 (ISO 14004) (Environmental management systems -- General guidelines on principles, systems and support techniques). Originally developed in 1996, both standards were revised by ISO's Technical Committee 207 - Environmental Management (ISO/TC 207) and published in 2004 to ensure that the standards represent the state of the art. Both standards are consistent with each other and are applicable to any organization that wishes to establish an environmental management system regardless of size, location, type and level of maturation (International Organization for Standardization, 2009).

ISO 14001 is often seen as the corner stone of the ISO 14000 series that specifies the requirements of an EMS. It includes all the necessary elements of an EMS that organizations are required to conform for registration, after an independent third-party audit. ISO 14004 on the other hand is not designed for registration purposes and provides only supplementary information. This standard includes examples, descriptions and practical suggestions as an aid for implementing an EMS. It can only be used to *guide* organizations that are just beginning to implement an EMS or to optimize the existing systems (Cascio, Woodside & Mitchell, 2005, pp. 31-45).

ISO 14001 applies to a whole organization. It does not specify levels of environmental performance. Instead, it gives generic requirements for an environmental management system. Since the levels of environmental performance are not specified, the scheme can be implemented by a wide variety of organizations with varying level of environmental maturities. It is especially suitable as a single standard EMS for multinational companies (MNC). MNCs are often faced with an important strategic decision of deciding whether to adopt a global company EMS standard or adapt several standards to meet the specific local requirements of each location. The ISO 14000 framework is a flexible system which can be implemented either as a global integrative or local adaptive environmental strategy (Epstein & Roy, 1998).

Comparison of EMAS and ISO 14001

EMAS and ISO 14001 are compatible, so it is possible to get accreditation from both schemes simultaneously or one by one. However, there are specific differences between the two environmental management systems. These differences are summarized in Table 1.

EMAS is a European government regulation whereas ISO 14001 is an international standard issued by a non-governmental organization. Entities and sites can be registered with EMAS only within the boundaries of member states. Every member state has designated a "Competent Body" (European Commission, 2009) which is responsible for registering organizations and for maintaining the list of registered organizations in their country.

ISO 14001 is considered less strict than EMAS. EMAS is required to be controlled by state authorities for legal compliance whereas ISO 14001 requires only commitment to comply with applicable legal requirements. The audit cycle of compliances must be at intervals of no more than three years (European Commission, 2009) whereas no such frequency is explicitly stated for ISO 14001. ISO 14001 is designed primarily as an internal management tool for organizations to improve their environmental performance,

Table 1. Comparison of EMAS and ISO 14001

	EMAS	ISO 14001
Status	Legal status (based on a regulation of EU)	No legal status (private standard of a non-governmental organization)
Coverage	European standard (applies to EU Member States and EEA countries)	International standard (applies to all countries worldwide)
Information of environmental performance	Obligation to provide information to the public regarding environmental performance	No obligation to provide information to the public
Compliance-audit	Control by state authorities for legal compliance	Commitment to comply with applicable legal requirements
Audit cycle	Audit cycle of no more than 3 years	No specific frequency of audit cycles specified
Demonstration of compliance	Entering into the register and logo	Certification

whereas EMAS places a further focus on external stakeholders. EMAS requires organizations to establish an open dialogue between the public and other interested parties. For example, organizations registered to EMAS have to publish an environmental statement on its activities to the public, while such a requirement does not exist for ISO 14001.

According to a recent study by KPMG (2008), the ISO 14001 is the most widely used EMS standard globally. The sample of over 2200 companies includes the Global Fortune 250 (G250) and the 100 largest companies by revenue (N100) in 22 countries. Over 50 percent of G250 and over 40 percent of N100 companies have implemented ISO 14001 as EMS standard. On the other hand, only 7 percent of G250 and 5 percent of N100 companies have selected EMAS. Other companies in the study have implemented sector-specific management systems or other EMS standards.

Besides ISO 14001 and EMAS there exist other EMS standards such as the British Standard BS8555 to manage environmental performance evaluation, which is especially suitable for smaller and medium sized businesses. It is the world's first standard for environmental management systems, which was developed and published by the British Standard Institution (BSI Group, 2009). Another frequently used standard is the AccountAbility 1000 (AA 1000) (The Institute for Social and Ethical Accountability, 2009), which is focused on securing the quality of social and ethical accountability, auditing and reporting. Furthermore, there exists an ethical global standard Social Accountability 8000 (SA8000), which is developed based on the Universal Declaration of Human Rights. It addresses the rights of the workers and is applicable to all companies regardless of size and industry (Social Accountability International (SAI), 2009).

CORPORATE ENVIRONMENTAL REPORTING

To demonstrate compliance with laws and regulations, organizations report to various administrative bodies including governmental agencies. In addition, more and more organizations are also reporting to the public on their environmental performance to outline the activities carried out in terms of their environmental responsibilities. In this section we summarize the role of environmental reporting for organizations and typical contents of reports.

The Role of Environmental Reporting for the Organizations

The first environmental reports were published in the late 1980s and early 1990s (Tischner & Charter, 2001, p. 80) in the chemical industry by companies having serious image problems (Nash, 2000). Other sectors such as oil, energy, electronics and consumer products have also started to communicate using environmental reports in the 1990s. The EMS Standards like EMAS and ISO have influenced the rapid spread of environmental reporting globally. Moreover, the change in attitudes of companies regarding increasing transparency and willingness for disclosure of information about internal operations of the company has fostered voluntary environmental reporting.

Under heavy pressure from environmental groups and local communities, the chemical industry has been the leader in undertaking CSR activities (The Associated Chambers of Commerce and Industry of India, 2009), implementing advanced environmental management systems and utilizing environmental reports as an important communication tool with its stakeholders. Due to its potential risk of damaging the environment, the information and reporting requirements of organizations operating in this sector are also quite high. For example, in Germany an organization in chemical industry is subject to 255 legal information and reporting duties, most of which being obligatory. They are based on national –local, state, federal– and EU laws and regulations (Schulze, 2009, p. 17).

Environmental reports serve as a medium to comply with mandatory reporting duties for several organizations such as environmental and fiscal reporting. Besides their role in complying with legal requirements, more and more organizations make use of the collected data with the objective of delivering information about the operations of the organization and promoting cooperation with the various stakeholders, who are concerned about environmental issues. Environmental reports serve as a medium of communication with their various stakeholder including customers, suppliers, employees, citizens, governmental and regulatory bodies, environmental groups, local communities, insurers and shareholders. These stakeholders exert pressure on companies to comply with the environmental regulations and to continuously improve their environmental performance of production processes, products and logistics.

Legal Reporting Duties

In the European Union, environmental and sustainability initiatives have increased in the last decades. Technische Universität München (Technische Universität München & Siemens IT Solutions and Services, 2009a) has performed a comprehensive research analyzing the reporting duties of businesses operating in Germany. According to this study, environmental data management is not a new area for the businesses operating in Germany. Many organizations already utilize CEMIS to manage their environment-related data and to generate reports based on their reporting obligations towards administration and the public. In addition to their compulsory legal requirements for documenting and reporting, the growing public interest in potentially polluting activities of companies is a critical motivation for this trend.

For this reason, large enterprises with production facilities, which can cause environmental impacts, have been using CEMIS to get an overview and to manage different ratios such as emissions, waste and resource utilization. These organizations use the evaluations received from these systems not only to meet their legal obligations but also to receive environmental certifications, such as EMAS or the Blue Angel (Umweltbundesamt), as well as informing the public about the deployed environmental protection measures. The Federal

Table 2. Classification of environmental business to government processes in Germany. (Technische Universität München & Siemens IT Solutions and Services, 2009a, p. 71, 2009b, pp. 2-36)

	Waste	Waste Water	Emission, Immission	Production factor	Water
Application	2	2	2	3	2
Report	33	4	22	17	3
Notification	27	-	8	20	2
Register/Achieve	17	-	4	8	-
Total	**79**	**6**	**36**	**48**	**7**

Environment Agency (Umweltbundesamt) has defined the Blue Angel as the first and oldest environment-related label for products and services in the world.

In the study of Technische Universität München, environmental reporting duties and processes between business and governmental agencies have been analyzed. Table 2 summarizes the distribution of processes according to the type of substance in the process. The processes analyzed in the project are based on over 70 local, state, federal laws in Germany and EU level regulations.

It can be seen that the highest number of processes is in the area of waste. An analysis of the archiving, reporting and informing requirements of organizations in the field of industrial waste shows that a high number of organizations already have implemented CEMIS. Especially for the process of "European Data Interchange for Waste Notification System" ("Elektronisches Abfallnachweisverfahren"), specific solutions of information systems have been implemented to support application, reporting and archiving requirements associated with the transportation of hazardous waste.

However, waste management in Germany presents an area of optimization for combination of several reports, as different types of reports about waste are based on the same data. Providers of CEMIS in the area of waste management have already recognized this overlap and consider integrating such client systems into their solutions, which enables integrated management of all the data related to waste. Like in this example there are many other areas where businesses can profit from an integrated view of different reporting duties concerning similar data. The goal must therefore be to identify these areas, to optimize the related processes and to develop interfaces on the side of administration, so that information and reports can be delivered from organizations to administration without any media breaks.

Content of the Reports

The content of environmental reports developed to comply with regulations (environmental compliance reports) can be quite different from CSR reports. Even though based on the same data, their structure, range of target users and detail level usually differ considerably. Environmental compliance reports are generally prepared more specifically, including one or a few aspects of environmental performance such as waste, waste water, production factor, emissions and immissions in detail. They are targeted to experts in government or environmental agencies therefore the commentary part is either missing or described only briefly.

CSR reports on the other hand are targeted to a broader range of stakeholders, some of which cannot be expected to have expert knowledge in environmental performance. Therefore, CSR reports mostly include explanatory graphics, commentary and discussion parts, in order to support comprehension and underline specific messages. In addition, CSR reports are generally less-focused and include a broad overview of several aspects related to the environmental performance of an organization.

It is not possible to define a specific structure for environmental compliance reports, since there are various types of reports depending on the focus of the report, substances to be included, organizations to be reported to and related regulations. CSR reports on the other hand usually have comparable structures. They are similar to annual reports of organizations including commentary and presentation parts. The commentary part includes the discussion and summary, while the presentation part consists of mainly the quantitative information. The typical contents of qualitative and quantitative information of CSR reports are analyzed in Table 3.

In order to prepare a CSR report, it is important to develop a clear and consistent reporting strategy with defined target groups and content. Typically there exists a wide variety of stakeholders with different needs and interests, therefore organizations need to prioritize their audiences or generate different versions of reports to target a large audience effectively. One of the challenges companies face with reporting is determining the style and content of reports, which reflects all the important issues but is also easy to understand and to navigate. Environmental reports commonly reflect the company's overall strategy and objectives, cover issues material to the company and stakeholders and deliver summary information as well as details. As a part of the environmental communication strategy, environmental managers also have to decide which type of data to include – whether or not to give the *tough* news and facts as well as the *good* ones. A survey by KPMG (2008) shows that generally a number of factors determine what to include in the reports: Nearly 60 percent of companies select the content of reports based on their own strategy and objectives. Nearly 40 percent of the companies cite stakeholder consultation as a key determinant for selecting indicators. About 60 percent of companies mention the Sustainability Reporting Guidelines of GRI as the framework they use to select their report contents. A recent analysis of Spada Research (2008) with Financial Times Stock Exchange (FTSE) 100 Index companies in Britain identifies seven themes, which the stakeholders might expect to see in reporting: "corporate responsibility, environment, climate change, sustainability, renewable energy, waste and recycling, and resource and supply chain" (Spada Limited, 2008, p. 36).

The analysis of the basic conditions and requirements for environmental compliance reports shows that enterprises report similar data to several authorities but in varying formats. Although the reports are structured differently, they are often composed of the same basic information. This increases the error-proneness of the data, creates redundancy and causes inefficiency. In order to reduce the burden on businesses caused by heterogeneous reporting in the field environmental data management, there exists a need to optimize the data generation and reporting processes by increasing the reusability of the data and abolishing the fragmentation of report requirements, as well as enabling automatic delivery without any media breaks.

Systematic Approaches for Sustainability Reporting

Thousands of companies over the world publish CSR reports voluntarily to disclose the sustainability impacts of their activities. Without a generally accepted reporting framework they would lack credibility, consistency and comparability. The Sustainability Reporting Guidelines of GRI is the first and most commonly known global framework for comprehensive sustainability reporting. Launched in 2000 and updated regularly, the reporting framework provides guidance on how organizations can disclose their sustainabil-

Table 3. Typical qualitative and quantitative contents of CSR reports. (Adapted from van der Molen 2009, pp. 7-14)

Typical categories	**Example content**
Qualitative Information	
Company description	• Company size and activities • Description of the main environmental issues related to production and distribution
Environmental policy	• Summary of corporate environmental policy • Expected achievements
Environmental Management Systems	• Programs for environmental policy implementation • Implementation level of environmental management system and certifications (EMAS, ISO or UNI)
Risk management	• Audits, measures taken and achievements regarding risk management • Description of major accidents
Compliance with environmental legislation	• Description of the way the company ensures compliance with environmental regulations • Description of measures adopted to comply with new environmental regulations (EU, national)
Product policy	• Description of products life cycle and of the related impacts • Co-operation programs with consumers and clients • Eco-label (where applicable)
Conservation of natural resources	• Energy and water saving programs • Other programs for the protection of natural heritage
Stakeholder relations	• Participation in voluntary agreement schemes • Relations with stakeholders
Certification	• External certification
Quantitative Information	
Environmental expenditures	• Data on environmental expenditures • Explanation of accounting criteria
Emissions and consumption of raw materials	• Raw materials and energy as input • Wastes, air emissions, water, discharges and soil pollution and other pollutants relevant for company's activity • Impacts related to production activity
Environmental performance indicators	• Environmental performance indicators compared with previous periods

ity performance. The framework is applicable to organizations of any size, constituency or location and has been used already by many organizations around the world.

Most of the organizations use information technology to support strategic and operative management of environmental issues. There are even software-based reporting tools developed specifically for one single reporting duty according to 13. Bundes-Immissionsschutzverordnung of the federal immission control law in Germany (Goscimski, 2007). CEMIS are information systems that include a variety of tools and technologies to facilitate storing, managing, analyzing and archiving of environment related information of the organizations. In advanced systems, performance data such as the energy usage required for processes and waste generation, the result of environmental accounting and site environmental audits can also be registered and centrally managed. Although the basic calculations required for the environmental reports can be made by a standard application, the reports have to be specifically customized depending on the organization and the authority to be delivered. In other words CEMIS allow the conversion of environmental data into environmental information. Accordingly many enterprises have already established environmental management information systems for the management of environmental data and the generation of different reports and declarations requested by law. There exist sophisticated solutions which allow a customizable and target-oriented generation of reports with trends, direction and magnitude of change in several formats including MS Excel, XML, PDF and Postscript (Fujitsu, 2009; WESTON, 2009). Many companies use a combination of both PDF and web versions presenting data online.

The organizations use CEMIS to generate the necessary reports, especially in compliance with the requirements of local environmental authorities. For example, CEMIS typically include a module for emission monitoring which displays the current levels of concentrations and possible excess values, as well as trend-analysis. Since emissions reports are generally required by environmental authorities, they generate the necessary data for emissions reports which represent the summary of emissions values on a daily, monthly or yearly basis. Other typical modules of CEMIS are waste reporting, eco-balance calculations and monitoring, CO_2 monitoring and reporting, authority reporting, air quality monitoring, environmental performance indicators and corporate reporting. Although most of the companies use sophisticated environmental information systems for the management of environmental data and generation of different reports, a close analysis clearly demonstrates that the process of gathering relevant information for the reports needs to be optimized.

The research of Technische Universität München (Technische Universität München & Siemens IT Solutions and Services, 2009a) involving businesses in Germany clearly demonstrates that many enterprises have already established information systems for the management of environmental data and the generation of reports requested by law. However, the reporting process between the governmental organizations and enterprises needs to be optimized by eliminating media breaks: Interfaces enabling automatic reporting and message delivery would greatly improve the processes.

There exist several other studies in literature, which recognize the need to optimize the reporting processes between private companies and government. One example is the development of a model for Data- and Information-management (DIRA) to simplify the communication between private companies and the administration in the area of waste (Lehmann, 2008). DIRA introduces a reference model for the data- and information-management in the waste management together with its all necessary system-components and possibly required extensions.

LIFE CYCLE ASSESSMENT (LCA) AS AN APPROACH TO ENVIRONMENTAL MANAGEMENT

There are different tools and approaches which can be used by organizations to structure environmental management such as LCA. Life Cycle Thinking enables organizations to take into account all environmental impacts associated with their business processes. It is used to evaluate environmental burdens associated with a process or product by identifying and quantifying relevant inputs and outputs and assessing their potential impacts to the environment. Although it is accepted as an operational approach, it has also several limitations. In this section LCA is introduced and its limitations are discussed.

Sustainability influences all aspects of industrial processes starting with the extraction of raw materials from the earth and tracing all operations until the final disposal of these materials as wastes back into the earth. This task requires completely new approaches to strategic decision making processes. The methodologies to assist decision support are still under development. The LCA approach is "an environmental assessment tool that intends to quantify impacts of processes, products and services over the complete sequence of a process chain" (Bortone & Palumbo, 2007, p. 145). The Life Cycle Assessment is also known as Life Cycle Analysis and Ecobalance (Ökobilanz) (Krcmar, Dold, Fischer, Strobel & Seifert, 2000, p. 16).

LCA offers a theoretical framework for understanding material flows and potential impacts involved with providing services or products in a closed loop. It is primarily focused on evaluating the potential environmental impacts of a product, a service, process or activity throughout its entire life cycle by quantifying the use of resources (inputs such as energy, raw materials, water) and environmental emissions (outputs to air, water and soil). LCA is based on reducing waste and inefficiency in production processes. This helps to save money and contribute to the environment protection at the same time. The potential environmental impact of a product, process or activity is evaluated throughout its entire life cycle from the extraction of raw materials through production of the materials which are used in manufacturing of the product, over the use of the product, to its recycling and/or ultimate disposal of some of its constituents. In addition to enterprises it is also used by governments e.g. for establishing eco-labeling criteria for certain product groups in Germany (Scholl & Nisius, 1998).

LCA is a powerful tool for analyzing commensurable aspects of quantifiable systems. However, it is criticized that not every factor can be reduced to a number and inserted into a model. Besides, the outcomes of LCA depend on the scope and depth of analysis which leads to problems with comparison of outcomes. The main problems of LCA are seen in parameters (considering paper productions for example, should the type of saw used for tree felling be considered?), in comparison of data (is one extra part per million of an air pollutant more or less damaging than an extra kilogram of a waterborne waste given the same toxic level?), in combination of issues (what is the total amount of damage if different types of wastes are combined?), in disposal and decomposition (what is long-term impact of disposal and decomposition?) and in assignable cause (which product(s) is/are exactly responsible for the damage occurred?) (Welford, 1996, p. 148).

Addressing the above listed problems at the planning stage of LCA and being aware of its limitations may increase its effectiveness. Being a very promising tool, it should still be kept in mind that LCA is a tool still under development. Further research is expected to introduce advanced approaches to address the problems listed above and make life cycle assessments more feasible.

SUGGESTED APPROACHES FOR AN EFFICIENT GENERATION OF ENVIRONMENT-RELATED DATA FOR ORGANIZATIONAL REPORTING

Based on the analysis of literature and recent projects, environmental reports include a high variety of information of several categories. The notification and reporting obligations in the field of environment are aimed at limiting and controlling the harmful effects of entrepreneurial activities on the environment. For this purpose, businesses are obligated to report about their potentially polluting activities. In other words, the environmental management of the organization *creates* information-flows along with the processed material-flows.

To control and manage the environmental impacts, an organization needs to know what these impacts are. We suggest two approaches based on LCA which can support organizations during data gathering and for the generation of environmental reports:

1. Environmental domain model: Generation of environmental data by utilizing an environmental model
2. Site/Facility centered environmental management: Generation of environmental data

Figure 2. Information and material-flow for a production process (Adapted from Krcmar, et al., 2000, p. 41)

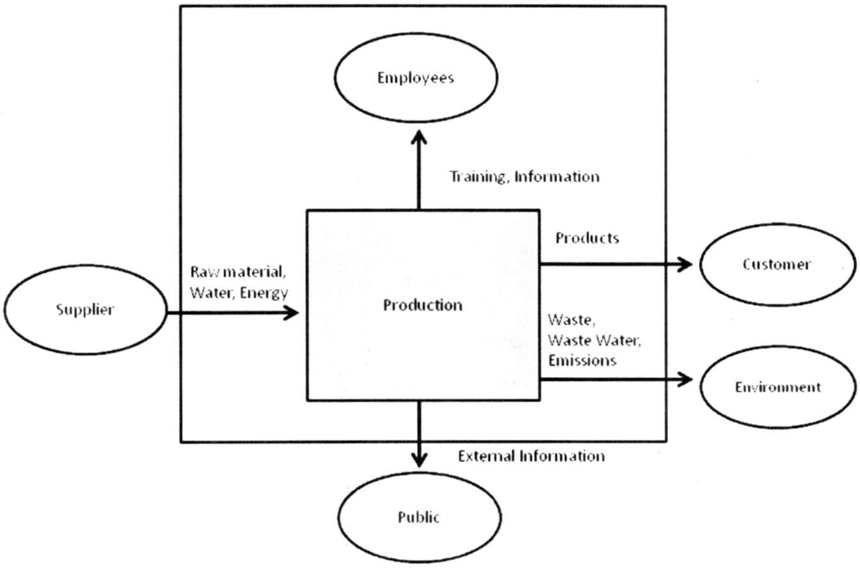

specific for each facility based on the analysis of environmental impacts

Environmental Domain Model (Model of Information and Material Flows)

A domain model is "a model of the domain within which an enterprise conducts its business" (Oldfield, 2002, p.3). Generally domain models describe the various entities and components involved in the system with their relationships. Domain models provide a structural view of systems by identifying the relationships among all major entities within the system as well as its specific domain-vocabulary (Gottesdiener, 2002).

One usage area of such a domain model for environment – environmental domain model – is the identification of environmental aspects for an organization. The environment related information and material flows of a production process are demonstrated by an environmental domain model as follows:

Environmental domain models are also used for environmental controlling and LCA purposes. In addition, they are also perfectly suitable to structure environmental data. This data can then be used for several purposes, e.g. generating different types of environmental reports discussed in section 2. The elements of an information- and material-flow for a production process can be described as follows (Krcmar, et al., 2000):

1. **Environmental impacts:** Environmental impacts of waste, waste water and emissions can be directly attributed to information- and material-flows.
2. **Energy management:** Energy management refers to using, selection and saving of energy. In particular, a structured and content-based control of the energy-flows is required for increasing the efficiency of energy.
3. **Raw materials and water:** An analysis of material-flows is required for management, saving, selection and transportation of raw

Figure 3. Site/facility based environmental management (Adapted from Schaaf, 2009, p. 4)

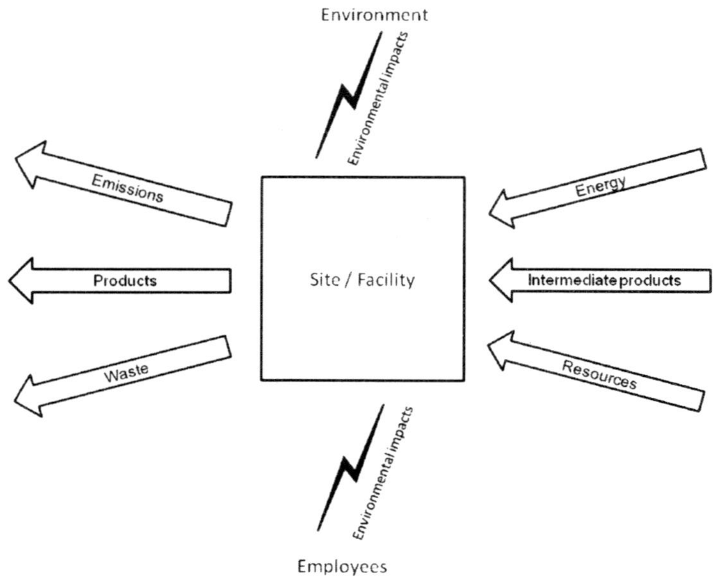

materials as well as for management of water supplies.

4. **Waste:** An analysis of material-flows is required for prevention, recycling and reuse of waste.
5. **Production process:** Production processes are directly involved in the environmental processes that affect the use and efficiency of material-flows.
6. **Design of products:** The design of the products has a direct impact on information- and material- flows.
7. **Informing and training of employees:** Information-flows required by the employees as well as their training needs should be considered.
8. **External information:** Information-flows should be made available to various stakeholders including the public.

There are different methods for identifying the elements of information- and material-flows. Interviews, questionnaires or process descriptions can be used as a basis for the generation of the domain model.

Site/Facility Centered Environmental Management

Most of the environmental reports are based on sites or facilities (e.g. production facility) (Bundesregierung, 2004, 2004a, 2006; The European Commission, 2008). For an efficient generation of data for organizational reporting, environment management should be based on sites or facilities.

As shown in Figure 3, the site/facility is placed on the center of environmental management. As example input factors, energy, intermediate products and resources are given. As output, the products, waste, emissions as well as other possible environmental impacts are covered. It is possible to include other input and/or output factors depending on the characteristics of the site or facility.

The above described approach enables organizations to control input and output factors specific to a site/facility, which in turn supports the generation of environmental reports.

FUTURE RESEARCH DIRECTIONS

The results of our research demonstrate that the field of environmental data management is not new for many organizations. There already exist advanced integrated models –such as DIRA– which support communication of businesses with administration. Meanwhile Corporate Environmental Management Information Systems have been developed and become more sophisticated. Advanced solutions of CEMIS offer possibilities to customize the system according to the organizational requirements and preferences to support the internal and external reporting duties of companies.

Future target in the area of environmental management should be the optimization of the processes as well as the elimination of media breaks. We would suggest, therefore, that further research be undertaken to create conceptual and technical premises in order to enable report and message data to be automatically delivered to the authorities without any media breaks. Evaluation and rating systems should also be introduced not only to further motivate the organizations and but also to provide a clear understanding for the members of public who cannot be expected to have a good command of the environmental terminology.

CONCLUSION

Recognizing the serious global concerns such as climate change and environmental pollution, many global organizations set clear strategies to reduce the environmental impact of their operations, products and processes. As a sign of their commitments to contributing to a sustainable development and 'green production' they issue various environmental sustainability reports to customers, shareholders and communities in which they operate. Environmental reports present an official, comparable and credible medium for communication. In addition, they serve a wide range of purposes – from regulatory compliance to informing various stakeholders. Reporting on operations can enhance a company's public image but it also presents a valuable opportunity to locate inefficiencies and waste. More than 80 percent of the Fortune global top 250 companies issue environmental, social or sustainability reports, most of them being voluntary. Recognizing their benefits, in the recent future, we expect an increase in the number of organizations which decide to report due to the increased public awareness. Organizations have already begun to accept it as a part of a legitimate process to success in a global world that is increasingly sensitive to issues of sustainable development. To support structured development of reports, most of them utilize EMS standards such as ISO 14001 and EMAS. The global reporting guidelines enable the comparability and consistency of them.

We believe that this trend will continue. Not only CSR reports will be an indispensable part of the policies of organizations but also they will communicate their commitment through their websites, brochures, press releases, company environmental policies and various types of advertisements. We also expect an increased usage of CEMIS as they are helpful tools for legal compliance and CSR reporting as well as continuous improvement. Moreover by utilizing LCA based methodologies –such as environmental domain model and site/facility centered environmental management– organization can enhance the data gathering and report generation process for environmental reporting significantly.

REFERENCES

Bassen, A., Jastram, S., & Meyer, K. (2005). Corporate Social Responsitility. Eine Begriffserläuterung. *Zeitschrift für Wirtschafts- und Unternehmensethik, 6*(2), 231-236.

Biloslavo, R., & Trnavcevic, A. (2009). Web sites as tools of communication of a "green" company. *Management Decision, 47*(7), 1158–1173. doi:10.1108/00251740910978359

Bonini, S. M. J., & Hintz, G., & Mendonca, Lenny T. (2008). Addressing consumer concerns about climate change. *The McKinsey Quarterly*, (2): 52–61.

Bortone, G., & Palumbo, L. (Eds.). (2007). *Sustainable management of sediment resources: Sediment and Dredged Material Treatment* (*Vol. 2*). Amsterdam: Elsevier.

Bundesregierung (2004). 11. BImSchV: Elfte Verordnung zur Durchführung des Bundes-Immissionsschutzgesetzes (Verordnung über Emissionserklärungen und Emissionsberichte). Retrieved August 10, 2009, from http://bundesrecht.juris.de/bundesrecht/bimschv_11_2004/ gesamt.pdf

Bundesregierung (2004a). 13. BImSchV: Elfte Verordnung zur Durchführung des Bundes-Immissionsschutzgesetzes (Verordnung über Großfeuerungs- und Gasturbinenanlagen). Retrieved September 1, 2009, from http://www.gesetze.juris.de/bundesrecht/ bimschv_13_2004/gesamt.pdf

Bundesregierung (2006). Verordnung über die Entsorgung gebrauchter halogenierter Lösemittel (HKWAbfV). Retrieved August 15, 2009, from http://www.gesetze.juris.de/bundesrecht/ hkwabfv/gesamt.pdf

Cascio, J., Woodside, G., & Mitchell, P. (2005). *ISO 14000 guide: the new international environmental management standards* (2nd ed.). McGraw Hill.

Commission of the European Communities. (2007). *Commission Staff Working Document: Accompanying document to the Communication from the Commission to the Council*. The European Parliament, The European Economic and Social Committee and the Committee of the Regions.

Darabaris, J. (2008). *Corporate Environmental Management*. Boca Raton, FL: CRC Press.

Darnall, N., Jolley, G. J., & Handfield, R. (2008). Environmental Management Systems and Green Supply Chain Management: Complement for Sustainability? *Business Strategy and the Environment*, 18.

Deloitte & Touche LLP, & Grocery Manufactures Association (GMA) (2009). Green Shopper Study.

Deming, W. E. (1986). *The New Economics: For Industry, Government and Education* (2nd ed.). Cambridge, MA: Massachusetts Institute of Technology Center for Advanced Engineering Study.

Epstein, M., & Roy, M. J. (1998). Managing Corporate Environmental Performance: A Multinational Perspective. *European Management Journal, 16*(3). European Commission. Eco-Management and Audit Scheme. Retrieved July 22, 2009, from http://ec.europa.eu/environment/emas/

European Commission. (2009). *The State of Sustainability Reporting in Europe: Commission Statement*. Fujitsu. Environmental Management Information Systems. Retrieved August 12, 2009, from http://www.fujitsu.com/global/about/ environment/management/ems/information-sys/

Global Reporting Initiative (GRI) (2006). *Sustainability Reporting Guidelines*.

Global Reporting Initiative (GRI) (2008). *European Sustainability Reporting Association Report from GRI*.

Goscimski, J. (2007). Development of a Software-based Environmental Reporting According to the "Bundes-Immissionsschutzgesetz". In Gomez, J. M., Sonnenschein, M., Müller, M., & Welsch, H. (Eds.), *Information Technologies in Environmental Engineering* (pp. 567–574). Berlin, Heidelberg: Springer Verlag. doi:10.1007/978-3-540-71335-7_55

Gottesdiener, E. (2002). *Requirements by Collaboration*. Boston: Pearson Education, Inc.

Group, B. S. I. BSI: Standards, Training, Testing, Assessment & Certification. Retrieved July 26, 2009, from http://www.bsi-global.com/

Hicks, J. R. (1946). *Value and Capital: An Inquiry into Some Fundamental Principles of Economic Theory*. Oxford: Clarendon Press.

International Organization for Standardization. ISO 14001:2004 - Environmental management systems. Retrieved July 10, 2009, from http://www.iso.org/

International Organization for Standardization. TC207 Environmental Management. Retrieved July 21, 2009, from http://www.tc207.org/

Kolk, A. (1999). Evaluating corporate environmental reporting. *Business Strategy and the Environment*, *8*(4), 225–237. doi:10.1002/(SICI)1099-0836(199907/08)8:4<225::AID-BSE206>3.0.CO;2-4

KPMG International (2008). *KPMG International Survey of Corporate Responsibility Reporting 2008*.

Krcmar, H., Dold, G., Fischer, H., Strobel, M., & Seifert, E. K. (Eds.). (2000). *Informationssysteme für das Umweltmanagement*. München: Oldenbourg Wissenschaftsverlag.

Lang, C. V. (2007). Modeling of a Corporate Environmental Management Information System (CEMIS) for Production Processes. In Gomez, J. M., Sonnenschein, M., Müller, M., & Welsch, H. (Eds.), *Information Technologies in Environmental Engineering* (pp. 231–240). Berlin, Heidelberg: Springer Verlag. doi:10.1007/978-3-540-71335-7_24

Lehmann, J. M. (2008). *Modell für das Daten- und Informationsmanagement in der Abfallwirtschaft*.

Marshall, S. R., & Brown, D. (2003). Corporate environmental reporting: What's in a metric? *Business Strategy and the Environment*, *12*(2), 87–106. doi:10.1002/bse.354

Nash, J. (2000). Voluntary Codes of Practice: Non-Governmental Institutions for Promoting Environmental Management by Firms.

Oldfield, P. (2002). Domain Modelling. Retrieved July 10, 2009, from http://www.aptprocess.com/whitepapers/DomainModelling.pdf

Prugh, T., Costanza, R., & Cumberland, J. H. (1999). *Natural Capital and Human Economic Survival* (2nd ed.). Crc Pr Inc.

Rawlins, B., Paine, K., & Kowalski, P. (2008). *Measuring the Transparency of Environmental Sustainability Reporting Through Websites of Fortune 50 Companies*.

Schaaf, U. (2009). Die Zukunft betrieblicher Umwelt-Informationssysteme. Retrieved October 10, 2009, from http://www.umweltcluster.net/getResource/18370/6_Zukunft-BUIS_ Schaaf_ Ulrich.pdf

Scholl, G. U., & Nisius, S. (1998). The environmental benefits to German companies through application of LCA. *Journal of Cleaner Production*, *6*, 247–252. doi:10.1016/S0959-6526(98)00025-0

Schulze, G. G. (2009). *Bürokratie- und Regulierungskosten in der chemischen Industrie: Potenziale zu ihrer Reduktion.* Social Accountability International (SAI). Overview of SA8000. Retrieved October 12, 2009, from http://www.sa-intl.org/

Spada Limited (2008). *Environmental Reporting: Trends in FTSE 100 Sustainability Reports.*

Strauss, R., & Bird, S. (2009). The State of Sustainability Reporting in Europe: Commission Statement. Retrieved July 26, 2009, from http://www.sustainabilityreporting.eu/general/ downloads/ec08.pdf

Technische Universität München. (2009a). *Siemens IT Solutions and Services.* Machbarkeitsstudie Prozessketten Umwelt.

Technische Universität München. (2009b). *Siemens IT Solutions and Services.* Prozessbibliothek zur Machbarkeitsstudie Prozessketten Umwelt.

The Associated Chambers of Commerce and Industry of India (2009). *ASSOCHAM Eco Pulse Study: Corporate Social Responsibility 2008-09.*

The European Commission. (2008). The European Pollutant Emission Register (EPER) and the European Pollutant Release and Transfer Register (E-PRTR). Retrieved October 14, 2009, from http://ec.europa.eu/environment/air/pollutants/stationary/eper/index.htm

The Institute for Social and Ethical Accountability. AccountAbility. Retrieved July 26, 2009, from http://www.accountability21.net/

Tischner, U., & Charter, M. (2001). *Sustainable Solutions: Developing Products and Services for the Future.* Sheffield: Greenleaf Publishing.

Umweltbundesamt. Der Blaue Engel. Retrieved July 26, 2009, from http://www.blauer-engel.de/

United Nations World Commission on Environment and Development. (1987). *Our Common Future.* Oxford: Oxford University Press.

U.S. Environmental Protection Agency. Environmental Management Systems: Key Management System Concepts Retrieved October 07, 2009, from http://www.epa.gov/ems/info/keyconcepts.htm

van der Molen, F. The International Corporate Sustainability Reporting Site. Retrieved July 21, 2009, from http://www.enviroreporting.com/others/feem.htm

Weiß, P., & Bentlage, J. (2006). *Environmental Management Systems and Certification.* The Baltic University Press.

Welford, R. (1996). *Corporate Environmental Management.* London: Earthscan Publications Ltd.

Wenk, M. S. (2005). *The European Union's Eco-management and Audit Scheme (EMAS)*: Springer Science & Business. WESTON. Environmental Management Information Systems (EMIS). Retrieved August 15, 2009, from http://www.weston-solutions.com/Services/environmental_solutions/health_safety/ems/ emis/ index.htm

Wisconsin Department of Natural Resources EMAS and ISO 14001. Retrieved July 16, 2009, from http://www.dnr.state.wi.us/org/caer/cea/environmental/advisors/documents/20070306EMASandISO14001.pdf

ADDITIONAL READING

Aerts, W., Cormier, D., & Magnan, M. (2008). Corporate environmental disclosure, financial markets and the media: An international perspective. *Ecological Economics*, *64*(3), 643–659. doi:10.1016/j.ecolecon.2007.04.012

Allenby, B. (2001). Clean products in a complex world. *Clean Products and Processes, 2*, 189–191. doi:10.1007/s100980000084

Atkinson, G. (2000). Measuring Corporate Sustainability. *Journal of Environmental Planning and Management, 43*(2), 235–252. doi:10.1080/09640560010694

Benett, R. M., Phipps, R. H., & Strange, A. M. (2006). An Application of Life-Cycle Assessment for Environmental Planning and Management: The Potential Environmental and Human Health Impacts of Growing Genetically-Modified Herbicide-Tolerant Sugar Beet. *Journal of Environmental Planning and Management, 49*(1), 59–74. doi:10.1080/09640560500373139

Bergeson, L. L. (2009). 2009 and Beyond: Outlook for Environmental Issues. *Environmental Quality Management, 18*(4), 73–86. doi:10.1002/tqem.20227

Biloslavo, R., & Trnavcevic, A. (2009). Web sites as tools of communication of a "green" company. *Management Decision, 47*(7), 1158–1173. doi:10.1108/00251740910978359

Brécard, D., Hlaimi, B., Lucas, S., Perraudeau, Y., & Salladarré, F. (2009). Determinants of demand for green products: An application to eco-label demand for fish in Europe. *Ecological Economics, 69*(1), 115–125. doi:10.1016/j.ecolecon.2009.07.017

Canadian Center of Science and Education. (2008-2009). Journal of Sustainable Development. Retrieved October 01, 2009, from http://ccsenet.org/journal/index.php/jsd/article/viewFile/ 88/1324

Cormier, D., & Magnan, M. (2007). The revisited contribution of environmental reporting to investors' valuation of a firm's earnings: An international perspective. *Ecological Economics, 62*(3-4), 613–626. doi:10.1016/j.ecolecon.2006.07.030

Cruz, L. B., & Pedrezo, E. A. (2009). Corporate social responsibility and green management: Relation between headquarters and subsidiary in multinational corporations. *Management Decision, 47*(7), 1174–1199. doi:10.1108/00251740910978368

Darabaris, J. (2008). *Corporate Environmental Management*. Boca Raton, FL: CRC Press.

Dold, G. (Ed.). (1996). *Computerunterstützung der produktbezogenen Ökobilanzierung*. Wiesbaden: Gabler Verlag, Deutscher Universitäts Verlag.

Donnelly, K., Salemink, A., Blechinger, F., Schuh, A., & Boehm, T. (2004). A Product-Based Environmental Management System. *Greener Management International* (46), 57-72.

Ekins, P., & Vanner, R. (2007). Sectoral sustainability and sustainability assessment methodologies: A review of methodology in light of collaboration with the UK oil and gas sector. *Journal of Environmental Planning and Management, 50*(1), 87–111. doi:10.1080/09640560601048440

European Commission (2009). *The State of Sustainability Reporting in Europe: Commission Statement*.

Fortunski, B. (2008). Does the environmental management standard ISO 14001 stimulate sustainable development?: An example from the energy sector in Poland. *Management of Environmental Quality: An International Journal, 19*(2), 204–212. doi:10.1108/14777830810856582

Frondel, M., Horbach, J., & Rennings, K. (2008). What triggers environmental management and innovation? Empirical evidence for Germany. *Ecological Economics, 66*(1), 153–160. doi:10.1016/j.ecolecon.2007.08.016

Garrido, N., & Alvarez del Castillo, M. Dolors. (2007). LCA Case Studies: Environmental Evaluation of Single-Use and Reusable Cups. *International Journal of Life Cycle Assessment, 12*(4), 252–256. doi:10.1065/lca2007.05.334

Gerbens-Leenes, P. W., Moll, H. C., & Schoot Uiterkamp, A. J. M. (2003). Design and development of a measuring method for environmental sustainability in food production systems. *Ecological Economics*, *46*(2), 231–248. doi:10.1016/S0921-8009(03)00140-X

Haddock-Fraser, J. E., & Tourelle, M. (2009). *Corporate Motivations for Environmental Sustainable Development: Exploring the Role of Consumers in Stakeholder Engagement.* Business Strategy and the Environment.

Hertin, J., Berkhout, F., Wagner, M., & Tyteca, D. (2008). Are EMS environmentally effective? The link between environmental management systems and environmental performance in European companies. *Journal of Environmental Planning and Management*, *51*(2), 259–283. doi:10.1080/09640560701865040

Inderscience Publishers. (1979-2009). International Journal of Environment and Sustainable Development (IJESD). Retrieved October 01, 2009, from http://www.inderscience.com/ browse/index.php?journalID=10

Interscience, W. (1993-2009). Sustainable Development. Retrieved October 01, 2009, from http://www3.interscience.wiley.com/journal/5346/toc?CRETRY=1&SRETRY=0

Krcmar, H., & Dold, G. (Eds.). (1996). *Aspekte der Ökobilanzierung.* Wiesbaden: Gabler Verlag, Deutscher Uniersitäts Verlag.

Krcmar, H., Dold, G., Fisher, H., Strobel, M., & Seifert, E. (Eds.). (2000). *Informationssysteme für das Umweltmanagement: Das Referenzmodell ECO-Integral.* München: R. Oldenbourg Verlag.

Lehmann, J.-M. (2008). *Modell für das Daten- und Informationsmanagement in der Abfallwirtschaft.*

Mooney, H., Larigauderie, A., Cesario, M., Elmquist, T., Hoegh-Guldberg, O., & Lavorel, S. (2009). Biodiversity, climate change, and ecosystem services. *Current Opinion in Environmental Sustainability*, *1*(1), 46–54. doi:10.1016/j.cosust.2009.07.006

Papageorgiou, A., Barton, J. R., & Karagiannidis, A. (2009). Assessment of the greenhouse effect impact of technologies used for energy recovery from municipal waste: A case for England. *Journal of Environmental Management*, *90*(10), 2999–3012. doi:10.1016/j.jenvman.2009.04.012

Parsons, D. (2007). LCA Case Studies: The Environmental Impact of Disposable Versus Re-Chargeable Batteries for Consumer Use. *International Journal of Life Cycle Assessment*, *12*(3), 197–203. doi:10.1065/lca2006.08.270

Pojasek, R. B. (2009). Using Leader Indicators to Drive Sustainability Performance. *Environmental Quality Management*, *18*(4), 87–93. doi:10.1002/tqem.20228

Rennings, K., Ziegler, A., Ankele, K., & Hoffmann, E. (2006). The influence of different characteristics of the EU environmental management and auditing scheme on technical environmental innovations and economic performance. *Ecological Economics*, *57*(1), 45–59. doi:10.1016/j.ecolecon.2005.03.013

Sarkis, J., & Sroufe, R. (2004). Strategic Sustainability: The State of the Art In Corporate Environmental Management Systems. *Greener Management International* (46), 5-9.

Scrase, J. I., & Sheate, W. R. (2002). Integration and integrated approaches to assessment: what do they mean for the environment? *Journal of Environmental Policy and Planning*, *4*(4), 275–294. doi:10.1002/jepp.117

Sneddon, C., Howarth, R. B., & Norgaard, R. B. (2006). Sustainable development in a post-Brundtland world. *Ecological Economics*, *57*(2), 253–268. doi:10.1016/j.ecolecon.2005.04.013

Solomon, A., & Lewis, L. (2002). Incentives and Disincentives for Corporate Environmental Disclosure. *Business Strategy and the Environment*, *11*, 154–169. doi:10.1002/bse.328

Technische Universität München. (2009). *Siemens IT Solutions and Services*. Machbarkeitsstudie Prozessketten Umwelt.

Ulku, O., Phil, L., Deborah, D., James, R. H., & Thomas, P. (2004). EMS and Sustainable Development: A Model and Comparative Studies of Integration. *Greener Management International* (46), 11-28.

Weiß, P., & Bentlage, J. (2006). *Environmental Management Systems and Certification*. The Baltic University Press.

Welford, R. (1996). *Corporate Environmental Management*. London: Earthscan Publications Ltd.

Will, M. (2008). Talking about the future within an SME?: Corporate foresight and the potential contributions to sustainable development. *Management of Environmental Quality: An International Journal*, *19*(2), 234–242. doi:10.1108/14777830810856618

Chapter 15
Cooperative Inter-Municipal Waste Collection:
A Multi Agent System Approach

Vitoantonio Bevilacqua
Politecnico di Bari, Italy

Francesca Intini
Università della Basilicata, Italy

Silvana Kühtz
Università della Basilicata, Italy

Paolo Renna
Università della Basilicata, Italy

ABSTRACT

The cooperative inter-municipal waste collection can be a real added value in terms of costs reduction and high performance services. The chapter proposes a Multi Agent Approach to support the inter-municipal infrastructure. The Multi Agent Systems (MAS) is an approach suitable to implement a distributed physically problem as the inter-municipal waste collection. The architecture of the approach is formalized by work-flow analysis: a static view by IDEF0 diagram and a dynamic view by UML activity diagram. This analysis promotes the cooperation among municipalities to manage the waste collection service in an optimal way. According to Italian laws, the municipalities are responsible for organizing the management of municipal waste in agreement with the principles of transparency, efficiency, effectiveness and inexpensiveness. The coordination protocol among the agents allows to divide the costs among the municipalities in an efficient way. Finally, a discrete event simulation environment is developed to test the proposed MAS architecture.

DOI: 10.4018/978-1-61520-981-1.ch015

INTRODUCTION

A municipal solid waste (MSW) management system is a very complex system: there are multi-objectives to be achieved. Planners must develop the best practicable and environmentally sustainable waste management strategies and this task could be very difficult to carry out. The different objectives are not all related to economic costs and must therefore be considered in a proper multi-objective framework.

In this chapter we have carried out a study in order to estimate and allocate the costs related to separate waste collection in an inter-municipal area located in the province of Bari (Italy). This analysis promotes the cooperation among municipalities to the waste collection service management. Actually the municipalities are responsible to waste collection in accordance with principles of transparency, efficiency, effectiveness and inexpensiveness.

For this reason we have built a model of separate waste collection management, highlighting the cost functions, based on Multi-Agent Theory (Li, 2006; Xiao, 2006). MAS is an approach suitable to implement a distributed physically problem as the inter-municipal waste collection. The search of waste collection path can be interpreted as a Travelling Salesman Problem TSP and it is solved with the use of genetic algorithms. The total cost of the service has been divided among the individual municipalities using the theory of cooperative games, stressing that local authorities are not interested in paying off more than they would pay if they were organized independently. The proposed simulation environment has been developed using the Java package and it can be used to support the decision of a municipal area to participate in a network.

In summary, the chapter deals with:

- The formalization of the MAS architecture, obtained using the IDEF0 and UML diagrams. The former describes the processes' static view, including inputs, outputs, controls and mechanisms. IDEF0 diagrams allow us to describe static view, while UML activity diagram the dynamic views of the MAS architecture.
- The cooperative approach proposed allows integrating several municipal areas through the MAS architecture. The innovative aspects concern two levels:
- At level of waste collection organization, the approach allows to adapt to real production waste rate by varying the waste collection frequency for each kind of waste.
- At computational level. The MAS architecture knows in quasi real-time the real state of the containers, therefore the TSP problem can be reduced.
- The simulation environment, based on a multi-agent architecture. The information provided by the simulation environment leads to a quantitative evaluation about the best strategies to be used by agents and the advantage for the municipal areas participating to the cooperative approach.

The conclusions can be located at two levels: design and operative. At design level the proposed approach is based on three kinds of technologies that, to the authors' best knowledge, are essential for added value services developing: agents, work-flow management techniques and open source IT tools.

At operative level the research underlines how, through the development of a simulation environment, real added value can be evaluated and the real costs reduction for the participants achieved.

BACKGROUND

In the last decade, waste management issues have gained importance. The production solid waste (MSW) in Italy has increased considerably: between 2003 and 2007 the volume of MSW in-

Table 1. The separate waste collection rate in Italy between 2003 and 2007

	2003	2004	2005	2006	2007
North	33.5%	35.5%	37.9%	39.9%	42.4%
Centre	17.1%	18.3%	19.2%	20%	20.8%
South	6.7%	8.1%	8.8%	10. 2%	11. 6%
Italy	**21.1%**	**22.7%**	**24.4%**	**25.8%**	**27.5%**

creased by 8.4%, whereas the per capita annual waste production increased from 524 to 546 kg (APAT, 2008).

A positive response to pressure from the waste on the environment is the percentage of separate waste collection that, in 2007, has reached a national level, equal to 27.5% of the total production of municipal waste. This value, although showing an increment compared to the value in 2003 (21.1%), appears, however, still significantly below the target of 40% before 31/12/2007, introduced in 2006 by the Italian N°296/2006 Law.

296/2006 law sets, in fact, the following targets for the separate waste collection:

a. At least 40% until December 2007.
b. At least 50% until December 2009.
c. At least 60% until December 2011.

The situation appears, however, different from one Italian geographical area to another because, while the North, with a collection rate amounted to 42.2% in 2007, the Centre and South, with percentages, respectively, equal to 20.8% and 11.6%, are still far from that goal.

In 2007, the national average cost of waste management per kg amounts to 0.24 €/ kg. In percentage terms the cost of separate waste management accounts to 31.7%. The average costs of separate waste management is about 0.08 €/kg for paper and paper board, 0.07 €/kg for glass, 0,2 €/ kg for plastic.

Considerable research efforts have been directed towards developing economics-based optimization models for MSW flow allocation. Several mathematical programming models have been developed for MSW management planning,

Table 2. Economics-based optimization models for MSW flow allocation

Author's name	Scope	Tools	Case study	Limits
Minciardi & al (2008)	Optimal flows of solid waste sent to landfill, recycling and different types of treatment plants	A non-linear, multi-objective formulation	Planning the MSW system in the municipality of Geneva (Italy)	The proposed approach is not suitable for a formalization of the decision process within a multi-person framework
Chang & al (1997)	Evaluate a regional program for solid waste management in a metropolitan region	GIS and optimization models to identify the cost–effective expansion plans	Solid waste management plans for the Taipei metropolitan region in Taiwan	Number of system variables
Li & al (2006)	Supporting long-term planning of waste management activities	An interval-parameter two-stage mixed integer linear programming (ITMILP) model	Waste management activities in the City of Regina, Canada.	Extension of the ITMILP to a more general scope of waste management for both residential and non-residential sectors

such as reported in Minciardi (2008), Chang (1977) and Li (2006). Tools and scope of the literature review are shown in Table 2, with some limits and case study identified.

In this chapter the MSWflow allocation problem is solved through the Multi-Agent Theory. In specifically, Multi-Agent System is being used in environmental modelling for many reasons that have already been discussed in the literature (e.g. Bousquet, 2001; Judson, 1994; Taylor, 1994). MAS provides a framework in which tractable techniques can be implemented with match various requirements of environmental management modelling (Hare, 2004). Namely, MAS permits the coupling of environmental models to the social systems that are embedded in them, such that the roles of social interaction and adaptive, disaggregated (micro-level) human decision making in environmental management can be modelled. It also permits the study of the interactions between different scales of decision-maker, as well as the investigation of the emergence of adaptive, collective responses to changing environments and environmental management policies. The efficient and effective use of MAS for environmental modelling is hindered by the fact that there is no fixed and clear definition of what an MAS is or even what an agent should be. About applying the software agents' paradigm to environmental monitoring informational system created by a three-layered MAS is reported in Athanasiadis et al. The aim is to provide measurements of meteorological information and air pollution data, to analyse them and to generate alarm signals (Athanasiadis, 2005).

In another paper the authors present the framework of a decision support system for water management in the Mediterranean islands coupling a multi-agents system with a geographic information system (Urbani, 2005). The platform developed makes it possible for users to better understand the current operation of the system, to apprehend the evolution of the situation, and to simulate different scenarios according to the selected water policies and the climatic changes hypothesis. Guerrin et al. studies an animal waste management that explores possible negotiating strategies and outcomes used by simulated actors involved in managing the removal, transportation and processing of animal wastes (Guerrin, 1999). Ting-hong Zhao et al. propose a control system based on Multi-Agent Theory, including a management agent, communication agent, control agent, echo agent, and so on. These agents are able to harmonize automation and intelligence to provide effective control of the running of a hydro power station. The end goal is a real control system that can operate independently of human intervention (Ting-hong Zhao, 2007).

Gnansounou et al. propose, in a decision-making perspective, a new multi-agent architecture specifically designed to support planning activities in decentralized electricity markets, with a certain level of flexibility (Gnansounou, 2007). In this model, synthetic agents are created allowing flexible representations of the multi-functional market players and possible mergers and coalitions in the electricity market. In summary the literature review is showed in Figure 1, classified by environmental sectors.

Figure 1. The literature review classified by environmental sectors

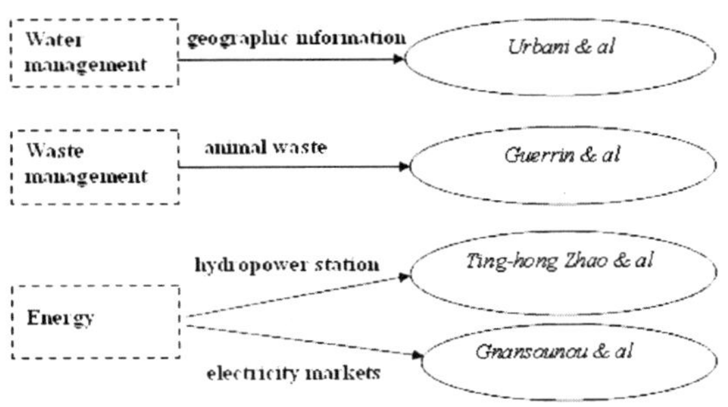

MULTI AGENT ARCHITECTURE

The development of Distributed Artificial Intelligence (DAI) (Bond, 1988) began in the early 90's, gave rise to the theory of computational agents. Multi Agent System (MAS) is a branch in DAI, it refers to a collect of agents that can collaborate in order to obtain a global objective. In literature there are many definitions about agents (Babiceanu, 2006; Luck, 2003). Two concepts are common proposed among authors:

- An agent is a computational system that is situated in a dynamic environment and is capable of exhibiting autonomous and intelligent behaviour.
- An agent may have an environment that includes other agents. The community of interacting agents, as a whole, operates as a multi-agent system.

The MAS approach was proposed for several fields like economics problem, manufacturing system, supply chain, traffic control, distributed computing, etc.

The advantages of MAS are the following: Computational efficiency; Reliability; Scalability; Robustness; Maintainability; Responsiveness; Flexibility; Reuse.

The disadvantages are: MAS coordination mechanism to reach the final target; No global vision of the world; Collaboration or Competition; Sub-Optimal solution Distributed Structure.

For the above reasons, MAS is a method suitable to the inter-municipal waste collection.

The proposed approaches are based on MAS; in particular for the specified problem the following agents have been developed:

- **Municipal agent:** the agent manages a local database about the information of the municipal area (container localization, costs, people number, etc.). Moreover, the agent holds a set of algorithms to support the decision at local level.
- **Collection agent:** the agent manages a local database about the information of the waste collection system (waste typology trucks, costs, availability, etc.). Moreover, the agent holds a set of algorithms to support the decision at waste collection level.
- **Waste collection agent:** the agent manages a local database about the information of the waste collection transporters (trucks' capacity, costs, availability, etc.). Moreover, the agent holds a set of algorithms to support the decision at local level.

Figure 2 shows the basic representation of the agents' interaction during the coordination mechanism. As the reader will notice, in the IDEF0

Figure 2. IDEF0 diagram

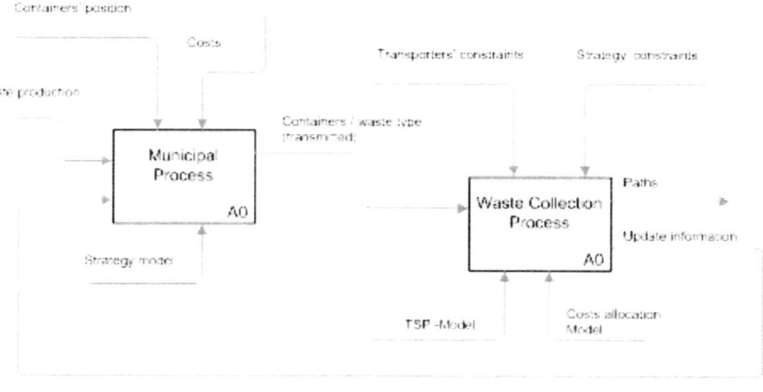

diagram in the figure, it is possible to identify the Municipal and the Waste Collection processes.

The Municipal process is triggered by the waste production computed by forecast model and it is constrained by the Containers position and by costs constraint. The output of this process is the position and kind of the containers that have to be needed for electronic transmission to the waste collection agent.

The Waste Collection process is triggered by the Municipal containers information and it is constrained by the transporters' constraint, strategy constraints. The Waste Collection process evaluates the paths for each transporter and transmits the information to the Municipal process. Such a process is undertaken by using the Travelling Salesman Problem Algorithms and Cost Allocation Model.

THE TRAVELING SALESMAN PROBLEM ALGORITHMS

The search of waste collection least path is interpreted as a Travelling Salesman Problem TSP and it is solved with the use of genetic algorithms. Known the containers' position, it is necessary to calculate the minimum paths in order to optimize the time and space and minimise the costs of collection.

The generic problem is: given a geographical area where a number N of nodes (containers' position) are linked together by a complex road network, find the minimum path to visit each node once, starting from the storage and returning to it.

The research area for the TSP is the set of permutations of n containers (Carter, 2006). Every single permutation produces a solution or a complete tour of n containers. The optimal solution is the permutation that produces the minimum cost of travel. The dimension of the research area is $n!$, then, increasing the number of containers, the research area generates an explosion combinatorial problem.

The application of genetic algorithms for combinatorial optimization problems was already intensively studied. Genetic algorithms (GAs), invented by John Holland in the 1960s, are the most widely used approaches to computational evolution. The genetic algorithms are an optimization technique based on natural evolution. They include the survival of the stronger. The GAs are a method of search which does not need to explore every possible solution in the feasible region to obtain a good result. In this area the rules are typically those of natural selection, with changes due to crossover and/or mutation.

In biology the enormous set of possibilities is established of all gene sequences and the top solutions are those with a strong ability to survive and reproduce.

Genetic algorithms are an evolutionary technique able to transfer within the computer systems the natural mechanisms of adaptation. It is a method to switch from a population of chromosomes represented by strings of one and zero (or bits), a new population using a kind of natural selection with operators of crossover, mutation and inversion. The selection operator chooses some chromosomes in the population for breeding purposes, and on average the chromosomes with high fitness produce more than one with lower fitness. The crossover changes parts of chromosomes, more or less imitating the biological recombination. The mutation changes at random the values of certain positions of the chromosome. Finally, the inversion changes the order of a section of chromosome, and then changes the order in which the genes are arranged.

It was taken in the analysis an inter-municipal area located in the province of Bari. There is a single private operator responsible for waste separate collection in each municipality. The AG enables management through the extensive analysis of the problem: a single operator for the entire area.

The coding of the problem was made through the sequence of bins. For example, 12 containers

(5 12 6 11 4 10 8 2 9 1 7 3)

is the path

5-12-6-11-4-10-8-2-9-1-7-3.

The genotype is a component of the population and it is a structure with the following variables:

- vector of integers of size equal to the number of cities;
- fitness of the genotype;
- relative fitness of the genotype;
- cumulative fitness of the genotype.

The genetic algorithm process consists of the following steps:

- random initialization of the chromosomes;
- calculation of Euclidian distances between cities, represented by pairs of Cartesian coordinates (x, y);
- evaluation of each chromosome by the fitness function;
- creation of a new population of individuals by applying the operators selection, crossover and mutation;
- application of the method of elitism that copies the best chromosome in the new population.

It is difficult to define a value of the probability of mutation and crossover that can avoid the stagnation in a local minimum. This problem was overcome by increasing the probability of mutation and decreasing the probability of crossover and by increasing the number of generations. The selection of a new population is based, respect to the probability distribution, on the values of fitness, using the technique of Roulette Wheel. The function of mutation is to change a gene on chromosome with a certain probability, typically very low. Thus, this phenomenon adds a noise in the entire procedure. It was used the special operator Judgment Day which modifies each chromosome of the population, except the optimum. The edge crossover recombination explores the best possible connections between cities in parents, then keep the memory of the position and order of the cities.

The genetic algorithm was successfully implemented and the population evolved in many generations so that the fitness of best individual and the average in each generation decreased towards the global minimum. A good rule suggested in literature to assess gene convergence is when 95% of the population shares the same value. The population converges when all the genes converge.

ECONOMIC MODEL FOR INTER-MUNICIPAL WASTE MANAGEMENT

The economic model created takes into account the information and the structure of the waste collection model in 2004, not much different from today. The attention was focused only on the selective collection organized with road containers. The percentage of selected waste is supposed equal to:

- 13% paper.
- 8% glass.
- 10% plastic.

In fact, the number of containers and their disposal on land are already known and it is, therefore, calculated the number of vehicles and the cost of management.

The total annual cost for each municipality is defined from the calculation of the following parameters:

- Number of hours in a shift.
- Vehicles and employees reserve coefficient.
- Time to land waste in landfill.
- Time of discharge of waste containers.
- Time to stop for traffic lights.
- Maintenance coefficient.
- Fuel cost.

- Lubricant cost
- Pneumatics cost.
- Pneumatics number for vehicle.
- Fuel, lubricant and pneumatics consumption.
- Workers' annual cost.
- Maximum and Average speed.
- Profit Rate.
- Expected life of the container.
- Expected life of the vehicle.
- Filling rate.
- Paper, plastic and glass density.

Each municipality has its own vehicles and containers. It is assumed, for each vehicle, only one operator.

The amortization coefficient is calculated:

$$amort\_coeff = \frac{r \cdot (1+r)^l}{(1+r)^l - 1}$$

where

- r is the profit rate;
- l is the expected life of the container or the vehicle.

Multiplying the amortization coefficient for the cost of purchasing, the annual cost of amortization is obtained.

To calculate the annual cost of a container, it is necessary to consider the following items: cost of amortization on the purchasing and on the first installation and maintenance cost. To calculate the annual cost of a vehicle, it is necessary to consider the following items: cost of amortization, fuel cost, pneumatic cost, lubricant cost, personal cost and maintenance cost. So the cost of operating of a system collection is

$$C = \sum_{b \in B} \begin{pmatrix} number\_vehicle * \cos t\_vehicle\_year \\ +number\_cont * \cos t\_container\_year \end{pmatrix}$$

where the set B contains all types of materials differentiable taken into consideration.

Cost Allocation Model

The total cost of the service has been divided among the individual municipalities using the theory of cooperative games, stressing that local authorities are not interested in paying off more than they would pay if they organized independently. To achieve this goal, we have created a model of aggregation of quantitative information on equipments and specialized personnel (and their costs).

The problem of the cost allocation is interpreted as an example of transferable utility games and it is resolved with the technique of Shapley values that are included in the nucleolus of the inter-municipal game (Moretti,2002; Shapley,1953; Bevilacqua, 2008).

The Shapley theory values the strength of a player in a cooperative game. There is a set *N* (of *n* players) and a function v that goes from subsets of players to reals and is called a value function. The amount that actor *i* gets if the gain function *v* is being used is $\Phi_i(v)$

$$\Phi_i(v) = \sum_{S:i \in S} \frac{(|S|-1)!(n-|S|)!}{n!}\left(v(S) - v(S \setminus \{i\})\right)$$

where *S* is a coalition of players ($S \subseteq N$) which agree to cooperate, then *v*(*S*) describes the total expected gain from this cooperation, independent of what the actors outside of *S* do. The notation |S| indicates the number of elements of *S*. The idea for the assessment of the strength of *i* in the Shapley index is given by the term (v(S)- V(S \ {i})), which clearly represents the marginal contribution that player *i* brings cooperating with other player of *S*. To find the Shapley value, it is analyzed which properties must meet a reasonable criterion for allocation of v (N) between the players. A first criterion is the anonymity: a player must not depend in who is this player, but only because the player is able to achieve alone or with others.

In addition to the condition of anonymity, it requires that for every game v, Φ(v) is a pre-allocation, so it must be $\sum_{i \in N} \Phi(v) = v(N)$. If you have that $v(S \cup \{i\}) - v(S) = v(i)$ for every coalition S that not containing i, the player is called the dummy player.

Finally there is the axiom of additivity

$\Phi_i(v + w) = \Phi_i(v) + \Phi_i(w)$, for each i ϵ N

Shapley's theorem states that there is and it is only Φ: G(N) → R^n that satisfies the previous definitions.

The cooperative game is characterized by

- N = number of cities.
- c(S), $S \subseteq N$ is the cost function.

To ensure the cooperation, the municipalities must agree on how the cost should be shared. This idea indicates the concept of core and allocation of a cooperative game. The one-point solution of a game is the only division that still exists (not necessarily in the core of the game). The one-point solution is the Shapley value, which takes into account the role of each player to increase (or decrease) the cost of each coalition.

In the cost's analysis of stability ownership is expressed as:

$$\sum_{i \in S} x_i \le c(S)$$

x is an *allocation* and it is a vector *x* ϵ RN. If *x* is in the core, then no coalition S has an incentive to split off if *x* is the proposed cost allocation in *N*, since the total amount $x(S) = \sum_{i \in S} x_i$ allocated to *S* is not larger than the amount *c*(*S*) which they should pay by forming the sub-coalition. In other words, allocations not in the core will be reasonably considered not acceptable for any players.

Coordination Approach

The dynamic behaviour of the system presented in section 3 is described by using UML activity diagram formalism, in particular the information flow involving the three agents Municipal Agent (MA), Collection Agent (CA) and Waste Collection Agent (WA). As well known from the UML activity diagram notation, each diagram, describing a specific process, is divided into so many swim lanes how many the involved parts of the system are; in this way, each activity is placed in the swim lane correspondent to class of the system that plays that action. The UML activity diagram of Figure 3 shows the global activities of the entire system. The diagram represents all the processes performed by the Municipal Agent, Collection Agent and Waste Collection Agent at the highest level of abstraction.

Municipal Agent

The Municipal system works out through the following activities:

- **Check level**: the first activity of the municipal system consists in check the level of the containers in its area. This activity can be performed by forecast methodology or by real-time control. The forecast approach is performed using the following information: the extension of the municipal area and the number of habitants. The real time control involves investments in Information Technology. The output of the activity is the level of paper, plastic and glass production and which containers have to be served.
- **Send centre information**: the MA sends to the Collection Agent (CA) the informa-

Figure 3. UML activity diagram

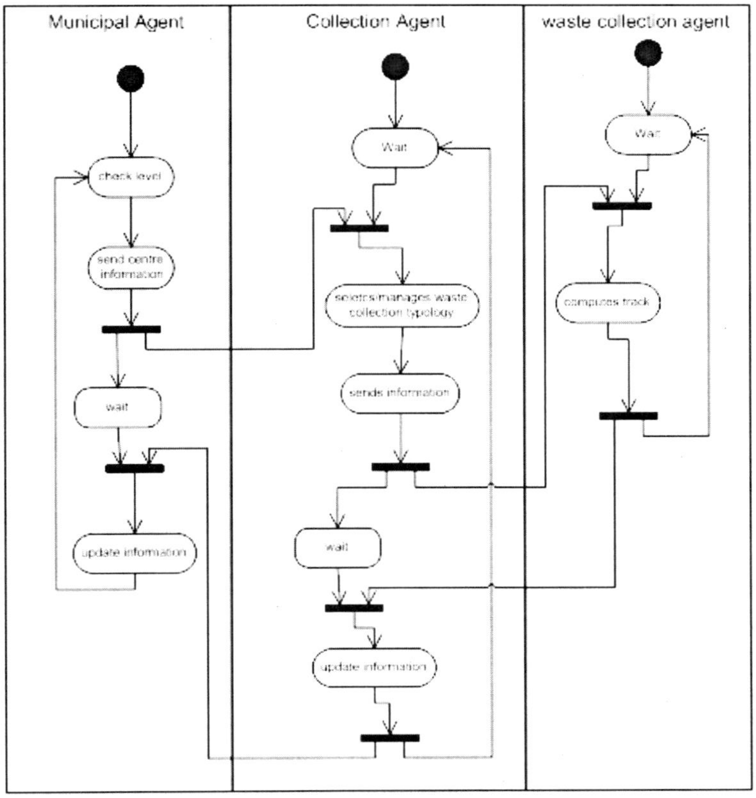

tion concerning the centres that require the service. The information is: centres position; typology of waste; capacity of the containers.

- **Wait**: after the data transmission, the MA waits for the service by the waste collection system.
- **Update information**: the MA update information on waste collection system. The information concerns the service level (wait time) in order to evaluate the costs of the service.

Collection Agent

The collection system performs the following activities:

- **Wait**: the CA is in initial state of waiting for a requester by a municipal agent.

Selects/manages waste collection typology: the CA collects all the inquire by the MA agents, after that, it detects what collection system will be activated. The CA agent is provided by the information on costs and characteristics of the transporters.

- **Send information**: the CA sends to Waste Collection Agent (WCA) the information on the centres to visit.
- **Wait:** the CA waits for the path information computed by the WCA.
- **Update information:** the CA acquires the information of paths computed by each WCA; these information are used to share the costs to allocate among the municipal areas.

Waste Collection Agent

The waste collection system performs the following activities:

- **Wait**: the WCA is in initial state of waiting for a requester by a collection agent.
- **Computes track**: The WCA computes the path of its collection typology and sends it to the CA. The path is computed by an opportune algorithm provided to this agent.

Simulation Environment

It has been developed a distributed simulation environment based on the Multi Agent Architecture proposed. It consists of a simulation environment that can be used to test the functionality of the proposed approaches and to understand advantages of added value services in an inter-municipal waste collection.

In order to cut times and costs for the development of the architecture, the simulation environment has been developed directly in open source architecture by using Java development kit package.

The modelling formalism here adopted is a collection of independent objects interacting via messages. This formalism is quite suitable for Multi Agent Systems development. In particular, each object represents an agent and the system evolves through a message sending engine managed by a discrete event scheduler.

In particular, the following agents have been developed: the MA, the CA, the WCA, the scheduler agent and model agent. The former three agents have been deeply previously described. The scheduler agent is in charge with system evolving by managing the discrete event of the simulation engine and the model agent is in charge with the suppliers and customers interaction.

Moreover, the waste collection agent has been provided with a local genetic algorithm in order to optimize the path of the trucks. A proper interface has been developed to connect the Java code to genetic algorithm and the Shapley value approach. In particular, the Municipal Agent is connected to the genetic algorithm to define the path of the truck resolving the travelling salesman problem and the Model Agent is connected to the Shapley value approach in order to distribute the costs among the municipal areas.

Figure 4 describes the objects that compose the simulation environment by a class diagram.

The proposed simulation environment can be used to represent the participation of a municipal area in a network and the decision of a waste collection system to decide the typology and number of transporters.

The simulations have been conducted in two scenarios:

- ***Scenario 1***: in each municipal area the route of the transporter go through the start point until the end point. Between these two points, the municipal area communicates which containers have to be served. The containers to be served are extracted by a uniform distribution.
- ***Scenario 2***; in the second scenario, the start point and the end point is extracted by a uniform distribution in order to emulate a variable path.

The simulations are conducted for ten periods, in each period it is performed an extraction of the distribution.

DATA

The data taken into consideration in the study were collected directly by the managers of the waste collection service (Table 3). The cities are designated as *X, Y, Z*.

The geographical layout is described in Figure 5.

Figure 4. Simulation environment class diagram

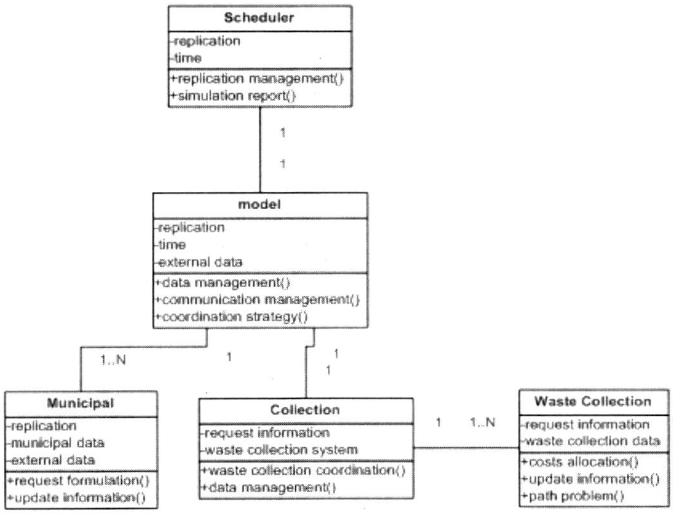

Each municipality has its own fleet and containers. The equipment and vehicles of the municipality *X* is took as a reference for the analysis of *inter-municipal* system. There are the following costs:

- purchase of the container – paper: 700 Euro;
- purchase of the container – plastic: 700 Euro;
- purchase of the container – glass: 400 Euro;
- cost of installation of the container – paper 45 Euro;
- cost of first installation of the container – plastic 45 Euro;
- cost of installation of the container – glass 45 Euro;
- purchase compactor 110,000 Euro;
- purchase truck 85,000 Euro.

For the annual cost of a vehicle was considered the cost of workers provided by the model adopted in the collection.

Table 3. Information on the inter-municipal area

	X	Y	Z
Population	27590	16288	10929
Urban area (km^2)	99.13	67.96	70.75
Waste Production (t)	10500	7174	5139
Number containers - paper	33	8	30
Number containers - plastic	31	19	32
Number containers - glass	38	24	42
Frequency of paper collection	7	7	7
Frequency of plastic collection	7	7	7
Frequency of glass collection	7	7	7

RESULTS

Table 4 reports the simulations results obtained by the multi agent architecture described above for ten replications.

In each simulation, the Shapley values are in the core of the inter-municipal game, in fact for each coalition the property of stability and efficiency $\sum_{i=1}^{N} x_i = c(N)$ is valid.

In scenario 1 the start point and final point of the path is always the same; therefore the costs are the maximum values for the number of containers considered for each typology waste. In fact, the costs are proportional to the number of points of the municipal areas. The standard deviation points out that the municipal areas with higher length of path are characterized by higher fluctuation of the performance.

The Scenario 2 concerns the variable paths for each municipal area. The total costs are (as the scenario 1) proportional to the number of points of the municipal areas. The costs are minor of scenario 1 because, in this case the path can be short; the path is extracted uniformly between the minor path possible and maximum length that is the scenario 1.

Figure 5. Geographical layout

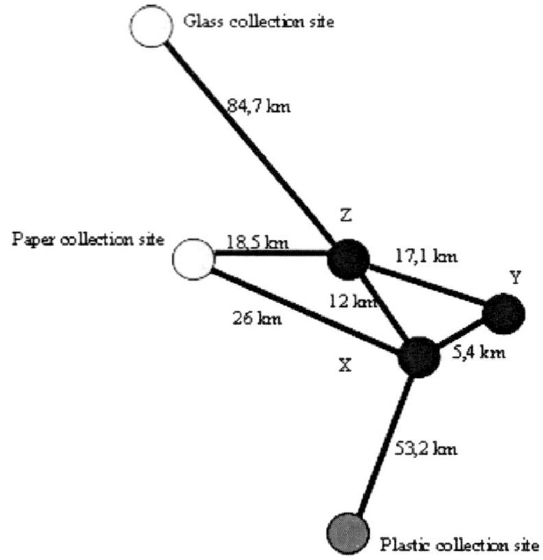

Table 5 reports the scenario 2 costs over the ten periods.

The standard deviation of the scenario 2 points out that the variability of the path is a factor that

Table 4. Simulation results

Replication no.	Putignano		Turi		Castellana	
	Costs	Shapley	Costs	Shapley	Costs	Shapley
1	€ 125,066	€ 77,638	€ 124,671	€ 77,731	€ 91,810	€ 44,595
2	€ 124,691	€ 77,263	€ 124,375	€ 77,434	€ 92,048	€ 44,832
3	€ 124,253	€ 76,825	€ 124,821	€ 77,881	€ 92,105	€ 44,890
4	€ 125,071	€ 77,643	€ 124,326	€ 77,386	€ 91,611	€ 44,395
5	€ 124,573	€ 77,145	€ 124,319	€ 77,379	€ 91,810	€ 44,594
6	€ 125,053	€ 77,625	€ 124,309	€ 77,369	€ 92,217	€ 45,002
7	€ 124,770	€ 77,342	€ 124,342	€ 77,402	€ 91,977	€ 44,762
8	€ 124,890	€ 77,462	€ 124,831	€ 77,891	€ 91,895	€ 44,680
9	€ 124,608	€ 77,180	€ 124,449	€ 77,509	€ 91,835	€ 44,619
10	€ 124,793	€ 77,365	€ 124,537	€ 77,596	€ 91,861	€ 44,646
Average	€ 124,776.8	€ 77,348.8	€ 124,498	€ 77,557.8	€ 91,916.9	€ 44,701.5
Standard deviation	260.63	260.63	207.06	207.11	174.16	174.39

Table 5. Simulation results – scenario 2

Replicazione no.	Putignano		Turi		Castellana	
	Costs	Shapley	Costs	Shapley	Costs	Shapley
1	€ 123,960	€ 76,532	€ 123,495	€ 76,555	€ 92,155	€ 44,940
2	€ 123,491	€ 75,981	€ 123,142	€ 76,202	€ 92,033	€ 44,818
3	€ 123,695	€ 76,267	€ 122,984	€ 76,044	€ 91,565	€ 44,350
4	€ 124,244	€ 76,816	€ 123,314	€ 76,374	€ 91,761	€ 44,546
5	€ 124,014	€ 76,586	€ 123,414	€ 76,474	€ 91,984	€ 44,769
6	€ 124,563	€ 77,135	€ 123,267	€ 76,327	€ 91,710	€ 44,495
7	€ 123,654	€ 76,226	€ 123,548	€ 76,608	€ 91,848	€ 44,633
8	€ 125,120	€ 77,692	€ 123,482	€ 76,542	€ 91,792	€ 44,576
9	€ 124,446	€ 77,018	€ 123,637	€ 76,697	€ 91,398	€ 44,183
10	€ 124,256	€ 76,828	€ 122,854	€ 75,914	€ 91,793	€ 44,577
Average	€ 124,144.30	€ 76,708.10	€ 123,313.70	€ 76,373.70	€ 91,803.90	€ 44,588.70
Standard deviation	489.98	502.65	254.38	254.38	221.83	221.84

affect the performance more than the number of container with fixed start and end points of the path.

FUTURE RESEARCH DIRECTIONS

Further researches will investigate the following aspects in depth:

- The design of a proper design of experiment in order to test the proposed architecture in different environmental conditions. It can be considered the periodicity of the waste typology production; the robustness of the approach when peaks occur; the robustness to exceptions as failures of trucks, errors and so on.
- The possibility to negotiate among municipalities and the waste collection to acquire the services in order to obtain a better service level. In this case the priority of the municipal areas can be negotiated for each period. Then a municipal area can pay higher price in order to obtain a better service. This negotiation process can be used as a coordination mechanism that involves multi-objective approach.
- How the number of municipal areas can influence the performance and the costs of the waste collection services. This research path concerns the number of municipal areas that participate in a cooperation network and the dynamic behaviour of the participants in the network.

CONCLUSION

The paper deals with real added value services in waste collection applications. In particular, the cooperation in inter-municipal areas has been investigated. The approach proposed is based on Multi Agent System methodology and on an open source simulation tool. The Multi Agent Architecture has been formalized by IDEF and UML activity diagram in order to highlight the static and dynamic context. The proposed architecture is able to support and automate the work-flow among the different municipal areas involved. The proposed approach is able to support transaction, information sharing and collaboration among municipal areas. The coordination mechanism is performed by information sharing among the municipal areas that allows optimizing the path of the waste typology transporter.

Then the cost allocation is obtained by using a game theory approach, in particular, Shapley value approach.

In general, given a cooperative game, the Shapley value provides an allocation that satisfies the properties of efficiency and the following principles:

- The allocation is fixed to change the name of the players.
- If the cost function can be divided into different categories (for example the cost of containers and the cost of vehicles), then the Shapley value of cooperative game, is equal to the sum of Shapley values calculated on games designed on individual categories.
- Must not be charged to the player an item of cost which the player does not use.

The results of the functionality test are quite interesting, since they demonstrate that the proposed agent architecture and work-flows are effectively able to support all the collaboration mechanism phases among municipal areas.

The numerical results show the distribution of the costs among the municipal areas in steady conditions (path length constant) and when the path can change over the periods. Moreover, the numerical results are obtained considering a real case study.

Moreover, the simulation tool can be a valid tool in order to highlight the value added by a coordination mechanism for the participants. In this way, the potential participants can improve their satisfaction and interest in staying in a network of municipal areas. The practical implication concerns the possibility for the municipal areas that should cooperate to evaluate the real advantages obtained. This allows to improve the efficiency of waste collection by the cooperation in a regional area.

The limitations of the proposed approach are the common limits of the distributed application by Multi – Agent Architecture. The distributed approach doesn't assure the optimal objectives because there is a cooperation among independent units. The Multi Agent needs to an opportune information and Technology structure in order to support the cooperation mechanism.

REFERENCES

Apat (2008). *Rapporto Rifiuti*. Italy.

Athanasiadis, I. N., Mentes, A. K., Mitkas, P. A., & Mylopoulos, Y. A. (2005). A hybrid agent-based model for estimating residential water demand. *Simulation*, *81*(3), 175–187. doi:10.1177/0037549705053172

Babiceanu, R. F., & Chen, F. F. (2006). Development and applications of holonic manufacturing systems: A survey. *Journal of Intelligent Manufacturing*, *17*(1), 111–131. doi:10.1007/s10845-005-5516-y

Bevilacqua, V., Intini, F. & Kühtz, S. (2008). Applicazione della teoria di Shapley ad un sistema di gestione della raccolta intermunicipale dei rifiuti. *Economia delle fonti di energia e dell'ambiente, 3.*

Bond, A. H., & Gasser, L. (1988). *Readings in Distributed Artificial Intelligence*. San Mateo, CA: Morgan Kaufmann Publishers.

Bousquet, F. (2001). Multi-agent simulations and ecosystem management. In Ghassemi, F., & Post, D. (Eds.), *M.*

Carter, A., & Ragsdale, C. (2006). A new approach to solving the multiple traveling salesperson problem using genetic algorithms. *European Journal of Operational Research*, *175*(1), 246–257. doi:10.1016/j.ejor.2005.04.027

Chang, N. B., & Lin, Y. T. (1997). Economic evaluation of a regionalization program for solid waste management in a metropolitan region. *Journal of Environmental Management*, *51*, 241–274. doi:10.1006/jema.1997.0144

Gnansounou, E., Pierre, S., Quintero, A., Dong, J., & Lahlou, A. (2007). A multi-agent approach for planning activities in decentralized electricity markets. *Knowledge-Based Systems*, *20*, 406–418. doi:10.1016/j.knosys.2006.06.004

Guerrin, F., Courdier, R., Calderoni, S., Paillat, J. M., Soulié, J. C., & Vally, J. D. (1999). Biomas: un modèle multi-agents pour aider à la gestion négociée d'effluents d'élevage. In Ferrand, N. (Ed.), *Modèles et systèmes multi-agents pour la gestion del'environnement et des territoires*. Paris: Cemagref.

Hare, M., & Deadman, P. (2004). Further towards a taxonomy of agent-based simulation models in environmental management. *Mathematics and Computers in Simulation*, *64*, 25–40. doi:10.1016/S0378-4754(03)00118-6

Jennings, N., Sycara, K., & Wooldridge, M. (1998). A roadmap of agent research and development. *Autonomous Agents and Multi-Agent Systems*, *10*(2), 199–215.

Judson, O. P. (1994). The rise of the individual-based model in ecology. *Trends in Ecology & Evolution*, *9*, 9–14. doi:10.1016/0169-5347(94)90225-9

Li, Y. P., & Huang, G. H. (2006). An inexact two-stage mixed integer linear programming method for solid waste management in the City of Regina. *Journal of Environmental Management*, *81*(3), 188–209.

Luck, M., McBurney, P., & Preist, C. (2003). Agent Technology: Enabling Next Generation Computing. A Roadmap for Agent-Based Computing. Southampton: AgentLink.org.

Minciardi, R., Paolucci, M., Robba, M., & Sacile, R. (2008). Multi-objective optimization of solid waste flows: Environmentally sustainable strategies for municipalities. *Waste Management (New York, N.Y.)*, *28*(11), 2202–2212. doi:10.1016/j.wasman.2007.10.003

Moretti, S. (2002). A model for cooperative inter-municipal waste collection: cost evaluation toward fair cost allocation. In C. Carraro, V. Fragnelli (Eds.), *Game Practice and the Environment – Proceedings of the International Meeting held in Alessandria on 12-13 April 2002*. Edward Elgar Publishing.

Shapley, L. S. (1953). A Value for n-Person Games. In Kuhn, H. W., & Tucker, A. W. (Eds.), *Contributions to the Theory of Games, Annals of Math. Studies* (*Vol. 28*, pp. 307–317). Princeton, NJ: Princeton University Press.

Sivapalan, & R. Vertessy (Eds.), Proceedings of MODSIM 2001 – International Congress on Modeling and Simulation: IntegratingModels for Natural ResourcesManagement Across Disciplines, Issues and Scales. Vol. 1. Natural systems (Part 1) *(pp. 43-52).*

Taylor, C., & Jefferson, D. (1994). Artificial life as a tool for biological inquiry. *Artificial Life*, *1*, 1–13.

Urbani, D., & Delhom, M. (2005). Water management policy selection using a decision support system based on a multi-agent system. (. *LNCS*, *3673*, 466–469.

Xiao, X. & Cai, J. (2006). Monitoring and diagnosis based on multi-agent system model. *Micro-Computer Information*, 212-214.

Zhan, J., & Gao, L. (2004). Multi-agent technology in advanced manufacturing. Beijing: the Application of Scientific Publishers.

Zhao, T., Qi, X., & Man, Z. (2007). An intelligent control hydropower system based on multi-agent theory. *Data Science Journal*, *6*, S435–S440. doi:10.2481/dsj.6.S435

Zhou, J. & Sun, Y. (2003). The Distributed Control System Based on Multi-Agent Technology. *Micro Computer Information*, 15-16.

Chapter 16
Management Instruments for Sustainable Information Systems Management

Koray Erek
Berlin Institute of Technology, Germany

Nils-Holger Schmidt
University of Göttingen, Germany

Rüdiger Zarnekow
Berlin Institute of Technology, Germany

Lutz M. Kolbe
University of Göttingen, Germany

ABSTRACT

The increasing dissemination of information systems (IS) into all areas of business and personal life has drawn attention to its economic, environmental and social effects. IS organizations are becoming aware that they have to take up their responsibility by thinking seriously about sustainability management for information systems. While measures for using computing resources efficiently have received considerable attention, the topic of sustainability in IS management is still lacking theoretical and conceptual foundation. As a contribution to the ongoing discussion of "Green IT", the purpose of this chapter is to apply the concept of sustainability into the field of IS management using practical concepts such as a procedural model, the balanced scorecard and a maturity model.

INTRODUCTION

The increasing dissemination and growing dependency on information technologies (IT) and related services create new unconsidered ecological and social challenges for information systems (IS) management. IS management is confronted with new demands from business units, customers and employees. A sustainable IS management covers not only the economical, but also the ecological and social perspective, extending traditional concepts of IS management.

DOI: 10.4018/978-1-61520-981-1.ch016

The ecological impact of the IS business has been discussed under the headline of "Green IT". The global ICT industry is claimed to account for approximately two percent of global carbon dioxide (CO_2), a figure equivalent to the aviation industry (Gartner, 2007). IT service providers, such as Google, whose 450 000 operating servers consume approximately 800 gigawatt hours electricity per year, account for tremendous amounts of indirect CO_2 emissions (Chou, 2008, p. 93). The energy consumption of all servers worldwide approximately equates to the consumption of the entire Polish economy (Koomey, 2007).

High technological intensity, rapid technological progress and short life time cycles of IT products contribute significantly to the waste stream of electronic products (e-waste). Information and communication equipment as well as monitors make up 25 percent of the approximately 20 to 50 million tons of e-waste generated each year (UNEP, 2007), an amount comparable to the weight of almost 9000 fully loaded Airbus A380 passenger planes containing dangerous metals, such as lead, mercury and cadmium.

The social responsibility of IS management is outlined by the frequent reports about data misuse connected to IT, in which companies, employees or customers are affected. The handling of data within many companies is described as being challenging (BSI, 2009, p. 7). Hence, IS management is coming under increasing pressure from external stakeholders. The social dimension of sustainable IS management includes topics of IT utilization by individuals and organizations, but also comprises the challenges of generating, preserving and safeguarding knowledge, information and data.

The above facts not only point to a huge need, but also to a great complexity of sustainable management in IS. Porter and Reinhardt (2007) argue that companies have no other choice than to deal with sustainability and that the challenge has moved from "whether" to "how" to integrate corporate sustainability into day-today management decisions. Despite the hype in trade press, especially concerning "Green IT", the topic of sustainability in IS management is still lacking practical and theoretical foundation. The purpose of this paper is to provide a theoretical basis with key definitions and contexts on the one hand and to illustrate initial steps towards operational planning and controlling of sustainability in IS managements otherwise.

SUSTAINABILITY AND INFORMATION MANAGEMENT

In the following sections a clear view on IS management and on the concept of sustainability and Green IT will be worked out. The proposed concept is based on the St. Gallen model of "industrialized information management", whose explicit consideration of external interfaces seems to be suitable to describe the IS management in the context of its environment.

The Concept of Sustainability

Sustainability has been extensively discussed within corporate management under the synonyms of corporate social responsibility, greening the business, eco-efficiency or eco-advantage (Epstein & Roy, 2001; Esty & Winston, 2006; Porter & Van der Linde, 1999; Schaltegger & Wagner, 2006). The predominant understanding of sustainability was shaped by the definition of the Brundtland Commission in 1987, which defined "sustainable development" as a "development that meets the needs of the present without compromising the ability of future generations to meet their own needs" (WCED, 1987).

At the business level, the concept of sustainability has emerged, based on the objectives of resource conservation and environmental protection, as an equitable and simultaneous consideration of economical, ecological and social objectives, known as the triple-bottom-line concept of sustainability. In this context, sustainable management can be defined as a concept of long-term simultaneous optimization of economical, ecological and social objectives to generate a lasting superior financial performance for the business (Elkington, 1997). The triple-bottom-line concept provides a framework for companies to measure and report their performance and organizational success according to these three pillars.

Addressees of a sustainable management are particularly internal (e. g. business units, employees) and external (e. g. customers, owners, suppliers, investors) stakeholders who exert tangible or intangible influence on the organization through various mechanisms of action, thereby, encouraging environmental and social responsible value creation (Freeman, 1984). Sustainable IS management responds to the needs of all these stakeholders through the balanced consideration of economic, environmental and social aspects. By doing so, it contributes to the companies' strategic objectives as well as to IS management's critical resources.

The Industrialized Information Management

The basis of industrialized information management forms the meta-model of business engineering, which divides companies into the operating levels of strategy, process and system (Oesterle & Blessing, 2000). The IS business consists of internal (in-house) and external organizations that provide products and services, such as hardware, software and services that can be assigned to IS organizations. These types of organizations generally follow the processes source, make, deliver, and return through which the value creation takes place. The management of these processes defines the scope of IS management. The foundation for this process oriented concept originated from the Supply Chain Operations Reference (SCOR) model (Supply Chain Council, 2006), a well-known value chain concept in industrial management, which makes it applicable for IS hardware providers. The transfer of the SCOR model to IS software and IS service providers have been done by Zarnekow et al. by developing the industrialized information management (IIM) model (Zarnekow, Brenner & Pilgram, 2006). The IIM model focuses on the whole IS value chain including customer and supplier relationship, while traditional IS management concepts are focusing on the management of applications (Hochstein, Brenner & Uebernickel, 2006). Figure 1 illustrates the value chain of IS business, including a return process and the stakeholders' interests:

Figure 1. The industrialized information management model

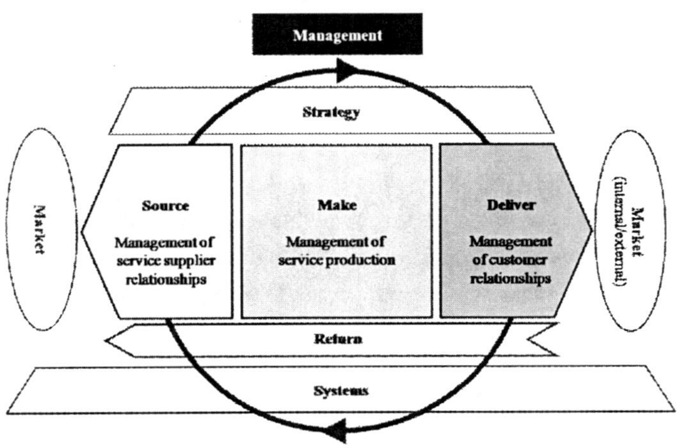

The strategy encompasses procedures and measures which ensure that allocated IS products and services contribute to the business objectives. In particular, it determines the supervisory functions, organizational structures, and processes.

The source process covers all tasks within the supplier relationship management. Usually, IS organizations purchase hardware components, software solutions, personnel or other technological resources. These resources are used in the production phase and are transformed to marketable IS services.

The make process comprises all tasks for the management of IS service production. In this paper, the focus is put on the two main places of IS service production: the data center and the office environment. Attention is therefore drawn to the efficient planning, development and production of IS services in these two areas.

The delivery process is responsible for the management of internal and external relationships. The main objective is to meet all types of internal and external demands in an adequate manner. This does not only comprise IS services but also demands for compliance or transparency. The delivery process can be seen as a mediator function between the internal make and the following source process.

Based on the original SCOR model we included a return process into the IS value chain. The return phase depicts the processes of recycling, preserving and reusing tangible and/or intangible resources. It ensures a lifecycle oriented view on IS services, including a waste management and reutilization of products in the value chain.

Summing up, the model cuts the value chain into four core processes which have to be considered simultaneously for implementing sustainability in IS management. All parts of the process are connected by an overarching management, combining the strategic and technical level with the value chain processes. For each process a continuum of "green" measures and solutions are applicable.

Green IT within the Concept of a Sustainable Information Systems Management

Even though Green IT has been used extensively by marketing departments to label their IT products and services as environmentally friendly, the term and its underlying measures have stayed rather vague and have not been well described (Buhl et al., 2009). In practice, no common definition has been found for Green IT, thus, hampering a clear view on the topic. The conciseness and the media coverage of the term with which environmental messages are communicated to customers and other stakeholders are, however, undisputed. It is also clear, that Green IT often refers to the "resource" IT infrastructure.

Green IT comprises a very large area with many measures and perspectives. The term encompasses not only technical solutions but also communication and coordination measures at the interfaces of IS organizations. Misleadingly, many organizations are focused on energy consumption, neglecting the significance of materials and behavioral aspects in IT. However, there is a consensus that Green IT is aimed to increase the energy efficiency of the operated IT infrastructure as well as to the sustainable usage of materials in the production of IT hardware, and, therefore accounts to the environmental dimension of sustainable information management (see Figure 2). In addition, the efficiency enhancements also contribute to the economic sustainability through saving costs.

It remains disputable, whether Green IT includes measures and solutions which affect other operational functions such as the logistics or the energy sector. However, Green IT covers all measures and solutions that contribute to a more efficient use of energy through the IT infrastructure and to an environmental friendly production and recycling of IT hardware including the accompanying activities for control and communication. In an optimum way, Green IT represents the

Figure 2. Interrelation of sustainability management, information management and Green IT

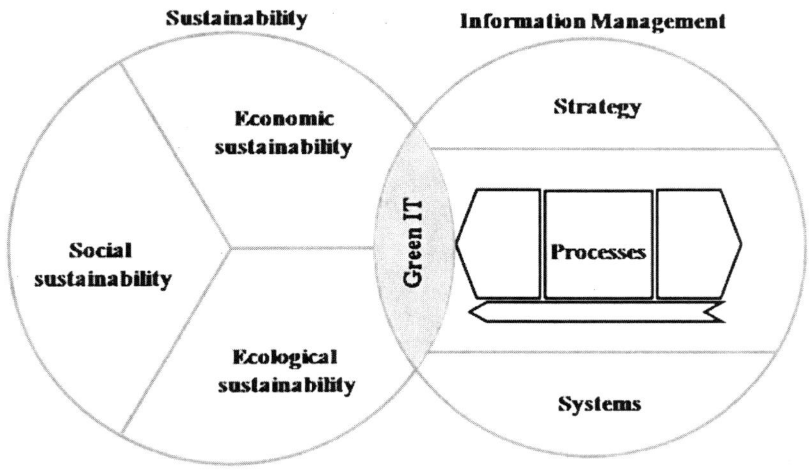

intersection of information management with the environmental and economical dimension of corporate sustainability.

Benefits of Ecological Oriented Information Management

IS organizations use measures of Green IT for different reasons. The main benefits cover risk avoidance, increased efficiency and image enhancement or improved reputation (see Figure 3). Thus, the objective of cost reduction at the operational level can be seen as one of the main reasons for going green in IS management.

Regulative and reputational risks pose an additional threat to IS management besides the problem of volatile and in the long-run rising prices for natural resources. Many companies see a risk that the legislator could determine binding de jure standards for IS organizations because of missing commitment and public pressure in the context of Green IT. Thus, CIOs, IT managers and environmental experts are forced to rethink the way they manage their IS. The introduction of mandatory guidelines, such as the "European Code of Conduct on Data Centers", is generally considered cost-intensive. On the other hand, many companies participate in the development of future standards in various Green IT initiatives, such as

Figure 3. Objectives, domains and value drivers of Green IT

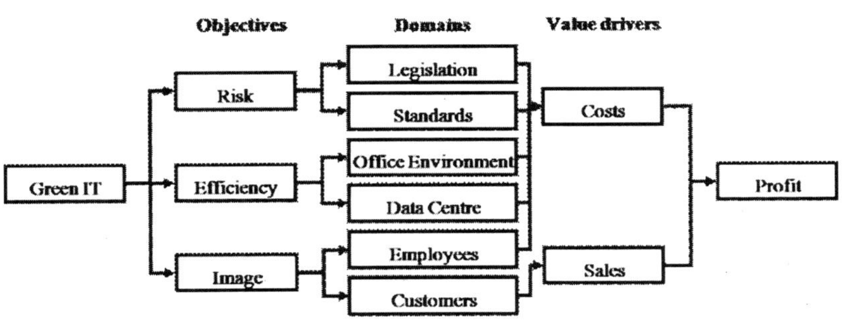

the Green Grid, to ensure that their interests are taken into account. According to many practitioners a commitment to Green IT leads to reduced risk costs for the company (Erek et al., 2009). It can be stated that most IS organizations poses a high level of maturity in the scope of greater energy efficiency within the data centres and the office environments. Especially popular are server and storage virtualization and optimizations regarding the cooling of the data centre, the network and additionally auxiliary equipment. Lower electricity and material consumption directly save costs and avoid or delay necessary investments in assets.

In addition to the enhanced efficiency through operations, some companies are using their Green IT activities for marketing purposes. This is primarily done to improve the corporate reputation, the competitive advantage, and the attractiveness to investors and customers through demonstrating a corporate commitment to environmental awareness.

The approaches described above illustrate that Green IT mainly influences the costs as a value driver and will become more attractive in times of ever-growing energy consumption, waste streams, performance expectations and difficult market conditions.

PLANNING AND CONTROL CONCEPTS OF A SUSTAINABLE INFORMATION MANAGEMENT

In the following sections we will go through the question how the potential benefits of a sustainability orientation within IS management could be realized by suggesting practical concepts that demonstrate the applicability and implementation process of sustainability in IS organizations. Therefore we propose a procedural model for the implementation of sustainable IS management that gets applied over the entire value-chain of IS (Figure 4).

Figure 4. Procedural model for sustainable information systems management

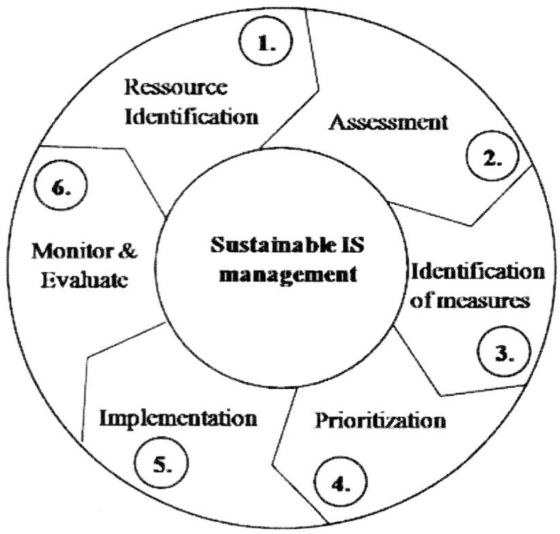

Starting point are the resources of IS. They get evaluated concerning their impact on the economic success, the ecology and the social relevance. The cycle consists of six consecutive steps, beginning with the identification of resource information management.

Resource Identification

There is a vast variety of approaches to identify IS resources: McKeen and Smith (2006) divided IS resources in technology, people and processes, which are needed to meet the challenges of the firm. Bharadwaj et al. (1998) suggested six dimensions: IT/business partnerships, external IT linkages, business IT strategic thinking, IT business process integration, IT management, and IT infrastructure. Wade and Hulland (2004) analyzed a broad variety of IS studies dealing with the resource based view and extracted eight key IS resources: external relationship management, market responsiveness, IS business partnerships, IS planning and change management, IS infrastructure, IS technical skills, IS development and cost effective operations. Practitioners from the

Office of Government Commerce (OGC, 2007) distinguish between capabilities such as management, organization, processes, knowledge and assets such as information, applications, infrastructure, financial capital, which are combined to create goods or services of value. In general, it can be said that resources of IS infrastructure include tangibles, such as buildings, machinery, IS hardware, electrical equipment and any kind of office installations, as well as intangibles that enable their usage, such as electricity, water, paper or location.

Knowledge resources can be seen as capabilities which include the insights, understandings, and practical know-how of employees (Galliers & Leidner, 2004). This knowledge can be classified into tacit and explicit knowledge (Nonaka, 1994). Tacit knowledge is connected to people and is deeply rooted in action, commitment, and involvement in a specific context, which makes it hard to externalize (e.g. skills, talents, the way of thinking, attitude, manners, and cultural competence). Explicit refers to knowledge that is transmittable in formal, systematic language and was generated by combination or externalization (e.g. applications, manuals, reference models) (Nonaka, 1994). IS governance is defined by Weill and Ross (2004) as "specifying the decision rights and accountability framework to encourage desirable behavior in the use of IT". Resource of IS governance therefore subsume capabilities dealing with management, organization or processes.

It has to be noted, as Hart (1995) states, the interconnectedness between certain resources. Meaning the accumulation, generation, deployment and securing of certain resources might depend upon having already developed other resources before.

Assessment of IS Resources

Following the identification of resources, the assessment of individual resources can be done by considering the contribution of certain resources to the strategic position of the IS organization. Therefore, the first step of the assessment is the characterization of each IS resource as core, threshold, or unnecessary (Johnson & Scholes, 1999):

- **Core resources** have to be preserved in order to remain competitive in the present and future. They lead to a competitive advantage over competitors.
- **Threshold resources** might not lead to a competitive advantage, but there might be no possibility to get rid of them either (e.g. electricity, local authorities). They are essential to be able to compete on a market.
- **Unnecessary resources** are not inevitably useless to IS, they might even generate a certain amount of benefits, but they are not essential for survival and might get sold, outsourced, or just neglected in the future.

Helpful questions to determine the type of each resource provide Weill and Ross (2004): "What is the unique and valuable position targeted by the firm?" and "What core processes embody the organization's unique market position?"

In the next step the ecological and social impacts that determine the amount of externalities have to be evaluated. A high amount of externalities by a resource increases the potential risk from stakeholders, offers ways to differentiate from competitors and makes external incentives more likely. A low amount of externalities makes sustainable management less advisable. Generally, portfolio planning models represents a two-dimensional, matrix-based framework that can be used to evaluate business unit performance, to formulate business unit strategies, and to set performance targets (Grant, 2005). The significance of the IS resource and its externalities can be positioned in a portfolio to generate strategic orientation to which degree sustainable measures should be taken or not (Figure 5).

As shown in the portfolio, three strategic directions can be derived: "keep it running", "selective

Figure 5. Assessment of resources

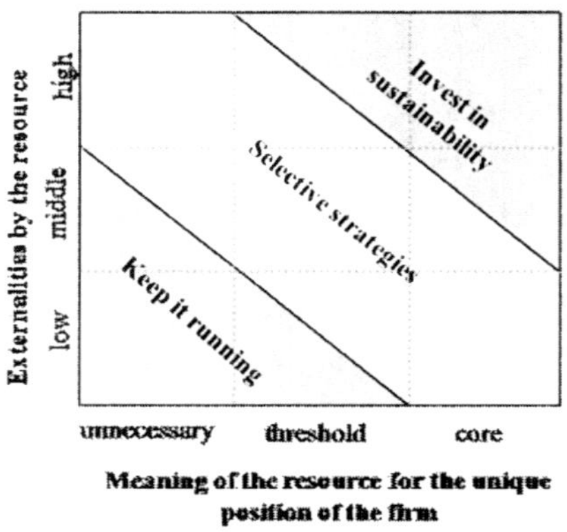

strategies", and "invest in sustainability". While "keep it running" matches a lower importance of the resource with a low externality, the strategy "invest in sustainability" represents a major impact on the performance by the resource and high externalities as well. Resources categorized in this section can be defined as core resources that need to be managed sustainable.

Identification of Measures

The next step is to identify measures that support the ecological and social dimensions of a resource to control or minimize its externalities. Applying the concept of sustainability into the field of IS management requires an integrated view on the entire value chain of IS organizations. For each of the phases of IS organizations providing hardware, software or services we open up an initially continuum of appropriate measures.

Individual measures can be assigned to the levels of IS management. Server virtualization in the data center for example, primarily touches the levels of IS operations processes and systems, whereas more complex measures such as grid or cloud computing, require change to the overall strategy, the processes and the systems of IS management. In this way, current measures can be classified and results in a variety of possible combinations (Table 1). Therewith, it can be shown which influence a measure can have besides the single-focused economic dimension. As shown, the table gives an exploratory overview, and depicts some already existing concepts that are currently under discussion. "Grid computing" for instance, is a concept for the collaboration of computers to perform very large computing tasks together. Its objective is to provide the maximum of service output with a minimum of computing power input, which leads to lower energy con-

Table 1. Exemplary measures and their contribution to the social and ecological dimension of sustainability

Process level of information management	Social dimension	Ecological dimension
IS sourcing (Source)	Employee selection Software selection Audits of suppliers Negotiation of SLAs	Check for eco-labels (e.g. Energy Star) Check for certification TCO analyzes
IS operations (Make)	Compliance to data privacy and data security Knowledge management (e.g. Web 2.0) Knowledge generation Use of lasting standards (e.g. ITIL) Workstation concepts (Shared Desk) Communication management (e.g. instant messaging)	Virtualization concepts Grid computing Cloud computing Thin Clients Cooling concepts in data centers Wake-on-LAN Compliance to standards and laws
IS delivery (Deliver)	Social marketing Training of customers and employees Documentation of projects Stakeholder relationship management	Eco-marketing Publication of an ecological balance sheet Stakeholder relationship management

sumption in total. Therefore we positioned "grid computing" in the make phase.

Prioritization and Implementation

In the next step the selected measures assigned have to be prioritized with respect to feasibility, importance and cost-effectiveness. The decision for pursuing specific measures within certain resources can be based on costs, values and risks resulting from those measures. Many techniques are already present for prioritizing projects that can be also used in this case: Some well-known methods are the cost-benefit or value benefit analysis, the portfolio analysis, the analytic hierarchy process or the prioritization via specific criteria in a checklist.

Regardless of the method of choice it is essential to take a top-down approach. The prioritization process should be aligned to the actual business strategy (e.g. revenue increase, expense reduction, efficiency gains etc.). In addition, the strategic position of the firm affects the decision: A first mover or an innovator for instance will have other preferences than a fast follower. Furthermore, the dependencies between several resources should be considered, so that the sustainable measures for one resource can have a positive or negative impact on others. One way to come to a solution is to use the value benefit analysis which is similar to the analytic hierarchy process (Jian & Klein, 1999).

In this case, certain criteria have to be identified and selected. Such criteria can be "minimization of risk" or "economic impact" of the resource. Hereupon, the decision makers have to assess each chosen criteria for its contribution to the firm's performance and strategic direction. This is a critical step because improper selection of weights can influence the decision. The next step is to score each resource across all defined parameters in order to determine the overall resource score. The resources should be scored by executives for their degree of agreement on a specific scale. As those priorities change because of the altered strategic relevance of IS to an organization, the weights can be adjusted correspondingly, so that the score for each resource is always in line with the business strategy. When all selected resources are scored they can be ranked to determine those that have the highest score. Finally, the number of resources that will be selected can be based on total investments available or other constraints the firm is operating under. Once the measures are prioritized, they can be implemented.

Monitor and Evaluate

In this step, the applied sustainability actions have to be measured and evaluated with appropriate indicators. This approach can help business managers to continuously monitor the efforts towards sustainable IS management. Indeed, the reporting is an essential part within the concept of corporate sustainability. Whilst it highlights inefficiencies in operations to managers, it can be also used for showcasing the sustainability efforts that have been undertaken by the company to reduce risks and seize opportunities for improving competitive advantage. This increase of transparency can improve the attractiveness of the company to investors and customers. The reporting guidelines published by the Global Reporting Initiative (GRI) is the most widely used sustainability reporting framework and provides principles and indicators that can be used by organizations to measure and report their economic, environmental, and social performance (GRI, 2009). These standardized guidelines make it possible to benchmark organizational performance with respect to regulators such as lawmakers or industry oversight committees. Moreover, it forms the basis to communicate organizational commitment to sustainable development and to satisfy the information needs of internal and external stakeholders.

In order to define appropriate metrics, the sustainability measures have to be translated into measurable goals. The goals have to be in accord with the corporate strategy as well as with the basic conditions within each value chain phase (e.g. sourcing strategy). An example for such metrics within the source process could be the number of ISO 14001 certified suppliers or the percentage of suppliers with green or eco-labeled products such as the TCO label for IT equipment or the energy star label that defines certain energy efficiency criteria for each product (Proto et al., 2007).

For translating sustainability strategy into specific performance indicators, existent management systems such as the Balanced Scorecard by Kaplan and Norton can be widened with a sustainability perspective. Another possibility for reporting the effectiveness towards sustainable IS management is to create a sustainability maturity model. The conceptual arrangement of these two methodological approaches is presented in the following two sections.

The Sustainability IT Balanced Scorecard

In order to implement sustainability into the daily business, it is necessary to deal with it at organizations strategic level. If a long-term orientation is insufficiently executed a significant misallocation of resources is possible. The operational implementation of a sustainability strategy can be done by using the Balanced Scorecard (BSC) which can helps IS managers to identify the key performance indicators and value driving factors that link their efforts to the company's strategic objectives. This section illustrates how a Sustainability IT BSC can be developed.

The BSC is a performance management tool that links operational corporate activities with causal relations to the firm's long-term strategy by transferring the strategy to the operational level through strategic objectives and key performance indicators (Kaplan & Norton, 1992). Due to problems of past orientation in management accounting, the BSC supports the alignment of corporate activities according to their strategic relevance, whereas traditional financial measures are supplemented with non-monetary indicators and driving factors. The traditional model focuses on four dimensions which are aligned to the strategy and core values of the company (financial, customer, internal business processes, and organizational learning and growth). Each perspective consists of the relevant goals, indicators and measures to achieve them. For internal IS organizations, the IT Governance Institute suggests the following perspectives: Business Contribution, User Orientation, Future Orientation, and Operational Excellence (IT Governance Institute, 2003).

There has been much research work done in the field of designing and implementing a Sustainability Balanced Scorecard (Bieker et al., 2001; Figge et al., 2002; Möller & Schaltegger, 2005).

Based on the theoretical foundations of the BSC and the IT BSC, a Sustainability IT BSC seeks to incorporate all significant environmental and social aspects into the main management systems of IS organizations. The goal is to improve organizations performance in all three dimensions of sustainability simultaneously (Figge et al., 2002).

Conceptually, there are three possibilities to integrate sustainability into the IT BSC: First, sustainability aspects can be integrated into the existing four perspectives. Second, an additional non-market perspective can be added to take environmental and social aspects into account. Third, a specific environmental and/or social scorecard can be derived (Bieker et al., 2001). The methodological steps when defining a Sustainability IT BSC is demonstrated for the case of an internal IS organization as follows (Bieker, 2003; Schaltegger & Wagner, 2006):

The starting point is the IT strategy of the internal IS organization that usually is aligned to the overall corporate strategy.

In the second step the environmental and social exposure that affects the IS organization must be identified. The result of this step is a detailed profile of all environmental and social aspects in order to obtain a comprehensive list of all possibly

Figure 6. Steps when defining a sustainability IT balanced scorecard

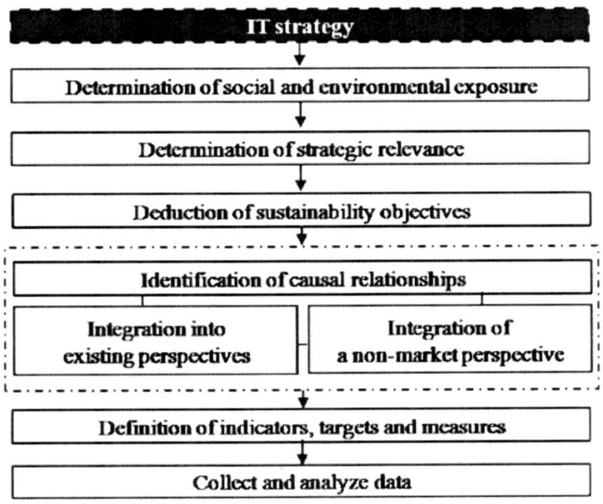

strategically relevant sustainability aspects. For example, if the IS organization purchases as part of its procurement process IT services or staff resources from a low-wage country such as India or China this will represent a social aspect that has to be taken into account. On the other hand the ever-growing energy consumption in data centers results indirectly to increased CO_2 emissions, which in turn highlights an ecological aspect.

In order to ensure that mainly the strategic relevant aspects are taken into account, the third step requires that the environmental and social aspects have to be classified and integrated into the scorecard system according to their strategic relevance. According to the conventional approach of developing a BSC, the identified environmental and social aspects are reviewed systematically in a top-down approach to identify the strategic relevance in all perspectives. By going through the perspectives in a cascade like process starting from the financial perspective as indicated in Figure 1, the hierarchical and causal linkage of the strategically relevant aspects is guaranteed. This serves to align all strategically relevant aspects of a business unit towards the successful conversion of the strategy and thus towards long-term economic success. For example, if the company is actively pursuing a sustainability strategy and all business units have to be aligned to this overall strategy, environmental and social aspects should be considered within the perspective "Business Contribution". The business strategic objective "Reduction of CO_2 emissions" have to be transferred by the IS organization as a highly strategic relevant environmental aspect.

In the next step the strategic objectives of the identified environmental and social aspects have to be defined, whereupon the fifth step builds the causal relationships in the form of a strategy map. Thus, the purpose is to translate the formulated sustainability strategy into causally linked strategic environmental and social objectives. Finally, appropriate indicators, targets, and measures have to be identified. For the example mentioned above the metric "CO_2 emissions within the data center" could be an appropriate indicator to measure the environmental performance in the "Operational Excellence" perspective.

The BSC provides a strong tool to integrate and control sustainability management into conventional financial based management systems. It helps significantly to show the business contribution of IS organizations towards value-based sustainability management. Furthermore, the identification of causal links between environmental and social issues and economic performance will ensure a more efficiently management in the whole value chain (Schaltegger & Wagner, 2006). The investigation of the relationship between the sustainability BSC and the eco-efficiency analysis as a component of an environmental information system has been done by Möller and Schaltegger (2005). In particular, the formulation of a Sustainability BSC depends on information and data sources generated by tools for strategic planning (Figge et al., 2002).

A Maturity Model for Sustainable Information Systems Management

In order to assess the effectiveness of sustainable economic activity in information management a maturity model is suggested. Maturity models are of great importance to IS management and exist in numerous variants. They give IS organizations guidance to evaluate their strategy and processes with regard to sustainability and enables them to discover potential improvement opportunities (Becker et al., 2009). Therefore it should be able to provide the basis for a status quo analysis of the IS organizations internal ecological and social initiatives. Thus it gives the first approach of a strategic realignment in terms of the triple bottom line model. In addition, the model provides support to select the right measures to tap the full potential of a sustainability alignment. Maturity models and self-assessment models are widely used in practice. They serve as a basis for a certification according to specifically accredited standards (e.g. ISO 9000), the outlining of potentials for excellent economic activities (e.g. the EFQM Excellence model for self-assessment) or are used as instruments for assessing and improving the quality of business processes or whole organizations (e.g. the SPICE- or CMM-model for evaluating software development processes). Using defined levels of maturity it is analyzed which maturity and capabilities the organization or its' single processes possess.

The following suggested maturity model is based on the ideas of the "Capability Maturity Model" (CMM) and the "Software-Process-Improvement-and-Capability-Determination" (SPICE) model for quality assurance of software development projects and associated processes. These models are especially qualified because they can systematically map the requirements for constant improvement. The CMM measures the level of maturity of a software development process using five levels ("initial process" until "optimized process") (Balzert, 1998). By contrast the SPICE model assesses the single processes using process attributes and the corresponding management activities. The SPICE model is defined by six maturity levels ("incomplete" until "optimizing").

Table 2. Sustainability maturity levels for an IS organization

Sustainability maturity level	Description or attribute
0 – none	Sustainability is not taken into account in the IT. The IS organization is not aware of its ecological and social impacts and does not evaluate them.
1 – ad hoc	First ideas and suggestions for the sustainable development of the IS organization already exist but are not followed through systematically. The IS organization has no observable sustainability activities in its processes.
2 – defined	First sustainability targets are formalized for particular process sections but they are connected to the commitment of individual employees. The focus is put on short term orientated efficiency gains. A sustainability process is being planned and controlled. Relevant activities are documented. Potential obstacles are being identified.
3 – established	A standard operating procedure for the application of environmental and social aspects in value chains is defined. Sustainability is being communicated and actively realized.
4 – quantitatively managed	Active commitment of the IS organization with comprehensive programs. Sustainability initiatives are quantitatively measured and managed. Impacts of the IS organization on ecological and social systems are predictable and controllable. IS organizations are focussed on long term alignment of the sustainability principles. The connection between ecological and social commitment with economical targets is set and utilizable.
5 – optimized	Sustainability is a fundamental part of the IT strategy. The IS organization has a leading role in ecological and social initiatives. Improvements are being selected and implemented systematically. Possible barriers are being analyzed and eliminated on the basis of the quantitative measures from level four. The procedure is being improved constantly.

The following Table 2 shows according to the CMM and the SPICE model a first outline of a maturity model which provides support for IS organizations to evaluate their sustainability activities.

The model is based on six consecutive maturity levels. There are no sustainability initiatives at level "zero" in the IS organizations. At the first level general ideas and suggestions are being collected without getting realized in a systematic way.

At the second maturity level the IS organization is aware of its ecological and social impacts and tries to selectively control it in several processes. Measures are not being documented so that the success depends on the commitment of single employees. In this case there is no long-run plan. The focus is rather set on short-run gains or measures due to external circumstances. Exemplary for this maturity level are IS organizations which act in the scope of typical Green IT activities. The popular measure "server virtualization" seems to be at first sight an adequate answer to the increasing prices for energy. But in the long-run there are far-reaching measures necessary which also pursue social aspects in sense of the triple bottom line model of sustainability.

In contrast to this, the next level encompasses standard procedures which are defined in several processes for realizing sustainability measures. The results will be documented and provided for other IT departments. An active commitment by the IS organization is obvious on the fourth maturity level. This commitment is being communicated openly and evaluated on the basis of appropriate key performance indicators. Sustainability initiatives are being quantitatively managed and the enterprises effect on environmental and social aspects are known and optimized. An IS organization which is situated on this level has aligned its processes with the three sustainability dimensions and is able to detect variations and environmental influences rapidly because of its utilization of quantitative performance indicators. Thereby the IS organization is able to counteract with qualified measures.

Finally the IS organization has a sector wide leading role on the fifth maturity level. Sustainability is an integral part of the IT strategy to which all processes of IT service provision are aligned to. At this level the objective is to establish structures to achieve continuous improvements of the sustainability assessment and evaluation process. Sustainability is part of the corporate sourcing and distribution policy and is being communicated internally and externally.

It is possible to define specific key performance indicators for each maturity level. These should include not only qualitative information but also quantitative indicators for the performance assessment. Furthermore it is possible to increase the applicability of the assessment on the basis of process attributes analogue to the SPICE model for mapping the respective requirements of one level.

The proposed maturity model offers an evaluation of how sustainable the performance of the IS organization is and points out where actions are needed. So the IS organization is provided with a tool which makes it possible to assess systematically its sustainability initiatives and also to discover the efficiency potentials. Additionally the maturity model can serve as a performance indicator for customers and other stakeholders.

The proposed model does not claim to be complete. There is a need for further upgrading and customizing the model because of changing general requirements (e.g. regulations, customer requirements, target markets, etc.). The evaluation and improvement of the model will be done using case study research.

CONCLUSION

In this chapter we have shown the relevance of sustainability within IS management. While the concept of sustainability has been successfully adopted in several sectors, the ICT industry is challenged to develop an own view on the topic of sustainability. This research is a first initial approach to describe the current environmental aspects of sustainability in IS. Furthermore, the elaborated structure of Green IT provides a common base for communication and future projects in this field.

We provided theoretical foundation to the topic and suggested conceptual models such as a procedural model, a sustainability IT Balanced Scorecard, and a maturity model for implementing sustainability in IS management. These approaches can be adopted by IS managers and CIOs for applying and coordinating sustainability and Green IT practices within the organization.

To refine the suggested models, which primarily have been derived theoretically, our future research will follow these next steps:

1. Empirical investigations using a large-scale of survey with a representative sample of CIOs and IS managers to proof or disprove causal relationships and propositions concerning sustainability and Green IT.
2. Further elaboration of the maturity model and exemplary benchmarking of IS organizations on the basis of the maturity model.

IS organizations have to be aware that sustainable measures are no longer a question of choice, it is a necessity in order to remain competitive in the future. The potential business benefits of sustainable IS management can be seen in terms of reduced costs, streamlined processes, and more efficient collaboration with suppliers and customers. In addition to the enhanced efficiency through operations, sustainability in IS management can improve the corporate reputation, the competitive advantage, and the attractiveness to investors and customers through demonstrating a corporate commitment to environmental awareness. Given the rising prices for energy and other resources the relevance of sustainability is destined to gain even more importance in the future. Hence, the concept of sustainability has an increased relevance for policy makers, practitioners, and researchers. As a result, we reason that sustainability is applicable in IS business and can have a positive impact on the IS business performance.

REFERENCES

Balzert, H. (1998). *Lehrbuch der Software-Technik. Software-Management, Software-Qualitätssicherung, Unternehmensmodellierung.* Heidelberg, Berlin, Germany: Spektrum Akademischer Verlag.

Becker, J., Knackstedt, R., & Pöppelbuß, J. (2009). Developing Maturity Models for IT Management. *Buisness & Information Systems Engineering, 1*(3), 213–222. doi:10.1007/s12599-009-0044-5

Bharadway, A. S., Sambamurthy, V., & Zmud, R. W. (1998). IT Capabilities: Theoretical perspectives and empirical operationalization. In R. Hirschheim, M. Newman, & J. I. Gross (Eds.), *Proceedings of the 19th International Conference on Information Systems* (pp. 378-385). Helsinki, Finland.

Bieker, T. (2003). Sustainability Management with the Balanced Scorecard. In *Proceedings of the International Summer Academy on Technology Studies, IFZ*, Graz. Retrieved July 25, 2008, from http://www.ifz.tugraz.at/index_en.php/filemanager/download/71/Bieker_SA03.pdf

Bieker, T., Dyllick, T., Gminder, C. U., & Hockerts, K. (2001). Towards a Sustainability Balanced Scorecard. Linking environmental and social sustainability to business strategy. In ERP Environment (Ed.), *Conference Proceedings of the 2001 Business Strategy and the Environment, University of Leeds* (pp. 22-31). Shipley, UK: ERP Environment.

BSI (Bundesamt für Sicherheit in der Informationstechnik). (2009). *Die Lage der IT-Sicherheit in Deutschland 2009.* Retrieved April 20, 2001, from http://www.bsi.bund.de/literat/lagebericht/Lagebericht2009.pdf

Buhl, H. U., Laartz, J., Löffler, M., & Röglinger, M. (2009). Green IT reicht nicht aus! *Wirtschaftsinformatik & Management, 1*(1), 54–58.

Chou, T. (2008). *Seven Software Business Models*. USA: Active Book Press.

Elkington, J. (1997). *Cannibals with forks. The triple Bottom Line of 21st century business*. Oxford, UK: Capstone.

Epstein, M. J., & Roy, M. J. (2001). Sustainability in Action: Identifying and measuring the key performance drivers. *Long Range Planning Journal, 34*, 585–604. doi:10.1016/S0024-6301(01)00084-X

Erek, K., Zarnekow, R., Schmidt, N. H., & Kolbe, L. M. (2009). *Sustainability in Information Systems – Assessment of Current Practices in IS Organizations.* Paper presented at the 15th Americas Conference on Information Systems (AMCIS 2009), paper 123, San Francisco, CA.

Esty, D. C., & Winston, A. S. (2006). *Green to Gold. How smart companies use environmental strategy to innovate, create value, and build competitive advantage*. New Haven, London: Yale University Press.

Figge, F., Hahn, T., Schaltegger, S., & Wagner, M. (2002). *The Sustainability Balanced Scorecard. Theory and application of a tool for value-based sustainability management*. Paper presented at the Greening of Industry network Conference 2002, Gothenburg.

Freeman, R. E. (1984). *Strategic Management: A Stakeholder Approach*. Boston: Financial Times Prentice Hall.

Galliers, R. D., & Leidner, D. E. (2004). *Strategic Information Management*. Rochester, UK: Butterworth Heinemann.

Gartner Inc. (2007). *Gartner Estimates ICT Industry Accounts for 2 Percent of Global CO2 Emissions*. Retrieved March 31, 2008, from http://www.gartner.com/it/page.jsp?id=503867

Grant, R. M. (2005). The Resource-Based Theory of Competitive Advantage. Implications for Strategy Formulation. *California Management Review, 33*(1), 114–135.

GRI (Global Reporting Initiative). (2006). Sustainability Reporting Guidelines. Version 3.0. Amsterdam, Netherlands.

Hart, S. L. (1995). A natural resource based view of the firm. *Academy of Management Review, 20*(4), 986–1014. doi:10.2307/258963

Hochstein, A., Brenner, W., & Uebernickel, F. (2006). *Operations Management and IS: Using the SCOR-Model to Source, Make, and Deliver IS Services*. Paper presented at the 12th Americas Conference on Information Systems (AMCIS 2006), Acapulco, Mexico.

IT Governance Institute. (2003). *Board Briefing on IT Governance* (2nd ed.). Rolling Meadows, IL: IT Governance Institute. Retrieved from http://www.itgovernance.org

Jian, J. J., & Klein, G. (1999). Project selection criteria by strategic orientation. *Information & Management, 36*, 63–75. doi:10.1016/S0378-7206(99)00009-9

Johnson, G., & Scholes, K. (1999). *Exploring corporate strategy. Text and Cases*. London: Prentice Hall.

Kaplan, R. S., & Norton, D. P. (1992). The Balanced Scorecard – measures that drive performance. *Harvard Business Review*, (Jan/Feb): 71–79.

Koomey, J. G. (2007). *Estimating Total Power Consumption by Servers in the U.S. and the World.* Final report, Stanford University. Retrieved from http://enterprise.amd.com/Downloads/svrpwrusecompletefinal.pdf

McKeen, J. D., & Smith, H. A. (2006). *Making IT happen*. UK: Wiley & Sons Ltd.

Möller, A., & Schaltegger, S. (2005). The Sustainability Balanced Scorecard as a Framework for Eco-Efficiency Analysis. *Journal of Industrial Ecology*, *9*(4), 73–83. doi:10.1162/108819805775247927

Nonaka, I. (1994). A Dynamic Theory of Organizational Knowledge Creation. *Organization Science*, *5*(1), 14–37. doi:10.1287/orsc.5.1.14

Oesterle, H., & Blessing, D. (2000). Business Engineering Model. In Oesterle, H., & Winter, R. (Eds.), *Business Engineering: Auf dem Weg zum Unternehmen des Informationszeitalters*. Berlin, Germany: Springer.

Office of Government Commerce. (2007). *ITIL - Service Design*. Crown, UK: The Stationery Office Ltd.

Porter, M. E., & Reinhardt, F. L. (2007). Grist: A Strategic Approach to Climate. *Harvard Business Review*, (October): 1–5.

Porter, M. E., & Van der Linde, C. (1999). Green and Competitive, Ending the Stalemate. *Journal of Business Administration and Policy Analysis*, *1999*, 215.

Proto, M., Malandrino, O., & Supino, S. (2007). Eco-labels. A Sustainability Performance in Benchmarking? *Management of Environmental Quality: An International Journal*, *18*(6), 669–683. doi:10.1108/14777830710826702

Schaltegger, S., & Wagner, M. (2006). *Managing the Business Case for Sustainability*. Sheffield, UK: Greenleaf Publishing.

Supply Chain Council (2006). *Supply-Chain Operations Reference-model (SCOR): Overview Version 8.0*. Pittsburgh, Washington DC: Supply-Chain Council Inc.

UNEP (United Nations Environment Programme). (2007). *Global Environment Outlook – GEO 4*. Retrieved May 17, 2008, from http://www.unep.org/geo/geo4/report/GEO-4_Report_Full_en.pdf

Wade, M., & Hulland, J. (2004). The Resource-Based View and Informations Systems Research. Review, Extension, and Suggestions for Future Research. *Management Information Systems Quarterly*, *28*(1), 107–142.

WCED (World Commission on Environment and Development). (1987). *Our Common Future*. New York: Oxford University Press.

Weill, P., & Ross, J. W. (2004). *IT Governance*. Massachusetts: Harvard Business School Press.

Zarnekow, R., Brenner, W., & Pilgram, U. (2006). *Integrated Information Management, Applying Successful Industrial Concepts in IT*. Berlin, Germany: Springer.

ADDITIONAL READING

Berkhout, F., & Hertin, J. (2001). *Impacts of ICT on Environmental Sustainability: Speculations and Evidence*. Report to the OECD. Brighton, United Kingdom. Retrieved May 25, 2008, from http://www.oecd.org/LongAbstract/0,3425,en_2649_34499_1897149_119666_1_1_1,00.html

Boudreau, M. C., Watson, R. T., & Chen, A. (2008). From Green IT to Green IS. *Cutter Benchmark Review*, *8*(5), 5–11.

Chen, A. J. W., Boudreau, M. C., & Watson, R. T. (2008). Information Systems and ecological Sustainability. *Journal of Systems and Information Technology*, *10*(3), 186–201. doi:10.1108/13287260810916907

Eder, S. W. (2009). Green Computers. *Business & Information Systems Engineering*, *1*(1), 123–125. doi:10.1007/s12599-008-0012-5

Elliot, S. (2007). Environmentally Sustainable ICT: A Critical Topic for IS Research. In F. Tan & J. Thong (Eds.), *Proceedings of PACIS 2007*. Auckland, New Zealand: AIS.

Elliot, S., & Binney, D. (2008). Environmentally sustainable ICT: Developing corporate capabilities and an industry-relevant IS research agenda. In *Leveraging ICT for Resilient Organizations and Sustainable Growth in the Asia Pacific Region* [July, Suzhou, China.]. *Proceedings of PACIS, 2008*, 4–7.

Erek, K., Zarnekow, R., Schmidt, N. H., & Kolbe, L. M. (2009). *Sustainability in Information Systems – Assessment of Current Practices in IS Organizations.* Paper presented at the 15th Americas Conference on Information Systems (AMCIS 2009), paper 123, San Francisco, CA.

Kawamoto, K., Yoshiyuki, S., & Minoru, M. (2004). Energy saving potential of office equipment power management. *Energy and Building*, *36*(9), 915–923. doi:10.1016/j.enbuild.2004.02.004

Lane, M. S., Howard, A., & Srecko, H. (2009). The Energy Inefficiency of Office Computing and Potential Emerging Technology Solutions. *Journal of Issues in Informing Science & Information Technology*, *6*(1), 795–808.

Molla, A. (2009). An Exploration of Green IT Adoption, Drivers and Inhibitors. In *Annual Conference on Information Science and Technology Management (CISTM 2009)*, July 13-15, 2009. DC: Information Institute Publishing.

Molla, A. (2009). Organizational Motivations For Green It: Exploring Green It Matrix And Motivation Models. In *Pacific Asia Conference on Information Systems (PACIS 2009)*, Hyderabad, India July 10-12, 2009, paper 13.

Molla, A., Cooper, V., Corbitt, B., Deng, H., Peszynski, K., Pittayachawan, S., & Teoh, S. Y. (2008). E-readiness to G-readiness: Developing a green information technology readiness framework. *In Proceedings of the 19th Australasian Conference on Information Systems*, Christchurch, New Zealand, December 3-5, 2008.

Murugesan, S. (2008). Harnessing Green IT: Principles and Practices. *IT Professional*, *10*(1), 24–33. doi:10.1109/MITP.2008.10

Roth, K. W. (2004). Information Technology and Energy Use. In *Encyclopedia of Energy* (pp. 425-438). New York: Elsevier. Retrieved 2008 from http://www.sciencedirect.com/science/article/B7GGD-4CM9GC0-60/2/692390883906a63851eaf6843831b8b0

Schmidt, N. H., Erek, K., Kolbe, L. M., & Zarnekow, R. (2009). *Towards a Procedural Model for Sustainable Information Systems Management.* Paper presented at the 42nd Hawaii International Conference on System Sciences, 2009 (HICSS-42), Big Island, Hawaii. Los Alamitos, CA: IEEE Computer Society.

Schmidt, N. H., Erek, K., Kolbe, L. M., & Zarnekow, R. (2009). Sustainable Information Systems Management. *Business & Information Systems Engineering*, *1*(5), 400–402. doi:10.1007/s12599-009-0067-y

Socolof, M. L., Overly, J. G., & Geibig, J. R. (2005). Environmental life-cycle impacts of CRT and LCD desktop computer displays. *Journal of Cleaner Production*, *13*(13-14), 1281–1294. doi:10.1016/j.jclepro.2005.05.014

Velte, T., Velte, A., & Elsenpeter, R. C. (2008). *Green IT: Reduce Your Information System's Environmental Impact While Adding to the Bottom Line. Illustrated edition.* USA: Mcgraw-Hill Professional.

Webber, L., & Wallace, M. (2009). *Green Tech: How to Plan and Implement Sustainable IT Solutions.* New York: Amacom Books.

Section 4
Applications

Chapter 17
Factory Planning Based on Environmental Information: Concept and Prototype Evaluation

Christian Grünwald
Volkswagen AG, Germany

ABSTRACT

The high complexity and a multitude of constraints in today's industrial manufacturing require a detailed planning of techniques as well as processes even before the building of production plants. Apart from technique- or process-related planning parameters, environmental aspects are separately considered in the task of planning. The approach of an integration of environmental information into a tool for planning production processes pursues the combination of both points of view. As a result, the expected generation of substances causing environmental hazards during production can hereby be uncovered even before an industrial plant is built. In this way actions for protecting employees and environment will early be considered and later high-cost conversions of plants are avoidable. The described concept is related to business practise by the development of a prototype in connection with a case study and shows the potential of the integration of both planning views.

INTRODUCTION AND MOTIVATION

A steady increasing competitive pressure in connection with the target of cost savings in companies requires a development of innovative solutions for products, plants and production methods in manufacturing industry. To achieve an efficient handling of the high complexity of the developed new methods and techniques, a detailed planning has to be processed already before realization.

According to the definition of REFA, the term of planning involves the systematic search and determination of targets as well as tasks and resources to reach these targets (REFA, 1985). The procedure of planning is supported by several specific software solutions (Beck, 1990; Fischer, 1990). In this connection the virtual product (Gausemeier, Ebbesmeyer & Kallmeyer, 2001) is developed in the task of Digital Manufactur-

DOI: 10.4018/978-1-61520-981-1.ch017

ing and Production (Walter, 2002). The virtual product exists in the form of a realistic, integrated computer model. Depending on the respective context, it may represent a singular part up to an entire assembly and includes all required functions for the support of design, engineering, planning, simulation, production as well as service. Apart from this definition, the term of Digital Manufacturing and Production is described as a realistic, integrated computer model of a production site containing singular processes up to the entire factory. It further includes all necessary functions for the support of planning, simulation, engineering, production as well as control and maintenance (Walter, 2002).

Task of production planning is to develop not only the product itself. Production planning further concerns the development of the production process (Gausemeier, Ebbesmeyer & Kallmeyer, 2001). Several existing regulations are valid for running production plants and even have to be considered in the state of planning (Schmigalla, 1995): Plants requiring monitoring, for instance, are defined in trade regulations. Furthermore, regulations related to the prevention of accidents are specified by the Association of Commercial and Industrial Workers' Compensation Insurance Carriers. A consideration of significant constraints of these regulations is even possible in the state of planning plants and business units. Further, several regulations concerning the operation of electrical plants or the use of inflammable liquids influence the planning of plants and production processes (Schmigalla, 1995).

Apart from the mainly technical view, production planning over and above that proceeds referred to environment, taking related laws and regulations into account. In this respect the German law "Bundes-Immissionsschutzgesetz" represents an example, as a significant part of this act contains the aspect of building and running plants that require official authorization (Marx Gómez, Grünwald, Griese, Petri, Rosenau-Tornow & Eppers, 2004; von Blumenthal, 2002). Further fields of application constitute the usage of hazardous substances or water-polluting substances that are regulated by specific environmental laws as well: Typical examples are the German regulation concerning hazardous substances (GefStoffV) and the regulation for plants concerning water-polluting substances (VAwS). Requirements related to industrial safety and health care additionally have to be considered in the planning process. The term of industrial safety contains all the actions for protecting life and health of the working employees, to preserve their working capacity as well as to organize the work in a human way. A main target in this connection is the prevention of accidents at work as well as occupational illness that can especially be achieved by a safe design of the technical equipment and precautions in employing. Precautions concerning dangerous plants, material or radiation represent examples in this case (von Blumenthal, 2002; Frolov, 2003).

BACKGROUND

Point of Origin for the Conception

The task of planning plants and production processes before their realization represents the point of origin for the idea of integrating environmental information into a tool for the task of planning. In this point of view plants are the objects in the focus. On the one hand these objects are related to the technical form of their realization, on the other hand the regarding plant is involved in a certain manufacturing process. Figure 1 shows the fundamental correlation of the views of operating technology and factory planning being the foundation for the integration of environmental information into factory planning.

I n view of the aspect of factory planning a manufacturing plant embodies a resource or a tool. As described before, it is directly related to a production process. Furthermore, a manufacturing plant is always bound to a specific requirement

Figure 1. Point of origin for an integration of environmental information with planning systems

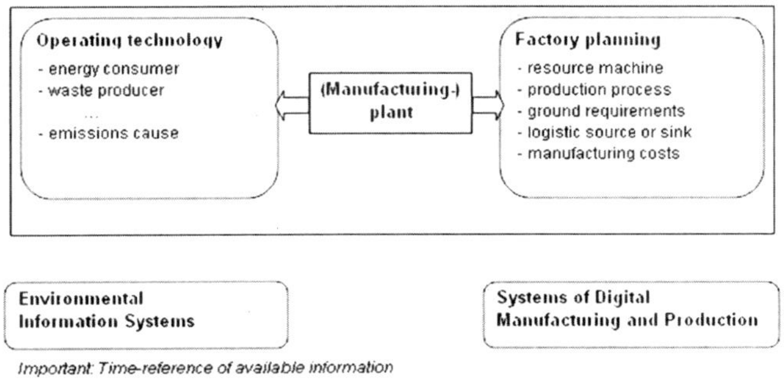

of ground that depends on its measurements, the layout at its location as well as form and procedure of its motion in running manufacturing. A manufacturing plant over and above that figures a logistic source or sink, from which material is taken or into which it is transported. Further, the operation of a plant is connected to certain manufacturing costs. All described factors are considered in the task of factory planning. The individual steps of planning are supported by specific systems of Digital Manufacturing and Production, partly based on complex 3D-models that enable planning and calculation close to reality.

Apart from that, several aspects of operating technology exist. In view of operating technology on the other hand a manufacturing plant represents an energy consumer, a producer of waste as well as a source of emissions. Hence, planning of future manufacturing processes particularly proceeds in an environment related view. While the previous described aspects of Digital Manufacturing and Production are managed in systems for factory planning, environment related data, particularly the amount of generated emissions and waste, is primary stored in Environmental Information Systems.

Motivation and Definition of Factory Planning

A major target of factory planning represents the optimization even of the start of production. Today up to date storage-, processing- and transportation facilities as well as the use of more flexible manufacturing systems allow a higher technical flexibility in industrial manufacturing. An effective conversion of this flexibility is realized by the use of suitable organization-, planning- and disposition concepts (Fischer, 1990). Since in industrial manufacturing obtaining the highest sales each time is possible at the beginning of a new model series (Walter, 2002), companies try to reach a high output of production as early as possible as well as to reduce production costs (Fritz, Kovač & Frank, 2005). The graph of the production curve in figure 2 shows a lower gradient than aimed at the start of a product series. One reason for the lower production curve gradient compared to the target graph are manufacturing processes that have not been validated adequate and result in long ramp-up times of production systems (Gausemeier, Schäfer, Eckes & Wagner, 2005). Minor faults concerning products and production processes are identified and removed only after start of production in this case.

The use of methods of Digital Manufacturing and Production however allows an early identification and elimination of those faults and obtaining minimal manufacturing costs (Avgoustinov & Bley, 2003). Testing alternative manufacturing strategies in a factory model, this model "...in simulation mode would run thousands of times faster than real factory operations and would probably cost much less as well..." (Banerjee &

Figure 2. Start-up curve at the start of a series as well as the entire progress of production

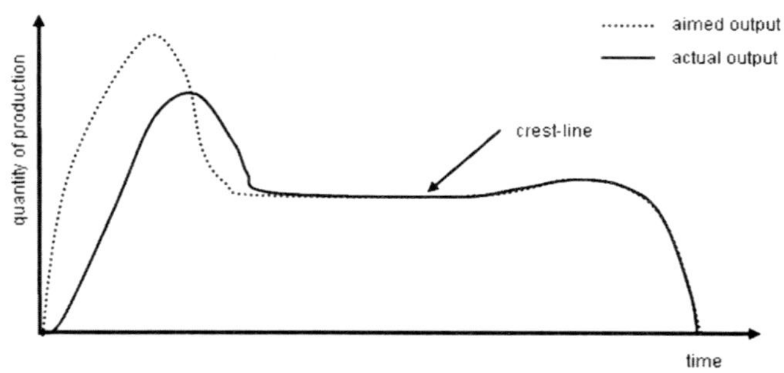

Zetu, 2001, p. 10). As a result, the actual production graph will be brought more into line with the target curve. Further, series- and mass-production require a detailed planning and optimisation of manufacturing processes and factory (Lemke & Heinisch, 2004). The increasing pressure of competition represents an additional factor having a direct effect on production. In this context, product development has steady been adapted, and consequently the digitalization of planning tools has increased.

Viewing the entire process of production planning, a classification of Digital Manufacturing and Production is possible. In this respect, long-term planning including factory planning has to be distinguished from operational planning and control. While long-term planning already starts before building production plants, operational planning only occurs after the realization of a production system. In this respect Günther (1998) describes the approach of an environmental production planning and control system. The early phase of long-term planning generates the output of target concepts, build- and run-projects as well as action plans. On the other hand, operational planning proceeds after the realization of a specific plant. It contains the tasks of production planning and control. Results of the task of operational planning are production plans, work plans and flow charts (Schmigalla, 1995).

Legal Requirements

A multitude of laws and regulations of various areas of responsibility have to be considered in the context of Digital Manufacturing and Production: Specific regulations related to the building of facilities determine requirements concerning the execution of building plants as well as the prevention of danger. One of these decrees represents the German building regulation "Bayerische Bauordnung" BayBO (von Blumenthal, 2002). Further laws and regulations for factory planning show a relation to the task of industrial safety. Industrial safety contains actions concerning labour organization in a human way as well as the prevention of accidents during work and danger to health caused by work (von Blumenthal, 2002).

The entire system of industrial safety consists of three essential parts (von Blumenthal, 2002): Civil law-industrial safety demands the protection of the employees against danger to life and health by an appropriate design of rooms, devices as well as plants and resources, as far as it is possible to realize these requirements in connection with the respective work. Public legal-industrial safety represents the second aspect where supervisory bodies control the compliance of specific regulations. In this regard, the requirements of the law concerning machinery safety determine the design of machine tools. In the following paragraph, as an example, government law of industrial safety will

Table 1. Laws and regulations concerning industrial safety in the context of factory planning (von Blumenthal, 2002; Schmigalla, 1995)

Law/ act	Respective regulations and contents
Law concerning industrial safety	Regulations concerning health and safety Usage of personal safety equipment at work Manual handling of load Work at video display units Usage of work equipment
Trade, Commerce and Industry Regulation Act	Regulations concerning workplaces Specific industrial safety-requirements related to outdoor work Working with compressed air
Equipment and Product Safety Act	Ensuring safety and health in placing products on market as well as installation and operation of plants requiring monitoring
Law concerning occupational health and safety	Law related to works doctors, safety engineers and further specialists for occupational health and safety
Chemicals Act	Hazardous substances
Law concerning genetic engineering	Regulations concerning authorization- and declaration-methods
Atom Act	Regulation concerning X-Ray Radiation Control Law
Law concerning explosives	Altogether four regulations as well as a general administrative regulation

be described: While the aspect of social industrial safety regulates the protection of specific groups of employees against danger, technical industrial safety is related to the following tasks (Schmigalla, 1995; von Blumenthal, 2002):

- Safety of hazardous plants
- Machinery safety
- Workplaces
- Protection against harmful immissions (chemicals, noise etc.) at the workplace
- Organization of industrial safety in companies
- Organization of labour in a human way

In the following table an overview of relevant laws of German legislation concerning technical industrial safety is given that have to be considered in Digital Manufacturing and Production (Schmigalla, 1995; von Blumenthal, 2002).

The aspect of safety of plants represents an important aspect in relation to the German law Equipment and Product Safety Act (GPSG). In this context plants requiring monitoring are bound to specific requirements related to the tasks of building and running plants that are part of the regulations of GPSG: The builder, producer or operator of the respective plant has to ensure the compliance with these regulations. Further, plants requiring monitoring may not be run, if they contain faults that endanger employed or third persons. As a consequence, supervisory bodies managing the monitoring of the compliance with these regulations are legitimated to counteract violations with fines or even shut down the respective plant. The law GPSG contains a list of these plants requiring monitoring. In many industrial countries companies over and above that have to generate detailed reports on activities having a significant environmental impact (Günther, 1998).

In addition to the requirements of legal guidelines, performance characteristics defined by the respective company exist in business practice. The given requirements and the characteristics of a factory realized on that basis usually show considerable differences if no planning methods are executed. The development of a factory concept adapted to the given requirements in the task of factory planning aims to reduce this difference. Factory planning additionally supports monitoring and conversion of this concept and considers several regulations concerning the process of transformation of production inside the factory.

Planning Categories

In production process a specific input containing the factors of raw material, personnel and assets results in a defined output of the factors amount of items, cycle time and variants. Several parameters like product characteristics, product technology and quality requirements as well as type of application are assigned to the task of production. Depending on the level of detail, the results of factory planning can reach from elementary feasibility studies up to detailed planning appropriate for a conversion. The documentation of these results is realized in the form of layouts, process plans, organigrams, database tables up to entire IT-models (Bergholz, 2005). Planning is further managed in different points of view: In this connection, a factory represents an entire system or is alternatively planned in the form of individual elements. Additional perspectives are focussed on existing structures and associated processes of the respective factory (Schmigalla, 1995). In case of a high complexity of the planning object, factory planning over and above that is possible in a modular way: Depending on the chosen point of view, the object factory can be separated into individual elements, substructures or process parts.

In connection with the process of planning several fundamental terms exist that will be described in the following paragraph (Schmigalla, 1995). Factory planning is characterized by the existence of unique intentions featuring unique planning conditions. These planning conditions are related close to the particular planning tasks. The form of possible planning organization in companies contains specific planning departments, depending on type and size of the regarding company. If planning departments even realize management tasks, these units are called planning instances. Further, employees of different planning departments operate together in planning projects in the form of project teams. In large scale enterprises however specific planning departments exist for the task of factory planning.

Being a part of company planning, factory planning is linked to additional areas of planning. In a view of company planning, planning fields can be separated by the two categories of planning horizon as well as the respective factual context (Schmigalla, 1995). According to the planning horizon, long-term (strategic), medium-term (tactical) and short-term (operational) planning are distinguished. A differentiation by the factual context separates between planning of distribution (sales and marketing), products (research, engineering and construction), production (preparation of work and manufacturing) as well as procurement. On the other hand, personnel-, financial- and investment planning as well as the task-crossing field of factory planning belong to the category of long-term planning. Even inside the category of factory planning different fields of planning can be distinguished, depending on the considered aspect of factory planning (Schmigalla, 1995). If the factory is considered in the form of a system, planning of production systems and planning of works structure are separated. In a view related to the individual elements of a factory, the categories of building-, plant-, facility- as well as personnel planning exist. Furthermore, if the focus is on individual processes, the categories of manufacturing-, transport-, storage-, supply-, disposal- as well as information process planning are distinguished. Planning of layout and logistics however show a relation to structural aspects.

According to the method of planning, four dimensions of planning can be separated that have already been described before in connection with the aspects of factory planning:

- systems
- elements

- process
- structure

A differentiation of three fundamental planning phases contains:

- target planning
- project studies
- execution planning

Planning Methods

Digital Manufacturing and Production is supported by several methods. In the development of complex products meeting high quality standards, e.g. in aircraft- and automobile industry, tests and optimization of real prototypes are causing high costs. The modification of a certain part type often requires a change of operating resources that are technological costly, as well as even manufacturing processes. In this connection, Digital Factory (Virtual Manufacturing, VM) offers a platform that supports modelling and simulation. On this platform further a computer-based representation of product manufacturing and the related processes is possible. Analogous, an integrated computer model of the product exists in the form of the digital product, virtual product or Digital Mock Up (DMU). In this computer model a representation of the product ranging from a singular part up to compound parts is possible. Additionally, the tasks of design, engineering, planning, simulation and production are supported by the respective software (Walter, 2002).

However, the support of the planning process by systems of Digital Factory does not implicate a completely automatic processing. Several process parts in the field of planning exist, in which decisions may not be made without the know-how of the planner. These cases require an exchange of information between planner and system (Beck, 1990). In this connection an allocation of information being relevant for planning is performed by Engineering Data Management (EDM) systems that administrate essential data related to the product lifecycle (Walter, 2002).

Various methods exist, supporting the process of factory planning: In the field of digital systems for factory planning the following basic instruments are used (Walter, 2002):

Work breakdown structure: Today working in project teams has been established. This requires separating the project into particular projects and work packages as well as the assignment of a responsible person in many cases. Working in project teams over and above that proceeds more efficient with the help of the critical path method, bar charts or Gantt charts.

Critical path method: Network plans consist of a directed graph, whose elements are nodes and arrows and allow the representation of operations as well as connections between them. These plans are further characterized by a defined start and end node as well as a sequential or parallel arrangement of activities.

Tools for the determination of execution times: Several methods exist for the determination of execution times. For the method of estimation a high degree of experience and a detailed description of the operation are required. As an alternative, the method for planned time values depends on inspected similar operations as well as the processing of data related to past. The results of this method are calculated based on mathematic or geographic functions. The approach of systems of predetermined times separates operations and assigns determined times to transaction elements. One result is the target time for the respective operation that is determined by summation of those times across the transaction elements.

Transport matrix: Target of this method is the reduction of transport costs as well as a decrease of material stock in production systems. The optimum arrangement of the resources and the required buffers are determined with the help of entering material flows in the matrix between objects for resources.

Simulation: Complex material flow systems show a dynamic behaviour in most cases. Planning of these systems is effectively realized by specific simulation methods. In this connection, the task of workflow simulation represents a typical application area for systems supporting simulation. Applying this method, resources and their linking are mapped in this model. Specific parameters for the resources are stored in the system. Additionally a change of the behaviour of resources can be configured by the user via parameter change, e.g. the cycle time of a processing step. A workflow simulation consists of three essential steps (Gausemeier, Ebbesmeyer & Kallmeyer, 2001):

- Creation of a simulation model
- Execution of experiments based on the simulation model
- Valuation of the results of the experiments

The application of time-discrete simulation methods allows a determination of simulation results concerning the flow rate of alternative conveying flows, breakdowns or conflicts during operation as well as the resulting production capacity. The motivation of virtual manufacturing is "... to predict potential problems and inefficiencies in product functionality and manufacturability before real manufacturing occurs." (Banerjee & Zetu, 2001, p. 2). In the task of cell planning an optimum arrangement of all considered resources is determined, minimizing cycle times and considering aspects of industrial safety, ergonomics and maintenance. On the other hand, an optimization of the layout of manufacturing cells is supported by tools for manufacturing cell simulation using 3D-models and methods of time continuous simulation (Gausemeier, Ebbesmeyer & Kallmeyer, 2001). The principle especially becomes transparent in the example of robot control: The generation of a control program for a welding robot is possible in an interactive way, using a system for manufacturing cell simulation, based on a graphical 3D representation of the robot. After translation the program created in the simulation system can be loaded in the real, non-simulated robot control and can be executed even in the real welding process (Gausemeier, Ebbesmeyer & Kallmeyer, 2001). Especially for working steps at high risk an analysis via simulation system is recommended (Fischer, 1990). Modules for manufacturing cell simulation even allow the planning and optimisation of manual working steps concerning aspects or ergonomics, based on human-models (Gausemeier, Ebbesmeyer & Kallmeyer, 2001).

In addition to 3D- and CAD methods virtual reality technologies are applied for a graphic visualization of work places and parts. Besides the given representation these systems allow an interaction based on the graphic information. Apart from this, planning systems are linked to systems of facility management in many cases to realize an exchange of information concerning buildings, plants and facilities, (Henn & Winter-Sattler, 1998). Further, product data management (PDM) systems support the administration of product related information in connection with Digital Factory planning.

MAIN FOCUS

Challenges of the Concept Idea and Potential Planning Evaluations

Considering the described two points of view of operating technology and factory planning, the target of the approach of integrating environmental information into factory planning contains two fundamental aspects that represent the main challenges of the described conception:

- Ensuring an information exchange between Environmental Information Systems and systems of Digital Factory

- Integration of both planning processes: Factory planning and planning in the environment related view.

The realization of this target is combined with several benefits: Following this approach, production processes could be represented more consistent, transparent and comprehensive in the phase of planning, if environmental data was considered additional to the primary technical data. Furthermore, the existing technical parameters in the complex models of Digital Factory would function as an assistant basis for planning in focus of environment. On this foundation environmental effects could be approximated with the help of calculations additional based on the technical parameters of the planning model of Digital Factory. Besides these environment related evaluations, the 3D graphic visualization of the tools of Digital Factory are extendable to support even a graphical representation of environmental effects at the workplace. Moreover, a system supported automatic display of environmental factors and hints on danger would be possible. On the basis of this more comprehensive processed data, extended by information about environment-related costs, a more complete calculation of planned costs for set-up and operation of a manufacturing plant is possible in a system allowing a combined point of view. Adding relevant environmental data, factory planning is enabled more close to reality.

Findings: Conception of an Environment Related Planning System

Concerning the task of factory planning, several requirements exist in a technical as well as in an environment related view that have been described in the paragraphs before. Considering this information, an approach of a more complete support of the task of factory planning was developed. The presented concept especially focuses on planning under environmental aspects. It is related to business practise in form of a case study in cooperation with the German car manufacturer Volkswagen AG. Further requirements received from business practise as well as a possible conversion of the approach have been considered this way. In the given scenario of the case study the software Tecnomatix eM-Planner is used for the task of process planning in long-term planning (Grünwald & Marx Gómez, 2007). In the planning model of the system production processes are defined in the form of objects for products, resources and operations. Existing links between these elements are realized via relations in the data model that allow a connection of product-related data with process-related data.

To obtain an effective support of planning processes in a concept integrating environmental data with the existing planning system, several challenges had to be mastered:

- Identification of a possible optimization in the support of various planning tasks
- Matching available environmental data and data required by the target system (data mapping, differences in scale, consistent frequency of measurements of source data as well as data format) (Günther, 1998)
- Using compatible interface techniques for data transfer between environment-related source- as well as (target) planning system
- Generation of new information meeting the requirements of planning tasks (calculation steps etc.)

Besides these aspects existing limitations had to be considered in conception

- Existing techniques of non-state-of-the-art source systems
- Extended data model requires consistent time-reference of environmental data
- Existing quality and quantity of (environmental) source data

Figure 3. Relevant environmental information for integration with a system for production planning

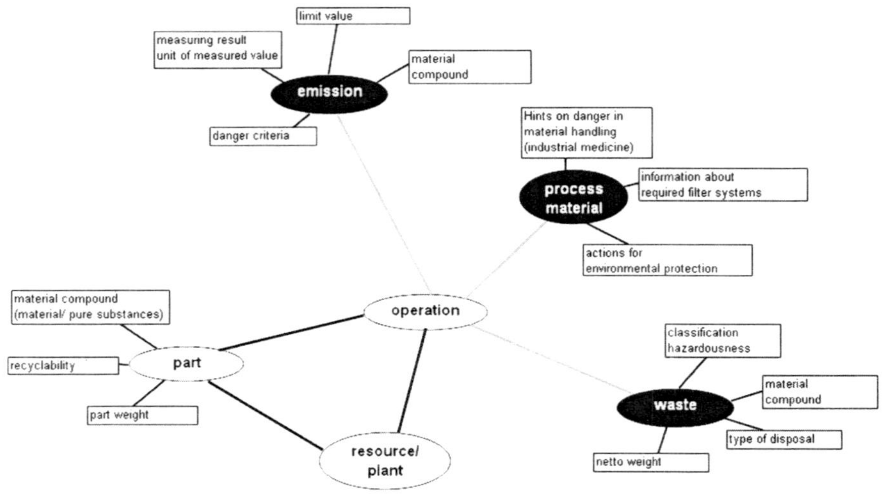

- Data model of a standard system for the task of factory planning

As a first step in the development of the concept, types of environmental information that could influence and optimize the planning of plants and related processes were determined. This information served as a basis for a possible correlation of environmental information with data of planning systems. A selection of this environmental information is shown in figure 3. The graphic shows three possible central objects of a planning system highlighted in white: part, operation and resource. The concept further considers a correlation of these objects to environmental information by an extension of the structure in the form of objects for emissions, process material as well as waste. Additional process parameters in this context are represented in gray boxes. The concept includes environmental information assigned to the described objects as process parameters in the form of attributes.

Based on this described structure an answer to several kinds of questions is possible by a system combining the technical with the environment related view:

- In which operations do substances appear that are hazardous or dangerous to health? What kind of plants is involved in this case?

    Correlating danger criteria as well as information concerning health care to the specific operation in the planning system, evaluations of environmental aspects related to production plants are possible.

- At which level has to be the performance of a required filter system in a specific production process to absorb generated substances that are dangerous to health? Which spatial positions of the respective filter system are possible, considering the dimension of this system as well as the respective plant?

    If quantity data as well as further attributes concerning the used material are correlated to a specific operation of the planning model, a calculation of the arising emissions in a production process is possible. Getting this information via system, the planner is able to directly counteract: The planning of a filter system with a filter volume derived from the information of the planning system represents an example for a possible planning action. The respective filter volume is planned based on technical and environmental information of the system and will consequently neither be much too high nor too much low. Connecting the integrated planning tool to a module for planning industrial halls even makes a consideration of the spatial position of production plants and filter systems possible.

- What kind of regulations and warnings have to be observed using a certain material in a specific production process? Is the use of an alternative material required at this point, as the original material causes high costs for actions of health care and industrial safety?

  Providing handling-information for materials used in a specific production process allows an estimation of costs for industrial safety and health care: The use of one-way-gloves in a work operation and the related costs represent a typical example in this case.
- Which volume of waste arises in a specific step of processing? Which costs result?

  The described data structure even supports the correlation of waste data to the attributes of an operation. This correlation allows, among other things, a determination of costs for disposal.
- Which amount of emissions arises in a group of plants? Will legal limit values be exceeded? Is it necessary to counteract? Which are the possible effects of these actions?

  The calculated amount of arising emissions can further be used for system supported comparisons with limit values. This generated information supports decisions concerning counteractions or production alternatives. An example in this case is the usage of a more environment-friendly plant-type. In this respect, modelling different variants of plants and processes under environmental aspects is possible in the planning environment.

All evaluations generated in a system for production planning are realizable in the early phase of planning plants and processes. In this connection, the developed concept supports a comparison of different types of plants and production processes under technical and environmental aspects. The concept further supports a more holistic point of view in modelling a factory before the phase of realization, considering additional environmental information. Correlating cost factors with the additional environmental data, even a valuation of different manufacturing concepts under environmental aspects is realizable. In this case a relation of cost factors to data of generated waste or additional equipment for industrial safety is possible. Consequently, an environment related planning tool supports decision making in the task of valuation as well as selection of alternative production plants and processes.

The integration of environmental information with systems of factory planning is not realizable without the respective data sources. A main data source for environmental information are Environmental Information Systems. Among further points of view, a classification auf Business Environmental Information Systems in the form of a morphologic box separates six aspects that are considered by the respective systems. The extract of this classification by the criterion aspect is shown in Figure 4.

Analogous to figure 4, the developed planning model of the concept divides six objects that allow a correlation to environmental information received from typical Environmental Information Systems: Appropriate data of the Environmental Information Systems related to the aspect of

Figure 4. Extract of the morphologic box of Business Environmental Information Systems

aspect	waste	emissions	energy	hazardous substance	plants	substance/ material

emissions in this way can directly be assigned to the object emission in the planning model. In the same way, systems concerning the aspect of waste allow a correlation to the planning object waste. As an essential part of process material belongs to the category of hazardous substances, systems related to the aspects of hazardous substances as well as substance or material are potential data sources for a linkage to the object process material in the planning model. The aspect of substance or material even shows a relation to the object part. Systems considering the aspect of plants store suitable data for an assignment to the object plant in the planning model. As a characteristic of the developed extended data structure the object operation represents a central element that is correlated to each of the other objects of the planning model. Further possible data sources are systems concerning the aspect of energy. To consider this particular case in the model, an extension of the data structure of the planning model by an object energy containing assigned attributes like the amount of consumed energy or the related energy costs is required. The assigned attributes in the planning model in figure 3 show relevant examples for possible transferred information of the assigned systems according to the classification of Environmental Information Systems.

Research Method: Prototype Implementation

In connection with a case study at Volkswagen AG a prototype-based conversion of the described concept was implemented. In the initial state of the case study the software Tecnomatix eM-Planner is used as a planning tool and was chosen as a basis platform for this project. This primary standard software represents an essential part of an integrated planning system that is connected with further software solutions for planning vehicles, tools and industrial halls. This kind of data integration involves the consideration of changes of one planning variable, for example the product, in all referred parts of the entire planning process. Apart from the existing systems of factory planning, several Environmental Information Systems support a multitude of tasks for environmental protection in the case study. In this respect, environment-related data that is primary relevant for the integration with a planning system is managed in the task fields of immission control and water protection, waste management as well as material data management.

To evaluate the developed approach, a prototype conversion based on realistic data was realized in connection with the case study. For this evaluation a production process of automobile industry is taken as an example. As the entire basis system described before is realized in the form of an integrated planning system, possible effects on the parts of the vehicle, the shape of tools and plants as well as the layout of the working stock in the halls of the factory are simultaneously considered, apart from a modification of the process. The integration of environmental information in the planning software however requires a customisation of the software. In the prototype implementation the first step of a process example is supported, containing the selection of an emission factor and the calculation of the entire amount of emissions at a workplace. Figure 5 shows the respective process model and the concerning process steps.

Figure 5. Implemented process example

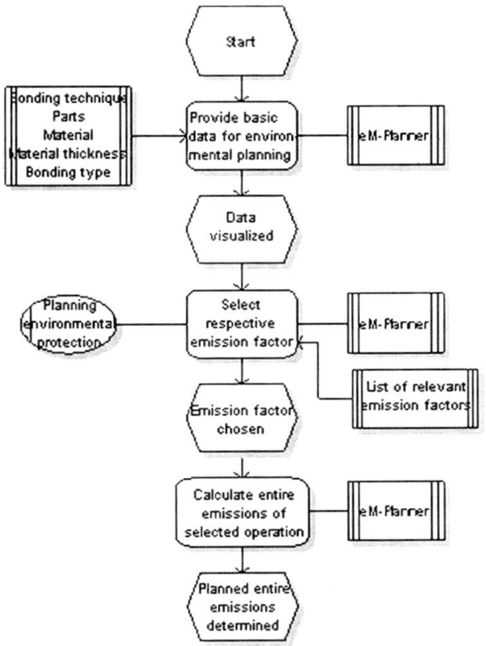

In the first process step several relevant parameters are provided for the respective object operation and the related part-objects. In further proceeding the parameters assigned to the operation will manually be compared with default combinations of operation parameters given by system that are related to a specific emission factor. The provided information allows the selection of an emission factor by the planner, based on the related parameter combinations. An example of possible combinations of operation parameters is given in table 2.

In a separate tab the described technical information of manufacturing planning, e.g. the amount of planned weld points in the currently chosen operation of the planning model, the amount of combinations of sheet metal or the material thickness of the parts involved in the operation, as well as environmental information linked to the operation, e.g, the material compound of the parts or its coating, are visualized. The planner is able to compare this information with the respective given combinations of operation parameters displayed in an additional table in the tab and to determine an emission factor on this basis. If the parameters are matching, he selects the respective emission factor from the table via mouse click. With the help of the details about the amount of weld points in the respective operation the system calculates the entire amount of emissions of all considered weld points. A screenshot of the implemented tab as well as the table of the given parameters and the assigned emission factor is shown in figure 6. The prototype implementation shows that using a specific fitting method and considering respective fitting parameters, the expected amount of arising emissions at a workplace can be determined with the help of integrating environmental information into planning systems.

Table 2. Parameters and related emission factor

Parameter	Example
Material 1	Zink coated sheet
Material thickness 1	1,6
Material 2	Zink coated sheet
Material thickness 2	1,2
Material 3	-
Material thickness 3	-
Bonding technique	spot welding
Bonding type	2-sheet
Bonding geometry	overlapping
Seam length	-
Emission factor (mg/ welding point or mm seam length)	0,21

CONCLUSION

The integration of environmental information into systems of Digital Factory allows a consideration of aspects of environmental protection not just after beginning of production. Even before the installation of manufacturing plants an estimation of environmental effects like arising emissions at

Figure 6. Prototype implementation for an integration of environmental information in planning systems

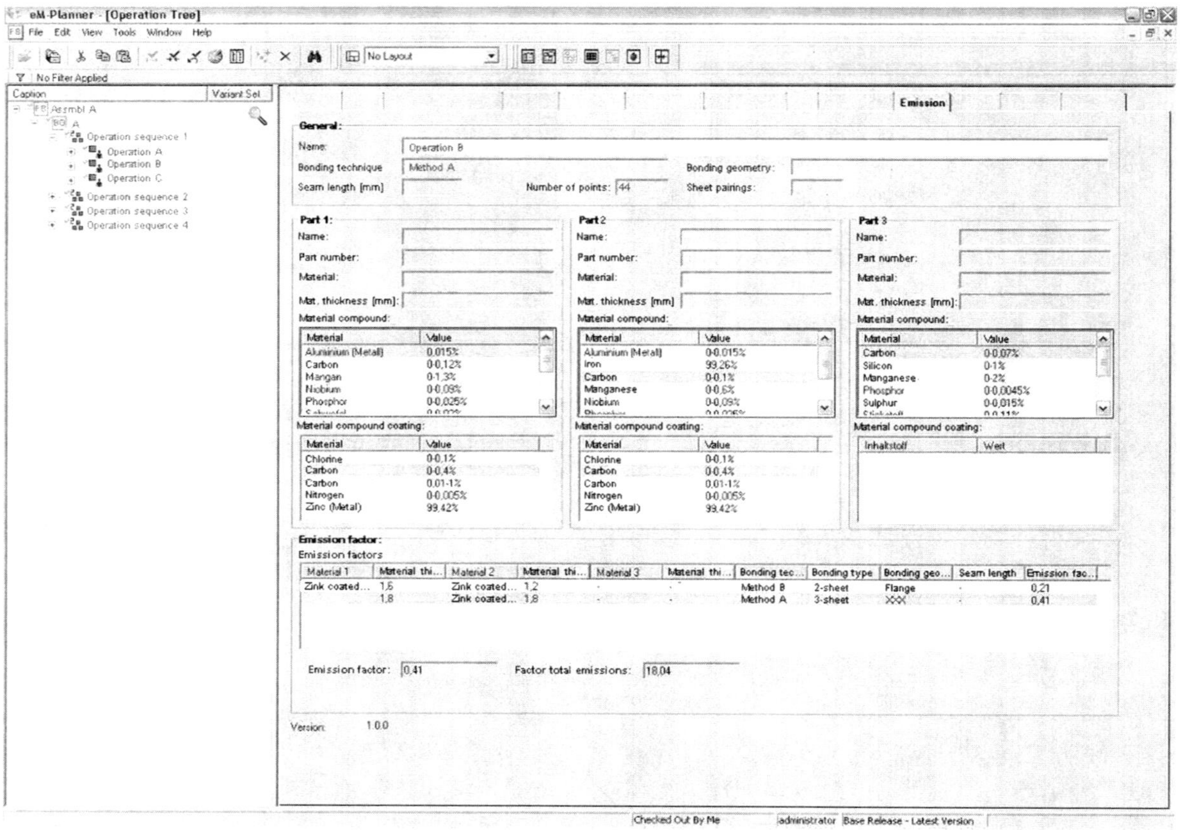

the workplace is possible, assigning information of Environmental Information Systems to data of the detailed models of Digital Manufacturing and Production. This way an aimed, early planning of actions for environmental protection is possible and later costly conversions after plant installation are avoidable. The potential of a concept conversion was shown by an implemented prototype supporting the determination of the expected emissions at a workplace in a fitting method.

FUTURE RESEARCH DIRECTIONS

In connection with the integration of environmental information with systems of factory planning a scheme of possible data references between technical information and environmental aspects has been developed. The considered environmental information is based on a classification of environmental information systems by environmental aspects. In further research an integration of additional environmental information into the data scheme has to be analyzed. Moreover, the data scheme contains a number of typical examples of related environmental information for each environmental aspect. An extension of these example data would result in a high detailed concept.

The prototype evaluation concerns the planning of emission values based on technical information of a future manufacturing process as well as environmental information in the form of emission factors. Besides the prototype implementation a process model for deriving planned emission values has been developed. Analogous, a creation of process models for a planning of further environmental aspects, such as waste or process material, is possible.

This chapter describes the conception and conversion of a prototype for a specific use case. Possible future tasks represent statistical evaluations as well as a specification of the experiences using planning systems extended by environmental data in business practice.

In view of a later implementation, interfaces to potential source systems for environmental data have to be defined. In the concept, a specific XML format was considered for the data transfer of environmental information related to the product data of the vehicle parts, taking the scenario of the case study into account. Apart from the case study, possible additional data formats and related transfer processes have to be determined, e.g. in connection with standard systems for environmental information like SAP EH&S or the transmission of data from individual software via web services. As product data management (PDM) systems support the administration of product related information, these systems represent a further data source for product related planning under environmental aspects.

Besides the pure data administration and processing, planning systems allow a visualization of geometry data of CAD models. In this connection, the additional representation of environmental effects as well as metadata is possible. A first approach concerning the height of planned emission values is described in Grünwald (2009) and has to be extended for the visualization of further planned environmental aspects.

REFERENCES

Avgoustinov, N., & Bley, H. (2003). Distributed Virtual Enterprises (DVE) in Modelling, Simulation and Planning. In C. Weber, H. Bley, & G. Hirt (Eds.), *Proceedings of the 36th CIRP International Seminar on Manufacturing Systems* (pp. 123-129). Series of production engineering, volume 29. Saarbrücken: Saarland University.

Banerjee, P., & Zetu, D. (2001). *Virtual Manufacturing*. New York: John Wiley & Sons, Inc.

Beck, T. M. (1990). *EDV-gestützte Planungssysteme zur optimalen Belegung von Fertigungslinien*. Doctoral dissertation, University of Karlsruhe, Germany.

Bergholz, A. (2005). *Objektorientierte Fabrikplanung*. Doctoral dissertation, Rheinisch-Westfälische Technische Hochschule Aachen, Germany.

Fischer, H. (1990). *Verteilte Planungssysteme zur Flexibilitätssteigerung der rechnerintegrierten Teilefertigung*. München: Carl Hanser.

Fritz, W., Kovač, I., & Frank, A. (2005). Virtual Simulation and Off-line Programming of Robot Guided Reconfiguration Systems. In M. Zaeh, & G. Reinhart (Eds.), *1st International Conference on Changeable, Agile, Reconfigurable and Virtual Production (CARV 2005)* (pp. 181-186). München: Herbert Utz Verlag.

Frolov, K. V. (2003). The Role of Mechanical Engineering in the 21st Century. In Dashchenko, A. (Ed.), *Manufacturing Technologies for Machines of the future – 21st Century Technologies* (pp. 3–29). Berlin, Heidelberg: Springer.

Gausemeier, J., Ebbesmeyer, P., & Kallmeyer, F. (2001). *Produktinnovation - Strategische Planung und Entwicklung der Produkte von morgen*. München, Wien: Carl Hanser.

Gausemeier, J., Schäfer, W., Eckes, R., & Wagner, R. (2005). Ramp-Up and Maintenance with Augmented Reality in Development of Flexible Production Control Systems. M. Zaeh, & G. Reinhart (Eds.), *1st International Conference on Changeable, Agile, Reconfigurable and Virtual Production (CARV 2005)* (pp. 201-206). München: Herbert Utz Verlag.

Grünwald, C. (2009). *Konzeption eines integrierten Betrieblichen Umweltinformationssystems – Fallstudie Volkswagen AG. Oldenburger Schriften zur Wirtschaftsinformatik* (*Vol. 2*). Aachen: Shaker-Verlag.

Grünwald, C., & Marx Gómez, J. (2007). Integrating Environmental Information with systems of Factory Planning. In J. Marx Gómez, M. Sonnenschein, M. Müller, H. Welsch, & C. Rautenstrauch (Eds.), *Information Technologies in Environmental Engineering, ITEE 2007 – Third International ICSC Symposium* (pp. 203-210). Berlin, Heidelberg: Springer.

Günther, O. (1998). *Environmental Information Systems*. Berlin, Heidelberg: Springer.

Henn, S., & Winter-Sattler, U. (1998). Facility Management – Schnittstellen zum Umweltmanagement. In L. Schimmelpfeng, S. Henn & C. Jansen (Eds.), Integrierte Umweltmanagementsysteme (pp.109-122). Taunusstein: Eberhard Blottner Verlag.

Lang, C., & Jürgens, G. (2003). Aufgaben betrieblicher Umweltinformationssysteme. In M. Kramer, J. Brauweiler, & K. Helling (Eds.), Internationales und interdisziplinäres Umweltmanagement. Vol. II: Umweltmanagementinstrumente und –systeme (pp. 77-100). Wiesbaden: Gabler Verlag.

Lemke, J., & Heinisch, A. (2004). *Durchgängiger und übergreifender Konstruktionsdatenzugriff als Baustein eines wirksamen PLM*. Düsseldorf: Springer.

Marx Gómez, J., Grünwald, C., Griese, S., Petri, T., Rosenau-Tornow, D., & Eppers, R. (2004). *Konzeption eines integrierten Systems für Umweltinformationen – Fallstudie Volkswagen AG*. Clausthal-Zellerfeld: Papierflieger.

REFA. (1985). *Methodenlehre der Planung und Steuerung. 5 volumes*. München, Wien: Carl Hanser.

Schmigalla, H. (1995). *Fabrikplanung – Begriffe und Zusammenhänge*. München: Carl Hanser.

Von Blumenthal, A. (2002). *Fabrikplanung Schwerpunkt Recht*. Aachen: Shaker.

Walter, T. J. (2002). *Einsatz von Methoden der Digitalen Fabrik bei der Planung von Produktionssystemen für die Automobilindustrie*. Aachen: Shaker.

ADDITIONAL READING

Arndt, H. K. (1997). *Betriebliche Umweltinformationssysteme: Gestaltung und Implementierung eines BUIS- Kernsystems*. Wiesbaden: Gabler.

Arndt, H. K., Fugmann, T., & Günther, O. (1999). Umweltmanagementinformationssysteme: Der Arbeitsplatz. In C. Rautenstrauch, & M. Schenk (Eds.), *Umweltinformatik '99 – Umweltinformatik zwischen Theorie und Industrieanwendung. 13. Internationales Symposium „Informatik für den Umweltschutz" der Gesellschaft für Informatik (GI), Magdeburg 1999* (pp. 244-255). Marburg: Metropolis Verlag.

Arndt, H. K., Geisler, K., & Günther, O. (1998). Betriebliche Umweltschutzsoftware – Ein Kriterienkatalog zur Beurteilung. In H. D. Haasis, & K. C. Ranze (Eds.), *Umweltinformatik '98 – Vernetzte Strukturen in Informatik, Umwelt und Wirtschaft. 12. Internationales Symposium „Informatik für den Umweltschutz" der Gesellschaft für Informatik (GI), Bremen 1998, volume I* (pp. 83-96). Marburg: Metropolis-Verlag.

Blümel, C., & Gamweger, J. (1999). Betriebswirtschaftliche Bewertung eines betrieblichen Umweltinformationssystems zur industriellen Abfallbewirtschaftung in Theorie und Praxis. In C. Rautenstrauch, & M. Schenk (Eds.), *Umweltinformatik '99 – Umweltinformatik zwischen Theorie und Industrieanwendung. 13. Internationales Symposium „Informatik für den Umweltschutz" der Gesellschaft für Informatik (GI), Magdeburg 1999* (pp. 310-320). Marburg: Metropolis Verlag.

Brauweiler, J., Helling, K., & Kramer, M. (2003) Grundsätzliche Kennzeichen von Umweltmanagementsystemen. In M. Kramer, J. Brauweiler& K. Helling (Eds.), Internationales Umweltmanagement. Band II: Umweltmanagementinstrumente und -systeme (pp. 117–134). Wiesbaden: Gabler Verlag.

Eppers, R., Marx Gómez, J., Grünwald, C., & López Francàs, S. (2005). Benchmarking of Waste Management Software based on a process and requirements analysis – Case study Volkswagen AG. In J. Hrebicek (Ed.), *Proceedings of the 19th International Symposium on Environmental Informatics – EnviroInfo 2005, Brno, Czech Republic* (pp. 398-405). Aachen: Shaker.

Griese, S., Grünwald, C., Meyer, C., & Schrul, G. (2006). Konzeption und Einsatz Umweltrelevanter Systeme in der Volkswagen AG. In Rey, U., Lang-Koetz, C., & Tuma, A. (Eds.), *Betriebliche Umweltinformationssysteme – System- und unternehmensübergreifender Daten- und Informationsaustausch* (pp. 157–181). Aachen: Shaker.

Grünwald, C. (2007). Konzeption einer integrierten GIS-Komponente für Umweltinformationen bei der Volkswagen AG. *Elektronische Zeitschrift für Agrarinformatik, 2*, 1–14.

Grünwald, C., & Marx Gómez, J. (2008). Factory planning with regard to Environmental Information. *International Journal of Information Technologies in Environmental Engineering, 1*, 23–31.

Haasis, H. D. (1994). Möglichkeiten und Grenzen betrieblicher Umweltinformations- und -managementsysteme. In L. M. Hilty, A. Jaeschke, B. Page, & A. Schwabl (Eds.), *Informatik für den Umweltschutz – 8. Symposium, Hamburg 1994. Vol. II: Anwendungen für Unternehmen und Ausbildung* (pp. 41-46). Marburg: Metropolis-Verlag.

Haasis, H. D., Hackenberg, D., & Hillenbrand, R. (1989). Betriebliche Umweltinformationssysteme. *Information & Management, 4*, 46–53.

Kaib, M. (2002). *Enterprise Application Integration – Grundlagen, Integrationsprodukte, Anwendungsbeispiele*. Wiesbaden: DUV.

Kramer, J. (1994). Betriebliche Umweltinformatik: Informationssysteme verdrängen Insellösungen. In L. M. Hilty, A. Jaeschke, B. Page, & A. Schwabl (Eds.), *Informatik für den Umweltschutz – 8. Symposium, Hamburg 1994. Band II: Anwendungen für Unternehmen und Ausbildung* (pp. 55-65). Marburg: Metropolis-Verlag.

Kraus, M. (1997). *Informationsmanagement im betrieblichen Umweltschutz – Strategien und Architekturen Betrieblicher Umweltinformationssysteme*. Doctoral dissertation, University of Saarbrücken.

Kraus, M., & Scheer, A. W. (1997). Integrationsaspekte Betrieblicher Umweltinformationssysteme. *Umwelt Wirtschafts Forum, 5*(3), 12–16.

Kürzl, H. (1999). BUIS der 2. Generation – von funktionalen Lösungen zur Prozessintegration. In In C. Rautenstrauch, & M. Schenk (Eds.), *Umweltinformatik '99 – Umweltinformatik zwischen Theorie und Industrieanwendung. 13. Internationales Symposium „Informatik für den Umweltschutz" der Gesellschaft für Informatik (GI), Magdeburg 1999* (pp. 13-20). Marburg: Metropolis Verlag.

Kürzl, H., & Machner, C. (1994). Informatikkonzept für ein integriertes Umweltsystem und seine Realisierung in einem Industriebetrieb. In L. M. Hilty, A. Jaeschke, B. Page, & A. Schwabl (Eds.), *Informatik für den Umweltschutz – 8. Symposium, Hamburg 1994. Band II: Anwendungen für Unternehmen und Ausbildung* (pp. 23-32). Marburg: Metropolis-Verlag.

Kutsche, R. D., & Röttgers, J. (1999). Praxisgerechte Entwicklungsmethoden für Umweltinformationssysteme: Perspektiven für UIS 2000++. In *Umweltinformatik '99 – Umweltinformatik zwischen Theorie und Industrieanwendung. 13. Internationales Symposium „Informatik für den Umweltschutz" der Gesellschaft für Informatik (GI), Magdeburg 1999* (pp. 149-162). Marburg: Metropolis Verlag.

Löchelt, H. (2000). *Computergestütztes betriebliches Umweltinformationssystem: Konzeption und Realisierung*. Wiesbaden: DUV.

Rautenstrauch, C. (1993). *Integration Engineering – Konzeption, Entwicklung und Einsatz integrierter Softwaresysteme*. Bonn, Paris, Reading, Mass: Addison-Wesley.

Rautenstrauch, C. (1999). *Betriebliche Umweltinformationssysteme – Grundlagen, Konzepte und Systeme*. Berlin, Heidelberg: Springer.

Röttgers, J., & Günther, O. (1998). Nutzeranforderungen an Umweltinformationssysteme: Die Fallstudie VKS-Umwelt. In H. D. Haasis, & K. C. Ranze (Eds.), *Umweltinformatik '98 – Vernetzte Strukturen in Informatik, Umwelt und Wirtschaft. 12. Internationales Symposium „Informatik für den Umweltschutz" der Gesellschaft für Informatik (GI), Bremen 1998: Vol. II* (pp. 435-446). Marburg: Metropolis-Verlag.

Schmidt, H. (2002). *Beitrag zum Variantenmanagement und zur Prozessoptimierung im Wagenkastenbau von Schienenfahrzeugen*. Doctoral dissertation, Technische Universität Berlin.

Schmidt, K. (2003). *Methodik zur integrierten Grobplanung von Abläufen und Strukturen mit digitalen Fabrikmodellen*. Doctoral dissertation, Rheinisch-Westfälische Technische Hochschule Aachen.

Stumpe, J., & Orb, J. (2005). *SAP Exchange Infrastructure*. Bonn: Galileo Press GmbH.

Chapter 18
Progression in Corporate Sustainability Reporting:
XBRL Taxonomy for Sustainability Reports

Ralf Isenmann
Fraunhofer Institute for Systems and Innovation Research (ISIR), Germany

ABSTRACT

In corporate reporting, greater internet use, reports available on the world wide web (WWW) and movements towards a more balanced reporting approach have become the most noticeable trends since the inception of sustainability reporting in the late 1980's and early 1990's. While early sustainability reports merely have been available on print media, today most are accessible on the WWW as HTML (Hypertext Markup Language) files. Such a layout oriented data format, however, does not seem to be sufficient any longer, especially in terms of content-syndication, harmonization, efficiencies, future ICT requirements, stakeholders' reporting expectations, and data exchange, be it inside and outside the companies. Hence, reference architecture for sustainability reports built on XBRL (eXtensible Businesses Reporting Language) is proposed. This development is based on a research initiative embedded in the German Environmental Informatics community. The proposed document structure within the reference architecture particularly meets the requirements of the Global Reporting Initiative's (GRI) sustainability reporting guidelines (G3). While developing the document structure, an existing XBRL FRTA (Financial Reporting Taxonomies Architecture) - common for business financial reporting- was used. Such a unifying document structure is a key for advanced reporting systems, particularly for current ICT applications like (web) content management systems. Using the reference architecture offers an impressive array of benefits, e.g. it helps: to facilitate data exchange between reporters and report users, to improve a company's information management, to support its reporting workflow, and to refine communication with its target groups in a meaningful way.

DOI: 10.4018/978-1-61520-981-1.ch018

INTRODUCTION

Corporate sustainability reporting has its roots both in environmental and in non-financial reporting (IISD, Deloitte & Touche & BCSD, 1992; DTTI, IISD, & SustainAbility, 1993; UNEP & SustainAbility, 1994). It follows a development path towards a concept of balanced reporting, usually communicating the three pillars of environmental, social, and economic performance and its mutual interrelations. This concept is in business terms often called the triple bottom line approach (Elkington, 1997). Sometimes, this approach is put in popular terms like "making values count" (ACCA, 1998), or "linking values with value" (KPMG, 2000), or described as "creating value and optimizing prosperity according to the Triple P bottom line" (SER, 2001: This concept highlights three dimensions of a company's value creation: profit, people, and planet; DCCA, 2006). The latter is understood as combining shareholder value, eco-efficiency, and corporate citizenship, or being part of corporate social responsibility (CSR Europe, 2000).

In the 10 years since sustainability reporting first became a topic of broader interest in academia, business, and government, it has rapidly grown to a field of research with increasing relevance for companies (Kolk, 2004) and capital markets (Flatz, 2003; Hesse, 2007), even in the eyes of investors (Australian Government, 2003; BSR, 2008). At present, sustainability reporting seems to become part of companies' daily affairs, even entering (to a certain extent) the business mainstream. Hence, for a growing number, not just for some pioneering companies, the question is now how to report on sustainability issues, and no longer whether to report at all (Marshall & Brown, 2003).

Regardless of nationality or other differences in country results, this is not only true for leading edge companies in corporate sustainability and few sector leaders, but also for global players and multinationals (KPMG, 2005), stock-quoted and publicly traded companies (Raar, 2002), as well as for a number of medium-sized (Clausen, Loew, Klaffke, Raupach & Schoenheit, 2001) or small companies (EC, 2002). This trend is evidently a worldwide phenomenon (Kolk, 2004; KPMG, 2008), with North America and Europe coming first, followed by the Asia-Pacific region, and even spreading to Africa (Visser, 2002).

Within several industrial sectors, there is further empirical evidence that environmental and sustainability reporting today has become of competitive relevance (Fichter, 1998) and strategic importance (Larsen 2000), with an impact on brand value (Interbrand, 2008). Today, "greenwashing" (Futerra, 2008), i.e. provision of "green glossy brochures" (UNEP & SustainAbility, 1994), does not seem to be sufficient any longer; a substantial amount of information is required. Further, sustainability reporting is only successful if the underlying management systems are appropriate and the associated processes are effective and operational. For example, goals have to be set, responsibilities have to be assigned to reach the goals, and outcomes must be assessed and used as the basis for forthcoming efforts.

Following Mesterharm (2001), comprehensive environmental or sustainability reports are regarded as the primary and leading vehicles and thus the pivotal instruments of such communication (Brophy & Starkey, 1996) because of its unique claim to credibility and reliability external stakeholders ascribe to it, containing quantitative and qualitative data. These reports are usually addressing a wide range of target groups, are often produced as single documents and issued for a certain period of time. Companies use such reports for disclosing environmental activities and integrated performance, often including the following topics: top management statement, management policy and system as well as input-output-inventory of impacts of production processes and products in terms of sustainability.

While the field is still evolving, as sustainability reporting matures and practice develops into a more sophisticated stage, companies have to realize that the "honeymoon period" (DTTI, IISD, & SustainAbility, 1993) in which comprehensive non-financial reports received media and public attention just for the fact that they publish reports at all rather than for what was disclosed is over. Nowadays, advanced reporting approaches with substantial information are required. However, further to the relevance of contents, also issues of communication style become of greater importance (Beattie & Pratt, 2003; Hund, Engel-Cox & Fowler, 2004; ACCA, 2004), in particular:

- interactivity (Teo, Oh, Liu & Wei, 2003; Isenmann & Kim, 2006)
- target group tailoring (Jensen & Xiao, 2001; Isenmann & Marx Gómez, 2004), and
- stakeholder dialogue (WBCSD, 2002; Unerman & Bennett, 2004).

These different trends seem to be converging to push the field towards sustainability reporting using the support of the internet and its associated technologies and services. Due to cross media availability and other innovative opportunities offered by the internet and its associated technologies and services, companies are entering a new transitional stage of online reporting (SustainAbility & UNEP, 1999; Clarke, 2001; Wheeler & Elkington, 2001; Isenmann, Bey & Welter, 2007).

For example, in "The 2001 Benchmark Survey of the State of Global Environmental and Social Reporting" carried out by the CSR network (Line, Hawley & Krut, 2002), internet-based reporting and a more balanced reporting approach are seen as the top reporting priorities. Just a short time later, many sustainability communication vehicles and reporting instruments are already available on the WWW, or – at least – benefit from internet support (ACCA, 2001; Shepherd, Abkowitz & Cohen, 2001; Isenmann & Lenz, 2002; Scott & Jackson, 2002; Rikhardsson, Andersen & Bang, 2002; Andrew, 2003; Lodhia, 2004; Isenmann, 2004): Reports, brochures, leaflets, newsletters, press releases, slides, presentations, audio sequences, video clips etc. are accessible via download and/or online, or can be "pulled" or automatically disseminated via email or other current "push" technologies (Isenmann & Lenz, 2001).

This chapter provides an outline of how to benefit from ICT-based (information and communication technologies) reporting for communicating sustainability issues, while developing from early reporting stages towards a more sophisticated digital sustainability approach:

- First, *emerging trends* are identified affecting decisions on which medium or access to provide for sustainability information.
- Second, the amount of opportunities the internet and its associated technologies and services offer for sustainability reporting is arranged in a *generic classification*.
- Third, following from this classification, a four-dimensional *framework* for advanced sustainability reporting is presented, intended to provide a guideline on how to exploit the internet-specific capabilities for communicating sustainability issues.
- Lastly, *limitations* of such ICT-based reporting approach are discussed that might be overlooked in the light of the array of its media-specific benefits.

As the overall aim, the chapter attempts to bridge the gap between the business-driven field of sustainability reporting and its different facets on the one hand and on the other, the technology-intensive area of business information systems and environmental informatics applications at corporate level. Although research in both domains is still quite disparate, recent progress in ICT enables an array of unique capabilities to be employed for closing this gap. The internet in particular and its associated technologies, services, and markup languages like XML (eXtensible Markup Language, e.g. W3C, 2004; Glushko & McGrath, 2005), XBRL (eXtensible Business Reporting Language,

Table 1. Converging trends in sustainability reporting

Traditional Reporting Approach	Sophisticated reporting approach
Managerial closed shop procedure	Quasi public effort
One-way company controlled exercise	Stakeholder involvement
Monologue	Dialogue
One-way communication	Two-way communication
One size fits all reports	Customized reports
Ad-hoc distribution of information	Continual exchange of ideas
Few opportunities for response	Many mechanisms for feedback and criticism
Hard copies	Computer-based media
Print media fixation	Cross-media availability

e.g. DiPiazza & Eccles, 2002; XBRL, 2006) and EML (Environmental Markup Language, e.g. Arndt & Günther, 2000) provide powerful tools, to the benefit of all groups involved in or affected by sustainability reporting (GRI, 2004), be they managers, accountants, employees, members of the financial community, customers, suppliers, local authorities, non-governmental institutions, pressure groups, or organizations focused on benchmarking, rating and ranking.

CURRENT TRENDS IN SUSTAINABILITY REPORTING

Corporate sustainability reporting is a multi-faceted, rapidly *developing field* that is influenced by a number of driving forces, outside and inside companies (Skillius & Wennberg, 1998; Kaptein & Wempe, 1999; Morhardt, 2002; Marx Gómez & Isenmann, 2004; Isenmann & Bey, 2007, Isenmann & Marx Gómez, 2008). Due to these complexities, predicting current trends in all their details is not a simple process. Among other trends that are to be considered (SustainAbility & UNEP, 1996; Clarke, 2001; KPMG & UNEP, 2006) and despite certain difficulties companies are struggling at present, a few trends are highlighted that seem to be of relevance for strategic ICT decisions (Table 1).

For example, how to communicate in general and to report in particular? Which media should be used for advanced reporting? How to manage the reporting workflow and its underlying core processes? How to design reports available on the WWW? Via which channels should reports be distributed? On what devices should these be available? How to better reach the target groups addressed? How can reporters communicate sustainability issues appropriately, at present and in the near future? All these media-relevant questions involve aspects of ICT, its operating information systems and issues of information management.

The latter are to a large extent responsible for potential benefits and total costs of sustainability reporting. Due to company-wide implications across certain departments, business units, sites, supply chains, or other inter-organisational networks and partnerships, companies should consider these aspects carefully because they influence the overall reporting capabilities. Furthermore, these aspects also define provision, added value, and facilities to design reporting online instruments and other communication vehicles in form and content in an efficient manner.

One trend (in Table 1) highlights that sustainability reporting is developing towards a "quasi public effort" of engaging and involving stakeholders (Hund, Engel-Cox & Fowler, 2004). Information supply evolves from a strict monologue and one-way company-controlled exercise towards a more *interactive* reporting approach, while communicating with a larger audience and initiating dialogues, trying to get feedback and stakeholder commentary from a number of target groups, or even to engage interested parties providing a "challenger report" (IfEU, imug & IÖW, 2001).

Further to the development of valuing stakeholder relationships, another trend is towards a more *customized* approach (Brosowski & Lenz, 2004; Isenmann & Kim, 2006). For such target group tailored reporting, it is characteristic to consider requirements of several standards and guidelines, as well as to take into account different needs of a number of users and then to produce reports exactly meeting all these requirements and needs. Such a process of fine tuning results from the fact that key target groups and other stakeholders are more critical towards and better informed of companies' activities, sometimes willing to initiate activism, to start campaigns, or to take up other forms of exerting pressure or challenging companies.

A third trend is the step beyond a reporting "monologue" towards a *dialogue* with stakeholders. Companies and whole industry sectors undertake considerable efforts to identify their stakeholders, and to understand their issues and concerns. Prominent examples are the stakeholder involvement guidebook for US cement facilities (WBCSD, 2002), a research project on stakeholder expectations and core indicators in the European aluminium industry striving for sustainability (Kuhndt, Geibler & Liedtke, 2002), and the communication campaign of the European steel manufacturers (European Steel Industry, 2004). Based on stakeholder analysis and information requirement analysis, companies could use reports to initiate dialogues, and to establish learning mechanisms to continually exchange ideas and knowledge. Such dialogue-oriented forms require two-way communication instead of monologues as this was usually done when just disseminating good news through hard copy reports as communication channels with only very limited opportunities for feedback or criticism.

Closely linked with cross media availability, computer-based media, and other innovative opportunities offered by the internet, the key trends above are setting the scene for any forward-looking approach in the field. The trends clearly illustrate that corporate communication in general and in particular sustainability reporting evolves rapidly or has already developed towards a sophisticated and digital stage and hence raises a number of challenges.

BENEFITS USING THE INTERNET FOR SUSTAINABILITY REPORTING

Within sophisticated environmental and sustainability reporting, reports available on the WWW and using the internet have become one of the most fashionable topics since its inception (Isenmann & Lenz, 2001; Isenmann & Lenz, 2002). The driving force that underlies this trend and promotes its use is the rapid development of the internet and other technologies and services associated. Together, these technical means offer unique capabilities that could be employed to improve current reporting practices either along efficiencies and strategic opportunities or in terms of new perspectives through interactive, tailored and dialogue-oriented sustainability reporting.

EFFICIENCIES AND STRATEGIC OPPORTUNITIES

In pursuing greater conceptual clarity, a comprehensive *classification* of ICT-based benefits is proposed and summarised in Table 2. The classification is based on a review of current approaches found in literature dealing with internet-based environmental reporting. Methodically, the classification rests on two heuristics, and it has

Table 2. Classification of internet-specific benefits for sustainability reporting

Technical benefits	**Possible realizations**				
Benefits concerning reporting purposes	Resource controlling	Information, disclosure	Dialogue, two-way-communication	Engagement for transactions	...
Benefits concerning reporting processes	Rationalization		Customization		...
	Easy administration of reporting elements	Efficient preparation of reports	Fast distribution of reports	Smart presentation of reports	...
Benefits concerning reporting contents	Reports		Additional information		...
	Customized selection (data view)	Topical selection, retrieval	Internal links: e.g. environmental division	External links: e.g. stock exchange, ranking	...
Benefits concerning reporting design	Online-, offline-availability	Navigation	Hypermedia	Enhanced communication	...

shown its usefulness in several empirical studies (Isenmann, Lenz & Müller-Merbach, 2001). It constitutes a helpful scheme for surveying the impressive array of benefits the internet could provide for environmental reporting in a broader sense. It may also be used to determine how to progress towards sustainability reporting.

The multitude of benefits can be organised in terms of a *three-step-strategy*:

- **Step 1:** The internet facilitates *incorporating complementary information* into free-standing reports, e.g. the incorporation of financial and social issues into environmental reports.
- **Step 2:** The internet provides *skilful connection* and *smart cross-linking* between stand-alone single environmental, financial and social reports in the sense of a virtual compound document, featured with hyperlinks. These hyperlinks are employed to assist user navigation so that they feel comfortable without "being lost in cyberspace" when browsing through such virtual reports.
- **Step 3:** The internet can help provide *customized sustainability reports*. Some target groups may perhaps wish to get a short divisional sustainability report. Some others may prefer a sustainability report in a more detailed fashion.

Computer scientists (Arndt & Günther, 2000), IT experts (Glushko & McGrath, 2005) and other reporting professionals (DiPiazza & Eccles, 2002) recommend that employing XML helps to realise the internet-specific benefits outlined above. Due to its multitude of technologies associated, XML could be understood as a collective term that incorporates all the items shown in Figure 1.

For example, XML has several advantages over HTML, and thus it is considered the preferred data format for any advanced reporting approach for a period of time, especially for sustainability reporting. The suitability of XML is based on its characteristics of multiple-usability, exchangeability and the separation between contents (semantics), report structure (logical order) and representation (layout and style) (Figure 2).

XML is structure-oriented and appropriate for advanced internet applications. XML documents consist of plain text, which can be validated by machine processing. Furthermore, XML offers a number of opportunities to improve the reporting workflow and allocation of human and organisational resources more efficiently. It does this by supporting all core processes from automated preparation and effective administration towards

Figure 1. XML technologies, used for advanced sustainability reporting

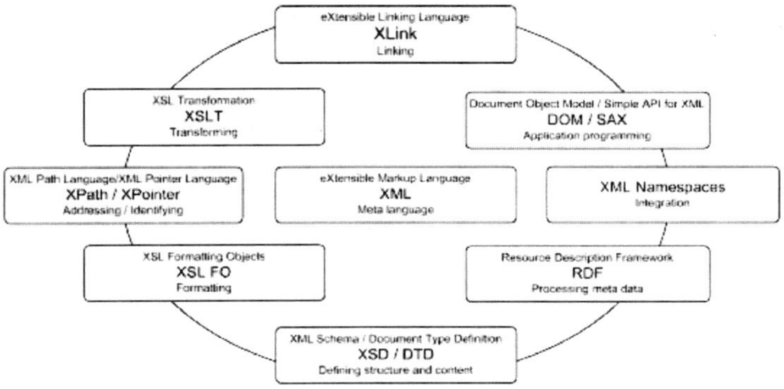

fast distribution and smart presentation, and also facilitating the teamwork along the reporting procedures, inside and outside the company (Table 3).

The idea behind reporting supported by the internet is that this computer-based method overcomes the limitations of paper-based communication like one size fits all reports, hard copies, print media fixation, and one-way-communication. In contrast, a fully ICT-supported approach offers a number of features to improve sustainability communication. It finally elevates the field to a more sophisticated stage by adding value for reporters and report users. Because of its overall *added value creating opportunities*, the internet is already used by several reporting companies and target groups as the *pivotal platform* to provide or to access information on environmental, social, and economic performance or other related issues of sustainability (Rikhardsson, Andersen & Bang, 2002; Jungle Rating, 2007). As Alan Benjamin

Figure 2. Separation between contents, structure, and layout of a report using XML

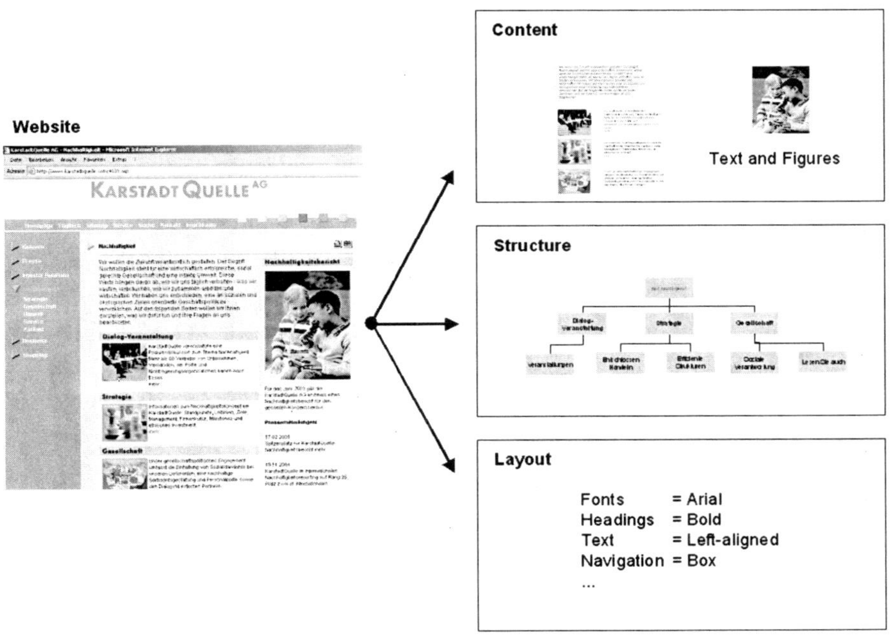

Table 3. XML specific benefits for sustainability reporting

Core processes	ICT-specific challenges	XML-specific benefits	XML-technologies
Preparation	• Data stored in documents • Need for teamwork • Trend for standardization	• Standardized document structure • Automated generation • Powerful hyperlinks	• Schema(XSD), document type definition (DTD) • Xlink, XPointer, XPath • XML parser (DOM/SAX)
Administration	• Data stored in documents • Need for teamwork	• Clear datastructure • Markup via metadata • Single source cross media publishing	• XML database • RDF
Distribution	• Demand for customization • Multitude of accessibility	• Integrated communication • Cross media distribution • Push and pull principle	• XSLFO • Data formats suitable for XML processing
Presentation	• Demand for customization • Smart presentation	• Hypermedia features • Customized presentation • Presentation independent from structure and contents	• XSLT and XSLFO • XSL parser

(1998), chairman of QSP Holdings plc, argues: "The Web site will be the prime communications vehicle of the 21st century – largely interactive. It will host a permanent dialogue as the gateway to the company" (p. 13).

NEW PERSPECTIVES FOR CUSTOMIZATION AND STAKEHOLDER-DIALOGUE

The way companies are communicating sustainability issues are decisive on users' perceived satisfaction, value, and overall attitude on sustainability reporting, perhaps whether users actually pay attention to sustainability reports, how readers assess reliability and value of these documents, and to what extent stakeholders are willing to make use of such communication vehicles for decision making. Further, companies' communication style may have an impact on users' media preferences, e.g. whether they tend to favour primarily hard copies or computer-based reports. Employees and customers but also suppliers and investors usually have different information needs (Azzone, Brophy, Noci, Welford & Young, 1997; Pleon Kohtes & Klewes, 2005; Isenmann & Marx Gómez, 2008). Hence, they want fine tuned information and expect tailor-made reports exactly meeting their specific needs in content, form, media, and information supply. Reporting merely through one size fits all hard copies or simple electronic duplicates without any added value may hardly fulfil emerging requirements and future expectations.

Contributing to a more user-driven reporting development makes clear that such an approach mirrors not only a 'passing fashion', but rather a shift in the way forward-looking companies are going to report on sustainability issues. In that sense, the issues highlighted here are probably becoming crucial reporting requirements in the near future. The transition phase may be described as a process that moves reporting away *from a rather "managerial closed shop procedure" towards a "quasi public effort"* of engaging and involving stakeholder, even to a certain extent (Spencer-Cooke, 1995). Information supply evolves from a strict monologue and one-way company controlled exercise towards a more interactive and tailored reporting approach, while communicating with a greater audience and making more use of the internet, trying to get feedback and stakeholder commentary from a number of target groups, or even to engage interested parties providing a "challenger report" (IfEU, imug & IÖW, 2001). Such a transition calls also for online communication actually facilitating engagement, involvement, and other mechanisms of learning. Companies realize that they cannot act alone to achieve their sustainability reporting objectives.

The issues of policy and practice and their mutual interrelations, which underlie the "triple bottom line" (Clarke, 2001), are too complex and usually divisive. They require involvement of different interests and continuous exchange of knowledge, from inside and outside the companies. Hence, companies are faced to develop *from strict confrontation to stakeholder engagement*. For example, pressure groups or other critical stakeholders which have primarily be seen as watchdogs could also be considered from a more open-minded perspective, perhaps valued as potentially constructive partners. Some partnerships with former critics have proved to be tremendous opportunities to open new lines of communication, e.g.: Nature Conservancy–International Paper, or Conservation International–Starbucks Coffee. Non governmental institutions could do more than strong activism; they could actually co-operate and even become a company's collaborator.

From a co-operative perspective, interactive reporters can make use of the stakeholders' existing expertise and profound knowledge. A prominent example was the co-operation between Hoechst AG – since 2004 incorporated into the Sanofi Aventis Group – and the Institute for Applied Ecology (Ewen, Ebinger, Gensch, Grießhammer, Hochfeld & Wollny, 1997). In a fruitful process of learning, they both developed a "product sustainability assessment" tool and implemented this instrument into the Hoechst sustainability management. Such successful examples illustrate: Interactive, target group tailored, and dialogue-oriented sustainability reporting is more than just a temporary 'hype'. In contrast, it may create real value and – when arranged to a concept and incorporated to organisation, structures and processes –, it even becomes a necessity and thus a part of companies' daily affairs. Further, when sustainability reporting is supported by an underlying ICT infrastructure and also implemented into information management systems, the outcomes and results can improve operating practices and certainly enhance the ongoing decision-making.

The *internal and external value* that companies are expecting to gain through stronger stakeholder relationships and tailored, dialogue-oriented reporting may be described along four ways (Ernst & Young, KPMG, PricewaterhouseCoopers & House of Mandag Morgen, 1999; Stratos, 2003; Hund, Engel-Cox & Fowler, 2004):

- The first benefit is to prevent and avoid *shareholder risk*. Such risk may occur if a company fails to establish or does not take enough care of stakeholder relationships. Ignoring real stakes, emerging concerns, or reasonable interests seems to be a risky communication strategy, just see the example of Brent Spar.
- Another benefit that companies could exploit is inspiration for *innovation*. Strong relationships with employees, along supply chains, and within other business networks are a fertile surrounding far more than a prerequisite to create innovative products, or to improve efficiency of processes.
- Closely related, a third benefit lays in the pool of *ideas, knowledge,* and other *resources* available in a network of relationships. Such a network provides valuable resources and crucial information necessary for the development of new markets and other business opportunities.
- As *reputation* is rather based on stakeholders' perceptions, good relationships are a vital source of intangible assets such as superior reputation and enhanced brand value, both of which generate a number of competitive advantages.

Generally, companies are recommended to see sustainability reporting and progression in communication no longer as an extra cost or burden on hard-pressed management, as from a long-term perspective the attainable benefits may exceed its costs by far. Hence, it is argued here that companies weigh the costs and benefits of such advanced reporting against the target groups' information needs and the companies' resource capabilities to satisfy them.

CUSTOMIZATION

Customization or target group tailoring respectively is rooted in the fact that stakeholders interested in sustainability issues usually have heterogeneous needs and preferences. More recently, it could be observed that they are becoming more critical on companies' business (Ahmed & Hardaker, 1999). Therefore, it is evident that attention must be paid best to produce reports truly meeting various – and perhaps conflicting – needs through a clearly *customized reporting approach* (Lenz, 2003). By doing so, users certainly realise that their concerns are truly taken into consideration. Nevertheless, companies have difficulties in identifying relevant target groups and discovering their certain needs. Axelrod (1998) pointed out: The "dilemma facing environmental reporting since its inception – how to cater to the varied interests of different target groups – still remains today" (p. 12).

Customization opens a window to improve sustainability communication, because tailored reports prevent information overload. Such a tailored approach likely results in ongoing communication, constructive dialogue, and further steps of engagement. Approaching target group tailoring and providing fine tuned reports companies should use the internet as an excellent instrument. Otherwise it would be very laborious – and probably expensive as well – to produce a great number of tailored reports on print media through an orthodox practice. In a more detailed fashion, target group tailoring based on the internet could be implemented through three different methods (Lenz, 2003), perhaps starting with stereotyping and then developing to individualization and personalization (Lenz, 2003; Brosowski & Lenz, 2004; Isenmann & Marx Gómez, 2004):

- The first approach is called *stereotyping,* a basic method employing standard user-profiles. These profiles record information needs that are thought of as characteristic for a specific group of users. Stereotypes are usually based on an analysis of empirical studies and then refined for a certain company via questionnaires and interviews with its key target groups. Using stereotypes, a tailored reporting approach provides different, but frequently static views of a report, perhaps dependent on a certain target group users are assigned to. For example, employees have a view of a report different from customers, and thus a company may prepare a set of tailored reports. This is the way that a number of users may prefer: They are provided with a pre-selected report, probably meeting their needs and likely to suit their preferences.
- One step beyond, the second method of customization is described as *individualization.* Through this more sophisticated method, users are able to create their own reports. They are becoming "reporters" themselves, just selecting the information they need, either according to their current preferences or in line with a certain guideline. Individualization offers more interactivity. Tailored reports that users request for, however, have to be produced dynamically through a (web) content management system. In order to manage its administration well, it is helpful to employ user-profiles. These profiles record users' preferences perhaps regarding their target groups, density, media, breadth, depth, time and the form in which the report is to be prepared.

Figure 3. Types of communication that can be adopted for stakeholder dialogue

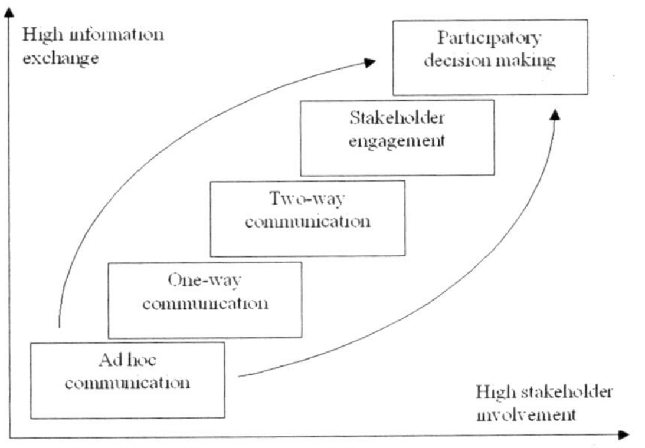

- The third method target group tailoring can be accomplished is *personalization.* Personalization is seen as the most sophisticated approach because it records personal data in addition to users' preferences. Recording personal data, e.g. like name and address, however is a sensitive issue that needs to be treated very carefully to prevent misuse. For that reason, any procedure of recording personal data should be voluntary, reversible, and made transparent to the user. Furthermore, its employment should be strictly limited to fine tuning communication vehicles. Implementing personalization mirrors an insight stated early in the field (CICA, 1994): "The choice of audience will directly affect the presentation of information, its tone, sophistication, emphasis, etc." (p. 40).

STAKEHOLDER DIALOGUE

Corresponding to customization, the second core element emphasised here is *stakeholder dialogue*. When providing stakeholder dialogue, companies can demonstrate openness and honesty in reporting, especially if communication with participating parties is meaningful, open, and fair. Such communication makes clear that reporters take users' needs and preferences into account, e.g. through feedback loops or other mechanisms for learning, finally linking to the management as an important input for reflection.

Following the guidebook on sustainability communication and stakeholder involvement (WBCSD, 2002; Hund, Engel-Cox & Fowler, 2004), stakeholder dialogues can take every form of a continuum, from passive and non-participatory to active and fully participatory; put in business terms, the spectrum includes: information, consultation, involvement, collaboration, and empowerment. Emphasizing the vital importance of stakeholder dialogue as a critical issue of reporting, the guidebook describes different types in a five-stage model, along degree of information exchange and degree of stakeholder involvement (Figure 3): ad hoc communication, one-way communication, two-way communication, stakeholder engagement, and partnership, understood as participatory fashion of decision making.

While the early stages have been focused primarily on ad hoc and one-way communication, advanced sustainability reporting is also on using the more sophisticated communication types. Support by the internet offers a number of opportunities to make such an approach work. This scenario may not be irrelevant or meaningless at all. On the contrary, customized and stakeholder-oriented reporting could make *good business sense*, at least for two main reasons: first, as sustainability reporting is becoming increasingly relevant for professional users in the financial community and decision making (Flatz, 2003); and second, since multiple inquiries companies are receiving from a ranking and rating institutions are a really time-consuming and costly exercise (Axelrod, 2000). Rather than endure these procedures, companies are recognising the value in having a readily available tool for providing the information needed.

Based on the development model above, the guidebook further illustrates how to use these types and points out the vehicles available. This catalogue of communication vehicles includes a number of written and verbal tools. Many of these reporting instruments could be made available on the WWW, or – at least – benefit from internet support: reports, brochures, leaflets, newsletters, press releases, slides, presentations, audio sequences, and video clips are accessible via download and/or online, prepared for being pulled or automatically disseminated via email or other current push technologies (Isenmann & Lenz, 2001).

Stakeholder dialogue can be a *fruitful method* to be taken along the phases of sustainability reporting:

- at the *beginning* of a reporting cycle, perhaps to draw stakeholders' attention to reports, or invite target groups to articulate what they need and expect to read;
- *along* the reporting processes, e.g. to provide opportunities for feedback, or criticism on reports;
- *subsequently* to the publication and release, e.g. through stakeholder consultation as an input for forthcoming efforts and the next reporting cycle.

Using the internet helps to break down barriers of information between companies and stakeholders. The bridge of this reporting medium without boundaries however has positive and negative impacts on companies. On the one hand, growing sensitivity in the public for sustainability issues linked with increasing demand for corporate transparency and credibility could influence companies to think hard about their way of doing business and thus to provide more interactivity. On the other hand, more and more critical customers tend to give feedback when they miss companies' commitment for environmental and social responsibility. In this respect, interactive sustainability online reporting could also be a reasonable defensive action companies may take against being stigmatized as insensitive for rising environmental and social issues.

Moreover, *online communities* will play an increasing role in forcing companies to become more sensitive to sustainability issues. Here, the internet helps bringing this about primarily by facilitating more effective and transparent communication (Ahmed & Hardaker, 1999). While the focus of customization is more on information supply and of particular relevance when reports are to be published, stakeholder dialogue is understood as an element throughout the whole reporting processes. Nevertheless, the two core elements of advanced sustainability reporting are complements. For that reason, stakeholders' heterogeneous needs could be best analysed through ongoing stakeholder dialogues.

FRAMEWORK FOR ADVANCED SUSTAINABILITY REPORTING

A framework for advanced internet-based environmental reporting is illustrated using four elements (Isenmann & Marx Gómez, 2004; Isenmann, 2005):

- stakeholder analysis,
- analysis of stakeholder information requirements,
- XML-based document engineering, and
- ICT architecture.

The framework serves as a *guideline* on how to exploit the media-specific capabilities that the internet and its associated technologies and services provide, perhaps when developing towards sustainability reporting, but surely leading to improvements in the areas of sustainability communications, information management, and organization.

STAKEHOLDER ANALYSIS

The starting point of any advanced sustainability reporting system is a stakeholder analysis identifying the primary users and typically asking: Who are the *relevant* stakeholders (including the critical ones), which key target groups inside and outside the company require information via environmental reporting (Figge & Schaltegger, 2000)? Generally, there are two ways of identification, either a deductive approach or an inductive approach combined with a deductive approach.

According to the deductive approach, initially all stakeholders could be considered relevant or called a target group who are involved in or affected by a company's impacts and activities along sustainability. Perhaps, as certain stakeholders claim some exclusive information rights, they may be seen as specific users (Lange, von Ahsen & Daldrup, 2001). For example, this is true for companies' top managers who hold ultimate liability, for local authorities who have a specific right to know and also for banks and insurers who require confidential information. Regardless of certain information rights, it could be fruitful anyway addressing these groups as users, too.

Despite its proven usefulness, the deductive approach should be combined with an inductive one for this task. Stakeholder analysis represents a company-specific task influenced by certain circumstances, e.g. size, industry, products, processes, location, environmental impacts, stakeholder relations, communication strategy, management systems, and strategic goals. Hence, an empirical analysis could validate the number of relevant stakeholders that are found through the deductive approach. Lenz (2003) provides a comprehensive stakeholder analysis. He reviewed a multitude of empirical studies that identified key target groups and primary users' needs in the field. Resulting from his in-depth survey he identified 12 key target groups, arranged in a stakeholder map with four groups:

- *Financial community,* including investors, insurance agents and financial analysts;
- *business partners,* including employees, customers and suppliers;
- *diffuse groups,* including media representatives, neighbors and consultants;
- *normative groups,* including local authorities, respective legislators, pressure groups and standard setting institutions.

To some extent, the users within a certain target group can be indicated through relatively homogeneous information needs.

ANALYSIS OF STAKEHOLDER INFORMATION REQUIREMENTS

Following stakeholder analysis and identification of primary users, a reporting organisation should study information needs and other preferences expected to be met in report form and content. Such an analysis of stakeholder information requirements are meant to determine relevant contents that target groups expect and the preferences they require regarding form, layout, design, media and distribution channel. There is consensus that meeting users' needs is needed for successful elaborated environmental and sustainability reporting (Isenmann & Kim, 2006). In contrast to its wide acceptance in frameworks and guidelines, however, current practice shows another picture, with significant room for improvements, even for the best reporters.

At present, little work has been done to conceptualise users' information needs, especially concerning distribution channels, presentation styles, and media preferences. Hence, van Dalen (1997) mentions a lack of more profound insights on users' information needs and preferences. Answering this need, Lenz (2003) provides a considerable analysis on stakeholder information requirements.

- For example, *employees* are interested in environmental and social performance of their employers and companies. They want to be informed about targets and activities related to the environmental management system. Further, they want to understand how companies are seen by local community groups. Employees wish to see their company as a going concern, recognizing that environmental performance might have some influence on this.
- In supply chains and other manufacturing networks, *suppliers* exchange information with participating business partners (Lippman, 2001). Establishing partnerships implies extensive environmental communication along the whole supply chain or network. These groups need environmental information regarding resource efficiency, regulatory compliance, new product and service opportunities, especially in terms of extended product stewardship, and other environmental liabilities.
- *Investors,* including institutional and private shareholders, financial analysts and investment consultants, are increasingly interested in environmental issues and their financial interrelations since they notice that sustainability reports make good business and environmental sense (Australian Government, 2003; Hesse, 2007). A number of investors expect that environmental performance influences financial performance and shareholder value. For example, in November 2000 a group of 39 financial investors, managing combined assets excess of $140 billion, sent a letter to CEOs of the 500 largest U.S. companies urging them to provide sustainability reports (SocialFunds, 2000).

Together, the analysis of stakeholder information requirements clearly demonstrates that employees, customers, suppliers, local authorities, legislators, neighbours, consultants, financial analysts, investors, insurance agents, media representatives and members of rating and ranking organisations have *heterogeneous information needs*. These different needs cannot be fully satisfied or easily met just by "reporting as usual" through orthodox practice, via one universal document (on print media), mostly produced as a "one size fits all" report. Users expect more and more customized reporting instruments (Isenmann, Brosowski & Lenz, 2003). It is necessary to determine what target groups want, and to identify their needs and preferences.

The results of the two analyses discussed above lend themselves to the creation of specific user profiles. For each of the core target groups, a profile of their information needs will be established that comprises content requirements, preferences as to the reporting form and secondary requirements such as the distribution channel.

XML-BASED DOCUMENT ENGINEERING

The results of stakeholder analysis and deeper insights of stakeholder information requirements are used for XML-based document engineering, indicating the ICT-laden area where contents, structures, procedures and design of reporting instruments and other communication vehicles are defined. This leads to the questions: What should an advanced sustainability report prepared as an XML document look like? What contents should be included? Who should be addressed? On what devices should the report be available? Which standards or guidelines need to be adhered to? Here, certain aspects of report structure, contents and layout are explicitly considered.

The core of XML-based document engineering is to develop standardized document structures for a certain type of documents (i.e. sustainability reports). This is usually done in the form of an XML schema, or more advanced, in the form of an XBRL taxonomy: A schema defines the semantics and overall pool of contents in a basic structure for a certain group of documents, in this case, for sustainability reports. Of this pool of structured contents, customized reports exactly meeting the requirements of certain user, user groups or guidelines respectively can be prepared in an automated fashion by machine processing. In terms of document engineering, a schema consists of several elements representing the contents and their corresponding attributes, specifying the semantics and indicating the elements. Consequently, a schema determines what elements can be used within a XML document. Further, a schema describes how elements can be arranged, and which attributes certain elements may carry.

Embedded in a research initiative in the German Environmental Informatics community, the existing XML schema for sustainability reports is blended in a standardized reference architecture for sustainability reports built on XBRL (Isenmann, Arndt, Bey, Marx Gómez & Solsbach, 2008; Arndt, Isenmann, Brosowski, Thiessen & Marx Gómez, 2006). This proposal is developed on three basics:

- In terms of *materiality and contents,* the XBRL taxonomy meets the requirements of the sustainability reporting guidelines (G3) of the Global Reporting Initiative (GRI, 2006).
- In terms of *design and configuration,* an existing XBRL FRTA (Financial Reporting Taxonomies Architecture; e.g. Hamscher, 2005) is applied. As the FRTA is common for business financial reporting, it helps that the XBRL taxonomy for sustainability reports may be used in the well-established field of business financial reporting.
- In terms of underlying *methodology,* a generic process-model for the development of schemas was used.

GRI-G3 SUSTAINABILITY REPORTING GUIDELINES

The GRI-G3 specify basic contents of a sustainability report which are of relevance to reporters and report users (GRI, 2006):

- *Strategy and profile* items set the overall context for understanding organizational performance such as strategy, profile, and governance;
- *management approach* items cover how an organization addresses a given set of issues to provide context for understanding the performance in a certain area;
- *performance indicators* provide comparable information along the economic, environmental, social, and integrative performance.

FINANCIAL REPORTING TAXONOMIES ARCHITECTURE

The FRTA provides a reference architecture for business financial reporting. It is characterized through a number of so-called taxonomy schemas and linkbases. A taxonomy schema is an XML schema, usually a standardized schema (XSD) and contains XBRL concepts. A concept is a definition on how to report about the activities or nature of a business entity. Taxonomies contain XBRL concepts represented by XML schema element definitions.

Using the design principles of the FRTA delivers specifications for a proper development and overall structure of an XBRL taxonomy for sustainability reports. These specifications are crucial for data exchange and information management as they ensure consistency between different XBRL taxonomies at different levels, e.g. in terms of correct representation, modularity, and evolution.

Figure 4. XBRL framework

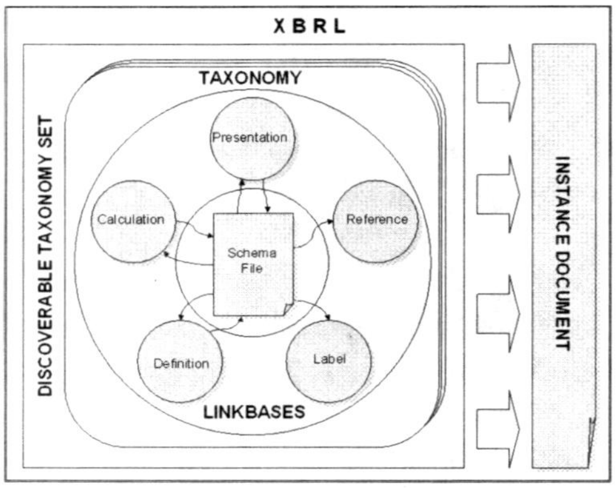

XBRL TAXONOMY FOR SUSTAINABILITY REPORTS

Following the FRTA, an XBRL taxonomy for sustainability reports consists of five elements (Figure 4):

- The *XML schema* is the core and represents the pivotal document of the taxonomy for sustainability reports. The schema contains all GRI disclosure items which are represented as XML elements and specified through certain data types.
- The *labelLinkBase* links all XML schema elements to certain literal meaning. For example, labels in English and German may be assigned to all XML schema elements if the sustainability report should be available in two languages.
- The *definitionLinkBase* defines a hierachical order within the labelLinkBase how to structure the overall contents and where to fix certain XML schema elements in the sustainability report.
- The *presentationLinkBase* makes it possible to arrange elements in any hierarchical order without changing the overall structure defined in the definitionLinkBase.

Figure 5. Process model for the development of XML schemas

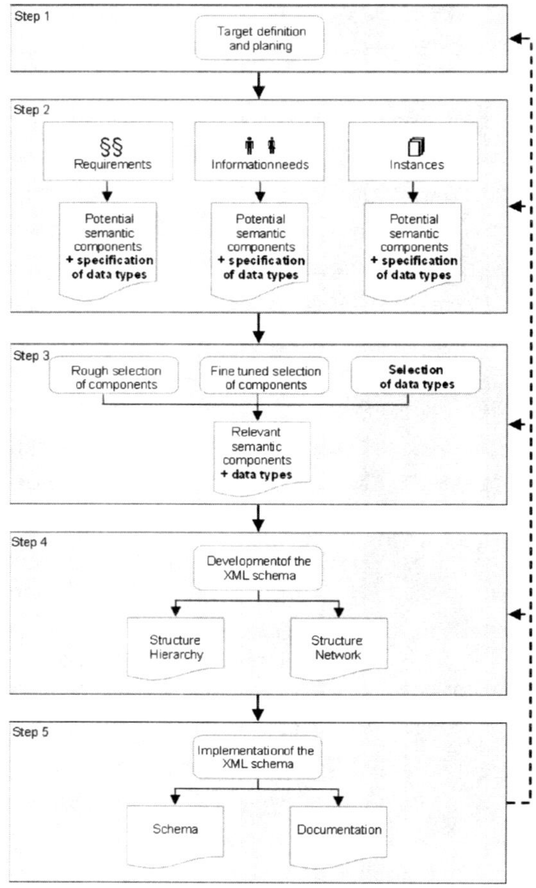

- The *referenceLinkBase* provides the opportunity to link XML schema elements with further information like regulations, guidelines, and comments, and hence to facilitate the overall understanding.

According to the XBRL framework, there is a sixth conceptual element, i.e. *calculationLinkBase*. Up to now, however, the GRI-G3 has not provided a method for the calculation of performance indicators. The calculationLinkBase defines rules on how to calculate performance indicators and other data.

PROCESS-MODEL USED AS UNDERLYING METHODOLOGY

The development of a schema for sustainability reports is a sophisticated work because a number of different requirements and heterogeneous needs have to be taken into account. The process-model used here was initially proposed by Schraml (1997) and then refined and elaborated by Lenz (2003) and Brosowski, Isenmann, Beisel & Marx Gómez (2004). It is structured in five major steps (Figure 5):

- **Definition of the main target (step 1):** The target is to develop a XML schema for sustainability reports. The schema has to simultaneously incorporate a variety of issues on sustainability, and the requirements of relevant regulations, standards, guidelines and manuals, especially at the European level.
- **Identification of possible semantic components (step 2):** According to the target, a multitude of resources need to be analyzed to extract possible contents from relevant regulations, standards, guidelines, already available reports and users' needs and preferences, e.g. the GRI (2002) "sustainability reporting guidelines", the revised European "Eco Management and Audit Scheme" (EC, 2001), the international standard ISO 14001 on "environmental management systems" (DIN, 1996), the German standard DIN 33922 "environmental reports for the public" (DIN, 1997), the early international guideline on "company environmental reporting" (UNEP and SustainAbility, 1994), its German counterpart "environmental reports – environmental statements" (future and IÖW, 1994), and a publicly available specification (PAS) on "data exchange between enterprise resource planning (ERP) systems and environmental information systems" (Lang, Rey, Wohlgemuth, Genz & Pawlytsch, 2003). This task identifies the pool of possible semantic components the schema may contain. Further, for all resources taken into account, the data types have to be identified and specified.
- **Selection of relevant semantic components (step 3):** From the pool of possible semantic components, a catalogue of actually relevant contents needs to be developed through a verification procedure. Using the full GRI (2002) content, the result is a total of 395 semantic components (using the full G3 content, the result will decrease to about 260 components). If any sector supplements may be included, then the total amount will increase up to 415-466, depending on the industry sector. All components incorporated are classified as "must be" (required) or "might be" (optional), and on which resource they are rooted. In addition, all data types used for a certain semantic component have to be determined and analyzed through a verification procedure in terms of redundancy. The result is a catalogue of relevant contents specified by certain data types.
- **Design of the schema (step 4):** Based on the catalogue above, the schema has to be designed. Therefore, all selected components can be organized in a hierarchy, typical for XML documents (Figure 6).
- **Implementation of the document type model (step 5):** Finally, the schema needs to be implemented, i.e. noted according to XML and transformed into an XML schema definition (XSD). Further, a manual needs to be prepared for documentation, further development and regular updates.

Employing an XML schema offers an impressive array of benefits, improves a company's information management, supports its reporting workflow, and helps to communicate with its target

Figure 6. Schema for advanced sustainability reports, illustration

groups in a meaningful way, that is, providing interactivity, producing tailor-made reports, and facilitating stakeholder dialogue. In total, on the basis of the schema, companies are enabled to provide integrated and customized sustainability reports, prepared by machine processing and generated in an automated manner.

ICT ARCHITECTURE

Reaping the media-specific benefits that the internet and XML may carry requires a proper ICT architecture, suitable to operate XML documents and appropriate to provide single source cross media publishing. For that reason, a three-tiered web application architecture is proposed:

- The basic *data layer* (I) contains several sources where the schema, style sheets, user profiles and a number of other XML documents are stored. These sources include relevant data, metadata and thesauri. The data layer is managed through a database server.
- The *application layer* (II) contains different services and applications to generate and distribute reports in an automated manner by machine processing. This complex layer is used as a data integrator responsible for system management and is accessed through an application server.
- The *presentation layer* (III) represents an interactive user interface that is used for submitting users' information needs as well

Figure 7. Web application for advanced sustainability reporting, illustration

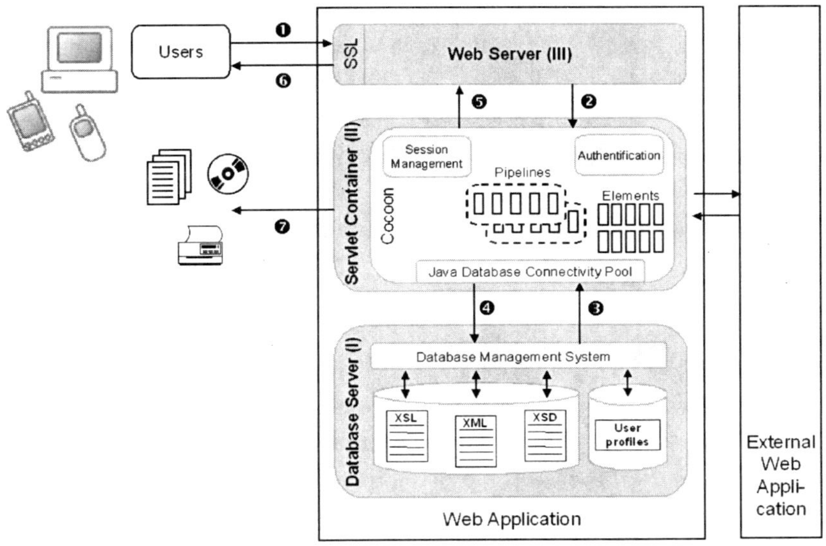

as for presenting reports. The presentation layer provides easy access via a standard internet browser, e.g. Netscape Navigator or Microsoft Internet Explorer.

For example, the procedure of an advanced reporting system is depicted in Figure 7.

For demonstration, we developed a set of XSL (eXtensible Stylesheet Language) style sheets (Table 4), providing a total of nine combinations: This set of style sheets demonstrates how certain contents can be extracted from the same underlying XML-based report, and how these contents might be arranged and presented according to certain user preferences or exactly meeting the requirements of regulations or guidelines in an automated fashion.

Together, the framework describes a comprehensive and ICT-based reporting approach in a broader sense, including its variety of value added features. Due to its fully supported underlying ICT infrastructure, an internet-based reporting system of this kind provides a set of important *contents,* different *media*, corresponding *distribution principles* and various *presentation styles*.

The ICT architecture discussed above has been realized in a software prototype as a practical application (Isenmann, Beisel, Brosowski & Marx Gómez, 2004; Isenmann, 2008). At the heart of its ICT architecture lies Cocoon (application

Table 4. Set of different views based on an underlying XML-based sustainability report through specific XSL style sheets

Content/Layout	Print Media	Computer-based media	Processing in Environmental Informaton Systems
Satisfying **investors'** needs Fulfilling the requirements of **E MAS II** Meeting the **GRI** guidelines	• Plain text • Table of contents • PDF	• Hypertext structure • Multimedia features • Navigation • HTML	• Plain Text • Marked with tags • XML

layer, II), a Java-based, modular structured, open source publishing software (Apache, 2008), able to perform the schema (see Figure 6) and other XML documents, and suitable to provide customized reports *on the fly*. Today, the prototype can be considered an *adaptable* reporting system providing *individualized* reports. The next step is the development towards personalization and an adaptive stage. In sum, companies are in a position to make progress in customization step by step, starting with stereotyping and next moving towards a sustainability reporting system able to provide individualized or even personalized reports. Perhaps soon the prototype may be implemented in a number of trail-blazing small and medium sized German enterprises.

CONCLUSION

Despite its overall usefulness for communicating sustainability issues, online reporting cannot solve a number of *current problems* discussed in the field (Gray, 2002; Gray & Milne, 2002; Unerman & Bennett, 2004): e.g. should sustainability reporting still be voluntary or must it be mandatory? Is it meaningful to disclose sustainability issues through well established annual and financial reports, or should information be covered just in (standalone) sustainability reports? How could companies' sustainability performance be conceptualized? What are proper methods of measurement? Which are the most meaningful indicators? Should stakeholders be involved, and what may audit, accounting control, and verification look like? No less importantly, where are the system boundaries, defining which effects are within the reporting scope and which are not?

Further, online reporting opens up a host of *new questions*, e.g. with respect to the target groups addressed and those actually reached. Among technical aspects of online communication and matters of efficient information management, a credible effort in sustainability reporting will have to address issues such as the digital divide, restricted access etc. On both ends of the communication link appropriate ICT infrastructure is needed; not just with the companies communicating (reporters), but more importantly with the stakeholders that need to be actually reached (report users). ACCA (2001) compiled some "cardinal sins" of online reporting in order to make its limitations clear.

Looking at the variety of methods firms are adopting for sustainability communication, CSR Europe (2000) point out that reporting belongs to the *least focused and coherent means of communication*, compared to standards and labels, awards and events, stakeholder consultation, or cause-related marketing. Although an institutional infrastructure around corporate sustainability – resulted in the evolution of initiatives such as the GRI, the social investment movement, and related efforts placing more emphasis on corporate responsibility, accountability and transparency – has emerged (Waddock, 2008), it is evident: sustainability reporting has some way to go before becoming a reliable and trustworthy activity. It is obvious, though, that the aim of providing a "clear and fair view" such as is (supposedly) attained in financial reports is illusory owing to the nature of sustainable development as a social process, where measurable "hard" data will never tell the whole story. From a reporter's perspective, sustainability is a notoriously complex issue to report. From a report user's point of view, this makes performance comparisons, benchmarking, rating and ranking rather difficult.

In contrast to the binary logic of recommending either print media or computer-based media as the only forms of a sustainability report, it is argued here for a *cross media reporting approach* that relies on an underlying ICT infrastructure. Such an approach may be based on the internet, preferably uses the benefits of XML, and provides powerful support along the whole reporting workflow. Further, such advanced reporting keeps companies in a position to provide sustainability reports and other communication vehicles on a variety of media, based on a single data source that serves as a shared publishing basis.

DiPiazza & Eccles (2002) state that "corporate information, in all its growing quantity and complexity can be – and in reality must be – communicated more effectively with the use of new technology. Reported information needs to break away from the constraints of paper-based formats" (p. 127). Numerous target groups are no longer satisfied solely with reports on print media or mere electronic duplicates. Sustainability reporting is becoming increasingly relevant for decision-making, and responding to multiple inquiries that a variety of stakeholder groups are making to companies is really time-consuming and costly (Axelrod, 2000). Rather than endure these procedures, companies are recognizing the value in having a readily available tool for providing the information needed.

Pioneering companies have started or will start to implement internet-based applications in the near future. Verie Sandborg, Baxter International's manager of environmental health and safety requirements regards a good environmental or sustainability report as an excellent source for responding to formalized requests for environmental or sustainability information (Axelrod, 2000).

Many of the questions asked are already answered in comprehensive reports. However, it would be helpful to have a fully ICT-based online reporting system: users could extract the information they need from a publishing database, and create an automatically generated customized report themselves, i.e. users are generate their own "reports à la carte", simply selecting keywords, clicking on preferences on a menu or choosing a certain guideline – perhaps creating a sustainability report in accordance with the GRI-guidelines at one's fingertips (Isenmann, 2008).

For some companies, advanced sustainability reporting might seem like a nice extra or just a buzzword in comparison to orthodox practice, traditional reporting focused on print media. The unique capabilities and benefits of such reporting approach, however, elevate it beyond the status of a mere "gadget". Internet technologies and services employed with XML and performed through web content management systems or other sophisticated software tools can do more than just offer new channels for report distribution or presentation.

The WWW is a service for *distributing* and *presenting* reports, including hypermedia-features, online information and global access around the clock. Furthermore, *information management* can be improved in various ways: data are captured from different data sources, combined despite different data formats, analyzed for decision making, professionally mastered and hypermedia-featured, tailored according to specific information needs and certain guidelines, distributed and presented, e.g. via email, cross media, fax, or ordinary mail.

Furthermore, *contents* and *design* of reports will be transformed: online availability, downloads, additional documents, interactivity, feedback opportunities, contact details, automatic order forms, electronic forums, hyperlinks, graphically designed websites, navigation, search engines, web rides, regular updates, and site promotion are some of the form and content capabilities that are already realized to a certain extent.

All in all, the internet is considered as a "reporting facilitator". Sensing that traditional standalone and single reporting might have limitations; a growing number of companies are considering improving their reporting practice and increase the use of reports in general. On improving sustainability reporting, Volkswagen (2003) makes the point: "Glossy brochures which are not real are worthless'. A classic glossy brochure makes little sense in this context. What is required here is to harness modern, flexible and cost-effective information technologies and channels – meaning which are also within the reach of small and medium-sized companies, and not just the global players. The internet provides numerous possibilities along these lines." With this in mind, one major challenge seems to be using ICT properly.

ICT-based reporting supports companies in moving away from traditional practice towards more advanced sustainability reporting.

The goal of this chapter was to elucidate how to move away, bringing to the surface tacit opportunities using the internet and the benefits of its associated technologies as a reporting backbone for companies' underlying ICT infrastructure. Such an approach might be a harbinger for a groundbreaking shift in the field, but at least will lead to progress in terms of reporting along multiple dimensions:

- Companies' *workflow* could be performed more efficiently, supporting all the core processes from automated preparation and streamlined administration towards fast distribution and appropriate presentation. ICT-based reporting can also facilitate the teamwork of different departments involved in text editing and other procedures, be it internally or externally, when co-operating with suppliers, intermediaries and rating or ranking institutions.
- The scope of the reports' *contents* could be expanded gradually, integrating economic, environmental and social issues according to companies' capabilities and communication strategies, but also to meet stakeholder needs. The typical evolution would move from an environmental report towards a fully integrated sustainability report, very often in line with the triple bottom line approach.
- Companies could improve their *communication* on sustainability issues, moving away from simple monologue and merely providing information towards an intensified stakeholder dialogue, user interactivity, information on demand, and thus developing from "one size fits all" publications on print media towards customized or even personalized reports available on different media.
- From a research perspective, a more balanced approach leading to fully integrated sustainability reporting based on the internet as a backbone for companies' underlying ICT infrastructure is considered a pioneering effort. As such, it may contribute to more conceptual clarity uncovering unique capabilities associated with the internet, especially when progressing in the field of sustainability reporting. From a practitioner's point of view, helpful guidance is provided on how to employ the internet productively and to make use of its associated technologies like XML for applications in the field of sustainability reporting.

REFERENCES

Ahmed, P. K., & Hardaker, G. (1999). The role of on-line communities on the internet for sustainable development. *Business Strategy and the Environment*, *8*(1), 75–81. doi:10.1002/(SICI)1099-0836(199901/02)8:1<75::AID-BSE186>3.0.CO;2-S

Andrew, J. (2003). Corporate governance, the environment, and the internet. *Electronic Green Journal, 19* (December). Retrieved April 4, 2004, from http://egj.uidaho.edu/egj19/andrew1.html

Apache (2008). *Apache Cocoon Project*. Retrieved April 24, 2008, from http://cocoon.apache.org

Arndt, H. K., & Günther, O. (Eds.). (2000). Environmental markup language (EML). First workshop Berlin 1999. Marburg: Metropolis.

Arndt, H. K., Isenmann, R., Brosowski, J., Thiessen, I., & Marx Gómez, J. (2006). Sustainability reporting using the eXtensible Business Reporting Language (XBRL). In Tochtermann, K., & Scharl, A. (Eds.), *Managing Environmental Knowledge* (pp. 75–82). Aachen: Shaker.

Association of Chartered Certified Accountants (ACCA). (1998). *Making values count: contemporary experience in social and ethical accounting, auditing, and reporting*. London: The Certified Accountants Educational Trust.

Association of Chartered Certified Accountants (ACCA). (2001). *Environmental, social and sustainability reporting on the world wide web: A guide to best practice*. London: The Certified Accountants Educational Trust.

Association of Chartered Certified Accountants (ACCA). (2004). *Towards transparency: Progress on global sustainability reporting 2004*. London: Certified Accountants Educational Trust.

Australian Government Department of the Environment and Heritage. (2003). *Corporate sustainability – an investor perspective. The Mays Report*. Canberra: Environmental Protection Branch, Department of the Environment and Heritage. Retrieved April 3, 2004, from http://deh.gov.au/industry/finance/publications/index.html

Axelrod, R. A. (1998). Ten years later: The state of environmental performance reports today. *Environmental Quality Management, 8*(2), 1–13. doi:10.1002/tqem.3310080202

Axelrod, R. A. (2000). Brave new words. The financial value of environmental communications. *Environmental Quality Management, 9*(4), 1–11. doi:10.1002/1520-6483(200022)9:4<1::AID-TQEM1>3.0.CO;2-J

Azzone, G., Brophy, M., Noci, G., Welford, R., & Young, W. (1997). A stakeholders' view of environmental reporting. *Long Range Planning, 30*(5), 699–709. doi:10.1016/S0024-6301(97)00058-7

Beattie, V., & Pratt, K. (2003). Issues concerning web-based business reporting: An analysis of the views of interested parties. *The British Accounting Review, 35*(2), 155–187. doi:10.1016/S0890-8389(03)00016-7

Benjamin, A. (1998). Prototype plc – the 21st century annual report. In The Institute of Chartered Accountants in England & Wales (Ed.), The 21st century annual report corporate governance (pp. 12-17). London: The Institute of Chartered Accountants in England & Wales.

Brophy, M., & Starkey, R. (1996). Environmental reporting. In Welford, R. (Ed.), *Corporate environmental management. Systems and strategies* (pp. 177–198). London: Earthscan.

Brosowski, J., Isenmann, R., Beisel, M., & Marx Gómez, J. (2004). XML schema for sustainbility reports meeting the needs of the GRI guidelines. In P. Minier, A. Susini (Eds.), *Sh@ring. Proceedings EnviroInfo 2004. 18th International Conference Informatics for Environmental Protection* (pp. 184-193). Genève: Editions du Tricorne.

Brosowski, J., & Lenz, C. (2004). Customised environmental reporting. *International Journal of Environment and Sustainable Development, 3*(1), 18–33. doi:10.1504/IJESD.2004.004687

Business for Social Responsibility (BSR). (2008). *Environmental, social and governance: Moving to mainstream investing?* Retrieved August 28, 2008, from http://bsr.org

Canadian Institute of Chartered Accountants (CICA). (1994). *Reporting on environmental reporting. Carried out in association with Canadian Standards Association, Financial Executives Institute Canada and International Institute for Sustainable Development (IISD)*. Toronto: CICA.

Clarke, T. (2001). Balancing the triple bottom line: Financial, social and environmental performance. *Journal of General Management, 26*(4), 16–27.

Clausen, J., Loew, T., Klaffke, K., Raupach, M., & Schoenheit, I. (2001). *The INEM sustainability reporting guide – a manual on practical and convincing communication for future-oriented companies*. Hamburg: International Network for Environmental Management (INEM). Retrieved April 22, 2002, from http://www.inem.org/free_downloads

Danish Commerce and Companies Agency (DCCA). (2006). *People & Profit. A practical guide to corporate social responsibility*. Retrieved September 22, 2008, from http://www.eogs.dk/sw28291.asp

Deloitte Touche Tohmatsu International (DTTI), International Institute for Sustainable Development (IISD), & SustainAbility Ltd. (1993). *Coming clean - corporate environmental reporting, opening up for sustainable development*. London: DTTI.

DiPiazza, S. A., & Eccles, R. G. (2002). *Building corporate trust. The future of corporate reporting*. New York: Wiley.

Elkington, J. (1997). *Cannibals with forks: The triple bottom line of 21st century business*. Oxford: Capstone.

Ernst & Young. KPMG, PricewaterhouseCoopers, & House of Mandag Morgen (1999). The Copenhagen Charter. A management guide to stakeholder reporting. Copenhagen: Mandag Morgen.

Europe, C. S. R. (2000). *Communicating corporate social responsibility*. Brussels: CSR Europe.

European Commission (EC) (2002). *European SMEs and Social and Environmental Responsibility*. Observatory of European SME 2002/No. 4, prepared by KPMG Special Services and EIM Business & Policy Research in the Netherlands in co-operation with European Network for SME Research (ENSR), and Intomart Luxembourg, Office for official publications of the European Communities.

European Communities (EC). (2001). Regulation (EC) No. 761/2001 of the European Parliament and of the Council of 19 March 2001 allowing voluntary participation by organisations in a Community eco-management and audit scheme (EMAS). *Official Journal of the European Communities*, *L*, 114.

European steel industry (2004). *Made of steel. The steel image campaign*. The joint initiative by steel companies from Europe to promote the image of steel. Retrieved October 25, 2004, from http://www.made-of-steel.com/html_en/informations/index.html

Ewen, C., Ebinger, F., Gensch, C.-O., Grießhammer, R., Hochfeld, C., & Wollny, V. (1997). *HoechstNachhaltig. Sustainable Development – Vom Leitbild zum Werkzeug* [Sustainable Development – From vision to an operational instrument]. Freiburg: Institute for Applied Ecology.
eXtensible Business Reporting Language (XBRL) (2006). *Extensible business reporting language 2.1*, recommendation -2003-12-31 and corrected errata -2005-11-07. Retrieved January 17, 2006, from http://www.xbrl.org/Specification/XBRL-RECOMMENDATION-2003-12-31+Corrected-Errata-2005-11-07.htm

Fichter, K. (1998). *Umweltkommunikation und Wettbewerbsfähigkeit. Wettbewerbstheorien im Lichte empirischer Ergebnisse zur Umweltberichterstattung von Unternehmen* [Environmental communication and competitiveness. Concepts of competition in the light of empirical results on corporate environmental reporting]. Marburg: Metropolis.

Figge, F., & Schaltegger, S. (2000). *What is "stakeholder value"? Developing a catchphrase into a benchmarking tool*. Lüneburg: University of Lüneburg & UNEP.

Flatz, A. (2003). Screening for sustainability. A case study of the Dow Jones Sustainability Index. In Waage, S. (Ed.), *Ants, Galileo, and Gandhi. Designing the future of business through nature, genius, and compassion* (pp. 144–168). Sheffield: Greenleaf.

Futerra Sustainability Communications. (2008). *The greenwash guide*. Retrieved September 17, 2008, from www.futerra.co.uk

Future e.V., & Institute for Ecological Economy Research (IÖW) (1994). *Environmental reports – environmental statements. Guidelines on preparation and distribution*. Osnabrück: future e.V.

German Institute for Standardisation e. V. (DIN) (1996). Environmental management systems – specifications with guidance for use. Berlin: Beuth.

German Institute for Standardisation e. V. (DIN) (1997). DIN 33922. Environmental reports for the public. Berlin: Beuth.

Global Reporting Initiative (GRI). (2002). *Sustainability reporting guidelines*. Retrieved October 15, 2002, from http://www.globalreporting.org

Global Reporting Initiative (GRI). (2004). *GRI software development. GRI enters digital age.* Retrieved May 18, 2004, from http://www.globalreporting.org/software

Global Reporting Initiative (GRI). (2006). *Sustainability reporting guidelines. Version 3.0.* Amsterdam: GRI.

Glushko, R. J., & McGrath, T. (2005). *Document engineering. Analyzing and designing documents for business informatics and web services*. Cambridge, MA: MIT.

Gray, R. (2002). Social and environmental responsibility, sustainability and accountability: Can the corporate sector deliver? *The Corporate Citizen*, *2*(3), 9–16.

Gray, R., & Milne, M. (2002). Sustainability reporting: Who's kidding whom? *Chartered Accountants Journal of New Zealand*, *81*(6), 66–70.

Hamscher, W. (Ed.). (2007). *Financial reporting taxonomies architecture 1.0.* Recommendation dated 2005-04-25. Retrieved December 14, 2007, from http://www.xbrl.org/technical/guidance/FRTA-RECOMMENDATION-2005-04-25.htm

Hesse, A. (2007): *Sustained added value. Information of investors and analysts for sector-specific "Sustainable Development Key Performance Indicators" (SD-KPIs) in management commentaries in German companies*. Study prepared for Deloitte Touche Tomatsu, issued 1/2007. Retrieved June 21, 2007, from http://deloitte.com/de

Hund, G., Engel-Cox, J., & Fowler, K. (2004). *A communications guide for sustainable development. How interested parties become partners*. Columbus: Battelle.

Institut für Energie und Umweltforschung (IfEU). Institut für Markt-Umwelt-Gesellschaft (imug), Institut für ökologische Wirtschaftsforschung (IÖW), & Öko-Institut (2001). *Challenger report.* Four institutes IfEU, imug, IÖW, Öko-Institut. Berlin: IfEU. Retrieved September 18, 2002, from http://www.ifeu.de/allgemein/pdf/Challenger-Report-Final.pdf

Interbrand (2008). *Best global brands 2008. Creating and managing brand value*. Retrieved September 29, 2008, from http://www.interbrands.com

International Institute for Sustainable Development (IISD). Deloitte & Touche, & Business Council for Sustainable Development (1992). Business strategy for sustainable development. Leadership and accountability for the 90's. Winnipeg: IISD.

Isenmann, R. (2004). Internet-based sustainability reporting. *International Journal of Environment and Sustainable Development*, *3*(2), 145–167. doi:10.1504/IJESD.2004.004700

Isenmann, R. (2005). Corporate sustainability reporting – a case for the internet. In Hilty, L. M., Seifert, E. K., & Treibert, K. (Eds.), *Information systems for sustainable development* (pp. 164–212). Hershey: Idea Group.

Isenmann, R. (2008). Environmental management information systems – illustrations from online communication and sustainability peporting. In M. Sánchez-Marrè, J. Béjar, J. Comas, A. E. Rizzoli, & G. Guariso (Eds.), *Proceedings of the iEMSs. Fourth Biennal Meeting. International Congress on Environmental Modelling and Software (iEMSs 2008), Barcelona, Catalonia, July 2008, vol. 3* (pp. 1636-1644). International Environmental Modelling and Software Society.

Isenmann, R., Arndt, H.-K., Bey, C., Marx Gómez, J., & Solsbach, A. (2008). XBRL-Taxonomie für Nachhaltigkeitsberichte – Vorschlag einer harmonisierten Dokumentstruktur zur Online-Kommunikation von Organisationen.In Bichler, M., Hess, T., Krcmar, H., Lechner, U., Matthes, F., & Picot, A. (Eds.), *Multikonferenz Wirtschaftsinformatik 2008* (pp. 601–613). Berlin: GITO.

Isenmann, R., Beisel, M., Brosowski, J., & Marx Gómez, J. (2004). Software tool for single source multiple media sustainability reporting. In P. Minier, & A. Susini (Eds.), *Sh@ring. Proceedings EnviroInfo 2004, 18th International Conference Informatics for Environmental Protection* (pp. 152-162). Genève: Editions du Tricorne.

Isenmann, R., & Bey, C. (2007). Environmental reporting on the internet – from a technical tool to a strategic necessity. In Sroufe, R., & Sarkis, J. (Eds.), *Strategic sustainability: The state of the art in corporate environmental management systems* (pp. 123–143). Sheffield: Greenleaf.

Isenmann, R., Bey, C., & Welter, M. (2007). Online reporting for sustainability issues. *Business Strategy and the Environment, 16*(7), 487–501. doi:10.1002/bse.597

Isenmann, R., Brosowski, J., & Lenz, C. (2003). Target group tailored corporate environmental reporting – stereotyping, individualisation, personalisation. In A. Gnauck, & R. Heinrich (Eds.), *The information society and enlargement of the European Union. Proceedings EnviroInfo 2003, 17th International Conference Informatics for Environmental Protection* (pp. 533-540). Marburg: Metropolis.

Isenmann, R., & Kim, K. (2006). Interactive sustainability reporting – developing towards more target group tailoring and stakeholder dialogue. In Schaltegger, S., Bennett, M., & Rikhardsson, P. (Eds.), *Sustainability Accounting and Reporting* (pp. 533–555). Amsterdam: Kluwer. doi:10.1007/978-1-4020-4974-3_24

Isenmann, R., & Lenz, C. (2001). Customized corporate environmental reporting by internet-based push- and pull-technologies. *Eco-Management and Auditing, 8*(2), 100–110. doi:10.1002/ema.153

Isenmann, R., & Lenz, C. (2002). Internet use for corporate environmental reporting: Current challenges – technical benefits – practical guidance. *Business Strategy and the Environment, 11*(3), 181–202. doi:10.1002/bse.329

Isenmann, R., Lenz, C., & Müller-Merbach, H. (2001). Betriebliche Umweltberichterstattung im Internet. Der aktuelle Stand für Deutschland [Corporate environmental reporting on the internet. Current practice in Germany]. *Praxis der Wirtschaftsinformatik, 38*(218), 97–107.

Isenmann, R., & Marx Gómez, J. (2004). How to provide customized environmental reports properly. In Scharl, A. (Ed.), *Environmental online communication* (pp. 173–182). London: Springer.

Isenmann, R., & Marx Gómez, J. (Eds.). (2008). *Internetbasierte Nachhaltigkeitsberichterstattung. Maßgeschneiderte Stakeholder-Kommunikation mit IT* [Internet-based sustainability reporting. Tailored stakeholder communication with IT]. Berlin: Erich Schmidt.

Jensen, R. E., & Xiao, J. Z. (2001). Customized financial reporting, networked databases, and distributed file sharing. *Accounting Horizons*, *15*(3), 209–222. doi:10.2308/acch.2001.15.3.209

Jungle Rating. (2007). *Online sustainability research 2007*. Research report November 2007. Amsterdam: Jungle rating – internet consultants. Retrieved December 3, 2008, from http://www.junglerating.com

Kaptein, M., & Wempe, J. (1999). *Sustainability management: Balancing and integrating economic, social and environmental responsibilities. Management report no. 51-1999*. Erasmus Universiteit Rotterdam.

Kolk, A. (2004). A decade of sustainability reporting: developments and significance. *International Journal of Environment and Sustainable Development*, *3*(1), 51–64. doi:10.1504/IJESD.2004.004688

KPMG. (2000). *Beyond the numbers: How leading organizations are linking values with value to gain competitive advantage. KPMG's Assurance & Advisory Services Center (AASC)*. KPMG.

KPMG. (2005). *KPMG international survey of corporate responsibility reporting 2005. University of Amsterdam (The Netherlands), KPMG global sustainability service*. Amsterdam: KPMG.

KPMG, & United Nations Environment Programme (UNEP) (2006). *Carrots and sticks for starters. Current trends and approaches in voluntary and mandatory standards for sustainability reporting*. Parktown: KPMG.

KPMG (2008). *International survey of corporate responsibility reporting 2008*. Amstelveen: KPMG Sustainability Services.

Kuhndt, M., Geibler, J., & Liedtke, C. (2002). *Towards a sustainable aluminium industry: Stakeholder expectations and core indicators. Final report*. Wuppertal: Wuppertal Institute for Climate, Environment, Energy.

Lang, C., Rey, U., Wohlgemuth, V., Genz, S., & Pawlytsch, S. (2003). *Data exchange between ERP-systems and environmental information systems. Publicly available specification (PAS) 1025*. Berlin: Beuth.

Lange, C. Ahsen von, A., & Daldrup, H. (2001). Umweltschutzreporting. Umwelterklärungen und –berichte als Module eines Reportingsystems [Environmental reporting, environmental statements and reports as modules of a reporting system]. München, Wien: Oldenbourg.

Larsen, L. B. (2000). Strategic implication of environmental reporting. *Corporate Environmental Strategy*, *7*(3), 276–287. doi:10.1016/S1066-7938(00)80122-0

Lenz, C. (2003). Empfängerorientierte Unternehmenskommunikation – Einsatz der Internet-Technologie am Beispiel der Umweltberichterstattung [Customised environmental communication – use of internet illustrated through corporate environmental reporting]. Köln: Eul.

Line, M., Hawley, H., & Krut, H. (2002). The development of global environmental and social reporting. *Corporate Environmental Strategy*, *9*(1), 69–78. doi:10.1016/S1066-7938(01)00159-2

Lippman, S. (2001). Supply chain environmental management. *Environmental Quality Management*, *11*(2), 11–14. doi:10.1002/tqem.1301

Lodhia, S. (2004). Corporate environmental reporting media: A case for the world wide web. *Electronic Green Journal, 20* (spring). Retrieved November 23, 2004, from http://egj.lib.uidaho.edu/egj20/lodhia1.html

Marshall, S. R., & Brown, D. (2003). Corporate environmental reporting: What's in a metric? *Business Strategy and the Environment, 12*(2), 87–106. doi:10.1002/bse.354

Marx Gómez, J., & Isenmann, R. (Eds.). (2004). Developments in environmental reporting. International Journal of Environment and Sustainable Development (IJESD), special issue 3(1/2).

Mesterharm, M. (2001). *Integrierte Umweltkommunikation von Unternehmen. Theoretische Grundlagen und empirische Analyse der Umweltkomunikation am Beispiel der Automobilindustrie* [Integrated environmental communication at corporate level. Conceptual foundation and empirical analysis, illustrated by the automotive sector]. Marburg: Metropolis.

Pleon Kohtes & Klewes. (2005). *Accounting for good: The global stakeholder report 2005*. Amsterdam, Bonn: Pleon.

Raar, J. (2002). Environmental initiatives: Towards triple-bottom line reporting. *Corporate Communications, 7*(3), 169–183. doi:10.1108/13563280210436781

Rikhardsson, P., Andersen, A. J. R., & Bang, H. (2002). Sustainability reporting on the internet. A study of the Global Fortune 500. *Greener Management International, 40*, 57–75.

Schraml, T. (1997). *Operationalisierung der ökologieorientierten Berichterstattung aus Sicht des Informationsmanagements* [Specification of environmental reporting from an information management perspective]. Unpublished dissertation thesis, Technische Universität Dresden.

Scott, P., & Jackson, R. (2002). Environmental, social and sustainability reporting on the web. Best practices. *Corporate Environmental Strategy, 9*(2), 193–202. doi:10.1016/S1066-7938(02)00016-7

Shepherd, K., Abkowitz, M., & Cohen, M. A. (2001). Online corporate environmental reporting: Improvements and innovation to enhance stakeholder value. *Corporate Environmental Strategy, 8*(4), 307–315. doi:10.1016/S1066-7938(01)00136-1

Skillius, Å., & Wennberg, U. (1998). *Continuity, credibility and comparability. Key challenges for corporate environmental performance measurement and communication*. The International Institute for Industrial Environmental Economics at Lund University.

Sociaal Economische Raad (SER) (2001). *Corporate social responsibility. A Dutch approach.* Assen: Koninklijke Van Gorcum.

SocialFunds. (Socially responsible investing information concerning corporations, mutual funds, and more) (2000). *Investors prod CEO's to adopt new reporting standards*. Retrieved December 16, 2000, from http://socialfunds.com/news/article

Spencer-Cooke, A. (1995). Engaging stakeholders: The next challenge in corporate environmental reporting. *IÖW/VÖW-Informationsdienst, 10*(3-4), 4-5.

Stratos Inc. (2003). *Building confidence. Corporate sustainability reporting in Canada.* Ottawa: Stratos. Retrieved September 18, 2003, from http://www.stratos-sts.com/sts_files/BC%20Building%20Confidence.pdf

SustainAbility Ltd., & United Nations Environment Programme (UNEP) (1996). *Engaging stakeholders. Vol. 1: The benchmark survey.* London: Polar.

SustainAbility Ltd., & United Nations Environment Programme (UNEP) (1999). *Engaging stakeholders 1999. The internet reporting report.* London: Beacon.

Teo, H. H., Oh, L. B., Liu, C., & Wie, K. K. (2003). An empirical study of the effects of interactivity on web user attitude. *International Journal of Human-Computer Studies, 58*(3), 281–305. doi:10.1016/S1071-5819(03)00008-9

Unerman, J., & Bennett, M. (2004). Increased stakeholder dialogue and the internet: Towards greater corporate accountability or reinforcing capitalist hegemony? *Accounting, Organizations and Society, 29*(7), 685–707. doi:10.1016/j.aos.2003.10.009

United Nations Environment Programme Industry and Environment (UNEP). & SustainAbility (1994). *Company environmental reporting. A measure of the progress of business & industry towards sustainable development.* Technical report 24. Paris: UNEP.

van Dalen, M. (1997). *Company environmental reporting. Conditions for the optimal information structure of environmental reports.* Unpublished doctoral dissertation, University of Humberside and Zeeland Polytechnic Flushing.

Visser, W. (2002). Sustainability reporting in South Africa. *Corporate Environmental Strategy, 9*(1), 79–85. doi:10.1016/S1066-7938(01)00157-9

Volkswagen, A. G. (2003). *Mobility and responsibility. Improving social performance reporting.* Retrieved April 4, 2003, from http://www.vw-ag.de/english/defaultIE.html

Waddock, S. (2008). Building a new institutional infrastructure for corporate responsibility. *The Academy of Management Perspectives, 22*(3), 87–108.

Wheeler, D., & Elkington, J. (2001). The end of the corporate environmental report? Or the advent of cybernetic sustainability reporting and communication. *Business Strategy and the Environment, 10*(1), 1–14. doi:10.1002/1099-0836(200101/02)10:1<1::AID-BSE274>3.0.CO;2-0

World Business Council for Sustainable Development (WBCSD). (2002). *Communications and stakeholder involvement guidebook for cement facilities.* Report prepared by the Battelle Memorial Institute (Ohio) and Environmental Resources Management (London). Retrieved April 18, 2003, from http://www.wbcsdcement.org/pdf/final_report1_2.pdf

World Wide Web Consortium. (W3C) (2004). *Extensible Markup Language (XML) 1.0 (3rd ed.).* W3C recommendation 04 February 2004. Retrieved July 12, 2004, from http://www.w3.org/TR/REC-xml/

Chapter 19
Development of an Information System for the Assessment of Different Bioenergy Concepts Regarding Sustainable Development

Meike Schmehl
University of Göttingen, Germany

Swantje Eigner-Thiel
University of Göttingen, Germany

Jens Ibendorf
University of Göttingen, Germany

Martina Hesse
University of Göttingen, Germany

Jutta Geldermann
University of Göttingen, Germany

ABSTRACT

From an environmental, economic, social, and technical perspective, this chapter focuses on a sustainability assessment of concepts for the energetic use of biomass in order to provide decision support for different options of biomass use. In rural areas, bioenergy concepts are of particular interest in this context. These can for example be biogas plants which are operated by electric service providers, or a biogas plant owned by one farmer, or bioenergy villages. The topic relates to the development of suitable criteria and to the adaption of existing indicator systems to the special requirements of sustainable biomass use for energy. The results of this sustainability assessment consider the different biomass concepts' advantages and disadvantages, which are illustrated by multi-criteria valuation methods. Furthermore, the sustainability assessment of bioenergy concepts has specific requirements with regard to an information system in terms of data and information's demand and supply side.

DOI: 10.4018/978-1-61520-981-1.ch019

INTRODUCTION

The use of biomass for energy is gaining attention among policy-makers, energy supply companies, and the public (BMU, 2009; Leitl, 2007). There are several motives for this increased attention: firstly, due to bioenergy's potentially lower carbon dioxide emissions, it is expected to contribute less to climate change than the use of fossil energy resources. Secondly, biomass use for energy would preserve fossil energy reserves. Thirdly, it could strengthen rural development by giving the farmers an alternative source of income besides food production. Finally, by using local biomass for energy, the domestic energy supply will be stabilized, thus reducing dependency on other – potentially unstable – countries for the import of energy resources (oil, uranium, natural gas, etc.) (IEA, 2004; Van Loo & Koppejan, 2008).

However, in discussions on sustainable development in terms of the use of biomass for energy, not only positive effects are mentioned. There are also concerns that the use of mono-cultures will increase due to a higher demand for energy crops, which would result in massive land-use changes to accommodate more high-productive crops like maize. In addition, an increase in transport activity is expected in rural areas, which would aggravate air pollution and disturbance. Another point relates to the direct emissions of energy plants, such as fine dust and sulfur dioxides, which could be hazardous to the local human health. The designation of areas for energy crop production is a highly controversial issue, too. In cases where areas for food production, nature conservation or grassland are used for the production of energy crops, criticism is to be expected with regards to the ethical aspects and the environmental effects (e.g., more carbon dioxide emissions through the ploughing of grassland and a reduction in the biodiversity) (Jessel, 2008; Fritsche et al., 2009).

With this as a backdrop, several concepts for biomass use for energy have been realized or are in the planning stage in Germany. However, economic, ecological, and social aspects have to be considered when following the principles of sustainable development. Therefore, the decision process concerning the biomass plant's type and dimension has become increasingly complicated and multi-criteria-decision models may need to be applied to arrive at the best agreement (Bucholz, Rametsteiner, Volk & Luzardis, 2009). Linked to the decision model is the crucial management of considerable amounts of diverse data. The coordination of these data and their processing to arrive at different visualized results pose a challenge for the decision model's central information system. The requirements and challenges of this information system are the same as those demanded by a corporate environmental information system. The latter is a system for the acquisition, processing, and communication of relevant environmental data, which originate from different scientific fields (biology, physics, chemistry, geology, meteorology, psychology, social and economic sciences). Furthermore, such data are extensive as well as time and space dependent (see Rautenstrauch, 1999; Page & Rautenstrauch, 2001). Thus, the information management should provide suitable methods to collect and condense data in different formats and from heterogeneous sources.

BACKGROUND

Over the past years, many concepts for bioenergy alternatives have been developed on a local scale in Germany. The idea of an energy-self-sufficient village emerged from a group of scientists at the Interdisciplinary Centre for Sustainable Development (IZNE, in German: Interdisziplinäres Zentrum für Nachhaltige Entwicklung) at the University Göttingen in 1998. The main aim was to have a village produce at least as much electric energy as needed by the residents and the local industry. The production of heat had to cover at least two-third of the demand. Another requirement was that the heat customers and the farmers providing the biomass would actively participate in the planning process of the village energy supply's conversion. With this idea in mind, the scientists chose a suitable village in the Göttingen district as a pilot project from 17 appropriate and interested villages. Ultimately, the village Jühnde was chosen as the model village. Jühnde has 780 inhabitants, nine farmers, an agricultural area of 1,300 ha and a forest area of 800 ha (Ruppert et al., 2008). Jühnde's advantages were its suitable size – which was important economically: if it was too small, building biomass plants would not be profitable –, a sufficient area for biomass production, and the farmers' willingness to use their land for biomass production, and, finally, a good village community with many active associations, which was important to spread the idea within the village and to motivate enough households to participate in the project (Eigner-Thiel, 2005).

The planning of a bioenergy village needs data from different sources. Firstly, technical data on the biomass plant's output are required. Furthermore, geographical data are needed to identify suitable crops for the location and to calculate potential yields. In addition, economic data on the investment and operating costs must be calculated. But the most important are social factors like the people's motivation to engage in the planning process and the social networks' quality, because as many people as possible have to be and kept informed during all the planning stages. Without people's willingness, such a project cannot be implemented.

After diverse planning stages (informing the inhabitants, closing contracts with farmers and heat consumers, building and operating licenses, etc.) during 2001–2004, construction started. The technical concept's central component is the biogas plant, in which microorganism turn liquid manure and other wet biomass to biogas by means of wet fermentation. In the combined heat and power plant (CHP), the biogas is turned into electricity and heat: electricity is fed into the public grid; heat is used for warming water, which is piped to the connected households by the district's heating network. To cover the high demand for heat in winter, the plant is augmented by a woodchip heating plant and an oil heating plant as contingency reserves.

Heat distribution started in September 2005. Today, 75% of Jühnde households receive about 2,800 MWh heat per year from the biogas plant. The rest of about 1,500 MWh heat per year is supplied by the woodchip heating plant. The production of electricity is about 4,000 MWh electricity per year, which the local energy supply company purchases. The price of the electricity is regulated by the EEG (Renewable Energy Sources Act).

There have been different impacts on the individuals, society, economy, and ecology in the wake of the substitution of biomass for oil in the bioenergy village Jühnde. With regard to the greenhouse effect, the ecological benefit can be quantified by a 70% per person reduction in the carbon dioxide emissions. After a financial deficit in the year of installation and start-up in 2005, the operating company recorded a positive annual surplus. Since then, the heat customers have saved about €800.00 per year. Psychological research has shown that people who were actively engaged in the planning process experienced a more interesting 'village community' and 'individual learning experiences.' In this context, different methods of public relations, participatory planning, and planning workshops were realized and documented (Eigner-Thiel, 2005). The inhabitants of Jühnde are predominantly very satisfied with the heat supply (Ruppert et al., 2008). However, during the decision process for the optimal bioenergy concept in Jühnde, ecological, economical, and social objectives were opposed in a few situations (Eigner-Thiel & Geldermann, 2009).

The idea of the bioenergy village spread to other parts of Germany and even to other countries (Ahl et al., 2007). Nevertheless, potential initiators can only draw on the limited experiences from existing bioenergy concepts. Diverse life-cycle assessment studies were compiled for a methodological analysis of environmentally relevant material and energy flows for biomass use for energy. However, natural scientists criticize the assessment of the impacts, as the interrelations are usually too complex to be modeled by linear impact factors. Besides these aspects, these studies do not support the impact on the affected local stakeholders, as economic and social perspectives as well as local aspects are usually underrepresented. The assessment from a social perspective and the linkage of the three spheres (ecology, economy, society) were just analyzed simplistically (see Hofstetter, 1998 as an early, comprehensive study).

For a comprehensive assessment of different bioenergy concepts pertaining to all three mentioned aspects, sustainability's general criteria can be used as a first source. Their actual application may, however, lead to very different and even conflicting results. Chapter 40 of Agenda 21 (United Nations, 1993), states that the usual indicators like a country's gross national product or unemployment rate do not suffice to describe the development status of sustainability. Therefore, beyond the existing economic characteristics, further indicators have to be developed to represent the three dimensions of sustainable development as accurately as possible.

There are, however, significant difficulties defining such indicator systems; possible indicators might not be precise, specific, or comprehensive enough to reflect the sustainability of local and regional developments (see Heiland, Tischer, Döring, Pahl & Jessel, 2003; Fleury, 2005). In order to make more specific statements with regard to the establishment of bioenergy villages and other bioenergy projects, the specific focus should be on the area of biomass as a renewable energy resource. After preliminary theoretical considerations regarding the definition and formulation of sustainability criteria, actual significant and quantifiable criteria should be chosen for the specific area of biomass use for energy. The obtained original, qualified data must be converted into quantifiable data to use them as a criterion. Currently, there is no general system for the specification of the indicators, due to the specificity and the complexity of relevant issues. Thus, in addition to the orientation to the principles of sustainability (see Agenda 21), it is crucial to transparently describe the requirements of the indicator system (see, e.g., Reul, 2002; Werheit, 1996).

In the first place, the mounting requirements regarding sustainable development due to an increasing awareness of climate change impacts, mandate the consultation of interdisciplinary expert groups to consider the numerous, and partly opposing, objectives and criteria within a bioenergy assessment. In most existing decision situations, there is no dominating alternative that meets all the objective criteria of sustainable development and which could thus be unanimously chosen from all other alternatives. In fact, most alternatives have characteristic strengths and weaknesses requiring some kind of trade-off. In figure 1, it is clear that common sense can be easily overwhelmed if one has to choose the most sustainable alternative, because too many aspects have to be taken into account and their varying priorities weighted against one another. A central biogas plant, one farmer's biogas plant and a bioenergy village are examples of possible bioenergy concepts. The bars' different heights display the various values of attributes within the criteria catalog on each concept. In contrast to other sustainability indicator catalogues, some technical criteria are considered explicitly (see the section "Criteria-developing process").

During the process of balancing and condensing information, many aspects are considered, which can quickly lead to a situation in which common sense no longer suffices (Dörner, 2003; Vester, 2003; Miller, 1956). The larger the number of people involved in the decision process, the more the support needed to objectively and efficiently arrive at complicated decisions. Decision models with several objectives often describe reality better than models with only one objective, which has

Figure 1. Schematic presentation of conflicting utility values of different bioenergy concepts

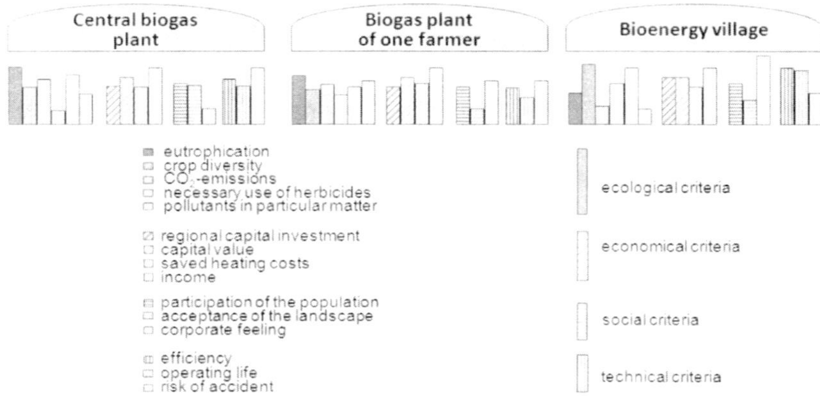

led to numerous new approaches to multi-criteria decision support having been developed in the last 30 years (Figueira, Greco & Ehrgott, 2005; Hwang & Yoon, 1981; Yue & Li, 1998; Munda, 1995). Oberschmidt, Ludwig, & Geldermann (2009) analyzed concepts for regional energy supply with a multi-criteria decision model. The study focused on the objectives: economic efficiency, security of supply, and environmental effects.

In the theory of decision support and multi-criteria analysis, weighting is one of the most disputed steps due to its relatively subjective character. Decision trees and objective hierarchies can, however, be used to operationalize ecological, economical, social and technical criteria, and represent them through certain attributes (e.g., CO_2 emissions as an attribute of the ecology criteria, see also figure 1).

DECISION SUPPORT FOR CONCEPTS FOR SUSTAINALBLE BIOMASS USE FOR ENERGY

Structure of the Theoretical Model for Multi Criteria Decision Analysis (MCDA)

The simulation of the complex group decision process regarding sustainable biomass use for energy in a defined rural area is realized in a multi-criteria decision model.

Multi Criteria Decision Analysis (MCDA) has been widely applied in environmental and in bioenergy contexts. Mustajoki (2003) describes the usage of this method in the field of lake regulation policy; Malczewski (1999) established a link between spatial approaches (GIS) and MCDA; while Buchholz, Rametsteiner, Volk and Luzardis (2009) provide a comprehensive overview of the application of MCDA in the context of bioenergy.

The MCDA process can be divided into four stages. In the first stage, the overall objective, which is to be specified in more detail in the criteria hierarchy, has to be defined. Alternatives that can meet the defined objective are compiled in the lowest level of the criteria hierarchy (second stage). The modeling and the information processing occur in the third stage, in which the values of the attributes are calculated for the alternatives. In this stage, the weighting process is considered: Depending on each attribute's relevance, the value is taken into account with a related weight of importance. Finally, the results are made visible with graphs and charts to assess the alternatives and choose one alternative.

In the first stage, one relevant element of this model is the criteria hierarchy to structure the decision group's objectives. One way to do this is the top-down approach by starting with

Figure 2. Criteria hierarchy of sustainable biomass use for energy

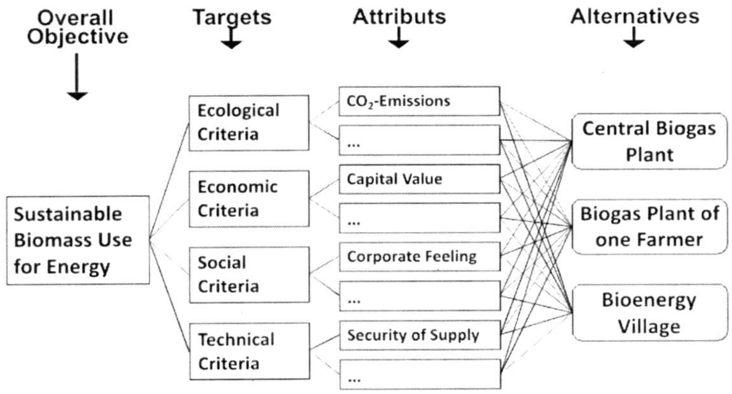

the overall objective (sustainable biomass use for energy) and expanding it with more detailed targets, which should adequately cover all ecological, economic, social and technical aspects but not create redundancy. The targets on the undermost level are represented by certain attributes, which can operationalize the objective on an ordinal or cardinal scale (see figure 2) (Belton & Stewart, 2003). Furthermore, each criterion is assigned to a grade of relevance regarding its importance for the special decision-maker or stakeholder group (weighting process).

Based on this information, the different concepts for biomass use for energy can be assessed on the grounds of their compliance with the primary objective "sustainable development". The implementation of various data sets in the decision model's information system is associated with this process. The data sets are required to calculate the values of all the considered bioenergy alternatives' attributes. Since bioenergy extends to many areas like agriculture, social sciences, economics, and earth sciences, the data bases are very heterogeneous (see section "Data sets"). Secondly, the visualization of the results, which relates to the requested information, is a challenge for the information system (see section "Visualization").

The Criteria-Developing Process

Framework of an Exemplary Project

The research project will be used as an example to describe the development of criteria and the application of MCDA in the field of bioenergy. The three-year project "Sustainable use of bioenergy: bridging climate protection, nature conservation and society" started in February 2009 (www.bioenergie.uni-goettingen.de). Consequently, the criteria-developing procedure presented in this chapter is preliminary, while the entire decision process is iterative. Nevertheless, the information-developing procedure is already applicable and will be realized in the subsequent steps.

Within this research project, 17 scientists study a wide variety of aspects from very different disciplines like economy, earth sciences, social sciences, psychology, and agronomy, which are all relevant for the planning of bioenergy concepts. The actual work packages are structured into six sub-projects. Naturally, each scientific discipline will employ its own methodological toolkit and will produce different kinds of data, information, and knowledge. The challenge for both the project management and decision support is the amalgamation of the relevant data. Both tasks are the subject of the interlinking sub-project "Development and testing of assessment criteria and methods". In this chapter, the demands for the development of an information system for the assessment of different bioenergy concepts for sustainable development are presented. In the following, the four steps are described:

- The definition of sustainable development,
- the compiling of a criteria list,
- the defining of biomass alternatives, and
- the establishing of a criteria hierarchy.

Definition of Sustainable Development

In order to assess the different bioenergy alternatives regarding their effects on sustainable development, a suitable definition is required. There are many different definitions of sustainable development. Some only refer to ecologic aspects like the indicator system SCOPE (1995). The most comprehensive system of indicators, which also considers social and economic aspects, is the UN Commission's Sustainable Development (CSD) indicator system. With its approximate 130 indicators, it is also a good basis for the comparison of bioenergy concepts.

In the scientific literature, strong and weak sustainability are distinguished: Weak sustainability means that the value of a single dimension can be substituted by another (e.g., high ecological values can substitute low economic ones), whereas strong sustainability means that there is no substitution possible between the dimensions (Wuppertal-Institut für Klima, Umwelt, Energie, 1997; Daly, 1999).

The definition of strong sustainability was chosen to compare bioenergy concepts. The technical conversion of biomass is one of the distinct criteria for the assessment of different bioenergy concepts. Therefore, to enhance the criteria development and assessment's transparency the technical dimension was added to the ecological, social, and economical dimensions.

Compiling of a Criteria List

From the different disciplines' perspective, criteria for the evaluation of bioenergy concepts were collected from experiences gained in local bioenergy projects (mainly the project "Bioenergy village Jühnde" and other village projects in the Göttingen district in Lower Saxony (Ruppert et al., 2008), from the literature, and from discussions with experts (project-internal and external experts).

The literature review concerned the many indicator systems for assessing sustainable development as described in, for example, Breitschuh, Breitschuh and Eckert (2008), Gamba (2008), Hoffmann (2007), Rösch, Skarka, Raab and Stelzer (2009) and German Advisory Council on Global Change (WBGU, 2008).

Moderated discussions were organized in different groups:

- ecology experts: geographers, earth scientists, agronomists, soil scientists, forestry scientists, and plant scientists;
- economy experts: business economists, agricultural economists, and industrial engineers;
- social aspects experts: psychologists and sociologists;
- technology experts: practitioners and scientists with experience in the field of bioenergy

The greatest challenge was to make everybody in the discussion groups understand that a criterion is only appropriate for the list if it differs from comparative alternatives, for example, geographic data like the soil type or the air temperature of a particular agricultural area will remain the same although different bioenergy concepts are compared for this area. Finally, since the geographic data cannot distinguish between the different concepts, the differentiating function is important when selecting criteria. It is important to mention

Figure 3. Different spatial dimension for the comparison of different bioenergy concepts

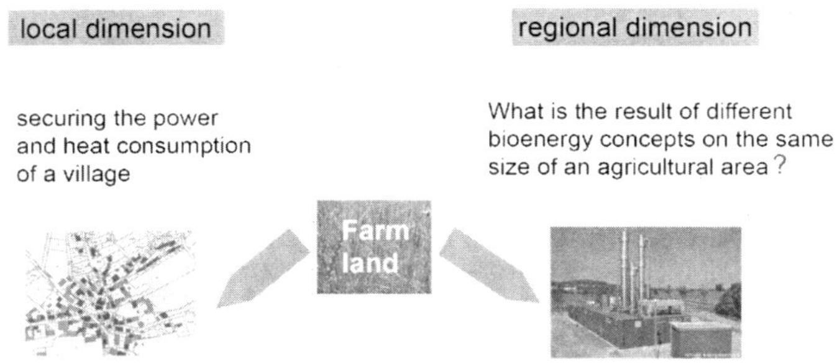

that these indistinguishable data are used in a pre-test to distinguish between different agricultural areas for possible use. However, the comparison of various bioenergy concepts will focus on the same section of agricultural land.

The next step of the development procedure is to test the identified evaluation criteria in an iterative process in terms of their applicability and significance for the evaluation of concepts for biomass use. In this case, the data for the assessing the criteria will originate from the scientists of the other sub-projects (see below, section "Data sets").

Bioenergy Alternatives

The overall aim of the research effort is to compare the sustainability of different bioenergy concepts regarding agricultural land of a specifically defined size (e.g., 300 hectares). The calculations for the comparison are related to a well-defined area of farmland in Lower Saxony. This area should have special natural characteristics like climate, soil type, elevation, air temperature, etc., which need to be taken into account for the comparison of the bioenergy concepts. Within these preconditions, two spatial dimensions are considered (figure 3):

1. different kinds of bioenergy villages as local bioenergy concepts (local dimension)
2. alternative regional bioenergy concepts (regional dimension)

For the local dimension, the following presumptions have to be met for a comparison of different approaches to bioenergy villages: The approaches are based on the bioenergy village Jühnde's concept. Therefore, the technical components will be a biogas plant, a combined heat and power station, a heating plant fuelled by wood chips, a hot-water grid, and a boiler fuelled by oil or biodegradable diesel (as a contingency reserve). Furthermore, it is assumed that 70% of the households have a connection to the local hot-water grid.

The alternatives are developed by combining one choice from the following four aspects:

- the kind of crop cultivation for the biogas plant: conventional vs. organic vs. crops from contaminated soils,
- the biomass fuel for the heating plant: wood, straw or wood from contaminated soils,
- the operating company: one investor from outside the village or a corporation with collective investors, with the majority originating from the village, and
- the possibility that the people could participate: yes or no.

On the regional scale, the result of the calculation of the most sustainable alternative of the bioenergy village concepts is compared with other possible bioenergy concepts related to this

Table 1. Alternative regional bioenergy concepts

Alternative	Biomass Input	Conversion Technology	Products
B1	Energy Crop	Anaerobic digestion	Biogas → Power, Heat
B2	Energy Crop	Anaerobic digestion	Biogas → Fuel; Biogas → Supply into the gas grid
B3	Energy Crop	Pressing/Extraction and esterification	Biodiesel → Liquid fuel
B4	Energy Crop	Alcohol fermentation	Bioethanol → Liquid fuel
B5	Energy Crop	Pyrolysis	BtL (Biomass-to-Liquid) → Liquid fuel
B6	Wood	Combustion	Heat
B7	Straw	Combustion	Heat

special farmland. The defined alternatives are listed in table 1.

The results could be statements like, "The bioenergy village concept yx is the most sustainable alternative for this special farmland" (this would be a local solution), or "The most sustainable solution for this farmland would be to cultivate 10% of the biomass for a central biogas plant from which to obtain biogas fuel" (this would be a regional solution).

The specification of the attributes needs to be collected and documented for the different alternatives. At this point, the structure of the central database for the information management is particularly important. In the described project, the data will be obtained from the other sub-projects.

Bioenergy concepts so far are intentionally not compared with other forms of renewable energy because the scope would then be too broad and an in-depth differentiated comparison for users would be impossible. Nevertheless, Oberschmidt, Geldermann, Ludwig and Schmehl (2010) offer an exemplary comparison of different forms of renewable energy.

The Weighting Process

Once the data have been collected, the criteria hierarchy for this sub-project is systematically and transparently compiled in workshops. The workshops are important for the prospective participants to gain comprehensive awareness of the problem. This will support an efficient discussion and a transparent and pleasant decision-making process. Besides the consensus orientation, the criteria hierarchy's transparency is relevant for the application of multi-criteria decision methods in a moderated workshop setting (Geldermann, Zhang & Rentz, 2002). The workshops also allow for an iterative definition of the relevant decision criteria: If one of the other involved scientific disciplines has found a more significant criterion or a criterion that can be measured much easier, the criteria hierarchy can be adjusted accordingly. Effective structuring, systematic management, as well as decision-making transparency are guaranteed by the application of different moderation methods (incl. the metaplan method). In addition to presenting means of visualizing (pin boards, charts in different forms and colors as well as glue dots), a moderator will facilitate the decision-making process by, for example, using value dots, argumentation, and decision charts. These methods will ensure that all the decision-makers have a consistent level of information. The relevant data and information need to be tracked by and stored in an information system. The structure and organization of the hierarchy of criteria form the basis of a systematic and quantitative assessment. Information must be recorded adequately in the information system without compromising the interdependencies of the data.

Table 2. Overview of the participating disciplines in this exemplary bioenergy project and the diverse quality of data used in the MCDA

Disciplines	Quality of data	Quantitative or quantifiable data	Qualitative results
Geography	Spatial data (GIS), temporal data (climate data)	X	
Chemistry	Numerical chemical analysis (concentration)	X	
Soil sciences	Numerical chemical analysis (concentration)	X	
Environmental sciences	Spatial data (habitat, biodiversity)	X	X
Psychology	Interviews, questionnaires (motivation, acceptance)	X	X
Economy	Numerical analysis (cash value)	X	
Crop cultivation	Numerical analysis (crop yield, amount of fertilizer)	X	
Agricultural Economics	Numerical analysis (contract design), questionnaires (acceptance)	X	X

Data Sets

Types of Data for the Comparison of Bioenergy Concepts within an Information System

As outlined, a comprehensive assessment of various bioenergy concepts is only possible by means of an interdisciplinary effort. Table 2 shows the scientific disciplines contributing to the mentioned research project, and indicates the type of data they usually deliver: natural scientists and engineers most often produce quantitative or quantifiable data, while the humanities and social sciences can deliver qualitative results. The different natures of these data will be illustrated by the following examples, which require appropriate information system support.

Analysis of Site-Specific Biomass Potentials and Optimization of the Energy Crop Production

In the context of local and regional bioenergy concepts knowledge about the local availability of biomass for energy is an important aspect. Estimations of the national biomass potential are usually not sufficient. Thus, the site-specific biomass growth's yield potential has to be investigated and simulated in Geoinformation Systems (GIS). Therefore geo-referenced input data regarding radiation, precipitation, evapotranspiration, temperature, and soil properties need to be compared with the cultivation-specific requirements on the site to allow the biomass production yield to be modeled (Bauböck, 2009). Consequently, a special modeling software is required to handle the comprehensive data sets and should offer a user-friendly interface for analysis. However, the data will be obtained on the local site and modeled up to the regional site with statistical extrapolation procedures. The outputs are databases and maps to illustrate the biomass potential of distinct agricultural land and in selected counties in Lower Saxony. These spatial data are necessary for the multi-criteria decision analysis of the bioenergy concepts on both the local and regional levels.

Especially the organic cultivation of biomass requires the agricultural sector to make a more significant contribution to nature and landscape through mixed cultivation or a reduced application of fertilizer and pesticides than in conventional cultivation. Thus, a suitable evaluation tool is needed for consultants and farmers to estimate agricultural processes' performance from a nature conservation point of view. Criteria for evaluation take into consideration agricultural activities' impact with regards to the protection of species and biotopes, the landscape, protection against erosion, and other environmental impacts (von Haaren & Bathke, 2007; Wiehe, Ruschkowski, Rode, Kanning & von Haaren, 2009).

Consensus-Oriented Expansion of Bioenergy

Biomass use for energy is not always met with broad acceptance. There are barriers, which complicate the realization of biomass projects. The utilization competition between the production of energy crops and food production is one aspect that inhibits the acceptance of bioenergy concepts. Besides economic reasons, farmers' willingness to cultivate energy crops depends on many behavioral factors like environmental awareness, attitude to risks, knowledge, involvement, and others. Thus, the decision-support tool should take the drivers and barriers into account that interviews, questionnaires, and subsequent statistical analyses reveal.

The plant operator's long-term management of the biomass input and the farmers' acceptance of the offered price are relevant elements for an efficient bioenergy project. Models can support the process of arriving at a contract and should consider information on the contract period, define the terms of the coordination, the price escalation clause, options for cancellation, and rewarding ecological performance benefits. The origin data can be qualitative as well as quantitative. For example, opinion making, which is influenced by the social environment, is better described verbally, while critical price limits can be better described numerically (Granoszewski, Reise, Spiller & Mußhoff, 2009).

Aspects of Specific Bioenergy Concepts

An example of a specific bioenergy concept is the use of biomass from contaminated sites for energy. Contaminated sites that may be polluted with hazardous substances (e.g., heavy metals) due to mining activities or by flooding with contaminated water, thus complicating food and fodder production at these sites, offer an interesting option for energy conversion (Deicke, Ruppert & Schneider, 2006). In this case, the phytoremediation (cleaning of contaminated soils by means of plants) is not an objective. On the contrary, the cultivated energy crops should not absorb the hazardous, toxic substances. The use of biomass from contaminated sites can require special arrangements to guarantee they are handled correctly and can influence farmers and the inhabitants' acceptance of bioenergy. These attributes of acceptance will flow into the calculations of the MCDA. Moreover, the chemical analyses of the digestate, which will be used as fertilizer afterwards, have to be taken into account. Consequently, further alternatives, which go beyond the normal set of alternatives and criteria for non-contaminated sites on the local and regional levels, need to be defined.

Furthermore, the emission of fine dust due to the burning of straw and wood (e.g., in wood pellet heating) may result in limited acceptances of bioenergy concepts. In order to assess the hazardous potential of the exhausted air, particle-size simultaneous analysis of the organic and inorganic components and an electron-microscopical characterization of the fine dust are performed. Relevant parameters, which are associated with a measurement's result, have to be distilled. The extensive results of such an analysis are stored in databases and can be evaluated by means of multivariate data analysis. From this, environmental as well as acceptance attributes will be derived for the combustion of wood, straw, and biogas.

Optimization of the Production and Distribution System

Before a bioenergy village's economic criteria can be compared with those of an optimized, centralized bioenergy concept run by a commercial heat

Figure 4. Variety of data formats

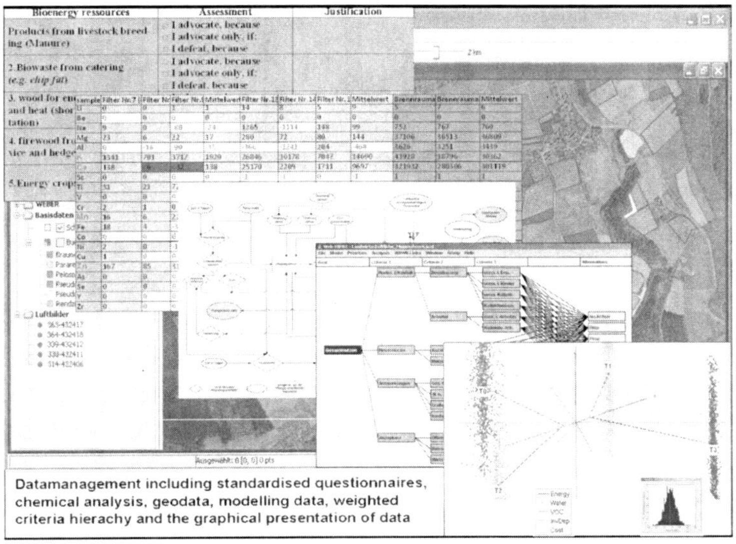

supplier, the production and logistics need to be optimized through suitable operations research approaches. On the one hand, the agricultural and forestry sectors with their corresponding infrastructure form the production system which supplies the needed resources to the biomass plant. On the other hand, the distribution of heat and electricity supplied by the biomass plant has to be planned.

Both the production and the distribution system can be modeled and the optimal costs be derived, which will depend on the specific local situation and the existing constraints. For example, configurable parameters are the dimensioning and structure of the local hot-water grid, or the area of agriculture and grassland required for the cultivation of energy crops for one village's energy supply. The model of the production and distribution system is described as a linearized system of equations. The simplex procedure is one possibility to solve such mathematical problems (Neumann, 1975; Zimmermann, 1987). Further optimization approaches can be realized by "branch & bound" and graph-theoretical methods. The constraints of these models may be the potential of biomass or logistical restrictions. All of these models need decision-relevant data and will deliver economic criteria.

Data Consolidation

The consolidation of data from the diverse scientific fields has to consider several aspects: The data have different reference values (site-related yields, plant-specific operating cost per year, share of the population, etc.), and are stored in different formats (shapefile, spreadsheets, text file, etc.). Figure 4 illustrates some of the diverse data structures and formats applied in this project and, finally: Figure 5 presents the graphical presentation of an MCDA. Moreover, the data quality can vary, as the data from a chemical analysis could have small ranges, while data on the operating level could have a much higher margin of deviation. In this context, the challenge is the data transmission into the system's specific data format since information is a very critical actor in decision and opinion making (Visser, Stuckenschmidt, Wache & Vögele, 2001; Page & Rautenstrauch, 2001).

Figure 5. Example of a possible graphical presentation of a comparison of six alternatives (A-F) with regard to five criteria and under consideration of the uncertainties by means of Monte-Carlo Simulation

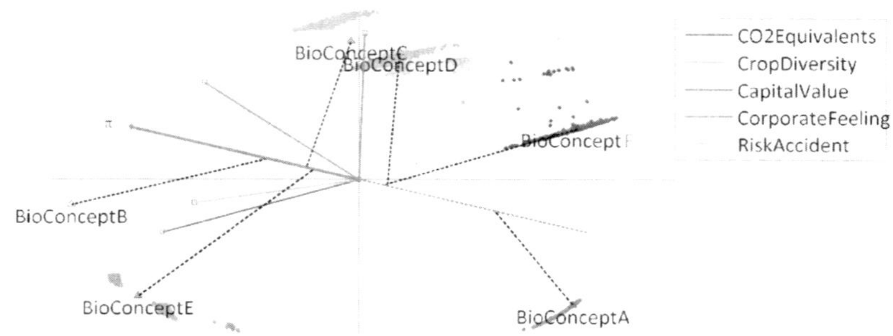

For the decision support within an MCDA model, the decision-relevant data need to be available in a decision table containing cardinal or ordinal values. Consequently, decisive qualitative data must be converted into quantitative data. Thus, it is essential to develop a database and a data dictionary for the utilization of all crucial data in the MCDA and for tracking and tracing the transformation of the raw data. As long as an all-embracing information system is not yet fully functioning, a data dictionary will compile all the metadata and information relevant for the different purposes within the assessment of bioenergy concepts. In contrast to the actual database, a data dictionary will not contain the actual data, but rather the structure of the data (European Environmental Agency, 2007). An important issue for the consolidation of the data is, for instance, the equalization of the data structure at the same geo-referenced site. Thus, ecological data (e.g., climate data, habitat data, crop production data), economic data (e.g., investment, operating costs, costs for logistics), social data (acceptance by the population, possibility to participate in the planning process) and technical data (e.g., degree of efficiency) must have at least the same data structure (data format), table properties, and characteristics to combine them in the MCDA. All the corresponding metadata (e.g., source of information, processor, storage place, administrator, and user rights) will be stored in the dynamic data dictionary.

Similar challenges are relevant for the development of a consistent life cycle inventory database. Hischier and Gilgen (2005) emphasize the relevance of standardized, comprehensive, and actual life cycle inventory databases. In their ECOINVENT project, a clearly defined and comprehensive data exchange format is used, which includes meta-information, modeling, and validation as well as administrative information. Furthermore, there are already approaches to implement geographic information in life-cycle databases and vice versa. On the one hand, the inventory data can be site-specifically assigned in the geographic information system. On the other hand, the geographic data can be used to identify the correct characterization and weighting factors for the life-cycle assessment (Wei & Carlson, 2002).

Visualization

Profiles for Different Concepts of Biomass Use for Energy

Modern information systems do not only store and process data and information, but also display them in a user-friendly manner. Currently, visual representations of data tables, such as bar charts, pie charts or trend lines, are widely used.

Especially in interdisciplinary research topics, the derived research results need to be presented to many lay-persons in the respected scientific disciplines. For instance, social scientists and natural scientists have to communicate their results to each other, but also to the interested public, like the village community or the local administration seeking advice on building a bio-energy village. Thus, it is essential to present the analyzed bioenergy concept's expected benefits and disadvantages for the specific village or region in an understandable way.

An open scientific question is the visualization of specific aspects of the problem to represent the fact that some aspects are characterized by considerably more assessment criteria than others. In decision theory, this is referred to as 'bias,' which is generated by highly unsymmetrical criteria hierarchies (Hämäläinen & Alaja, 2008).

For the assessment of the different bioenergy concepts, profiles will be generated to depict the impacts of sustainable development's three pillars for direct comparison. Utilizing methods from operations research and from main component analysis, a high dimensional solution space can be graphically illustrated (Bertsch, Treitz, Geldermann & Rentz, 2007; Bertsch, Geldermann, Rentz & Raskob, 2006; Treitz, Bertsch, Schollenberger, Geldermann & Rentz, 2008; Geldermann et al., 2007) (see figure 5).

Psychological Aspects

Cognitive aspects lead to people perceiving graphically visualized evaluation results in different ways. Exposure to graphical representations is not self-evident or elemental and must therefore be learned (Cox & Brna, 1995; Petre & Green, 1993; Weidenmann, 1994; Ainsworth, 1999). The use of graphics for the visualization of non-spatial, abstract information, most prominently economic data, has only been in common practice in the West since the 18th century (Tversky, 2000; Roth & Bowen, 1999). Consequently, graphical representations can easily be misunderstood, especially by inexperienced persons and are therefore prone to superficial interpretations (Weidenmann, 1994; Cheng, Lowe & Scaife, 2001). It is therefore important to edit the results of the multi-criteria decision support graphically so that perception-psychological knowledge is taken into consideration. This is open for further research.

Representation is the illustration of an issue in the mind (Palmer, 1978). According to Larkin and Simon (1989), the concept can be differentiated into propositional (similar to language and to logical statements, linearly arranged information) and graphical representations (use of spatial relations, availability of information at a glance). On the other hand, individuals' different cognitive styles are also relevant. There are 'verbalizers' and 'visualizers,' i.e. people with different preferences for the kinds of illustrations and, therefore, with a different understanding of them (Cox, Stenning & Oberlander, 1994). The first studies were undertaken by Schmuck, Eigner, Kaufhold, and Kraproth (1998) on the understandability of various symbols for specific product and company groups' assessment according to sustainable development aspects. It was shown that various symbols can have very different effects on the speed and the clarity of perception. The best way to visualize the outcome of the MCDA concerning the biomass alternatives described in this article will be the result of specific psychological studies, which will be part of this research project in the next weeks.

CONCLUSION

The development of an information system for the assessment of different bioenergy concepts concerning sustainable development has to take into account the requirements needed to support local and regional decision-makers in choosing suitable and sustainable concepts for the context conditions in their villages and regions.

An information system for the assessment of different bioenergy concepts concerning sustainable development has to manage data on ecological, economical, social and technical aspects. On the synthesis side, there are data on geo-referenced environmental information, surveys on acceptance, the technical characteristics of biomass plants, the documentation of interviews and questionnaires, chemical analyses' results, etc. The challenge is not only the vast amount of data in very inhomogeneous formats, but especially the mastering of the logical coherence of the data from different scenarios.

To date the spatial and temporal scaling problem has been unsolved. Specifically, in the field of interdisciplinary research, in which economists, natural scientists, and social scientists work together and collect data on different spatial and temporal scales, further research is needed to extrapolate and model the data from one scale to another in the different research fields and to combine them properly.

It is strongly recommended that such complex questions are put to interdisciplinary experts involved in sustainable development.

ACKNOWLEDGMENT

The authors would like to thank the Ministry for Science and Culture of Lower Saxony and the Volkswagen Foundation for the financial support of the research association "Sustainable use of bioenergy: bridging climate protection, nature conservation and society". Special thanks go to the projects coordinator Hans Ruppert and to all involved colleagues from geosciences, agricultural science, agricultural economics, production research, environmental science and psychology. The authors are also very grateful for the valuable comments by the anonymous reviewers.

REFERENCES

Ahl, C., Eigner-Thiel, S., Girschner, W., Karpenstein-Machan, M., Roland, F., & Ruppert, H. (2007). *Bioenergiedörfer - Dörfer mit Zukunft. Information brochure*. Göttingen, Germany: Interdisciplinary Centre for Sustainable Development.

Ainsworth, S. (1999). *Designing effective multi-representational learning environments* (Report No. 58). Nottingham, United Kingdom: University of Nottingham, ESRC Centre for research in Development, Instruction and Teaching.

Bauböck, R. (2009). Bioenergie im Landkreis Göttingen – GIS-gestützte Biomassenpotenzialabschätzung anhand ausgewählter Energiepflanzen, Triticale und Mais. In Kappas, M. (Ed.), *Erdsicht – Einblicke in geographische und geoinformationstechnische Arbeitsweisen* (*Vol. 18*). Stuttgart, Germany: Ibidim-Verlag.

Belton, V., & Stewart, T. J. (2002). *Multiple criteria decision analysis: an integrated approach*. Dordrecht, Netherlands: Kluwer Academic Publishers.

Bertsch, V., Geldermann, J., Rentz, O., & Raskob, W. (2006). Multi-criteria decision support and stakeholder involvement in emergency management. *International Journal of Emergency Management*, *3*(2/3), 114–130. doi:10.1504/IJEM.2006.011163

Bertsch, V., Treitz, M., Geldermann, J., & Rentz, O. (2007). Sensitivity analyses in multi-attribute decision support for off-site nuclear emergency and recovery management. *International Journal of Energy Sector Management*, *1*(4), 342–365. doi:10.1108/17506220710836075

BMU. (Federal Ministry for the Environment, Nature conservation and Nuclear Safety) (2009). German cabinet has approved national biomass action plan. Press release no. 122/09. Berlin, Germany.

Breitschuh, G., Breitschuh, T., & Eckert, H. (2008). Einfluss einer erhöhten Biomasseproduktion auf die Nachhaltigkeitsparameter landwirtschaftlicher Betriebe. In Kuratorium für Technik und Bauwesen in der Landwirtschaft e.V. (KTBL) (Ed.), Ökologische und ökonomische Bewertung nachwachsender Energieträger (pp. 104-116). Darmstadt, Germany: KTBL.

Buchholz, T., Rametsteiner, E., Volk, T. A., & Luzardis, V. A. (2009). Multi-criteria analysis for bioenergy systems assessments. *Energy Policy*, *37*(2), 484–495. doi:10.1016/j.enpol.2008.09.054

Cheng, P. C. H., Lowe, R. K., & Scaife, M. (2001). Cognitive science approaches to understanding diagrammatic representations. *Artificial Intelligence Review*, *15*, 79–94. doi:10.1023/A:1006641024593

Cox, R., & Brna, P. (1995). Supporting the use of external representations in problem solving: the need for flexible learning environments. *Journal of Artificial Intelligence in Education*, *6*(2/3), 239–302.

Cox, R., Stenning, K., & Oberlander, J. (1994). Graphical effects in learning logic: reasoning, representation and individual differences. *Proceedings of the 16th Annual Conference of the Cognitive Science Society*. Hillsdale, NJ: Lawrence Erlbaum Associates.

Daly, H. (1999). *Wirtschaft jenseits von Wachstum: Die Volkswirtschaftslehre nachhaltiger Entwicklung*. Salzburg, Austria: Pustet.

Deicke, M., Ruppert, H., & Schneider, J. (2006). Mining and smelting in the Harz Mountains (Germany) – a neverending environmental story. *Schriftenreihe der Deutschen Gesellschaft für Geowissenschaften*, *45*, 237–256.

Dörner, D. (2003). *Die Logik des Misslingens - Strategisches Denken in komplexen Situationen*. Hamburg, Germany: Rowohlt.

Eigner-Thiel, S. (2005). *Kollektives Engagement für die Nutzung erneuerbarer Energieträger - Motive, Mobilisierung und Auswirkungen am Beispiel des Aktionsforschungsprojektes „Das Bioenergiedorf*. Hamburg, Germany: Kovac.

Eigner-Thiel, S., & Geldermann, J. (2009). Entscheidungsunterstützung bei der Planung eines Bioenergiedorfes. In Geldermann, J., & Lauven, L. (Eds.), *Einsatz von OR-Verfahren zur Entscheidungsunterstützung*. Aachen, Germany: Shaker.

European Environmental Agency. (2007). *User guide, Data Dictionary.* Retrieved November 20, 2009, from http://dd.eionet.europa.eu/DD-User-Guide.pdf

Figueira, J., Greco, S., & Ehrgott, M. (2005). *Multiple criteria decision analysis – State of the art. Surveys*. New York: Springer.

Fleury, A. (2005). Eine Nachhaltigkeitsstrategie für den Energieversorgungssektor - dargestellt am Beispiel der Stromversorgung in Frankreich. Karlsruhe, Germany: University of Karlsruhe (TH), French-German Institute for Environmental Research.

Fritsche, U. R., Hennenberg, K., Hermann, A., Hünecke, K., Schulze, F., Wiegmann, K., et al. (2009). *Sustainable bioenergy: Current status and outlook.* Darmstadt/Heidelberg, Germany. Retrieved July 13, 2009, from http://www.umweltdaten.de/publikationen/fpdf-l/3741.pdf

Gamba, L. (2008). *Erste Modellentwicklung zur nachhaltigen Nutzung von Biomasse*. Doctoral dissertation, Technical University Berlin, Germany.

Geldermann, J., Bertsch, V., Treitz, M., French, S., Papamichail, K.N., & Hämäläinen, R.P. (2007). Multi-criteria decision support and evaluation of strategies for nuclear remediation management. *OMEGA – The International Journal of Management Science, 37* (1), 238-251.

Geldermann, J., Zhang, K., & Rentz, O. (2002). *Entwicklung eines integrierten multikriteriellen Gruppenentscheidungsunterstützungssystems (MGDSS) - Fallstudie: Hierarchische Planung in der Industrielackierung*. Frankfurt, Germany: Verlag Peter Lang.

Granoszewski, K., Reise, C., Spiller, A., & Mußhoff, O. (2009). *Entscheidungsverhalten landwirtschaftlicher Betriebsleiter bei Bioenergie-Investitionen* (Discussion paper No. 0911). Göttingen, Germany: University of Göttingen, Department of Agricultural Economics and Rural Development.

Hämäläinen, R. P., & Alaja, S. (2008). The threat of weighting biases in environmental decision analysis. *Ecological Economics*, *68*(1/2), 556–569. doi:10.1016/j.ecolecon.2008.05.025

Heiland, S., Tischer, M., Döring, T., Pahl, T., & Jessel, B. (2003). *Indikatoren zur Zielkonkretisierung und Erfolgskontrolle im Rahmen der Lokalen Agenda 21*. Berlin, Germany: Umweltbundesamt.

Hischier, R., & Gilgen, P. W. (2005). Life cycle assessment databases as part of sustainable development strategies: The example of Ecoinvent. In Hilty, L. M., Seifert, E. K., & Treibert, R. (Eds.), *Information systems for sustainable development* (pp. 15–24). Hershey, PA: Idea Group Publishing.

Hoffmann, D. (2007). *Regionale Wertschöpfung durch optimierte Nutzung endogener Biomassepotenziale.* Doctoral dissertation, Saarland University, Germany.

Hofstetter, P. (1998). *Perspectives in life cycle impact assessment; A structured approach to combine models of the technosphere, ecosphere and valuesphere*. Dordrecht, Netherlands: Kluwer Academic Publishers.

Hwang, C. L., & Yoon, K. (1981). *Multiple Attribute Decision Making, Methods and Applications - A State-of-the-Art Survey*. Heidelberg, Germany: Springer.

IEA (International Energy Agency). (2004). *Biofuels for transport: an international perspective*. Paris, France: IEA.

Jessel, B. (2008). *Biodiversity and Bioenergy*. Presentation at the 9th meeting of the Conference of the Parties (COP 9), 19.-30.05.2008. Bonn, Germany.

Larkin, J. H., & Simon, H. A. (1987). Why a diagram is (sometimes) worth ten thousand words. *Cognitive Science*, *11*, 65–99.

Leitl, T. (2007). *Biomasse, Bestandteil der RWE-Strategie im Bereich erneuerbare Energien*. Presentation at the 2nd BioEnergy Conference Carinthia, 06.11.2007. Velden, Austria.

Malczewski, J. (1999). *GIS and multicriteria analysis*. New York: Wiley.

Miller, G. A. (1956). The magic number seven plus or minus two: some limits on our capacity for communicating information. *Psychological Review*, *63*, 81–97. doi:10.1037/h0043158

Munda, G. (1995). *Multicriteria evaluation in a fuzzy environment: Theory and Applications in Ecological Economics*. Heidelberg, Germany: Physika-Verlag.

Mustajoki, J., Hämäläinen, R. P., & Martunen, M. (2003). Participatory multicriteria decision analysis with Web-HIPRE: a case of lake regulation policy. *Environmental Modelling & Software*, *19*(6), 537–547. doi:10.1016/j.envsoft.2003.07.002

Neumann, K. (1975). *Operation Research Verfahren* (*Vol. I*). München, Germany: Hauser.

Oberschmidt, J., Geldermann, J., Ludwig, J., & Schmehl, M. (2010. (accepted)). Modified PROMETHEE approach to assessing energy technologies. Speciel issue: Uses of frontier efficiency methodologies and multi-criteria decision making for performance measurement in the energy sector. *International Journal of Energy Sector Management.*

Oberschmidt, J., Ludwig, J., & Geldermann, J. (2009). Ein modifizierter PROMETHEE-Ansatz zur Lebenszyklus-orientierten Bewertung der Strom- und Wärmeversorgung. In Geldermann, J., & Lauven, L. (Eds.), *Einsatz von OR-Verfahren zur Entscheidungsunterstützung*. Aachen, Germany: Shaker.

Page, B., & Rautenstrauch, C. (2001). Environmental informatics-methods, tools and applications in environmental information processing. In Rautenstrauch, C., & Patig, S. (Eds.), *Environmental information systems in industry and public administration* (pp. 2–11). Hershey, PA: Idea Group Publishing.

Palmer, S. E. (1978). Fundamental aspects of cognitive representation. In E. Rosch & B. B. LLoyd (Eds.), Cognition and categorization (pp. 259-303). Hillsdale, N.J.: Erlbaum.

Petre, M., & Green, T. R. G. (1993). Learning to read graphics: some evidence that 'seeing' an informational display is an aquired skill. *Journal of Visual Languages and Computing, 4*, 55–70. doi:10.1006/jvlc.1993.1004

Rautenstrauch, C. (1999). *Betriebliche Umweltinformationssysteme, Grundlagen, Konzepte und Systeme*. Berlin/Heidelberg, Germany: Springer.

Reul, F. (2002). *Entwicklung einer Nachhaltigkeitsstrategie für den Stadtverkehr - das Beispiel Berlin*. Doctoral dissertation, Humboldt-University Berlin, Germany. Retrieved July 13, 2009, from http://edoc.hu-berlin.de/dissertationen/reul-frithjof-2002-12-17

Rösch, C., Skarka, J., Raab, K., & Stelzer, V. (2009). Energy production from grassland – Assessing the sustainability of different process chains under German conditions. *Biomass and Bioenergy, 33*(4), 689–700. doi:10.1016/j.biombioe.2008.10.008

Roth, W.-M., & Bowen, G. M. (1999). Of cannibals, missionaries, and converts: graphing competencies from grade 8 to professional science inside (classrooms) and outside (field/laboratory). *Science, Technology & Human Values, 24*(2), 179–212. doi:10.1177/016224399902400201

Ruppert, H., Eigner-Thiel, S., Girschner, W., Karpenstein-Machan, M., Roland, F., & Ruwisch, V. (2008). *Wege zum Bioenergiedorf – Leitfaden für eine eigenständige Wärme- und Stromversorgung auf Basis von Biomasse im ländlichen Raum*. Gülzow, Germany: Fachagentur Nachwachsende Rohstoffe.

Schmuck, P., Eigner, S., Kaufhold, A., & Krapoth, S. (1998). *Psychologische Aspekte von Unternehmensbewertung* (*Vol. 13*). Göttingen, Germany: Schriftenreihe des Koordinations- und Studienzentrums Frieden und Umwelt.

SCOPE (Scientific Committee on Problems of the Environment). (1995). *Environmental indicators: systematic approach to measuring and reporting on the environment in the context of sustainable development*. Discussion paper presented at the workshop "International Consultation of Sustainable Development Indicators", Ghent. Bruxelles, Belgium: Bureau du Plan.

Treitz, M., Bertsch, V., Schollenberger, H., Geldermann, J., & Rentz, O. (2008). Multi-criteria decision support for process design. *International Transactions in Operational Research* (accepted), Vol. Special, Issue of the IFORS Conference in Hawaii 2005, 10.-15.July Honolulu, Hawaii.

Tversky, B. (2000). Some ways maps and diagrams communicate. In Freksa, C., Brauer, W., Habel, C., & Wender, K. F. (Eds.), *Spatial cognition II*. Berlin, Germany: Springer. doi:10.1007/3-540-45460-8_6

United Nations. (1993). *Agenda 21: programme of action for sustainable development*. New York: United Nations.

Van Loo, S., & Koppejan, J. (Eds.). (2008). *Handbook of biomass combustion and Co-firing*. London, United Kingdom: Earthscan.

Vester, F. (2003). Die Kunst, vernetzt zu denken. Ideen und Werkzeug für einen Umgang mit Komplexität. Der neue Bericht an den Club of Rome. München, Germany: dtv.

Visser, U., Stuckenschmidt, H., Wache, H., & Vögele, T. (2001). Using environmental information efficiently: Sharing data and knowledge from heterogeneous sources. In Rautenstrauch, C., & Patig, S. (Eds.), *Environmental information systems in industry and public administration* (pp. 2–11). Hershey, PA: Idea Group Publishing.

Von Haaren, C., & Bathke, M. (2007). Integrated Planning and remuneration of agri-environmental goods and services for the management of sustainable landscapes – results of a case study in the Fuhrberg region of Germany. *Journal of Environmental Management*, *89*, 209–221. doi:10.1016/j.jenvman.2007.01.058

WBGU. (2008). *Wissenschaftlicher Beirat der Bundesregierung Globale Umweltveränderungen. Zukunftsfähige Bioenergie und nachhaltige Landnutzung*. Berlin: Springer.

Wei, B., & Carlson, R. (2002). *Practical Pre-Study of GIS application with LCA database SPINE*. Presentation at the fifth International Conference on Ecobalance, 06-08.11.2002. Tsukuba, Japan.

Weidenmann, B. (Ed.). (1994). *Wissenserwerb mit Bildern*. Bern, Switzerland: Huber.

Werheit, M. (1996). Indikatoren für eine nachhaltige Entwicklung. Information letter No. 29 of the Independent Institute for Environmental Concerns (UfU), Berlin, Germany.

Wiehe, J., Ruschkowski, E. V., Rode, M., Kanning, H., & Haaren, C. v. (2009). Auswirkungen des Energiepflanzenanbaus auf die Landschaft am Beispiel des Maisanbaus für die Biogasproduktion in Niedersachsen. *Naturschutz und Landschaftsplanung*, *41*(4), 107–113.

Wuppertal-Institut für Klima. Umwelt, Energie (1997). Zukunftsfähiges Deutschland – ein Beitrag zu einer global nachhaltigen Entwicklung. Basel, Switzerland: Birkhäuser.

Yue, C. Y., & Li, H. (1998). Multi-attribute evaluation for environment, resource and sustainable development. *Monitoring and Assessment*, *12*, 28–30.

Zimmermann, H. J. (1987). *Fuzzy Sets, Decision Making, and Expert Systems*. Boston: Kluwer.

ADDITIONAL READING

French, S., & Geldermann, J. (2005). The varied contexts of environmental decision problems and their implications for decision support. *Environmental Policy and Science*, *8*(4), 378–391. doi:10.1016/j.envsci.2005.04.008

Geldermann, J., & Rentz, O. (2005). Multi-Criteria Analysis for Technique Assessment: Case Study from Industrial Coating. *Journal of Industrial Ecology*, *9*(3), 127–142. doi:10.1162/1088198054821591

Chapter 20
The German Environmental Information Portal PortalU

Stefanie Konstantinidis
Lower Saxony Ministry of Environment and Climate Protection, Germany

Fred Kruse
Lower Saxony Ministry of Environment and Climate Protection, Germany

Martin Klenke
Lower Saxony Ministry of Environment and Climate Protection, Germany

ABSTRACT

In Germany, public environmental data are in the responsibility of several different public organisations and institutions. The German Environmental Information Portal PortalU® (www.portalu.de) is a web service operated by the environmental administrations to make digital environmental information easier accessible, usable and exploitable for both citizens and environmental experts. The fruitful long-time co-operation between the environmental administrations is an example for a well working organisational structure within a federal state. In this chapter the PortalU technology and the content of the portal are presented. Due to the current discussion referring to INSPIRE, a special focus is set on publishing INSPIRE conform metadata.

INTRODUCTION

Finding and using relevant digital information are getting more and more difficult in times of the overwhelming range of information in the World Wide Web. Search engines like Google or Yahoo will thereby be helpful to solve general questions. But are these search results in fact always relevant? And what is about the quality of the results? In the field of public environmental information, the German Environmental Information Portal PortalU offers an alternative to Google and co. In Germany, public environmental information are widespread over many public organisations and institutions and thereby collected and preserved in different ways, both technically and semantically. This makes it difficult to find, exploit and analyse environmental information in a broader context. The web service PortalU, operated by the German environmental administrations on federal and state level, aims at making digital environmental information easier accessible, us-

DOI: 10.4018/978-1-61520-981-1.ch020

able and exploitable for experts and non-experts. Thus, the portal enables information providers as well as users to improve the potential of digital environmental information. The chapter aims at giving an inside in the technology behind PortalU and the current content of the portal. Due to the current discussion referring to INSPIRE, a special focus is set on the InGrid®Catalog, which can be used to publish information about spatial data and services in terms of INSPIRE.

BACKGROUND

The central web application PortalU offers access to publicly owned environmental information especially on federal and state level, but also increasingly on municipal level in Germany. The portal aims at establishing a fast and reliable survey of all relevant public environmental information. PortalU plays an important role within the strategy of the environmental administration in reference to the Aarhus Convention, the EU Directive 2003/4/EC and the INSPIRE Directive.

The Aarhus Convention is a convention of the United Nations Economic Commission for Europe Committee on Environmental Policy from 1998 with focus on access to information, public participation in decision-making and access to justice in environmental matters (UNECE 2009). The convention aims at strengthen the rights of access to information, public participation in decision-making and access to justice in environmental matters in order to contribute to the protection of right of present and future generations to an environment adequate to his or her health and well-being. The Aarhus Convention is the first contract according to international law which assigns each person rights referring to environmental protection. It was signed by 35 nations, including Germany, and the European Union. Based on the Aarhus Convention the European Parliament and the Council passed the EU Directive 2003/4/EC on public access to environmental information in 2003, which is shortly called the Environmental Information Directive (EU 2003). This directive aims at guaranteeing the right of access to public environmental information and setting out the basic terms and conditions of and practical arrangements for its exercise. Above this the directive aims at ensuring that environmental information is progressively made available and disseminated to the public to achieve the widest possible systematic availability and dissemination to the public. A further EU directive which concerns environmental information was passed by the European Parliament and the Council in 2007: the EU Directive 2007/2/EC for establishing an infrastructure for spatial information in the European Community, which is shortly called the INSPIRE Directive (EU 2007). As the title of the directive already implies, the directive aims at establishing an infrastructure for spatial information. The INSPIRE Directive thereby defines 34 spatial data themes, which are described in the three annexes of the directive. In order to implement the INSPIRE Directive, separate implementing rules for metadata, network services, data specifications, data sharing as well as monitoring and reporting are defined. The implementing rules for metadata for instance are already passed in December 2008. The corresponding metadata for the spatial data themes, which are described in annex I and II of the INSPIRE Directive, has to be provided until December 2010. Metadata for INSPIRE annex III spatial data themes has to be provided until December 2013.

Due to these legal obligations, one important focus of PortalU is the evidence of environmental information according to the Environmental Information Directive. Moreover PortalU will be the central nodal point for collecting environmental metadata in Germany referring to INSPIRE. So especially the active dissemination of environmental information as well as the discovery of

Figure 1. Main aspects of the development, maintenance and dissemination of PortalU

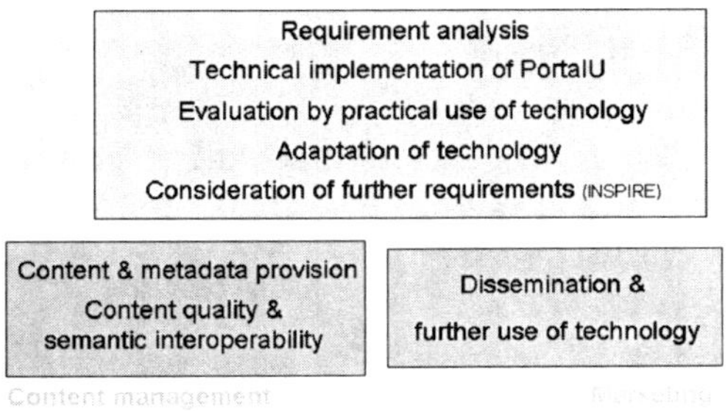

existing environmental data through metadata are important tasks of PortalU.

The idea of setting up a common technology to improve the access to environmental data traces back to 1991. At that time a research and development project started at the Ministry for Environment and Climate Protection of Lower Saxony with focus on improving access to public environmental information by structured descriptions of these data in terms of metadata. In this regard the first version of the environmental data catalogue software UDK was developed (Lessing & Schuetz, 1994). After the end of the project, UDK was further developed through a federal/state co-operation which was established in 1996. A second important step was taken by the development of the German Environmental Information Network GEIN® in 1998. Developed by the German Environmental Agency, the web application GEIN made environmental web pages and data bases from public institutions accessible (Bandholz et al., 2000).

Both systems aimed at improving the access to environmental data, so the idea was born to combine the systems by creating a one-stop-portal for all environmental information. Thus the existing UDK federal/state co-operation was expanded in 2003. The new one-stop-portal PortalU combines the demands from the former technologies UDK and GEIN with new demands which came up especially referring to EU Directive 2003/4/EC. The new portal was set up by using up-to-date technology. Figure 1 provides an overview of the most important aspects of the development, maintenance and dissemination of the environmental information portal PortalU.

The overall management of PortalU consists of three parts: the project coordinator, the steering committee PortalU and the working group for technical and content issues of PortalU. The project coordinator, which is executed by the Coordination Center PortalU, is thereby responsible for the overall coordination including the monitoring of all technical and content aspects of the portal. Technical developments and content issues are discussed firstly in the working group to have a foundation for the decision-makers in the steering committee. The members of the steering committee and the working group are representatives from the federal level and from all 16 German federal states. With this structure, a sustainable network was established where both consensus building and awareness rising referring to different interests of partners play an important role.

THE FEATURES OF PORTALU

Before the one-stop-portal PortalU was developed a requirement analysis was carried out. The following requirements took thereby center stage. The environmental information portal shall be a technical tool referring to EU Directive 2003/4/EC

- which provides access to environmental information in a comprehensible, accurate and comparable way,
- for active and systematic dissemination of environmental information to the public and
- which provides free access to public-owned environmental information (metadata and data).

Figure 2. The architecture of the PortalU software InGrid; DB: data base, DSC: data source client, IGC: InGridCatalog, SE: search engine, SNS: semantic network service (www.semantic-network.de)

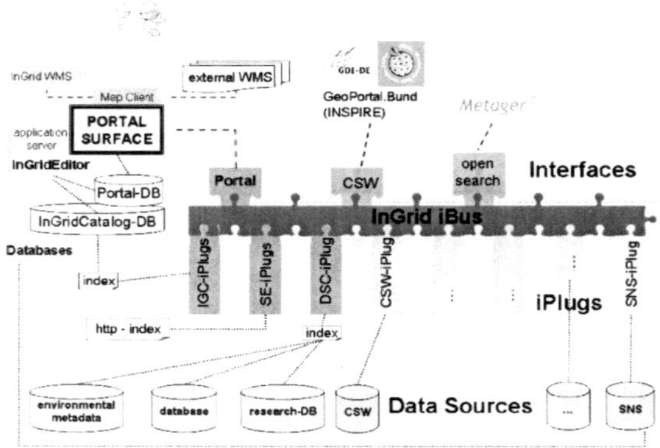

Furthermore

- the technology shall provide short response times for search queries,
- results shall be clearly arranged in sorted result lists,
- provided information shall be as up-to-date as possible,
- the information shall be stored only at one place,
- the technology shall be flexible in order to add features in future if necessary and
- last but not least the system shall be cost efficient and should not cause licence fees.

In order to meet these demands, the modular, service oriented, distributed software InGrid® was developed. The software consists of several open source software components which were combined and modified according to the corresponding requirements. InGrid is an acronym for information grid, which shall emphasize the modular structure of the software. The software is java-based and consists of several building blocks (Figure 2):

1. The information broker, called iBus, is the central component of InGrid. It can be queried via the web portal or via generic interfaces like Catalog Service Web or OpenSearch. The iBus transfers search queries to the connected data sources (web pages, data bases, catalogs, etc.), collects the results and delivers them to the query client.
2. The search engine is based on the Nutch framework. It includes a web crawler and Apache Lucene indexing technology.
3. The InGridCatalog is an ISO 19115/19119 and INSPIRE compliant web catalog.
4. The map component integrates and visualises web mapping services (WMS) and web feature services (WFS).
5. Several interfaces (iPlugs) are available to connect diverse data sources including external data bases ("hidden web").
6. Above that, further interfaces are available to transfer information to external information systems like GeoPortal.Bund or the German metadata search engine Metager (www.metager.de).

Short response times for search queries are reached by omitting cascading. Moreover the use of an index accelerates the response time and permits the sorting of results in a result list.

The environmental information are integrated and made accessible in PortalU via standardized interfaces, so called iPlugs. The most important iPlugs are the SE-, CSW-, DSC- and IGC-iPlug. The search engine iPlug (SE-iPlug) is used to provide result lists for search queries. For this purpose an http-index, which contains essential text information about diverse environmental information from several data sources, is generated and searched through. The CSW-iPlug is an OGC conform CSW-2-0 interface to connect external CSW (catalog service web) data sources like the WSV data catalog of the German federal water and shipping administration (Wasser- und

Figure 3. Entry mask of the InGridEditor

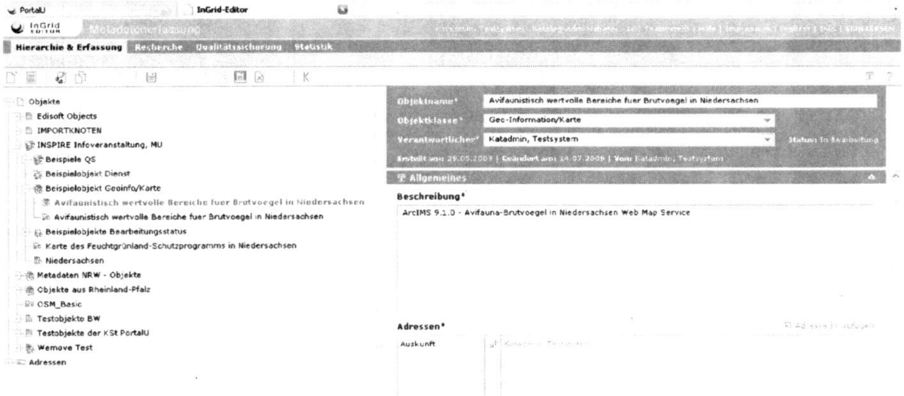

Schifffahrtsverwaltung). Data bases with different kind of data structure are connected by the data source client iPlug (DSC-iPlug). The IGC-iPlug connects the iBus with all environmental data catalogues which are based on InGridCatalog (IGC) technology. The development of new interfaces is oriented along the practical needs to make further important data sources available.

The web application InGridCatalog is the successor system of the former desktop UDK technology. With the InGridCatalog metadata can be recorded, updated and discovered easily. Recording and updating of metadata are carried out in a web editor, the InGridEditor (Figure 3). The metadata profile of the catalog is ISO 19115, ISO 19119 and INSPIRE conform. Six different classes are provided to describe different kind of environmental information:

- spatial data,
- services,
- data series & data bases,
- documents, reports & literature,
- projects & programs and
- organisational structures & thematic tasks.

In all classes less then twenty fields have to be filled in mandatory to describe a new metadata object. Information about the contact address, spatial reference and keywords are thereby inherited by the hierarchical higher ranked object. Beside this, different kinds of wizards are provided to assist the metadata editor by filling in the fields. When environmental information (e.g. a specific project or report) is already described on a web page, the common entry wizard can be used to fill in the object fields title, description, keywords, spatial and time reference. However, the getCapabilities wizard assists the editor by describing services (WMS, WFS, WCS, WCTS und CSW). As a result, the effort for generating new metadata is altogether relatively low. Metadata which are published once in an InGridCatalog can be found in several systems: in PortalU, MetaGer and before long in the geo portals of GDI-DE and INSPIRE. Consequently the information is available for a wide range of potential users within public administration and economy as well as for citizens.

As mentioned before, the software InGrid consists of several open source software components. Due to this, the federal/state co-operation PortalU does not have to pay any external licence fees. Table 1 provides an overview of the particular open source components. The Federal Ministry for the Environment, Nature Conservation and Nuclear Safety holds the copyrights for InGrid. The software can be used without any licence fees on all levels of administration (federal, state

Table 1. Integrated open source tools in InGrid

Component / feature	Open source tool
Portal user interface	Jetspeed
Search engine	Nutch & Lucene
Map server	UMN-Map-Server
Map viewer / integrated WMS	MapBender
Indexing of data bases	Lucene
Supported data bases	MySQL, PostgreSQL & several proprietary data bases (Oracle, Tamino, etc.)

and municipal level) within Germany. Hence the web catalog InGridCatalog can be used within the German on all levels of administration to enlarge and build up corresponding catalogs to prove environmental spatial data and services through metadata, in order to meet the corresponding demands of INSPIRE.

ENVIRONMENTAL INFORMATION IN PORTALU

In PortalU all environmental information, web pages, databases as well as data catalogs can be searched by different kinds of search queries according to the requirements of the user: spatially, temporally and semantically filters are available. The results of a query are displayed in a ranked result list independent from the data source. Besides this, PortalU offers a separate access to service pages, web pages with environmental monitoring data and selected web pages which serve as easy access point to diverse environmental topics (Figure 4). Moreover the portal offers access to maps in terms of WMS and an environmental almanac. Furthermore current environmental news are displayed on the PortalU start page in a common list from different institutions.

PortalU provides currently access to over 2.9 million environmental information from the public

Figure 4. Start page of PortalU (www.portalu.de)

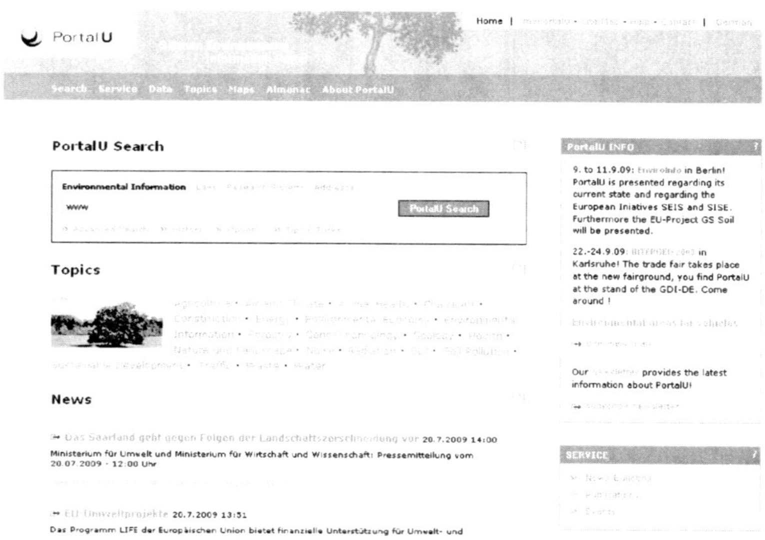

Figure 5. Embedded environmental information (search results) in PortalU

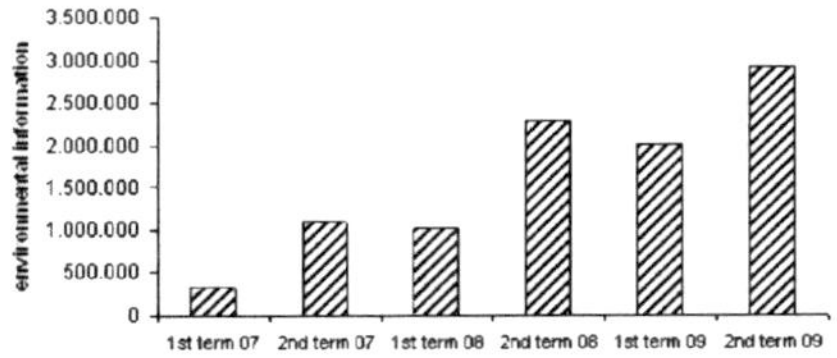

administration in Germany including web pages and about 500,000 data base entries. Within the last years the amount of environmental information is growing continuously (see Figure 5): from almost 500,000 pieces of information in the first term of 2007 to over 1 Mio. in the second term of 2007 and over 2 Mio. pieces of information until the second term of 2008. The increase of available information in PortalU can be traced back to different factors like:

- an increase of pieces of environmental information within already connected data sources (e.g. web pages, catalog entries, data base entries)
- the integration of further data bases and
- the integration of web pages of further environmental data providers

Thus the amount of integrated data bases increased from nine in May 2006 to 28 until now. Eighteen of the 28 data bases, which are currently accessible via PortalU, are environmental data catalogs from the federal environmental administration and several German states (Bundeslaender). These catalogs contain about 5,000 INSPIRE relevant metadata entries. Besides these, further data bases from state or federal environmental agencies, such as DNL-online (a literature data base from the German Federal Agency for Nature Conservation) or UFORDAT (the environmental research data base from the German Federal Environmental Agency) are integrated in PortalU.

Figure 6. Information providers in PortalU

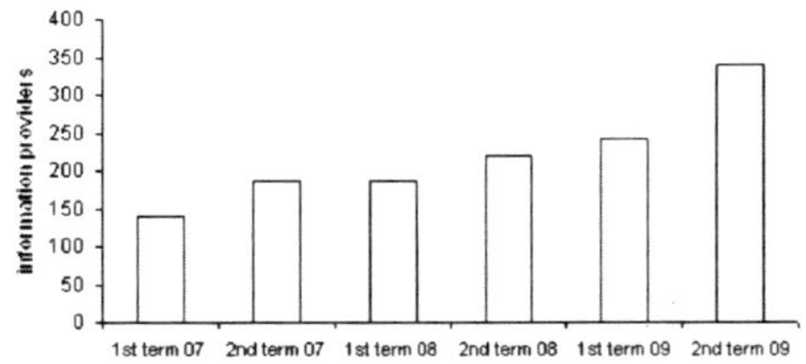

Above that, the amount of PortalU data providers increased from about 90 in May 2006 to over 340 until now (Figure 6). Fifteen percent of the data providers are thereby from the federal level: from federal ministries like the Federal Ministry of Environment, Nature Conservation and Nuclear Safety or the Federal Ministry for Food, Agriculture and Consumer Protection, from federal agencies and institutes like the Federal Nature Conservation Agency of the Federal Institute of Hydrology as well as from special initiatives and permanent working groups like the federal state working group water. About 58 percent of the data providers are from institutions and organisations on state level, including information from the three town states Berlin, Bremen and Hamburg. Information providers on this level are in particular state ministries, agencies, special initiatives, academies as well as national and nature parks and research institutes. The remaining seventeen percent information providers are municipal providers. Currently two initiatives have started to include municipal environmental information in PortalU: in Lower Saxony and Saxony. Until now information from 68 towns and communes in Lower Saxony and from 26 towns and communes in Saxony are integrated in PortalU. The single environmental information from web pages to data base entries, which can be searched through by the PortalU search, is recalled from the information source.

PortalU offers further features, besides the search functionality. Such as a merge from up-to-date environmental news on the PortalU start

Figure 7. PortalU page views

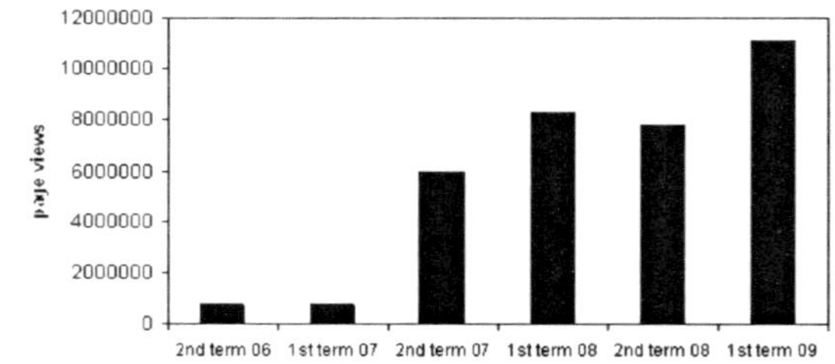

page. These news are merged RSS-feeds with environmental relevance from several federal and state institutions. The service rubric offers access to 145 service pages from press releases, publications to information about events on federal and state level. The rubric data offers access to about 100 different kind of environmental monitoring data from federal and state level. Especially information about monitoring data related to radiation, air and water can be found, such as monitoring data about the ozone concentration or about environmental radioactivity in Germany.

The rubric topics offers a special access to single environmental web pages, which have high relevance for a special environmental topic. Altogether 21 environmental themes from A like Agriculture, Air and Climate or Animal Health to W like Waste or Water and six functional categories from Concepts over Legislation to State-of-the-Environment are distinguished. The classification is thereby geared to the topics mentioned in the Environmental Information Directive. The rubric topics aims at providing an easy access point to relevant environmental topics for non-experts. The topic "waste / legislation" offers par example links to special web pages from federal and state level to websites were corresponding legal texts are listed.

Besides the increase of environmental information and information providers, the number of visitors increased significantly during the last years as well. The amount of page views rose from less than 1 million per half year (term) in 2006 and the first term of 2007 up to 8 million in the second term of 2008 (Figure 7). In the first term of 2009 more than 11 million PortalU pages were viewed. During the same period the amount of visitors and the amount of visits (sessions) significantly increased as well.

In conclusion, PortalU offers an easy access to various German public environmental information. Currently the focus is set on the integration of additional public institutions, which are not part of the environmental administration but provide environmental data relevant to the EU Directive 2003/4/EC such as forest management etc. In order to involve these institutions in PortalU regular information events are offered for new potential information providers. Finally, the involvement of municipal information providers is also an important issue to follow up.

PERSPECTIVE

The German Environmental Information Portal PortalU has been and will be continuously improved and extended referring to its technology and content. The environmental portal was nominated 2007 as one of the 53 finalist (from 311 cases) for the EU eGovernment Award (www.epractice.eu/cases/portalu). With the award the European Commission assigns innovative projects of the public administration in order to foster the exchange of good practice. In addition, PortalU was mentioned in the SEIS communication 2008 (EU 2008) as initiative at national level which will help to make the Share Environmental Information System for Europe (SEIS) reality. SEIS is an initiative of the European Commission (Directorate General Environment) and the European Environmental Agency (EEA) to establish together with the Member States an integrated and shared EU-wide environmental information system in order to modernise reporting obligations (EU 2009). In this connection PortalU was integrated in the NESIS Best Practice Catalog of ICT solutions for managing environmental data. NESIS (www.nesis.eu) is a network to enhance a European environmental shared and interoperable information system (Saio et al., 2009), which is funded by the European Commission. The network can be seen as preparing project for implementing SEIS.

The continuous technical development of PortalU is a reaction on the dynamic development of information and communication technologies and the demands of the users of public environmental information. Currently the Catalog Service Web (CSW), the Data Source Client (DSC) and the map viewer of the InGrid software will be updated. Moreover new components referring to numerical measurement data are discussed with special focus on the upcoming demands according to EU initiative SEIS.

In order to implement the Environmental Information Directive, different approaches were traced in the single European member states. Austria par example established the Environmental Portal Austria (http://reference.e-government.gv.at/Umweltinformation.1024.0.html) as a central public access point to environmental information. The Environmental Portal Austria is technically a web presence, where especially background information to the Environmental Information Directive is presented. However a technical tool comparable with PortalU which makes different kinds of distributed data sources accessible, does not exist yet. According to INSPIRE several advanced systems were established within the last years like Geoportal.Bund (http://geoportal.bkg.bund.de) in Germany, Geoland.at (www.geoland.at) in Austria or Geoportail.fr (http://www.geoportail.fr) in France. These spatial data infrastructures (SDIs) are specialised on the discovery and visualization of spatial data and corresponding services. In comparison to PortalU some similarities and some differences can be outlined. The SDIs do not focus exclusively on environmental information like PortalU, but on all 34 spatial data themes including themes like statistical units, buildings and utility and government service. Besides this, PortalU offers a huger amount of features (e.g. news, monitoring data and separate topic pages) and a broader spectrum of environmental information (web sites, data bases ect.).

Both, the whole InGrid technology as well as single components can be seen as added-value products which have been built up for PortalU but can also be used for building up further portals on regional or local administrative level in Germany, in other countries or on European level. InGrid is currently used not only for operating the German Environmental Information Portal PortalU, but for operating three state and one municipal environmental information portals: the state portal of Saxony (http://portalu.smul.sachsen.de), the state portal of Rhineland-Palatinate (www.portalu.rlp.de), the state portal Saarland (http://portalu.saarland.de) and the municipal InGrid portal of Lower Saxony (www.portalu.niedersachsen.de). Beyond that the InGrid technology is currently used as basic platform to build up an European Soil Portal within the EU-funded project GS Soil (Uhrich et al. 2009). The three years project (www.gssoil.eu) started in June 2009 and aims at making INSPIRE compliant spatial soil data and services available. The consortium consists of 34 partners from 18 European member states.

REFERENCES

Bandholtz, T., Bös, R., & Ruether, M. (2000). The German Environmental Information Network (GEIN). In A. B. Cremers & K. Greve (Eds.), *Proceedings of the 14th International Symposium „Computer Science for Environmental Protection '00", Vol. 2* (pp. 632-646). Marburg: Metropolis.

EU (2003). Directive 2003/4/EC of the European Parliament and of the Council of 28 January 2003 on public access to environmental information and repealing Council Directive 90/313/EEC. *Official Journal of the European Union*, L 41, 26.

EU. (2007). Directive 2007/2/EC of the European Parliament and of the Council of 14 March 2007 establishing an Infrastructure for Spatial Information in the European Community (INSPIRE). *Official Journal of the European Union. L&C, L*, 108.

EU. (2008). *Communication from the Commission to the Council, the European Parliament, the European Economic and Social Committee and the Committee of the Regions – Towards a Shared Environmental Information System (SEIS). COM/2008/0046 final*. Retrieved July 2009, from http://eur-lex.europa.eu/LexUriServ/LexUriServ.do?uri=COM:2008:0046:FIN:EN:PDF

EU. (2009). *Website from the European Commission's DG Environment about SEIS*. Retrieved November 2009, from http://ec.europa.eu/environment/seis/index.htm

Lessing, H., & Schuetz, T. (1994). Der Umwelt-Datenkatalog als Instrument zur Steuerung von Informationsfluessen. In L.M. Hilty, A. Jaeschke., B. Page, & A. Schwabl (Eds.), *Informatik für den Umweltschutz, 8. Symposium. Vol. 1* (pp. 159-167). Marburg: Metropolis.

Saio, G., Vandenbroucke, D., & Wawer, R. (2009). NESIS – a Network to enhance a European Environmental Shared and Interoperable Information System. In J. Hřebíček, J. Hradec, E. Pelikán, O. Mírovský, W. Pillmann, I. Holoubek, & T. Bandholtz (Eds.), *Proceedings of the European conference of the Czech Presidency of the Council of the EU TOWARDS eENVIRONMENT. Opportunities of SEIS and SISE: Integrating Environmental Knowledge in Europe* (pp. 258-264). Brno, Czech Republic: Masaryk University.

Uhrich, S., Klenke, M., Kruse, F., & Giffei, C. (2009). Approach to Build a Soil Information Portal for Europe Based on the PortalU Technology. In J. Hřebíček, J. Hradec, E. Pelikán, O. Mírovský, W. Pillmann, I. Holoubek, & T. Bandholtz (Eds.), *Proceedings of the European conference of the Czech Presidency of the Council of the EU TOWARDS eENVIRONMENT. Opportunities of SEIS and SISE: Integrating Environmental Knowledge in Europe* (pp. 266-268). Brno, Czech Republic: Masaryk University.

UNECE (United Nations Economic Commission for Europe). (2009): *Publication of the Aarhus Convention*. Retrieved June 2009, from http://www.unece.org/env/pp/documents/cep43e.pdf

Chapter 21
Environment–Enterprise Integration:
Networked Entrepreneurial Opportunities

R.C. Michelini
DIMEC, University of Genova, Italy

R.P. Razzoli
DIMEC, University of Genova, Italy

ABSTRACT

Part of manufacturers' responsibility when bringing out new products is to consider their environmental footprint. The legal supply chain combines hardware/software delivery, granting on-duty conformance to use preservation, and end-of-life take-back, with compulsory recovery targets. These entrepreneurial competencies appear externally, in respect to old manufacturing practices, which were internal. Networking options provide fundamental technological aids. This chapter analyses some technologically-driven solutions which stand out for the exploitation of net concerns at these three integration levels: business project co-operation, through spot-wise agreements; the factually united organisation or virtual corporation; joint and several liability, or extended corporation. The checks are centered on the bottom up series of appraisals, to evidence the return on investment from below so that the partnership permanently spurs motivation and fosters competition through properly established facilities/functions integration into unified competitive entrepreneurial organisations.

INTRODUCTION

Ecology requires dramatic changes in industrial economic trends. The affluent society paradigm, based on manufacturing efficiency, transforming raw materials into mass products, quickly increases pollution and waste and is facing imminent limitations to safeguard mankind's future. It is difficult to accept the today's population approach that it is their absolute privilege to exploit the earth's resources. They seem to feel their entitlement is based on being the first to obtain possession. The impending eco-regulation is an entangled issue made rather critical in times of economic recession, as mandatory restraints are seen as severe changes and forbidding full access to immediately spendable riches.

DOI: 10.4018/978-1-61520-981-1.ch021

In this chapter we outline the knowledge entrepreneurship way out of this issue (Michelini, 2008), based on value added intangibles and assured by two main opportunities:

- the resort to product-service deliveries, imposed as the lifestyle manufacturers' responsibility;
- and the net-concerns efficiency, obtained by clustering facility/function fit-for-purpose capacities.

The issue is a technology-driven construct, offered by information and communication aids, aimed at advanced entrepreneurial settings. The emerging net-concerns have to incorporate the Information and Communication Technology as instrumental business support of lifestyle supply chains. The technicalities cover a series of prospects showing the readily available mix of opportunities:

- design, manufacture, trade, service, and bookkeeping fusion
- net-enhanced product-service deployment organisation
- forward/backward logistics information flow integration
- resource productivity management and imbalance recording
- customers relationship and certification establishment
- supervisors' accreditation and eco-vaulting administration
- entrepreneurial project and partnership clustering appraisal
- facility/function market and broker negotiation/incorporation
- interoperability ruling and in-progress achievement assessment
- networking value added and return on the collaborative course

- design, manufacture, trade, service, and bookkeeping fusion
- net-enhanced product-service deployment organisation
- forward/backward logistics information flow integration
- resource productivity management and imbalance recording
- customers relationship and certification establishment
- supervisors' accreditation and eco-vaulting administration
- entrepreneurial project and partnership clustering appraisal
- facility/function market and broker negotiation/incorporation
- interoperability ruling and in-progress achievement assessment
- networking value added and return on the collaborative course.

The *product-service* delivery is definitely a duty to be accomplished during the design phase. The unified liability falls on the main manufacturer even if it integrates components, technologies, and expertise of different origins. The lifestyle commitment requires extended ranges of skills, beyond the core competencies of most manufacturers. For effectiveness, resorting to fitting facilities and functions becomes imperative, making it important to aggregate apt partners each time the business project is defined.

The advanced enterprise challenge consequently develops based on three successful occurrences:

- the compulsory lifestyle transformation of the manufacturing entrepreneurship towards the product-service delivery;
- fitting facility/function integration with regards to networking agility and the pervasiveness of developing the best-suited and efficient methods;

- the profitably transparency of co-operative production and business projects to assess the best integration setting.

The analyses derive from a series of studies recently conducted to explain the strict correlation stemming from durable growth with service engineering and reverse logistics. These studies also examine the maximally intangible value chain and the complete visibility of the tangibles' productivity. The closing remarks provide suggestions for short-term accomplishments.

PRODUCT-SERVICE AND ECO-PROVISION

Lifestyle provisioning is deemed to be standard issue in the future of industrialism, foreshadowed by the «externalities» to «internalities» interlacing supply chains where the *net concern* settings become a forced solution in view of incorporating the facilities and functions to make the delivery feasible. The analysis aims to define the metrics and compare related performance in terms of intra-organisational ties since the legal, administrative, and other aspects allow independently reaching enacted bylaws (Acaccia, 2007 a; Michelini & Razzoli, 2007).

The analysis on these grounds does not look at technology-driven guesses. Instead it looks at factual set-ups required by manufacturers each time a product is put on the market. The lifestyle entrepreneurship is presently motivated at two levels (Michelini & Razzoli, 2004 a-b):

- The on-duty conformance-to-use certification, after proper maintenance and regulation, is basically ruled by means of voluntary agreements, binding suppliers to purchasers.
- The end-of-life take-back and recovery (reuse, recycle) accomplishments, according to the enacted compulsory targets, are fulfilled and recorded by the authorised treatment facilities.

Both levels entail *externalities*, namely, actions outside the point-of-sale, when the items are fully enjoyed to the buyers' profit but their lawful operation needs to satisfy eco-protection acts. Environmental safeguard requires choices, taken at the design step, and a series of accomplishments which are a standard completion of each provision are suitably detailed in the PLM, *product lifecycle manager*.

The eco-defence exemplifies the main *externalities*, as compared with the earlier *internalities* of the manufacturing business. It portrays engagements taken by consumers (producers and users), as allowed, withdrawing the given natural capital, namely, borrowing raw material, transformed to pollution and waste. The consumers' debt is ambiguous (fraudulent), because the sponged-off natural capital is downgraded (with entropy increase), and the damages up to now are vague, even if the overall appraisal is performed by independent third parties (governmental authorities or notified certification bodies), (Michelini & Razzoli, 2007). As a result, eco-protection is an emerging activity, needing regulation and enacted by the national authorities according to EU directives and harmonised to assure worldwide equivalence. The promising business will profit through co-operative nets, according to different schemes:

- the manufacturers stay in charge of all services: provision, lifecycle conformance, and disposal deeds, so that the trade regulation depends on single indentures;
- independent actors profit by the safety rules and environment acts expansion, to become service dealers, with technology-oriented qualification and infrastructure-based organisations.

Figure 1. The PLM-SE set-up, managed by advanced enterprises

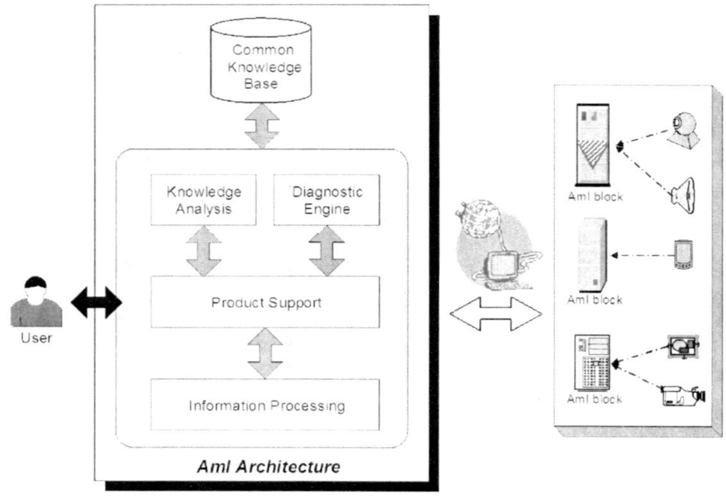

The schemes exploit suitable PLM information aids, *service-engineering* oriented, i.e., PLM-SE, in the first case, or *reverse-logistics* oriented, i.e., PLM-RL, in the second one. The entrepreneurial set-up involves several competencies. However, the lifestyle supply chain asks for the best-suited design pre-setting necessary to complete the manufacturer's task. The company without proper know-how is compelled to out-source major duties, lowering its competitiveness, in front of qualified competitors.

Eco-protection is a growing domain, with a number of impending bylaws. As preliminary glance, we might quote (Acaccia, 2008; Michelini & Kovàcs, 2002):

- the conformance-to-use preservation and certification is rightfully assured by voluntary agreements to guarantee the buyers through self-consistent product-service delivery;
- the end-of-life take-back, today included in the manufacturer's responsibility for given durables accomplishes the enacted recovery (reuse, recycle) compulsory targets.

The situations in existing industrial contexts are well-exemplified by advanced enterprises in which lifecycle *externalities* have become part of the business' mission, Figure 1, turning the company's skills into lifelong service delivery (Anufriev, 2007; Kopàcsi, 2006; Michelini & Razzoli, 2009). Remote service duty is highly enhanced by resourceful and friendly interfaces which incorporate ambient intelligence, AmI, and aids (see Figure 2) to support users' pleasant access (Michelini & Razzoli, 2008 a). The ability to take profit from the existing technologies and transform the eco-defence acts into business assignments is a challenge faced by innovative and motivated companies ready to draw focused contracts and widen the conventional trade course.

Figure 2. The AmI aids functional modules in real-life missions

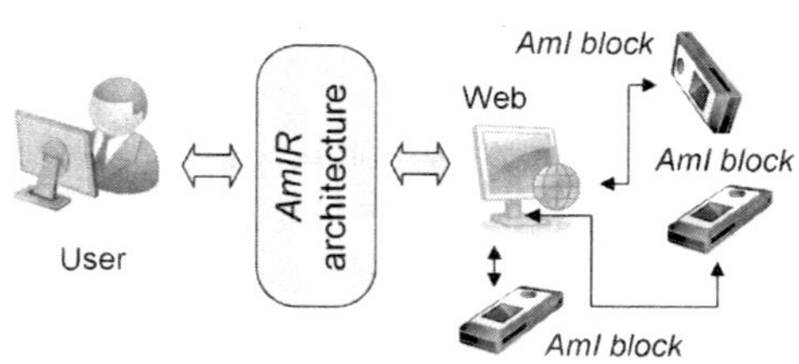

Figure 3. The knowledge build-up in ELV reverse logistics

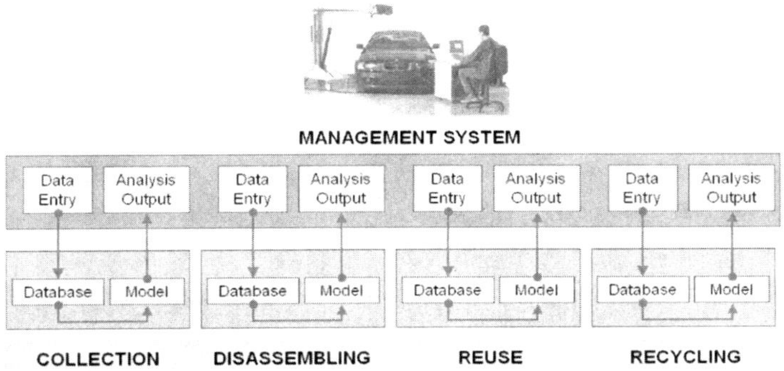

Ahead of mandatory bylaws, the chance to remain in the market requires strict policies where added commissions have to play the enacted role, should the company become equipped accordingly or not. In the first instance, e.g., reverse logistics, it is beyond the conventional manufacturer's capabilities, Figure 3, and (conservative) carmakers might prefer concentrating their efforts on their core activities and leaving the *end-of-life* vehicle (ELV) treatment to external organisations.

This choice is not without risk, whether competing carmakers will oppose with offers, having dissimilar overall (call-back included) costs. The producer's responsibility leaves little respite once the actual charges' visibility cannot be disguised by local administrative inefficiency. This critical instance deserves careful analysis (Acaccia, 2007 b-c), combining material and information flow efficiency with the negotiation, incorporation, and exploitation of the special facilities/functions each time it is necessary. Knowledge management (see Figure 4) broadly profits by networked operation nodes, sharing the *product-service* data-base, linked to provide optimal processing effectiveness of the industrial efficiency.

The eco-charges' transparency is a primary enabler of the business's effectiveness. The capability of creating entrepreneurial organisations fully encompassing lifestyle *externalities* within standard business *internalities* is a challenge to come in the face of pervasive eco-acts, impelling companies to shift business models to those whose return shall maximally depend on knowledge management aids due to embedded information and communication technologies.

FUNCTION-FACILITY ASSEMBLY INCORPORATION

The mentioned example set-ups are consistent with *controlled* collaborative net-concerns, linking suppliers and clients with value added chains which make the *product-service* course transparent to the certifying bodies through checks and conformance

Figure 4. The reverse logistics flow simulation/ appraisal tool

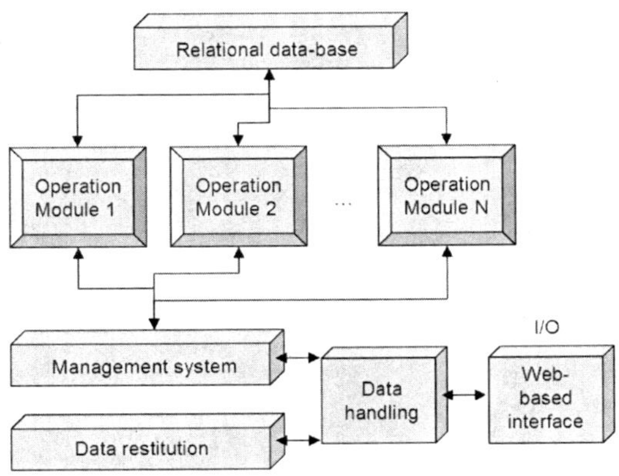

assessments. This might all be appreciated as an extraordinary job creation mechanism. However it has different potential issues:

- Governmental agencies opt for the administrative ruling without free competition.
- Net-concerns aim at opportunistic task arrangements under the oversight of a third party.
- Virtual enterprises perform the duties under the service ruler on a self-consistent basis.
- Extended enterprises maintain the duties as the firm's lifestyle provision accomplishments.

The first does not include the enterprise's risk, and pricing is chiefly affected by political biases. In the second, efficiency is confined within the networking options, above all because of process visibility. Subsequent ones (virtual and extended enterprise) profit by computer technology aids, though at different integration levels. The *virtual* enterprise (Michelini, 2008) is the distributed assembly of facilities/functions linked by the common project to expand the business and enhance the partners' profitability. It operates as a single company when the *externalities* are viewed by the clients, without however, full interplay with the producer's *internalities*. The *extended* enterprise is the next step, if the *product-service* is entirely conceived and delivered in a timely manner by the main manufacturer in regards to pertinent partners assuring complementary competencies.

The networking advantage is a complex issue with overall prerequisites at the project range due to the knowledge involved.

At the project range:

- *Knowledge dissemination: the information flow and decision-support tools acknowledgement and evaluation are managed, in order to appreciate the networking effectiveness*
- *Operation programming: the business is stated, setting the partnership strength and accepting interest to fix the set-up details, duty schedules, node responses, audit plans, etc.*

At the concern range:

- *Net-concern participation: the negotiation and setting of the listed series of accomplishments are run to account for the individual intra-organisational requirements*
- *Co-ordination acceptance: the assessments, advice, and guidelines of the collaboration frames are addressed to guarantee the pertinent integration sharing*

At the node range:

- *Involvement obligations: given the supplier/receiver and inner/outer lists, the task allotment is applied to verify all the involved nodes' competencies and provisions*
- *Audits/reviews schemes: the audit/review schemes are acknowledged to establish the periodic and emergency measurement schedules and on-duty acceptation tests.*

At the partners' co-operation level, the roles require feasibility and leanness checks. Then each participant has to acknowledge the team's relationships. Dealing with the eco-defence, the project knowledge covers the product, process, environment, enterprise, and the **2P2E** frames with the extension of the old **2P** simultaneous engineering practices. It also takes in the lifestyle *externalities* to incorporate the needed service-oriented facilities/functions:

- Standard product data: physical representation; producibility; operation management, quality, cost and affordability; lifecycle requirements; use and maintenance directions; dismissal instructions

- Standard manufacturing data: materials procurement and processing, assembly and disassembly; quality testing and conformance assessment; packaging; re-manufacturing
- Standard environment data: voluntary agreements for low pollution and high remediation; mandatory targets to cover recovery (reuse, recycle) and safe dumping
- Standard enterprise data: business functions: trading strategies, finance/resource management, etc.; operation functions: facility and job management, scheduling and planning, etc.; other project data.

The net concerns pertain to new technologies with many stakeholders: users, net-workers and developers, service-providers, equipment manufacturers, software producers, access managers, etc., all actively engaged in conceiving new options and issues. The intangibles' provision directly and indirectly co-ordinates with the value added increase. The indirect features help modifying users' habits all over the supply chain, adding transparency to the allotted goods and functions and their related eco-impacts. Consumers start recognising the differences in competing alternatives. Visibility becomes the initiative for conservation choices. The net organisation covers three areas:

- the inner cluster, to link nodes collaborating in the manufacturing and managing of the product-service
- the outer lines, for the buyers' assistance and conformance appraisal at the point-of-operation
- the selective bonds for the overseeing bodies' access and the eco-certification/accounting duty.

The first area affects the suppliers' infrastructures. The other two are *service* features, which at present are ruled by *voluntary agreements* or *mandatory functions* in the producers' *lifestyle* responsibility schema. The *extended* enterprise typifies the self-sufficient information frames with a unifying context to fulfil the *product-service* delivery:

- Co-operative development of the technical construction files, with regards to virtual prototyping and predisposing the lifecycle overseeing, call-back and recovery duties
- Decision support during manufacturing by simultaneous engineering aiming at scope economy for buyers' satisfaction on-duty and end-of-life service included
- Facility/function updating, suitably driven by the lifestyle product-service eco-footprint control, all along the supply chain's emerging requirements
- On-duty observation for control, diagnostics, maintenance, repair, etc., through conformance-to-specification checks, functions assurance, and impact assessment
- Monitoring help for the supply chain eco-management, with data transparency of provisioning, maintenance, recovery, recycle, reclamation, and dumping
- Off-process ascertainment channels, to measure resources consumption and remediation requirements on the entire (forward/backward) supply chain.

The example of characterising capabilities is crucial in achieving the best-suited eco-conservativeness through fully-structured entrepreneurial profitability. They help explain why the net organisation's technology is necessary.

The benefits of interactive communication networks, in addition to linking people anywhere in the world come from their capability of granting the job «visibility» and enabling the direct control of the organisation's efficiency and the transaction's real usefulness. Both aspects were in the background of most bureaucratic accomplishments, leading to masking productivity if the cost was simply transferred to the citizens through fiscal measures. The knowledge society, from this standpoint, qualifies progress at least through the operation's transparency and instrumental neutrality.

The knowledge infrastructure characterises a set of aspects (Michelini & Razzoli, 2008 b) having a unifying motivation on the business project, even if enforced by mandatory bylaws:

- Varying-geometry boundaries expand over every view specifying the products-services
- Embedded simulation-emulation tools allow virtual behavioural experimentations
- Co-operative infrastructure supports problem-solving issues, and is open to multiple-domain experts
- Automatic propagation of changes with consistent updating of the super-model data-frame
- Straightforward evaluation of alternatives, trends, risks, etc., based on reliable relational schemes
- Rapid producibility, affordability, etc. and analyses performed via intelligent decision support
- Fast and accurate exploration of lifecycle occurrences to broaden concept-to-production figures
- Efficient archival of globally accessible knowledge bases, readily available for current activity
- Ubiquitous service through the extended enterprise, enabling effective, inter-operable tools
- Any similar opportunities of advanced PLM surroundings that present IT tools can provide.

On such premises the advanced enterprise's solution is achieved after the incorporation of all *externalities* into the company's accomplishments. Certainly, the usual manufacturing process does not yet cover the SE and RL duties which end at the *point-of-sale*, and are not involved in *point-of-service* and *end-of-life* tasks. Thus the *extended* enterprise challenge is worth investigating.

The idea is to distinguish the technicalities, namely, the facilities/functions needed for the timely *product-service* delivery from the actual corporate assembly. The «buy or do» axiom suggests the ability to look at the «enterprise's capability» as a dynamic allocation of facilities/functions to be developed into the 2P2E frames and continually modified, depending on the lifestyle demand. The 2P2E integration is just one step ahead of the earlier 2P practice. The advanced enterprise develops as a cluster of nodes, interfaced to fulfil each arising business project demand. The partnership exploits a balanced scorecard to fulfil the information *planner*-to-*supplier* cross-flow with local-to-global perspectives planning, as seen in Figure 5. The local tier plans the *two-port* cross-flow using the *inner-outer* scheduler in view of intra-organisation prospects.

The focus of the *planner* is to handle the input requests. The case reverses for the *supplier*, which has to deal with the subsequent nodes, assuring they are correct. Every local tier sorts out many relationships. The node fixes its inner setting, amalgamates the planner/supplier work-flow, and generates the schedules for the aggregation of duties. The net concern allows:

- the team partner to establish the value delivery flow; create the mission-driven service change; explore self-mending measurements; ensure the behaviour accountability and recording; allow the allotted tasks negotiation; help define trends and detect out-of-bound threats; retain liability for calling and running reviews and executing any decisions; etc.
- the business ruler (dominant trader): intervenes when the nodes run into problems; ensures the consistency of overall assessments; defines policies and decides corrective actions; negotiates contracts; es-

Figure 5. The two-port local planner/supplier node, with inner/outer scheduler

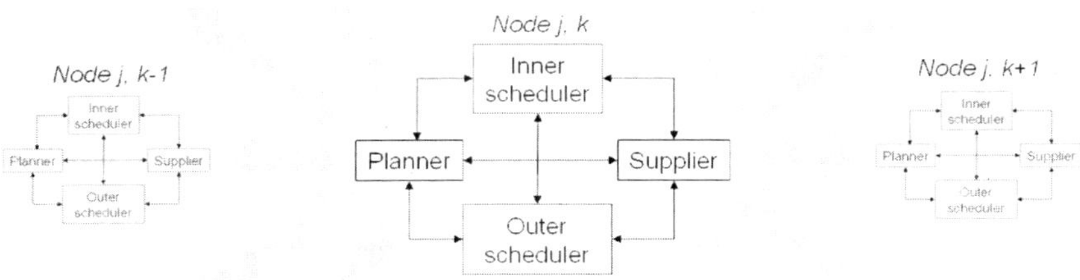

tablishes any general rules and assures the project's progression.

In abstract, the business ruling means managing the supply chain, transmitting the rising deeds to the partners, and enabling bottom-up collaboration aimed at fulfilling the business project:

- The transition fixes the local tier behaviour, giving the planner/supplier schedules conditioned by the inner/outer perspectives
- The inner perspectives show the local performance through standards taken from the shared measures list, and expresses the assessments after cross-examination
- The planner schedules, giving the joint assessments of the node and each of its feeders, which is eventually averaged through measures drawn from the standard performance measures list
- The supplier schedules, providing the integrated output interface, jointly weighing with each client and using the shared performance measures list from the averaged cross-flow raw data
- The outer perspectives adapt the pooled requirements drawn from the shared performance measures list and produce the output affecting the involved net-concern nodes.

The *net-concern* value added appraisal is established in the deliberate self-ruling frame, by quickly specifying the supply constraints raised at the project stage between co-operating partners or at more structured stages of *virtual/extended* enterprises with the lawful responsibility on the delivered *products-services*.

The performance assessment permits an understanding of the networking value added. The appraisal, at the unstructured stage, of course only makes sense at the node level. Even so, the remarks that follow suggest using a method consistent with the surroundings' *complexity*. At the *virtual* or *extended* structure stage, the bottom up appraisal permits distinguishing each partner's benefit from the overall project profitability. The method is sketched in the following, to promote the entrepreneurial spirit toward the advanced enterprise's solution, once the return on investment is assessed.

BUSINESS INFRA-ORGANISATION APPRAISAL

The assessment method is based on two assumptions (Cunha & Putnik, 2006; Michelini, 2009):

- the existence of the appropriate facility/function market, where each time partners are picked up, assuring the requested competences and capabilities

- the availability of lawful and smart negotiation, assemblage, and management aids, through which dynamic corporate up-dating becomes a standard option.

For explanatory purposes, we distinguish three infrastructural levels (Michelini & Razzoli, 2005):

- the networked affiliation links (independent) partners co-operating without sole and permanent bonds, with the value added information and communication technology tools
- the virtual enterprise net-concern builds on the unique business project, with partners' bonds, perpetually oriented at the product-service provision, under binding legal constrictions
- the extended enterprise net-concern establishes the responsibility of the manufacturer or equivalent representative, who maintains the product-service provision's total liability.

The bottom up performance measurement deals with node and network properties. The node is the unit of service responsible for formulating, detailing, and distributing the information concerning the locally allotted directions and requirements of the co-operating partners. At the lowest stand, the efficiency depends on the networking virtues (out of the all product-service conceptions and rulings), permitting value added deployment. The examination covers a set of accomplishments used as a self-assessment check of the business' profitability:

At the node range:

- *assessment aids: the facilities set-up evaluation of decision support tools, to deal with the feeder/receiver and inner/outer perspectives*
- *impact certification: the eco-consistency is assessed, and conformance-to-use checks are assigned to (third-party) accredited bodies*
- *issues monitoring: the co-operation (cost, time, conformance, quality, etc.) which is granted full visibility and the predicted compatibility is shown*
- *shared metrics: the nodes standards are taken from the agreed measurements list, with the ability to establish, revise, or cancel out the metrics.*

At the concern range:

- *control and govern: each node operates autonomously, performing decision-keeping and issues communication that allows on-process interaction*
- *deployment trend: the ability to create 'value' goes beyond the performance measurement, by training/learning aids based on the up-graded net-concern setting*
- *duty organisation: clear-cut responsibility management for allocation, co-operation, achievement, etc. assigning tasks, specifying goals and clout, and developing and managing the business*
- *integration modes: the facility/function market is accessed to find out, negotiate, and assemble the partner cluster that grants enhanced deliveries.*

At the project range:

- *policy and objectives: the business consistency and appropriateness are analysed as overall outcome, using market-driven cost/benefit figures*
- *strategy choice: the performance figure is dealt with for strategic resetting, guaranteeing the involvement (and assent) of all (active) partners*

- *tactical setting: the current facilities/functions steering is done by the business ruler (dominant trader), according to the chosen policy and objectives*
- *up-grading planning: the net concern is thought out with an evolving structure, through new partners and facility/function incorporation.*

The weight and rank of each of the twelve self-assessment tests depends on the application and changes made when the policies and/or objectives were modified. The overall figure is important to assess the networking value added, notably, when the eco-service duties are performed within administrative regimes under governmental authorities.

The assessment procedure is the most important procedure for partners operating within *virtual* enterprises to fulfil the analysis in respect to competitors, in order to adjust the cluster «instantiation» up to the most effective functions or facilities incorporated. The evaluation of entrepreneurial know-how becomes instrumental in deriving and propagating the new forms of network-based industrial organisations. The eco-duties, fixed by administrative bylaws, aims at infra-organisational settings, with organisational managers and integration brokers (Michelini & Razzoli, 2008 c):

At the node range:

- *efficiency: the entrepreneurship value is affected by the information hurriedness, completeness, and reliability exchanging/managing among the business partners*
- *involvement: the partnership aims at co-designing, co-producing, co-selling, and co-supporting the delivery to customers' satisfaction and third-parties' protection*
- *partnership: the net-concern nodes may or may not be linked hierarchically, dominated by the market objectives and co-operation abilities*
- *technologies: the core-competency compatibility allows organisation effectiveness, by net and decision tools to make the integration work.*

At the concern range:

- *collaboration: each one treats the other as a business partner, allowing and accepting the other's requests in view of the chosen business*
- *duration: within the project scope, the nodes share a unified vision and work to accomplish the product-service delivery*
- *integration: the business ruler (configuration manager or dominant trader only) resorts to brokers' help for facilities/functions negotiation and incorporation*
- *ruling: the decision-making aims at the best use of the partners' competencies and accounts for the scheduled common goal subscribed at the cluster setting/resetting.*

At the project range:

- *communication: the information sharing, on-line and in real-time, needs to grant in-progress collaboration up-dating between autonomic units*
- *drivers: the supply chain complexity, covering multi point-of-service engagements, requires the manufacturer and provision clustering comparable sophistication*
- *size: the setting occurs among the nodes and across the value chain, dynamically adapting the partnership to the on-progress supply chain*
- *structure: the fitting will take the form of net concern, where each partner is a node (with one or more input and output links).*

The lifestyle provisioning requires a responsive trader allied with all pertinent partners with a view of optimising the business opportunity, the buyers' satisfaction, and environmental protection. The networking effectiveness, Figure 5, depends on the interplay with the control agency, or the service integration of the supply manager. The project's overall betterment needs a series of accomplishments at the intra-organisational setting, typically ruled by the main manufacturer, when the network configuration manager oversees the entire product-service value chain:

At the node range:

- *involvement: service provision is a standard duty because the right facility/function competencies inclusion is fully defined by the ruling manufacturer*
- *partnership: the three-party scheme binds the suppliers (product/service dealers), the buyers, and the certifying body (for the results of overseeing and recording).*

At the concern range:

- *integration: lifelong responsiveness admits business assistants out of the main manufacturer operating under proper accreditation*
- *ruling: the provider's commitment is fixed through voluntary agreements with clients and when requested compulsory achievements with governmental authorities.*

At the project range:

- *drivers: the stipulation covers the product lifecycle, fully engaging for the conformance-to-use service and end-of-life take-back, accounting for enacted eco-regulations*
- *structure: the net-concern has to reach self-consistent lay-out, confining the «virtual» setting to brokers/agencies only for facilities/functions choice and appraisal.*

The transition from the net-concern and *virtual* setting to *extended* enterprise involves revising the business integration at the entrepreneurial level. Then it is based on the overall supply chain's unified responsibility to incorporate *externalities* carried within the scope of *internalities*. Becoming a permanent achievement, the *extended* enterprise has the company ruler managing the necessary facilities and functions with a view of optimising the unified provision and eco-protection duties.

The permanent supply of on-duty and end-of-life eco-services obviously needs to turn towards the *extended/virtual* enterprise levels, since the government administered level has hidden costs which are not easy to remove. The *virtual* vs. *extended* enterprise choice depends on the local entrepreneurial context. If no advanced enterprise develops, factual replacement encourages outcome. The efficiency in this dilemma requires the distinguishing of the internal viewpoints, where the self-assessments are carried on at the bottom-up base from the external viewpoints where (by the top-down project/concern/node logic) the single partner ranking is accomplished to appraise the entire infra-organisation value added. Additionally, the evaluation discerns the *extended* and *virtual* enterprise cases in terms of intra-organisational features along with the above outlined checks:

At the project range:

- *brokerage aid: the business ruler and on-the-market facilities/functions intermediation can be carried by a domain broker or forced by governmental agencies*
- *function/facility market: the core-competencies to be incorporated by net-concern are accessed from the facility/function market after specific enquiry*
- *facilities assembly: the entrepreneurial assembly will identify the (stable) extended enterprise, by addressing the current supply chain virtual set-up*
- *re-setting rules: the supply chain servicing and end-of-life call-back imply constant*

up-dating of the net-concern partnership to include the pertinent facilities.

At the concern range:

- *information system: the scope and organisation are ranked by competitive comparisons, using benchmarking indices*
- *business ruler: the business opportunity is made up to entail worldwide leadership, having vision of the sought market share*
- *net management: the productive lay-out, support services, and business processes are sustained and ruled by the transparent partners' co-operation*
- *strategic enhancer: the included and timely core-competencies are ranked by the innovative jobs synthetic figures and the resulting net-concern complex outcomes.*

At the node range:

- *local leadership: manufacturer's responsibility requires defining the reference dealer, even if specific/shared charges are managed according to contract rules*
- *notification duties: environmental protection is subjected to enacted mandatory targets and the issues are brought to the attention of the overseeing authority*
- *operation achievements: the on-duty monitoring and conformance-to-use assessment require co-operation in order to make transparent the responsibility attribution*
- *customer satisfaction: current and final approval is ruled by voluntary agreement protocols in addition to the enacted compulsory targets.*

External viewpoints are helpful indicators for estimating the intra-organisational entrepreneurial deeds and listing the business integration's main features. Dissimilar lists are possible. The choices are suggested based on the selected economy of scope policy. The combined top-down/bottom-up networking value-added benefits evaluation shows the potential of the partnership build up. This is important from the 'node' standpoint, to appreciate the temporary aggregation/merging that takes place to answer a given business problem or question. The process is deemed to evolve from the bottom up, as the single function/facility provider is supposed to have self-sufficiency, autonomy, and to negotiate the partnership after the advantages are properly weighed.

The bottom-up performance appraisal needs to be comprised of all the measures made between the group of *planners* and those of the group of *suppliers*, along with the overlapping risk which always affects complex structures. The value added measurement at the tier's cross-flow depends on the local viewpoints and shall be appropriately balanced by the intra-organisational prospects. The top-down finding is less sensitive to complexity drawbacks, but cannot exploit sharply defined metrics. Regardless, the devised procedure provides preliminary guesses.

The partnership dynamic negotiation, integration, and up-dating are wholly linked to the on-going *product-service* delivery. The business does not end at the point-of-sale. It expands at the points-of-service (for control, maintenance, conformance assessment, restoration, etc.) and includes the take-back of the end-of-life items (for recovery-reuse-recycle targets and waste dumping duties). Today, manufacturers' affairs end mainly at the point-of-sale, with the tiny exception of the operation instructions and maintenance data sheets, given by the product lifecycle management, PLM, and other aids.

The net-concern new business opportunities largely go beyond traditional manufacturing duties. It permits linked partners to co-operate within the common project, assemble expertise, and add matching capabilities whether or not they are required. The function/facility assembly allows lifestyle supply chains' efficient answer, maintaining the core activity even when non-proprietary processes are involved and accomplishments are enforced by law. The business project leads to the addition of competencies to be built around (as closely as possible to) the supply chain for the buyers' satisfaction and environmental protection. Networking at the concern range implies effectiveness through information infrastructures and a series of opportunities in data-base management, communication transparency, and collaborative ruling.

The evolution from the *networked* affiliation to the *extended/virtual* enterprise organisation will develop when technology-driven actors exist, having the best-suited ICT competence and capabilities. A further condition for this development is the improvement of an economically sound answer to proper socio-political requests. The framework will settle the pertinent function/facility market with annexed backing and brokerage aids to potentially assemble complementary organisations. The assessment procedure is just a step of the interplay and is critical for showing the return on investment.

The example cases discussed in the investigation suggest that the lifestyle business should separately tackle the *on-duty* backing. Advanced enterprises could eventually deploy based on efficient PLM-SE tools, drawing them up on a *voluntary agreement* basis. The *end-of-life* duties are a rather different situation. Here, the specified recovery (reuse, recycle) targets are enacted due to compulsory bylaws. The administrative ruling of governmental agencies happens to be a heavy burden, with a huge opacity in the cost build up which is only slightly mitigated by *networked* affiliation nodes. The *extended* enterprise solution maximally depends on the manufacturers' capacity to fit in the full *externalities* as the current economy of scope accomplishments. The *virtual* enterprise alternative is a transitional step, to be carefully appraised if it is to be profitably reached.

CONCLUSION

The «service» value added in the future is important to channel wealth build-up towards «intangibles» following the « de-materialise» axiom by which in lieu of «material goods» trading of «functions» takes place. Here, the opportunity is moved a step ahead, looking at market changes promoted by the additional manufacturers' responsibilities requiring their involvement in the lifelong supply chains for the provisions of conformance-to-use certification and end-of-life recovery (reuse and recycle). These changes entail looking at the advantages of networking. Hence, the outlined study looks at the different possible outcomes of: *governmental agencies*, *net-concerns*, and *virtual/extended* enterprises. The evaluation of the cost/benefit ratio each time a relevant requirement is achieved, both in the immediate term and for longer terms, fall-out, has to be done.

Explanatory suggestions are obtained considering the regulations foreshadowed by EU directives. The eco-protection against on-duty common durables (cars, home cauldrons, etc.) requires periodic conformance-to-use checks charged to the users as the producers' responsibility ends at the point-of-sale. The fee is fixed at the administrative level, incorporating the governmental tax. Recently, the *free* take-back of *end-of-life vehicles* and of *waste-electrical-electronic-equipment* is an obligation to include in the items' markets, with mandatory recovery (reuse, recycle) pre-set targets. The assembly of accidental *net*-concerns eventually assuring the on-duty conformance-to-use certification is then out-of-date and for the *end-of-life vehicles*, three issues emerge:

- the deposit-refund scheme (Sweden model): the cost is fixed by the governmental agency which oversees the lawful accomplishment of the compulsory reverse logistic demands

- the visible-fees scheme (Dutch model): the duty is ruled by the area foundation, acting as a broker to engage the right partners taken from the existing function/facility market
- the extended enterprise scheme (German model): the product-service provision includes the end-of-life call-back, since carmakers guarantee reverse logistic duties.

The charge analysis is instructive. The first and second schemes address the *virtual* enterprise setting, with rulers outside the manufacturers. The big disparity of costs shows the administrative lack of efficiency, with large users getting penalized. In any event, all the charges are even bigger when no overseeing ruler exists and the reverse logistic is managed on fortuitous arrangements adding administrative taxes to the businesses' impromptu reclamation. Quite often, this situation leads to the unlawful rejection of wrecks, the (actual) consumers' profit, and community damage. The *extended* enterprise scheme internalises the reverse logistic costs, and this choice fosters competition among producers to optimise all of their *product-services*.

In any case, the pre-emptive appraisal of lifestyle provisioning is fundamentally required. The alternative suggested here combines the bottom-up procedure of the nodes' self-assessment (to clearly show each partner's benefit), with the stepwise appraisal of the networking, the *virtual*, and the *extended* partnership's value added. The evaluation is further shown in standard contexts by the top-down rule, to provide third party rates. The *extended* enterprise has the chance of optimal *product-service* delivery fixed at the design stage through the coherent fourfold interplay of the **2P2E** frames.

ACKNOWLEDGMENT

The chapter is based on the material presented in the paper:

Michelini, R.C., Razzoli, R.P. (2009, October). *Lifecycle design supply chain: net value-added appraisal.* International Conference on Enterprise Information Systems, Ofir, Portugal.

We gratefully acknowledge conference organisers' acceptance of republishing part of the text and figures.

REFERENCES

Acaccia, G. M., Kopàcsi, S., Kovàcs, G., Michelini, R. C., & Razzoli, R. P. (2007 a). Service engineering and extended artefact delivery. In Putnik, G. D., & Cunha, M. M. (Eds.), *Knowledge and Technology Management in Virtual Organisations: Integration: Issues, Trends, Opportunities and Solutions* (pp. 45–77). Hershey, PA: IGI Global.

Acaccia, G. M., Michelini, R. C., Penzo, L., & Qualich, N. (2007 b). Reverse logistics and resources recovery: modelling car dismantling facilities. *World Review of Science. Technology and Sustainable Development*, *4*(4/5), 284–332.

Acaccia, G. M., Michelini, R. C., & Qualich, N. (2007 c). Sustainable engineering management: end-of-life vehicles with recycling in mind. *World Review of Science. Technology and Sustainable Development*, *4*(2/3), 105–125. doi:10.1504/WRSTSD.2007.013578

Acaccia, G. M., Michelini, R. C., Qualich, N., & Razzoli, R. P. (2008). Logistica inversa: dalla dismissione, al recupero, riuso, riciclo. In R. Mosca (Ed.), Teoria, Metodi e Modelli per la Logistica e la Logistica Inversa (pp. 219-285). Milano, IT: Franco Angeli.

Anufriev, A., Kopàcsi, S., Kovàcs, G., & Michelini, R. C. (2007). Ambient intelligence as enabling technology for modern business paradigms. *Journal of Robotics and Computer Integrated Manufacturing, 23*(2), 242–256. doi:10.1016/j.rcim.2006.01.002

Cunha, M. M., & Putnik, G. D. (2006). *Agile virtual enterprises: implementation and management support*. Hershey, PA: IGI Global.

Kopàcsi, S., Kovàcs, G., Haidegger, G., & Michelini, R. C. (2006). Ambient intelligence in product lifecycle design. *Journal of Engineering Applications of Artificial Intelligence, 19*(8), 953–965. doi:10.1016/j.engappai.2006.01.017

Michelini, R. C. (2008). *Knowledge entrepreneurship and sustainable growth*. New York: Nova Science Pub. Inc.

Michelini, R. C. (2009). *The robot age knowledge changeover*. New York: Nova Science Pub. Inc.

Michelini, R. C., & Kovàcs, G. (2002). Integrated design for sustainability: intelligence for eco-consistent products-and-service. *The Estonian Business School Review, 15*, 81–95.

Michelini, R. C., & Razzoli, R. P. (2004 a). Product-service eco-design: knowledge-based infrastructures. *International Journal of Cleaner Production, 12*(4), 415–428. doi:10.1016/S0959-6526(03)00036-2

Michelini, R. C., & Razzoli, R. P. (2004 b). Product-service for environmental safeguard: a metric to sustainability. *International Journal of Resources. Conservation and Recycling, 42*(1), 83–98. doi:10.1016/j.resconrec.2004.02.005

Michelini, R. C., & Razzoli, R. P. (2005). Collaborative networked organisations for eco-consistent supply-chains. In Putnik, G. D., & Cunha, M. M. (Eds.), *Virtual Enterprise Integration: Technological and Organisational Perspectives* (pp. 45–77). Hershey, PA: IGI Global.

Michelini, R. C., & Razzoli, R. P. (2007, June). *Take-back of end-of-use vehicles, part/material recovery and landfill management*. Paper presented at the XVI ADM International Conference on Tools and Methods Evolution in Engineering Design, Perugia, Italy.

Michelini, R. C., & Razzoli, R. P. (2008 a). Ubiquitous computing & communication for product monitoring. In Khosrow-Pour, M. (Ed.), *Encyclopaedia of Information Science and Technology* (2nd ed., pp. 3851–3857). Hershey, PA: IDEA Group.

Michelini, R. C., & Razzoli, R. P. (2008 b, June). *Modelling and simulation features for products-services*. Paper presented at the International EUROSIS Industrial Simulation Conference, Lyon, France.

Michelini, R. C., & Razzoli, R. P. (2008 c). Innovation for sustainability in product lifecycle design. In Cascini, G. (Ed.), *Computer-Aided Innovation* (pp. 217–228). Boston, MA: Springer. doi:10.1007/978-0-387-09697-1_18

Michelini, R. C., & Razzoli, R. P. (2009). The service net facility integration appraisal. *Int. J. Services. Economics and Management, 1*(4), 371–392.

ADDITIONAL READING

Abels, S., Brehm, N., Hahn, A., & Gómez, J. M. (2006). Change management issues in Federated ERP systems: an approach for identifying requirements and possible solutions. *International Journal of Information Systems and Change Management, 1*(3), 318–335. doi:10.1504/IJISCM.2006.011202

Antonelli, C. (1995). *The economics of localised technological change and industrial dynamics*. Boston, MA: Kluwer.

Baskin, A. B., Kovacs, G., & Jacucci, G. (1999). *Cooperative knowledge processing for engineering design*. Boston, MA: Kluwer.

Best, M. H. (2001). *The competitive advantage*. Oxford, UK: Oxford Press. doi:10.1093/0198297459.001.0001

Blumberg, D. F. (2004). *Introduction to management of reverse logistics and closed loop supply chain processes*. Boca Raton, FL: CRC Press.

Borg, J. C., Farrugia, Ph. J., & Camilleri, K. P. (2004). Knowledge-intensive design technology. London, UK: Springer, IFIP Series.

Cascini, G. (Ed.). (2008). *Computer-aided innovation*. Boston, MA: Springer. doi:10.1007/978-0-387-09697-1

Dickhoff, H., Lackes, R., & Reese, J. (2004). *Supply chain management and reverse logistics*. Berlin, DE: Springer.

Forey, D. (2004). *The economics of knowledge*. Cambridge, MA: MIT Press.

Friedman, T. L. (2005). *The world is flat: a brief history of the twenty-first century*. New York: Farrar Straus and Giroux.

Lambert, A. J. D., & Gupta, S. M. (2004). *Disassembly modelling for assembly, maintenance, reuse and recycling*. Boca Raton, FL: CRC Press.

Liu, J. X. (2005). *New developments in robotics research*. Nova Science.

Mo, J. P. T., & Nemes, L. (Eds.). (2001). *Global engineering, manufacturing and enterprise networks*. New York: Kluwer Academic.

Muller, E. (2001). *Innovation interactions between knowledge-intensive business services and small-and-medium sized enterprises: an analysis in terms of evolution, knowledge and territories*. Berlin, DE: Springer.

Nevins, J. L., Whitney, D. E., & DeFazio, T. L. (1989). *Concurrent design of products and processes*. New York: McGraw Hill.

Oesterle, H., Fleisch, E., & Alt, R. (2001). *Business networking: shaping collaboration between enterprises*. Berlin, DE: Springer.

Olling, G. J., & Kimura, F. (Eds.). (1992). Human aspects in computer integrated manufacturing. Amsterdam, NL: North-Holland.

Parker, S. (2006). *The lifecycle of entrepreneurial ventures*. London, UK: Springer. doi:10.1007/978-0-387-32313-8

Parsaei, H., Usher, J., & Roy, U. (1998). *Integrated product and process development: methods, tools, and technologies*. New York: John Wiley.

Schoensleben, P. (2004). *Integral logistics management: planning and control of comprehensive supply chains*. Boca Raton, FL: CRC Press.

Sherman, H. D., & Zhu, J. (2006). *Service productivity management: improving service performance by data envelopment analysis*. London, UK: Springer.

Suhas, H. K. (2001). *From quality to virtual enterprise: an integrated approach*. Boca Raton, FL: CRC Press.

Teuteberg, F. (2003). Experimental evaluation of a model for multilateral negotiation with fuzzy preferences on an agent-based marketplace. *International Journal of Electronic Commerce & Business Media, 13*(1), 21–32.

Weber, M. K., & Hemmelskamp, J. (2004). *Toward environmental innovation systems*. Berlin, DE: Springer.

Wingand, R., Picot, A., & Reichwald, R. (1997). *Information, organisation & managing: expanding markets and corporate boundaries*. Chichester, UK: John Wiley.

Womack, J. P., Ross, D., & Jones, D. T. (1990). *The machine that changed the world*. New York: Rawson.

Chapter 22
Effective Stakeholder Relations:
Sustainability Reporting Topic Maps

Hans-Knud Arndt
Otto-von-Guericke University Magdeburg, Germany

Henner Graubitz
Otto-von-Guericke University Magdeburg, Germany

ABSTRACT

Compared to the DIN EN ISO Standard 14001 every organization has to create – in respect to environmental aspects and environmental system – processes so that internal communications between different organization levels and function, or proper questions and answer coming from outer site could be guaranteed. One of the possibilities to realize these requirements is the introduction of an organization wide GRI-guideline, created by the idea of the Global Reporting Initiative (GRI), which can easily be published in the Internet. But normally not all environmental information is necessary for everybody, resulting in an information flood. Following the idea to represent special information to special interest groups we present an idea of how to convert these sustainability reports into a Topic Maps by using eXtensible Business Reporting Language (XBRL).

RELATED WORK

Regarding the economical success for global acting organizations[1] the sustainability reporting plays an importing role in future time. Three things are responsible for these reasons. First of all these organizations are confronted with lawful duties created by its domestic governments. Domestic governments are in a worldwide competition to reduce environmental pollution because there might be the possibility to loose positive environmental reputation globally. Additionally organizations get the chance to publish volunteered environmental facts about their organization to reveal weak ecological points. Nonetheless - correlated to decades before - with the growing up Internet these organizations get the chance to publish their sustainability report worldwide by creating documents which can be downloaded from their Internet sites. That means that on the one hand these organization get a low cost tool to keep their positive environmental reputation, on the other

DOI: 10.4018/978-1-61520-981-1.ch022

hand instead of producing paper made brochure they deliver these information in environment-friendly efficient way.

Looking onto the history a few organizations started to distribute their reports in 1992 following the rules of (IISD, 1992) or later with (UNEP, 2002) which resulted in subjectively positive reports because these concerns could publish whatever they wanted. With the publication of the Global Reporting Initiative (GRI) guidelines (cf. below) these habits changed. Organizations were not anymore allowed to voluntary publish environmental facts, with the GRI guidelines these concerns got a tool which describes "how" they can publish these facts (Marshall & Brown, 2003).

But publishing sustainable reports means distributing paper-bound reports via transport systems which also produces environmental damages and which - in sum - stands for a conflict between a "green" reputation and a organization which will inform about its environmental facts. The raising growth of the Internet gave a solution for this problem. According to KPMG 2008 more than 90% of the queried persons answered that they "want to understand the specific sustainability issues of the company" while additionally 70% answered that they "use it for general understanding of the company". In fact, about 50% of the queried persons answered that they inform their self because they "want to buy the products or services of the company".

Associated to the study of IÖW & future (2007) that could be one reason why – in contrast to the ranking of 2005 – all DAX-30-organizations started to create sustainability reports in 2008. That means that all major German organizations, which are traded in the blue chip stock market index at the Frankfurt Stock Exchange, follow the goal to publish their environmental acting. But IÖW future (2007) also mentions that these organizations publish in a some how form which means that these organizations are unsure about the format of the sustainability report. Like (Arndt et al., 2004) there is the chance to build up sustainability reporting on an XML standard while (Arndt et al., 2006) starts to convert XBRL to a topic map which is not Internet compatible. But these conversion are not flexible and stands in contrast to KPMG (2008) where more than 50% of the queried persons stands for the opinion that they "don't have time to navigate deep websites or lengthy reports to find the information" they need and are "not aware of the possible value of sustainability reports". These queried persons just want to get a small overview about their personal interests.

Compared to Isenmann et al. (2006) or Isenmann et al. (2009) there is a chance to create "sustainability reporting a la carte" (Isenmann et al., 2008) but these solution needs manual effort for users and nearly impossible to "navigate" through a special interest values. That's why a more flexible solution should be build up.

THE EXTENSIBLE BUSINESS REPORTING LANGUAGE (XBRL)

Published and pushed by the American Institute of Certified Public Accountants (AICPA), the largest professional organization of Certified Public Accountants (CPAs) in the United Stated of America, the eXtensible Business Reporting Language (XBRL) is an XML-standard for storing financial information in different organizations. For example XBRL can be used to store financial information in headquarters, or its subsidiaries. But normally the detailed financial information, its quality, and its formats are different which results in making it more difficult to manage the information exchange between a organization and its affiliated organizations. To enable the exchange of financial reporting in all its different procedures the standards of the approved eXtensible Markup Language (XML), e.g. the XBRL standard, can be used. It gives organizations the chance to inform shareholders, banks, investors, or other interested parties about common organization's projects. Additionally XBRL, as all XML standards, can easily be delivered via networks and analyzed with common software products. Looking onto other similar exchange formats following the same goal (e.g. Open Financial Exchange (OFX), Research Information Exchange Markup Language (RIXML), Markup Language for the Financial Information eXchange (FIX), Market Data Definition Language (MDDL), or Application Message Layer (FIXML)) the XBRL standard can be described as the modern standard to exchange financial information, mainly used by international acting organizations which is mostly used by organizations in North America. In 2006 the XBRL community published a standard, which can be defined as a number of report concepts as well as its respective contents (XBRL, 2006a). These two things can be separated into instances and taxonomies (XBRL, 2006b). Instances use xlinks (eXtended links, W3C Xlink 2001) to a corresponding taxonomy which consists of a W3C XML Schema modeling descriptions. Depending on which taxonomy is used these files have the following content:

- **Labels:** Beside of using different multilingual descriptions a label gives the element in an instance a name. While using a language attribute in its element a corresponding foreign language and label can be mentioned. This makes it easy to display elements multilingual.
- **References:** While using a linkbase references make it possible for users to add information to, or delete information from a label. For instance a label which contains information about a law can be explained better if a linkbase to an external description of this law exists.
- **Definition:** Definition linkbases make it possible to bring variant labels into a ranked order. For example typical XML father-child or child-father hierarchies can be created. E.g. this linkbase give you the option to split an accounting "sum" into "sub-instances" and "subtotals".
- **Presentation**: This linkbase follows the concept to make a better granular order available for child elements. The presentation linkbase can be described as an extension of the definition linkbase which makes brother-sister relationship available.
- **Calculation:** For XBRL the calculation linkbase can be described as the base of all linkbases. It contains information about relationships between elements and its corresponding operators, e.g. plus, minus, division, or multiply. Additional Binstock et al. (2005) mention that this linkbase enables to create semantic relations in XBRL files.

Summarized all taxonomy files give instance files the possibility to display its content in the right format at the right place (XBRL, 2006c). Compared to XBRL (2006c) a set of specific taxonomy files is also called Discoverable Taxonomy Set (DTS) which can be separated into three levels: recommended taxonomies must have the same official status of the XBRL specification itself. Approved ones are taxonomies which are compliant the XBRL specification and have been developed by the XBRL interest group. In contrast acknowledged taxonomies are taxonomies which are used compliant to the XBRL specification but are developed by other interest groups.

THE STANDARDIZATION IN SUSTAINABILITY REPORTING

Developed to provide environmental knowledge, sustainability reports contain information about environmental sustain developments of specific organizations. Usually, after financial reports,

Figure 1. Overview of GRI Standard Disclosures (Source: GRI 2006, 19)

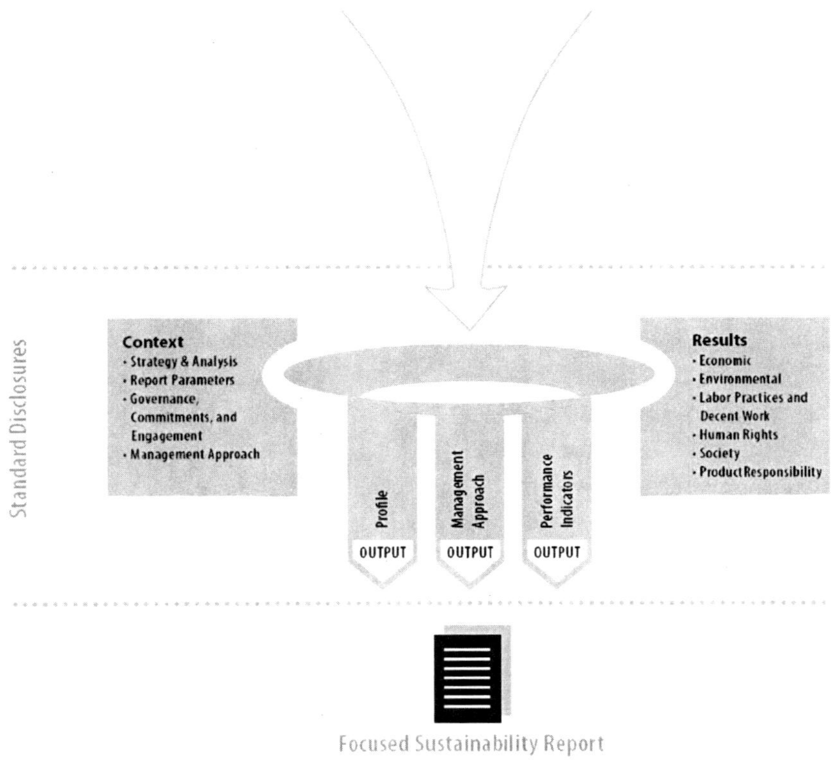

these sustainability reporting are one of the most important tools to distribute information about environmental developments in organizations.

For instance global acting major corporations use this possibility to publish their social respective duties to interested groups. Additionally it gives major corporations the possibility to provide an additional marketing tool for itself.

Influenced by the Global Reporting Initiative (GRI), a non-governmental international organization launched in 1997 as a joint initiative of the Coalition for Environmentally Responsible Economics (CERES) and the United Nations Environment Program (UNEP), sustainability reports are build on an environmental, a social, and an economic performance. Each of these performances can be described a pillar which interact and effect each other. One of the GRI's visions about reporting has been illustrated with the statement "that reporting on economic, environmental, and social performance by all organizations becomes as routine and comparable as financial reporting."

Like Morhardt (2002) this can be done by distributing global applicable guidelines expects that "its guideline will become the de facto standard for sustainability reporting worldwide."

Based on a worldwide acting community from all areas of business and civil society the third generation (G3) of guidelines has been released and changed after the GRI G3 conference from a former "draft version" to a "ready for use" one (GRI, 2006). Taking the last draft the G3-Guidelines can be divided into three main parts: Part 1 defines report content, boundary, and quality, while Part 2 describes standard disclosures. Part 3 contains general reporting notes.

G3-GUIDELINES PART 1: DEFINING REPORT CONTENT, QUALITY, AND BOUNDARY

Part 1 contains ten basic topics which should be included into a sustainability report. These topics form the basic of the report and can be described the essentials of a report:

1. **Stakeholder Inclusiveness:** The organization has to concentrate on its stakeholders and their feedbacks. That's why all players inside and outside of an organization should be identified and mentioned in the report.
2. **Materiality:** All subject matter and signals which influences economic, environmental, and social impacts or stakeholders decisions should be mentioned. Additionally materiality represents at which threshold topics and indicators should be remarked.
3. **Sustainability Context:** One of the goals of creating these reports can be seen in representing the environmental sustainable acting of an organization. That's why topics and signals should be described with a clear and wide context of sustainability. Relationships between sustainability subjects and non-subjects will be cleared.
4. **Completeness:** There are a lot of things which can cause the economic, environmental, and social performance and which should be mentioned in the report. One of the goals should be seen in the complete description of all boundaries, scopes, and its corresponding time periods.
5. **Balance:** The environmental characteristics can not only be seen in positive facets: also the negative ones should be described in a report. The organization should try to give a balanced report, consisting of positive and negative environmental facets. Only this guarantees a non-biased view of the organization.
6. **Comparability:** The organization has to mention a harmonious uniformity with its boundary and scopes of its reports, e.g. by discover any changes, and restate of previously reported in-formation.
7. **Accuracy:** With the accuracy principle the organization focus on a concentration of a high degree of exactness. That means that business partners will make quicker decisions while they can trust this information.
8. **Timeliness:** Like financial annual reports also sustainability reports should be published frequently in predefined periods. Normally both, the stakeholders "timetable" and the schedule of the information should be respected and inline.
9. **Clarity:** The quality of being believable or trustworthy should be one of the highest goals of an organization. That's why reports should be written capable of being apprehended. Additionally it should include all processes, procedures, and assumptions.
10. **Reliability:** Reported information should be gathered, recorded, compiled, analyzed, and disclosed in a way that would resist every examination, internally and externally.

G3-GUIDELINES PART 2: STANDARD DISCLOSURES

The Part 2 references to the basic content which should be represented in a sustainability report:

1. **Strategy and Analysis:** All sustainability must add a part containing a nonverbal message of the representatives of an organization e.g. the chief executive officer (CEO). The representative should report the organization's key impacts, risk involving danger, and possibilities due to the current favorable combination of circumstances which are involved in the publication of the report.

2. **Organizational Profile:** Assorted knowledge about an organization must be added to the sustainability report, which should include regional, national and international roles while also organizational Meta information like the organizations name, its brands, or commodities offered for sale should be mentioned.
3. **Reported Parameters:** Normally the guideline of the reported parameter is divided into four parts: the first part consists of the report profile which expects information about the date the report has been written, its periodical returns, and contact information for questions or feedbacks. The second part called "Report Scope and Boundary" gives comprehensible information of what will be reported and to which community these information belongs to so that the this part shows it boundaries. "GRI Content Index" is added as the third part into the Reported Parameters and tells about certain report refers to the G3-guidelines. The Reported Parameters closes with "Assurance" which informs about the sustainability report's internal and external assurances.
4. **Governance, Commitments, and Engagement:** Also this guideline is divided into parts: beginning with the first one, "Governance" formalizes the policy, responsibilities, and competencies of the organization. Followed up by "Commitments to External Initiatives" which gives a general summary about non-organizational/external social, economic and environmental initiatives of the reporting organization. This guideline closes with "Stakeholder Engagement" which specifies the stakeholders' involvement beside during the reporting period.
5. **Management Approach and Performance Indicators:** The standard disclosures ends with a description of the economic (like economic conditions), environmental (like on living and non-living natural systems, including all ecosystems), and social indicators (like Human Rights or Society), advances of the executives, and statement about the used performance indicators.

G3-GUIDELINES PART 3: GENERAL REPORTING NOTES

The G3-Guidelines finalize with general reporting notes. It includes advices of how to gather data, the report form and its frequency, and advices of how to choose assurances.

Topic Maps

Following the goal to reach a big audience, organizations publish their sustainability reports via their Internet presence while publishing via ad-hoc messages, print like newspaper, magazines and brochures or news-ticker become negligible. Usually the content of a sustainability report is arranged by its topics, e.g. environmental strategies. But this arrangement produces one disadvantage: the audience of the sustainability report is addressed to lose the overview while informing themselves about one sustainability of one topic. Typically all topics of a sustainability report can be described as a net with a cause and effect. All topics are connected to or influence each other.

The computer science offers a standard to avoid this disadvantage: the ISO/IEC 13250:2000, also known as Topic Maps (TM). These TMs, published as purpose of the Davenport Group (Pepper, 2000), offer you an idea of how to represent knowledge via information technology. Concentrating onto a topic and visualizing all topic relationships to other topics the audience which is interested into the sustainability report gets a better representation what is going on. Nonetheless TMs can be seen as a new way of e-learning: because digital files are used these files can easily be converted into other formats so that interested persons can interact with TMs.

All topics of a TM represent knowledge as a node where each node has a relationship to other nodes where information can be completed. In addition occurrence elements are used. These occurrences inform the viewer which other media (e.g. pictures) can be used to fulfill the information content. TMs can also be subscribed as a specification of the semantic web. Like the semantic web TMs use information technology to build up thesauri, classify topics or create indexes for quicker search.

Following the goal to design TMs more suitable for the Internet TMs have been uplifted in the year 2002. The standard ISO/IEC 13250: 2000 has been improved by the TopicMaps.org author group to the new standard ISO 13250: 2003 (Park, 2002). In contrast to the old standard the new one used the proofed eXtensible Markup Language (XML) and changed its file structure to an eXtensible Markup Topic Map (XTM). With this measurement user of XTMs got the possibility to merge other information sources with the current XTM so the information content could be fulfilled additionally. For example a law could be fulfilled with the full law text or different decisions of justice courts via the Internet.

A large benefit of the new standard is the usage of the element scope. This element can be used to represent a tailored view for different interest groups without recomputing the whole TM. If a person is interested in special topics, e.g. in the CO2 emission the element scope helps to represent a distinct sustainability report. The person is not confronted with an immense information flood which is out of the interest of this person. But while playing with these scope elements readers still have the chance to receive all other information the topic map contains. Readers can receive information e.g. about financial measurements and all relations between the CO2 emission and the financial acting.

TRANSFORMATION PROCESS: GENERATING AN SUSTAINABILITY REPORTING TOPIC MAP (SRTM)

All transformations are based on a created XBRL taxonomy using sustainability reports. These reports are based on Thiessen (2006) and Arndt et al. (Arndt et al., 2006; Arndt et al., 2007a; Arndt et al., 2007b).

The process of how to create a Topic Map out of XBRL files can be done in three steps: the first step is the generation of a general valid XTM out of the box, while the second fulfils this XTM with information step by step using the XBRL taxonomy. Part 3 uses external or internal files to visualize different scopes of the created XTMs.

Because of that TMs are a perfect tool to represent sustainability XBRL. Different information will be distributed to different interest groups without rewriting the whole sustainability report or losing information (Arndt &Günther, 2004). In addition these TMs can be fulfilled with information while using external sources.

The ISO/EC Topic Maps standard 13250 is a standard for describing information structures and associating them with information resources. The enabling of multiple, current views of set of information resources is one of the benefits of topic maps. The development of a topic map for sustainability reporting can help to support the stakeholder inclusiveness.

The process of how to create a Sustainability Reporting Topic Map (SRTM) can be done in three steps: the first step is the generation of a general valid XTM out of the box, while the second fulfills this XTM with information step by step using the SRTA taxonomy. Part three uses external or internal files to visualize different scopes of the created XTMs.

Figure 2. Creating a Sustainability Reporting Topic Map (SRTM)

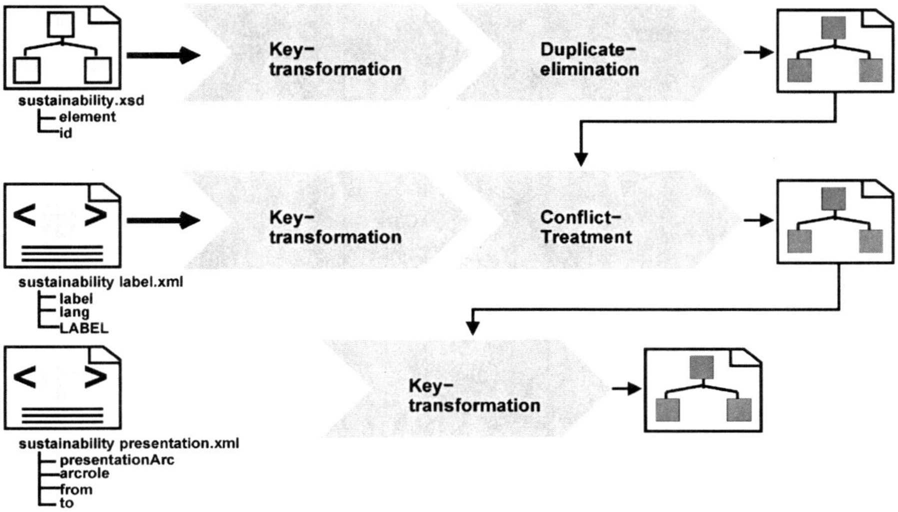

CREATION OF THE XTM

As explained before and in (XBRL 2006b) XBRL taxonomies are divided into two layers: the syntactical and semantic one. Concentrating onto the syntactic layer we can assume that every linkbase has a corresponding element and a locator. Therefore – for all elements – the locator can be linked to an equivalent of the schema file which can be done one by one or together. But what does it mean to link together? Following the eXtensible Markup Language (XML) Standard and its thinking it could mean using the father-child relation on the one hand or the child-father relation on the other hand. Additionally schema offers another feature: it contains XBRL root elements so that an initial starting point for the XBRL to XTM transformation is given.

For a necessary unique topic identifier (ID) an element's attribute can be used: they will be transformed for the resulting XTM. Offered by the XBRL specification an attribute can contain combined strings, e.g. the father-child-node names. A good idea we propose is to use an ending part on an attribute name. Remarked earlier in this article one of the problems could be the deduplication of attribute which can exists. They will be replaced with a unique entry containing all concatenated available information of the same attribute. Because information like a data type is not so important for our XTM this information will be left out.

FULFILL INFORMATION AND EXTRACTION OF THE BASE NAME

The previous section has shown how we can receive predicted IDs. By the usage of the label linkbase we are now able to extract legible multilingual labels because locators for each element in the label linkbase are connected to an element in the schema file. Because the unique ID has been extracted (as described before) we are now able to supply additional names. On the one hand these names can be used as scopes or as multilingual displays. The presentation and definition linkbase can be usage as a utility to obtain child-father relations. Each presentationArc which comes first can be used to establish a hierarchical SRTM

Figure 3. Extracting the Identifiers (IDs)

```
< element
  name =" sustainReport "
  id =" sustainReport "
  type =" xbrli:tupleType "
  substitutionGroup =" xbrli:tuple "/>
< element
  name =" sustainReport
      . strategyAndAnalysis "
  id =" sustainReport
    . strategyAndAnalysis "
  type =" xbrli:tupleType "
  substitutionGroup =" xbrli:tuple "/>
```

```
→ < topic id =" sustainReport "/>
  < topic id =" strategyAndAnalysis "/>
```

structure. In opposite brother-sister relations can be established by using meta-information like "from" and "to".

SPECIALIZATION OF DIFFERENT SCOPES FOR DIFFERENT STAKEHOLDERS

Special views for special interested groups can be built up by adding specialized scopes to the elements in the last creation step. But this can result into name conflict because same names are used. Because topic names, topic anchors, and the topics references are used the idea is to use topic characteristics to add scopes (cf. Figure 4). As mentioned earlier a scope is responsible for giving an application the information which information should be shown to which organization, group, or individual interested person.

E.g. for large TMs this means that a scope filter can be used to reduce the graphical resource which will be used by the application. Additionally user rights can be added while using these filters techniques. For example it would not be a good idea to bring out the quote of how many employees will be fired at the end of the months. Normally this information should be addressed to the organizations execute part and should only be visualized for the "executive level" by using the scope "EXECUTIVE". But an additionally scope "SECRETARY" should avoid the appearance. On the other hand creators of a TM should not create TMs twice, e.g. for different technical terms. For example there could be the possibility that TM creators need special biological terms which should also be understandable for the commonality. In this case they could use the technical term with the scope "biologist" while using a common expression for the scope "commonality". Summarized the scope of a topic map should be chosen very carefully and for the following cases:

- Different languages and different terminology;
- Different access rights;
- Different special target groups;
- Topics (topic maps including different topics should declare the scope of the topic);
- Time: topics which are valid for only a period of time should declare their time scope.

Figure 4. Adding different members to the scopes

```
< association >
  < scope >
    < topicRef xlink:href =" #insurance "/>
    < topicRef xlink:href =" #aktionaer "/>
  </ scope >
  < member >
    < topicRef xlink:href =" #sustainReport "> </ topicRef >
    < topicRef xlink:href =" #ist-in-statementCEO "> </ topicRef >
  </ member >
</ association >
```

Figure 5. Screenshot of the SRTM-Transformer

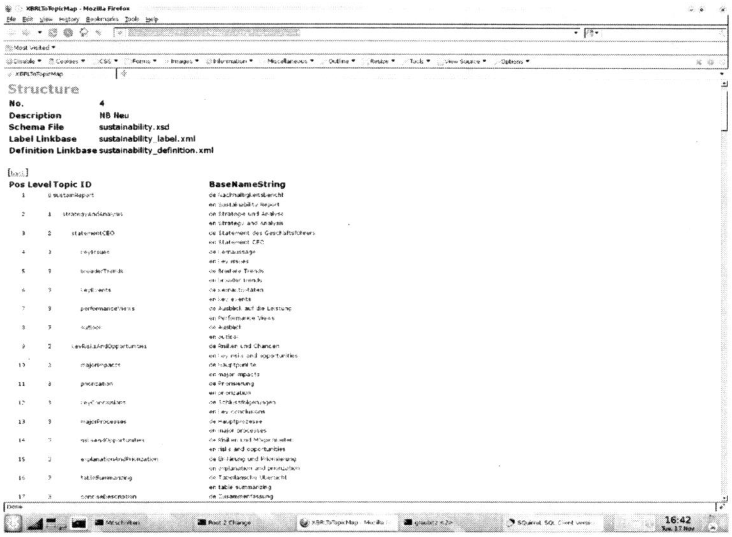

THE APPLICATION

The application consists of two parts: the SRTM-Transformer and WikiTM. Both applications has been implemented as web service. Looking onto the SRTM-Transformer the hardware platform has been realized as a distributed system which consists of a client-part, an application server and a database server. The application server represents a normal physical server with a connection to a network. Its job can be seen as the kernel system where computer programs can be run, which connects the client with the application and which also provides the interface between the application and a database. The application itself has been realized with PHP-5 and an executing Apache Web Server. As mentioned, the application also provides a database server as an independence instance in this system. Our system is based onto the database MySQL. As client a browser can be used (cf. Figure 5).

The SRTM-Transformer itself helps organizations to realize software-based the steps which are described above. User can upload their organization-specific XBRL and automatically – by using standard GRI-XML-Schemas – a Sustainability Reporting Topic Map (SRTM) will be created. Additionally user can enrich the output SRTM with scopes. The output of the application will be provided as downloadable valid eXtensible Topic Maps (XTM), version 1.0, which includes the Sustainable Report as Topic Map.

Because there are no tools to display XTMs "on the fly" another Internet-based application has been realized: WikiTM (http://bauhaus.cs.uni-magdeburg.de/wikitm). WikiTM helps interested people to visualize the live content of the German Wikipedia as Topic Map on the one hand, or upload self-created XTMs, which can be validated against the standard XTM 1.0, and display these XTMs. By drag and drop of the topic onto the search field user get the chance to go through the topics in an effective way, additionally associations or scopes can be visualized (cf. Figure 6).

CONCLUSION

Actual discussion in prints like newspapers or on TV, especially about global warming or CO2

Figure 6. Screenshot of WikiTM, the Internet-based Topic Map Visualizer

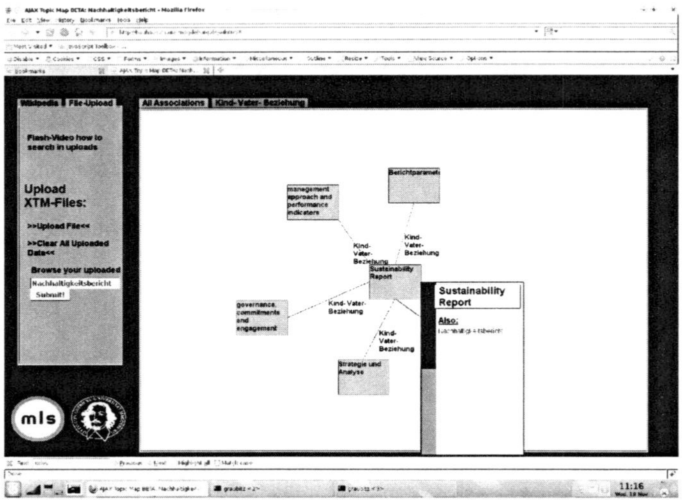

emission, gives us the evidence that organizations consciousness about environment pollution changed or should change in the near future. Especially organizations which are global industry player become a main target for these observations.

Because customers behavior changed as they want to be environment-friendly acting persons and are interested about sustainability of products organizations started to publish their sustainability reports on their Internet sites. Using the GRI-guidelines (GRI, 2006) organizations can use a perfect tool which tells them how to structure these reports.

In this publication we presented an approach of how to transform sustainability reports and make them available via Internet. Our purpose is a further development of a XBRL taxonomy specially used for sustainability reports (Arndt et al., 2006; Arndt et al., 2007a; Arndt et al., 2007b).

Commonly – if you look onto sustainability reporting Internet sites – these Internet sites are packed full with sustainability information separated from other information like financial one. Our suggested format XTM in this article can help organizations to tackle this information flood, produce relationships between sustainability and financial information and using scopes to provide only the information which is requested. Additionally external information (e.g. paragraphs, specifications, pictures) from the Internet can be added to the nodes of the SRTM. Nonetheless organizations use a format which is readable with every software which can display ASCII code and which can easily be exchanged between different offices via Internet.

REFERENCES

Arndt, H. K., Graubitz, H., & Klesinski, R. (2007a). Using Topic Maps for Sustainability Reporting. In J. Marx Gómez, M. Sonnenschein, M. Müller, H. Welsch, & C. Rautenstrauch (Eds.), *Information Technologies in Environmental Engineering – 3rd International ICSC Symposium, Oldenburg 2007, 29.03.-30.03.2007* (pp. 47-59). Berlin/Heidelberg: Springer.

Arndt, H. K., Graubitz, H., & Klesinski, R. (2007b). Sustainability Reporting Topic Maps: An Approach to Support Stakeholder Inclusiveness. In O. Hryniewicz, J. Studzinski, & M. Romaniuk (Eds.): *Environmental Informatics and System Research – 21rst International Conference on Informatics for Environmental Protection, Warsaw 2007, 12.09.-14.09.2007* (pp. 79-86). Aachen: Shaker.

Arndt, H. K., & Günther, O. (2004). Environmental Reporting of Organizations – Extending the XML-based Standardization Using Topic Maps. In P. Minier, & A. Susini (Eds.), *Sh@ring – 18th International Conference Informatics for Environmental Protection, EnviroInfo 2004 CERN Geneva 2004, 21.10.-23.10.2004, Part 2* (pp. 172-183). Geneva: CERN Press.

Arndt, H. K., Isenmann, R., Brosowski, J., Thiessen, I., & Marx Gómez, J. (2006). Sustainability Reporting Using the eXtensible Business Reporting Language (XBRL). In K. Tochtermann, & A. Scharl (Eds.), *Managing Environmental Knowledge – 20th International Conference on Informatics for Environmental Protection, EnviroInfo 2006, Graz 2006, 06.09.-08.09.2006* (pp 75-82). Aachen: Shaker.

Binstock, C., Hoffman, C., Egmond, R. V., & Walenga, W. (2005). Comparing XML and XBRL (Version 2005-06-06). Retrieved January 17, 2006, from http://www.ubmatrix.com/Documents/XBRLComparedToXML-2005-07-06%20(4).pdf

eXtensible Business Reporting Language (XBRL) (2006a). XBRL FAQ. Retrieved January 17, 2006, from http://www.xbrl.org/Faq.htm

eXtensible Business Reporting Language (XBRL) (2006b). Extensible Business Reporting Language 2.1, Recommendation -2003-12-31 and Corrected Errata-2005-11-07. Retrieved January 17, 2006, from http://www.xbrl.org/Specification/XBRL-RECOMMENDATION-2003-12-31+Corrected-Errata-2005-11-07.htm

eXtensible Business Reporting Language (XBRL) (2006c). Guidance on XBRL Instance Documents and Reports. Retrieved January 05, 2006, from http://www.xbrl.org/InstanceGuidance/

Financial Reporting Taxonomies Architecture (FRTA). (2005). Financial Reporting Taxonomies Architecture (FRTA) 1.0 - Recommendation dated 2005-04-25, Corresponding to XBRL 2.1 Recommendation. Retrieved January 17, 2006, from http://www.xbrl.org/technical/guidance/FRTA-RECOMMENDATION-2005-04-25.htm

Global Reporting Initiative (GRI) (Ed.). (2006). *Sustainability Reporting Guideline – Version 3.0*. Amsterdam: Global Reporting Initiative Press.

Institut für ökologische Wirtschaftsforschung (IÖW), & future e.V. (Eds.) (2007). *Nachhaltigkeitsberichterstattung in Deutschland. Ergebnisse und Trends im Ranking*. Retrieved August 31, 2009, from http://www.ioew.de/uploads/tx_ukioewdb/Ergebnisbericht_Ranking_2007_final.pdf

International Institute for Sustainable Development. Deloite & Touche, & Business Council for Sustainable Development (Eds.) (1992). Business Strategy for Sustainable Development. Leadership and Accountability for the 90'. Winnipeg, MB: International Institute for Sustainable Development (IISD) Press.

International Organization for Standardization ISO, & International Electrotechnical Commission IEC (Eds.) (2002). *ISO/IEC 13250 Topic Maps – Information Technology Document Description and Processing Languages (ISO/IEC 13250:2002 (2nd edition)*. Geneva: ISO Press.

Isenmann, R., & Kim, K. (2006). Interactive sustainability reporting. In Schaltegger, S., Bennett, M., & Burritt, R. T. (Eds.), *Sustainability Accounting and Reporting* (pp. 533–555). Berlin, Heidelberg: Springer. doi:10.1007/978-1-4020-4974-3_24

Isenmann, R., Marx Gómez, J., & Süpke, D. (2008). Sustainability Reporting à la carte – Concept and Implementation of a Software Tool with Shopping Cart Functionality. In A. Möller, B. Page, & M. Schreiber (Eds.), *Environmental Informatics and Industrial Ecology – 22nd International Conference on Environmental Informatics Envio-Info 2008, Leuphana University Lüneburg 2008, 10.09.-12.09.2008* (pp. 36-41). Aachen: Shaker.

Isenmann, R., Süpke, D., & Marx Gómez, J. (2009). Stakeholder interaction in sustainability reporting with Web 2.0. In: I. N. Athanasiadis, P. A. Mitkas, A. E. Rizzoli, & J. Marx Gómez (Eds.), *Information Technologies in Environmental Engineering – Proceedings of the 4th International ICSC Symposium Thessaloniki, Greece, May 28-29, 2009* (pp. 387-398). Berlin/Heidelberg: Springer.

KPMG (Ed.). (2008). Count me in: The readers' take on sustainability reporting. Retrieved August 31, 2009, from http://www.sustainability.com/researchandadvocacy/reports_article.asp?id=1489

Marshall, S. R., & Brown, D. (2003). Corporate environmental reporting. *Business Strategy and the Environment, 12*(2), 87–106. doi:10.1002/bse.354

Morhardt, E. J. (2002). *Clean, green, and read all over. Ten rules for effective corporate environmental and sustainability reporting.* Milwaukee, WI: ASQ Quality Press.

Park, J., & Huntington, S. (2002). *XML Topic Maps: Creating and Using Topic Maps for the Web.* Amsterdam: Addison Wesley Longman.

Pepper, S. (2000). The TAO of Topic Maps – Finding the Way in the Age of Infoglut. In XML Europe 2000 (Ed.), *Conference Proceedings, 12-16 June 2000, Le Palais des Congrès de Paris.* Retrieved January 17, 2006, from http://www.gca.org/papers/xmleurope2000/papers/s11-01.html

Thiessen, I. (2006). *Konzept und Implementierung eines XBRL Schema zur computergestützten Unternehmensberichterstattung.* Unpublished Diploma Thesis, Technische Universität Kaiserslautern.

United Nations Environment Program (UNEP) (Ed.). (2002). *SustainAbility Ltd. United Nations Environment Program – Trust us: The global reporters 2002 survey of corporate sustainability reporting.* London: Beacon Press.

World Wide Web Consortium (W3C) (Éd.) (2001). *XML Linking Language (*Xlink) Version 1.0 (document dated: 2001). Retrieved January 17, 2006, http://www.w3.org/TR/xlink

ENDNOTE

1 Organization: "Company, firm, enterprise, authority or institution, or part or combination thereof, whether incorporated or not, public or private, that has its own functions and administration." (DIN EN ISO 14001: 1996)

Section 5
Case Studies & Pilot Projects

Chapter 23
Sustainable Supply Chain Management:
Cases and Models of RFID and Information Systems use in Green Logistics

Iskra Dukovska-Popovska
Aalborg University, Denmark

Malcolm Bertoni
University of Tasmania, Australia

Hans-Henrik Hvolby
Aalborg University, Denmark

Paul Turner
University of Tasmania, Australia

Kenn Steger-Jensen
Aalborg University, Denmark

ABSTRACT

Integrating environmental considerations into supply-chain management has become an increasingly important issue for industry, government and academic researchers. Supply chain managers are being required to respond to the challenges of new legislation, standards and regulations; changing customer demands; drivers for efficiency, cost effectiveness and return on investment; while simultaneously being 'green'. The fundamental tension between business and environmental drivers is difficult, but critical to understanding how to effectively re-engineer and re-design existing supply chains in a manner that is sustainable both financially and environmentally. Information systems have a significant role to play in supporting corporate responses to environmental management and the development of holistic green logistic solutions. This chapter examines contemporary discussions on the current state of sustainable supply-chain management and green logistics. It presents a case study from the Fujitsu Corporation in Japan and explores models of information systems and RFID use in green logistics. Combining insights from the case and existing models the chapter explores an example of how a combined model can be used to explore the potential of a specific emerging technology (RFIDs) in 'greening' supply chains.

DOI: 10.4018/978-1-61520-981-1.ch023

INTRODUCTION

Industry increasingly recognises the challenges of responding to concerns about the environment. These challenges include both how to respond to compliance with emerging climate policies such as the EU Emission Trading Scheme and to changing consumer demands for carbon neutral products and/or environmentally friendly and sustainable production processes. These issues directly impact on production processes and supply chain management. In order for organisations to minimise their impact on the environment, it has been argued that they need to evaluate and act from a total system perspective (Wu & Dunn, 1995). The supply chain represents such a holistic system and is a strong candidate for far-reaching greening initiatives. Supply chains link various types of organisations and extend across multiple boundaries before reaching the consumer. The volume of goods and produce being carried across the globe continues to grow. This is due in part to higher productivity, increased efficiency in primary industries, cheaper freight costs and the rapid expansion of the BRIC (Brazil, Russia, India, and China) nations.

Conventional approaches to supply chain management continue to encounter the challenge of how to balance being effective and cost efficient on one hand, whilst becoming more environmentally friendly on the other (Rodrigue, Slack & Comtois, 2001). Technology has been presented as a means to resolve this tension between the need for cost efficiency in SCM and improved quality, safety, and environmental sustainability. Many current technology scenarios for cutting emissions are focused on large-investment solutions like electrical vehicles, aircrafts running on bio fuels, and ships running on hydrogen fuel cells, or hybrid fuel cells (Stangeland, 2008). An alternative to evolution towards green supply management can be seen in several emerging technologies that can assist companies in achieving cost efficiency, value advantage (Rundh, 2008) and environmental sustainability. One candidate technology is Radio Frequency IDentification (RFID). However, the evidence of the return on investment (ROI) in terms of cost efficiencies or effectiveness of these responses to improve moves to carbon neutrality are lacking for most current technologies (O'Connor, 2005). From a research perspective there is also a challenge in how to approach this tension and the generation of insights that can be used meaningfully by multiple stakeholders (industry, governments, community and consumers). Aside from the challenges of a lack of evidence of ROI, the use of technology such as RFIDs presents issues around standardisation in global supply chains.

RFID technology provides automated identification and information gathering from objects and people which are not necessarily within a short range and at an optically visible disposition. An RFID system can also communicate with products and update the data on RFID tags simultaneously, which makes it possible to capture process data as well. The technology provides opportunities in the automation of the data capture and monitoring of time, temperature, product location, etc. and compliance verification across the whole supply chain. Integrating these processes into an Information System that is available to all partners in the supply chain, facilitates a useful tool for logistics managers. A number of researchers and practitioners have already considered the application of RFID in certain areas of green supply chain, for example in reverse logistics (Lee & Chan, 2009; Payaro, 2004). In reverse logistics, RFID is adopted for example to increase the service level to the customers so as to complete the recovery service in a certain period of time. In forward logistics, RFID helps replenish the goods in a timely manner so as to satisfy customer needs.

This chapter examines contemporary discussions on the current state of sustainable supply-chain management and green logistics. It presents a case study from the Fujitsu Corporation in Japan and explores models of information systems use in green logistics. Combining insights from the case and existing models the chapter explores an example of how a combined model can be used to explore the potential of a specific emerging technology (RFIDs) in 'greening' supply chains.

GREEN SUPPLY CHAIN MANAGEMENT

Green supply-chain management is defined as "integrating environmental thinking into supply-chain management, including product design, material sourcing and selection, manufacturing processes, delivery of the final product to the consumers as well as end-of-life management of the product after its useful life" (Srivastava, 2007, pp.54-55). Such definition implies establishing closed-loop logistics systems. The advantage of the holistic perspective can be found by looking at the (direct and indirect) interconnections that an organization has with other participants in the supply chain. This means that the environmental effect of a business is not only a result from its own actions, and the actions of its first tier suppliers (direct effect), but also a result from suppliers up the supply chain (indirect effect) (Darnall, Jolley & Handfield, 2008), as well as customers, and parties interacting with the end of lifecycle down the supply chain. Cases from the automobile and computer industry, beside other sectors, provide examples of manufacturers who are considering the environmental aspects of their suppliers, and, thus evaluating the potential environmental problems that may be transmitted from the suppliers. Such manufacturers are beginning to pay attention to designing green products, and also demonstrate commitment to initiate recycling of products. In this way businesses can take a more proactive approach, which should be differentiated from the reactive approach where a company's activities focus mainly on "end of pipeline" initiatives to lower the environmental impact of production (Srivastava, 2007). Finally, companies may undertake a third, *value-seeking approach*, by making the greening perspective as part of their competitive strategy since such perspectives can bring resource saving, waste elimination, and productivity improving, and thus create competitive advantage. Reviewing the literature, three generic perspectives on the green supply chain that support the value-creation approach have been identified.

The first perspective is related to the *scope of the supply chain*. Previous research provided reviews of different problem contexts dealt within the green supply chain area (Srivastava, 2007), as well as several functional models of environmentally friendly chain (Sarkis, 2003; Wu & Dunn, 1995). These models have contributed to the green supply chain theory by extending the focus of the greening initiatives from the end of the manufacturing processes (for example, filtering of the wastes) and the recycling of the waste, to the whole supply chain perspective (including the design of product). These models offer a number of aspects that different actors in the supply chain need to consider in order to decrease the total environmental footprint. An illustrative example of the importance of considering the wider scope is drawn from the food industry. The most significant environmental effects are not achieved by treating the end-of-pipeline or transportation waste, but rather the inherent upstream wastes related to cultivation of crops and livestock, processing of these, production of additives etc. When food is wasted, all activities upstream and their related emissions are in vain (Nereng, Ramsdal & Brekke, 2009). What remains challenging in this holistic supply chain perspective is how to establish the cross-functional and cross-company approach in order to achieve the synergetic effect on the environmental issues. Information and communications technologies are likely to play a key role in the co-ordination and integration of green SCM (Dekker, Fleischmann, Inderfurth & Van Wassenhove, 2004).

Table 1. Evaluation of greening efforts throughout the supply chain (Adapted from Van Hoek, 1999)

Performance measures	• Emission rates and energy efficiency per material % of virgin material • Volume of goods disassembled per hour • Degree of utilization transport equipment • Amount of "air" in package • Volume selected for recycling

The second perspective on the greening initiatives in the supply chain is related to the *generic activities* that need to be considered by each actor in the supply chain. Carter and Ellram (1998) propose a hierarchy of strategies where *resource reduction* should have the top priority. This refers to minimization of materials, energy and waste spent in the process of handing the product. In this way the focus is placed at the source and through the process, and not only at the end-of-pipeline. The other two strategies, *reuse* and *recycle* are also supporting the resource reduction strategy, but they are placed in the reverse logistics if the product. *Disposal* strategy should be the last option remained after the first three have been employed.

The third perspective includes the *performance measures* of the green initiatives through the supply chain (Table 1). The main presumption is that the supply chain footprint needs to be evaluated against specific indicators – performance measures, example of which is listed in Table 1. These are just a few "green" performance indicators, and a more complete list needs to be developed in the future.

The three perspectives presented above embrace the environmental aspects or "greening business process" of a supply chain since they deal with *who* is involved through the supply chain, *what* activities are undertaken, and *how* the greening process performs. Therefore these perspectives need to be considered when analysing and/or improving the supply chain management seen from greening perspective. Noticeably however, these perspectives still need to be developed. An overarching potential is seen in exploring the value creation approach - not only minimizing ecological damage, but also leading to overall economical profit, competitive advantage, and larger scope sustainability (not only environmental, but also social and economical aspects of it (Green Logistics, 2009)). Therefore, green supply management could have the potential to be driver of innovation, job creation, and energy conservation, as well as CO2 reduction.

GREEN LOGISTICS

Although there are many definitions, the Council of Supply Chain Management Professionals (CSCMP) defines logistics as: "Logistics management is that part of supply chain management that plans, implements, and controls the efficient, effective forward and reverses flow and storage of goods, services and related information between the point of origin and the point of consumption in order to meet customers' requirements. " (Council of Supply Chain Management Professionals, n.d.). Logistics management typically includes inbound, outbound, internal, and external movements, both physical and importantly information flows. Significantly, the above definition acknowledges the holistic nature of the logistics process. This implies control and organization across supply chain management, manufacturing, warehousing, distribution and retailing.

Green logistics would imply environmentally-friendly and efficient transport and distribution system (Rodrigue et al., 2001). While traditional logistics has focused on forward (producer to consumer) logistics and efficiency, the environmental considerations opened up new market opportunities for logistics – transport and storage of waste and used materials. In fact, waste disposal were considered the leading environmental issues related to logistics operations contrary to congestion and land use which were considered as least important. Furthermore, inventory control, customer service, and production scheduling has also been seen to have negligible environmental implications (Rodrigue et al., 2001).

However, environmental perspective has taken on a new meaning. It implies not just the recycling of waste but also the reduction of harmful by-products such as carbon dioxide and monoxide, as well as minimization of the use of fossil fuels. As Rodrigue, Slack and Comtois (2001) describe, there is a paradox regarding adding the greening aspect on logistics, and suggests that the application of green logistics could be more difficult than might be expected.

Rodrigue et al. (2001) list these paradoxes and they are briefly summarized here:

- **Costs.** The purpose of logistics is efficiency gains and thus reducing costs. Some of the strategies to achieve these objectives are related to using cheaper gasoline (diesel), consolidation of passengers and fright at hubs, etc. However, such solutions could be least environmentally friendly.
- **Time/Speed.** Increased flexibility and delivery time reduction, especially for high value products as well as JIT manufacturing is a strategic goal for logistics providers. Flexibility draws higher usage of logistics, while speed is achieved by most polluting transportation modes.
- **Service Reliability.** In a competitive market, customer service viewed through delivery on time and no quality degradation is very important. However, these aspects are mostly accomplished by least environmentally friendly modes of transport such as air and road.
- **Warehousing systems** are focusing on the reduction of inventories which is enabled by the speed and reliability of deliveries. However, with this reduction in inventories, they are actually moved i transit, thus contributing to congestion and pollution.
- **E-Commerce.** Electronic commerce is a burgeoning market sector. This is due to integrated systems between manufacturers, suppliers, distributors, transporters, etc. The number of small parcels and cartons being shipped is staggering. However, once again the most efficient transport systems are air and road; the most environmentally unfriendly modes of transportation.

The above overview suggests that there is a great challenge for logistics operations to ensure being environmentally friendly. In this context, the next section combines a number of cases and frameworks to examine green logistic issues and challenges from a holistic perspective. In particular, the next section overlays Zhou's (2009) Forward Logistics model with three other considerations: Reverse Logistics, Substitution & Re-Design, and Information Logistics.

GREEN SUPPLY CHAIN/LOGISTICS REFERENCE MODEL AND CASES

The necessity of greening the logistics industry is not debatable. The main issue is how it is to be realized.

One way to advance this issue will be via a top-down approach. Different government interventions such as higher road costs, mandatory collection and recycling, controlled movement of hazardous materials, are some of polices that support green logistic. However, a bottom-up industry approach is needed as well to support the greening of logistics. This approach should create value for the customers and a competitive advantage to organizations. This section is divided in two parts: cases that exemplify greening initiatives, and models that can guide a green logistics bottom-up approach.

There are currently not many case studies that can be used to illustrate a green logistics initiative that has produced measurable and quantifiable results. An excellent example of green logistics activity is found in Fujitsu's initiatives for green logistics (Niwa, 2009). Fujitsu's initiatives were started by the Green Logistics Committee at the same month when the Japanese Energy Conservation Law was revised requiring transporters and shippers to protect the environment in their logistics activities. Fujitsu's goal was a reduction of transport-related CO2 emissions for 30% from 2000 levels by 2010, even though Japan's target was just a 6% reduction from 1990 levels by 2010. Some companies in Japan had targets of as little as 4%, while some also had high targets of 30%.

One result of the Green Logistics Committee was the integration of logistics functions of all business groups into a Logistics Division, aiming to optimise all logistics functions. The aim was to create environment-friendly logistics that could maintain a balance of cost, time and quality. In cooperation with transporters, Fujitsu worked to make logistics processes more efficient and to reduce environmental impact.

Fujitsu's focused on making logistics more efficient by rationalising distribution centres, reducing transport distances and simplifying routes, and reducing the truck fleet. These measures had a two-fold benefit of reducing both costs as well as CO2 emissions. However to reduce CO2 emissions further required new measures and this was a modal shift in transport by switching from truck and aircraft transport to rail and ship transport. Road transport generates six times more CO2 emissions compared to rail and air transport, air 75 times more than sea. Although switching from road to rail and from air to sea makes sense, there are issues such as cost, time and quality. Fortunately Fujitsu does not make perishable or time-critical products, and is attempting to get customers to accept a slightly longer delivery time. To use rail more effectively, Fujitsu had a fixed number of containers ordered to reduce fees and introduced new, smaller pallets so that eight and not six pallets could be loaded into a container. These improvements meant that rail transport grew to 20%. Fujitsu also began to optimize and minimize the number of transport vehicles by rationalization of distribution centres, standardized shipping instructions, modification and streamlining of operations systems with logistics partners and optimizing of vehicles. Full-scale operations of these improvements began in February 2007 in the Tokyo region. The project was praised as groundbreaking and received a commendation from the Minister of Economy, Transport and Industry in December 2007.

These logistic processes improvements meant that by the end of 2007, Fujitsu estimated that they had reduced CO2 by 29% from their 2000 estimates; well on target to meet the 2010 target of 30%. Future activities are focusing on introduction of the Toyota Production System to eliminate waste and free up floor space, more efficient use of shipping, reducing the truck fleet further and using smaller, high-frequency modes of transport and more use of the rail system. Fujitsu is also developing a new logistics system. Since 2007 Fujitsu has collaborated on the Green Logistics Partnership Promotion Project with DHL. DHL which is the world's leading express and logistics company currently provides Fujitsu with an integrated, end-to-end logistics solution.

Another case that illustrates the environmental benefits of supply chain re-design involves considering GHG emission tradeoffs and water scarcity (Reich-Weiser & Dornfeld, 2009). Location decisions are based on the global warming potential of electricity consumed and of transport, as well as on the water availability in the region. Data used for analysis is extracted from generic databases on GHG emissions. However, proper assessment and collecting specific data of the green aspects across the whole supply chain are challenges. Other initiatives include reporting CO_2 emissions decreases related to a reduction of empty truck movements as a result of improvements in fleet management and freight distribution. Such activities are enabled by growing sophistication of fleet management (by for example using GPS) and Information Systems for scheduling and routing (McKinnon, 1998).

A systematic analysis of the whole supply chain is needed in order to determine the environmental impacts related to certain organizations. One model that can support such an analysis is seen in the Supply Chain Operations Reference (SCOR) Model – a supply chain analysis tool that incorporates performance measurements, process modelling and best practices associated to all phases of satisfying customer's demand. Some of the key performance indicators are related to delivery performance, fill rate, perfect order fulfilment, order fulfilment lead time, Supply Chain response time, production flexibility, cash-to-cash cycle time, inventory days of supply, net asset turns. However, SCOR model does not directly measure green logistics and green supply chains (Sanchez-Rodrigues, 2006). Therefore it is important to align the Key Performance Indicators (KPIs) with green logistics and if required, to develop a new set to assess the performance of transport from a holistic green supply chain perspective (Sanchez-Rodrigues, 2006).

Zhou (2009) developed a system diagram to show a green supply chain system for textiles. In this diagram Zhou explicitly tried to undertake a holistic approach to green supply chains: "In the green textile supply chain management, the management objects become into the strategic partners among enterprises through many basic flows such as green plan, green stock, green manufacturing, green distribution, green logistics, green consumption and green reclaim" (Zhou, 2009). Although, this diagram was developed for the textile industry by being explicit about this holistic perspective, it provides a useful basis for adaption and combination with other aspects that need to be included in a more holistic conceptualisation of green logistics that aims to adopt a value-creation perspective. Figure 1 adapts Zhou's model and overlays consideration of three other elements: Reverse Logistics; Re-Design & Substitution, and Information Logistics.

These four dimensions all need to be considered to effectively conceptualise green logistics. These are briefly listed below:

1. **Forward Logistics:** includes manufacturing, assembly, distribution and warehousing, retailing and end user.
2. **Reverse Logistics:** includes recycling, returned good and damaged goods, legislative requirements and disposal.
3. **Re-Design & Substitution:** includes product and rare material substitution, redesign and the use of the four natural capitalism principles.
4. **Information Logistics:** includes an environmental scorecard and benchmarks to evaluate and assess supply chains. Criteria could include
   - Carbon footprint
   - Product miles or food miles
   - Fuel consumption, cost and efficiency
   - Waste disposal costs
   - Reuse and recycle costs
   - Renewable energy

The model presented identifies four dimensions for holistically conceptualising green logistics. Later in this chapter this model is used to explore the potential of RFID technologies to provide support for value-creation in each of these dimensions.

USING RFID TO SUPPORT 'GREENING' OF THE SUPPLY CHAIN

RFIDs can be used to ensure that products can reach the consumer in good condition and to monitor the

Figure 1. Green Supply Chain System Conceptual model (adapted from Zhou, 2009)

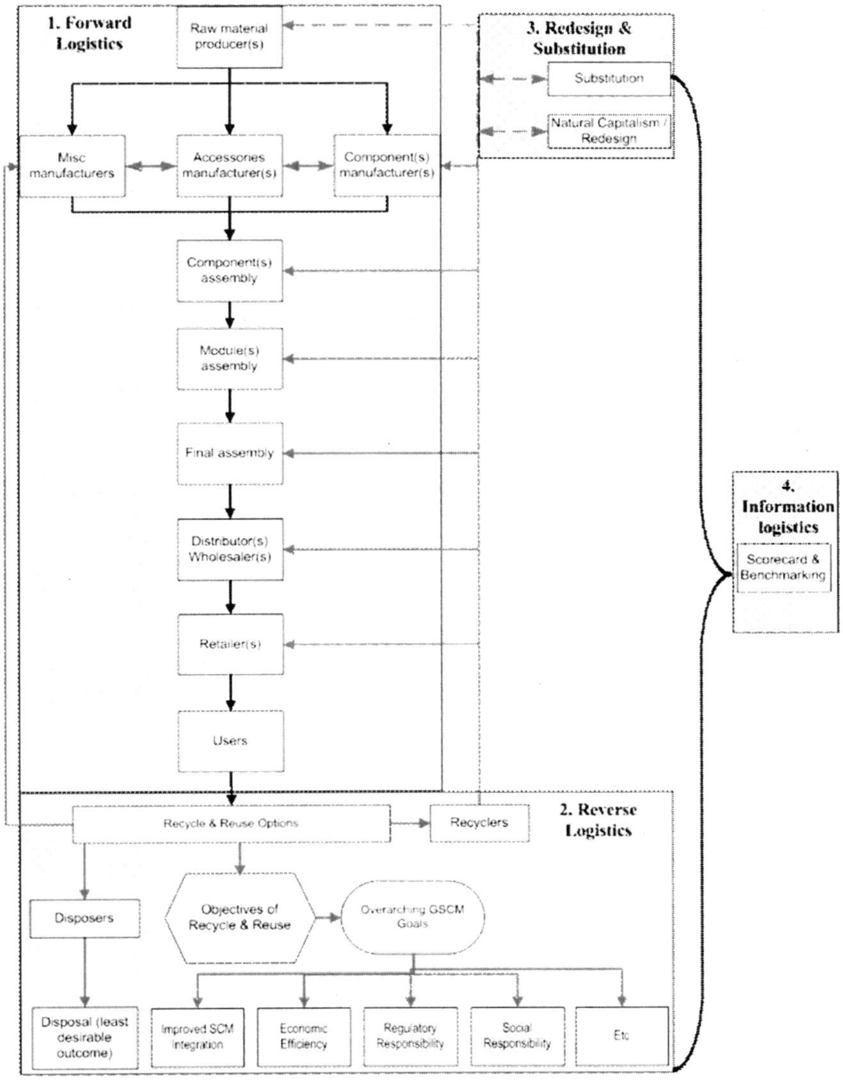

environmental parameters of a product, thus having in place a system that enables close monitoring, regulation and recording of these environmental conditions. Supply chain benefits that are often promoted by RFID vendors include: real-time product tracking, decreased labour costs, security against counterfeiting (authenticity tracking) and improved accuracy in distribution (Lapide, 2004). Many of these benefits are as a result of products can be moved around faster and cheaper, and are tracked in a more timely fashion. RFID readers require less manual labour, and less prone to reading errors with the ability to read large amounts of information compared to barcode and other manual methods currently used for shipping, handling and receiving. RFID tags can also make recall operations easier (Sullivan, 2005).

From a technological perspective, the ability to monitor environmental factors including time, temperature and shock as well as product

Table 2. The four main RFID frequency bands and their application

Band	Typical Operating Range		Typical Application	Relative Data Transfer Rate	Comment
	Read Only	Read Write			
Low Frequency (LF)	Up to 2m	Few cm	• Animal identification • Car immobiliser • Access control & swipe cards • Manufacturing processes • POS applications	Slow Non -concurrent multiple access	• Expensive tag • Susceptible to electrical noise • First RFID frequency range, in use since 1980s
High Frequency (HF)	Up to 1m	Up to 0.5m	• Access control swipe cards and smart cards • Smart labels • Electrical white goods • Library books • Healthcare patients • Airline baggage • Item level tracking in factory & warehouse	Medium Multiple concurrent read <50 items	• Worldwide RFID frequency • Different reader for North America – Europe • Medium t o low cost
Ultra High Frequency (UHF)	Up to 5m	Up to 0.5m	• Item level tracking in factory, warehouse and supply chains • Supply chain tracking • Tollway collection • Parking access • Specialist animal & asset tracking	Fast Multiple concurrent read >100 items	• High ability to simultaneously read multiple tags • Highly integrated manuf. • Inexpensive tag • Different frequencies and power levels in North America, Europe, Japan • Low cost • Interference from liquids • EPC standard • Uses a battery (limited life) • Active tags
Microwave	Up to 10m	Up to 1m	• Tollway collection • Prepaid travel cards & phone cards • Asset tracking • Airline baggage	Fast	• Active tags • Bluetooth and WiFi • Highly integrated manuf. • Inexpensive tag • Uses a battery (limited life)

location and compliance verification across the whole supply chain is now possible through the deployment of active RFIDs. Numerous projects involving pilot tests have illustrated how active RFIDs can offer opportunities for supply chain participants to acquire benefits; but adoption of active RFIDs remains slow. A review of the research literature indicates that most of the pilot tests continue to be conducted in the retail and manufacturing sectors (O'Connor, 2005; Saran & Mohamed, 2005). On the other hand, another study finds that RFID offers a significant benefit and can provide companies with competitive advantage only when fully deployed across the whole supply chain (Visich, Li, Khumawala, & Reyes, 2008).

Unlike static bar code technology, active RFID technology and systems can identify, communicate, update and process data and environmental characteristics (such as time, temperature, shock, product location, weight, etc) on tags on remote products. Another advantage of RFID is the potential for information visibility and automation of information processing to all the participants throughout the supply chain. Besides active and passive technology, RFID also use different frequencies for different purposes and these are briefly presented in as described in Table 2.

RFID clearly outperforms barcode systems but has, however, not yet become the primary approach to collect data from the supply chain activities. This is partly due to the (relative) high cost, partly due to the fact that not all of the expectations of this new technology have been met, especially the ability to identify single items in a batch. As well systems integration in and across supply chains remains an issue.

Despite considerable recognition within the research literature of the need to develop a substantial theory on the economic impact of active RFID technology for quality assurance and for clear business models that identify ROI/pay back, these have not been fully developed to date. Decisions on whether and how to implement RFID are confronted with large up-front investments, with payoffs that look small in the short term and uncertain in out years (Laubacher, Kothari, Malone & Subirana, 2005).

Furthermore, the evidence of the return on investment of RFIDs in terms of cost efficiencies or effectiveness of response towards environmental issues (carbon neutrality) is lacking and under-researched. How these technologies can be used, and what benefits arise from their deployment to 'green' supply chains remains under-researched (Fontanella, 2004; Intermec, 2007).

A number of researchers and practitioners have already considered the application of RFID in certain areas of green supply chain, for example in recovery process (Lee & Chan, 2009; Payaro, 2004). In reverse logistics, RFID has been adopted to increase the service level to the customers to complete the recovery service. In forward logistics, RFID helps replenish the goods in a timely manner to satisfy customer needs.

As stated earlier, RFID technology is considered as one of enablers for greening of the supply chain. Therefore, some of the previous implementations of this technology in (green) supply-chain management are presented.

RFID-based systems, either at organization's internal operations or across the supply chain, are mainly used as an automatic data collection mechanism. The data recorded ranges from a basic code of a product to certain characteristics of a product (weight, ect.) as well as characteristics of a process (time, phases, temperature, etc.).

The most widespread area where RFID is implemented is inventory management (including warehousing). Furthermore, RFID has frequently aided improvements of production processes, of workers performance, as well as optimizations of logistic systems. Most of these improvements have been based on the potential of RFID to liberate considerable human labour from certain workflows (offer "process freedom" (Angeles, 2005), as well as to decrease the possibilities of human errors in repetitive activities. Another, significant advantage of RFID is the potential for information visibility to all the participants through the supply chain. Further on, four business processes, which are part of a supply chain and have benefited from both advantages of RFID, are presented.

Distribution processes. RFID is used to automatically update inventory as cartons and pallets enter a distribution centre. The discrepancies between purchased order and incoming items can be identified easily. Furthermore, putaway workers can easily find the correct locations and the load dropped at that location will be automatically adjusted in the inventory system. Similarly, the replenishment operators can be freed from scanning products and verification procedures. Order filling is another area where RFID directs the pickers to the correct location and automatically verifies that correct product in the correct quantities has been removed. In addition, the inventory files can be automatically updated. In all cases, alerts can be activated if inappropriate items or quantities are handled. Similar advantages can be obtained in the shipping department enabling the speeding up of the conveyor system made possible due to the increased read speeds of RFIDs (comparing to barcode technology). In all the cases, the system can automatically generate increasingly error-free documents. (Angeles, 2005)

Transportation. The main idea with application is to track products and assets as they pass through critical points of the supply chain where reader portals have been installed. Retailers will be able to track shipment movements from the time of release by the supplier until it arrives at the retailer's receiving dock. The time at each point can be recorded at the RFID tag and alerts can be generated if shipments stay longer than expected. This can prompt parties involved to explore the matter and ensure timely delivery. Lower safety stock inventory levels are expected as the products move more swiftly through inspection points. Furthermore, the retailers can save as much as 80 percent of detention and demurrage charges for third-party-owned assets since they can track their products and different products handling assets. (Angeles, 2005)

Reverse logistics. There are cases that present advantages for the use of RFID in handling reverse logistics better. Such a use requires placing a tag on each product at the manufacturer, and further updating the data at the retailer, as well as at the customer if a certain service has been conducted on the product (Payaro, 2004). The data from the RFID tag is later used in the reverse logistics to assist the Collection and Sorting Center in deciding which components can be remanufactured, refurbished or send to landfill or incinerator. The advantages of implementing an RFID-based system are through the: increase of recovered products, tracking of returned products, simplification of the operations of collecting, sorting, and disassembly, as well as reduction of the quantities of toxic components in the environment. The weaknesses of RFID implementation are the: need for a unique identification system, need for shared system of coding among all the manufacturers of a particular product (integration), need for organizational change, need for a high level of modularity of products. Overall, the RFID enables minimization of the complexities of the reverse logistics processes that comes mainly from irregular material flow as well as inventories that are in different conditions (repaired, defective, damaged, etc.). RFID combined with other computational intelligence techniques (Lee & Chan, 2009) can help determine the economical transportation from collection points to collection centers. It minimizes the holding time and depreciating value for the returned products at the same time. Therefore, an improved reverse information flow (supported by RFID) would reduce resource consumption (e.g. transportation, storage, obsoleteness) and thus reduce the environmental impact in the total product lifecycle.

Product safety. Besides storing the product identity, the RFID tag could be used for storing other product or process information that can increase the safety of the product. For example, domestic animals in Denmark can have a read-only tag injected under their skin. If the tag is read-write and carries an animal's injection history, it can be updated by the veterinarian at the check-out. The authorities can later assess whether the compulsory injection scheme criteria has been fulfilled. Similar techniques can be applied to other goods such as food, flight maintenance, cars, and pharmaceutical products. This aspect is especially important if the goods have been handled by several parties (for example, in export and import of food), so the handling history can be recorded on the RFID tag, and safety problems can be identified. Such information can additionally be used in the reverse processes (recycling, remanufacturing).

From this representation of current applications of RFID use in the supply chain, a model (Figure 2) was developed that presents the use of RFID in greening the supply chain.

The three main axes represent the three perspectives of green supply chain (discussed in the second section above), and the points in the diagram present how different RFID applications fulfil the different perspectives. From this model it can be determined that only one of the RFID applications, Reverse logistics, has more explicit environmental performance effects such as waste reduction. The use of RFID in this context could

Figure 2. RFID application effects in green supply chain

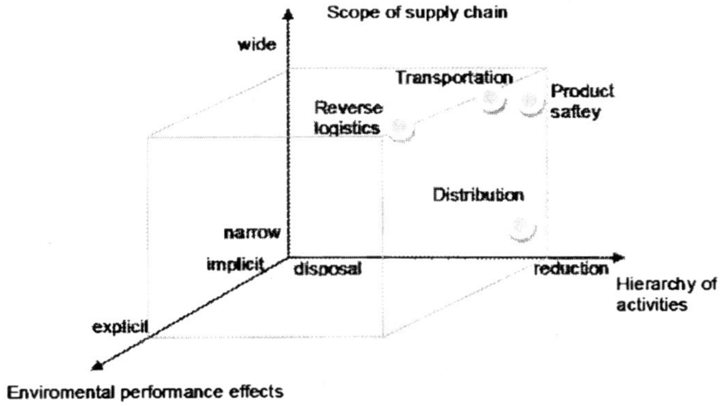

increase the number of products returned, and provide greater process efficiency. The application of RFID in transportation, as presented in the case above, has some implicit environmental performance advantages (enabling economical and thus environmental transportation). It can be speculated that RFID can enable significant reductions in logistic-related costs by helping eliminating unnecessary transportation and finding the optimal mode of transportation for all shipping. This can provide significant carbon benefit and can be perceived as being "green". The current case examples of RFID application in distribution and product safety, do not have explicit environmental performance effect, but implicit effects can be speculated.

The next section focuses on possible future opportunities for RFID in green supply chains.

OPPORTUNITIES FOR RFID IN GREEN LOGISTICS

RFID as a Diagnostic Tool

The opportunities presented in this section are drawn on the bases of two main directions. One direction comes from the model of RFID application effects in green supply chain (Figure 2). What has been evident from the model is that there is a need (gap in the application area) for considering more explicit environmental performance effects from out of RFID applications. The other direction comes from the previously argued weakness of RFID, which is related to investment costs.

The main premise is to develop an ad hoc RFID system for diagnostic purposes in green supply chain management. Here the term ad hoc reflects the fact that the RFID system can be rapidly deployed, without a pre-existing communication infrastructure, in order to monitor some part of the supply chain process.

The ad hoc system should be considered in at least two different scenario types. In the first scenario it is assumed that the subjects are having the tags placed by the manufacturer or other party in the chain and not all the supply-chain actors need to have RFID readers. This creates a proper context for ad hoc deployment of RFID systems, where the objective is to identify certain process environmental performance.

For the second scenario the premise is to create a system where the tags would be ad-hoc as well (ad-hoc RFID tags). The concept of ad-hoc tags is useful if scenarios/processes are considered in which the items are originally not tagged (or at least not all of them are tagged, such as e. g. if a truck is tagged but not the items inside) and the ad hoc tags are introduced for the purpose of recording/identifying certain parameters that are pertinent to that process (for example temperature, time, etc).

From the examples above as well as from the large body of literature and practice on RFID-enabled supply chains, it is evident that the canonical usage of RFID systems is focused on the items and products, their traceability and integrity, inventory control etc. There could be conjecture that there is great potential for RFID, and in particular ad hoc RFID systems, to monitor/regulate the processes and the resource consumption, where a real environmental impact can be achieved. RFID can, for example, help companies quickly assess their facility's emissions associated to a product or group of products. In generic terms, RFID can be instrumental in correlating the presence/action of a certain object or product with resource consumption. This potentially enables the use of RFID technology to improve planning and process design with respect to resource consumption and for example carbon emissions.

Based on the concept of an ad hoc RFID system, the performance measures in Table 1 could be used to identify possible applications that will strengthen the environmental contribution of the RFID technology.

One of the key performance measures, not only upstream, but through the whole supply chain, is the emission rates and energy efficiency per material percentage of virgin material. An ad hoc RFID application can be theorized that will enable screening different processes through the chain, for a certain period of time (few days or weeks), in order to identify the emission rates and energy efficiency of different parts of the process.

Regarding degree of utilization of transport equipment which is also related to other performance – degree of "air" in package – a tag can be envisaged which carries the information about the dimensions or volume of the package. A tag could also be placed at the container carrying the information about the volume/dimensions of the container. In such way, an explicit contribution is created from the use of RFID technology, by enabling higher utilization of the transport equipment.

It is instructive to put the above observations on the different usages of the RFID technology in the perspective of the Deming's process improvement circle – PDCA (plan-do-check-act). The usual usage of RFID in the supply chain (e. g. inventory control) seems to be focused on the check-act part of the circle. Conversely, the savings in resource consumption occur at the larger scale of the process, through re-planning and re-designing the operations. Therefore, the diagnostic usage of an ad hoc RFID system can be understood to affect the plan-do part of Deming's circle. The analogy with the process improvement systems can be taken a step further. Statistical Process Control (SPC) should be employed before initiating costly processes. As the low carbon emission becomes a costly provision, the detailed snapshot of the resource/energy consumption of different parts of the process, collected through RFID tags, may be adopted as a mandatory operation before fully activating the process.

RFIDs across the Four Dimensions of Green Logistics

Four business processes, which are part of green supply chain (Figure 1), and how they can benefit from advantages of RFID, are briefly presented next.

RFID and Green Forward Logistics

Up to now the main usage of RFID in forward logistics has been related to timely delivery to the customer. New applications of RFID need to be searched which can enable environmentally friendly forward logistics. RFID can enable gathering data about environmental emissions and energy efficiency in different parts of the supply chain.

Such information could be used in re-planning and re-designing of different processes and the supply chain as a whole with the aim of reducing resource consumption and GHG emissions. Furthermore, in logistics, a trade-off between warehouse size and increased transportation needs to be evaluated, and RFID can help in diagnosing different situations. Although the general logic has been towards decreasing stocks at different points, such philosophy leads to increased inventories in transport, which is affecting the environment negatively. RFID can enable significant reductions in logistic-related costs by helping eliminating unnecessary transportation and finding the optimal mode of transportation for all shipping. This can provide significant carbon benefit and can be perceived as being "green", and thus contribute to the price of the product or the carbon tax of the product.

RFID and Green Reverse Logistics

Most of the existing applications of RFID mainly cover the reverse logistics aspect. However, they mainly contribute to the reuse and recycle strategies. Further applications need to address the emission and energy efficiency aspect in a greater manner. They need to focus more on resource reduction strategy instead, and make the reverse logistics greener.

RFID and Green Re-Design & Substitution

Natural capitalism presumes increased resource productivity, industry redesign producing zero waste and toxicity, leasing rather than selling products and using organisational profits to invest in natural capitalism. Examples include building redesign, hyper vehicles, and the use of natural materials for manufacture. Natural capitalism requires a whole new business model that harnesses environmental performance as a mechanism for competitive advantage.

RFID and Green Information Logistics

In order to ensure the order of various flows and maximize the performance of the whole green supply chain, much technical support, and information support such as decision-making support system, information management system, and green evaluation system should be established. RFID is not worth much without being synchronized with the other information systems in the supply chain. The challenge is how to get meaningful information out of the data. Furthermore, greening the supply chain can be seen as a common objective of all parties involved. They all need to participate not only in sharing information, but also in developing the system.

CONCLUSION

The research presented in this chapter is focused on giving and overview on the current green supply chain and logistics practises, as well as their support by RFID technology. Furthermore, innovative opportunities of RFID in green supply-chain management were proposed. Based on previous literature, the paper discusses the current state of green supply-chain management and the associated current use of RFID technology.

The use of RFIDs is by no means the only solution to the issue of green logistics due to the many factors that can influence the supply chain. But, along with other technology and efficiency enhancements, substantial progress can be made towards "greener" logistics.

The paper identifies three main perspectives when considering the green supply-chain management: the scope of the supply chain (how many actors would be involved in greening the supply chain), the generic activities related to greening, and the performance measures related to greening. Furthermore, the paper translates the current RFID supply chain applications into these three main greening perspectives, and discusses how RFID has been utilized in relation to greening. There is an evident gap of RFID dealing with explicit environmental performance measures in the supply chain area. Another challenge that pertains in the literature is the cost efficiency of the RFID systems, which is believed to slow down or block the wider implementation of RFID. Based on the identified gap in the RFID application literature, and the cost efficiency challenge, the paper identified opportunities throughout the green supply chain that can be subject of RFID implementation. Motivated by process improvement literature, the paper proposes larger focus of the future RFID applications on diagnostic of processes, in order to initiate the creation of new operational modes with significantly improved environmental performance. An ad hoc RFID system for diagnostic purposes in green supply chain management will enable temporary process scanning. Furthermore, the investment costs, which are one of the main challenges for current RFID systems, will be much decreased in ad hoc RFID system.

A measure of the emission rates and energy efficiency of virgin material could be a key performance measures. RFID technology can be utilised to enable screening of different processes through the supply chain over any period of time of time of days or weeks in order to identify the emission rates and energy efficiency of different components of the process.

The usual use of RFIDs in supply chains are mostly focused forward and reverse logistics and savings in resource consumption could occur at the re-planning and re-designing process.

Further research will focus on developing and testing of an ad hoc RFID diagnostic system. In addition to this, the following questions need to be further investigated:

- What is the system (from the technical perspective) that can enable ad hoc RFID implementations through the supply chain?
- How can ad hoc RFID diagnostic system be implemented through the supply chain, and what will be the environmental and cost related effects of such a system? Will such systems increase the usage of RFID across organizations?
- What are the major commercial, technological, and regulatory inhibitors to the use of RFIDs in the green supply chains?
- Where are RFIDs most effective in greening, and in which part of particular supply chain?

REFERENCES

Angeles, R. (2005). RFID technologies: supply-chain applications and implementation issues. *Information Systems Management*, *22*(1), 51–65.

Carter, C. R., & Ellram, L. M. (1998). Reversed logistics: A review of the literature and framework for future investigation. *Journal of Business Logistics*, *19*(1), 85–102.

Council of Supply Chain Management Professionals. (n.d.). *CSCMP supply chain management definitions.* Retrieved December 9, 2009, from http://cscmp.org/aboutcscmp/definitions.asp

Darnall, N., Jolley, G. J., & Handfield, R. (2008). Environmental management systems and green supply chain management: Complements for sustainability? *Business Strategy and the Environment*, *17*(1), 30–45.

Dekker, R., Fleischmann, M., Inderfurth, K., & Van Wassenhove, L. N. (Eds.). (2004). *Reverse logistics: quantitative models for closed-loop supply chains*. Berlin, Germany: Springer.

Fontanella, J. (2004). Finding the ROI in RFID. *Supply Chain Management Review*, *8*(1), 13–14.

Green Logistics. (2009) *What is Green Logistics?* Retrieved December 9, 2009, from http://www.greenlogistics.org/PageView.aspx?id=97

Intermec. (2007, February). *Supply chain RFID: How it works and why it pays?* Retrieved December 9, 2009, from http://epsfiles.intermec.com/eps_files/eps_wp/SupplyChainRFID_wp_web.pdf

Lapide, L. (2004). RFID: What's in it for the forecaster? *The Journal of Business Forecasting*, *23*(2), 16–19.

Laubacher, R., Kothari, S.P., Malone, T.W., & Subirana, B. (2005). What is RFID worth to your company? Measuring performance at the activity level. *MIT Center for eBusiness Research Brief*, *7*(2).

Lee, C. K. M., & Chan, T. M. (2009). Development of RFID-based reverse logistics system. *Expert Systems with Applications*, *36*(5), 9299–9307.

McKinnon, A. (1998). Logistical restructuring, freight traffic growth and the environment. In Banister, D. (Ed.), *Transport policy and the environment* (pp. 97–109). London, England: Routledge.

Nereng, G., Romsdal, A., & Brekke, A. (2009). Can innovations in the supply chain lead to reduction of GHG emissions from food products? A framework. Retrieved December 9, 2009, from http://gin.confex.com/gin/2009/webprogram/Paper2373.html

Niwa, K. (2009). Fujitsu activities for green logistics. *FUJITSU Scientific Technology Journal*, *45*(1), 28–32.

O'Connor, M. C. (2005, July 22). Most RFID users believe RFID lacks ROI. *RFID Journal.* Retrieved December 9, 2009, from www.rfidjournal.com/article/articleprint/1753/-1/1

Payaro, A. (2004). The role of ICT in reverse logistics: A hypothesis of RFID implementation to manage the recovery process. In P. Cunningham & M. Cunningham (Eds.), *The Proceedings of eChallenges 2004 Conference: eAdoption and the Knowledge Economy: Issues, Applications and Case Studies, IOS Press.* Retrieved December 9, 2009, from http://www.reloaderitalia.it/doc/download/payaro_rfid.pdf

Reich-Weiser, C., & Dornfeld, D. A. (2009). A discussion of greenhouse gas emission tradeoffs and water scarcity within the supply chain. *Journal of Manufacturing Systems*, *28*(1), 23–27. doi:. doi:10.1016/j.jmsy.2009.04.002

Rodrigue, J. P., Slack, B., & Comtois, C. (2001). Green logistics. In Brewer, A. M., Button, K. J., & Hensher, D. A. (Eds.), *The Handbook of logistics and supply-chain management, Handbooks in transport #2* (pp. 339–351). London, England: Pergamon/Elsevier.

Rundh, B. (2008). Radio frequency identification (RFID): Invaluable technology or a new obstacle in the marketing process? *Marketing Intelligence & Planning*, *26*(1), 97–114.

Sanchez-Rodrigues, V. (2006, November). *Supply chain management, transport and the environment – A review*, Retrieved December 9, 2009, from http://www.greenlogistics.org.uk/SiteResources/7a76ee40-f62d-4efe-9d4e-47ac2a2a9211_WM1%20-%20Cardiff%20-%20Supply%20Chain%20Management.pdf

Saran, C., & Mohamed, A. (2005, January 31). *Lack of standards and high cost hinders RFID. Computer Weekly*, Retrieved December 9, 2009, from http://www.computerweekly.com/Articles/2005/02/01/208032/Lack-of-standards-and-high-cost-hinders-RFID.htm

Sarkis, J. (2003). A strategic decision framework for green supply chain management. *Journal of Cleaner Production, 11*(4), 397–409.

Srivastava, S. K. (2007). Green supply-chain management: A state-of-the-art literature review. *International Journal of Management Reviews, 9*(1), 53–80.

Stangeland, A. (Ed.). (2008). How to combat global warming - An ambitious but necessary approach to reduce greenhouse gas emissions. *Working paper prepared by the Energy and Climate Department of the Bellona Foundation.* Retrieved December 9, 2009, from http://www.bellona.org/reports/How_to_Combat_Global_Warming

Sullivan, L. (2005, January 3). RFID: The plot thickens. *Information Week.* Retrieved December 9, 2009, from http://www.informationweek.com/news/mobility/RFID/showArticle.jhtml?articleID=56800166

Van Hoek, R. I. (1999). From Reversed Logistics to Green Supply Chains. *Supply Chain Management, 4*(3), 129–134.

Visich, J. K., Li, S., Khumawala, B. M., & Reyes, P. M. (2008). *Empirical evidence of RFID impacts on supply chain performance.* Retrieved December 1, 2009 from http://www.decisionsciences.org/Proceedings/DSI2008/docs/441-4907.pdf

Wu, H.-J., & Dunn, S. C. (1995). Environmentally responsible logistics systems. *International Journal of Physical Distribution & Logistics Management, 25*(2), 20–38.

Zhou, F. (2009). Study on the implementation of green supply chain management in textile enterprises. *Journal of Sustainable Development, 2*(1), 75–79.

Chapter 24
Eco-Industrial Parks and Application of Corporate Environmental Management Information System in China

Juan Wen
Tianjin Academy of Environmental Sciences, China

Xueqiang Lu[1]
Tianjin Academy of Environmental Sciences, China

ABSTRACT

The history, current situation, policy system and three typical cases for eco-industrial parks in China have been described and analyzed systematically. On the basis of this, application of CEMIS to EIPs has been discussed. A CEMIS framework for EIPs has been proposed according to the Chinese policy system. Furthermore, a schematic control diagram for EIPs has been suggested using box model.

INTRODUCTION

The EIP definition proposed by the Indigo Development Team in 1993 has been widely accepted, which is "An eco-industrial park or estate is a community of manufacturing and service businesses located together on a common property" (Lowe, 2001). Cote & Hall (1995) suggested that an eco-industrial park, an industrial system could conserve natural and economic resources, reduce costs and debts incurred by production, materials, energy, insurance and handling, promote operation efficiency and quality, improve workers' health and public image, and provide people with opportunities of making profit through utilization and sales of wastes. The President's Council on Sustainable Development of USA (1996) identified an EIP as combination of the market community for effective cooperation and resources sharing (information, raw materials, water, energy, infrastructure and natural environment) and the industrial system for exchange of raw materials and energy. In the *Guideline for Planning of Demonstration Eco-industrial Parks (on trial)* promulgated by the former State Environmental Protection Administration (SEPA) of China in 2003, an EIP is defined as a new type of industrial

DOI: 10.4018/978-1-61520-981-1.ch024

park designed and established in accordance with the concept of circular economy, the principles of industrial ecology and the requirements of cleaner production. Lowe & Warren (2008) pointed out that EIPs were characterized as the interaction between enterprises and the nature, and among themselves. In a study in Kalunborg Industrial Symbiosis System located to the west of Copenhagen, the characteristics were described as optimized utilization of resources with the cooperation between various enterprises, particularly through waste recycling (Erkman, 1999).

In addition to economic profits, an EIP also pursues a beautiful, attractive and heavenly work and life style, ideal and benign ecological circulation, and sustainable development of community. Comparing to a traditional industrial park, an EIP is characterized as:

a. An EIP has an obvious core enterprise or a theme, and the whole park is established and operated on the basis of one or more such core enterprises;
b. An EIP pays attention to harmonious development with community;
c. An EIP has a cleaner production and by-products/wastes exchange network based on supply and demand relationships in order to reduce environmental pollution, instead of simple conglomeration of environmental technology corporations or corporations producing green products;
d. An EIP maximizes energy efficiency through symbiosis and superposition, and realizes sustainable utilization of materials through recovery, regeneration and recycling;
e. An EIP is established based on the theories of circular economy, regional cleaner production and industrial ecology;
f. An EIP has efficient and concentrated environmental infrastructure or facilities, and the environment of enterprise, industrial park and the whole community can be improved continuously;
g. The investment for the enterprises within the ecological chain have priority for an EIP;
h. An EIP has a standardized ecological management and evaluation system.

The main factors for an EIP include system, cooperation, interaction, efficiency, resources and environment. CEMIS is an extensive environmental-protection-oriented information system including systematic collecting, recording and processing of environmentally relevant information. Therefore, corporate environmental management information system (CEMIS) is obviously an information platform to integrate such information of each factor for an EIP. Although information technologies have been widely used in environmental management (e.g., Xin et al., 1999), the application of CEMIS is rare for an EIP. In recent years, the application of CEMIS is increasing with the requirement of corporate environmental management. Lang (2007) proposed a CEMIS framework for production process. However, the studies on CEMIS for EIPs are still relatively rare. The objectives of this chapter are: a) to clarify the development of EIPs in China; and b) to establish a CEMIS framework for EIPs.

EIPS IN CHINA

History: EDA, HIP and EIP

In China, industrial parks have boomed after the nation's reform and opening to the outside world. The development history of China's industrial park can be classified into three phases: economic and technological development area (EDA), high-tech industrial park (HIP), and eco-industrial park (EIP).

The EDA, the first generation of industrial park, is a comprehensive economic development zone located in a designated area, and mainly engaged in manufacturing and business with the aim of importing foreign capitals, increasing export and developing modern industries through focused construction of infrastructure, improved legislation system concerning economy with foreign elements, establishment of efficient management mechanism and execution of preferential economic policies (Peng, 1998). The EDAs focus on promotion of economic development in quantity. In July, 1979, China approved the establishment of tentative special economic zones in Shenzhen, Zhuhai and Shantou in Guangdong Province, and Xiamen in Fujian Province. In April, 1994, on the basis of the experience in the special economic zones, the first 14 EDAs were established in 14 coastal cities. Up to date, 49 national-level EDAs have been approved in China.

The HIPs as the second generation of industrial park, aim to develop high technology and realize its industrialization through preferential policies (Ren, 2000). It focuses on promotion of economic development in quality. In 1983, the Chinese government made the strategic decision of developing high-tech industries. In 1984, the State Council of China approved and promulgated Summary of Report on New Technological Revolution and Our Nation's Countermeasures, which deemed the tentative establishment of new technology- and economy- intensive area as one of the important measures to confront the challenges of new technological revolution. Therefore, the first HIP was built in Shenzhen with the cooperation between Shenzhen Municipal Government and the Chinese Academy of Sciences. China has by far approved 53 national-level HIPs.

There are essential differences between EDAs and HIPs. In location, the EDAs are mainly located in coastal areas, and HIPs mainly rely on the cities with advanced technologies and culture and solid industrial foundations, instead of mere coastal cities. In identification of functions, the EDAs are mainly engaged in developing export-oriented economy on the basis of utilizing foreign capitals. And HIPs are social organizations mainly relying on our nation's scientific and technological strength, industrial technological foundations, available international funds, technologies and production conditions, aiming to develop China's high-tech industries, which is also the most obvious difference between the first generation and the second generation of industrial park.

The third generation of industrial park is the EIP, the form of which is now being spread rapidly in China. This type of park is improved and optimized on the basis of the two above-mentioned development zones, which is an important measure to solve the conflict between the economic development in industries-concentrating area and the limitation of resources and environment (Xiang et al., 2009).

Prior to the import of EIP concepts to China, Chinese enterprises, such as Guangxi Guigang Group Co., Ltd and Lubei Chemical Plant, had made attempt in reduction, reutilization and recycling of resources. However, such experiences had not been summarized in words like industrial ecology or EIP. At the same time, during the rapid development of industrialization, the harmonious relationship between population, resources and environment was somehow damaged, and the continuous expansion of industrial parks induced numerous problems such as occupation of farmland, air pollution, soil pollution, water pollution and noise pollution. Due to the lag effect of undertaken environmental protection measures, the pollution still trended to more and more serious.

Since understanding and acceptance of industrial ecology theory and the EIP concept, the first EIP in China, Guangxi Guigang Eco-Industrial (Sugar Refinery) Park was approved to construct under the guidance of SEPA in 2001. In the subsequent eight years, 33 national demonstration EIPs were approved to construct. In 2009, three national demonstration EIPs, Suzhou High-tech Industrial Park, Suzhou Industrial Zone and Tianjin Economic and Technological Development Area (TEDA) past through the acceptance inspection and were nominated as National Demonstration EIP. It should be noted that Chinese government played a significant role in the promotion of

EIPs. As the manager and operator of the park, government exerted a major influence on EIPs in establishment of strategic planning, formulation of laws and regulations, supply of technologies and fund support, organization and coordination etc. To some extent, combined the knowledge contribution from various research institutions and individuals, it accelerated the development of EIPs in China (Wang, 2007).

CLASSIFICATION OF EIPS IN CHINA

According to the establishment status, the EIPs can be divided into upgrading type, newly-planning type and virtual symbiosis type.

The EIPs of upgrading type are upgraded from the old industrial park, through eco-melioration of the industries with obsolete technologies and improper layout. Based on this improvement, a complementary ecological industry chain between different industries and enterprises can be established so as to upgrade industries, optimize layout, rationalize resource allocation and realize energy conservation and reduction of cost and emission. This type of EIPs is mostly national-level EDAs, HIPs, bonded zones, and export processing zones, or provincial-level industrial parks and old industries aggregation areas. Most of the 33 EIPs abovementioned belong to this category, for example TEDA, Suzhou HIP and Suzhou Industrial Park.

The EIPs of newly-planning type is constructed with a new plan. An industry chain is gradually established through building outstanding infrastructure and attracting enterprises with green manufacturing technologies. The examples for this type of EIPs include Naihai Industrial Park in China and Choctaw EIP in US.

The EIP of virtual symbiosis type is a loose and incompact system or network composed of different enterprises or corporations in related regions. This type of EIPs does not require the members should be in the same area. Instead, they establish materials or energy connections between members through information system, i.e. establishing computer demonstration and database, and then implement these connections in the real world through supply-demand contract. Therefore, the enterprises inside the park can be connected with those outside the park. For the EIP of virtual symbiosis type, the high land-purchasing cost, difficult enterprise moving, and complex network systems such as park channels can be avoided and business partners can be selected more flexibly in accordance with market fluctuation. Thus the impact of market risks can be reduced and the enterprises becoming more flexible. However, the shortcoming is higher transportation expenses. Typical parks include Brownsville EIP in US.

In the *Guideline for Planning of Demonstration EIP (on trial)* promulgated by SEPA in December 2003, two kinds of classification were proposed. For the first one, EIPs can be divided EIP with industrial features or regional features, such as Guangxi Guigang National Demonstration EIP (Sugar Refinery) and the upgraded EDAs or HIPs, respectively. For the second one, in accordance with the construction status and the connectivity between park units, the EIPs can be divided into: a) the industrial zone or park with sound rudiments of ecological industry, b) the park under construction or not in a large-scale, c) the industrial zone or park with various industries and numerous enterprises (such as large quantities of national and local scientific and technological parks and EDAs), and d) virtual park.

In practice, the EIPs have been classified into three types by the Ministry of Environmental Protection (MEP), which are sector-integrate type, sector specific type, and venous industry based type, respectively. It is also adopted by the Ministry of Science and Technology (MOST), and the Ministry of Commerce (MOC) in establishment and management of EIPs.

A sector-integrate EIP is composed of enterprises of different industries, and is upgraded from the old industrial parks such as HIPs or

EDAs. This type of park is mostly formulated upon design, eco-melioration or industry upgrade on the basis of the existing industrial aggregation area in accordance with the concept of circular economy, principle of ecological industry and requirement of clean production. Most of EIPs in China belong to this type.

A sector-specific EIP is established on the basis of one or more core enterprises in one specific sector. Typical parks include Guigang Sugar Refinery Base, Baotou Aluminum Manufacturing Base, and Fushun Mining Group.

A venous industry based EIP is primarily composed of enterprises engaged in manufacturing of venous industries. In *Standards of Venous Industry Based Eco-Industrial Parks (on trial)* (HJ/T275-2006), a venous industry is defined as the industry, in which the wastes produced in manufacturing and consumption are transformed into resources and products that can be reused. It includes two phases: transforming wastes into regenerated resources, and processing regenerated resources into products. Qingdao New World Industrial Park is a typical park of this type.

CURRENT SITUATION OF EIPS IN CHINA

In accordance with the statistics of *Report of Construction Progress of National Eco-Industrial Demonstration Park in 2008* promulgated by MEP, 33 Demonstration EIPs have been approved to construct by the end of January, 2009. These parks are concentrated in eastern coastal area, where China has established numerous EDAs, bonded zones, processing zones and HIPs.

Geographically, there are 25 EIPs in the eastern China (2 in Guangdong, 6 in Shandong, 2 in Liaoning, 7 in Jiangsu, 2 in Zhejiang, 2 in Tianjin, 1 in Fujian, 2 in Shanghai, 1 in Beijing). There are 3 EIPs in the central China (1 in Hunan, 1 in Henan and 1 in Shanxi). And there are 5 EIPs in the western China (2 in Inner Mongolia, 1 in Guizhou, 1 in Guangxi and 1 in Yunnan). The distribution of EIPs in China is related to the factors such as the opening degree, geographical location, land-use conditions, level of industrial structure, and external traffic capability (Zhong, 2007). The relative sophisticated industrial technologies, convenient transportation, and good ecological environment in the eastern area induce fast development of large-scale EIPs there.

Among the 33 EIPs, there are 23 sector-integrate parks, 9 sector-specific parks and 1 venous industry based park. The sector-integrate parks are composed of 4 national HIPs, 11 national EDAs, 1 national bonded zone, 1 environmental protection industry park and 6 provincial industrial parks. The sector-specific EIPs include sugar refinery, electrolytic aluminum, salt chemistry, mining, phosphorous coal chemistry, marine chemistry, and steel & coal chemistry. The venous industry based park is Qingdao New World Industrial Park established in 2006.

THE CHINESE POLICY SYSTEM FOR EIPS

Policies

In December, 2003, SEPA issued *Guideline for Planning of Eco-industrial Parks (on trial)* and *Regulations on the Application, Nomination and Management of Eco-industrial Parks (on trial)*. The former document detailed the concept of EIPs, the principle, method, indicator system and procedures in preparation of the EIP planning; whereas the latter focused on specifying the procedure of application, planning, approval and nomination, supervision and management, and organization and implementation. The launch of the two documents provided sound technical basis for China to advance the construction of EIPs in the early stage and identified the responsibility division from the management angle and optimized the management at the same time.

In 2005, the State Council issued the *Decision on Implementing Scientific Development Concept and Strengthening Environmental Protection* (Guofa No. 39 [2005]), *Measures of the State Council on Accelerating the Development of Recycling Economy* (Guofa No. 22 [2005]) and *Notice of the State Council on the Comprehensive Work Plan for Energy Conservation and Emission Reduction.* The construction of national demonstration EIPs were therefore promoted through the actions to build the environment-friendly society.

In 2007, SEPA, MOC and MOST jointly issued the *Management Measures for National Demonstration Eco-industrial Parks (on trial)*. The management measures are the further amendment and perfection based on that in 2003. The application, management, plan preparation, examination, acceptance and construction performance evaluation for EIPS are systematically regulated. Meanwhile, not only SEPA but also another two ministries has been involved in the promotion of EIPs. At the national level, a coordinative leading group is established for the construction of the parks by MEP, MOC and MOST. Under it, an administrative office is set up. The leading group is responsible for the review, nomination and comprehensive work for the park and the administrative branches of MEP, MOC and MOST at different levels are responsible for the daily supervision work.

In May 2008, MEP, MOC and MOST jointly held a working conference on EIP construction to accelerate the construction of the EIPs in national EDAs, national HIPs and other industrial assemblies. In August of the same year, the *Act on Promoting the Recycling Economy* was issued. According to the act, industry parks shall organize the enterprises to promote the development of recycling economy. The state encourages enterprises in different types of industrial parks to reuse the waste in the way of exchanging, energy cascade utilization, land consolidation utilization, classified and recycled use of water and share of infrastructures and other related facilities. All of those are for promoting the development of EIPs.

A relative complete management system for EIPs such as laws, management measures, plan formulation, park construction, management, and evaluation has been established in China. Each year, the demonstration EIPs under construction should report their progress and situation of the year to the leading group. The leading group also organizes random inspection on the parks. For the nominated parks, evaluation of the construction performance will be performed once every 3 years. The launch of such policies, laws and management measures effectively pushed the development progress of the EIPs in China.

STANDARDS

Up to date, there are three standards for the sector-integrate, sector-specific and venous industry based EIPs in China.

- **Standard for Sector-integrate Eco-industrial Parks(HJ274-2009):** The standard has 26 indicators, including economic development, resource recycling and utilization, pollution control and park management. The economic development indicators include per capita industrial value added, and growth rate of industrial value added per year; The material reduction and recycling indicators include industrial value added per unit of industrial land, comprehensive energy consumption per unit of industrial value added, comprehensive energy consumption elasticity coefficient, fresh water consumption per unit of industrial value added, fresh water consumption elasticity coefficient, amount of produced wastewater per unit of industrial value added, amount of solid waste per unit of industrial value added, repeating utilization factor of industrial water, industrial solid waste comprehensive utilization factor and treated waste water reuse rate; The pollution control indicators include COD emission per unit of industrial value added, COD emission elasticity factor, SO_2 emission per unit of industrial value added, SO_2 emission elasticity factor, hazardous waste disposal rate, sewage collective treatment rate, house refuse harmless treatment rate, waste collection and collective treatment and disposal ability; The park management indicators include environment management system and capability, ecological industrial information platform perfection system, environment report preparation condition, sanitary production review execution rate of major enterprises, satisfaction of the public with the environment and public awareness of the eco-industry.

- **Standard for Sector-specific Eco-industrial Parks (on trial) (HJ/T273-2006):** The standard contains 19 indicators in total, including economic development, resource recycling and utilization, pollution control and park management. The economic development indicators include growth rate of industrial value added; The material reduction and recycling indicators: comprehensive energy consumption per unit of industrial value added, fresh water consumption per unit of industrial value added, amount of produced waster water per unit of industrial value added, repeating utilization factor of industrial water, and industrial solid waste comprehensive utilization factor; The pollution control indicators include COD emission per unit of industrial value added, SO_2 emission per unit of industrial value added, hazardous waste disposal rate, industry characterized pollutant emission total amount, industry characterized pollutant emission standard-meeting rate, waste collection and collective treatment and disposal facilities and environmental management system; The park management indicators include workmanship and technology level, perfection degree of information platform, environment report preparation condition, the satisfaction of neighboring communities with the parks and the staff's awareness of eco-industry.
- **Standard for Venous Industry Based Eco-industrial Parks (HJ/T275-2006):** The standard has 20 indicators, including economic development, resource recycling and utilization, pollution control and park management. The economic development indicators: per capita industrial value added and contribution rate of the venous industry based EIP to the industrial value added; The resource recycling and utilization: waste disposal amount, waste home appliance resource rate, waste automobile resource rate, waste tire resource rate, waste plastic resource rate and other waste resource rate; The pollution control indicators: hazardous waste safe disposal rate, waste water discharge per unit of industrial value added, pollutant discharge standard-meeting rate of enterprises in the park, waste collective treatment and disposal facilities and collective sewage treatment facilities; The park management indicators: environment supervision system in the park, waste disposal and production and processing technology of the enterprises in the park, the greening coverage rate in the park, perfection system of the information platform, tour and sightseeing in the park, the number of persons who come for visiting and learning and the environment report preparation condition of the park.

PLANNING FOR EIPS

As previously-mentioned, *Guideline for Planning of EIPs (on trial)* and *Management Measures for National Demonstration Eco-industrial Parks (on*

Table 1. Contents of a construction plan and construction technological report for an EIP in China

Construction plan	Construction technological report
1. Abstract **2. Construction significance and advantageous conditions** – Background of society, economy and environment – Construction significance – Constraints, problems and analysis – Advantages **3. General design** – General concept (including orientation, construction framework, industry chain construction and material circulation analysis) – Overall objectives and specific indicators – Planning scope – Planning principle **4. Eco-industrial development planning for each industry** – Status quo analysis – Development objectives and specific indicators – Cleaner production measures – Eco-industry design **5. Major pollutant control plan** – Water pollution control and water reuse plan – Air pollution control plan – Solid waste control plan **6. Major projects and benefit analysis** – Park entry conditions for projects – Major supports (including industrial projects, infrastructures and service facilities) – Benefit analysis (economic, social and environmental benefits) **7. Safeguard system** – organization and management system – Economic policies – Policy assurance – Environment risk emergency management system – Environmental management tools	**1. Analysis for current natural, social and ecological situation** – Overview – Natural conditions – Social economy – Ecological environment **2. Necessities and advantageous conditions for EIP construction** – Retrospective analysis on environmental impact assessment – Necessities and significance – Advantageous conditions – Constraints **3. General design** – Guiding ideology and planning principles – Planning scope and basis – Overall objectives and specific indicators (including the analysis on the achievability for the major indicators) – General framework (including the general description of the ecological chain in the EIP) **4. Eco-industrial development planning for each industry** – Status quo analysis – Development objectives and specific indicators (short-term and middle-term) – Pollution control – Industrial ecological system design – Waste metabolism chain construction and perfection **5. Pollution control plan** – Air pollution control – Water pollution control – Solid waste control **6. Major projects and benefit analysis** – Key projects entering the park (including industrial projects, infrastructure and service facilities) – Benefit analysis (including economic, ecological environment and social benefits) **7. Safeguard systems** – Organization – Environmental management – Industry and economic policies – Technical safeguard system (such as information network system, new technology development and enterprise incubator) – Other measures (such as talent cultivation and introduction, public participation, publicity and education, international exchange, and infrastructure construction.)

trial) are the two key documents, which should be followed in the plan-making for EIPs in China. Planning for EIPs in China includes preparation for two reports called construction plan and construction technological report. The contents for the plan and report are listed in Table 1. It should be noted that the contents can be changed with the situation for a specific EIP.

In general, the construction plan for an EIP focuses on the overall aspects including general concept, development objectives, construction projects and safeguard mechanism. The construction technological report for an EIP should analyze the feasibility of the specific plans and measures and assess the environmental impact historically (at least from 5-10 years before) and currently.

The detailed analysis includes the number and distribution of pollution sources, the discharge characteristics of major pollutant, potential environment risks and action plan for emergencies, the consumption level of major energy and resources, changes of regional environmental quality, the execution and implementation of environment laws and regulations, investment in environment protection, and environment management.

TYPICAL EIPS IN CHINA

Sector-Specific Case: Guigang Demonstration EIP

Guangxi Guigang National Demonstration EIP (Sugar Refinery), the first EIP in China has been well-developed. The sugar output in Guangxi occupies more than 40% of that in China. Guigang is located in the middle of Guangxi, surrounded by the majority of sugar manufacturers of Guangxi within a scope of 300km. The wastewater discharged from the sugar industry approaches to 80% of the total wastewater discharge in Guigang. Such structural pollution has become the bottleneck confining the development of local economy and society. Guangxi Guitang Group Co., Ltd. lays emphasis on comprehensive utilization of resources during its development and becomes the core enterprise in Guiguang demonstration EIP. The Guiguang park had formed an eco-industrial symbiosis network made up by six subsystems such as sugar cane fields and sugar making. Through optimizing the combination, the input and output between the subsystems are mutually connected to achieve the optimum configuration and the effective utilization of the waste. Thus, it is expected that the pollution could be reduced to the lowest level through the construction of such a rather complete ecological system combining sugar industry and planting.

The six subsystems in Guigang EIP are:

a. **Sugar cane field system:** responsible for providing safe and stable sugar cane of high productivity and high sugar content to the production in the park to ensure sufficient supply of raw material to the manufacturing system in the park;
b. **Sugar making system:** through the technological transformation of sugar making and technological transformation of oligosaccharides, produce the common refined sugar and organic sugar and oligosaccharides of high added value;
c. **Alcohol system:** through energy alcohol projects and yeast extract projects, effectively make use of the byproducts in sugar making with sugar cane—waste molasses to produce products such as energy alcohol together with high value added yeast extract;
d. **Paper making system:** make full use of the byproducts in sugar making with sugar canes—bagasse to produce products such as high quality domestic paper and cultural paper as well as high value added CMC (carboxymethylcellulose sodium);
e. **Heat-power cogeneration system:** use the byproducts in sugar making with sugar cane--bagasse pith to replace part of fuel coal to co-generate heat and power and supply power and steams necessary for production to ensure the power supply to the whole production system in the park;
f. **Environment comprehensive handling system:** provide environmental service to the manufacturing system in the park, including waste water and gas handling, production of byproducts such as cement, light calcium and composite fertilizer and provide water to save water resource.

SECTOR-INTEGRATE CASE: TIANJIN ECONOMIC AND TECHNOLOGICAL DEVELOPMENT AREA

Tianjin Economic and Technological Development Area (TEDA) began to pay attention to the issues of eco-industry in the end of year of 2000. In 2001, Sino-Japanese Recycling Economy and Zero Emission Workshop was held to introduce the concept of recycling economy in TEDA. In 2002, TEDA participated in the joint project of SEPA and UNEP called "China Industrial Park Environmental Management Pilot Project" and made decision to develop towards an EIP. In 2003, the construction plan was finished. In 2004, TEDA was approved by SEPA to construct itself as a national demonstration EIP. In 2008, it became one of the first national demonstration EIPs formally nominated by the State.

Three chains for eco-industry, water ecosystem and waste recycling are the key components for the EIP construction in TEDA.

For the eco-industrial chain, a product metabolism network is constructed with four backbone industries: electronic information industry, biological pharmacy, automobile manufacturing industry and food and drink industry.

The water ecosystem chain includes dual-water supply, water reuse, conservative utilization and the use of unconventional water. For the dual-water supply, low quality reclaimed or seawater water pipelines are constructed in parallel with the existing tap water pipelines. For water reuse, water reuse plant is constructed to supply water for city vegetation, municipal use, enterprise cooling water, production process, groundwater supplementary and landscape lakes. For conservative utilization of water, water saving in households is mainly realized in the way of improving the efficiency of pipe fittings and appliances. Water saving in industry adopts the measures to improve water equipment and water use process and use cleaner production technology to reduce water consumption. For the unconventional water development and utilization, seawater is directly used for cooling and flushing toilet in homes and seawater indoor pools. Meanwhile, a seawater desalination plant is being constructed and a rain water system including collection, storage and use is also being constructed.

The waste recycling chain is established through construction of domestic waste recycling, waste greening, industrial waste chains and waste minimization club. For the domestic waste recycling, Shuanggang Domestic Waste Incineration Plant of Tianjing TEDA Environmental Protection Co. Ltd. with a waste treatment capacity to 1,200 t/d and an installed capacity of 18MW, can generate 351,000 kWh power per day and send 116 million kWh power to the grid in one year, which is equivalent to saving 4800 tons coal each year. For waste greening, fly ash and slag are promoted to be used in the greening projects. For the industrial waste chains, Taiding Electronic Waste Processing Co., Ltd with a treatment capacity of 10 thousand tons of electronic waste can produce metals such as copper, gold and zinc; Human Resource Co., Ltd, Honggang Cast Iron Co., Ltd and Toho Zinc Co., Ltd can recycle the waste from automobile industry; the feed and organic fertilizer enterprises are built to recycle the waste from food and biological pharmacy industry. Simultaneously, the administrative departments create an industrial waste exchange information platform through the activities in the waste minimization club.

VENOUS INDUSTRY BASED CASE: QINGDAO NEW WORLD EIP

Qingdao New World EIP in Shandong Province is the first professional venous industry based EIP in China. The park is engaged in the venous industry of disassembling of home appliance, automobiles, cables and wires and lead accumulators. A chain has been established with five segments: solid waste collection, transportation and storage, solid waste treatment and disposal, solid waste recycling, and polluted soil restoration. The park is divided into research region, testing region, service region and production region as four functional regions and 1 reserve region.

In the research region, the National Environmental Protection Research Center for Solid Wastes Reuse Technologies has been set up. The research of the Center focuses on solid wastes treatment technology, hazardous wastes identification technology, reuse technology of recycled materials, polluted soil restoration technology, and technology for new energy exploration. It will also serve to set up some testing methods, formulated and validate related technology standards and provide training. This center will provide technological support for solid wastes reuse and the development of recycling economy, and becomes a incubator for solid wastes disposal technologies in the Park to advance the science and technology for environmental protection industry.

In the service region, the Solid Waste Information Exchange Center of Shandong Province has been set up to provide timely and effectively information service to Qingdao Hazardous Waste Disposal Center and Shandong Hazardous Waste Disposal Center as well as the park itself. The center will collect and provide information on reclaiming, exchanging and disposing the hazardous waste, medical waste, solid waste and electronic waste to realize information and infrastructure share and make the waste be exchanged and disposed fast and efficiently.

In the production region, there exists a regional hazardous waste disposal center which can safely dispose various solid wastes produced by enterprises in the park and therefore no solid waste would be discharged from the park. In the region, a polluted soil restoration factory with an area of 100 Chinese mu and an investment of 63 million RMB was jointly funded by China and UK to carry out biological, plant and chemical restoration for the polluted soil. The used car dissembling factory with a disposal capacity of 10,000 sets/y is a safe disposal center for the used cars in the park. Demonstration project of comprehensive use of used home appliance and electronic products has been undertaken in the park since 2006. The total investment for this project is 83 million RMB and 200,000 sets of used home appliances per year in the first phase and 600,000 sets per year in the second phase can be dissembled. There is also a landfill site for industrial solid waste with an investment of 10 million RMB and a designed capacity of 10×10^4 m^3. In addition, Qingdao Medical Waste Disposal Center with an investment of 17.5 million RMB and an incineration capacity of 24t/d can treat the medical waste from more than 320 hospitals in five towns and 7 districts in Qingdao.

APPLICATION OF CEMIS TO EIPS IN CHINA

CEMIS Modeling for EIPs in China

As mentioned above, the indicator system for EIPs in China includes the aspects of economic development, resource recycling and utilization, pollution control and park management. The goals for a CEMIS are actually similar to those. Traditionally, there are structural life cycle method, prototype method, business system planning method and critical success factors method for construction of a management information system (Liu, 1995). Due to the complexity of both CEMIS and EIPs, combination of those methods should be applied to construct a CEMIS for an EIP.

Figure 1 shows the hierarchy plus input-process-output diagram of a CEMIS for an EIP. The values of each indicator can reflect how the park achieves the national EIP standards. Thus, the indicator data should be essential data for the system input. Certainly the support knowledge system such as relevant standards or background information of EIPs should be also included. Data processing is complex for a CEMIS, due to the

Figure 1. Schematic diagram of hierarchy plus input-process-output for a CEMIS in EIPs

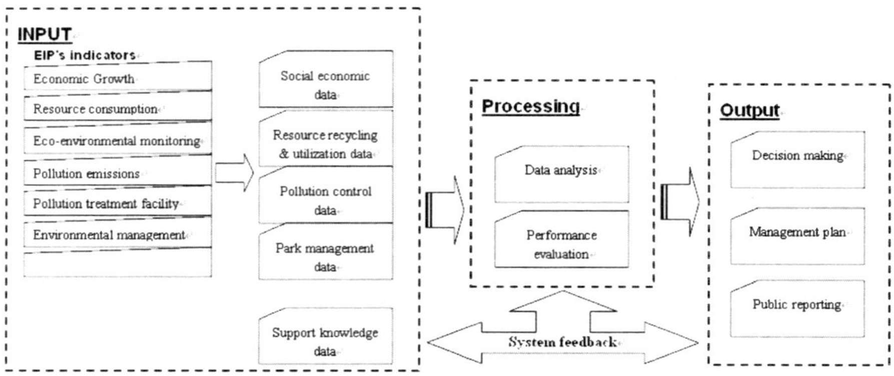

diversity of heterogeneous data. Not only multi-variable statistic analysis should be conducted, but also the EIP performance should be evaluated. Therefore an adjusted management plan should be performed with systematic decision targeted benign development of an EIP. Meanwhile, the performance data should be open to the community in order to increase public awareness and support. In addition, a feedback module is helpful to manage the information flow corporately.

It should be noted that the CEMIS data collection is related to various park departments such as environmental protection department, municipal construction department, statistic department and even questionnaire survey. A platform or mechanism for data and knowledge sharing is fundamental and essential for a successful CEMIS.

CEMIS CONTROL FOR EIPS IN CHINA

As a symbiosis network exists between companies in an EIP, the connection between companies

Figure 2. Schematic diagram of control for an EIP

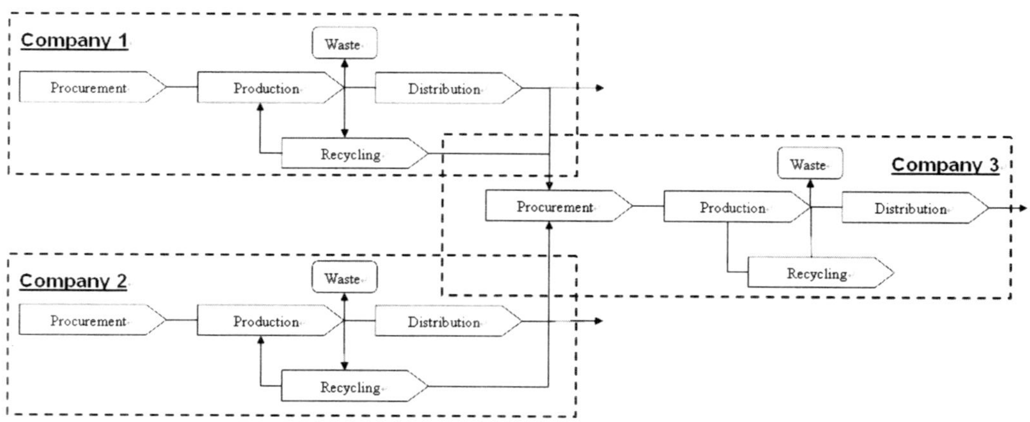

makes application of systems control theories be possible. The aim of controlling for EIPs is to make and adjust management strategies and measures based on simulation of the system performance and scenario as a part of CEMIS.

Provided that a company is a box, the box model can employed for the system simulation. For simplicity, an ideal eco-industrial chain with three companies is taken as an example herein (Figure 2). For one company in the chain, the input and output should be:

$$F_{in} = QC_{in}$$

$$F_{out} = QC_{out}$$

$$M_{res} = VC_{res}$$

where F_{in} is the input flux of material and energy from procurement and recycling; F_{out} is the output flux of material and energy of product and waste; Q is the flow rate of material and energy; V is the scale of production; C is concentration or density; and M_{res} is the material and energy within the production process. The system will be in steady state when F_{in} is equal to F_{out}. The production time or residence time (t) will be:

$$t = \frac{VC_{res}}{F_{out}}$$

Similarly, such box model can be established for other companies in an EIP. If there are n companies, a model with n boxes can be established using the input-output connections among companies.

The objective functions for such a box model are $\min(F_{waste})$ and $\max(F_{product})$. Obviously, establishment of a perfect symbiosis network is the most convenient way to minimize the waste and maximize the product. In addition, with development of environmental protection, the environmental management in CEMIS is becoming broader than before. In other words, environmental protection is not limited to traditional pollutants such as heavy metals or COD etc. but also green house gases such as CO_2. Therefore, the waste herein should take all of those "pollutants" into account.

CONCLUSION

Since the introduction of EIP in the 1990s, EIPs in China have developed rapidly with the promotion of Chinese government. In this chapter, the development of EIPs in China including classification, distribution, related policies and standards, planning, and three typical EIPs has been described. As the construction of eco-industrial chains is the core of EIP construction, a corporate environmental management information system (CEMIS) is necessary to make the industrial system efficiently. Therefore, a concept CEMIS model for EIPs in China has been proposed according to the management policies. Furthermore, as a part of CEMIS the control and simulation for EIPs has been discussed using the box model. With the concept CEMIS models for EIPs, the study on a practicable CEMIS for EIPs is needed for the future work.

REFERENCES

Cote, R. P., & Hall, J. (1995). Industrial parks as ecosystems. *Journal of Cleaner Production*, *1*(3), 41–46. doi:10.1016/0959-6526(95)00041-C

Erkman, S. (1999). *Industrial Ecology*. Beijing, China: Economic Daily Press.

Lang, C. V. (2007). Modeling of a corporate environment information system (CEMIS) for production processes. In Marx Gómez, J., Sonnenschein, M., Müller, M., Welsch, H., & Rautenstrauch, C. (Eds.), *Information Technologies in Environmental Engineering* (pp. 231–240). Berlin, Heidelberg, New York: Springer. doi:10.1007/978-3-540-71335-7_24

Liu, L. (1995). *Design Principle and Application of Information Systems*. Beijing, China: Beihang University Publishing House.

Lowe, E. A. (2001). *Eco-Industrial Park Handbook for Asian Developing Countries. Report to Asian Development Bank*. Retrieved from http://www.indigodev.com/ADBHBdownloads.html

Lowe, E. A., & Warren, J. L. (2008). The source of value: an executive briefing and source book on industrial ecology. *Northwest National Richland, 2*, 151–152.

Pen, Z. (1998). *Region Research and Planning*. Shanghai, China: Tongji University Press.

President's Council on Sustainable Development. (1996). *Eco-Industrial Park Workshop Proceedings*. Retrieved from http://clinton2.nara.gov/PCSD/Publications/Eco_Workshop.html

Ren, Z. (2000). *City Planning and Management in the 21st Century*. Nanjing, China: Southeast University Press.

Wang, Z. (2007). *Recycling Economy: Regional Industry Symbiosis Network – a theory and practice to the development of eco-industrial park*. Beijing, China: Economy and Science Press.

Xiang, X., Yang, Q., Zhou, J., & Wang, R. (2009). Eco-industrial park planning method research and prospect. *Environmental Science & Technology, 1*, 32.

Xin, Z., Lu, X., & Tang, Y. (1999). A study on management information system for environmental protection industry in Tianjin. *Urban Environment & Urban Ecology, 12*(6), 42–44.

Zhong, S. (2007). *Eco-industrial Park Construction and Management*. Beijing, China: People's Publishing House.

ADDITIONAL READING

Heeres, R. R., Vermeulen, W. J. V., & de Walle, F. B. (2004). Eco-industrial park initiatives in the USA and the Netherlands: first lessons. *Journal of Cleaner Production, 12*(8-10), 985–995. doi:10.1016/j.jclepro.2004.02.014

Jessup, L., & Valacich, J. (2008). *Information Systems Today: Managing in the Digital World* (3rd ed.). Upper Saddle River: Prentice Hall.

Marx Gómez, J., Sonnenschein, M., Müller, M., Welsch, H., & Rautenstrauch, C. (Eds.). (2007). *Information Technologies in Environmental Engineering*. Berlin, Heidelberg, New York: Springer. doi:10.1007/978-3-540-71335-7

Morrow, D., & Rondinelli, D. (2002). Adopting corporate environmental management systems: motivations and results of ISO 14001 and EMAS certification. *European Management Journal, 20*(2), 159–171. doi:10.1016/S0263-2373(02)00026-9

Sangwon, S. (Ed.). (2009). Handbook of Input-Output Economics in Industrial Ecology. Dordrecht, NL: Springer.

ENDNOTE

1 Corresponding author: Dr. and Prof. Xueqiang Lu, Address: 17 Fukang Road, Nankai District, Tianjin, 300191, China; Tel&Fax: +86-22-2305-1227; Email: xueqianglu@gmail.com

Chapter 25
Sustainable Scorecard as an Actionable Framework for Managing Sustainability:
The Case of Tube Brazil

Marlei Pozzebon
HEC Montréal, Canada

Paulina Arroyo
HEC Montréal, Canada

Angela Fleury
Fundação Dom Cabral, Brazil

ABSTRACT

This paper investigates how corporate sustainable practices can be supported by information management models and information and communication technology (ICT) applications. The empirical work is based on a single case study, a Brazilian company that is applying the concept of a sustainability balanced scorecard (SBSC) to put forward a triple bottom-line strategy. Our results suggest that (a) implementation and use of the SBSC, (b) integration of the triple-bottom line concept within the SBSC, and (c) the place occupied by the eco-efficiency indicator at the heart of the strategic map represented three key factors that helped to enhance sustainability management. Moreover, the development of a sustainability-oriented culture and the strong business intelligence (BI) platform put in place enabled successful implementation of the SBSC in this particular company.

INTRODUCTION

This paper investigates how social responsibility and sustainable practices in contemporary organizations can be supported by information management models and information and communication technology (ICT) applications. It is recognized by many analysts that ICT is not only one of today's most pervasive and ubiquitous phenomena, but also the motor of so-called societal "revolutions" like the information society and the network society (Castels, 2000). Undeniably, ICT has come to pervade human activities at all levels

DOI: 10.4018/978-1-61520-981-1.ch025

– individual, organizational and institutional. It is also evident that the fields of corporate social responsibility and sustainability have grown exponentially over the last decade. An increasing number of managers and companies worldwide have been engaging in serious efforts to integrate sustainability into their business practices (Jones, 2003). This emergence should be evaluated in the complex context of globalization, deregulation and privatization, wherein inequalities in terms of social, environmental and economic conditions continue to grow (UNIDO, 2004). Despite the explosion of interest in and concern with social responsibility and sustainability, their effective implementation faces serious obstacles.

Viewed separately, sustainability and ICT both represent relevant themes for investigation. Curiously, few management studies have considered these two themes together. The exception is the area known as CEMIS – corporate environmental management information systems – defined as organizationally technical systems that offer the possibility of systematically gathering, processing and making available environmentally relevant information (Lang, 2007). In line with this research area, we put forward the argument that the purposive use of information management models, supported by ICT applications, can help support sustainability management by improving the gathering, analysis and sharing of useful knowledge (including quantitative and qualitative information like socio-environmental indicators, measures, metrics, ideas, opinions, experiences) among employees, clients, partners and the community (Watson, 2007; Ferland 2009). By *information management models*, we mean models that conjoin interrelated activities – such as identification, gathering, organization, storage and sharing of information needs – to support decision making activities at the operational, tactical and strategic levels (Choo, 1998). ICT is seen as a critical support for organizational processes, and the knowledge we seek to generate relates to *how* ICT applications can support socially responsible corporate projects.

In this paper, we describe an information management model, successfully implemented by a Brazilian company, based on the concept of a *sustainability balanced scorecard (SBSC)*, and supported by an ICT application known as *business intelligence (BI)*. The evidence provided by this case study illustrates not only how an SBSC framework becomes extremely useful for facilitating integration of sustainability into business practices and strategy, but also how firms might overcome typical challenges confronted in these kinds of projects. In the following sections, we present: the literature review, encompassing the concepts of corporate social responsibility and sustainability, the emergence of the concept of sustainability balanced scorecard (SBSC) and business intelligence (BI) applications; our methodological approach; the case study; and the conclusions.

BACKGROUND

Corporate Social Responsibility (CSR) and Sustainability

Over the last 40 years, several definitions have been put forward to take into account more than economic concerns in the debate over corporate behavior and strategy. The concept of corporate social responsibility (CSR) is one of these concerns. One explanation for the explosion of interest in business ethics and CSR grows out of the increasing body of literature claiming that CSR does, in fact, have a positive impact on business economic performance (Miles & Munilla, 2004). Several studies claim that initiatives aimed at improving environmental performance (such as reducing emissions of gases that contribute to global climate change or reducing use of agrochemicals) also lower costs; that recycling initiatives cut waste-disposal costs and generate

Table 1. CSR: A multidimensional concept

Multiple dimensions	Multiple Stakeholders	Multiple levels of analysis
Social	Employees	Individual
Economic	Shareholders	Group
Environmental	Customers	Organizational
	Suppliers	Institutional
	Society	

income through sale of recycled materials; that, in the human resources arena, flexible scheduling and other work-life programs result in reduced absenteeism and increased retention of employees, often saving companies money through increased productivity and reduction of hiring and training costs (BSR, 2008). In addition, a company considered socially responsible is likely to benefit from an enhanced reputation among the general public as well as within the business community, increasing the company's ability to attract capital and trading partners (Miles & Munilla, 2004).

Over the last few years, the CSR research agenda has been shifting from 'why' and 'what' to 'how' to adopt strategies and processes that support CSR decisions within organizations (Basu & Palazzo, 2008). Aligned with that agenda, we define CSR as a comprehensive set of policies, practices and programs that are integrated into business operations, supply chains, and decision-making processes throughout a company, for the purpose of inculcating responsibility for current and past actions as well as future impacts (BSR, 2008). CSR is seen as a multidimensional concept, and examining it involves different dimensions, stakeholders and levels of analysis. As illustrated by Table 1: dimensions include social, economic and environmental aspects; often identified as leading stakeholders are employees, shareholders, customers, suppliers and the community or society at large; and levels of analysis span the individual, group, organizational and institutional or societal.

Stirring wide interest, the *1992 Earth* Summit held in Rio de Janeiro triggered a surge of visibility for the concept of sustainability, which became ever more widely discussed and analyzed by politicians, business leaders and NGOs, gaining increased relevance for such considerations in day-to-day business discussion. Nowadays, an increasing number of managers have accepted corporate sustainability as a precondition for doing business, forced by the need to comply with new environmental and social regulations (Dyllick and Hockerts, 2002). A growing number of firms are starting to realize the potential benefits of incorporating sustainability issues into their corporate strategies with a view towards eventual competitive advantages and improvements in their financial performance.

Although sustainability is widely discussed, finding a single consensual definition of sustainability is a difficult task. The predominant interpretation of *sustainable development* was introduced in the Brundtland Commission's report: meeting the needs of the present without compromising the ability of future generations to meet their own needs. From a corporate point of view, a strategy for corporate sustainability must meet the needs of the firm's stakeholders without compromising its ability to meet the needs of future stakeholders as well (Hockerts, 2001). However, this macroeconomic definition provides little guidance regarding sustainable development and cannot explain why managers are used to conflating the term corporate sustainability with the term corporate social responsibility. Epstein and Roy (2003) suggest that this amalgam might be based on the fact that both terms share the common premise that

Table 2. A summary of the three cases and the most important indicators

	Business Case		
	Eco-Efficiency	Socio-Efficiency	
Green Case	Eco-Effectiveness	Socio-Effectiveness	Social Case
	Sufficiency	Ecological Equity	

business and society are interconnected and that society has expectations in terms of appropriate business behaviours.

Elkington (1998) defines a sustainable enterprise as a company that contributes to sustainable development by delivering economic, social and environmental benefits simultaneously – the so called *triple bottom line* – concomitantly expanding the spectrum of values and criteria for measuring organizational (and societal) success. Meeting the needs of a firm's stakeholders in the future and today necessitates a long-term approach requiring that all three dimensions of sustainability be satisfied simultaneously: the economic, social and environmental. However, because addressing the three dimensions simultaneously is too complex for companies, some authors suggest thinking separately about the links within each of the two dimensions (Elkington, 1998).

First, we can analyze how environmental and social sustainability contribute to economic sustainability. This, known as the "business case" for sustainability, claims it is possible to prove that firms could improve shareholder value through *eco-efficiency* and *socio-efficiency strategies* (Table 2). *Eco-efficiency* means producing more (goods, services and aggregate value) with less (resources, waste and pollution) and most companies have opted for eco-efficiency as their guideline principle (Dyllick and Hockerts, 2002). The second component of the "business case" is *socio-efficiency*, which describes the relation between a firm's value added and its social impact (positive or negative). From an environmental point of view ("the green case"), the concepts of *eco-effectiveness* and *sufficiency* are key because ecological sustainability is concerned not only with relative improvements but with absolute thresholds as well. Finally, from a social point of view, *socio-effectiveness* and *ecological equity* are relevant to the "social case" for corporate sustainability (Dyllick & Hockerts, 2002).

Despite the complexity of the entire process, Möller and Schaltegger (2005) suggest that when *eco-efficiency* indicators are embedded within a sustainability balanced scorecard (SBSC), they become an important starting point, an instrument for estimating and controlling key measures – relating to environmental and economic issues that might evolve – to integrate other relevant concepts. The SBSC is, therefore, the subject of the next section.

The Emergence of the Concept of Sustainability Balanced Scorecard (SBSC)

Although standards like ISO 14031 and SA 8000, and principles like the Triple Bottom Line, have been introduced over the past decade, they have not been sufficient to support business, green or social cases for corporate sustainability. This explains the emergence of the *sustainability balanced scorecard* (SBSC) as a sub-field of research and one of the most important approaches to inclusion of environmental and social concerns as core strategic issues. In the ICT field, scorecards and dashboards are part of the area called *business intelligence (BI)*. BI implies a combination of methodologies for the definition of information, measures and indicators that are likely to support decision-making processes, and also a collection

Table 3. Five approaches to integrating social and environmental aspects within an SBSC

Type of approach	Main features
Partial SBSC	Integrates one or two socio-environmental indicators into a single and existing perspective.
Transversal SBSC	Integrates one or more socio-environmental indicators into all four perspectives
Additive SBSC	Integrates one or more socio-environmental indicators into a fifth perspective: social and environmental sustainability
Total SBSC	Both transversal and additive
Separate SBSC	Formulates a specific and separate scorecard for environmental and social issues (E&S scorecard).

of software and databases that support gathering, consolidation, analysis and diffusion of that information (Petrini, 2006).

The SBSC concept is based on the balanced scorecard (BSC) framework, a strategy implementation tool proposed by Kaplan and Norton (1996) that takes into consideration non-monetary strategic success factors (such as learning processes, quality improvement and employee motivation), which, in turn, lead to economic benefits for the company. Traditionally, a BSC has four dimensions: growth and learning, internal processes, clients and financial. An SBSC is a BSC that incorporates sustainability strategies into its strategic maps, objectives, targets, actions and indicators. Although Kaplan and Norton have not focused their research on how to incorporate sustainability issues into the BSC, they suggest that when they are vital for the success of the business unit's strategy, all stakeholder interests can be incorporated into the BSC (Kaplan & Norton, 1996). Moreover, these objectives should not be appended as an isolated set of measures but should be fully integrated into the cause-and-effect relationships that tell the story of the business unit's strategy.

Regarding the literature on SBSC, we can recognize two main branches of studies: (a) proposals that are based on Kaplan and Norton's framework with slight modifications to the original BSC approach; and (b) proposals that clearly go beyond Kaplan and Norton's framework. Studies based on Kaplan and Norton are focused mainly on the "business case" for sustainability, while those going beyond Kaplan and Norton expand their focus to build the three cases for sustainability, i.e. the business, green and social cases (van der Woerd & van den Brink, 2004; Dias-Sardinha & Reijnders, 2005).

Developing an SBSC helps a firm integrate social and environmental issues into corporate strategy. The configuration of an SBSC depends mainly on the identification and analysis of sustainability strategies that the firm is trying to pursue or intends to pursue (Bieker et al., 2001). We identified five different possibilities for integrating social and environmental issues in order to build an SBSC (Table 3).

The simplest strategy involves integration of one or two socio-environmental indicators into the BSC perspective which is more exposed to sustainability issues. This amounts to a first step in strategic management of sustainability, but is still considered a "partial SBSC" (Bieker et al., 2001). For instance, the *customer perspective* can be expanded to include other relevant groups of stakeholders such as NGOs, government agencies, local community, etc. (Johnson, 1998). Likewise, the *internal process perspective* can be revised to include an existing or new environmental management program in the value chain (Radcliffe, 1999). This approach allows a firm to integrate sustainability issues progressively and moderately.

A second approach proposes integrating socio-environmental indicators into not just one but all four perspectives, the "transversal SBSC" (Brown, 1996). Such an approach significantly increases integration of sustainable management as compared to the "partial SBSC" (Figge et al., 2002). In this modality, sustainability issues became fully integrated into the cause-and-effect relationship as well as hierarchically oriented towards the financial perspective, supporting the "business case" for sustainability.

A third approach represents a further step in terms of increasing the importance of socio-environmental issues. This approach proposes inclusion of a distinct fifth dimension specifically embracing social and environmental sustainability, an "additive SBSC". Such a solution might elevate sustainability's status within the company and would probably be found in companies with a high degree of exposure to sustainability issues. The weight given to this perspective would depend on the relative priorities of particular organizations (Epstein and Wisner, 2001). Among reasons that lead companies to adopt a fifth perspective, Epstein and Wisner mention recognition of social and environmental issues as a core component of strategy (creating competitive advantage), rather than just as a means of improving operational efficiency. A second reason is the intention to develop a better instrument for communicating management's strong concern about sustainability issues and highlighting the importance of these issues, especially after facing a number of problems in the environmental or social field.

The fourth approach is called "total SBSC", and is considered a combination of the two approaches discussed above ("transversal" and "additive" SBSC). The fifth dimension, sustainability, is related to trend indicators for all four dimensions, becoming part of the cause-effect relationship among them. Here, strategically relevant social and environmental issues included in the fifth perspective could impact the firm's performance in all four perspectives of the original BSC, whether directly, as in the financial perspective, or indirectly through the other perspectives. The fifth "sustainability dimension" would be linked to all of the other four dimensions, making the cause-and-effect relationships clear (Johnson, 1998).

Finally, a still different approach proposes formulation of a specific scorecard for environmental and social issues. A derived sustainable scorecard could be formulated once one of the previous approaches had been developed, because this particular scorecard is not an independent alternative for integration but merely an extension of the previous approaches. Formulating a separate environmental and social scorecard can serve to clarify relationships among internal service units and their scorecards (Figge et al., 2002).

We found in the concept of SBSC the ground rules for an *information management model* that can help companies integrate sustainability into their strategy and practices. A case study carried out in Brazil has enabled us to better understand the most important triggers for successful implementation of an SBSC, fully supported by an ICT application called *business intelligence (BI) application.* Although integration of sustainability with management models is present in management and accounting literatures, these models are not yet integrated into the *BI literature.*

BI Applications: ICT to Support Decision Making and Strategy Execution

From a historical standpoint, what we call business intelligence (BI) has evolved over the last 35 years. In the 1970s, initial versions of analytical software packages appeared on the market. The 1980s saw the release of spreadsheet software, e.g., Excel, which is still widely used today. By the mid-1980s and early 1990s, so-called executive information systems (EIS) were introduced and quickly grew in popularity by promising to provide top management with easy access to internal and external information relevant to decision-making needs, thereby placing "key information on the desktops of executives" (Rasmussen et al., 2002, p. 99). The 1990s witnessed a kind of revolution in analytical application scenarios, accounting for the emergence of business intelligence (BI) systems. Nowadays, BI is the accepted term for analytical and strategic information systems, including an array of applications classified under three broad headings: analytics (e.g., data mining), monitoring (e.g., dashboards and scorecards) and reporting.

A literature review around the theme *business intelligence* (BI) reveals "separation" between technical and managerial approaches, tracing two broad patterns. The managerial approach sees BI as a *process* in which data gathered from inside and outside the company are integrated in order to generate information relevant to the decision making process. The technical approach presents BI as a *set of tools* that support the process described above. Despite differences between technical and managerial approaches, we can recognize one basic idea shared by BI studies: the core of BI is the gathering, analysis and distribution of information with the goal of supporting the strategic decision-making process. By strategic decisions, we mean decisions related to implementation and evaluation of organizational vision, mission, goals and objectives, which are supposed to have medium- to long-term impacts on the organization, as opposed to operational decisions, which are day-to-day in nature and more related to execution (Petrini, 2006).

From a technical point of view, the stage is set for rapid growth in adoption of BI applications in the coming decades. Nowadays, BI technologies integrate a large set of diversified resources (packages, tools and platforms), and various products are being released aimed at fulfilling different needs related to the search for and use of information. The literature review also shows that knowledge advancements on the technical side have been higher than on the managerial side of BI. Although the volume of information available in data warehouses is increasing and the functionalities of analytical tools are becoming more and more sophisticated, this is not an automatic indicator that firms and individuals are able to derive value from them (Petrini, 2006).

RESEARCH APPROACH

Our research approach was based on a single in-depth case study. A Brazilian firm (here called TUBE,) was selected due to its exceptional characteristics that make it an unparalleled successful Brazilian initiative in implementing a SBSC. We followed Stake's (1998) concept of *instrumental* case study: a particular case is examined in order to provide insight into a research issue. One of the advantages of case-based research over other methodologies is the opportunity to use multiple sources and types of evidence to achieve triangulation (Stake, 1998). To guide data collection and analysis, we adopted a *historical approach*, as proposed by Mason et al. (1997), which offers a valuable perspective for understanding contemporary phenomena, i.e., how issues arose, which solutions have worked, which have not, and why. As Table 4 shows, we proceeded along five research steps (adapted from Mason et al., 1997).

THE CASE: BUILDING AN SBSC AT TUBE BRAZIL

TUBE is a Brazilian firm recognized as one of the leaders in sustainability in Brazil, continuously developing and improving socially responsible practices with its clients, employees, suppliers and local communities. TUBE was created in 2000 as a result of the merger of two smaller firms operating in the same sector: manufacture and sale of a complete line of hydraulic solutions for buildings, irrigation, geo-mechanical (well-drilling) and infrastructure segments. In October 2007, TUBE was a leader in the plastic tube sector in Brazil, with more than 2,000 products distributed across more than 50,000 stores and irrigation shops spanning Brazilian territory. With around

Table 4. Applying a historical approach in five steps

Step	Step	Description (research activities)
1	To identify a research goal	The general aim of the research project is to better understand the role of ICT in supporting management of sustainability. The particular goal of the current case study is to examine a sub-area of ICT, called information management models, in order to provide a clear illustration of strengths of and barriers to a successful project in implementing a model.
2	To specify a domain of inquiry	In order to specify a domain of inquiry with well-defined spatial and temporal boundaries, we designated as our primary unit of analysis the SBSC project developed by TUBE Brazil, retrospectively investigated from its creation in 2000 until October 2007.
3	To gather relevant data (documents and written records).	The main sources of data are interviews, archival research and observations. A number of visits to TUBE were carried out by one of the authors from July 2005 until October 2007. In addition to several informal discussions with TUBE's employees, formal interviews were carried out in July 2006 and in March 2007. The interviews were semi-structured, followed a research protocol, were conducted in Portuguese, and were tape-recorded and transcribed verbatim. The interviews were held with people directly involved in the implementation of sustainability practices at TUBE and in the SBSC project. The most important interviews involved: (a) the director of EHQ department), (b) the CIO (Chief Information Officer) and (c) one of the business analysts working at corporate level, with responsibility for analyzing the information provided by the SBSC and providing executive summaries to TUBE's board on a weekly basis. Our data collection includes articles, doctoral dissertations, project material and documents provided by the director of EHQ.
4	To create a historical narrative.	In this step, we have critically evaluated the empirical material, in order to assess the overall coherence of the historical data.
5	To analyze and interpret the historical data.	The outcome of a historical approach can be more than a mere chronology of facts. The researcher might assemble and interpret the reconstructed "facts" in order to assess their meaning and logic regarding the research goal. We use TUBE's historical data to illustrate the process of building an SBSC, with particular attention to how the concepts of CSR and sustainability were integrated into business strategy and how information management models and ICT applications contributed to effective management of sustainability and interaction with different stakeholders.

1,600 employees, and headquartered in Sao Paulo, TUBE operated four industrial units located in three different regions of Brazil.

The mission of TUBE is the profitable manufacture and sale of complete, innovative and world-class solutions for conducting and controlling fluids, while operating in an ethical, eco-efficient and socially responsible context. The great challenge for TUBE, as for thousands of other companies around the world, is to make the "deed match the word", that is, to conceive, manufacture, sell and deliver products, while respecting the long-term interests of the environment and society.

Key Managerial Initiatives to Build a Culture of Sustainability

The historical analysis allowed us to recognize a number of key managerial initiatives put in place by TUBE's board of directors in order to design, integrate, improve and disseminate a "culture for sustainability", not only within the firm (where employees are called collaborators) but across the entire chain of suppliers (called business partners), customers and the local community. The process started in 2000, shortly after the firm's creation, when the president invited all directors and managers to a series of meetings to discuss the firm's sustainability. One important decision resulting from those meetings was the creation of a formal sustainability area. Without this first key initiative, social and environmental issues would have played a secondary role. The creation of the EHQ (Environment, Health and Quality) department represented an important step in terms of putting in place a governance model to build a true sustainability program.

A second key managerial initiative was the formulation of a coherent collection of programs,

Table 5. Programs, projects and action plans at three levels

Strategic goal: Achieve minimal environmental impact				
Level		**Example**	**Time span**	**Responsible**
1	Strategic programs	Recycling and Residue Management Program	Three years	Firm's directors
2	Vital Projects and Campaigns	Recycling Project	One year	Firm's managers
3	Action Plans	Auditing actions	Three to four months	Processes' owners (analysts, technicians, engineers, coordinators).

projects and action plans, articulated at three levels from long- to short-term, with well-defined targets, owners and rewards. These programs, projects and action plans were associated with strategic goals which, in turn, were articulated within a corporate strategic map (described later), one of the core features of the balanced scorecard methodology. Table 5 illustrates the articulation of actions at three levels.

For example, one of the strategic goals defined by TUBE's board of directors was "minimal environmental impact". To help achieve this goal, a three-year strategic program was designed, the *Recycling and Residue Management Program.* This program defined a number of projects – *recycling projects, residue management projects*, etc. – all, on average, within the one-year time frame. Within each project, a number of specific short-term action plans were articulated, each having a duration of three to four months but renewable, *auditing actions* being one example. This articulation at three levels had a strong impact on all stakeholders' actions, perceptions and decisions. There are some programs in which all 1,600 collaborators participate, like those involving the environment, health and security. Others are more specific, such as the volunteering program, in which a particular number of collaborators are actively engaged.

Associated with the three-level framework, TUBE mounted a "remunerated participation program", where indicators are analyzed by various units and departments. For example, some of the indicators used to monitor the goal of "using international standards for quality, security and environment" are related to the number, frequency and severity of labor accidents; regarding "minimal environmental impact", indicators are related to usage of water and energy and generation of waste. These indicators are monitored at different levels – corporate, unit and departmental – and performance at the end of each period is linked to corresponding reward. This level of granularity (departmental) in the visualization of the information allows precise identification of areas to be improved, but may also encourage competition rather than cooperation. To avoid that, TUBE affirmed that collective values and goals are more important than individual performance, reinforcing the importance of analyzing these indicators at all levels as well as achieving positive results at the corporate level.

A third key managerial initiative was to promote synergy among all stakeholders around sustainability by means of strong communication and training programs. For instance, in launching the previously mentioned *Recycling and Residue Management Program,* "people involvement was key", according to the EHQ director. Through a strong communication campaign, using various materials - billboards, textbooks and internet shock waves - TUBE was able to create "an atmosphere of excitement" around the program. Presentations on the subject were given to 100% of the collaborators and 100% of the partners who acted outside the factory premises. Everyone in the company was involved in the program. In the words of the EHQ director: "The motivation was fantastic! People were feeling the need for practices that were coherent with their words."

Client involvement was also secured through distribution of catalogs highlighting environmental product orientation, health, security and the company's social projects. In 2003, the marketing area launched the "TUBE Award for a Better World" campaign, the first initiative of this kind in the Brazilian market, to recognize the nominee's social and environmental projects aimed at delivering a better place to live to future generations. To involve the local community around the firm's sustainability initiatives, TUBE created: (1) the "volunteering" program, involving numbers of employees in target social projects; (2) the "family visit to the factory" program, which seeks to strengthen bonds between collaborators and their families and the company's social projects, in which many of them work as volunteers; (3) the "child home" project, a partnership that builds and repairs social institutions which treat children with cancer; (4) the "cook Brazil" program, which allows collaborators and their families to get information on healthy, tasty eating that derives nutrients from food without waste; and (5) the "live better" program, which uses workplace exercise to achieve better integration of the internal workforce.

The fourth and final key managerial initiative reported relates to participation and knowledge sharing mechanisms. Between 2002 and 2003, TUBE created two programs to improve coherence between company discourse and practices, and to facilitate exchange of ideas and innovation. The first, called "TUBE wants to know what you think", is a program in which collaborators could send anonymous comments and criticism to management, thereby contributing to evaluation of the organizational environment. The second is the "Coffee and chat" program, a frequent activity in which employees were asked to formulate questions that needed to be formally responded to and explained by their respective managers or other concerned people.

Although TUBE was replete with examples of coherent and interrelated initiatives to promote the integration of social responsibility and sustainability into company business operations and strategy, in the first part of the analysis we identify four that we considered key. In the second part of the analysis, we focus on the contribution of information management models and ICT applications to the effectiveness of these four key initiatives.

The Role of a SBSC Model and of a BI Platform

The Global Compact was created in 1999 by the Secretary General of the United Nations, Kofi Annan, for the purpose of promoting alignment of the corporate sector, labor sector and civil society with nine goals in the areas of human rights, working rights and environmental protection. Coherent with its commitment to the principles of the Global Compact initiative, TUBE put the concept of SBSC into operation to support its sustainable business policies and practices. The approach adopted was the third approach described in the background section, known as "additive SBSC": the scorecard model retained the four traditional dimensions of a BSC and included a fifth dimension, specifically designed to integrate social and environmental goals. The underlying logic of the SBSC is to create a corporate strategic map wherein goals are defined for each dimension and interrelated in a cause-effect chain intended to promote proactivity. In the case of TUBE, a series of programs, projects and plans was defined for each goal on the strategic map, with indicators associated and monitored. The corporate strategic map summarizes TUBE's vision and goals (Figure 1).

A second pillar of TUBE's sustainability management is explicit integration of the triple-bottom line concept *within* the SBSC. The triple-bottom

Figure 1. The corporate strategic map of TUBE Brazil

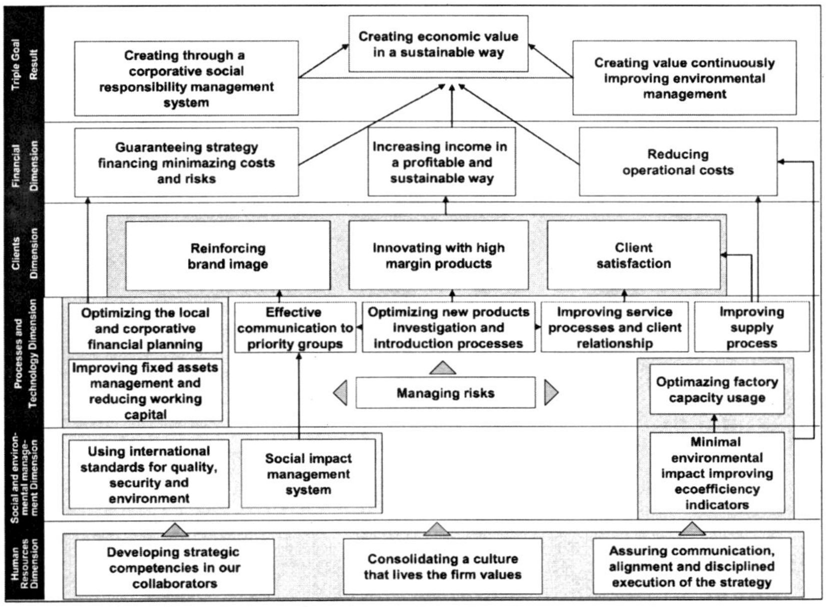

line ensures that, at the top of the cause-effect chain, economic goals are not ranked exclusively as the most important, but are interwoven with those of a social and environmental nature. As Figure 1 shows, at the top of the corporate scorecard TUBE consolidates the five dimensions under the rubric "triple goal results", which includes economic, environmental and social ultimate corporate goals. Due to inclusion of the "triple-bottom line" concept within the strategic map, the results are evaluated in all three dimensions – social, environmental and economic – and are supposed to involve all collaborators (employees) so as to produce positive results at the corporate level.

A third and no less important pillar of TUBE's sustainability management is the *eco-efficiency* indicator which lies at the heart of the cause-effect chain of the SBSC system. The main result is to focus the production system on truly decreasing its environmental impacts. Figure 2 is a chart of the SBSC system, where the eco-efficiency indicator can be visualized and monitored. The metaphor of a green, yellow and red light, widely used in BI applications, facilitates understanding of the current indicator status. For example, although the eco-efficiency indicator is green, indicating that it is achieving its target, the cause-effect chain shows that some indicators (red) warrant attention by collaborators, mainly scrap and scrap sold to other companies.

Regarding the ICT platform operating underneath the SBSC system, we recognize that TUBE created a strong BI architecture and infrastructure. First of all, the company invested in a robust data warehouse able to store all the information necessary to calculate the various socio-environmental indicators. This is not a negligible point, since most of the information necessary to monitor social and environmental performance is rarely available in databases. The data warehouse is at the core of any BI platform because it allows filtering, storage and retrieval of relevant data to support decision making. Second, TUBE has implemented user-friendly interfaces, with power-

Figure 2. The AIMS system: the eco-efficiency indicator and the cause-effect relationship

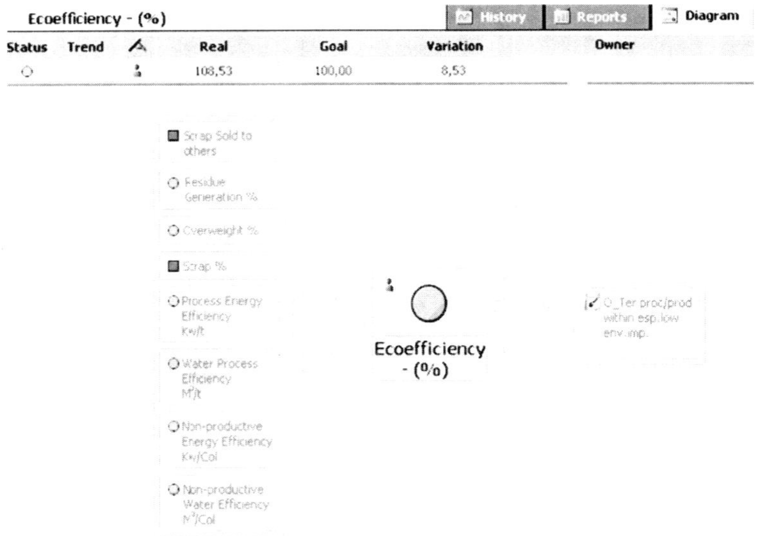

ful underlying functionalities, to allow different groups of stakeholders, especially collaborators, to monitor and analyze their performance on a daily, weekly or monthly basis (depending on the nature of the indicator). Thus, from the data warehouse, information cubes are constructed to feed different applications, where interactive graphic interfaces allow users to analyze corporate, unit and departmental information in a multidimensional way. The right choice of indicators seems to be one of the most important steps in the whole process, since everything that subsequently takes place is based on this definition. A good definition of indicators allows: (a) registering of conditions and trends; (b) comparison of places and situations; (c) evaluation of conditions and trends in relation to objective goals; (d) allowing for prior alert; and (e) anticipation of future conditions and trends.

Two basic characteristics emanate from TUBE's information management model, *transparency* and *proactivity*, and they seem related to the purposive use of ICT. Transparency can be associated with use of portals and other web-based systems that allow all stakeholders involved to access and monitor valuable information. Proactivity is related to the possibility of timely action regarding social responsibility indicators. Adoption of an SBSC supported by a BI platform lies at the heart of proactivity and merits further investigation.

FUTURE RESEARCH DIRECTIONS

Future research might build on the results reported here by composing and refining a conceptual model that facilitates successful SBSC implementation and use, by reflecting on the transferability of the proposed factors to different contexts, and by applying them in concrete situations (using action-research, for instance).

In addition, SBSC is just one possible model that helps in the support of sustainability initiatives. Corporate sustainable practices might be supported by several other information management models and ICT applications. Future research might explore different models and the adequacy of those models to different industries and sectors.

Table 6. Factors facilitating a successful SBSC implementation and use

Creating a culture for sustainability	Integrating social and environmental goals into corporate strategy	Supporting a information management model with a strong BI architecture and infrastructure
Creation of a sustainability formal area (governance)	Implementation of a SBSC and a strategic map	Investment in a robust data warehouse
Creation of programs, projects and action plans at three-level + remuneration strategy	Integration of triple-bottom line at the top of the strategic map	Implementation of user-friendly interfaces
Implementation of communication and training programs + participation and knowledge sharing mechanisms	Integration of eco-efficiency indicator at the heart of the strategic map	A meaningful selection of indicators
Leadership + Stakeholder involvement + Cross-functional collaboration		**Transparency + proactivity**

CONCLUSION

The main argument put forward in this study is that purposive use of information management models, supported by ICT applications, can help support sustainability management by improving the gathering, analysis and sharing of relevant information among employees, clients, partners and the community.

The TUBE Brazil case lends support to this argument by showing how the implementation and use of an SBSC enhanced sustainability management at TUBE Brazil. In effect, we identified three main building blocks permitting support of sustainable management in this company: implementation and use of an SBSC; integration of the triple-bottom-line concept within the SBSC; and placing the eco-efficiency indicator at the heart of the strategic map.

Moreover, this case illustrates how SBSC becomes a management tool that not only improves internal and external transparency but also provides accountability by explicitly including and interconnecting environmental and social indicators with corporate objectives. It is relevant to point out that in our study, the SBSC is not the "tool" that translates sustainability vision and strategies into action, a feature commonly trumpeted by BSC supporters. Actually, SBSC appears as the management instrument helping TUBE Brazil integrate its social and environmental values into its corporate strategies.

Moreover, this case study helps us better understand how to overcome the challenge of implementing and using a SBSC, a process in which leadership, stakeholder involvement and cross-functional collaboration seem to be the basic elements. In effect, we observe that these four basic elements are embedded in the two pillars at TUBE Brazil that we identify as having had a positive impact on implementation and use of SBSC, as presented in Table 6.

Leadership means securing commitment by management and developing a system of incentives to reward leaders that develop and push for the adoption of sustainability practices (Szekely & Knirsch, 2005). Moreover, an SBSC based on leadership and communication can also allow firms to achieve higher stakeholder involvement and more effective cross-functional collaboration because of the transparency and seriousness surrounding each initiative within and outside the organization.

Doubtless, promoting a culture of sustainability before implementation of the SBSC was a key factor in the success of the TUBE Brazil initiative. Indeed, the SBSC is perceived not as a management system that only provides reports on sustainability performance but as a proactive management tool that provides continuous learning and promotes new initiatives (Gibbs, 2007). In terms of key mechanisms that allow building a culture of sustainability, we identified adaptation of the governance structure and coherent articulation of strategy and daily practices as core mechanisms.

To sum up, organizations aiming at managing the social and environmental impacts of their operations must define and monitor social and environmental indicators, integrating them into their everyday practices and management systems (Walker et al., 2007). Information models can be purposefully designed and managed to improve the flow of information and show key indicators within and across companies, giving support to the process of visualizing and monitoring CSR indicators. TUBE is integrating social responsibility and sustainability into its everyday business practices, and linking them to long-range strategy using an integrated framework and architecture. SBSC is not a tool for formulating strategy but it has proven very useful as a framework for rendering those strategies explicit and for proving that a positive relationship exists between "sustainable responsibility" and profitability.

The adoption of SBSC has some barriers or limitations. It depends on the existence of an organizational culture open to integrating sustainability into corporate strategy and everyday practices, open to being more transparent regarding performance monitoring and open to empowering employees at all levels and functions to engage in innovative initiatives towards sustainability. The proposed model has, therefore, implications for research and for practice. One the one hand, the research community should be more aware of the potential link between sustainability and ICT, as represented by the SBSC model, in order to explore other means to nourish and reinforce those links and the necessary conditions for putting those conceptual models in operation. At the same time, top management should exhibit greater openness to social and technological innovations and to new kinds of corporate leadership able to make those conceptual models actionable.

ACKNOWLEDGMENT

We would like to thank FQRSC (*Fonds québécois de recherche sur la société et la culture*) for providing financial support to this project.

REFERENCES

Basu, K., & Palazzo, G. (2008). Corporate Social Responsibility: A Process Model of Sensemaking. *Academy of Management Review*, *33*(1), 122–136. doi:10.2307/20159379

Bieker, T., Dyllick, T., Gminder, C., & Hockerts, K. (2001). Towards a Sustainability Balanced Scorecard. Linking Environmental and Social Sustainability to Business Strategy. In ERP Environment (Ed.), *Proceedings of the 2001 business strategy and the environment conference, Leeds, UK* (pp. 22-31). Shipley (UK): ERP.

Brown, M. G. (1996). *Keeping Score*. New York: Quality Resources.

BSR. (2008). *Overview of Corporate Social Responsibility*. Retrieved December 2009 from http://www.wingsweb.org/documents/WINGS%20CSR%20mapping%202007%20FINAL.pdf

Castels, M. (2000). *The information age: economy, society and culture*. Cambridge, MA: Blackwell.

Choo, C. E. (1998). *Information Management for the Intelligent Organization: The art of scanning the environment* (2nd ed.). Medford, New Jersey: Information Today, Inc.

Dias-Sardinha, I., & Reijnders, L. (2005). Evaluating Environmental and Social Performance of Large Portuguese Companies. *Business Strategy and the Environment*, *14*(2), 73–91. doi:10.1002/bse.421

Dyllick, T., & Hockerts, K. (2002). Beyond the business case for corporate sustainability. *Business Strategy and the Environment*, *11*(2), 130–141. doi:10.1002/bse.323

Elkington, J. (1998). *Cannibals with forks: the triple bottom line of 21st century business*. Gabriola Island, British Columbia: New Society Publishers.

Epstein, M. J., & Roy, M. J. (2003). Making the Business Case for Sustainability. *Journal of Corporate Citizenship*, *9*, 79–96.

Epstein, M. J., & Wisner, P. S. (2001). Using a Balanced Scorecard to Implement Sustainability. *Environmental Quality Management*, *11*(2), 1–10. doi:10.1002/tqem.1300

Ferland, J. (2009). Environnement et société: les TI sont des agents de changement. *Direction Informatique Express*, Edition du 4 Novembre 2009 (www.directioninformatique.com).

Figge, F., Hahn, T., Shaltegger, S., & Wagner, M. (2002). The Sustainability Balanced Scorecard – linking sustainability management to business strategy. *Business Strategy and the Environment*, *11*(5), 269–284. doi:10.1002/bse.339

Gibbs, M. (2007). To Be Proactive or Not To Be? *Network World*, May 10, 2007. Retrieved December 2009 from http://www.networkworld.com/columnists/2007/051007-backspin.html

Hockerts, K. (2001). *What does corporate sustainability actually mean from a business strategy point of view?* Paper presented at the Greening of Industry Network Conference, Bangkok.

Johnson, S. (1998). Identification and Selection of Environmental Performance Indicators: Application of the Balanced Scorecard Approach. *Corporate Environmental Strategy*, *5*(4), 34–41. doi:10.1016/S1066-7938(00)80079-2

Jones, T. M. (2003). An integrating framework for research in business and society. *Academy of Management Review*, *8*(4), 559–564. doi:10.2307/258257

Kaplan, R. S., & Norton, D. P. (1996). *The Balanced Scorecard – Translating Strategy into Action*. Boston, Massachusetts: Harvard Business School Press.

Lang, C. V. (2007). Modeling of a Corporate Environmental Management Information System (CEMIS) for Production Processes. In Marx Gómez, J., Sonnenschein, M., Müller, M., Welsch, H., & Rautenstrauch, C. (Eds.), *Information Technologies in Environmental Engineering* (pp. 231–240). Berlin: Springer. doi:10.1007/978-3-540-71335-7_24

Mason, R., McKenney, J. L., & Copelan, D. G. (1997). An historical method for MIS research: steps and assumptions. *Management Information Systems Quarterly*, *31*(3), 307–320. doi:10.2307/249499

Miles, M. P., & Munilla, L. S. (2004). The potential impact of social accountability certification on marketing. *Journal of Business Ethics*, *50*(1), 1–11. doi:10.1023/B:BUSI.0000021139.94166.74

Möller, A., & Schaltegger, S. (2005). The Sustainability Balanced Scorecard as a Framework for Eco-efficiency Analysis. *Journal of Industrial Ecology*, *9*(4), 73–83. doi:10.1162/1088198057752479 27

Petrini, M. (2006). *Incorporando a sustentabilidade aos sistemas de inteligência de negócio*. Unpublished doctoral dissertation, FGV-EAESP, São Paulo, Brazil.

Radcliffe, M. (1999). Using the Balanced Scorecard to develop metrics for Sustainable Development. *Proceedings of the 8th International Conference of the Greening of Industry Network*, Chapel Hill, USA.

Rasmussen, N., Goldy, P., & Solli, P. P. (2002). *Financial Business Intelligence*. New York: John Wiley & Sons.

Stake, R. E. (1998). Case studies. In Denzin, N. K., & Lincoln, Y. S. (Eds.), *Strategies of Qualitative Inquiry* (pp. 86–109). Thousand Oaks, CA: Sage.

Szekely, F., & Knirsch, M. (2005). Responsible Leadership and Corporate Social Responsibility: Metrics for Sustainable Performance. *European Management Journal*, *23*(6), 628–647. doi:10.1016/j.emj.2005.10.009

UNIDO. (2004). http://www.unido.org/doc/5162

Van der Woerd, F., & van den Brink, T. (2004). Feasibility of a Responsive Business Scorecard – a pilot study. *Journal of Business Ethics*, *55*, 173–186. doi:10.1007/s10551-004-1900-3

Walker, D., Pitt, M., & Thakur, U. J. (2007). Environmental Management Systems: Information Management and Corporate Responsibility. *Journal of Facilities Management*, *5*(1), 49–61. doi:10.1108/14725960710726346

Watson, R. T. (Ed.). (2007). *Green IS: Building Sustainable Business Practices*. Global Text Project. Retrieved December 2009 from http://globaltext.terry.uga.edu/userfiles/pdf/Green.pdf

Compilation of References

Abraham, R. (2007).Mobile Phones and Economic Development: Evidence from the Fishing Industry in India. Information and Technologies and International Development, 4(1).

Acaccia, G. M., Kopàcsi, S., Kovàcs, G., Michelini, R. C., & Razzoli, R. P. (2007 a). Service engineering and extended artefact delivery. In Putnik, G. D., & Cunha, M. M. (Eds.), Knowledge and Technology Management in Virtual Organisations: Integration: Issues, Trends, Opportunities and Solutions (pp. 45–77). Hershey, PA: IGI Global.

Acaccia, G. M., Michelini, R. C., & Qualich, N. (2007 c). Sustainable engineering management: end-of-life vehicles with recycling in mind. World Review of Science. Technology and Sustainable Development, 4(2/3), 105–125. doi:10.1504/WRSTSD.2007.013578

Acaccia, G. M., Michelini, R. C., Penzo, L., & Qualich, N. (2007 b). Reverse logistics and resources recovery: modelling car dismantling facilities. World Review of Science. Technology and Sustainable Development, 4(4/5), 284–332.

Acaccia, G. M., Michelini, R. C., Qualich, N., & Razzoli, R. P. (2008). Logistica inversa: dalla dismissione, al recupero, riuso, riciclo. In R. Mosca (Ed.), Teoria, Metodi e Modelli per la Logistica e la Logistica Inversa (pp. 219-285). Milano, IT: Franco Angeli.

Adam, L. (1996). Electronic communications technology and development of Internet connectivity in Africa. Information Technology for Development, 7(3), 133–145.

Agbontalor, E. A. (2007). Overview of Various Biomass Energy Conversion Routes. American-Eurasian Journal of Agricultural & Environmental Sciences, 2(6), 662–671.

Ahl, C., Eigner-Thiel, S., Girschner, W., Karpenstein-Machan, M., Roland, F., & Ruppert, H. (2007). Bioenergiedörfer - Dörfer mit Zukunft. Information brochure. Göttingen, Germany: Interdisciplinary Centre for Sustainable Development.

Ahmed, P. K., & Hardaker, G. (1999). The role of on-line communities on the internet for sustainable development. Business Strategy and the Environment, 8(1), 75–81. doi:10.1002/(SICI)1099-0836(199901/02)8:1<75::AID-BSE186>3.0.CO;2-S

Aiken, R. J., Boroumand, J., & Wolff, S. (2004). Network and computing research infrastructure: Back to the future. Communications of the ACM, 47(1), 93–98. doi:10.1145/962081.962086

Ainsworth, S. (1999). Designing effective multi-representational learning environments (Report No. 58). Nottingham, United Kingdom: University of Nottingham, ESRC Centre for research in Development, Instruction and Teaching.

Akpan, P. I. (2003). Basic-needs to globalization: Are ICTs the missing link? Information Technology for Development, 10, 261–274. doi:10.1002/itdj.1590100405

Albersmeier, F., & Spiller, A. (2009). Das Ansehen der Fleischwirtschaft: Zur Bedeutung einer stufenübergreifenden Perspektive. In J. Böhm, F. Albersmeier, & A. Spiller (Eds.), Die Ernährungswirtschaft im Scheinwerferlicht der Öffentlichkeit (pp. 213-250). Lohmar, Köln: EUL Verlag.

Albertin, A. L., & Sanchez, O. P. (2008). Outsourcing de TI: impactos, dilemas, discussões e casos reais. Rio de Janeiro, Rio de Janeiro: FGV.

Alexander, J. A. (1991). Adaptive Change in Corporate Control Practices. Academy of Management Journal, 34(1), 162–193. doi:10.2307/256306

Alleven, M. (2008, April 2). Going Green. Wireless Week, 14-15.

Andersen, M. S. (2007). An introduction note on the environmental economics of the circular economy. Sustainability Science, 2, 133–140. doi:10.1007/s11625-006-0013-6

Andrew, J. (2003). Corporate governance, the environment, and the internet. Electronic Green Journal, 19 (December). Retrieved April 4, 2004, from http://egj.uidaho.edu/egj19/andrew1.html

Angeles, R. (2005). RFID technologies: supply-chain applications and implementation issues. Information Systems Management, 22(1), 51–65.

Angstenberger, L. (2000). Dynamic Fuzzy Pattern Recognition. Doctoral dissertation, RWTH Aachen. Retrieved July 18, 2007, from http://darwin.bth.rwth-aachen.de/opus/volltexte/2001/167/pdf/ Angstenberger_Larisa.pdf

Anonymous,. (2009). Green remediation information available on the Web. Hazardous Waste Consultant, 27(2), 1–5.

Antoni-Komar, I. (2009). Die Neudefinition von Lebensqualität: Kulturelle Implikationen ökonomischer Praxis. In I. Antoni-Komar, M. Beermann, C. Lautermann, J. Müller, N. Paech, H. Schattke, U. Schneidewind, & R. Schulz (Eds.), Neue Konzepte der Ökonomik. Unternehmen zwischen Nachhaltigkeit, Kultur und Ethik (pp. 329-347). Marburg: Metropolis Verlag.

Antoni-Komar, I., & Pfriem, R. (2009). Kulturalistische Ökonomik. Vom Nutzen einer Neuorientierung wirtschaftswissenschaftlicher Untersuchungen. WENKE2-Diskussionspapier 06/09. Oldenburg.

Antoni-Komar, I., Lautermann, C., & Pfriem, R. (2010). Kulturelle Kompetenzen. Interaktionsökonomische Erweiterungsperspektiven für den Competence-based View des Strategischen Managements. In M. Stephan, W. Kerber, T. Kessler, & M. Lingenfelder (Eds.), 25 Jahre ressourcen- und kompetenzorientierte Forschung. Der kompetenzbasierte Ansatz auf dem Weg zum Schlüsselparadigma in der Managementforschung (pp. 465-489). Wiesbaden: Gabler Verlag, (forthcoming)

Anufriev, A., Kopàcsi, S., Kovàcs, G., & Michelini, R. C. (2007). Ambient intelligence as enabling technology for modern business paradigms. Journal of Robotics and Computer Integrated Manufacturing, 23(2), 242–256. doi:10.1016/j.rcim.2006.01.002

Apache (2008). Apache Cocoon Project. Retrieved April 24, 2008, from http://cocoon.apache.org

Apat (2008). Rapporto Rifiuti. Italy.

ArcelorMittal. (2009). Building sustainable supply chains in Brazil. World Business Council for Sustainable Development (WBCSD), 1-3. Retrieved July 2009, from http://www.wbcsd.org/includes/getTarget.asp?type=d&id=MzI5OTI

Arndt, H. K., & Günther, O. (2004). Environmental Reporting of Organizations – Extending the XML-based Standardization Using Topic Maps. In P. Minier, & A. Susini (Eds.), Sh@ring – 18th International Conference Informatics for Environmental Protection, EnviroInfo 2004 CERN Geneva 2004, 21.10.-23.10.2004, Part 2 (pp. 172-183). Geneva: CERN Press.

Arndt, H. K., & Günther, O. (Eds.). (2000). Environmental markup language (EML). First workshop Berlin 1999. Marburg: Metropolis.

Arndt, H. K., Graubitz, H., & Klesinski, R. (2007a). Using Topic Maps for Sustainability Reporting. In J. Marx Gómez, M. Sonnenschein, M. Müller, H. Welsch, & C. Rautenstrauch (Eds.), Information Technologies in Environmental Engineering – 3rd International ICSC Symposium, Oldenburg 2007, 29.03.-30.03.2007 (pp. 47-59). Berlin/Heidelberg: Springer.

Arndt, H. K., Graubitz, H., & Klesinski, R. (2007b). Sustainability Reporting Topic Maps: An Approach to Support Stakeholder Inclusiveness. In O. Hryniewicz, J. Studzinski, & M. Romaniuk (Eds.): Environmental Informatics and System Research – 21rst International Conference on Informatics for Environmental Protection, Warsaw 2007, 12.09.-14.09.2007 (pp. 79-86). Aachen: Shaker.

Arndt, H. K., Isenmann, R., Brosowski, J., Thiessen, I., & Marx Gómez, J. (2006). Sustainability Reporting Using the eXtensible Business Reporting Language (XBRL). In K. Tochtermann, & A. Scharl (Eds.), Managing Environmental Knowledge – 20th International Conference on Informatics for Environmental Protection, EnviroInfo 2006, Graz 2006, 06.09.-08.09.2006 (pp 75-82). Aachen: Shaker.

Association of Chartered Certified Accountants (ACCA). (1998). Making values count: contemporary experience in social and ethical accounting, auditing, and reporting. London: The Certified Accountants Educational Trust.

Association of Chartered Certified Accountants (ACCA). (2001). Environmental, social and sustainability reporting on the world wide web: A guide to best practice. London: The Certified Accountants Educational Trust.

Association of Chartered Certified Accountants (ACCA). (2004). Towards transparency: Progress on global sustainability reporting 2004. London: Certified Accountants Educational Trust.

Athanasiadis, I. N., Mentes, A. K., Mitkas, P. A., & Mylopoulos, Y. A. (2005). A hybrid agent-based model for estimating residential water demand. Simulation, 81(3), 175–187. doi:10.1177/0037549705053172

Attadia, L. C. L., & Martins, R. A. (2003). Medição de desempenho como base para evolução da melhoria contínua. Revista Produção, 13(2).

Australian Government Department of the Environment and Heritage. (2003). Corporate sustainability – an investor perspective. The Mays Report. Canberra: Environmental Protection Branch, Department of the Environment and Heritage. Retrieved April 3, 2004, from http://deh.gov.au/industry/finance/publications/index.html

Avgerou, C. (1998). How can IT Enable Economic Growth in developing Countries? Information Technology for Development, 8(1).

Avgoustinov, N., & Bley, H. (2003). Distributed Virtual Enterprises (DVE) in Modelling, Simulation and Planning. In C. Weber, H. Bley, & G. Hirt (Eds.), Proceedings of the 36th CIRP International Seminar on Manufacturing Systems (pp. 123-129). Series of production engineering, volume 29. Saarbrücken: Saarland University.

Avison, D. E., Lau, F., Myers, M., & Nielsen, P. A. (1999). Action Research. Communications of the ACM, 42(1), 94–97. doi:10.1145/291469.291479

Axelrod, R. A. (1998). Ten years later: The state of environmental performance reports today. Environmental Quality Management, 8(2), 1–13. doi:10.1002/tqem.3310080202

Axelrod, R. A. (2000). Brave new words. The financial value of environmental communications. Environmental Quality Management, 9(4), 1–11. doi:10.1002/1520-6483(200022)9:4<1::AID-TQEM1>3.0.CO;2-J

Azzone, G., Brophy, M., Noci, G., Welford, R., & Young, W. (1997). A stakeholders' view of environmental reporting. Long Range Planning, 30(5), 699–709. doi:10.1016/S0024-6301(97)00058-7

Azzone, G., Noci, G., Manzini, R., Welford, R., & Young, C. W. (1996). Defining environmental performance indicators: an integrated framework. Business Strategy and the Environment, 5(2), 69–80. doi:10.1002/(SICI)1099-0836(199606)5:2<69::AID-BSE48>3.0.CO;2-W

Baark, E., & Heeks, R. (1998). Evaluation of Donor-Funded Information Technology Transfer Projects in China: A Life-Cycle Approach. Retrieved August 12, 2009, from http://idpm.man.ac.uk/wp/di/di_wp01.htm

Babiceanu, R. F., & Chen, F. F. (2006). Development and applications of holonic manufacturing systems: A survey. Journal of Intelligent Manufacturing, 17(1), 111–131. doi:10.1007/s10845-005-5516-y

Bacon, C. (1992). The use of decision criteria in selecting information systems/technology investments. Management Information Systems Quarterly, 16(3), 335–353. doi:10.2307/249532

Baliamoune-Lutz, M. (2003). An analysis of the determinants and effects of ICT diffusion in developing countries. Information Technology for Development, 10(3), 151–170. doi:10.1002/itdj.1590100303

Balzert, H. (1998). Lehrbuch der Software-Technik. Software-Management, Software-Qualitätssicherung,

Unternehmensmodellierung. Heidelberg, Berlin, Germany: Spektrum Akademischer Verlag.

Bandholtz, T., Bös, R., & Ruether, M. (2000). The German Environmental Information Network (GEIN). In A. B. Cremers & K. Greve (Eds.), Proceedings of the 14th International Symposium „Computer Science for Environmental Protection '00", Vol. 2 (pp. 632-646). Marburg: Metropolis.

Banerjee, P., & Zetu, D. (2001). Virtual Manufacturing. New York: John Wiley & Sons, Inc.

Barton, C., & Bear, M. (1999). Information and Communications Technologies: Are they the Key to Viable Business Development Services for Micro and Small Enterprises? Report for USAID as part of the Microenterprise Best Practices Project. Retrieved December 12, 2007, from http://www.mip.org/PUBS/MBP/ict.htm

Bassen, A., Jastram, S., & Meyer, K. (2005). Corporate Social Responsitility. Eine Begriffserläuterung. Zeitschrift für Wirtschafts- und Unternehmensethik, 6(2), 231-236.

Basu, K., & Palazzo, G. (2008). Corporate Social Responsibility: A Process Model of Sensemaking. Academy of Management Review, 33(1), 122–136. doi:10.2307/20159379

Bauböck, R. (2009). Bioenergie im Landkreis Göttingen – GIS-gestützte Biomassenpotenzialabschätzung anhand ausgewählter Energiepflanzen, Triticale und Mais. In Kappas, M. (Ed.), Erdsicht – Einblicke in geographische und geoinformationstechnische Arbeitsweisen (Vol. 18). Stuttgart, Germany: Ibidim-Verlag.

Beattie, B., & Taylor, R. (1985). The Economics of Production. New York: John Wiley & Sons.

Beattie, V., & Pratt, K. (2003). Issues concerning web-based business reporting: An analysis of the views of interested parties. The British Accounting Review, 35(2), 155–187. doi:10.1016/S0890-8389(03)00016-7

Beaumont, J. R. (1992). Managing the environment: Business opportunity and responsibility. Futures, 24(3), 187–205. doi:10.1016/0016-3287(92)90030-J

Beck, T. M. (1990). EDV-gestützte Planungssysteme zur optimalen Belegung von Fertigungslinien. Doctoral dissertation, University of Karlsruhe, Germany.

Becker, J., Knackstedt, R., & Pöppelbuß, J. (2009). Developing Maturity Models for IT Management. Buisness & Information Systems Engineering, 1(3), 213–222. doi:10.1007/s12599-009-0044-5

Becker, J., Lunardi, G., & Maçada, A. (2003). Análise de eficiência dos bancos brasileiros: um enfoque nos investimentos realizados em tecnologia de informação (TI). Revista Produção, 13(2), 70–81.

Beermann, M. (2009). Enterprise resilience: a concept for coping with climate change challenges. Theoretical considerations. Conference contribution from 15th Annual International Sustainable Development Research Conference. Utrecht/Netherlands.

Beermann, M., & Schattke, H. (2009). Innovationspotenziale für die Ernährungswirtschaft: Das Resilience-Konzept als Perspektivwechsel. In I. Antoni-Komar, M. Beermann, C. Lautermann, J. Müller, N. Paech, H. Schattke, U. Schneidewind, & R. Schulz (Eds.), Neue Konzepte der Ökonomik. Unternehmen zwischen Nachhaltigkeit, Kultur und Ethik (pp.119-141). Marburg: Metropolis Verlag.

Beirat für nachwachsende Rohstoffe (2005). Erklärung Bioenergie und Ethik (Statement). Hannover, Germany: Niedersächsisches Ministerium für Ernährung, Landwirtschaft, Verbraucherschutz und Landesentwicklung.

Belitz, H., & Schrooten, M. (2008). Innovationssystem – Motor der Wirtschaft. Vierteljahreshefte zur Wirtschaftsforschung, 77, 5–10. doi:10.3790/vjh.77.2.5

Belton, V., & Stewart, T. J. (2002). Multiple criteria decision analysis: an integrated approach. Dordrecht, Netherlands: Kluwer Academic Publishers.

Benjamin, A. (1998). Prototype plc – the 21st century annual report. In The Institute of Chartered Accountants in England & Wales (Ed.), The 21st century annual report corporate governance (pp. 12-17). London: The Institute of Chartered Accountants in England & Wales.

Bennete, M., & James, P. (1999). ISO 14031 and the future of environmental performance evaluation. In Bennett, M., & James, P. (Eds.), Sustainable measures: evaluation and reporting of environmental and social performance (pp. 76–97). Sheffield, UK: Greenleaf Publisher.

Bergholz, A. (2005). Objektorientierte Fabrikplanung. Doctoral dissertation, Rheinisch-Westfälische Technische Hochschule Aachen, Germany.

Berkhout, F., Hertin, J., & Gann, D. M. (2006). Learning to Adapt: Organisational Adaptation to Climate Change Impacts. Climatic Change, 78(1), 135–156. doi:10.1007/s10584-006-9089-3

Berlin, D., & Uhlin, H.-E. (2004). Opportunity cost principles for life cycle assessment: toward strategic decision making in agriculture. Progress in Industrial Ecology, 1(1/2/3), 187-202.

Berndes, G., Hoogwijk, M., & van den Broek, R. (2003). The contribution of biomass in the future global energy supply: a review of 17 studies. Biomass and Bioenergy, 25(1), 1–28. doi:10.1016/S0961-9534(02)00185-X

Bertsch, V., Geldermann, J., Rentz, O., & Raskob, W. (2006). Multi-criteria decision support and stakeholder involvement in emergency management. International Journal of Emergency Management, 3(2/3), 114–130. doi:10.1504/IJEM.2006.011163

Bertsch, V., Treitz, M., Geldermann, J., & Rentz, O. (2007). Sensitivity analyses in multi-attribute decision support for off-site nuclear emergency and recovery management. International Journal of Energy Sector Management, 1(4), 342–365. doi:10.1108/17506220710836075

Bevilacqua, V., Intini, F. & Kühtz, S. (2008). Applicazione della teoria di Shapley ad un sistema di gestione della raccolta intermunicipale dei rifiuti. Economia delle fonti di energia e dell'ambiente, 3.

Bezdek, J. C. (1981). Pattern Recognition with Fuzzy Objective Function Algorithms. New York: Plenum.

Bharadwaj, A. (2000). A resource-based perspective on information technology capability and firm performance: an empirical investigation. Management Information Systems Quarterly, 24(1), 169–196. doi:10.2307/3250983

Bharadwaj, A., Bharadwaj, S., & Konsynski, B. (1999). Information technology effects on firm performance as measures by Tobin's q. Management Science, 45(6), 1008–1024. doi:10.1287/mnsc.45.7.1008

Bharadway, A. S., Sambamurthy, V., & Zmud, R. W. (1998). IT Capabilities: Theoretical perspectives and empirical operationalization. In R. Hirschheim, M. Newman, & J. I. Gross (Eds.), Proceedings of the 19th International Conference on Information Systems (pp. 378-385). Helsinki, Finland.

Bia, M., & Kalika, M. (2007). Adopting an ICT code of conduct: An empirical study of organizational factors. Journal of Enterprise Information Management, 20(4), 432–446. doi:10.1108/17410390710772704

Bieker, T. (2003). Sustainability Management with the Balanced Scorecard. In Proceedings of the International Summer Academy on Technology Studies, IFZ, Graz. Retrieved July 25, 2008, from http://www.ifz.tugraz.at/index_en.php/filemanager/download/71/Bieker_SA03.pdf

Bieker, T., Dyllick, T., Gminder, C. U., & Hockerts, K. (2001). Towards a Sustainability Balanced Scorecard. Linking environmental and social sustainability to business strategy. In ERP Environment (Ed.), Conference Proceedings of the 2001 Business Strategy and the Environment, University of Leeds (pp. 22-31). Shipley, UK: ERP Environment.

Biloslavo, R., & Trnavcevic, A. (2009). Web sites as tools of communication of a "green" company. Management Decision, 47(7), 1158–1173. doi:10.1108/00251740910978359

Binstock, C., Hoffman, C., Egmond, R. V., & Walenga, W. (2005). Comparing XML and XBRL (Version 2005-06-06). Retrieved January 17, 2006, from http://www.ubmatrix.com/Documents/XBRLComparedToXML-2005-07-06%20(4).pdf

BMBF. (1997). Bundesministerium für Bildung, Wissenschaft, Forschung und Technologie. Bonn: Forschung für die Umwelt – Programm der Bundesregierung.

BMU. (Federal Ministry for the Environment, Nature conservation and Nuclear Safety) (2009). German cabinet has approved national biomass action plan. Press release no. 122/09. Berlin, Germany.

Bodo, B., & Unny, T. E. (1983). Sampling strategies for mass-discharge estimation. Journal of Environmental Engineering, 109(4), 812–829. doi:10.1061/(ASCE)0733-9372(1983)109:4(812)

Bohrer, P., Elnozahy, E., Keller, T., Kistler, M., Lefurgy, C., McDowell, C., & Rajamony, R. (2002). The Case for Power Management in Web Servers. In Graybill, R., & Melhem, R. (Eds.), Power Aware Computing (pp. 261–289). New York: Kluwer Academic/Plenum Publishers.

Bond, A. H., & Gasser, L. (1988). Readings in Distributed Artificial Intelligence. San Mateo, CA: Morgan Kaufmann Publishers.

Bonini, S. M. J., & Hintz, G., & Mendonca, Lenny T. (2008). Addressing consumer concerns about climate change. The McKinsey Quarterly, (2): 52–61.

Borgelt, C. (2005). Prototype-based Classification and Clustering. Professorial dissertation, Otto-von-Guericke-Universität Magdeburg. Retrieved March 07, 2008, from http://edoc.bibliothek.uni-halle.de/receive/HALCoRe_document_00005337?lang=de

Bortone, G., & Palumbo, L. (Eds.). (2007). Sustainable management of sediment resources: Sediment and Dredged Material Treatment (Vol. 2). Amsterdam: Elsevier.

Bortz, C. (2007). Conversation: An interview with Alyson Slater. Harvard Business Review, 85(10), 32–32.

Boulding, K. E. (1972). Toward the Development of a Cultural Economics. Social Science Quarterly, 53(2), 267–284.

Bourdieu, P. (1984). Distinction: A social critique of judgement of taste. London: Routledge and Kegan Paul.

Boursas, L., Hegering, H., & Hommel, W. (2009). Standards and new technology for systems and virtualization management: A report on SVM'08. Journal of Network and Systems Management, 17(1-2), 99–104. doi:10.1007/s10922-009-9117-5

Bousquet, F. (2001). Multi-agent simulations and ecosystem management. In Ghassemi, F., & Post, D. (Eds.), M.

BPMF. (2009). The Business Performance Management Forum: IT Sustainability Imperatives in Internet and eCommerce Business. Retrieved November, 12, 2009, from http://www.rackable.com/thinkecological/pdf/IT-Sustainability.pdf

Braczyk, H. J., Cooke, P., & Heidenreich, M. (1998). Regional innovation systems – the role of governances in a globalized world. London: UCL Press.

Bramer, M. (2007). Principles of Data Mining. London: Springer.

Brancheau, J. C., & Wetherbe, J. C. (1994). Key issues in information Systems. MIS Quaterly Executive, 10(2), 225–242.

Brattlebø, H. (2005). Towards a Methods Framework for Eco-Efficiency Analysis? Journal of Industrial Ecology, 9(4), 9–11. doi:10.1162/108819805775247837

Brehm, N., Mahmoud, T., Marx Gómez, J., & Memari, A. (2008). Towards Intelligent Discovery of Enterprise Architecture Services (IDEAS). Journal of Enterprise Architecture, 4(3), 26–37.

Breitschuh, G., Breitschuh, T., & Eckert, H. (2008). Einfluss einer erhöhten Biomasseproduktion auf die Nachhaltigkeitsparameter landwirtschaftlicher Betriebe. In Kuratorium für Technik und Bauwesen in der Landwirtschaft e.V. (KTBL) (Ed.), Ökologische und ökonomische Bewertung nachwachsender Energieträger (pp. 104-116). Darmstadt, Germany: KTBL.

Bremer, J. (2005). Modellierung und protoypische Realisierung von Komponenten für die Datenexploration und Reststoffvermittlung bei der kooperativen Konzeption eines Sekundärrohstoff-Marktplatzes. Unpublished Bachelor's Thesis, University of Oldenburg, Germany.

Bremer, J., Rapp, B., Vogel, U., & Sonnenschein, M. (2007). Metadata Driven Acquisition, Search and Procurement of Secondary Materials within an Internet-based Marketplace. In L. M. Hilty, X. Edelmann und A. Ruf (Eds.), Proceedings of the 8th World Congress on Integrated Resources Management. St. Gallen, Switzerland: Empa.

Bright, M. (2009). Data center: The next generation. Oracle Magazine, 29-34. Retrieved 8 March, 2009, from http://www.oracle.com/oraclemagazine

Brodbeck, A. F., & Hoppen, N. (2000, September). Modelo de alinhamento estratégico para implementação dos planos de negócio e de tecnologia de informação. Paper presented at the Xxiv Encontro Nacional da ANPAD. São Paulo.

Brookshire, R. G. (2001). Letter from the editor: Large scale computing and the technology curriculum. Information Technology, 24(2), i-iii.

Brophy, M., & Starkey, R. (1996). Environmental reporting. In Welford, R. (Ed.), Corporate environmental management. Systems and strategies (pp. 177–198). London: Earthscan.

Brosowski, J., & Lenz, C. (2004). Customised environmental reporting. International Journal of Environment and Sustainable Development, 3(1), 18–33. doi:10.1504/IJESD.2004.004687

Brosowski, J., Isenmann, R., Beisel, M., & Marx Gómez, J. (2004). XML schema for sustainbility reports meeting the needs of the GRI guidelines. In P. Minier, A. Susini (Eds.), Sh@ring. Proceedings EnviroInfo 2004. 18th International Conference Informatics for Environmental Protection (pp. 184-193). Genève: Editions du Tricorne.

Brown, A., & Grant, G. (2005). Framing the frameworks: a review of IT governance research. Communications of the Association for Information Systems, 15, 696–712.

Brown, D. H., & Lockett, N. (2004). Potential of critical e-applications for engaging SMEs in e-business: a provider perspective. European Journal of Information Systems, 13(2), 21–34. doi:10.1057/palgrave.ejis.3000480

Brown, D. L., Dillard, J. F., & Marshall, R. S. (2005). Strategically informed, environmentally conscious information requirements for accounting information systems. Journal of Information Systems, 19(2), 79–103. doi:10.2308/jis.2005.19.2.79

Brown, M. G. (1996). Keeping Score. New York: Quality Resources.

Bryden, M., & McCorkle, D. (2005). Virtual engineering: in powerful new workspaces, the next-generation power plant is only the beginning. Mechanical Engineering-CIME, 127(11), 38–41.

Brynjolfsson, E. (1993). The productivity paradox of information technology: review and assessment. Communications of the ACM, 36(12), 66–77. doi:10.1145/163298.163309

BSI (Bundesamt für Sicherheit in der Informationstechnik). (2009). Die Lage der IT-Sicherheit in Deutschland 2009. Retrieved April 20, 2001, from http://www.bsi.bund.de/literat/lagebericht/Lagebericht2009.pdf

BSR. (2008). Overview of Corporate Social Responsibility. Retrieved December 2009 from http://www.wingsweb.org/documents/WINGS%20CSR%20mapping%202007%20FINAL.pdf

Buchholz, T., Rametsteiner, E., Volk, T. A., & Luzardis, V. A. (2009). Multi-criteria analysis for bioenergy systems assessments. Energy Policy, 37(2), 484–495. doi:10.1016/j.enpol.2008.09.054

Buhl, H. U., Laartz, J., Löffler, M., & Röglinger, M. (2009). Green IT reicht nicht aus. Wirtschaftsinformatik & Management, 1(1), 54–58.

Bülow, M. V. (2009). The essentials in Copenhagen. COP15 Copenhagen 2009. Retrieved July 2009, from http://en.cop15.dk/news/view+news?newsid=876

Bundesregierung (2004). 11. BImSchV: Elfte Verordnung zur Durchführung des Bundes-Immissionsschutzgesetzes (Verordnung über Emissionserklärungen und Emissionsberichte). Retrieved August 10, 2009, from http://bundesrecht.juris.de/bundesrecht/bimschv_11_2004/ gesamt.pdf

Bundesregierung (2004a). 13. BImSchV: Elfte Verordnung zur Durchführung des Bundes-Immissionsschutzgesetzes (Verordnung über Großfeuerungs- und Gasturbinenanlagen). Retrieved September 1, 2009, from http://www.gesetze.juris.de/bundesrecht/ bimschv_13_2004/gesamt.pdf

Bundesregierung (2006). Verordnung über die Entsorgung gebrauchter halogenierter Lösemittel (HKWAbfV). Retrieved August 15, 2009, from http://www.gesetze.juris.de/bundesrecht/ hkwabfv/gesamt.pdf

Bunke, D., Gensch, C. O., Möller, M., Rüdenauer, I., Ebinger, F., & Graulich, K. (2003). Assessment of Toxicological Risks due to Hazardous Substances: Scoring of Risk Phrases. International Journal of Life Cycle Assessment, 8(1), 6–7.

Burritt, R., Hahn, T., & Schaltegger, S. (2002). Towards a Comprehensive Framework for Environmental Management Accounting. Australian Accounting Review, 12(2), 39–50. doi:10.1111/j.1835-2561.2002.tb00202.x

Busch, T., Liedtke, C., & Beucker, S. (2006). The Concept of Corporate Resource Efficiency Accounting. In Schaltegger, S., Bennett, M., & Burritt, R. (Eds.), Sustainability Accounting and Reporting. Dordrecht: Springer. doi:10.1007/978-1-4020-4974-3_5

Business for Social Responsibility (BSR). (2008). Environmental, social and governance: Moving to mainstream investing? Retrieved August 28, 2008, from http://bsr.org

Cagno, E., Tardini, L., & Trucco, P. (2007). EPIDesign: integrating corporate strategies into the development process of an environmental performance evaluation system. In Sroufe, R., & Sarkis, J. (Eds.), Strategic sustainability. The state of the art in corporate environmental management systems (pp. 20–42). Sheffield, UK: Greenleaf Publisher.

Caldeira, M. M., & Ward, J. M. (2003). Using resource-based theory to interpret the successful adoption and use of information systems and technology in manufacturing small and medium-sized enterprises. European Journal of Information Systems, 12, 127–141. doi:10.1057/palgrave.ejis.3000454

Canadian Institute of Chartered Accountants (CICA). (1994). Reporting on environmental reporting. Carried out in association with Canadian Standards Association, Financial Executives Institute Canada and International Institute for Sustainable Development (IISD). Toronto: CICA.

Carlisle, T. (2009). UK lays out low-carbon blueprint. The National, July 19. Retrieved July 2009, from http://www.thenational.ae/apps/pbcs.dll/article?AID=/20090719/BUSINESS/707199988

Carlson, R. (2002). Environmental Performance Indicators. Insight (American Society of Ophthalmic Registered Nurses), 5(2), 22–23.

Carlson, R. (2006a). Framework For Structuring Information For Environmental Management Of Industrial Systems. Göteborg, Sweden: CPM, Chalmers University of Technology.

Carlson, R. (2009). Eco-Efficiency. – The conceptual model, the concept model and an operational data structure. [Göteborg, Sweden: CPM, Chalmers University of Technology.]. CPM-report, 2009, 2.

Carlson, R. (Ed.). (2005). Establishing common primary data for environmental overview of product life cycles, Users, perspectives, methods, data, and information systems, Swedish EPA-report, Utg 2005-12 Nr 91-620-5523-2. Stockholm, Sweden: Naturvårdsverket.

Carlson, R., & Pålsson, A. C. (2000). PHASES Information models for industrial environmental control. Göteborg, Sweden: CPM, Chalmers University of Technology.

Carlson, R., & Pålsson, A. C. (2001). Industrial environmental information management for technical systems. Journal of Cleaner Production, 9, 429–435. doi:10.1016/S0959-6526(01)00002-6

Carlson, R., & Pålsson, A. C. (2002). Documentation of environmental impact assessment, compatible with SPINE and ISO/TS 14048, IMI-report 2002:1 (2nd ed.). Göteborg, Sweden: Department of Computer Science and Engineering, Industrial Environmental Informatics, Chalmers University of Technology.

Carlson, R., Erixon, M., Erlandsson, M., Flemström, K., Häggström, S., Pålsson, A. C., & Tivander, J. (2006b). Implementation of integrated environmental information systems [Göteborg, Sweden: CPM, Chalmers University of Technology.]. CPM Report, 2006, 18.

Carlson, R., Erixon, M., Forsberg, P., & Pålsson, A. C. (2001). System for Integrated Business Environmental Information Management. Advances in Environmental Research, 5(4), 369–375. doi:10.1016/S1093-0191(01)00088-0

Carlson, R., Häggström, S., & Pålsson, A. C. (2004a). Policy controlled environmental management work - Manual [Göteborg, Sweden: CPM, Chalmers University of Technology.]. CPM-report, 2004, 11.

Carlson, R., Häggström, S., & Pålsson, A. C. (2004b). Policy controlled environmental management work - Final report [Göteborg, Sweden: CPM, Chalmers University of Technology.]. CPM-report, 2004, 10.

Carlson, R., Löfgren, G., & Steen, B. (1995). SPINE, A Relation Database Structure for Life Cycle Assessment, IVL-Report B 1227. Göteborg, Sweden: Swedish Environmental Research Institute.

Carr, N. (2003). IT doesn't matter. Harvard Business Review, 81(5), 41–49.

Carr, N. G. (2005). The End of Corporate Computing. MIT Sloan Management Review, 46(3), 67–73.

Carter, A., & Ragsdale, C. (2006). A new approach to solving the multiple traveling salesperson problem using genetic algorithms. European Journal of Operational Research, 175(1), 246–257. doi:10.1016/j.ejor.2005.04.027

Carter, C. R., & Ellram, L. M. (1998). Reversed logistics: A review of the literature and framework for future investigation. Journal of Business Logistics, 19(1), 85–102.

Casazza, J. P., Greenfield, M., & Shi, K. (2006). Redefining server performance characterization for virtualization benchmarking. Intel Technology Journal, 10(3), 243–251. doi:10.1535/itj.1003.07

Cascio, J., Woodside, G., & Mitchell, P. (2005). ISO 14000 guide: the new international environmental management standards (2nd ed.). McGraw Hill.

Castels, M. (2000). The information age: economy, society and culture. Cambridge, MA: Blackwell.

Cecchini, S., & Scott, C. (2003). Can information and communications technology applications contribute to poverty reduction? Lessons from rural India. Information Technology for Development, 10, 73–84. doi:10.1002/itdj.1590100203

Chan, S. (2004). Sarbanes-Oxley: the IT dimension. The Internal Auditor, 61(1).

Chang, N. B., & Lin, Y. T. (1997). Economic evaluation of a regionalization program for solid waste management in a metropolitan region. Journal of Environmental Management, 51, 241–274. doi:10.1006/jema.1997.0144

Checkland, P. (1981). Systems Thinking, Systems Practice. New York: John Wiley & Sons.

Checkland, P. (1991). From Framework through Experience to Learning: The Essential Nature of Action Research. In H.-E. Nissen, H. Klein & R. Hirschheim (Eds.), Information Systems Research: Contemporary Approaches and Emergent Traditions (pp. 397-403). North Holland: Elsevier Publishers.

Cheng, P. C. H., Lowe, R. K., & Scaife, M. (2001). Cognitive science approaches to understanding diagrammatic representations. Artificial Intelligence Review, 15, 79–94. doi:10.1023/A:1006641024593

Chin, P., Brown, G., & Hu, Q. (2004). The impact of mergers & acquisitions on IT governance structures: a case study. Journal of Global Information Management, 12(4), 50–74.

ChipSensorsTM (2009). Retrieved November 18, 2009, from www.chipsensors.de

Choo, C. E. (1998). Information Management for the Intelligent Organization: The art of scanning the environment (2nd ed.). Medford, New Jersey: Information Today, Inc.

Chou, T. (2008). Seven Software Business Models. USA: Active Book Press.

Christini, G., Harzam, M. W., Mattews, D. H., & Hendrickson, C. (2007). A comparison of environmental system components and practices. In Sroufe, R., & Sarkis, J. (Eds.), Strategic sustainability. The state of the art in corporate environmental management systems (pp. 43–55). Sheffield, UK: Greenleaf Publisher.

Cieniawski, S., Ehart, J., & Ranjithan, S. (1995). Using genetic algorithms to solve a multiobjective groundwater monitoring problem. Water Resources Research, 31(2), 399–409. doi:10.1029/94WR02039

Cios, K. J., Pedrycz, W., Swiniarski, R. W., & Kurgan, L. A. (2007). Data Mining – A Knowledge Discovery Approach. Berlin, Heidelberg, New York: Springer.

Clarke, T. (2001). Balancing the triple bottom line: Financial, social and environmental performance. Journal of General Management, 26(4), 16–27.

Clausen, J., Loew, T., Klaffke, K., Raupach, M., & Schoenheit, I. (2001). The INEM sustainability reporting guide – a manual on practical and convincing communication for future-oriented companies. Hamburg:

International Network for Environmental Management (INEM). Retrieved April 22, 2002, from http://www.inem.org/free_downloads

Cleff, T., & Rennings, K. (1999). Determinants of Environmental Product and Process Innovation – Evidence from the Mannheim Innovation Panel and a Follow-Up Telephone Survey. European Environment, Special issue on Integrated Product Policy, 9(5), 191-201.

Cochran, W. G. (1963). Sampling Techniques (2nd ed.). New York: John Wiley.

Coelli, T. J., Rao, D. S. P., O'Donnell, C. J., & Battese, G. E. (2005). An Introduction to Efficiency and Productivity Analysis (2nd ed.). New York: Springer.

Collison, D., Lorraine, N., & Power, D. (2003). An exploration of corporate attitudes to the significance of environmental information for stakeholders. Corporate Social Responsibility and Environmental Management, 10(4), 199–212. doi:10.1002/csr.45

Commission of the European Communities. (2007). Commission Staff Working Document: Accompanying document to the Communication from the Commission to the Council. The European Parliament, The European Economic and Social Committee and the Committee of the Regions.

Commission of the European Communities. (2008). Addressing the challenge of energy efficiency through Information and Communication Technologies, Brussels, 13.5.2008. Retrieved July 2009, from http://ec.europa.eu/information_society/activities/sustainable_growth/docs/com_2008_241_1_en.pdf

Compamed (2009). Retrieved November 18, 2009, from www.compamed.de ecoTech (2009). Umwelt-Monitoring: enviLog Maxi Datenlogger. Retrieved November 18, 2009, from www.echotech-bonn.de/de/produkte/monitordaten/envilogmaxi.html

Consoli, F., Allen, D., Boustead, I., Fava, J. A., Franklin, W. E., Jensen, A. A., et al. (1993). Guidelines for Life-Cycle Assessment: A Code of Practice. Brussels, Washington, DC: Society of Environmental Toxicology and Chemistry (SETAC).

Corsten, H., Gössinger, R., & Schneider, H. (2006). Grundlagen des Innovationsmanagements. München: Verlag Vahlen.

Costanza, R., Cumberland, J., Daly, H., Goodland, R., & Norgaard, R. (2001). Einführung in die Ökologische Ökonomik. Stuttgart: Lucius & Lucius UTB.

Cote, R. P., & Hall, J. (1995). Industrial parks as ecosystems. Journal of Cleaner Production, 1(3), 41–46. doi:10.1016/0959-6526(95)00041-C

Council of Supply Chain Management Professionals. (n.d.). CSCMP supply chain management definitions. Retrieved December 9, 2009, from http://cscmp.org/aboutcscmp/definitions.asp

Cowherd, D. M., & Luchs, R. H. (1988). Linking Organization Structures and Processes to Business Strategy. Long Range Planning, 21(5), 47–55. doi:10.1016/0024-6301(88)90104-5

Cox, R., & Brna, P. (1995). Supporting the use of external representations in problem solving: the need for flexible learning environments. Journal of Artificial Intelligence in Education, 6(2/3), 239–302.

Cox, R., Stenning, K., & Oberlander, J. (1994). Graphical effects in learning logic: reasoning, representation and individual differences. Proceedings of the 16th Annual Conference of the Cognitive Science Society. Hillsdale, NJ: Lawrence Erlbaum Associates.

Cragg, P. B., & King, M. (1993). Small-Firm Computing: Motivators and Inhibitors. Management Information Systems Quarterly, 17(1), 47–60. doi:10.2307/249509

Cunha, M. M., & Putnik, G. D. (2006). Agile virtual enterprises: implementation and management support. Hershey, PA: IGI Global.

Daly, H. (1999). Wirtschaft jenseits von Wachstum: Die Volkswirtschaftslehre nachhaltiger Entwicklung. Salzburg, Austria: Pustet.

Damelio, R. (1996). The basics of process mapping. New York, New York: Productivity Press.

Danish Commerce and Companies Agency (DCCA). (2006). People & Profit. A practical guide to corporate social responsibility. Retrieved September 22, 2008, from http://www.eogs.dk/sw28291.asp

Darabaris, J. (2008). Corporate Environmental Management. Boca Raton, FL: CRC Press.

Darnall, N., Jolley, G. J., & Handfield, R. (2008). Environmental management systems and green supply chain management: Complements for sustainability? Business Strategy and the Environment, 17(1), 30–45.

Davis, S. C., Anderson-Teixeira, K. J., & DeLucia, E. H. (2008). Life-cycle analysis and the ecology of biofuels. Trends in Plant Science, 14(3), 140–146. doi:10.1016/j.tplants.2008.12.006

De Haes, S., & Van Grembergen, W. (2005). IT governance structures, processes and relational mechanisms: achieving IT/business alignment in a major Belgian financial group, Hawaii International Conference on System Sciences. Proceedings of the 38th Hawaii International Conference on System Sciences (pp.237b). Hawaii.

De Haes, S., & Van Grembergen, W. (2006). Information technology governance best practices in Belgian organizations, Hawaii International Conference on System Sciences. Proceedings of the 39th Hawaii International Conference on System Sciences (pp.195b). Hawaii.

de Jong, E., & van Ree, R. (2006). Biorefineries Co-production of Fuels, Chemicals, Power and Materials from Biomass (New Task Proposal). Retrieved July 15, 2009, from http://www.biorefinery.nl/iea-task-42/proposal/

de Mello, R. F. L. (1999). Em busca da sustentabilidade da organização antropossocial através da reciclagem e do conceito de auto-eco-organização. Curitiba, Paraná: UFPR.

de Mol, R. M., Jogems, M. A. H., van Beek, P., & Gigler, J. K. (1997). Simulation and optimization of the logistics of biomass fuel collection. Netherlands Journal of Agricultural Science, 45, 219–228.

de Morais Cordeiro, C., & Agrawal, D. P. (2006). Ad hoc & sensor networks: theory and applications. Singapore: World Scientific Publishing.

Dedrick, J., Gurbaxani, V., & Kraemer, K. (2003). Information technology and economic performance: a critical review of the empirical evidence. ACM Computing Surveys, 35(1), 1–28. doi:10.1145/641865.641866

Dehning, B., & Dow, K. E., & Stratopoulos. (2004). T. Information technology and organizational slack. International Journal of Accounting Information Systems, 5(1), 51–63. doi:10.1016/j.accinf.2004.02.003

Dehning, B., & Richardson, V. (2002). Returns on investments in information technology: a research synthesis. Journal of Information Systems, 16(1). doi:10.2308/jis.2002.16.1.7

Dehning, B., Richardson, V., & Zmud, R. (2003). The value relevance of announcements of transformational information technology investments. Management Information Systems Quarterly, 27(4).

Dehning, B., Richardson, V., & Zmud, R. (2007). The financial performance effects of ITbased supply chain management systems in manufacturing firms. Journal of Operations Management, 25(4), 806–824. doi:10.1016/j.jom.2006.09.001

Deicke, M., Ruppert, H., & Schneider, J. (2006). Mining and smelting in the Harz Mountains (Germany) – a neverending environmental story. Schriftenreihe der Deutschen Gesellschaft für Geowissenschaften, 45, 237–256.

Dekker, R., Fleischmann, M., Inderfurth, K., & Van Wassenhove, L. N. (Eds.). (2003). Reverse Logistics: Quantitative Models for Closed-Loop Supply Chains. Berlin: Springer.

Dekker, R., Fleischmann, M., Inderfurth, K., & Van Wassenhove, L. N. (Eds.). (2004). Reverse logistics: quantitative models for closed-loop supply chains. Berlin, Germany: Springer.

Deloitte & Touche LLP, & Grocery Manufactures Association (GMA) (2009). Green Shopper Study.

Deloitte Touche Tohmatsu International (DTTI), International Institute for Sustainable Development (IISD), & SustainAbility Ltd. (1993). Coming clean - corporate environmental reporting, opening up for sustainable development. London: DTTI.

Deming, W. E. (1986). The New Economics: For Industry, Government and Education (2nd ed.). Cambridge, MA: Massachusetts Institute of Technology Center for Advanced Engineering Study.

Desrochers, P. (2000). Eco-Industrial Parks and the Rediscovery of Inter-Firm Recycling Linkages (Working Paper). Retrieved July 13, 2009, from http://mises.org/journals/scholar/Eco6a.PDF

Devaraj, S., & Kohli, R. (2003). Performance impacts of information technology: Is actual usage the missing link? Management Science, 49(3), 273–289. doi:10.1287/mnsc.49.3.273.12736

Dewulf, W., et al. (2001). Integrating Eco-Efficiency in Rail Vehicle Design. Leuven, Belgium: Leuven University Press. ELCD, European Life Cycle Database. Retrieved August 10, 2009, from http://lca.jrc.ec.europa.eu/lcainfohub/datasetArea.vm.

Diamond, J. (2005). Collapse – How Societies Choose to Fall or Succeed. New York: Penguin.

Dias, M. B., & Brewer, E. (2009). How computer science serves the developing world. Communications of the ACM, 52(6), 74–80. doi:10.1145/1516046.1516064

Dias-Sardinha, I., & Reijnders, L. (2005). Evaluating Environmental and Social Performance of Large Portuguese Companies. Business Strategy and the Environment, 14(2), 73–91. doi:10.1002/bse.421

Diekema, W. H., de Mol, R. M., Annevelink, E., & Elbersen, H. W. (2005, October). Combining goals in the logistics bio-energy chains. Paper presented at the 14th European Biomass Conference, Paris, France.

Dignan, L., & Perlow, J. (2007). Green IT: Why it matters? ZDNet. Retrieved April 26, 2007 from http://blogs.zdnet.com/BTL/?p=4929

DiPiazza, S. A., & Eccles, R. G. (2002). Building corporate trust. The future of corporate reporting. New York: Wiley.

Dörner, D. (2003). Die Logik des Misslingens - Strategisches Denken in komplexen Situationen. Hamburg, Germany: Rowohlt.

Dragstra, P. (2005). Enterprise architecture: the select process of an Enterprise Architecture Toolset to support understanding and the governing enterprise. Unpublished master dissertation, Technische Universiteit Eindhoven, Netherlands.

Duncombe, R., & Heeks, R. (2003). An information systems perspective on ethical trade and self-regulation. Information Technology for Development, 10(2), 123–139. doi:10.1002/itdj.1590100206

Dyckhoff, H. (1994). Betriebliche Produktion. Theoretische Grundlagen einer umweltorientierten Produktionswirtschaft. Berlin, Heidelberg: Springer. (in German)

Dyllick, T., & Hockerts, K. (2002). Beyond the business case for corporate sustainability. Business Strategy and the Environment, 11(2), 130–141. doi:10.1002/bse.323

Ebinger, F., Cahyandito, M. F., von Detten, R., & Schlüter, A. (2006). Just a Paper Tiger? Exploration of Sustainability Reporting as a Corporate Communication Instrument. In Schaltegger, S., Bennett, M., & Burritt, R. (Eds.), Sustainability Accounting and Reporting. Dordrecht: Springer. doi:10.1007/978-1-4020-4974-3_23

Eder, P. (1994). Grüne Computer. Wirtschaftsinformatik, 36(6), 600–603.

Eigner-Thiel, S. (2005). Kollektives Engagement für die Nutzung erneuerbarer Energieträger - Motive, Mobilisierung und Auswirkungen am Beispiel des Aktionsforschungsprojektes „Das Bioenergiedorf. Hamburg, Germany: Kovac.

Eigner-Thiel, S., & Geldermann, J. (2009). Entscheidungsunterstützung bei der Planung eines Bioenergiedorfes. In Geldermann, J., & Lauven, L. (Eds.), Einsatz von OR-Verfahren zur Entscheidungsunterstützung. Aachen, Germany: Shaker.

Eisenhardt, K. M., & Martin, J. A. (2000). Dynamic capabilities: What are they? Strategic Management Journal, 21(10/11), 1105–1121. doi:10.1002/1097-0266(200010/11)21:10/11<1105::AID-SMJ133>3.0.CO;2-E

Eisert, U., Geiger, K., Hartmann, G., Ruf, H., Schindewolf, S., & Schmidt, U. (2001). mySAP Product Lifecycle Management. Bonn: Galileo Press (in German).

Elden, M., & Chisholm, R. F. (1993). Emerging Varieties of Action Research: Introduction to the Special Issue. Human Relations, 46(2), 121–142. doi:10.1177/001872679304600201

Elkington, J. (1997). Cannibals with forks: The triple bottom line of 21st century business. Oxford: Capstone.

Elkington, J. (2004). Enter the triple bottom line. In Henriques, A., & Richardson, J. (Eds.), The Triple Bottom Line: Does It All Add up? (pp. 1–16). London: Earthscan.

Elrad, T., Filman, R. E., & Bader, A. (2001). Aspect-Oriented Programming. Communications of the ACM, 44(10), 29–32. doi:10.1145/383845.383853

EPA. (2009). EPA – United States Environmental Protection Agency. About Energy Star. Retrieved November 19, 2009, from http://www.energystar.gov/index.cfm?c=about.ab_index

Epstein, M. J., & Roy, M. J. (2001). Sustainability in Action: Identifying and measuring the key performance drivers. Long Range Planning Journal, 34, 585–604. doi:10.1016/S0024-6301(01)00084-X

Epstein, M. J., & Roy, M. J. (2003). Making the Business Case for Sustainability. Journal of Corporate Citizenship, 9, 79–96.

Epstein, M. J., & Wisner, P. S. (2001). Using a Balanced Scorecard to Implement Sustainability. Environmental Quality Management, 11(2), 1–10. doi:10.1002/tqem.1300

Epstein, M., & Roy, M. J. (1998). Managing Corporate Environmental Performance: A Multinational Perspective. European Management Journal, 16(3). European Commission. Eco-Management and Audit Scheme. Retrieved July 22, 2009, from http://ec.europa.eu/environment/emas/

Erechtchoukova, M. G., & Khaiter, P. A. (2007). Uncertainty reduction in modelling of chemical load in streams. In L. Oxley & D. Kulasiri (Eds.), MODSIM 2007 International Congress on Modelling and Simulation. Modelling and Simulation Society of Australia and New Zealand, December 2007 (pp. 2445- 2451).

Erechtchoukova, M. G., & Khaiter, P. A. (2008). Role of models for building an efficient monitoring design. In M. Sànchez-Marrè, J. Béjar, J. Comas, A. Rizzoli, & G. Guariso (Eds.), iEMSs2008: International Congress on Environmental Modelling and Software. Integrating Sciences and Information Technology for Environmental Assessment and Decision Making, July 2008 (pp. 528-535).

Erechtchoukova, M. G., & Tsirkunov, V. V. (1989). Determination of sampling strategy for calculation of mass-discharge in streams with a given accuracy. In Proc. of the Conf. Problems of Surface Hydrology, February, 1987 (pp. 171-189). Leningrad: Gidrometeoizdat.

Erechtchoukova, M. G., Chen, S. Y., & Khaiter, P. A. (2009). Application of optimization algorithms for the improvement of water quality monitoring systems. In I. N. Athanasiadis, P. A. Mitkas, A. E. Rizzoli, & J. Marx Gómez (Eds.), Information Technologies in Environmental Engineering. Proceedings of the 4th International ICSC Symposium, Thessaloniki, Greece, May 28-29, 2009 (pp. 176-188). Berlin, Heidelberg: Springer.

Erek, K., Zarnekow, R., Schmidt, N. H., & Kolbe, L. M. (2009). Sustainability in Information Systems – Assessment of Current Practices in IS Organizations. Paper presented at the 15th Americas Conference on Information Systems (AMCIS 2009), paper 123, San Francisco, CA.

Erixon, M., Carlson, R., & Pålsson, A. C. (2003). Measuring the environmental impact of products. CPM report 2003:1, Swedish Environmental Protection Agency Report 5349. Stockholm, Sweden: Naturvårdsverket.

Erkman, S. (1999). Industrial Ecology. Beijing, China: Economic Daily Press.

Erlandsson, J. (2006). Company and Product Related Environmental Information Management – A pilot field study. Göteborg, Sweden: Chalmers University of Technology.

Ernst & Young. (2009). Green IT in kleinen und mittleren Unternehmen (KMU): Ein Blick auf das Thema aus Sicht von IT-Verantwortlichen in KMU. Retrieved November 12, 2009, from http://www.ey.com/publicationwwLUAssets/Green_TI/Green-IT in KMU.pdf

Ernst & Young. KPMG, PricewaterhouseCoopers, & House of Mandag Morgen (1999). The Copenhagen Charter. A management guide to stakeholder reporting. Copenhagen: Mandag Morgen.

Esty, D. C., & Winston, A. S. (2006). Green to Gold. How smart companies use environmental strategy to innovate, create value, and build competitive advantage. New Haven, London: Yale University Press.

EU (2003). Directive 2003/4/EC of the European Parliament and of the Council of 28 January 2003 on public access to environmental information and repealing Council Directive 90/313/EEC. Official Journal of the European Union, L 41, 26.

EU. (2007). Directive 2007/2/EC of the European Parliament and of the Council of 14 March 2007 establishing an Infrastructure for Spatial Information in the European Community (INSPIRE). Official Journal of the European Union. L&C, L, 108.

EU. (2008). Communication from the Commission to the Council, the European Parliament, the European Economic and Social Committee and the Committee of the Regions – Towards a Shared Environmental Information System (SEIS). COM/2008/0046 final. Retrieved July 2009, from http://eur-lex.europa.eu/LexUriServ/LexUriServ.do?uri=COM:2008:0046:FIN:EN:PDF

EU. (2009). Website from the European Commission's DG Environment about SEIS. Retrieved November 2009, from http://ec.europa.eu/environment/seis/index.htm

Europe, C. S. R. (2000). Communicating corporate social responsibility. Brussels: CSR Europe.

European Commission (2001). Regulation (EC) No 761/2001 of the European parliament and of the council of 19 March 2001 allowing voluntary participation by organizations in a Community eco-management and audit scheme (EMAS). L. 114, v. 44, 42 April 2001.

European Commission (EC) (2002). European SMEs and Social and Environmental Responsibility. Observatory of European SME 2002/No. 4, prepared by KPMG Special Services and EIM Business & Policy Research in the Netherlands in co-operation with European Network for SME Research (ENSR), and Intomart Luxembourg, Office for official publications of the European Communities.

European Commission. (2009). Smarter use of energy. Retrieved July 2009, from http://ec.europa.eu/information_society/activities/sustainable_growth/energy_efficiency/index_en.htm

European Commission. (2009). The State of Sustainability Reporting in Europe: Commission Statement. Fujitsu. Environmental Management Information Systems. Retrieved August 12, 2009, from http://www.fujitsu.com/global/about/ environment/management/ems/information-sys/

European Communities (EC). (2001). Regulation (EC) No. 761/2001 of the European Parliament and of the Council of 19 March 2001 allowing voluntary participation by organisations in a Community eco-management and audit scheme (EMAS). Official Journal of the European Communities, L, 114.

European Environmental Agency. (2007). User guide, Data Dictionary. Retrieved November 20, 2009, from http://dd.eionet.europa.eu/DD-User-Guide.pdf

European Space Agency (2009). Earthnet Online. Retrieved November 18, 2009, from envisat.esa.int

European steel industry (2004). Made of steel. The steel image campaign. The joint initiative by steel companies from Europe to promote the image of steel. Retrieved October 25, 2004, from http://www.made-of-steel.com/html_en/informations/index.html

Ewen, C., Ebinger, F., Gensch, C.-O., Grießhammer, R., Hochfeld, C., & Wollny, V. (1997). HoechstNachhaltig. Sustainable Development – Vom Leitbild zum Werkzeug [Sustainable Development – From vision to an operational instrument]. Freiburg: Institute for Applied Ecology. eXtensible Business Reporting Language (XBRL) (2006). Extensible business reporting language 2.1, recommendation -2003-12-31 and corrected errata -2005-11-07. Retrieved January 17, 2006, from http://www.xbrl.org/Specification/XBRL-RECOMMENDATION-2003-12-31+Corrected-Errata-2005-11-07.htm

Ewringmann, D., & Koch, L. (2006). Einleitung in die Problemstellung: Chemische Industrie, Nachhaltigkeit und Innovationen. In Koch, L., & Monßen, M. (Eds.), Kooperative Umweltpolitik und nachhaltige Innovationen (pp. 2–26). Heidelberg: Physica. doi:10.1007/3-7908-1661-2_1

eXtensible Business Reporting Language (XBRL) (2006a). XBRL FAQ. Retrieved January 17, 2006, from http://www.xbrl.org/Faq.htm

eXtensible Business Reporting Language (XBRL) (2006b). Extensible Business Reporting Language 2.1, Recommendation -2003-12-31 and Corrected Errata-2005-11-07. Retrieved January 17, 2006, from http://www.xbrl.org/Specification/XBRL-RECOMMENDATION-2003-12-31+Corrected-Errata-2005-11-07.htm

eXtensible Business Reporting Language (XBRL) (2006c). Guidance on XBRL Instance Documents and Reports. Retrieved January 05, 2006, from http://www.xbrl.org/InstanceGuidance/

Fama, E., & Jensen, M. (1983). Separation of ownership and control. The Journal of Law & Economics, 26, 301–327. doi:10.1086/467037

Farrell, I. J. (2003). Alignin IT to corporate objectives: organizational factores. Unpublished doctoral dissertation, Macquarie University, Sydney.

Ferguson, G. T. (1996). Strategy in the digital age. The Journal of Business Strategy, 17(6), 28–31.

Ferland, J. (2009). Environnement et société: les TI sont des agents de changement. Direction Informatique Express, Edition du 4 Novembre 2009 (www.directioninformatique.com).

Ferrer, G., & Whybark, D. C. (2001). Material Planning for a Remanufacturing Facility. Production and Operations Management, 10(2), 112–124.

Fichman, R. G. (2000). The diffusion and assimilation of information technology innovations. In Zmud, R. W. (Ed.), Framing the Domains of IT Management: Projecting the Future...Through the Past (pp. 105–128). Cincinnati, OH: Pinnaflex Educational Resources Inc.

Fichter, K. (1998). Umweltkommunikation und Wettbewerbsfähigkeit. Wettbewerbstheorien im Lichte empirischer Ergebnisse zur Umweltberichterstattung von Unternehmen [Environmental communication and competitiveness. Concepts of competition in the light of empirical results on corporate environmental reporting]. Marburg: Metropolis.

Fichter, K. (2005). Interpreneurship – Nachhaltigkeitsinnovationen in interaktiven Perspektiven eines vernetzten Unternehmertums. Marburg: Metropolis.

Figge, F., & Schaltegger, S. (2000). What is "stakeholder value"? Developing a catchphrase into a benchmarking tool. Lüneburg: University of Lüneburg & UNEP.

Figge, F., Hahn, T., Shaltegger, S., & Wagner, M. (2002). The Sustainability Balanced Scorecard – linking sustainability management to business strategy. Business Strategy and the Environment, 11(5), 269–284. doi:10.1002/bse.339

Figueira, J., Greco, S., & Ehrgott, M. (2005). Multiple criteria decision analysis – State of the art. Surveys. New York: Springer.

Financial Reporting Taxonomies Architecture (FRTA). (2005). Financial Reporting Taxonomies Architecture (FRTA) 1.0 - Recommendation dated 2005-04-25, Corresponding to XBRL 2.1 Recommendation. Retrieved January 17, 2006, from http://www.xbrl.org/technical/guidance/FRTA-RECOMMENDATION-2005-04-25.htm

Fink, D. (1998). Guidelines for the successful adoption of information technology in small and medium enterprises. International Journal of Information Management, 18(4), 243–253. doi:10.1016/S0268-4012(98)00013-9

Fischer, H. (1990). Verteilte Planungssysteme zur Flexibilitätssteigerung der rechnerintegrierten Teilefertigung. München: Carl Hanser.

Fischer-Kowalski, M., & Haberl, H. (Eds.). (2007). Socioecological Transitions And Global Change – Trajectories of Social Metabolism and Land Use. Cheltenham: Edward Elgar Publishing.

Fischer-Kowalski, M., & Hüttler, W. (1999). Society's Metabolism – The Intellectual History of Material Flow Analysis, Part II, 1970 – 1998. Journal of Industrial Ecology, 2(4), 61–78.

Fisher, M. A. (2005). Virtualised computing infrastructure. BT Technology Journal, 23(3), 52–58. doi:10.1007/s10550-005-0030-5

Fitzgerald, G. (1998). Evaluating information systems projects: a multidimensional approach. Journal of Information Technology, 13(1), 15–27. doi:10.1080/026839698344936

FIU (Forschungsverbund innovative Wirkungen umweltpolitischer Instrumente) (1997). Letter in September. Essen.

Flatz, A. (2003). Screening for sustainability. A case study of the Dow Jones Sustainability Index. In Waage, S. (Ed.), Ants, Galileo, and Gandhi. Designing the future of business through nature, genius, and compassion (pp. 144–168). Sheffield: Greenleaf.

Flemström, K., Carlson, R., & Erixon, M. (2004). Relationships between Life Cycle Assessment and Risk Assessment – Potentials and Obstacles. Naturvårdsverket Rapport 5379. Stockholm, Sweden: Naturvårdsverket.

Fleury, A. (2005). Eine Nachhaltigkeitsstrategie für den Energieversorgungssektor - dargestellt am Beispiel der Stromversorgung in Frankreich. Karlsruhe, Germany: University of Karlsruhe (TH), French-German Institute for Environmental Research.

Fontanella, J. (2004). Finding the ROI in RFID. Supply Chain Management Review, 8(1), 13–14.

Forrester Research. (2007). Umwelt ist ein wichtiger Faktor in der IT. Retrieved May 3, 2009, from http://www.computerwoche.de/knowledge_center/green-it/592768/

Forschungsgruppe Unternehmen und gesellschaftliche Organisation (FUGO) (Ed.). (2004). Perspektiven einer kulturwissenschaftlichen Theorie der Unternehmung. Marburg: Metropolis Verlag.

Fougère, M., & Solitander, N. (2009). Against corporate responsibility: critical reflections on thinking, practice, content and consequences. Corporate Social Responsibility and Environmental Management, 16(4), 217–227. doi:10.1002/csr.204

Foxon, T. J., Gross, R., Chase, A., Howes, J., Arnall, A., & Anderson, D. (2005). The UK innovation systems for new and renewable energy technologies. Energy Policy, 33(16), 2123–2137. doi:10.1016/j.enpol.2004.04.011

Frankl, P., & Rubik, F. (2000). Life Cycle Assessment in Industry and Business – Adoption Patterns, Applications and Implications. Berlin, Heidelberg: Springer.

Freeman, C. (1987). Technology Policy and Economic Reformance. Lessons from Japan. London: Pinter Pub.

Freeman, R. E. (1984). Strategic Management: A Stakeholder Approach. Boston: Financial Times Prentice Hall.

Frischknecht, R. (2004). Ecoinvent Database: Quality Control and User Interfaces for a Web-based Life Cycle Assessment Database. In Hilty, L. M., Seifert, E. K., & Treibert, R. (Eds.), Information Systems for Sustainable Development. Hershey, PA: Idea Group Publishing.

Fritsche, U. R., Hennenberg, K., Hermann, A., Hünecke, K., Schulze, F., Wiegmann, K., et al. (2009). Sustainable bioenergy: Current status and outlook. Darmstadt/Heidelberg, Germany. Retrieved July 13, 2009, from http://www.umweltdaten.de/publikationen/fpdf-l/3741.pdf

Fritz, W., Kovač, I., & Frank, A. (2005). Virtual Simulation and Off-line Programming of Robot Guided Reconfiguration Systems. In M. Zaeh, & G. Reinhart (Eds.), 1st International Conference on Changeable, Agile, Reconfigurable and Virtual Production (CARV 2005) (pp. 181-186). München: Herbert Utz Verlag.

Frolov, K. V. (2003). The Role of Mechanical Engineering in the 21st Century. In Dashchenko, A. (Ed.), Manufacturing Technologies for Machines of the future – 21st Century Technologies (pp. 3–29). Berlin, Heidelberg: Springer.

Frondel, M., Horbach, J., & Rennings, K. (2004). End-of-Pipe or Cleaner Production? An Empirical Comparison of Environmental Innovation Decisions Across OECD Countries. ZEW Discussion Paper, 04-82.

Frondel, M., Horbach, J., Rennings, K., & Requate, T. (2004). Environmental Policy Tools and Firm-Level Management Practices: Empirical Evidence for Germany. RWI Mitteilungen Quarterly, 54/55(2), 87–111.

Fuchs, C. (2008). The implications of new information and communication technologies for sustainability. Environment, Development and Sustainability, 10(3), 291–319. doi:10.1007/s10668-006-9065-0

Funk, B., Moeller, A., & Niemeyer, P. (2009). Integration of Environmental Management Information Systems an ERP systems using Integration Platform. In I. N. Athanasiadis, P. A. Mitkas, A. E. Rizzoli, & J. Marx Gómez (Eds.), Information Technologies in Environmental Engineering. Proceedings of the 4th International ICSC Symposium Thessaloniki, Greece, May 28-29, 2009 (pp. 64-77). Berlin, Heidelberg: Springer.

Furuholt, B., & Ørvik, T. U. (2006). Implementation of Information Technology in Africa: Understanding and Explaining the Results of Ten Years of Implementation Effort in a Tanzanian Organization. Information Technology for Development, 12(1), 45–62. doi:10.1002/itdj.20030

Futerra Sustainability Communications. (2008). The greenwash guide. Retrieved September 17, 2008, from www.futerra.co.uk

Future e.V., & Institute for Ecological Economy Research (IÖW) (1994). Environmental reports – environmental statements. Guidelines on preparation and distribution. Osnabrück: future e.V.

Gabrielli de Azevedo, J. S. (2009). The Greening of Petrobras. Harvard Business Review, 87(3), 43–47.

Gadatsch, A. (2009). IT controlling – concepts and transformation in practice. Business Information Systems and Engineering, 1(3), 254–262.. doi:10.1007/s12599-009-0043-6

Gadatsch, A., & Juszczak, J. (Eds.). (2009). Results of the short survey concerning the status of Green IT in German speaking countries (Green IT 2009). Schriftenreihe des Fachbereiches Wirtschaftswissenschaft Sankt Augustin, Hochschule Bonn-Rhein-Sieg, vol. 25. Sankt Augustin: Hochschule Bonn-Rhein-Sieg.

Galliers, R. D. (1992). Choosing Information Systems Research Approaches. In R.D. Galliers (Ed.), Information Systems Research: Issues, Methods and Practical Guidelines (pp. 144-162). Henley-on-Thames: Alfred Waller.

Galliers, R. D., & Leidner, D. E. (2004). Strategic Information Management. Rochester, UK: Butterworth Heinemann.

Gamba, L. (2008). Erste Modellentwicklung zur nachhaltigen Nutzung von Biomasse. Doctoral dissertation, Technical University Berlin, Germany.

Gartner (Ed.) (2008). Gartner identifies the Top 10 Strategic Technologies for 2009. Retrieved November 18, 2009, from http://www.gartner.com/it/page.jsp?id=777212

Gartner Inc. (2007). Gartner Estimates ICT Industry Accounts for 2 Percent of Global CO2 Emissions. Retrieved March 31, 2008, from http://www.gartner.com/it/page.jsp?id=503867

Gausemeier, J., Ebbesmeyer, P., & Kallmeyer, F. (2001). Produktinnovation - Strategische Planung und Entwicklung der Produkte von morgen. München, Wien: Carl Hanser.

Gausemeier, J., Schäfer, W., Eckes, R., & Wagner, R. (2005). Ramp-Up and Maintenance with Augmented Reality in Development of Flexible Production Control Systems. M. Zaeh, & G. Reinhart (Eds.), 1st International Conference on Changeable, Agile, Reconfigurable and Virtual Production (CARV 2005) (pp. 201-206). München: Herbert Utz Verlag.

Geldermann, J., Bertsch, V., Treitz, M., French, S., Papamichail, K.N., & Hämäläinen, R.P. (2007). Multi-criteria decision support and evaluation of strategies for nuclear remediation management. OMEGA – The International Journal of Management Science, 37 (1), 238-251.

Geldermann, J., Zhang, K., & Rentz, O. (2002). Entwicklung eines integrierten multikriteriellen Gruppenentscheidungsunterstützungssystems (MGDSS) - Fallstudie: Hierarchische Planung in der Industrielackierung. Frankfurt, Germany: Verlag Peter Lang.

German Institute for Standardisation e. V. (DIN) (1996). Environmental management systems – specifications with guidance for use. Berlin: Beuth.

German Institute for Standardisation e. V. (DIN) (1997). DIN 33922. Environmental reports for the public. Berlin: Beuth.

Gherardi, S. (2009). Introduction: The Critical Power of the 'Practice Lens'. Management Learning, 40, 115–128..doi:10.1177/1350507608101225

Gibbs, M. (2007). To Be Proactive or Not To Be? Network World, May 10, 2007. Retrieved December 2009 from http://www.networkworld.com/columnists/2007/051007-backspin.html

Giddens, A. (1984). The Constitution of Society: Outline of the Theory of Structuration. Cambridge: Polity Press.

Gillwald, K. (2000). Konzepte sozialer Innovation. Paper P00-519 der Querschnittsgruppe Arbeit und Ökologie des Wissenschaftszentrums Berlin.

Global Reporting Initiative (GRI). (2002). Sustainability reporting guidelines. Retrieved October 15, 2002, from http://www.globalreporting.org

Global Reporting Initiative (GRI). (2004). GRI software development. GRI enters digital age. Retrieved May 18, 2004, from http://www.globalreporting.org/software

Global Reporting Initiative (GRI) (Ed.). (2006). Sustainability Reporting Guideline – Version 3.0. Amsterdam: Global Reporting Initiative Press.

Global Reporting Initiative (GRI) (2008). European Sustainability Reporting Association Report from GRI.

Glushko, R. J., & McGrath, T. (2005). Document engineering. Analyzing and designing documents for business informatics and web services. Cambridge, MA: MIT.

Gnansounou, E., Pierre, S., Quintero, A., Dong, J., & Lahlou, A. (2007). A multi-agent approach for planning activities in decentralized electricity markets. Knowledge-Based Systems, 20, 406–418. doi:10.1016/j.knosys.2006.06.004

Goessling-Reisemann, S. (2008). What Is Resource Consumption and How Can it Be Measured? Journal of Industrial Ecology, 12(1), 10–25. doi:10.1111/j.1530-9290.2008.00012.x

Golinska, P., Fertsch, M., Marx Gómez, J., & Oleskow, J. (2007). The concept of Closed-loop Supply Chain Integration Through Agent-based System. In J. Marx Gómez, M. Sonnenschein, M. Müller, H. Welsch, & C. Rautenstrauch (Eds.), Information Technologies in Environmental Engineering, ITEE 2007, Third International ICSC Symposium (pp. 189-202). Berlin, Heidelberg: Springer.

Goscimski, J. (2007). Development of a Software-based Environmental Reporting According to the "Bundes-Immissionsschutzgesetz". In Gomez, J. M., Sonnenschein, M., Müller, M., & Welsch, H. (Eds.), Information Technologies in Environmental Engineering (pp. 567–574). Berlin, Heidelberg: Springer Verlag. doi:10.1007/978-3-540-71335-7_55

Gottesdiener, E. (2002). Requirements by Collaboration. Boston: Pearson Education, Inc.

Granoszewski, K., Reise, C., Spiller, A., & Mußhoff, O. (2009). Entscheidungsverhalten landwirtschaftlicher Betriebsleiter bei Bioenergie-Investitionen (Discussion paper No. 0911). Göttingen, Germany: University of Göttingen, Department of Agricultural Economics and Rural Development.

Grant, R. M. (2005). The Resource-Based Theory of Competitive Advantage. Implications for Strategy Formulation. California Management Review, 33(1), 114–135.

Gray, R. (2002). Social and environmental responsibility, sustainability and accountability: Can the corporate sector deliver? The Corporate Citizen, 2(3), 9–16.

Gray, R., & Milne, M. (2002). Sustainability reporting: Who's kidding whom? Chartered Accountants Journal of New Zealand, 81(6), 66–70.

Green Logistics. (2009) What is Green Logistics? Retrieved December 9, 2009, from http://www.greenlogistics.org/PageView.aspx?id=97

Green, A., & Ryan, J. J. (2005). A framework of intangible valuation areas (FIVA): Aligning business strategy and intangible assets. Journal of Intellectual Capital, 6(1), 43–52. doi:10.1108/14691930510574654

Grembergen, W. V. (2004). Strategies for information technology governance. Hershey, PA: Idea Group Publishing.

Greuel, V. (2009). Economic Benefits of Green IS. Unpublished thesis, Bonn-Rhein-Sieg University of Applied Science, Sankt Augustin, Germany.

GRI (Global Reporting Initiative). (2006). Sustainability Reporting Guidelines. Version 3.0. Amsterdam, Netherlands.

GRI. (2009). Global Reporting Initiative. Retrieved November 04, 2009, from http://www.globalreporting.org.

Groot, S., & Schilperoort, T. (1983). Optimization of water quality monitoring networks. Water Science and Technology, 16, 275–287.

Grosh, B., & Somolekae, G. (1996). Mighty oaks from little acorns: Can micro-enterprise serve as the seedbed of industrialization? World Development, 24(12), 1879–1890. doi:10.1016/S0305-750X(96)00082-4

Group, B. S. I. BSI: Standards, Training, Testing, Assessment & Certification. Retrieved July 26, 2009, from http://www.bsi-global.com/

Grünwald, C. (2009). Konzeption eines integrierten Betrieblichen Umweltinformationssystems – Fallstudie Volkswagen AG. Oldenburger Schriften zur Wirtschaftsinformatik (Vol. 2). Aachen: Shaker-Verlag.

Grünwald, C., & Marx Gómez, J. (2007). Integrating Environmental Information with systems of Factory Planning. In J. Marx Gómez, M. Sonnenschein, M. Müller, H. Welsch, & C. Rautenstrauch (Eds.), Information Technologies in Environmental Engineering, ITEE 2007 – Third International ICSC Symposium (pp. 203-210). Berlin, Heidelberg: Springer.

Guerrin, F., Courdier, R., Calderoni, S., Paillat, J. M., Soulié, J. C., & Vally, J. D. (1999). Biomas: un modèle multi-agents pour aider à la gestion négociée d'effluents d'élevage. In Ferrand, N. (Ed.), Modèles et systèmes multi-agents pour la gestion del'environnement et des territoires. Paris: Cemagref.

Guide Jr., V. D. R. (2003). Matching Demand and Supply to Maximize Profits from Remanufacturing. Manufacturing and Service operations Management, 5(4), 303-316.

Guide, V. D. R. Jr, & Van Wassenhove, L. N. (Eds.). (2003). Business Aspects of Closed-Loop Supply Chains. Pittsburgh, PA: Carnegie Mellon University Press.

Guide, V. D. R. Jr. (2000). Production planning and control for remanufacturing. Journal of Operations Management, 18, 467–483. doi:10.1016/S0272-6963(00)00034-6

Guinée, J. B. (final editor) (2002). Handbook on Life Cycle Assessment – Operational Guide to the ISO Standards. Boston: Kluwer Academic Publishers.

Gunasekaran, A., & Ngai, E., & McGaughey. (2006). Information technology and systems justification: A review for research and applications. European Journal of Operational Research, 173(3), 957–983. doi:10.1016/j.ejor.2005.06.002

Günther, E., Kirchgeorg, M., & Winn, M. (2007). Resilience Management: Konzeptentwurf zum Umgang mit Auswirkungen des Klimawandels. UmweltWirtschafts-Forum, 15, 175–182.

Günther, O. (1998). Environmental Information Systems. Berlin, Heidelberg: Springer.

Habermas, J. (1985). The Theory of Communicative Action: Vol. 2. Lifeworld and System: A Critique of Functionalist Reason (3rd ed.). Boston, MA: Beacon Press.

Hahn, T., & Wagner, M. (2001). Sustainability Balanced Scorecard. Lüneburg, Germany: Center for Sustainability Management.

Hämäläinen, R. P., & Alaja, S. (2008). The threat of weighting biases in environmental decision analysis. Ecological Economics, 68(1/2), 556–569. doi:10.1016/j.ecolecon.2008.05.025

Hamscher, W. (Ed.). (2007). Financial reporting taxonomies architecture 1.0. Recommendation dated 2005-04-25. Retrieved December 14, 2007, from http://www.xbrl.org/technical/guidance/FRTA-RECOMMENDATION-2005-04-25.htm

Hanson, J., & Edwards, S. (2002). Towards a Biobased Economy: Issues and Challenges Paper. Retrieved July 27, 2009, from http://www.pollutionprobe.org/Reports/biobased.pdf

Hardy, G. (2006). Using IT governance and COBIT to deliver value with IT and respond to legal, regulatory and compliance challenges. Information Security Technical Report, 55–61. doi:10.1016/j.istr.2005.12.004

Hare, M., & Deadman, P. (2004). Further towards a taxonomy of agent-based simulation models in environmental management. Mathematics and Computers in Simulation, 64, 25–40. doi:10.1016/S0378-4754(03)00118-6

Harmel, R. D., Cooper, R. J., Slade, R. M., Haney, R., & Arnold, J. G. (2006). Cumulative uncertainty in measured streamflow and water quality data for small watersheds. Transactions of the ASABE, 49(3), 689–701.

Hart, S. L. (1995). A natural resource based view of the firm. Academy of Management Review, 20(4), 986–1014. doi:10.2307/258963

Hart, S. L. (1997). Beyond greening: Strategies for a sustainable world. Harvard Business Review, 75(1), 66–76.

Hassis, H. D., Hilty, L. M., Hundscheind, J., Kuerzl, H., & Ratenstrauch, C. (1995). Umweltinformatik in der Production. Marburg: Metropolis.

Haworth, D., & Pietron, L. (2006). Sarbanes-Oxley: achieving compliance by starting with ISO17799. Information Systems Management, 23(1), 73–87. doi:10.1201/1078.10580530/45769.23.1.20061201/91775.9

Hazan, M. (2002). Virtual South: E-Commerce for unprivileged artisans. Retrieved December 12, 2008, from http://www.iicd.org/stories/

Hebdige, D. (1979). Subculture: The Meaning of Style. London: Taylor & Francis. doi:10.4324/9780203139943

Heier, H. Borgman, Hans P., & Mileos, C. (2009). Examining the Relationship between IT Governance Software, Processes, and Business Value: A Quantitative Research Approach, Hawaii International Conference on System Sciences. In Proceedings of the 42nd Hawaii International Conference on System Sciences (pp.1-11). Hawaii.

Heijungs, R. (1994). A generic method for the identification of options for cleaner products. Ecological Economics, 10, 69–81. doi:10.1016/0921-8009(94)90038-8

Heijungs, R., & Suh, S. (2002). The computational structure of life cycle assessment. Dordrecht, NL: Kluwer Academic Publishers.

Heiland, S., Tischer, M., Döring, T., Pahl, T., & Jessel, B. (2003). Indikatoren zur Zielkonkretisierung und Erfolgskontrolle im Rahmen der Lokalen Agenda 21. Berlin, Germany: Umweltbundesamt.

Heiskanen, E. (2001). Institutionalization of Life-Cycle Thinking in the Everyday Discourse of Market Actors. Journal of Industrial Ecology, 4(4), 31–46. doi:10.1162/10881980052541936

Hemmelskamp, J. (1999). Umweltpolitik und technischer Fortschritt. Heidelberg: Physica.

Hemmelskamp, J., Rennings, K., & Leone, F. (2000). Innovation-Oriented Environmental Regulation – Theoretical Approaches and Empirical Analysis. Heidelberg: Physica.

Henn, S., & Winter-Sattler, U. (1998). Facility Management – Schnittstellen zum Umweltmanagement. In L. Schimmelpfeng, S. Henn & C. Jansen (Eds.), Integrierte Umweltmanagementsysteme (pp.109-122). Taunusstein: Eberhard Blottner Verlag.

Hesse, A. (2007): Sustained added value. Information of investors and analysts for sector-specific "Sustainable Development Key Performance Indicators" (SD-KPIs) in management commentaries in German companies. Study prepared for Deloitte Touche Tomatsu, issued 1/2007. Retrieved June 21, 2007, from http://deloitte.com/de

Hicks, J. R. (1946). Value and Capital: An Inquiry into Some Fundamental Principles of Economic Theory. Oxford: Clarendon Press.

Hischier, R., & Gilgen, P. W. (2005). Life cycle assessment databases as part of sustainable development strategies: The example of Ecoinvent. In Hilty, L. M., Seifert, E. K., & Treibert, R. (Eds.), Information systems for sustainable development (pp. 15–24). Hershey, PA: Idea Group Publishing.

Hitt, L., & Brynjolfsson, E. (1996). Productivity, business profitability, and consumer surplus: three different measures of information technology value. Management Information Systems Quarterly, 20(2), 121–142. doi:10.2307/249475

Hochschule Karlsruhe. (2009). Retrieved November 18, 2009, from www.hs-karlsruhe.de

Hochstein, A., Brenner, W., & Uebernickel, F. (2006). Operations Management and IS: Using the SCOR-Model to Source, Make, and Deliver IS Services. Paper presented at the 12th Americas Conference on Information Systems (AMCIS 2006), Acapulco, Mexico.

Hockerts, K. (2001). What does corporate sustainability actually mean from a business strategy point of view? Paper presented at the Greening of Industry Network Conference, Bangkok.

Hoffmann, D. (2007). Regionale Wertschöpfung durch optimierte Nutzung endogener Biomassepotenziale. Doctoral dissertation, Saarland University, Germany.

Hofstetter, P. (1998). Perspectives in life cycle impact assessment; A structured approach to combine models of the technosphere, ecosphere and valuesphere. Dordrecht, Netherlands: Kluwer Academic Publishers.

Holling, C. S. (1973). Resilience and Stability of Ecological Systems. Annual Review of Ecology and Systematics, 4, 1–23. doi:10.1146/annurev.es.04.110173.000245

Honig, B. (1998). What determines success? Examining the human, financial, and social capital of Jamaican microentrepreneurs. Journal of Business Venturing, 13(5), 371–394. doi:10.1016/S0883-9026(97)00036-0

Höppner, F., Klawonn, F., Kruse, R., & Runkler, T. (1999). Fuzzy Cluster Analysis – Methods for Classification, Data Analysis and Image Recognition. Chichester: Wiley.

Hörning, K. H. (2004). Kultur als Praxis. In F. Jäger, & B. Liebsch (Eds.), Handbuch der Kulturwissenschaften (pp. 139-151). Stuttgart, Weimar: Akademie Verlag.

Hörning, K. H., & Reuter, J. (2004). Doing Culture: Neue Positionen zum Verhältnis von Kultur und sozialer Praxis. Bielefeld: transcript-Verlag.

Hu, Q., & Plant, R. (2001). An empirical study of the casual relationship between IT investment and firm performance. Information Resources Management Journal, 14(3), 15–26.

Huber, M. (1998). PVC im Kreuzfeuer der Kritik. Die publizistische Auseinandersetzung über den Werkstoff PVC nach dem Brand am Rhein-Ruhr-Flughafen. In Bentele, G., & Rolke, L. (Eds.), Konflikte, Krisen and Kommunikationschancen in der Mediengesellschaft. Berlin: Vistas. (in German)

Hübner, K., & Nill, J. (2001). Nachhaltigkeit als Innovationsmotor. Herausforderungen für das deutsche Innovationssystem. Berlin: Edition Sigma.

Hund, G., Engel-Cox, J., & Fowler, K. (2004). A communications guide for sustainable development. How interested parties become partners. Columbus: Battelle.

Hunt, T. L. (2007). Rethinking Easter Island's ecological catastrophe. Journal of Archaeological Science, 34, 485–502. doi:10.1016/j.jas.2006.10.003

Huppes, G., & Ishikawa, M. (2005a). Why Eco-Efficiency? Journal of Industrial Ecology, 9(4), 2–5. doi:10.1162/108819805775248052

Huppes, G., & Ishikawa, M. (2005b). A Framework for Quantified Eco-Efficiency Analysis. Journal of Industrial Ecology, 9(4), 25–42. doi:10.1162/108819805775247882

Huppes, G., & Ishikawa, M. (2005c). Eco-Efficiency and Its Terminology. Journal of Industrial Ecology, 9(4), 43–46. doi:10.1162/108819805775247891

Hwang, C. L., & Yoon, K. (1981). Multiple Attribute Decision Making, Methods and Applications - A State-of-the-Art Survey. Heidelberg, Germany: Springer.

Hyman, E. L., & Dearden, K. (1998). Comprehensive impact assessment systems for NGO Microenterprise Development Programs. World Development, 26(2), 261–276. doi:10.1016/S0305-750X(97)10022-5

IBGC. (2009). Linha do Tempo. Retrieved November 09, 2009, from http://www.ibgc.org.br/LinhaTempo.aspx.

IBM. (2009). A Comparative Review of Business Architecture. IBM Research Report. Retrieved November 01, 2009, from http://domino.research.ibm.com/library/cyberdig.nsf/papers/E3E920683AB1AEF6852576250052CD22/$File/rj10451.pdf

Icaga, Y. (2005). Genetic algorithm usage in water quality monitoring networks optimization in Gediz (Turkey) river basin. Environmental Monitoring and Assessment, 108, 261–277. doi:10.1007/s10661-005-4328-z

IDC (Ed.). (2008). IDC Predictions 2009: An Economic Pressure Cooker Will Accelerate the IT Industry Transformation. Retrieved November 18, 2009, from http://www.idc.com/getdoc.jsp?containerId=215519

IEA (International Energy Agency). (2004). Biofuels for transport: an international perspective. Paris, France: IEA.

INSADI. (2005). Apostila do Curso de Formação de Gestores de Processos. São Paulo, São Paulo: Insadi.

Institut für Energie und Umweltforschung (IfEU). Institut für Markt-Umwelt-Gesellschaft (imug), Institut für ökologische Wirtschaftsforschung (IÖW), & Öko-Institut (2001). Challenger report. Four institutes IfEU, imug, IÖW, Öko-Institut. Berlin: IfEU. Retrieved September 18, 2002, from http://www.ifeu.de/allgemein/pdf/Challenger-Report-Final.pdf

Institut für ökologische Wirtschaftsforschung (IÖW), & future e.V. (Eds.) (2007). Nachhaltigkeitsberichterstattung in Deutschland. Ergebnisse und Trends im Ranking. Retrieved August 31, 2009, from http://www.ioew.de/uploads/tx_ukioewdb/Ergebnisbericht_Ranking_2007_final.pdf

Interbrand (2008). Best global brands 2008. Creating and managing brand value. Retrieved September 29, 2008, from http://www.interbrands.com

Intergovernmental Panel of Climate Change (IPCC). (1988). 2009. Retrieved July 2009, from http://www.ipcc.ch/organization/organization.htm

Intermec. (2007, February). Supply chain RFID: How it works and why it pays? Retrieved December 9, 2009, from http://epsfiles.intermec.com/eps_files/eps_wp/SupplyChainRFID_wp_web.pdf

International Energy Agency. (2007). Bioenergy Project Development & Biomass Supply - Good Practice Guidelines. Paris, France: Author.

International Institute for Sustainable Development. Deloite & Touche, & Business Council for Sustainable Development (Eds.) (1992). Business Strategy for Sustainable Development. Leadership and Accountability for the 90'. Winnipeg, MB: International Institute for Sustainable Development (IISD) Press.

International Organization for Standardization ISO, & International Electrotechnical Commission IEC (Eds.) (2002). ISO/IEC 13250 Topic Maps – Information Technology Document Description and Processing Languages (ISO/IEC 13250:2002 (2nd edition). Geneva: ISO Press.

International Organization for Standardization. (2004). Environmental management systems – requirements with guidance for use (ISO 14001:2004). Jersey City, NJ: International Organization for Standardization.

International Organization for Standardization. ISO 14001:2004 - Environmental management systems. Retrieved July 10, 2009, from http://www.iso.org/

International Organization for Standardization. TC207 Environmental Management. Retrieved July 21, 2009, from http://www.tc207.org/

International Standardisation Organisation. (1996). Environemental Management – Life Cycle Assessment – Principles and Framework – ISO 14040, Paris.

Isenmann, R. (2004). Internet-based sustainability reporting. International Journal of Environment and Sustainable Development, 3(2), 145–167. doi:10.1504/IJESD.2004.004700

Isenmann, R. (2005). Corporate sustainability reporting – a case for the internet. In Hilty, L. M., Seifert, E. K., & Treibert, K. (Eds.), Information systems for sustainable development (pp. 164–212). Hershey: Idea Group.

Isenmann, R. (2008). Environmental management information systems – illustrations from online communication and sustainability peporting. In M. Sánchez-Marrè, J. Béjar, J. Comas, A. E. Rizzoli, & G. Guariso (Eds.), Proceedings of the iEMSs. Fourth Biennal Meeting. International Congress on Environmental Modelling and Software (iEMSs 2008), Barcelona, Catalonia, July 2008, vol. 3 (pp. 1636-1644). International Environmental Modelling and Software Society.

Isenmann, R., & Bey, C. (2007). Environmental reporting on the internet – from a technical tool to a strategic necessity. In Sroufe, R., & Sarkis, J. (Eds.), Strategic sustainability: The state of the art in corporate environmental management systems (pp. 123–143). Sheffield: Greenleaf.

Isenmann, R., & Kim, K. (2006). Interactive Sustainability Reporting. Developing Clear Target Group Tailoring and Stimulating Stakeholder Dialogue. In Schaltegger, S., Bennett, M., & Burritt, R. (Eds.), Sustainability Accounting and Reporting. Dordrecht: Springer. doi:10.1007/978-1-4020-4974-3_24

Isenmann, R., & Lenz, C. (2001). Customized corporate environmental reporting by internet-based push- and pull-technologies. Eco-Management and Auditing, 8(2), 100–110. doi:10.1002/ema.153

Isenmann, R., & Lenz, C. (2002). Internet use for corporate environmental reporting: Current challenges – technical benefits – practical guidance. Business Strategy and the Environment, 11(3), 181–202. doi:10.1002/bse.329

Isenmann, R., & Marx Gómez, J. (2004). How to provide customized environmental reports properly. In Scharl, A. (Ed.), Environmental online communication (pp. 173–182). London: Springer.

Isenmann, R., & Marx Gómez, J. (Eds.). (2008). Internetbasierte Nachhaltigkeitsberichterstattung. Maßgeschneiderte Stakeholder-Kommunikation mit IT [Internet-based sustainability reporting. Tailored stakeholder communication with IT]. Berlin: Erich Schmidt.

Isenmann, R., Arndt, H.-K., Bey, C., Marx Gómez, J., & Solsbach, A. (2008). XBRL-Taxonomie für Nachhaltigkeitsberichte – Vorschlag einer harmonisierten Dokumentstruktur zur Online-Kommunikation von Organisationen.In Bichler, M., Hess, T., Krcmar, H., Lechner, U., Matthes, F., & Picot, A. (Eds.), Multikonferenz Wirtschaftsinformatik 2008 (pp. 601–613). Berlin: GITO.

Isenmann, R., Arndt, H.-K., Brosowski, J., Marx-Gómez, J., & Schappert, M. (2007). Using Internet Technologies and Services for Sustainability Reporting: Research Initiative, Agenda, Early Results. In Hryniewicz, O., Studzinski, J., & Romaniuk, M. (Eds.), EnviroInfo 2007 – Environmental Informatics and Systems Research (Vol. 1). Aachen: Shaker.

Isenmann, R., Beisel, M., Brosowski, J., & Marx Gómez, J. (2004). Software tool for single source multiple media sustainability reporting. In P. Minier, & A. Susini (Eds.), Sh@ring. Proceedings EnviroInfo 2004, 18th International Conference Informatics for Environmental Protection (pp. 152-162). Genève: Editions du Tricorne.

Isenmann, R., Bey, C., & Welter, M. (2007). Online reporting for sustainability issues. Business Strategy and the Environment, 16(7), 487–501. doi:10.1002/bse.597

Isenmann, R., Brosowski, J., & Lenz, C. (2003). Target group tailored corporate environmental reporting – stereotyping, individualisation, personalisation. In A. Gnauck, & R. Heinrich (Eds.), The information society and enlargement of the European Union. Proceedings EnviroInfo 2003, 17th International Conference Informatics for Environmental Protection (pp. 533-540). Marburg: Metropolis.

Isenmann, R., Lenz, C., & Müller-Merbach, H. (2001). Betriebliche Umweltberichterstattung im Internet. Der aktuelle Stand für Deutschland [Corporate environmental reporting on the internet. Current practice in Germany]. Praxis der Wirtschaftsinformatik, 38(218), 97–107.

Isenmann, R., Marx Gómez, J., & Süpke, D. (2008). Sustainability Reporting à la carte – Concept and Implementation of a Software Tool with Shopping Cart Functionality. In A. Möller, B. Page, & M. Schreiber (Eds.), Environmental Informatics and Industrial Ecology – 22nd International Conference on Environmental Informatics EnvioInfo 2008, Leuphana University Lüneburg 2008, 10.09.-12.09.2008 (pp. 36-41). Aachen: Shaker.

Isenmann, R., Süpke, D., & Marx Gómez, J. (2009). Stakeholder interaction in sustainability reporting with Web 2.0. In: I. N. Athanasiadis, P. A. Mitkas, A. E. Rizzoli, & J. Marx Gómez (Eds.), Information Technologies in Environmental Engineering – Proceedings of the 4th International ICSC Symposium Thessaloniki, Greece, May 28-29, 2009 (pp. 387-398). Berlin/Heidelberg: Springer.

ISO 14031:1999Environmental management – Environmental Performance Evaluation – Guidelines. International Organization for Standardization.

ISO 14044:2006, Environmental management – Life cycle assessment – Requirements and guidelines. International Organization for Standardization.

ISO/TS 14048:2002, Environmental management – Life cycle assessment – Data documentation format. International Organization for Standardization.

IT Governance Institute. (2003). Board Briefing on IT Governance (2nd ed.). Rolling Meadows, IL: IT Governance Institute. Retrieved from http://www.itgovernance.org

IT Governance Institute. (2005). Cobit 4.0: control objectives, management guidelines, maturity models. Rolling Meadows, Illinois: IT Governance Institute.

Itaudit. (2007). Reaching Compliance through Foundational IT Controls. Institure of Internal Auditors, 10.

ITGI. (2003). Board briefing on IT governance. IT Governance Institute. Retrieved October 20, 2009, from www.itgi.org.

Jacobson, J. J., Searcy, E., Muth, D., Wilkerson, E., Sokhansanj, S., Jenkins, B., et al. (2009). Sustainable Biomass Supply Systems. In Proceedings of the 2009 AIChE Spring National Meeting.

Jain, S. C. (1984). Environmental scanning in U.S. corporations. Long Range Planning, 17(2), 117–128. doi:10.1016/0024-6301(84)90143-2

Jennings, N., Sycara, K., & Wooldridge, M. (1998). A roadmap of agent research and development. Autonomous Agents and Multi-Agent Systems, 10(2), 199–215.

Jensen, K. (1992). Coloured Petri Nets – Basic Concepts, Analysis Methods and Practical Use (Vol. 1). Berlin, Heidelberg: Springer.

Jensen, M. C., & Meckling, W. H. (1976). Theory of the firm: managerial behavior, agency costs and ownership structure. Journal of Financial Economics, 3(4). doi:10.1016/0304-405X(76)90026-X

Jensen, R. E., & Xiao, J. Z. (2001). Customized financial reporting, networked databases, and distributed file sharing. Accounting Horizons, 15(3), 209–222. doi:10.2308/acch.2001.15.3.209

Jessel, B. (2008). Biodiversity and Bioenergy. Presentation at the 9th meeting of the Conference of the Parties (COP 9), 19.-30.05.2008. Bonn, Germany.

Jian, J. J., & Klein, G. (1999). Project selection criteria by strategic orientation. Information & Management, 36, 63–75. doi:10.1016/S0378-7206(99)00009-9

Johnson, G., & Scholes, K. (1999). Exploring corporate strategy. Text and Cases. London: Prentice Hall.

Johnson, S. (1998). Identification and Selection of Environmental Performance Indicators: Application of the Balanced Scorecard Approach. Corporate Environmental Strategy, 5(4), 34–41. doi:10.1016/S1066-7938(00)80079-2

Jones, T. M. (2003). An integrating framework for research in business and society. Academy of Management Review, 8(4), 559–564. doi:10.2307/258257

Jouliet, O., Margni, M., Charles, R., Humbert, S., Payet, J., Rebitzer, G., & Rosenbaum, R. (2003). IMPACT 2002+: A New Life Cycle Assessment Methodology. International Journal of Life Cycle Assessment, 8(6), 324–330. doi:10.1007/BF02978505

Joutsenvirta, M., & Uusitalo, L. (2009). Cultural Competences: An Important Resource in the Industry–NGO Dialog. Journal of Business Ethics. doi:.doi:10.1007/s10551-009-0089-x

Judson, O. P. (1994). The rise of the individual-based model in ecology. Trends in Ecology & Evolution, 9, 9–14. doi:10.1016/0169-5347(94)90225-9

Jungle Rating. (2007). Online sustainability research 2007. Research report November 2007. Amsterdam: Jungle rating – internet consultants. Retrieved December 3, 2008, from http://www.junglerating.com

Kaarst-Brown, M., & Kelly, S. (2005). IT governance and Sarbanes-Oxley: the latest pitch or real challenges for the IT function? Hawaii International Conference on System Sciences. Proceedings of the 38th Hawaii International Conference on System Sciences (pp.236a). Hawaii.

Kalle, L., & Daniel, R. (1999). Learning failure in information systems development. Information Systems Journal, 9(2), 85–101. doi:10.1046/j.1365-2575.1999.00051.x

Kamm, B., & Kamm, M. (2004). Principles of biorefineries. Applied Microbiology and Biotechnology, 64(2), 137–145. doi:10.1007/s00253-003-1537-7

Kaplan, R. S., & Norton, D. P. (1992). The Balanced Scorecard – Measures that drive performance. Harvard Business Review, 70(1), 71–79.

Kaplan, R. S., & Norton, D. P. (1996). The Balanced Scorecard – Translating Strategy into Action. Boston, Massachusetts: Harvard Business School Press.

Kaplan, R. S., & Norton, D. P. (1997). A Estratégia em Ação: balanced scorecard. Rio de Janeiro, Rio de Janeiro: Campus.

Kaplan, R. S., & Norton, D. P. (2004). Strategy Maps – Converting Intangible Assets into Tangible Outcomes. Boston, MA: Harvard Business School Press.

Kaptein, M., & Wempe, J. (1999). Sustainability management: Balancing and integrating economic, social and environmental responsibilities. Management report no. 51-1999. Erasmus Universiteit Rotterdam.

Kauffman, R. J., & Kumar, A. (2008). Mapping the multi-tiered impacts on the growth of IT industries in India: A combined scale-and-scope externalities perspective. Information Technology for Development, 14(3), 225–252. doi:10.1002/itdj.20094

Kavanagh, R. (2009). IT virtualization helps to go green; businesses can use their green IT effort to enhance their public image, increase their agility and cut their operating costs. Information & Management, 19(2), 20–27.

Kempener, R. T. M. (2008). From Organisational Behaviour to Industrial Network Evolutions: Stimulating Sustainable Development of Bioenergy Networks in Emerging Economies. Unpublished doctoral dissertation, University of Sydney, Australia.

Kempf, P. (2008). Green, Greener, Greenest: the New Technology Horizon. Canadian Electronics, 23(2), 6–11.

Kendler, P. B. (2007, August 1). Virtualization Reality: by optimizing computing resources, virtualization can lower infrastructure operating costs while improving business agility and speed to market. Insurance & Technology, 42.

Kenny, C. J. (2000). Expanding Internet access to the rural poor in Africa. Information Technology for Development, 9(1), 25–32.

Keßeler, T. (2000). Kettenübergreifender Austausch von einzelbetrieblichen Umweltinformationen in Unternehmen der Land- und Ernährungswirtschaft. In L.M. Hilty, D. Schulthess, & T.F. Ruddy (Eds.), Strategische und betriebsübergreifende Anwendungen betrieblicher Umweltinformationssysteme (pp. 125-142). Marburg: Metropolis Verlag.

Keyes-Pearce, S. (2002). Rethinking IT governance in the eWorld. Pacific Asia Conference. Proceedings of the 6th Pacific Asia Conference (pp. 062). Tóquio.

Kilbourne, W. E., & Marshall, K. P. (2005). The transfer of for-profit marketing technology to the not-for-profit domain: Precautions from the theory of technology. Journal of Marketing Theory and Practice, 13(1), 14–25.

Kim, H. J., Severengiz, S., Skerlos, J., & Seliger, G. (2008). Economic and Environmental Assessment of Remanufacturing in the Automotive Industry. In Proceedings of the LCE 2008: 15th CIRP International Conference on Life Cycle Engineering, Sydney, Australia (pp. 195-200).

Kleindorfer, P. R., Singhal, K., & van Wassenhove, L. N. (2005). Sustainable operations management. Production and Operations Management, 14(4), 482–492.

Koch, C. (2000). Building coalitions in an era of technological change: Virtual manufacturing and the role of unions, employees and management. Journal of Organizational Change Management, 13(3), 275–289. doi:10.1108/09534810010330922

Koh, L. P., & Wilcove, D. S. (2008). Is oil palm agriculture really destroying tropical biodiversity? Conservation Letters, 1(2), 60–64. doi:10.1111/j.1755-263X.2008.00011.x

Kolk, A. (1999). Evaluating corporate environmental reporting. Business Strategy and the Environment, 8(4), 225–237. doi:10.1002/(SICI)1099-0836(199907/08)8:4<225::AID-BSE206>3.0.CO;2-4

Kolk, A. (2004). A decade of sustainability reporting: developments and significance. International Journal of Environment and Sustainable Development, 3(1), 51–64. doi:10.1504/IJESD.2004.004688

Kondratieff, N. D. (1926). Die langen Wellen der Konjunktur. Archiv für Sozialwissenschaft und Sozialpolitik, 56, 573–609.

Konrad, W., & Nill, J. (2001). Innovationen für Nachhaltigkeit. Schriftenreihe des IÖW, 157.

Koomey, J. G. (2007). Estimating Total Power Consumption by Servers in the U.S. and the World. Final report, Stanford University. Retrieved from http://enterprise.amd.com/Downloads/svrpwrusecompletefinal.pdf

Kopàcsi, S., Kovàcs, G., Haidegger, G., & Michelini, R. C. (2006). Ambient intelligence in product lifecycle design. Journal of Engineering Applications of Artificial Intelligence, 19(8), 953–965. doi:10.1016/j.engappai.2006.01.017

Korac-Kakabadse, N., & Kakabadse, A. (2001). IS/IT governance: need for an integrated model. Corporate Governance, 1(4), 9–11. doi:10.1108/EUM0000000005974

Korhonen, J. (2001). Some Suggestions for Regional Industrial Ecosystems – Extended Industrial Ecology. Eco-Management and Auditing, 8, 57–69. doi:10.1002/ema.146

KPMG (2008). International survey of corporate responsibility reporting 2008. Amstelveen: KPMG Sustainability Services.

KPMG (Ed.). (2008). Count me in: The readers' take on sustainability reporting. Retrieved August 31, 2009, from http://www.sustainability.com/researchandadvocacy/reports_article.asp?id=1489

KPMG International (2008). KPMG International Survey of Corporate Responsibility Reporting 2008.

KPMG, & United Nations Environment Programme (UNEP) (2006). Carrots and sticks for starters. Current trends and approaches in voluntary and mandatory standards for sustainability reporting. Parktown: KPMG.

KPMG. (2000). Beyond the numbers: How leading organizations are linking values with value to gain competitive advantage. KPMG's Assurance & Advisory Services Center (AASC). KPMG.

KPMG. (2005). KPMG international survey of corporate responsibility reporting 2005. University of Amsterdam (The Netherlands), KPMG global sustainability service. Amsterdam: KPMG.

Krausmann, F., Fischer-Kowalski, M., Schandl, H., & Eisenmenger, N. (2008). The Global Sociometabolic Transition: Past and Present Metabolic Profiles and Their Future Trajectories. Journal of Industrial Ecology, 12(5/6), 637–656. doi:10.1111/j.1530-9290.2008.00065.x

Kraut, R., Steinfield, C., Chan, A. P., Butler, B., & Hoag, A. (1999). Coordination and virtualization: the role of electronic networks and personal relationships. Organization Science, 10(6), 722–741. doi:10.1287/orsc.10.6.722

Krcmar, H., Dold, G., Fischer, H., Strobel, M., & Seifert, E. K. (Eds.). (2000). Informationssysteme für das Umweltmanagement. München: Oldenbourg Wissenschaftsverlag.

Kreeb, M., Dold, G., Enzler, St., Fischer, H., Hoffmann, A., Krcmar, H., Oettinger, M., Scheide, W., Seifert, E.K., Strobel, M., &Wagner, B. (1997). Fortschritt durch Eco-Intergral. Ökologisches Wirtschaften, 5, 16-18 (in German).

Krikke, H., le Blanc, I., & van de Velde, S. (2004). Product modularity and the design of closed-loop supply chains. California Management Review, 46(2), 23–39.

Krishna, S., & Walsham, G. (2005). Implementing Public Information Systems in Developing Countries: Learning from a Success Story. Journal of Information Technology for Development, 11(2).

Krishnapuram, R., & Keller, J. M. (1993). A Possibilistic Approach to Clustering. IEEE Transactions on Fuzzy Systems, 1(2), 98–110. doi:10.1109/91.227387

Krittwattanakhorn, J., Bauersfeld, M. L., Kovacs, A., Mescheder, U., Müller, B., Rademacher, S., & Wöllenstein, J. (2006). Optimization of Platinum Adhesion in Electochemical Etching Process for Multisensor Systems. In Enoksson, P. (Ed.), Proceedings of Eurosensors 20th Anniversary (Vol. II, pp. 376–377). Göteborg, Sweden.

Kroeker, K. (2009). The Evolution of virtualization. Communications of the ACM, 52(3), 18–20. doi:10.1145/1467247.1467253

Kromus, S., Wachter, B., Koschuh, W., Mandl, M., Krotscheck, C., & Narodoslawsky, M. (2004). The Green Biorefinery Austria – Development of an Integrated System for Green Biomass Utilization. Chemical and Biochemical Engineering Quarterly, 18(1), 7–12.

Kudyba, S., & Vitaliano, D. (2003). Information technology and corporate profitability: a focus on operating efficiency. Information Resources Management Journal, 16(1), 1–13.

Kuhndt, M., Geibler, J., & Liedtke, C. (2002). Towards a sustainable aluminium industry: Stakeholder expectations and core indicators. Final report. Wuppertal: Wuppertal Institute for Climate, Environment, Energy.

Kumar, S., & Putnam, V. (2008). Cradle to cradle: Reverse logistics strategies and opportunities across three industry sectors. International Journal of Production Economics, 115(2), 305–315. doi:10.1016/j.ijpe.2007.11.015

Kuosmanen, T. (2005). Measurement and Analysis of Eco-Efficiency. Journal of Industrial Ecology, 9(4), 15–18. doi:10.1162/108819805775248025

Landsiedel, R., & Saling, P. (2002). Assessment of Toxicological Risks for Life Cycle Assessment and Eco-Efficiency Analysis. International Journal of Life Cycle Assessment, 7(5), 261–268. doi:10.1007/BF02978885

Lang, C. V. (2007). Modeling of a Corporate Environmental Management Information System (CEMIS) for Production Processes. In Marx Gómez, J. C., Sonnenschein, M., Müller, M., & Welsch, H. (Eds.), Information Technologies in Environmental Engineering (pp. 231–240). Berlin, Heidelberg: Springer Verlag. doi:10.1007/978-3-540-71335-7_24

Lang, C., & Jürgens, G. (2003). Aufgaben betrieblicher Umweltinformationssysteme. In M. Kramer, J. Brauweiler, & K. Helling (Eds.), Internationales und interdisziplinäres Umweltmanagement. Vol. II: Umweltmanagementinstrumente und –systeme (pp. 77-100). Wiesbaden: Gabler Verlag.

Lang, C., Rey, U., Wohlgemuth, V., Genz, S., & Pawlytsch, S. (2003). Data exchange between ERP-systems and environmental information systems. Publicly available specification (PAS) 1025. Berlin: Beuth.

Lang, C., Steinfeld, M., Loew, T., Beucker, S., Heubach, D., & Keil, K. (2004). Konzepte zur Einfuehrung und Anwendung von Umweltcontrollinginstrumenten in Unternehmen. Endbericht des Forschungsprojekts INTUS.

Lange, C. Ahsen von, A., & Daldrup, H. (2001). Umweltschutzreporting. Umwelterklärungen und –berichte als Module eines Reportingsystems [Environmental reporting, environmental statements and reports as modules of a reporting system]. München, Wien: Oldenbourg.

Lang-Koetz, C., & Heubach, D. (2007). Umweltcontrolling Umsetzen – Erstellung von Kennzahlen für Stoff-Energieströme und deren Integration in die betriebliche IT. Stuttgart: Frauenhoffer IRB Verlag.

Lapide, L. (2004). RFID: What's in it for the forecaster? The Journal of Business Forecasting, 23(2), 16–19.

Larkin, J. H., & Simon, H. A. (1987). Why a diagram is (sometimes) worth ten thousand words. Cognitive Science, 11, 65–99.

Larsen, L. B. (2000). Strategic implication of environmental reporting. Corporate Environmental Strategy, 7(3), 276–287. doi:10.1016/S1066-7938(00)80122-0

Latchem. C. & Walker, D. (2001). Telecentres: Case Studies and Key Issues. Vancouver: The Commonwealth of Learning.

Laubacher, R., Kothari, S.P., Malone, T.W., & Subirana, B. (2005). What is RFID worth to your company? Measuring performance at the activity level. MIT Center for eBusiness Research Brief, 7(2).

Laudon, K. C., & Laudon, J. P. (2006). Management Information Systems: Managing the Digital Firm (9th ed.). New Jersey: Prentice Hall.

Laurin, L., Möller, A., Prox, M., & Schmidt, M. (2006). How Production-theory can Support the Analysis of Recycling Systems in the Electronic Waste Sector. In Proceedings of the 2006 IEEE International Symposium on Electronics & the Environment. San Francsisco, CA.

Lee, C. K. M., & Chan, T. M. (2009). Development of RFID-based reverse logistics system. Expert Systems with Applications, 36(5), 9299–9307.

Lee, J., Eom, M., Kim, B. O., & Katerattanakul, P. (2007). Virtual Organization: Resource-Based View. International Journal of E-Business Research, 3(1), 1–16.

Lefebvre, L., & Lefebvre, L. A. (1996). Information and Telecommunication Technologies: The Impact of their Adoption on Small and Medium-sized Enterprises. Retrieved December 12, 2007, from http://web.idrc.ca/en/ev-9303-201-1-DO_TOPIC.html

Lehmann, J. M. (2008). Modell für das Daten- und Informationsmanagement in der Abfallwirtschaft.

Lehni, M. (2000). Eco-Efficiency: Creating more value with less impact. World Business Council for Sustainable Development (WBCSD), 1-33. Retrieved July 2009, from http://www.wbcsd.org/web/publications/eco_efficiency_creating_more_value.pdf

Leifsit, R., & Lombardi, D. R. (1997). Who should pay and why? Some thoughts on the conceptual foundations for the assignment of extended producer responsibility. In Proceedings of the International Workshop on Extended Producer Responsibility, OECD, Ottawa.

Leitl, T. (2007). Biomasse, Bestandteil der RWE-Strategie im Bereich erneuerbare Energien. Presentation at the 2nd BioEnergy Conference Carinthia, 06.11.2007. Velden, Austria.

Lemke, J., & Heinisch, A. (2004). Durchgängiger und übergreifender Konstruktionsdatenzugriff als Baustein eines wirksamen PLM. Düsseldorf: Springer.

Lenz, C. (2003). Empfängerorientierte Unternehmenskommunikation – Einsatz der Internet-Technologie am Beispiel der Umweltberichterstattung [Customised environmental communication – use of internet illustrated through corporate environmental reporting]. Köln: Eul.

Lessing, H., & Schuetz, T. (1994). Der Umwelt-Datenkatalog als Instrument zur Steuerung von Informationsfluessen. In L.M. Hilty, A. Jaeschke., B. Page, & A. Schwabl (Eds.), Informatik für den Umweltschutz, 8. Symposium. Vol. 1 (pp. 159-167). Marburg: Metropolis.

Levin, S. A., Barrett, S., Aniyar, S., Baumol, W., Bliss, C., & Bolin, B. (1998). Resilience in natural and socioeconomic systems. Environment and Development Economics, 3(2), 222–234. doi:10.1017/S1355770X98240125

Levy, M., Powell, P., & Yetton, P. (2001). SMEs: Aligning IS and the Strategic Context. Journal of Information Technology, 16(3), 133–144. doi:10.1080/02683960110063672

Levy, M., Powell, P., & Yetton, P. (2002). The Dynamics of SME Information Systems. Small Business Economics, 19, 341–354. doi:10.1023/A:1019654030019

Lewis, G. J. (2004). Uncertainty and equivocality in the commercial and natural environments: the implications for organizational design. Corporate Social Responsibility and Environmental Management, 11(3), 167–177. doi:10.1002/csr.64

Li, C., & Bernoff, J. (2008). Groundswell: Winning in a world transformed by social technologies. Boston, Massachusetts: Harvard Business Press.

Li, M., & Ye, L. (1999). Information technology and firm performance: linking with environment, strategic and managerial contexts. Information & Management, 35(1), 43–51. doi:10.1016/S0378-7206(98)00075-5

Li, Y. P., & Huang, G. H. (2006). An inexact two-stage mixed integer linear programming method for solid waste management in the City of Regina. Journal of Environmental Management, 81(3), 188–209.

Lichtenstein, G. A., & Lyons, T. S. (2001). The entrepreneurial development system: Transforming business talent and community economies. Economic Development Quarterly, 15(1), 3–20. doi:10.1177/089124240101500101

Line, M., Hawley, H., & Krut, H. (2002). The development of global environmental and social reporting. Corporate Environmental Strategy, 9(1), 69–78. doi:10.1016/S1066-7938(01)00159-2

Lippman, S. (2001). Supply chain environmental management. Environmental Quality Management, 11(2), 11–14. doi:10.1002/tqem.1301

Liu, C., Sia, C., & Wei, K. (2008). Adopting organizational virtualization in B2B firms: An empirical study in Singapore. Information & Management, 45(7), 429–437. doi:10.1016/j.im.2008.06.005

Liu, L. (1995). Design Principle and Application of Information Systems. Beijing, China: Beihang University Publishing House.

Lockwood, C. (2006). Building the green way. Harvard Business Review, 84(6), 129–137.

Lodhia, S. (2004). Corporate environmental reporting media: A case for the world wide web. Electronic Green Journal, 20 (spring). Retrieved November 23, 2004, from http://egj.lib.uidaho.edu/egj20/lodhia1.html

Lopez-Fernandez, M. C., & Serrano-Bedia, A. M. (2007). Organizational consequences of implementing an ISO 14001 environmental management system. An empirical analysis. Organization & Environment, 20(4), 440–459. doi:10.1177/1086026607309388

Lowe, E. A. (2001). Eco-Industrial Park Handbook for Asian Developing Countries. Report to Asian Development Bank. Retrieved from http://www.indigodev.com/ADBHBdownloads.html

Lowe, E. A., & Warren, J. L. (2008). The source of value: an executive briefing and source book on industrial ecology. Northwest National Richland, 2, 151–152.

Luck, M., McBurney, P., & Preist, C. (2003). Agent Technology: Enabling Next Generation Computing. A Roadmap for Agent-Based Computing. Southampton: AgentLink.org.

Luftman, J., & McLean, E. (2004). Key issues for IT executives. MIS Quarterly Executive, 3(2), 89–104.

Luks, F. (2005). Innovationen, Wachstum und Nachhaltigkeit: Eine ökologisch-ökonomische Betrachtung. In F. Beckenbach, U. Hampicke, C. Leipert, G. Meran, J. Minsch, H. G. Nutzinger, R. Pfriem, J. Weimann, F. Wirl & U. Witt (Eds.), Jahrbuch Ökologische Ökonomik, Band 4: Innovationen und Nachhaltigkeit (pp. 41-62). Marburg: Metropolis.

Lunardi, G. L., Dolci, P. C., Becker, J. L., & Maçada, A. C. G. (2008, October). Governança de TI no Brasil: uma análise dos mecanismos mais difundidos entre as empresas nacionais. Paper presented at the SEGeT – Simpósio de Excelência em Gestão e Tecnologia, Rio de Janeiro.

Lund, R. (1983). Remanufacturing: United States Experience for Developing Nations. Washington, DC: The World Bank.

Lund, R. (1998). Remanufacturing: An American resource. In Proceedings of the 5th International Congress on Environmentally Conscious Design and Manufacturing. Rochester, NY: Rochester Institute of Technology.

Lundvall, B. A. (Ed.). (1992). National Systems of Innovation: Towards a Theory of Innovation and Interactive Learning. London: Pinter Pub.

Maçada, A., Becker, J., & Lunardi, G. (2005). Efetividade de Conversão dos Investimentos em TI na Eficiência dos Bancos Brasileiros. Revista Contemporânea de Administração, 9(1), 9–33.

MacLean, R. (2008). The green conversation. Harvard Business Review, 86(9), 58–62.

Malczewski, J. (1999). GIS and multicriteria analysis. New York: Wiley.

Mansell, R., & Wehn, U. (1998). Knowledge Societies: Information Technology for Sustainable Development. Oxford: Oxford University Press.

Marchand, D. (2005). Reaping the business value of IT. Business & Economic Review.

Marketing News (2008, February 1). Going Green. Marketing News, 15-18.

Marshall, S. R., & Brown, D. (2003). Corporate environmental reporting: What's in a metric? Business Strategy and the Environment, 12(2), 87–106. doi:10.1002/bse.354

Marx Gómez, J. C., Sonnenschein, M., Müller, M., & Welsch, H. (Eds.). (2007). Information Technologies in Environmental Engineering: ITEE 2007 – Third International ICSC Symposium. Carl-von-Ossietzky-Universität Oldenburg. Berlin, Heidelberg: Springer Verlag.

Marx Gómez, J., & Isenmann, R. (Eds.). (2004). Developments in environmental reporting. International Journal of Environment and Sustainable Development (IJESD), special issue 3(1/2).

Marx Gómez, J., Grünwald, C., Griese, S., Petri, T., Rosenau-Tornow, D., & Eppers, R. (2004). Konzeption eines integrierten Systems für Umweltinformationen – Fallstudie Volkswagen AG. Clausthal-Zellerfeld: Papierflieger.

Marx Gómez, J., Prötzsch, S., & Rautenstrauch, C. (2004). Data Defects in Material Flow Networks – Classification and Approaches; Cybernetics and Systems. Cybernetics and Systems, 35(5-6), 549–558. doi:10.1080/01969720490451931

Marx-Gómez, J. (2004). Automated Generation of Environmental Reports – a Case Study. International Journal of Environment and Sustainable Development, 3(1), 65–75. doi:10.1504/IJESD.2004.004689

Mason, R., McKenney, J. L., & Copelan, D. G. (1997). An historical method for MIS research: steps and assumptions. Management Information Systems Quarterly, 31(3), 307–320. doi:10.2307/249499

Matlin, G. (1979). What is the value of investment in information systems? Management Information Systems Quarterly, 3(3), 5–34. doi:10.2307/248786

Matthews, P. (2007). ICT Assimilation and SME Expansion. Journal of International Development, 19, 817–827. doi:10.1002/jid.1401

McKeen, J. D., & Smith, H. A. (2006). Making IT happen. UK: Wiley & Sons Ltd.

McKinnon, A. (1998). Logistical restructuring, freight traffic growth and the environment. In Banister, D. (Ed.), Transport policy and the environment (pp. 97–109). London, England: Routledge.

McLane, G. (2003). IT governance and its impact on IT management (a literature review). Unpublished master dissertation, University of Technology Sydney, Sydney.

McLaughlin, G. T., Liu, L. Y., DeGroff, D. J., & Fleck, K. W. (2008). IBM Power Systems platform: Advancements in the state of the art in IT availability. IBM Systems Journal, 47(4), 519–533. doi:10.1147/SJ.2008.5386517

Melville, N., Kraemer, K., & Gurbaxani, V. (2004). Review: information technology and organizational performance: an integrative model of IT business value. Management Information Systems Quarterly, 28(2), 283–322.

Mertens, P., Große-Wilde, J., & Wilkens, I. (2005). Die (Aus-)Wanderung der Softwareproduktion – Eine Zwischenbilanz. Arbeitsberichte des Instituts für Informatik, vol. 38, Nr. 3. Erlangen, Germany: Friedrich-Alexander-Universität Erlangen-Nürnberg.

Mescheder, U., Kritwattanakhorn, J., Kovacs, A., Müller, B., Ament, C., & Peter, A. (2007). Sensorarray zur Luftqualitätsmessung. Horizonte, 30, 3–8.

Mesterharm, M. (2001). Integrierte Umweltkommunikation von Unternehmen. Theoretische Grundlagen und empirische Analyse der Umweltkomunikation am Beispiel der Automobilindustrie [Integrated environmental communication at corporate level. Conceptual foundation and empirical analysis, illustrated by the automotive sector]. Marburg: Metropolis.

Meyer, H. (2000). The greening of corporate America. The Journal of Business Strategy, 21(1), 38–43. doi:10.1108/eb040058

Michalewicz, Z., & Fogel, D. B. (2000). How to solve it: modern heuristics. Berlin: Springer-Verlag.

Michelini, R. C. (2008). Knowledge entrepreneurship and sustainable growth. New York: Nova Science Pub. Inc.

Michelini, R. C. (2009). The robot age knowledge changeover. New York: Nova Science Pub. Inc.

Michelini, R. C., & Kovàcs, G. (2002). Integrated design for sustainability: intelligence for eco-consistent products-and-service. The Estonian Business School Review, 15, 81–95.

Michelini, R. C., & Razzoli, R. P. (2004). Product-service eco-design: knowledge-based infrastructures. International Journal of Cleaner Production, 12(4), 415–428. doi:10.1016/S0959-6526(03)00036-2

Michelini, R. C., & Razzoli, R. P. (2004). Product-service for environmental safeguard: a metric to sustainability. International Journal of Resources. Conservation and Recycling, 42(1), 83–98. doi:10.1016/j.resconrec.2004.02.005

Michelini, R. C., & Razzoli, R. P. (2005). Collaborative networked organisations for eco-consistent supply-chains. In Putnik, G. D., & Cunha, M. M. (Eds.), Virtual Enterprise Integration: Technological and Organisational Perspectives (pp. 45–77). Hershey, PA: IGI Global.

Michelini, R. C., & Razzoli, R. P. (2007, June). Take-back of end-of-use vehicles, part/material recovery and landfill management. Paper presented at the XVI ADM International Conference on Tools and Methods Evolution in Engineering Design, Perugia, Italy.

Michelini, R. C., & Razzoli, R. P. (2008). Ubiquitous computing & communication for product monitoring. In Khosrow-Pour, M. (Ed.), Encyclopaedia of Information Science and Technology (2nd ed., pp. 3851–3857). Hershey, PA: IDEA Group.

Michelini, R. C., & Razzoli, R. P. (2008, June). Modelling and simulation features for products-services. Paper presented at the International EUROSIS Industrial Simulation Conference, Lyon, France.

Michelini, R. C., & Razzoli, R. P. (2008). Innovation for sustainability in product lifecycle design. In Cascini, G. (Ed.), Computer-Aided Innovation (pp. 217–228). Boston, MA: Springer. doi:10.1007/978-0-387-09697-1_18

Michelini, R. C., & Razzoli, R. P. (2009). The service net facility integration appraisal. Int. J. Services. Economics and Management, 1(4), 371–392.

Miles, M. P., & Munilla, L. S. (2004). The potential impact of social accountability certification on marketing. Journal of Business Ethics, 50(1), 1–11. doi:10.1023/B:BUSI.0000021139.94166.74

Miller, G. A. (1956). The magic number seven plus or minus two: some limits on our capacity for communicating information. Psychological Review, 63, 81–97. doi:10.1037/h0043158

Minciardi, R., Paolucci, M., Robba, M., & Sacile, R. (2008). Multi-objective optimization of solid waste flows: Environmentally sustainable strategies for municipalities. Waste Management (New York, N.Y.), 28(11), 2202–2212. doi:10.1016/j.wasman.2007.10.003

Ministry of Climate and Energy of Denmark. (2009). 17 percent renewable energy – and on the way up. COP15 Copenhagen 2009. Retrieved July 2009, from http://en.cop15.dk/climate+facts/research/17+per+cent+renewable+energy+%E2%80%93+and+on+the+way+up

Minke, A., Ambrosi, K., & Hahne, F. (2009). Approach for Dynamic Problems in Clustering. In I. N. Athanasiadis (Ed.), Proceedings of the 4th International ICSC Symposium on Information Technologies in Environmental Engineering (pp. 373-386). Berlin: Springer.

Molinaro, L. F. R., et al. (2009, October). Governance and Management of Information Technology: Decomposing the Enterprise in Modular Building Blocks Based on Enterprise Architecture and Business Oriented Services. Paper presented at the CENTERIS-Conference Enterprise Information System.

Möller, A. (2000). Grundlagen stoffstrombasierter Betrieblicher Umweltinformationssysteme. Bochum: Projekt Verlag. (in German)

Möller, A. (2005). Dynamic Material Flow Analysis in the Life Cycle Assessment Tool Chain. In Geldermann, J., Treitz, M., Schollenberger, H., & Rentz, O. (Eds.), Challanges for Industrial Production. Karlsruhe, Germany: Universitätsverlag.

Möller, A., & Prox, M. (2008). Efficiency Engineering - Requirements for Tools from Industrial Practice. In Proceedings of the 2008 China Life Cycle Management Conference (CLCM 2008). Chengdu, China.

Möller, A., & Rolf, A. (2001). Eco Product Lifecycle Management. In Proceedings of the EcoDesign 2001: Second International Symposium on Environmentally Conscious Design and Inverse Manufacturing. Tokyo, Japan.

Möller, A., & Schaltegger, S. (2005). The Sustainability Balanced Scorecard as a Framework for Eco-Efficiency Analysis. Journal of Industrial Ecology, 9(4), 73–83. doi:10.1162/108819805775247927

Möller, A., & Viere, T. (2005). Material Flow Analysis between Dynamic Modeling and Life Cycle Assessment. In L. Filho, J. Marx-Goméz, & C. Rautenstrauch (Eds.), Proceedings of the 2nd International ICSC Symposium on Information Technologies in Environmental Engineering (ITEE 2005). Aachen, Germany: Shaker.

Möller, A., Prox, M., & Viere, T. (2006). Computer Support for Environmental Management Accounting. In Schaltegger, S., Bennett, M., & Burritt, R. (Eds.), Sustainability Accounting and Reporting. Dordrecht: Springer. doi:10.1007/978-1-4020-4974-3_27

Montiel, I. (2008). Common futures corporate social responsibility and corporate sustainability: separate pasts. Organization & Environment, 21(245), 245–269. doi:10.1177/1086026608321329

Moretti, S. (2002). A model for cooperative inter-municipal waste collection: cost evaluation toward fair cost allocation. In C. Carraro, V. Fragnelli (Eds.), Game Practice and the Environment – Proceedings of the International Meeting held in Alessandria on 12-13 April 2002. Edward Elgar Publishing.

Morhardt, E. J. (2002). Clean, green, and read all over. Ten rules for effective corporate environmental and sustainability reporting. Milwaukee, WI: ASQ Quality Press.

Morioka, T., Tsunemi, K., Yamamotu, Y., Vabar, H., & Yoshida, N. (2005). Eco-Efficiency of Advanced Loop-closing Systems for Vehicles and Household Appliances in Hyogo Eco-Town. Journal of Industrial Ecology, 9(4), 205–222. doi:10.1162/108819805775247909

Moyi, E. D. (2003). Networks, information and small enterprises: New Technologies and the ambiguity of empowerment. Information Technology for Development, 10, 221–232. doi:10.1002/itdj.1590100402

Munda, G. (1995). Multicriteria evaluation in a fuzzy environment: Theory and Applications in Ecological Economics. Heidelberg, Germany: Physika-Verlag.

Murugesan, S. (2008). Harnessing Green IT: Principles and Practices. IT Professional, 10(1), 24–33. doi:10.1109/MITP.2008.10

Mustajoki, J., Hämäläinen, R. P., & Martunen, M. (2003). Participatory multicriteria decision analysis with Web-HIPRE: a case of lake regulation policy. Environmental Modelling & Software, 19(6), 537–547. doi:10.1016/j.envsoft.2003.07.002

na. (2008). Netzkomponenten, 60 Prozent des IT-Stromverbrauchs außerhalb des Rechenzentrums, Experton Group: Green Office kommt. Retrieved December 15, 2008, from www.lanline.de

na. (2009). Journalisten haben gewählt: Die CeBIT – Trends 2009. Retrieved February 12, 2009, from http://www.ad-hoc-news.de/journalisten-haben-gewaehlt-die-cebit-trends-2009--/de/Wirtschaft-Boerse/Marktberichte/20037194

Naddeo, V., Zarra, T., & Belgiorno, V. (2007). Optimization of sampling frequency for river water quality assessment according to Italian implementation of the EU Water Framework Directive. Environmental Science & Policy, 10, 243–249. doi:10.1016/j.envsci.2006.12.003

Nash,J.(2000). Voluntary Codes of Practice: Non-Governmental Institutions for Promoting Environmental Management by Firms.

Naylor, J., & Williams, J. (1994). Successful Use of IT in SMEs. European Journal of IS, 3(1), 48–56.

Neely, A., & Adams, C. (2000). Perspectives on performance: the performance prism. Centre for Business Performance. Retrieved January 10, 2006, from http://www.exinfm.com/pdffiles/prismarticle.pdf

Nereng, G., Romsdal, A., & Brekke, A. (2009). Can innovations in the supply chain lead to reduction of GHG emissions from food products? A framework. Retrieved December 9, 2009, from http://gin.confex.com/gin/2009/webprogram/Paper2373.html

Neumann, A. (2008). Fuzzy Clustering in Dynamic Problems. Unpublished technical report: Universität Hildesheim.

Neumann, K. (1975). Operation Research Verfahren (Vol. I). München, Germany: Hauser.

Nidumolu, R., Prahalad, C. K., & Rangaswami, M. R. (2009). Why sustainability is now the key driver of innovation. Harvard Business Review, 87(9), 56–64.

Niedersächsisches Ministerium für Umwelt und Klimaschutz. (2009). Luftmessnetz Niedersachsen (LÜN). Retrieved November 18, 2009, from http://www.umwelt.niedersachsen.de/master/C21884990_N41769409_L20_D0_I598.html

Ning, S. K., & Chang, N. B. (2002). Multi-objective, decision-based assessment of a water quality monitoring network in a river system. Journal of Environmental Monitoring, 4, 121–126. doi:10.1039/b107041j

Niwa, K. (2009). Fujitsu activities for green logistics. FUJITSU Scientific Technology Journal, 45(1), 28–32.

Nonaka, I. (1994). A Dynamic Theory of Organizational Knowledge Creation. Organization Science, 5(1), 14–37. doi:10.1287/orsc.5.1.14

North, D. C. (1992). Institutionen, institutioneller Wandel und Wirtschaftsleistung. Tübingen: Mohr Siebeck.

O'Connor, M. C. (2005, July 22). Most RFID users believe RFID lacks ROI. RFID Journal. Retrieved December 9, 2009, from www.rfidjournal.com/article/articleprint/1753/-1/1

O'Farrell, C., Norrish, P., & Scott, A. (1999). Information and Communication Technologies (ICTs) for Sustainable Livelihoods. Burton Hall: Intermediate Technology Development Group.

Oberschmidt, J., Geldermann, J., Ludwig, J., & Schmehl, M. (2010. (accepted)). Modified PROMETHEE approach to assessing energy technologies. Speciel issue: Uses of frontier efficiency methodologies and multi-criteria decision making for performance measurement in the energy sector. International Journal of Energy Sector Management.

Oberschmidt, J., Ludwig, J., & Geldermann, J. (2009). Ein modifizierter PROMETHEE-Ansatz zur Lebenszyklus-orientierten Bewertung der Strom- und Wärmeversorgung. In Geldermann, J., & Lauven, L. (Eds.), Einsatz von OR-Verfahren zur Entscheidungsunterstützung. Aachen, Germany: Shaker.

Odum, E. P. (1971). Fundamentals of ecology (3rd ed.). Philadelphia: Brooks Cole.

OECD. (1992). Technology and the Economy: The Key Relationships. Paris: OECD.

OECD. (1997). Eurostat Oslo Manual. Proposed Guidelines for Collecting and Interpreting Technological Innovation Data. Paris: OECD.

Oesterle, H., & Blessing, D. (2000). Business Engineering Model. In Oesterle, H., & Winter, R. (Eds.), Business Engineering: Auf dem Weg zum Unternehmen des Informationszeitalters. Berlin, Germany: Springer.

Office of Government Commerce. (2007). ITIL - Service Design. Crown, UK: The Stationery Office Ltd.

Oktem, U., Lewis, P., Donovan, D., Hagan, J. R., & Pace, T. (2007). EMS and sustainable development: a model and comparative studies of integration. In Sroufe, R., & Sarkis, J. (Eds.), Strategic sustainability. The state of the art in corporate environmental management systems (pp. 56–75). Sheffield, UK: Greenleaf Publisher.

Oldfield, P. (2002). Domain Modelling. Retrieved July 10, 2009, from http://www.aptprocess.com/ whitepapers/DomainModelling.pdf

Oliveira Filho, J. (2004). Gestão Ambiental e Sustentabilidade: um novo paradigma eco-econômico para as organizações modernas. Domus On Line: Ver. Teor. Pol., soc. Cidad. Salvador, 1(1), 92–113.

Organisations, R. (2007). Resilience Management: A Framework for Assessing and Improving the Resilience of Organisations, Research Report 01/2007. Retrieved October 29, 2009, from http://www.resorgs.org.nz/pubs/Resilience%20Management%20Research%20Report%20ResOrgs%2007-01.pdf

Ott, K., & Döring, R. (2004). Theorie und Praxis starker Nachhaltigkeit. Marburg: Metropolis.

Overby, E. (2008). Process Virtualization Theory and the Impact of Information Technology. Organization Science, 19(2), 277–292. doi:10.1287/orsc.1070.0316

Overby, S. (2007, March 26). How Green Data Centers Save Money. CIO, 1-5.

Owen, W., & Darkwa, O. (1999). Role of Multipurpose Community Telecentres in Accelerating National Development in Ghana. First Monday, 5(1), 1–23.

Page, B., & Rautenstrauch, C. (2001). Environmental Informatics – Methods, Tools and Applications in Environmental Information Processing. In Rautenstrauch, C., & Patig, S. (Eds.), Environmental Information Systems in Industry and Public Administration. Hershey, PA: Idea Group Publishing.

Palmer, R. N., & MacKenzie, M. C. (1985). Optimization of water quality monitoring networks. Journal of Water Resources Planning and Management, 111(4), 478–493. doi:10.1061/(ASCE)0733-9496(1985)111:4(478)

Palmer, S. E. (1978). Fundamental aspects of cognitive representation. In E. Rosch & B. B. LLoyd (Eds.), Cognition and categorization (pp. 259-303). Hillsdale, N.J.: Erlbaum.

Pålsson, A. C., & Carlson, R. (1998). Maintaining Data Quality within Industrial Environmental Information Systems. In H. D. Haasis, K. C. Ranze (Eds.), Proceedings of the 12th International Symposium 'Computer Science for Environmental Protection', Bremen: Vol. 1. Computer Science for Environmental Protection (pp. 252-265). Marburg: Metropolis.

Pålsson, A. C., Enqvist, A., Karlsson, G., Loviken, G., Möller, Å., & Nilseng, A. B. (2005). Methodology for handling forest industry environmental data – Method report [Göteborg, Sweden: CPM, Chalmers University of Technology.]. CPM-report, 2005, 1.

Pålsson, A. C., Enqvist, A., Karlsson, G., Loviken, G., Möller, Å., & Nilseng, A. B. (2005). Methodology for handling forest industry environmental data – Manual [Göteborg, Sweden: CPM, Chalmers University of Technology.]. CPM-report, 2005, 2.

Park, J., & Huntington, S. (2002). XML Topic Maps: Creating and Using Topic Maps for the Web. Amsterdam: Addison Wesley Longman.

PAS 1025 (2003). Austausch umweltrelevanter Daten zwischen ERP-Systemen und betrieblichen Umweltinformationssystemen. Berlin: Beuth-Verlag (in German).

PAS 2050:2008– Specification for the assessment of the life cycle greenhouse gas emissions of goods and services. United Kingdom: British Standards Institute.

Patel, P., & Pavitt, K. (1994). The continuing, widespread (and neglected) importance of improvements in mechanical technologies. Research Policy, 23, 533–546. doi:10.1016/0048-7333(94)01004-8

Pateli, A. G., & Giaglis, G. M. (2004). A research framework for analyzing eBusiness models. European Journal of Information Systems, 13, 302–314. doi:10.1057/palgrave.ejis.3000513

Patzek, T. W. (2004). Thermodynamics of the Corn-Ethanol Biofuel Cycle. Critical Reviews in Plant Sciences, 23(6), 519–567. doi:10.1080/07352680490886905

Pavitt, K. (1984). Sectoral Patterns of Technical Change: Towards a Taxonomy and a Theory. Research Policy, 13, 343–373. doi:10.1016/0048-7333(84)90018-0

Payaro, A. (2004). The role of ICT in reverse logistics: A hypothesis of RFID implementation to manage the recovery process. In P. Cunningham & M. Cunningham (Eds.), The Proceedings of eChallenges 2004 Conference: eAdoption and the Knowledge Economy: Issues, Applications and Case Studies, IOS Press. Retrieved December 9, 2009, from http://www.reloaderitalia.it/doc/download/payaro_rfid.pdf

Pearce, D. W., & Turner, R. K. (1990). Economics of Natural Resources and the Environment. Baltimore: John Hopkins University Press.

Pearlson, K. E., & Saunders, C. S. (2006). Managing & Using Information Systems – A Strategic Approach (3rd ed.). Hoboken, NJ: John Wiley & Sons.

Pelanda, M. L. (2006). Modelos de governança de tecnologia da informação adotados no Brasil: um estudo de casos múltiplos Unpublished master dissertation, Universidade Metodista de São Paulo, São Bernardo do Campo.

Pen, Z. (1998). Region Research and Planning. Shanghai, China: Tongji University Press.

Pepper, S. (2000). The TAO of Topic Maps – Finding the Way in the Age of Infoglut. In XML Europe 2000 (Ed.), Conference Proceedings, 12-16 June 2000, Le Palais des Congrès de Paris. Retrieved January 17, 2006, from http://www.gca.org/papers/xmleurope2000/papers/s11-01.html

Pernici, B., Ardagna, D., & Cappiello, C. (2008). Business Process Design: Towards Service-Based Green Information Systems. In P. Forbrig, F. Paternò, & A. M. Pejtersen (Eds.), Human-Computer Interaction Symposium: Proceedings of the IFIP 20th World Computer Congress, Milano, Italy (pp. 195–203). Berlin: Springer.

Perrings, C. (1998). Resilience in the Dynamics of Economy-Environment Systems. Environmental and Resource Economics, 11(3-4), 503–520. doi:10.1023/A:1008255614276

Perrings, C. (2006). Resilience and sustainable development. Environment and Development Economics, 11, 417–427. doi:10.1017/S1355770X06003020

Peterson, R. (2004a). Integration strategies and tactics for information technology governance. In Van Grembergen, W. (Ed.), Strategies for information technology governance (pp. 37–80). Hershey: Idea Group Publishing.

Peterson, R. (2004b). Crafting information technology governance. Information Systems Management, 21(4), 7–22. doi:10.1201/1078/44705.21.4.20040901/84183.2

Petre, M., & Green, T. R. G. (1993). Learning to read graphics: some evidence that 'seeing' an informational display is an aquired skill. Journal of Visual Languages and Computing, 4, 55–70. doi:10.1006/jvlc.1993.1004

Petrini, M. (2006). Incorporando a sustentabilidade aos sistemas de inteligência de negócio. Unpublished doctoral dissertation, FGV-EAESP, São Paulo, Brazil.

Pflueger, J. (2008). Re-Defining the "green" data center. A dell technical white paper. Managing the data center by efficient use of IT resources. Retrieved November 22, 2009 from http://www.dell.com/downloads/global/vectors/dec_2008_redefining.pdf

Pfriem, R. (2006). Unternehmensstrategien: Ein kulturalistischer Zugang zum Strategischen Management. Marburg: Metropolis Verlag.

Pfriem, R., Schattke, H., & Uphoff, K. (2009). Nachhaltigkeit als kommunikationspolitische Herausforderung der niedersächsischen Fleischwirtschaft. In J. Böhm, F. Albersmeier, & A. Spiller (Eds.), Die Ernährungswirtschaft im Scheinwerferlicht der Öffentlichkeit (pp. 251-271). Lohmar, Köln: EUL Verlag.

Phahalad, C. K., & Krishnan, M. S. (2008). The new age of innovation: driving co-created value through global networks. New York: McGraw Hill.

Piscitello, L., & Sgobbi, F. (2004). Globalisation, E-Business and SMEs: Evidence from the Italian District of Prato. Small Business Economics, 22(5), 333. doi:10.1023/B:SBEJ.0000022208.34741.55

Pleon Kohtes & Klewes. (2005). Accounting for good: The global stakeholder report 2005. Amsterdam, Bonn: Pleon.

Porter, M. (1991). America's green strategy. Scientific American, 264(4).

Porter, M. E., & Reinhardt, F. L. (2007). Grist: A Strategic Approach to Climate. Harvard Business Review, (October): 1–5.

Porter, M. E., & van der Linde, C. (1995). Toward a new conception of the environment competitiveness relationship. The Journal of Economic Perspectives, 9(4), 97–118.

Porter, M. E., & Van der Linde, C. (1999). Green and Competitive, Ending the Stalemate. Journal of Business Administration and Policy Analysis, 1999, 215.

Porter, M., & Millar, V. (1985). How information gives you competitive advantage. Harvard Business Review, 63(4), 149–160.

Porter, M., & van der Linde, C. (1995). Green and Competitive – Ending the Stalemate. Harvard Business Review, 73, 120–134.

President's Council on Sustainable Development. (1996). Eco-Industrial Park Workshop Proceedings. Retrieved from http://clinton2.nara.gov/PCSD/Publications/Eco_Workshop.html

Pressman. (2006). Software Engineering: a practitioner`s approach. New York: McGraw Hill.

Proto, M., Malandrino, O., & Supino, S. (2007). Eco-labels. A Sustainability Performance in Benchmarking? Management of Environmental Quality: An International Journal, 18(6), 669–683. doi:10.1108/14777830710826702

Prugh, T., Costanza, R., & Cumberland, J. H. (1999). Natural Capital and Human Economic Survival (2nd ed.). Crc Pr Inc.

Pun, K. F., Hui, I. K., Lau, H. C. W., Law, H. W., & Lewis, W. G. (2002). Development of an EMS planning framework for environmental management practices. International Journal of Quality & Reliability Management, 19(6/7), 688–709. doi:10.1108/02656710210429573

Qiang, C. Z., Clarke, G. R., & Halewood, N. (2006). The Role of ICT. In Doing Business Information and Communications for Development – Global Trends and Policies. Washington, DC: World Bank.

Qureshi, S. (2005). How does Information technology effect Development? Integrating Theory and Practice into a Process Model. In Proceedings of the 11th Americas Conference on Information Systems (AMCIS), Omaha, NE.

Qureshi, S., Kamal, M., & Wolcott, P. (2009). Information Technology Therapy for Competitiveness in Micro-Enterprises. International Journal of E-Business Research, 5(1).

Raar, J. (2002). Environmental initiatives: Towards triple-bottom line reporting. Corporate Communications, 7(3), 169–183. doi:10.1108/13563280210436781

Radcliffe, M. (1999). Using the Balanced Scorecard to develop metrics for Sustainable Development. Proceedings of the 8th International Conference of the Greening of Industry Network, Chapel Hill, USA.

Rahman, M. M., & Schroer, B. J. (1998). Optimum Production Conditions for JIT, MRP, OPT. In 29th Annual Meeting of the Decision Sciences Institute (pp. 1158-1162). Las Vegas, NV: Decision Science Institute.

Rapp, B. (2005). Modellierung und protoypische Realisierung von Komponenten zur Interaktion zwischen Unternehmen und Marktplatz bei der kooperativen Konzeption eines Sekundärrohstoff-Marktplatzes. Unpublished Bachelor's Thesis, University of Oldenburg, Germany.

Rasmussen, N., Goldy, P., & Solli, P. P. (2002). Financial Business Intelligence. New York: John Wiley & Sons.

Rau, K. (2004). Effective governance of IT: design objectives, roles and relationships. Information Systems Management, 21(4), 35–42. doi:10.1201/1078/44705.21.4.20040901/84185.4

Raufflet, E. (2006). Re-mapping corporate environment management paradigms. International Studies of Management & Organization, 36(2), 54–73. doi:10.2753/IMO0020-8825360203

Rautenstrauch, C. (1994). Concepts for Integrated Production and Recycling Planning and Scheduling Systems. In K. Feldmannn (Ed.), Proceedings of the 2. International Seminar on Life Cycle Engineering RECY'94. Bamberg, Germany.

Rautenstrauch, C. (1999). Betriebliche Umweltinformationssysteme, Grundlagen, Konzepte und Systeme. Berlin/Heidelberg, Germany: Springer.

Rautenstrauch, C. (2007). Integration of MRP II and Material Flow Management Systems. In J. Marx Gómez, M. Sonnenschein, M. Müller, H. Welsch, & C. Rautenstrauch (Eds.), Information Technologies in Environmental Engineering, ITEE 2007, Third International ICSC Symposium (pp. 261-269). Berlin, Heidelberg: Springer.

Rawlins, B., Paine, K., & Kowalski, P. (2008). Measuring the Transparency of Environmental Sustainability Reporting Through Websites of Fortune 50 Companies.

Raymond, L., Bergeron, F. O., & Blili, S. (2005). The Assimilation of E-business in Manufacturing SMEs: Determinants and Effects on Growth and Internationalization. Electronic Markets, 15(2), 106–118. doi:10.1080/10196780500083761

Reckwitz, A. (2002). Toward a theory of social practices: A development in culturalist theorizing. European Journal of Social Theory, 5, 243–263. doi:10.1177/13684310222225432

Reckwitz, A. (2004). Die Reproduktion und die Subversion sozialer Praktiken: Zugleich ein Kommentar zu Pierre Bourdieu und Judith Butler. In K.H. Hörning, & J. Reuter (Eds.), Doing culture: Neue Positionen zum Verhältnis von Kultur und soziale Praxis (pp 40-54). Bielefeld: transcript-Verlag.

REFA. (1985). Methodenlehre der Planung und Steuerung. 5 volumes. München, Wien: Carl Hanser.

Rehfeld, K. M., Rennings, K., & Ziegler, A. (2004). Integrated Product Policy and Environmental Product Innovations: An Empirical Analysis. ZEW Discussion Paper, 04-71.

Reich, B. H., & Benbasat, I. (2000). Factors that influence the social dimension of alignment between business and information tecnology objectives. MIS Quarterly Executive, 24(1), 81–113.

Reich-Weiser, C., & Dornfeld, D. A. (2009). A discussion of greenhouse gas emission tradeoffs and water scarcity within the supply chain. Journal of Manufacturing Systems, 28(1), 23–27. doi:.doi:10.1016/j.jmsy.2009.04.002

Reinfeld, N. V., & Vogel, W. R. (1958). Mathematical Progamming. Englewood Cliffs: Prentice-Hall.

Reisig, W. (1985). Petri nets: an introduction. Berlin, Heidelberg: Springer.

Remmen, A., Jensen, A. A., & Frydendal, J. (2007). Life Cycle Management – A Business Guide to Sustainability. Paris: UNEP/SETAC Life Cycle Initiative Publications.

Ren, Z. (2000). City Planning and Management in the 21st Century. Nanjing, China: Southeast University Press.

Rennings, K. (2005). Innovationen aus Sicht der neoklassischen Umweltökonomie. In F. Beckenbach, U. Hampicke, C. Leipert, G. Meran, J. Minsch, H. G. Nutzinger, R. Pfriem, J. Weimann, F. Wirl & U. Witt (Eds.), Jahrbuch Ökologische Ökonomik, Band 4: Innovationen und Nachhaltigkeit (pp. 15-40). Marburg: Metropolis.

Report, B. (1987). Report of the world commission of environment. Retrieved October 29, 2009, from http://www.bne-portal.de/coremedia/generator/unesco/de/Downloads/Hintergrundmaterial_international/Brundtlandbericht.pdf.

Reul, F. (2002). Entwicklung einer Nachhaltigkeitsstrategie für den Stadtverkehr - das Beispiel Berlin. Doctoral dissertation, Humboldt-University Berlin, Germany. Retrieved July 13, 2009, from http://edoc.hu-berlin.de/dissertationen/reul-frithjof-2002-12-17

Rezende, D. A. (2002). Tecnologia da informação integrada à inteligência empresarial: alinhamento estratégico e análise da prática nas organizações. São Paulo, São Paulo: Atlas.

Ridley, G., Young, J., & Carroll. (2004). P. COBIT and its utilization: a framework from the literature. Hawaii International Conference on System Sciences. Proceedings of the 37th Hawaii International Conference on System Sciences (pp. 80233). Hawaii.

Riebel, P. (1990). Einzelkosten- und Deckungsbeitragsrechnung (6th ed.). Wiesbaden: Gabler. (in German)

Riebel, P. (1994). Core features of the 'Einzelkosten- und Deckungsbeitragsrechnung'. European Accounting Review, 3(3), 515–546. doi:10.1080/09638189400000034

Riemenschneider, C., Harrison, D., & Mykytyn, P. (2003). Understanding IT Adoption Decisions in Small Business: Integrating Current Theories. Information & Management, 40.

Rikhardsson, P., Andersen, A. J. R., & Bang, H. (2002). Sustainability reporting on the internet. A study of the Global Fortune 500. Greener Management International, 40, 57–75.

Rings, T., Caryer, G., Gallop, J., Grabowski, J., Kovacikova, T., Schulz, S., & Stokes-Rees, I. (2009). Grid and Cloud Computing: Opportunities for Integration with the Next Generation Network. Grid Computing, 7, 375–393. doi:10.1007/s10723-009-9132-5

Rodrigue, J. P., Slack, B., & Comtois, C. (2001). Green logistics. In Brewer, A. M., Button, K. J., & Hensher, D. A. (Eds.), The Handbook of logistics and supply-chain management, Handbooks in transport #2 (pp. 339–351). London, England: Pergamon/Elsevier.

Roosevelt Iv, T., & Llewellyn, J. (2007). Investors hunger for clean energy. Harvard Business Review, 85(10), 38–40.

Rösch, C., Skarka, J., Raab, K., & Stelzer, V. (2009). Energy production from grassland – Assessing the sustainability of different process chains under German conditions. Biomass and Bioenergy, 33(4), 689–700. doi:10.1016/j.biombioe.2008.10.008

Roth, W.-M., & Bowen, G. M. (1999). Of cannibals, missionaries, and converts: graphing competencies from grade 8 to professional science inside (classrooms) and outside (field/laboratory). Science, Technology & Human Values, 24(2), 179–212. doi:10.1177/016224399902400201

Rummler, G., & Brache, A. P. (1994). Melhores desempenhos das empresas. São Paulo, São Paulo: Makron Books.

Rundh, B. (2008). Radio frequency identification (RFID): Invaluable technology or a new obstacle in the marketing process? Marketing Intelligence & Planning, 26(1), 97–114.

Ruppert, H., Eigner-Thiel, S., Girschner, W., Karpenstein-Machan, M., Roland, F., & Ruwisch, V. (2008). Wege zum Bioenergiedorf – Leitfaden für eine eigenständige Wärme- und Stromversorgung auf Basis von Biomasse im ländlichen Raum. Gülzow, Germany: Fachagentur Nachwachsende Rohstoffe.

Ryan, E. (2008). Building Sustainable IT. Cutter IT Journal, 21(2), 6–12.

Sachs, S. (2000). Die Rolle der Unternehmung in ihrer Interaktion mit der Gesellschaft. Bern: Paul Haupt Verlag.

Saio, G., Vandenbroucke, D., & Wawer, R. (2009). NESIS – a Network to enhance a European Environmental Shared and Interoperable Information System. In J. Hřebíček, J. Hradec, E. Pelikán, O. Mírovský, W. Pillmann, I. Holoubek, & T. Bandholtz (Eds.), Proceedings of the European conference of the Czech Presidency of the Council of the EU TOWARDS eENVIRONMENT. Opportunities of SEIS and SISE: Integrating Environmental Knowledge in Europe (pp. 258-264). Brno, Czech Republic: Masaryk University.

Salem, H. (2003). Organizational Performance Management and Measurement: The Lebanese Experience, Beirut. Economic and Social Council. Retrieved October 04, 2009, from http://unpan1.un.org/intradoc/groups/public/documents/unescwa/unpan010860.pdf

Saling, P., Kicherer, A., Dittrich-Krämer, B., Wittlinger, R., Zombik, W., & Schmidt, I. (2002). Eco-Efficiency Analysis by BASF: The Method. International Journal of Life Cycle Assessment, 7(4), 203–218. doi:10.1007/BF02978875

Sambamurthy, V., & Zmud, R. (1999). Arrangements for information technology governance: a theory of multiple contingencies. Management Information Systems Quarterly, 23(2), 261–290. doi:10.2307/249754

Sambamurthy, V., & Zmud, R. (2000). Research Commentary: the organizing logic for na enterprise's IT activities in the Digital Era – a prognosis of practice and a call for research. Information Systems Research, 11(2), 105–114. doi:10.1287/isre.11.2.105.11780

Sambra, A., Sørensen, G., & Kristensen, E. F. (2008). Optimized harvest and logistics for biomass supply chain. In Proceedings of the 16th European Biomass Conference and Exhibition. (pp. 84-91). Valencia, Spain.

Sanchez, M. C., Brown, R. E., Webber, C., & Homan, G. K. (2008). Savings estimates for the United States Environmental Protection Agency's ENERGY STAR voluntary product labeling program. Energy Policy, 36(6), 2098–2108. doi:10.1016/j.enpol.2008.02.021

Sanchez, R. (2001). Resources, dynamic capabilities, and competences: Building blocks of integrative strategy theory. In Elfring, T., & Volberda, H. (Eds.), Rethinking strategy (pp. 143–157). Thousand Oaks, CA: Sage Publications.

Sanchez, R., & Heene, A. (1997). Reinventing Strategic Management: New Theory and Practice for Competence-based Competition. European Management Journal, 15(3), 303–317. doi:10.1016/S0263-2373(97)00010-8

Sanchez, R., & Heene, A. (Eds.). (1996). Strategic Learning and Knowledge Management. Chichester: John Wiley & Sons.

Sanchez-Rodrigues, V. (2006, November). Supply chain management, transport and the environment – A review, Retrieved December 9, 2009, from http://www.greenlogistics.org.uk/SiteResources/7a76ee40-f62d-4efe-9d4e-47ac2a2a9211_WM1%20-%20Cardiff%20-%20Supply%20Chain%20Management.pdf

Sanders, C. K. (2002). The impact of microenterprise assistance programs: A comparative study of program participants, nonparticipants, and other low-wage workers. The Social Service Review, 76(2), 321–340. doi:10.1086/339664

Saran, C., & Mohamed, A. (2005, January 31). Lack of standards and high cost hinders RFID. Computer Weekly, Retrieved December 9, 2009, from http://www.computerweekly.com/Articles/2005/02/01/208032/Lack-of-standards-and-high-cost-hinders-RFID.htm

Sarkis, J. (2003). A strategic decision framework for green supply chain management. Journal of Cleaner Production, 11(4), 397–409.

Satpix (2009). NOAA Satellitenbilder aus Tolk. Retrieved November 18, 2009, from www.satpix.de

Schaaf, U. (2009). Die Zukunft betrieblicher Umwelt-Informationssysteme. Retrieved October 10, 2009, from http://www.umweltcluster.net/getResource/18370/6_Zukunft-BUIS_ Schaaf_ Ulrich.pdf

Schäfer, H. (2005). International corporate social responsibility rating systems: Conceptual outline and empirical results. Journal of Corporate Citizenship, 20, 107–120.

Schaltegger, S., & Burritt, R. (2000). Contemporary Environmental Accounting – Issues, Concepts and Practice. Sheffield, UK: Greenleaf Publishing.

Schaltegger, S., & Sturm, A. (1989). Ökologieinduzierte Entscheidungsprobleme des Managements. Ansatzpunkte zur Umgestaltung von Instrumenten. WWZ-Discussion Paper No. 8914. Basel: WWZ (in German).

Schaltegger, S., & Wagner, M. (2006). Managing Sustainability Performance Measurement and Reporting in an Integrated Manner. Sustainability Accounting as the Link between the Sustainability Balanced Scorecard and Sustainability Reporting. In Schaltegger, S., Bennett, M., & Burritt, R. (Eds.), Sustainability Accounting and Reporting. Dordrecht: Springer. doi:10.1007/978-1-4020-4974-3_30

Schaltegger, S., & Wagner, M. (2006). Managing the Business Case for Sustainability. Sheffield, UK: Greenleaf Publishing.

Schaltegger, S., Burritt, R., & Petersen, H. (2003). An Introduction to Corporate Environmental Management – Striving for Sustainability. Sheffield, UK: Greenleaf Publishing.

Schattke, H. (2008). Nachhaltigkeit und Qualitätskommunikation in der niedersächsischen Fleischwirtschaft: Eine empirische Annäherung. Schriftenreihe des Lehrstuhls für Allgemeine Betriebswirtschaftslehre, Unternehmensführung und Betriebliche Umweltpolitik, 47, Oldenburg.

Schatzki, T. R. (1996). Social Practices. A Wittgensteinian Approach to Human Activity and the Social. Cambridge: Cambridge University Press. doi:10.1017/CBO9780511527470

Schauer, H. (2006). Vergleichende Buchbesprechung IT-Controlling. Wirtschaftsinformatik, 48(3), 212–218. doi:10.1007/s11576-006-0046-6

Scheer, A.-W. (1988). CIM Computer Integrated Manufacturing – Computer Steered Industry. Berlin, Heidelberg: Springer.

Scheier, R. L. (2007). Virtualization 101. Computerworld, (October): 15, 54–56.

Schendler, A. (2007). When being green backfires. Harvard Business Review, 85(10), 35–38.

Schmidt, M. (2005). A production-theory-based framework for analysing recycling systems in the e-waste sector. Environmental Impact Assessment Review, 25(5), 505–524. doi:10.1016/j.eiar.2005.04.008

Schmidt, M., Lambrecht, H., & Möller, A. (2007). Optimisation Approaches in Material Flow Models for Manufacturing Systems. In Hryniewicz, O., Studzinski, J., & Romaniuk, M. (Eds.), Environmental Informatics & Systems Research (Vol. 1). Aachen: Shaker.

Schmidt, M., Möller, A., Hedemann, J., & Müller-Beilschmidt, P. (1997). Environmental Material Flow Analysis by Network Approach. In Geiger, W. (Eds.), Environmental Informatics '97 (Vol. 2). Marburg, Germany: Metropolis.

Schmidt, S. J. (2005). Lernen, Wissen, Kompetenz, Kultur: Vorschläge zur Bestimmung von vier Unbekannten. Heidelberg: Carl-Auer Verlag.

Schmigalla, H. (1995). Fabrikplanung – Begriffe und Zusammenhänge. München: Carl Hanser.

Schmookler, J. (1966). Invention and Economic Growth. Cambridge: Harvard University Press.

Schmuck, P., Eigner, S., Kaufhold, A., & Krapoth, S. (1998). Psychologische Aspekte von Unternehmensbewertung (Vol. 13). Göttingen, Germany: Schriftenreihe des Koordinations- und Studienzentrums Frieden und Umwelt.

Scholl, G. U., & Nisius, S. (1998). The environmental benefits to German companies through application of LCA. Journal of Cleaner Production, 6, 247–252. doi:10.1016/S0959-6526(98)00025-0

Schraml, T. (1997). Operationalisierung der ökologieorientierten Berichterstattung aus Sicht des Informationsmanagements [Specification of environmental reporting from an information management perspective]. Unpublished dissertation thesis, Technische Universität Dresden.

Schreiner, M., & Woller, G. (2003). Micro-enterprise Development Programs in the United States and in the Developing World. World Development, 31(9), 1567–1580. doi:10.1016/S0305-750X(03)00112-8

Schuhmacher, T. (1997). West Coast Camelot. The Rise and Fall od an Organizational Culture. In Sackmann, S. A. (Ed.), Cultural Complexity in Organizations. Inherent Contrasts and Contradictions. Thousand Oaks, CA: Sage Publications.

Schulze, G. G. (2009). Bürokratie- und Regulierungskosten in der chemischen Industrie: Potenziale zu ihrer Reduktion. Social Accountability International (SAI). Overview of SA8000. Retrieved October 12, 2009, from http://www.sa-intl.org/

Schumpeter, J. (1964). Theorie der wirtschaftlichen Entwicklung. Göttingen: Duncker & Humblot.

Schwarz, A., & Hirschheim, R. (2003). An extended platform logic perspective of IT governance: managing perceptions and activities of IT. The Journal of Strategic Information Systems, 12(2), 129–166. doi:10.1016/S0963-8687(03)00021-0

SCOPE (Scientific Committee on Problems of the Environment). (1995). Environmental indicators: systematic approach to measuring and reporting on the environment in the context of sustainable development. Discussion paper presented at the workshop "International Consultation of Sustainable Development Indicators", Ghent. Bruxelles, Belgium: Bureau du Plan.

Scott, P., & Jackson, R. (2002). Environmental, social and sustainability reporting on the web. Best practices. Corporate Environmental Strategy, 9(2), 193–202. doi:10.1016/S1066-7938(02)00016-7

Seitz, M., & Peattie, K. (2004). Meeting the Closed-Loop Challenge: The Case of Remanufacturing. California Management Review, 46(2), 74–89.

Seliger, G. (Ed.). (2006). Sustainability in Manufacturing: Recovery of Resources in Product and Material Cycles. Heidelberg, Berlin: Springer.

Servon, L. J. (1998). Credit and social capital: The community development potential of US micro-enterprise programs. Housing Policy Debate, 9(1), 115–149.

SETAC. (1993). Guidelines for Life Cycle Assessment: A 'Code of Practice'. Proceedings of a Workshop in Sesimbra, Portugal. Brussels: Society of Environmental Toxicology and Chemistry (SETAC).

Severengiz, S., Sezgin, C., & Yonk, N. K. (2008). Automotive Remanufacturing in Europe: Survey Results. TU Berlin.

Shapley, L. S. (1953). A Value for n-Person Games. In Kuhn, H. W., & Tucker, A. W. (Eds.), Contributions to the Theory of Games, Annals of Math. Studies (Vol. 28, pp. 307–317). Princeton, NJ: Princeton University Press.

Shepherd, K., Abkowitz, M., & Cohen, M. A. (2001). Online corporate environmental reporting: Improvements and innovation to enhance stakeholder value. Corporate Environmental Strategy, 8(4), 307–315. doi:10.1016/S1066-7938(01)00136-1

Sivapalan, & R. Vertessy (Eds.), Proceedings of MODSIM 2001 – International Congress on Modeling and Simulation: IntegratingModels for Natural Resources-Management Across Disciplines, Issues and Scales. Vol. 1. Natural systems (Part 1) (pp. 43-52).

Skillius, Å., & Wennberg, U. (1998). Continuity, credibility and comparability. Key challenges for corporate environmental performance measurement and communication. The International Institute for Industrial Environmental Economics at Lund University.

Sliwa,C.(2008).GreenIT:Buzzwordorstrategy?TechTargets. Retrieved February 27, 2008 from http://searchcio.techtarget.com/tip/0,289483,sid182_gci1302716,00.html?track=NL-983&ad=626565&asrc=EM_NLT_3154136&uid=2470905The

Smith, H., & McKeen, J. (1993). How does Information Technology affect Business value? A reassessment and research propositions. Canadian Journal of Administrative Sciences, 10(3), 229–240.

Sociaal Economische Raad (SER) (2001). Corporate social responsibility. A Dutch approach. Assen: Koninklijke Van Gorcum.

SocialFunds. (Socially responsible investing information concerning corporations, mutual funds, and more) (2000). Investors prod CEO's to adopt new reporting standards. Retrieved December 16, 2000, from http://socialfunds.com/news/article

Sokhansanj, S., Kumar, A., & Turhollow, F. (2006). Development and implementation of integrated biomass supply analysis and logistics model (IBSAL). Biomass and Bioenergy, 30(10), 838–847. doi:10.1016/j.biombioe.2006.04.004

Sordi, J. O. (2003). Tecnologia da informação aplicada aos negócios. São Paulo, São Paulo: Atlas.

Southwood, R. (2004). ICTs and Small Enterprise: A Motor of Economic Development in Africa. IICD Research Briefs 9. The Hague.

Spada Limited (2008). Environmental Reporting: Trends in FTSE 100 Sustainability Reports.

Spencer-Cooke, A. (1995). Engaging stakeholders: The next challenge in corporate environmental reporting. IÖW/VÖW-Informationsdienst, 10(3-4), 4-5.

Speth, J. G. (2009). Doing business in a postgrowth society. Harvard Business Review, 87(9), 18–19.

Srivastava, S. K. (2007). Green supply-chain management: A state-of-the-art literature review. International Journal of Management Reviews, 9(1), 53–80.

Sroufe, R., & Sarkis, J. (2007). Strategic Sustainability: The state of the art in corporate environmental management systems. Sheffield: Greenleaf.

Stake, R. E. (1998). Case studies. In Denzin, N. K., & Lincoln, Y. S. (Eds.), Strategies of Qualitative Inquiry (pp. 86–109). Thousand Oaks, CA: Sage.

Stangeland, A. (Ed.). (2008). How to combat global warming - An ambitious but necessary approach to reduce greenhouse gas emissions. Working paper prepared by the Energy and Climate Department of the Bellona Foundation. Retrieved December 9, 2009, from http://www.bellona.org/reports/How_to_Combat_Global_Warming

Stapleton, P. J., Glove, M. A., & Davis, S. P. (2001). Environmental Management Systems: An Implementation Guide for Small and Medium-Sized Organizations. NSF International.

Starr, R., Newfrock, J., & Delurey, M. (2003). Enterprise Resilience: Managing Risk in the Networked Economy. Retrieved October 15, 2009, from http://www.boozallen.com/media/file/139766.pdf

Steinberg, J. (2003). Information Technology and Development Beyond Either/Or. The Brookings Review, 21(2), 45–48.

Steinhilper, R. (1998). Remanufacturing the ultimate form of recycling. Stuttgart: Frauenhoffer IRB Verlag.

Stennes, B., & McBeath, A. (2006). Bioenergy options for woody feedstock: are trees killed by mountain pine beetle in British Columbia a viable bioenergy resource? (Information Report BC-X-405). Ottawa, Canada: Canadian Forest Service.

Sterr, T., & Ott, T. (2004). The industrial region as a promising unit for eco-industrial development - reflections, practical experience and establishment of innovative instruments to support industrial ecology. Journal of Cleaner Production, 12(8-10), 947–965. doi:10.1016/j.jclepro.2004.02.029

Steurer, R. (2001). Paradigmen der Nachhaltigkeit. Zeitschrift für Umweltpolitik und Umweltrecht, 4, 537–566.

Strassman, P. (1997). The squandered computer: evaluating the business alignment of information technology. New Canaan, Connecticut: The Information Economics Press.

Stratopoulos, P., & Dehning, B. (2000). Does successful investment in information technology solve the productivity paradox? Information & Management, 38(2), 103–117. doi:10.1016/S0378-7206(00)00058-6

Stratos Inc. (2003). Building confidence. Corporate sustainability reporting in Canada. Ottawa: Stratos. Retrieved September 18, 2003, from http://www.stratos-sts.com/sts_files/BC%20Building%20Confidence.pdf

Strauss, R., & Bird, S. (2009). The State of Sustainability Reporting in Europe: Commission Statement. Retrieved July 26, 2009, from http://www.sustainabilityreporting.eu/general/ downloads/ec08.pdf

Sujitparapitaya, S., Janz, B., & Gillenson, M. (2003). The contribution of IT governance solutions to the implementation of data warehouse practice. Journal of Database Management, 14(2), 52–69.

Sullivan, B. C. (1985). Economics of Information Technology. International Journal of Social Economics, 12(1), 37. doi:10.1108/eb013983

Sullivan, L. (2005, January 3). RFID: The plot thickens. Information Week. Retrieved December 9, 2009, from http://www.informationweek.com/news/mobility/RFID/showArticle.jhtml?articleID=56800166

Süpke, D., Marx Gómez, J., & Isenmann, R. (2009). Web 2.0 for sustainability reporting: Approach to refining communication on sustainability. In Wohlgemuth, V., Page, B., & Voigt, K. (Eds.), EnviroInfo 2009 - Environmental Informatics and Industrial Environmental Protection: Concepts (pp. 219–229). Berlin, Germany: Methods and Tools.

Supply Chain Council (2006). Supply-Chain Operations Reference-model (SCOR): Overview Version 8.0. Pittsburgh, Washington DC: Supply-Chain Council Inc.

SustainAbility Ltd., & United Nations Environment Programme (UNEP) (1996). Engaging stakeholders. Vol. 1: The benchmark survey. London: Polar.

SustainAbility Ltd., & United Nations Environment Programme (UNEP) (1999). Engaging stakeholders 1999. The internet reporting report. London: Beacon.

Sutton, P. (2004). A Perspective on environmental sustainability? A paper for the Victorian Commissioner for Environmental Sustainability. The State of Victoria, 12-April [Version 2.b]. Retrieved July 2009, from http://www.green-innovations.asn.au/

Suurs, R. A. A. (2002). Long Distance Bioenergy Logistics: An assessment of costs and energy consumption for various biomass transport chains (Report NWS, Vol. E-2002-01). Utrecht, The Netherlands: Utrecht University, Copernicus Institute.

Svending, O. (2003). Industrial Management of Environmental Data – Suggested procedures for internal allocation based on stakeholder needs. Thesis to earn the degree of licentiate of engineering. Göteborg, Sweden: Chalmers University of Technology.

Synnot, W. R. (1987). Information Weapons. Information Strategy, 4(1), 12.

Szekely, F., & Knirsch, M. (2005). Responsible Leadership and Corporate Social Responsibility: Metrics for Sustainable Performance. European Management Journal, 23(6), 628–647. doi:10.1016/j.emj.2005.10.009

Tachizawa, T., Andrade, R. O. B., & Carvalho, A. B. (2002). Gestão ambiental: enfoque estratégico aplicado ao desenvolvimento sustentável. São Paulo: Pearson Education do Brasil.

Taprantzi, A. (2001). A Systematic Approach for Acquiring Industrial Data and Information for Environmental Applications. Procedures for modelling the communication of environmental inquiries within an organisational structure. Falun, Sweden: Stora Enso Research, Falun Research Centre.

Taylor, C., & Jefferson, D. (1994). Artificial life as a tool for biological inquiry. Artificial Life, 1, 1–13.

Taylor, F. W. (1911). The Principles of Scientific Management. New York: Harper & Brothers Publications.

Technidata, A. G. (2009). NMC Messzentrale für Umweltmonitoring. Retrieved November 18, 2009, from www.technidata.de/envinet/documents/ENVINET_NMC_D_000.pdf

Technische Universität München. (2009a). Siemens IT Solutions and Services. Machbarkeitsstudie Prozessketten Umwelt.

Technische Universität München. (2009b). Siemens IT Solutions and Services. Prozessbibliothek zur Machbarkeitsstudie Prozessketten Umwelt.

Teixeira Júnior, F., & Ponte, V. M. R. (2003). Alinhamento estratégico: estudo comparativo das percepções dos executivos de negócios e TI. Revista Eletrônica de Administração, 7(5).

Telle, K. (2006). "It Pays to be Green" – A Premature Conclusion? Environmental & Resource Economics, 35, 195–220. DOI 10.1007/s10640-006-9013-3

Teo, H. H., Oh, L. B., Liu, C., & Wie, K. K. (2003). An empirical study of the effects of interactivity on web user attitude. International Journal of Human-Computer Studies, 58(3), 281–305. doi:10.1016/S1071-5819(03)00008-9

Teo, T. S. H., & King, W. R. (1997). Integration between business planning and information systems planning: An evolutionary-contingency perspective. Journal of Management Information Systems, 14(1), 185–214.

Teuteberg, F., & Straßenburg, J. (2009). State of the art and future research in environmental management information systems – a systematic literature review. In I. N. Athanasiadis, P. A. Mitkas, A. E. Rizzoli, & J. Marx Gómez (Eds.), Information Technologies in Environmental Engineering. Proceedings of the 4th International ICSC Symposium Thessaloniki, Greece, May 28-29, 2009 (pp. 64-77) Berlin, Heidelberg: Springer.

The Associated Chambers of Commerce and Industry of India (2009). ASSOCHAM Eco Pulse Study: Corporate Social Responsibility 2008-09.

The European Commission. (2008). The European Pollutant Emission Register (EPER) and the European Pollutant Release and Transfer Register (E-PRTR). Retrieved October 14, 2009, from http://ec.europa.eu/environment/air/pollutants/stationary/eper/index.htm

The Green Grid (2009). The Green Grid Data Centre Power Efficiency Metrics: PUE and DCiE. Retrieved November 22, 2009 from http://www.thegreengrid.org/en/Global/Content/white-papers/The-Green-Grid-Data-Centre-Power-Efficiency-Metrics-PUE-and-DCiE

The Institute for Social and Ethical Accountability. AccountAbility. Retrieved July 26, 2009, from http://www.accountability21.net/

Thiessen, I. (2006). Konzept und Implementierung eines XBRL Schema zur computergestützten Unternehmensberichterstattung. Unpublished Diploma Thesis, Technische Universität Kaiserslautern.

Tiemstra, J. P. (2003). Environmental policy for business and government. Business and Society Review, 108(1), 61–69. doi:10.1111/1467-8594.00009

Tiernan, C., & Peppard. (2004). J. Information technology: of value or a vulture? European Management Journal, 22(6), 609–623. doi:10.1016/j.emj.2004.09.025

Timm, H. (2002). Fuzzy-Clusteranalyse: Methoden zur Exploration von Daten mit fehlenden Werten sowie klassifizierten Daten. Doctoral dissertation, Otto-von-Guericke-Universität Magdeburg. Retrieved July 25, 2006, from http://iws.cs.uni-magdeburg.de/~htimm/data/dissertation.pdf

Timm, H., Borgelt, C., Döring, C., & Kruse, R. (2001). Fuzzy Cluster Analysis with Cluster Repulsion. In: Proceedings of the European Symposium on Intelligent Technologies. Aachen: Verlag Mainz, CD-ROM.

Tinsley, S. (2002). EMS models for business strategy development. Business Strategy and the Environment, 11(6), 376–390. doi:10.1002/bse.340

Tischner, U., & Charter, M. (2001). Sustainable Solutions: Developing Products and Services for the Future. Sheffield: Greenleaf Publishing.

Tivander, J., Carlson, R., Erixon, M., & Pålsson, A. C. (2004a). OMNIITOX Concept Model Supports Characterisation Modelling for Life Cycle Impact Assessment. Intl. Journal of LCA, 9(5), 289–294. doi:10.1007/BF02979418

Tivander, J., Carlson, R., Erixon, M., & Pålsson, A. C. (2006). IMPRESS integrated data format [Göteborg, Sweden: CPM, Chalmers University of Technology.]. CPM Report, 2006, 15.

Tivander, J., Carlson, R., Erlandsson, M., Erixon, M., & Geiron, K. (2004b). Concept Model for the OMNIITOX Information System Including OMNIITOX Data Format Definition – OMNIITOX project report D20 and D26, 2004, EC contract G1RD-CT–2001–00501. Göteborg, Sweden: IMI, Chalmers University of Technology.

Treitz, M., Bertsch, V., Schollenberger, H., Geldermann, J., & Rentz, O. (2008). Multi-criteria decision support for process design. International Transactions in Operational Research (accepted), Vol. Special, Issue of the IFORS Conference in Hawaii 2005, 10.-15.July Honolulu, Hawaii.

Turban, E., Mclean, E., & Wetherbe, J. (2004). Tecnologia da informação para gestão. Porto Alegre, Rio Grande do Sul: Bookman.

Tversky, B. (2000). Some ways maps and diagrams communicate. In Freksa, C., Brauer, W., Habel, C., & Wender, K. F. (Eds.), Spatial cognition II. Berlin, Germany: Springer. doi:10.1007/3-540-45460-8_6

U.S. Environmental Protection Agency. Environmental Management Systems: Key Management System Concepts Retrieved October 07, 2009, from http://www.epa.gov/ems/info/keyconcepts.htm

UBA. (1997). Nachhaltiges Deutschland – Wege zu einer dauerhaft-umweltgerechten Entwicklung. Berlin: Erich Schmidt Verlag.

Udo de Haes, H. A., Hejungs, R., Suh, S., & Huppes, G. (2004). Three Strategies to Overcome the Limitations of Life-Cycle Assessment. Journal of Industrial Ecology, 8(3), 19–32. doi:10.1162/1088198042442351

Uhrich, S., Klenke, M., Kruse, F., & Giffei, C. (2009). Approach to Build a Soil Information Portal for Europe Based on the PortalU Technology. In J. Hřebíček, J. Hradec, E. Pelikán, O. Mírovský, W. Pillmann, I. Holoubek, & T. Bandholtz (Eds.), Proceedings of the European conference of the Czech Presidency of the Council of the EU TOWARDS eENVIRONMENT. Opportunities of SEIS and SISE: Integrating Environmental Knowledge in Europe (pp. 266-268). Brno, Czech Republic: Masaryk University.

Umweltbundesamt (2008). Daten zur Umwelt 2008. Retrieved November 18, 2009 from www.umweltbundesamt-daten-zur-umwelt.de

Umweltbundesamt (2009). Luftdaten. Retrieved August 13, 2009, from www.env-it.de/ luftdaten/trsyear.fwd?comp=PM1&state=UB&year=2009&month=8&boxed

=1&order=0 umwelt-monitoring-systeme (2009). Retrieved November 18, 2009, from www.ums-muc.de

Umweltbundesamt. Der Blaue Engel. Retrieved July 26, 2009, from http://www.blauer-engel.de/

UNECE (United Nations Economic Commission for Europe). (2009): Publication of the Aarhus Convention. Retrieved June 2009, from http://www.unece.org/env/pp/documents/cep43e.pdf

UNEP (United Nations Environment Programme). (2007). Global Environment Outlook – GEO 4. Retrieved May 17, 2008, from http://www.unep.org/geo/geo4/report/GEO-4_Report_Full_en.pdf

Unerman, J., & Bennett, M. (2004). Increased stakeholder dialogue and the internet: Towards greater corporate accountability or reinforcing capitalist hegemony? Accounting, Organizations and Society, 29(7), 685–707. doi:10.1016/j.aos.2003.10.009

UNFCCC. (2009). Kyoto Protocol. Retrieved July 2009, from http://unfccc.int/kyoto_protocol/items/2830.php.

UNIDO. (2004). http://www.unido.org/doc/5162

United Nations Environment Program (UNEP) (Ed.). (2002). SustainAbility Ltd. United Nations Environment Program – Trust us: The global reporters 2002 survey of corporate sustainability reporting. London: Beacon Press.

United Nations Environment Programme Industry and Environment (UNEP). & SustainAbility (1994). Company environmental reporting. A measure of the progress of business & industry towards sustainable development. Technical report 24. Paris: UNEP.

United Nations World Commission on Environment and Development. (1987). Our Common Future. Oxford: Oxford University Press.

United Nations. (1993). Agenda 21: programme of action for sustainable development. New York: United Nations.

Unruh, G. C. (2000). Understanding carbon lock-in. Energy Policy, 28(12), 817–830. doi:10.1016/S0301-4215(00)00070-7

Urbani, D., & Delhom, M. (2005). Water management policy selection using a decision support system based on a multi-agent system. (. LNCS, 3673, 466–469.

US Environmental Protection Agency (1997). Implementation guide for the Code of Environmental Principles for Federal Agencies. EPA-315-B-97-001.

US Environmental Protection Agency. (2003). Elements of a state water monitoring and assessment program (EPA 841-B-03-003). Retrieved June 19, 2009, from http://www.epa.gov/owow/monitoring/elements/index.html

van Dalen, M. (1997). Company environmental reporting. Conditions for the optimal information structure of environmental reports. Unpublished doctoral dissertation, University of Humberside and Zeeland Polytechnic Flushing.

van der Molen, F. The International Corporate Sustainability Reporting Site. Retrieved July 21, 2009, from http://www.enviroreporting.com/others/feem.htm

Van der Woerd, F., & van den Brink, T. (2004). Feasibility of a Responsive Business Scorecard – a pilot study. Journal of Business Ethics, 55, 173–186. doi:10.1007/s10551-004-1900-3

Van Hoek, R. I. (1999). From Reversed Logistics to Green Supply Chains. Supply Chain Management, 4(3), 129–134.

Van Loo, S., & Koppejan, J. (Eds.). (2008). Handbook of biomass combustion and Co-firing. London, United Kingdom: Earthscan.

van Ree, R., & Annevelink, B. (2007). Status Report Biorefinery 2007 (Report 847). Wageningen, The Netherlands: Wageningen University and Research Centre, Agrotechnology and Food Sciences Group.

Vandermerwe, S., & Oliff, M. D. (1990). Customers Drive Corporations Green. Long Range Planning, 23(6), 10–16. doi:10.1016/0024-6301(90)90096-M

Vargas, C. M. (2000). Community development and microenterprises: fostering sustainable development. Sustainable Development, 8(1), 11. doi:10.1002/(SICI)1099-1719(200002)8:1<11::AID-SD119>3.0.CO;2-7

Velazquez-Marti, B., & Annevelink, E. (2008, June). Mathematical algorithm to transform digital biomass distribution maps into linear programming networks in order to optimize bio-energy delivery chains. Paper presented at the International Conference on Agricultural Engineering. Hersonissos, Greece.

Verfaillie, H. A., & Bidwell, R. (2000). Measuring eco-efficiency: A guide to reporting company performance. World Business Council for Sustainable Development (WBCSD), 1-33. Retrieved July 2009, from http://www.wbcsd.org/web/publications/measuring_eco_efficiency.pdf

Verhoef, C. (2007). Quantifying the effects of IT-governance rules. Science of Computer Programming, 67(2-3), 247–277. doi:10.1016/j.scico.2007.01.010

Vester, F. (2003). Die Kunst, vernetzt zu denken. Ideen und Werkzeug für einen Umgang mit Komplexität. Der neue Bericht an den Club of Rome. München, Germany: dtv.

vHauff, M., & Solbach, D. (1999). Perspektiven integrierter Umweltschutztechnologie in der Bundesrepublik Deutschland. Zeitschrift für Umweltpolitik & Umweltrecht, 1, 67–86.

vHauff, M., Kleine, A., & Jörg, A. (2005). Förderung der Wettbewerbsfähigkeit in Kleinunternehmen durch Ökoeffizienz. Sternenfels: Verlag Wissenschaft und Praxis.

Videras, J., & Alberini, A. (2000). The appeal of voluntary environmental programs: Which firms participate and why? Contemporary Economic Policy, 18(4), 449–461. doi:10.1111/j.1465-7287.2000.tb00041.x

Visich, J. K., Li, S., Khumawala, B. M., & Reyes, P. M. (2008). Empirical evidence of RFID impacts on supply chain performance. Retrieved December 1, 2009 from http://www.decisionsciences.org/Proceedings/DSI2008/docs/441-4907.pdf

Visser, U., Stuckenschmidt, H., Wache, H., & Vögele, T. (2001). Using environmental information efficiently: Sharing data and knowledge from heterogeneous sources. In Rautenstrauch, C., & Patig, S. (Eds.), Environmental information systems in industry and public administration (pp. 2–11). Hershey, PA: Idea Group Publishing.

Visser, W. (2002). Sustainability reporting in South Africa. Corporate Environmental Strategy, 9(1), 79–85. doi:10.1016/S1066-7938(01)00157-9

Vitale. (2001, October). The dot.com legacy: governing IT on internet time. Paper presented at the Information Systems Research Call, Baurer College of Business, Houston.

Vlachos, D., Iakovou, E., Karagiannidis, A., & Toka, A. (2008). A strategic supply chain management model for waste biomass networks. In K. D. Bouzakis (Ed.), 3rd International Conference on Manufacturing Engineering (pp. 797-804).

VMWare. (2008). Green IT - reduces energy costs and goes green with VMWare virtualization. VMWare. Retrieved April 12, 2008 from http://www.vmware.com/

Voigt, K., Welzl, G., Brüggemann, R., & Pudenz, S. (2002). Bewertungsansatz von Umweltmonitoring-Informationssystemen in Ballungsräumen. Umweltwissenschaften und Schadstoff-Forschung. Berlin, Heidelberg: Springer.

Volkswagen, A. G. (2003). Mobility and responsibility. Improving social performance reporting. Retrieved April 4, 2003, from http://www.vw-ag.de/english/defaultIE.html

Von Blumenthal, A. (2002). Fabrikplanung Schwerpunkt Recht. Aachen: Shaker.

Von Haaren, C., & Bathke, M. (2007). Integrated Planning and remuneration of agri-environmental goods and services for the management of sustainable landscapes – results of a case study in the Fuhrberg region of Germany. Journal of Environmental Management, 89, 209–221. doi:10.1016/j.jenvman.2007.01.058

Waddock, S. (2008). Building a new institutional infrastructure for corporate responsibility. The Academy of Management Perspectives, 22(3), 87–108.

Wade, M., & Hulland, J. (2004). The Resource-Based View and Informations Systems Research. Review, Extension, and Suggestions for Future Research. Management Information Systems Quarterly, 28(1), 107–142.

Walker, D., Pitt, M., & Thakur, U. J. (2007). Environmental management systems: Information management and corporate responsibility. Journal of Facilities Management, 5(1), 49–61. doi:10.1108/14725960710726346

Walter, T. J. (2002). Einsatz von Methoden der Digitalen Fabrik bei der Planung von Produktionssystemen für die Automobilindustrie. Aachen: Shaker.

Wang, D. (2007). Meeting Green Computing Challenges. IEEE, 1244-1253.

Wang, X., Du, Z., Chen, Y., & Li, S. (2008). Virtualization-based autonomic resource management for multi-tier Web applications in shared data center. Journal of Systems and Software, 81(9), 1591–1608. doi:10.1016/j.jss.2007.11.719

Wang, Z. (2007). Recycling Economy: Regional Industry Symbiosis Network – a theory and practice to the development of eco-industrial park. Beijing, China: Economy and Science Press.

Warde, A. (2005). Consumption and Theories of Practice. Journal of Consumer Culture, 5, 131–153. doi:10.1177/1469540505053090

Warschauer, M. (2003). Demystifying the Digital Divide. Scientific American, 289(2), 42–48. doi:10.1038/scientificamerican0803-42

Water Quality Task Group. (2006). A Canada-wide framework for water quality monitoring. PN 1369. Retrieved June 19, 2009, from: http://www.ccme.ca/assets/pdf/wqm_framework_1.0_e_web.pdf

Waters, B. (2005). Software as a service: A look at the customer benefits. Journal of Digital Asset Management, 1(1), 32–39. doi:10.1057/palgrave.dam.3640007

Watson, R. T. (Ed.). (2007). Green IS: Building Sustainable Business Practices. Global Text Project. Retrieved December 2009 from http://globaltext.terry.uga.edu/userfiles/pdf/Green.pdf

Waverman, L., Meschi, M., & Fuss, M. (2005). The impact of telecoms on economic growth in developing countries. The Vodafone Policy Paper, Series 2.

WBGU. (2008). Wissenschaftlicher Beirat der Bundesregierung Globale Umweltveränderungen. Zukunftsfähige Bioenergie und nachhaltige Landnutzung. Berlin: Springer.

WCED (World Commission on Environment and Development). (1987). Our Common Future. New York: Oxford University Press.

Wei, B., & Carlson, R. (2002). Practical Pre-Study of GIS application with LCA database SPINE. Presentation at the fifth International Conference on Ecobalance, 06-08.11.2002. Tsukuba, Japan.

Weidema, B., Thrane, M., Christensen, P., Schmidt, J., & Loekke, S. (2008). Carbon Footprint – A Catalyst for Life Cycle Assessment? Journal of Industrial Ecology, 12(1), 3–6. doi:10.1111/j.1530-9290.2008.00005.x

Weidenmann, B. (Ed.). (1994). Wissenserwerb mit Bildern. Bern, Switzerland: Huber.

Weil, P., & Ross, J. W. (2004). It Governance: How Top Performers Manage It Decision Rights For Superior Results. Boston, Massachusetts: Harvard Business School Press.

Weill, P. (2004). Don't just lead govern: how top-performing firms govern IT. MIS Quarterly Executive, 3(1), 1–17.

Weill, P., & Olson, M. (1989). Managing investment in information technology: mini case examples and implications. Management Information Systems Quarterly, 13(1), 3–17. doi:10.2307/248694

Weill, P., & Ross, J. W. (2004). IT Governance. Massachusetts: Harvard Business School Press.

Weill, P., & Woodham, R. (2002). Don't just lead, govern: implementing effective IT governance. Center for Information Systems Research. Working paper n. 326. Retrieved August 10, 2009, from http://biblioteca.universia.net/ficha.do?id=21878

Weinert, F. E. (2001). A concept of competence: A conceptual clarification. In Rychen, D. S., & Salganik, L. H. (Eds.), Defining and selecting key competencies (pp. 45–65). Seattle: Hogrefe.

Weiß, P., & Bentlage, J. (2006). Environmental Management Systems and Certification. The Baltic University Press.

Welford, R. (1996). Corporate Environmental Management. London: Earthscan Publications Ltd.

Welsch, J. (2005). Innovationspolitik – eine problemorientierte Einführung. Wiesbaden: Gabler.

Wenk, M. S. (2005). The European Union's Eco-management and Audit Scheme (EMAS): Springer Science & Business. WESTON. Environmental Management Information Systems (EMIS). Retrieved August 15, 2009, from http://www.westonsolutions.com/Services/environmental_solutions/health_safety/ems/ emis/ index.htm

Werheit, M. (1996). Indikatoren für eine nachhaltige Entwicklung. Information letter No. 29 of the Independent Institute for Environmental Concerns (UfU), Berlin, Germany.

Werner, F. (2005). Ambiguities in Decision-oriented Life Cycle Inventories. Berlin, Heidelberg: Springer.

Wernerfelt, B. (1984). A resource-based view of the firm. Strategic Management Journal, 5(2), 171–180. doi:10.1002/smj.4250050207

Wheeler, D., & Elkington, J. (2001). The end of the corporate environmental report? Or the advent of cybernetic sustainability reporting and communication. Business Strategy and the Environment, 10(1), 1–14. doi:10.1002/1099-0836(200101/02)10:1<1::AID-BSE274>3.0.CO;2-0

Wiehe, J., Ruschkowski, E. V., Rode, M., Kanning, H., & Haaren, C. v. (2009). Auswirkungen des Energiepflanzenanbaus auf die Landschaft am Beispiel des Maisanbaus für die Biogasproduktion in Niedersachsen. Naturschutz und Landschaftsplanung, 41(4), 107–113.

Wildangier, A., & Jensen, J. (2006). Virtual infrastructures in GXP regulated industry. Journal of GXP Compliance, 11(1), 48–53.

Willcocks, L., Feeny, D., & Olson, N. (2006). Implementing core IS capabilities: Feeny- Willcocks IT governance and management framework revisited. European Management Journal, 24(1), 28–37. doi:10.1016/j.emj.2005.12.005

Williams, J., & Curtis, L. (2008). Green: The New Computing Coat of Arms. IEEE, 12-16.

Willis, P. (1990). Common Culture: Symbolic work at play in the everyday cultures of the young. Milton Keynes: Open University Press.

Winograd, T. (1986). A language/action perspective on the design of cooperative work. In Proceedings of the 1986 ACM conference on Computer-supported cooperative work. Austin, Texas.

Winograd, T., & Flores, F. (1986). Understanding Computers and Cognition. Reading, MA: Addison-Wesley Publishing.

Wisconsin Department of Natural Resources EMAS and ISO 14001. Retrieved July 16, 2009, from http://www.dnr.state.wi.us/org/caer/cea/environmental/advisors/documents/20070306EMAS andISO14001.pdf

Wohlgemuth, V. (2005). Komponentenbasierte Unterstützung von Methoden der Modellbildung und Simulation im Einsatzkontext des betrieblichen Umweltschutzes. Aachen, Germany: Shaker. (in German)

Wohlgemuth, V., Schnackenbeck, T., Mäusbacher, M., & Panic, D. (2009). Conceptual Design and Implementation of a Toolkit Plattform for the development of EMIS based on the Open Source Plugin-Framework Empinia. In Wohlgemuth, V., Page, B., & Voigt, K. (Eds.), Environmental Informatics and Industrial Environmental Protection: Concepts, Methods and Tools. Aachen: Shaker.

Wolcott, P., Kamal, M., & Qureshi, S. (2008). Meeting the Challenges of ICT Adoption by Micro-enterprises. Journal of Enterprise Information Management, 21(6). doi:10.1108/17410390810911212

Wolcott, P., Qureshi, S., & Kamal, M. (2007). Information Technology Therapy Approach to Microenterprise Adoption of ICTs. In Proceedings of the 13th Americas Conference on Information Systems (AMCIS), Keystone, Colorado.

World Business Council for Sustainable Development (WBCSD). (2002). Communications and stakeholder involvement guidebook for cement facilities. Report prepared by the Battelle Memorial Institute (Ohio) and Environmental Resources Management (London). Retrieved April 18, 2003, from http://www.wbcsdcement.org/pdf/final_report1_2.pdf

World Business Council for Sustainable Development (WBCSD). (2008). Sustainable Consumption: Facts and Trends from a Business Perspective. Retrieved from.http://www.wbcsd.org/includes/getTarget.asp?type=d&id=MzI2ODM

World Commission on Environment and Development. (WCED, 1987). Our common future. New York: Oxford University Press.

World Wide Web Consortium (W3C) (Éd.) (2001). XML Linking Language (Xlink) Version 1.0 (document dated: 2001). Retrieved January 17, 2006, http://www.w3.org/TR/xlink

World Wide Web Consortium. (W3C) (2004). Extensible Markup Language (XML) 1.0 (3rd ed.). W3C recommendation 04 February 2004. Retrieved July 12, 2004, from http://www.w3.org/TR/REC-xml/

Wu, H.-J., & Dunn, S. C. (1995). Environmentally responsible logistics systems. International Journal of Physical Distribution & Logistics Management, 25(2), 20–38.

Wuppertal-Institut für Klima. Umwelt, Energie (1997). Zukunftsfähiges Deutschland – ein Beitrag zu einer global nachhaltigen Entwicklung. Basel, Switzerland: Birkhäuser.

Xiang, X., Yang, Q., Zhou, J., & Wang, R. (2009). Eco-industrial park planning method research and prospect. Environmental Science & Technology, 1, 32.

Xiao, X. & Cai, J. (2006). Monitoring and diagnosis based on multi-agent system model. Micro-Computer Information, 212-214.

Xin, Z., Lu, X., & Tang, Y. (1999). A study on management information system for environmental protection industry in Tianjin. Urban Environment & Urban Ecology, 12(6), 42–44.

Xu, X., & Roland, K. G. (1995). Building market intelligence systems for environment scanning. Logistics Information Management, 8(2), 22–29. doi:10.1108/09576059510084975

Yue, C. Y., & Li, H. (1998). Multi-attribute evaluation for environment, resource and sustainable development. Monitoring and Assessment, 12, 28–30.

Zah, R., Böni, H., Gauch, M., Hischier, R., Lehmann, M., & Wäger, P. (2007). Ökobilanz von Energieprodukten: Ökologische Bewertung von Biotreibstoffen (Final Report). St. Gallen, Switzerland: EMPA.

Zarnekow, R., Brenner, W., & Pilgram, U. (2006). Integrated Information Management, Applying Successful Industrial Concepts in IT. Berlin, Germany: Springer.

Zee, J.T.M, & Van Der; Jong, B. D. (1999). Alignment is nor enough: integrating business and information technology management with the balanced business scorecard. Journal of Management Information Systems, 16(2), 137–156.

Zhan, J., & Gao, L. (2004). Multi-agent technology in advanced manufacturing. Beijing: the Application of Scientific Publishers.

Zhao, T., Qi, X., & Man, Z. (2007). An intelligent control hydropower system based on multi-agent theory. Data Science Journal, 6, S435–S440. doi:10.2481/dsj.6.S435

Zheng, L., Hui, C., Folan, P., Potter, D., & Browne, J. (2007). RFID-based Information Management in the Automotive Plastic Recycling Industry. In J. Marx Gómez, M. Sonnenschein, M. Müller, H. Welsch, & C. Rautenstrauch (Eds.), Information Technologies in Environmental Engineering, ITEE 2007, Third International ICSC Symposium (pp. 397-408). Berlin, Heidelberg: Springer.

Zhong, S. (2007). Eco-industrial Park Construction and Management. Beijing, China: People's Publishing House.

Zhou, F. (2009). Study on the implementation of green supply chain management in textile enterprises. Journal of Sustainable Development, 2(1), 75–79.

Zhou, J. & Sun, Y. (2003). The Distributed Control System Based on Multi-Agent Technology. Micro Computer Information, 15-16.

Zimmermann, H. J. (1987). Fuzzy Sets, Decision Making, and Expert Systems. Boston: Kluwer.

Zuber-Skerrit, O. (1991). Action Research for Change and Development. Aldershot: Gower Publishing.

About the Contributors

Frank Teuteberg has been head of the Research Group in Accounting and Information Systems, which is part of the Institute of Information Management and Corporate Governance (IMU) at the University of Osnabrück since 2008. In 1996 he received his degree in Business Administration with focus on Information Systems from Georg-August-Universität Göttingen/Germany. From 1996 to 2001 he worked as a research assistant to Prof. Dr. Karl Kurbel (holder of the Chair in Information Systems) at Europa-Universität Frankfurt (Oder), where he took up a postdoctoral position after his doctoral graduation in May 2001. From April 2004 to October 2007 Frank Teuteberg held a junior professorship of Business Administration/E-Business and Information Systems at the University of Osnabrück. He teaches at Virtual Global University (www.vg-u.de) and is a regular visiting professor at ESCEM (www.escem.fr) in Tours/Poitiers (France). Frank Teuteberg was the leader of a subproject on Mobile Supply Chain Management (run from April 2004 to the end of 2007) as part of the joint project "Mobile Internet Business" (www.mib.uni-ffo.de) which was funded more than 2 million Euros by the Federal Ministry of Education and Research. He has published more than 100 scientific papers, many of which have appeared in leading German and international journals. His main research interests are Semantic Business Process Management, Sustainable Supply Chain Management, Corporate Environmental Management Information Systems and IT Risk Management.

Jorge Marx Gómez studied Computer Engineering and Industrial Engineering at the University of Applied Sciences Berlin (Technische Fachhochschule). He was a lecturer and researcher at Otto-von-Guericke-Universität Magdeburg where he also obtained a PhD degree in Business Information Systems with a thesis on "Computer-based Approaches to Forecast Returns of Scrapped Products to Recycling". In 2004 he received his postdoctoral lecture qualification (Habilitation) from Otto-von-Guericke-Universität Magdeburg with a professorial dissertation on "Automated Environmental Reporting through Material Flow Networks". From 2002 to 2003 he was a Visiting Professor for Business Information Systems at the Technical University of Clausthal. In 2005 he became a Full Professor of Business Information Systems at Carl von Ossietzky University Oldenburg. He is head of the department of Business Informatics (Very Large Business Applications). Jorge Marx Gómez teaches at Virtual Global University (www.vg-u.de). His personal research interests include Environmental Management Information Systems, Material Flow Management Systems, Federated ERP-Systems, Enterprise Systems Engineering, Business Information Systems in Higher Education, Enterprise Tomography, Environmental Data Warehousing, Recycling Program Planning, Disassembly Planning and Control and Life Cycle Assessment. Jorge Marx Gómez is a member of the following associations and groups: German Association of Computer Science (Gesellschaft für Informatik e.V. – GI), OFFIS e.V. (Oldenburg Institute of Informatics), SAP

Roundtable for Business Intelligence, German Association of University Professors and Lecturers (Deutscher Hochschulverband – DHV), German Forum of Interoperability (DFI), German Oracle Users Group e.V. (DOAG). He also serves as a reviewer and expert in the DAAD selection committee for Latin-American research proposals.

***

Cigdem Akkaya has been working as a researcher and PhD student at the Chair for Information Systems at Technische Universität München (TUM) since August 2008. She received her B.Sc. Degree in Computer Engineering from Middle East Technical University Ankara/Turkey in 1999. From 1999 to 2001 she worked as a research assistant at Middle East Technical University, where she received her MBA Degree in 2001. During her 5 years of experience at Siemens Business Services she has managed various projects. Her main research interests include eGovernment, Process and Project Management.

Irene Antoni-Komar is a project coordinator and research assistant. Currently, she is working on the research project "WENKE2 – Transitions towards Sustainable Consumption – Energy, Alimentation" at Carl von Ossietzky University Oldenburg/Germany, Department of Business Administration, Economics and Law. The project is funded by the German Federal Ministry of Education and Research. Antoni-Komar lectured on Fashion and Aesthetics at the Technical University of Darmstadt. From March 2006 to August 2007 she was the coordinator for the Oldenburg research project „OSSENA – Alimentation Quality as Quality of Life". Her research foci are: cultural approach in economics, theory of social practices, sustainable consumption.

Hans-Knud Arndt received a Diploma in Business Administration from the University of Hamburg in 1990. He completed his PhD thesis on environmental information systems at Humboldt University of Berlin in 1997. From 1997 to the end of 2004 he was an Assistant Professor of Information Systems at Humboldt University. Since December 2004 Hans-Knud Arndt has been a Full Professor of Business Informatics at Otto-von-Guericke-University Magdeburg. Hans-Knud Arndt has conducted research projects in the areas of management information systems, as well as eco-balancing and environmental cost accounting. His list of publications includes books and papers on related topics.

Paulina Arroyo is a PhD candidate in Administration at HEC Montréal, a research assistant at the CMA International Centre for Studies of Business Processes, and a part-time lecturer of management accounting at HEC Montréal. She holds an MBA from HEC Montréal, a graduate diploma in Finance from the University of California, Berkeley Extension, and a Bachelor of Business Administration from the University of Chile. Her research interest is management accounting and control, with particular emphasis on management accounting and control change, environmental and social management accounting, and performance measurement systems. She has presented at various conferences across Canada and has participated actively in different research projects. Her doctoral thesis seeks to contribute a new conceptual framework that links sustainability, stakeholders and management control change through an institutional approach.

Marina Beermann works as a project coordinator on the research project "Northwest 2050: Perspectives for Climate Adaptive Innovation Processes in the Metropolitan Region Bremen – Oldenburg" in the research cluster "food industry" at Carl von Ossietzky University Oldenburg/Germany. The project is funded by the German Federal Ministry of Education and Research. After completing her studies in Oldenburg/Germany, Siena/Italy and Basel/Switzerland with a diploma in economics, she started as a doctoral candidate in business administration. Her research interests include resilience, climate adaptation strategies and sustainable business models.

Malcolm Bertoni is a lecturer at the School of Computing and Information Systems, University of Tasmania. He is a member of the logistics research group in the School working on supply chain technologies. He has qualifications in management, marine science, economics and computing. His current PhD research is in the logistics domain.

Vitoantonio Bevilacqua was born in Bari (Italy) in 1969 and obtained both the Bachelor Degree in Electronic Engineering and the PhD in Electrical Engineering from Polytechnic of Bari in 1996 and 2000 respectively. He is currently an Assistant Professor in Computing Systems at the Department of Electrical and Electronic Engineering of Polytechnic of Bari where he teaches C/C++ Programming, Expert Systems and Medical Informatics. Since 1996 he has been working and investigating in the field of image processing, neural networks, evolutionary algorithms, and hybrid expert systems. The main applications of his research are in real world, in biometry, in medicine and recently in bioinformatics and systems biology. In 2000 he was involved as Visiting Researcher in an EC-funded TMR (Trans-Mobility of Researchers) network (ERB FMRX-CT97-0127) called CAMERA (CAd Modeling Environment from Range Images) and worked in the field of geometric feature extraction and 3D objects reconstruction. He has published more than 60 papers in refereed journals, books, international conferences' proceedings and has chaired several sessions such as Speech Recognition, Biomedical Informatics, Intelligent Image Processing and Bioinformatics at international conferences. He won the Best Paper Award at the International Conference on Intelligent Computing held in Shanghai (ICIC 2008) and is Program Chair of ICIC 2009 held in Ulsan (Korea) in September 2009.

Jörg Bremer studied Environmental Informatics at Carl von Ossietzky University Oldenburg, Germany. In 2006 he received his degree in computing science with a thesis in the field of agent based simulation of household energy consumption in decentralized scenarios. Since 2006 he has been working as a research assistant to Prof. Sonnenschein (holder of the chair in Environmental Informatics) at the University of Oldenburg and at the OFFIS Institute for Computer Science in Oldenburg. In addition, he joined the department of Business Information Systems as a research assistant to Prof. Marx Gómez in 2009. Since 2007 Jörg Bremer has been teaching as an assistant lecturer at the University of Oldenburg. His teaching topics are advanced Java technologies and decentralized energy systems. He has worked on several projects in the field of decentralized energy resources. His main research interests are machine learning, environmental modelling and simulation and smart computing. Jörg Bremer has published several papers in leading conferences on environmental management, including the EnviroInfo conference and the R' World Congress.

Raul Carlson made his academic career within the Swedish competence center CPM (Center for environmental assessment of Product and Material systems) at Chalmers University of Technology in Gothenburg between 1996 and 2008. Between 1996 and 1998 he was project manager for the build-up of a joint academic and industrial environmental life cycle assessment database, and between 1998 and

2001 he was one of the strategic research leaders of the competence center. Between 2001 and 2008 he was head of the research department 'Industrial Environmental Informatics'. In parallel with managing the department Raul Carlson finalized his PhD in Environmental Sciences in 2006. In 2008 Raul Carlson left the university to start his own spin-off company eco2win, and he also took up a part-time position as senior researcher at the Swedish non-profit IT-research institute Viktoria in Gothenburg. Since 1998 Raul Carlson has been participating as an expert in the international standardization of environmental management systems (ISO/TC 207), with special focus on environmental information and data management aspects. Since 1998 Raul Carlson has also participated in several industrially focused European projects. Raul Carlson published ca. 25 papers in reviewed scientific journals and around 30 technical reports. Also, he contributed to 5 books in his field.

Edward T. Chen is a professor of Management Information Systems in the Operations and Information Systems Department at University of Massachusetts Lowell. He has published his research articles in scholarly journals such as *Information & Management, Journal of Computer Information Systems, Project Management, Comparative Technology Transfer and Society, Journal of International Information Management, and International Journal of Innovation and Learning.* Dr. Chen has been serving as vice-president, journal editor, board director, editorial reviewer, track chair, and session chair of many professional associations and conferences. He has received the Irwin Distinguished Paper Award at the Southwestern Federation of Administrative Disciplines conference and the Best Paper Award at the International Conference on Accounting and Information Technology.

Stephen Y. Chen is an Associate Professor of Information Technology at York University where he has been since 2001. He received his PhD in Robotics from Carnegie Mellon in 1999 under the supervision of Dr. Stephen F. Smith for a thesis focusing on the role of common components in genetic algorithms and heuristic search. His current research interests include financial market modeling, swarm-based algorithms, numerical optimization, and real-world applications. This research has been supported by two NSERC Discovery Grants.

Iskra Dukovska-Popovska is an Assistant Professor at the Centre for Logistics, Aalborg University. She holds a B.Sc. in Mechanical Engineering and a M.Sc. in Industrial Engineering from the Faculty of Mechanical Engineering, University 'Sts. Cyril and Methodius' in Skopje, Macedonia, and a PhD in Manufacturing Strategic Management from Aalborg University, Denmark. She has published articles in the field of Manufacturing Strategy Management, Supply Chain Strategy Management, interaction of strategic management, contingencies and performance, and human aspects in strategy design. She is a member of the International Manufacturing Strategy Survey project. Besides the above mentioned areas, her research focus is extending towards environmental aspects of logistics and supply chain management, and the use of RFID in such context.

Swantje Eigner-Thiel is a psychologist working in the field of ecological psychology. Since 2009 she has been involved in the research project "Sustainable use of bioenergy: bridging climate protection, nature conservation and society" at the Interdisciplinary Centre of Sustainable Development, which is part of the University of Göttingen/Germany. Within this project, she is coordinating the sub-project "Development and testing of assessment criteria and methods" (www.bioenergie.uni-goettingen.de). From 2000 to 2008 she worked as research assistant in the action research project "The bioenergy village Jühnde". Swantje Eigner-Thiel did her doctoral graduation in 2004, analyzing people's motivation to change over to biomass as a renewable energy source for their heating supply system, as exemplified by the village of Jühnde/Germany (www.bioenergiedorf.info/). Furthermore, within that pilot project she did research on motivation and communication strategies, environmental awareness, community feeling, self-efficacy conviction and well-being. From 2006 until today, she was involved in the scientific attendance of the motivation processes of further local community projects within the district of Göttingen/Germany. Among other issues, she analyzed the motivation for the use of bioenergy. From 1998 to 2000 she worked as a research assistant to Prof. Kruse-Graumann in the division of ecological psychology at Fernuniversität Hagen and for the German Advisory Council on Global Change (WBGU). Her further research interests are perceptional, cognitive, and organizational psychology within the field of sustainable development.

Flavio Elias Gomes de Deus received his BS in Electrical Engineering from Universidade Federal do Goiás in 1998, his MS in Electrical Engineering from Universidade de Brasília in 2001, and a PhD in Electrical Engineering from Universidade de Brasília in 2006. In 2004/2005 he was also a Visiting Scholar in Information Science and Telecommunications at the University of Pittsburgh, USA. In 2007, he was Coordinator of the Network and Support Services unit of the Data Processing Center at Universidade de Brasília. In 2008, he worked in software development projects, primarily on the following themes: electronic document management system, use case description and web services development. He is currently an Associate Professor at the Department of Electrical Engineering, Universidade de Brasília, Brazil. His research interests include information technologies, wireless and sensors networks, fault tolerant systems, software development process, and other related topics.

Marina G. Erechtchoukova is an Assistant Professor of Information Technology in the Faculty of Liberal Arts and Professional Studies, York University. She has been affiliated with York University, Canada since 2001. She received her BS and MS degrees in Applied Mathematics and a PhD in Computer Science. She is an author of more than 55 refereed research papers. Her research focuses on applications of information technology for sustainable development. Her scientific interests include optimization of environmental monitoring, data-driven and model-driven decision support, sustainable environmental resource management, environmental assessment, simulation modeling, environmental modeling and assessment under uncertainty.

Koray Erek received his diploma in Industrial Engineering from the Berlin Institute of Technology and the Haas School of Business at Berkeley (CA, USA) in 2006. During his studies he completed internships at Daimler AG, Siemens AG and Pirelli Tyres Ltd (UK). Since 2007 he has been working as research assistant to Prof. Dr. Rüdiger Zarnekow at the Chair of Information and Communication Management at the Berlin Institute of Technology. His research focuses on the areas of Green IT, ecological sustainability of information management and IT Sustainability.

Angela Fleury is an associate professor at Fundação Dom Cabral, Brazil. Her research interests are Information Technology Role and Knowledge Management, Leadership and Sustainability. Some key words are Leadership, Complex Systems, and Sustainability. Professionally, she specialized on training and consultancy in Information Technology Role and Organizational Knowledge Management. Angela has published many articles nationally and internationally.

Andreas Gadatsch is a professor of business information systems at the department of business administration at the Bonn-Rhein-Sieg University of Applied Sciences in Sankt Augustin, Germany. He has several years of experience as a consultant, project manager and IT manager. His main research fields are IT-Controlling, medical controlling, business process management, workflow management and ERP software (esp. SAP®). He published more than 160 papers. He is the author or co-author of 14 books; some have been published in a number of editions or have been translated into foreign languages.

Jutta Geldermann is a Professor for Production and Logistics at the University of Göttingen/Germany. She received her diploma in Industrial Engineering and Management and her PhD in Business Administration from the University of Karlsruhe/Germany (TH). From 1995 to 2006 she worked as a research assistant and assistant professor at the Institute for Industrial Production (IIP)/French-German Institute for Environmental research (DFIU/IFARE) at the University of Karlsruhe/Germany. Her major research areas are multicriteria decision aiding, development of emission reduction strategies on regional, national and supranational levels and industrial risk management. She is head of the working group "Decision Theory and Practice" in the German Society of Operations Research (GOR). Currently, she is significantly involved in the integrated research project "Sustainable use of bioenergy: bridging climate protection, nature conservation and society" (www.bioenergie.uni-goettingen.de), which is funded by the Ministry for Science and Culture of Lower Saxony and the Volkswagen Foundation.

Paulina Golinska has been working as an assistant professor at Poznan University of Technology (Poland) since September 2008. She received her PhD degree from the Faculty of Computing and Management at Poznan University of Technology, working in the field of "construction and exploitation of machines" with a specialization on "organization of production systems". She received the degree of "Executive Master of Business Administration" by taking part in a joint program at the University of Warsaw and the University of Illinois at Urbana Champaigne (USA). Her current fields of research include: sustainable production planning and control, closed loop supply chain management, the distributed and artificial intelligent application for manufacturing systems. She is the author and co-author of over 60 papers published in books, journals and conference proceedings about application of crisis management procedures in manufacturing systems, planning of production in conditions of uncertainty, material flow management in closed loop supply chains and application of artificial intelligence techniques for production planning and control. Since 2004 Paulina Golinska has been advising Polish Small and Medium Enterprises, as well as R+D Institutions on application for EU funds. She has prepared over 20 feasibilities studies for projects financed by European Funds.

Henner Graubitz is a research associate and PhD candidate. While working as an undergraduate research assistant he finished his diploma thesis in Economy at Humboldt University of Berlin in 2003. After managing a university research project and working as an IT consultant in Sydney/Australia, he became a member of the research group "Management Information Systems" at the University of Magdeburg/Germany. His PhD thesis is about automatic derivation of Balanced Scorecards from financial key performance indicators, which also summarizes his research interests.

Christian Grünwald has been working in the field of product data management at the IT department of Volkswagen AG since the fall of 2007. In January 2004 he graduated in Business Informatics from TU Clausthal/ Germany. Afterwards he started working on a doctorate supervised by Prof. Jorge

Marx Gómez of Carl von Ossietzky University Oldenburg. During this time Christian Grünwald was involved in the organization of scientific conferences, e.g. as a member of the program committee and session chair at the ITEE conference in Magdeburg in 2005. Furthermore, he has authored 10 publications in the area of Environmental Business Informatics. In 2009 he received his doctoral degree from the University of Oldenburg.

Karoll Haussler Carneiro Ramos received a B.Sc. degree in Business Administration from Universidade de Brasília (UNB) in December 2006. She is specialized on Public Administration. In December 2009 she received her M.Sc. degree in Electrical Engineering from UNB. She worked for some Public Administration Departments as a consulter and trainer for Business Process Management. She is currently a researcher at the Department of Electrical Engineering of UNB, Brazil. Her research interests include strategic planning, information technologies, enterprise architecture design, component business model, IT human resource, management of change.

Martina Hesse received her degree in Forest Sciences from Dresden University of Technology/ Germany in December 2008. Since February 2009 she has been working as a research assistant to Prof. Dr. Jutta Geldermann, who holds the Chair of Production and Logistics at the University of Göttingen/ Germany. She is involved in the sub-project "Development and testing of assessment criteria and methods" of the project "Sustainable use of bioenergy: bridging climate protection, nature conservation and society" (www.bioenergie.uni-goettingen.de). Her main research interest is the multicriteria assessment of cultivation methods of bioenergy plants with focus on fast growing tree species.

Hans-Henrik Hvolby (hhh@production.aau.dk) is a professor at the Centre for Logistics at Aalborg University in Denmark and a visiting professor at the University of South Australia. He holds a PhD in Manufacturing Information Systems, has published more than 100 peer-reviewed papers and serves as an associate European editor of two international journals and as an editorial board member of 5 international journals. He has been the originator of or a partner in 13 research projects, raising national research funding to a value of 14.7 million DKK (2 million €) and European research funding to a value of 14 million DKK (1.9 million €). He has organized more than 30 seminars and workshops, e.g. the SMESME International Conference in 2001. He accepted to organize the MITIP International Conference in 2010. He has published 97 peer-reviewed publications since 1993. His research areas include manufacturing information systems (MRP, ERP, APS, VMI), Logistics, Supply Chain Planning, Supply Chain Integration, Value Chain Management, Order Management (BPR).

Jens Ibendorf has been the project coordinator of the project "Sustainable use of bioenergy: bridging climate protection, nature conservation and society" at the Interdisciplinary Centre for Sustainable Development, University of Göttingen/Germany since March 2009. In 2003 he received his degree in Geoecology with focus on carbon storage in arctic and alpine soils from the University of Potsdam/Germany. From 2005 to 2009 Jens Ibendorf held the position of project coordinator for the junior research group "Ecosystem Dynamics" at the Botanical Institute of Ernst-Moritz-Arndt-University Greifswald/ Germany. His main interest is research coordination in interdisciplinary and international groups with a focus on sustainability, ecology and society.

Francesca Intini graduated in Management Engineering at Politecnico di Bari (Italy), specializing in environmental management of production systems. Currently, she is a PhD student in Industrial and Innovation Engineering at Università della Basilicata. Her research topics include the assessment of the environmental, social and economic life cycle of products and services, Carbon Footprint Management and sustainability reporting to companies, as well as application of operational research techniques for the solution of optimal problems.

Ralf Isenmann joined the Fraunhofer Institute for Systems and Innovation Research (ISI), Karlsruhe, in 2008. He is an associate professor and a senior lecturer at the Faculty 07, Economics and Business Studies, of the University of Bremen and a senior researcher at artec | Research Center for Sustainability Studies, University of Bremen. In 2002 he gained his PhD from the University of Kaiserslautern with a thesis on environmental economics and management. In 2006 he acquired a postdoctoral lecture qualification (venia legendi) in business administration and management studies from the University of Bremen with a professorial dissertation (Habilitation) on internet-based sustainability reporting. He teaches corporate communications, management of innovation, sustainability management, and industrial ecology at the University of Bremen and technology management at the University of Kassel. His research interests are the interfaces between sustainability management, information management, and innovation management. His publication record includes more than 170 contributions: 8 books, 3 special issues, and more than 10 papers in academic journals, as e.g. *Journal of Industrial Ecology, Business Strategy & the Environment, Eco-Management and Auditing, International Journal of Sustainable Development, Sustainable Development, and International Journal of Technology Intelligence and Planning*. He studied Industrial Engineering (Master of Business and Engineering (MBE)/MBA for Science and Technology) at the University of Kaiserslautern where he also received a professional teaching and training degree in Educational Science.

Andrea Jörg studied Economic Mathematics at the University of Kaiserslautern and received her PhD (Dr. rer. pol.) from the Technical University of Kaiserslautern in 2006. The subject of her thesis was: "Economic growth and environment – an environmental implication". In her research she mainly focuses on the economic theory of economic growth, environmental economics and sustainability. She was significantly involved in the creation of a water framework directive monitoring program in connection with the sustainability strategy for Rhineland-Palatinate.

Ana Carolina Kalume Maranhão has been part of the Research Group "Núcleo de Multimídia e Internet" at the Department of Electrical Engineering, which is part of the Faculdade de Tecnologia at Universidade de Brasília since August 2009. In 2003 she received her degree in Communication with focus on journalism studies from Centro Universitário de Brasília (Uniceub). In 2004 she received her specialization title in Bioethics from Universidade de Brasília, and in 2008 she gained her degree in master communication from Universidade de Brasília. She worked as a reporter for Correio Brazilienze and Journal of Brasília, and as a press advisor in Brazil, e.g. for the Ministry of Health. Her research interests include Information and Communication Technologies, Enterprise Architecture Design, IT Governance, models of learning in technology.

Mehruz Kamal is an Assistant Professor at the Department of Computer Science at The College at Brockport, State University of New York. She earned her PhD in Information Technology at the

University of Nebraska at Omaha in 2009. Her current research interests include IT adoption in small businesses, IT for development, and knowledge networking. Her research work has been presented at various prestigious Information Systems conferences such as AMCIS, HICSS, and MWAIS. Her work has also been published in *International Journal of E-Business Research, Journal of Enterprise Information Management*, and other proceedings.

Peter A. Khaiter is an Assistant Professor of Information Technology in the Faculty of Liberal Arts and Professional Studies, York University, Canada. He has been affiliated with York University since 2000. Prior to that, he worked as an Associate Professor in the Department of Economic Informatics at Rostov State Economic Academy and in the Department of Economic Theory at Rostov State University (Russian Federation). In 1995-1996 he held a position of Professor and Chair in the Department of Economic Theory and Information Technology at Rostov Institute of Management and Marketing. He received his BS and MS degrees in Economic Cybernetics, MS in Environmental Studies and PhD in Mathematical Modeling/Information Technology. He is an author of more than 60 research papers. His scientific interests are in the areas of mathematical modeling and optimal control of complex systems, mathematical and ecological stability, information systems for environmental monitoring, sustainable development and management, and environmental economics.

Martin Klenke studied Geography at the University of Bremen. He earned the degree "Diplom-Geograph" in 1995. From 1995 to 1999 he worked as a research fellow at the chair for Geohydrology and Geoinformatics at Friedrich-Schiller-University Jena. In 1999, Martin Klenke received the doctoral degree from the School of Chemical and Earth Sciences at the University of Jena. From 1999 to 2004 he worked as postdoctoral research fellow in the Bathymetry Working Group of the Alfred Wegener Institute (AWI) for Polar and Marine Research in Bremerhaven. In 2004 he took the position of technical project lead at the Coordination Center PortalU in Hannover, managing the operation and further development of the PortalU software systems. Since 2009, he has been working as an advisor for the Lower Saxon Ministry of Environment and Climate Protection in Hanover. He is responsible for the advancement of Lower Saxony's environmental information systems with regard to the EU-INSPIRE and Environmental Information directives.

Lutz M. Kolbe (born 1966) completed an apprenticeship in banking and received his degree in Information Systems from the Technical University of Braunschweig, Germany. From 1994 to 1997 he worked as a research assistant to Prof. Dr. Walter Brenner at the Technical University of Freiberg, Germany and earned his PhD in Business Administration. Subsequently, he lead various divisions of IT Management at Deutsche Bank AG, his last post being that of Managing Director reporting to the CIO in New York (USA). In 2002 he moved on to the Institute of Information Systems at the University of St. Gallen, Switzerland, as head of several competence centers. He was also a visiting scholar at the University of Rhode Island and at New York University (USA). In June 2006 he completed his post-doctoral thesis and was appointed to associate level. Since 2007, Lutz M. Kolbe has been holding the Chair of Information Management at Georg-August-University Goettingen, Germany. He has published more than 60 refereed academic papers. His main research interests are IT Security, IT Sustainability, IT Performance Measurement and IT Innovation Management.

Stefanie Konstantinidis works for the Coordination Center PortalU at the Lower Saxony Ministry of Environment and Climate Protection. PortalU (www.portalu.de) is the German Environmental Information Portal for public environmental information. The central portal is an initiative of German environmental administration authorities at both federal and state level. Mrs. Konstantinidis studied Geography at the universities of Göttingen and Bonn (Germany) and received her diploma with focus on hydrological modeling from the University of Bonn in 1999. From 1999 to 2000 she worked as a research assistant to Prof. Dr. Bernd Diekkrueger at the University of Bonn, being involved in the European Commission Interreg-IIC project IRMA Sponge (www.irma-sponge.org). Afterwards she worked at the University of Cologne as a lecturer and research assistant to Prof. Dr. Karl Schneider. Since 2007 Stefanie Konstantinidis has been responsible for content quality and marketing at the Coordination Center PortalU.

Helmut Krcmar has been holding the Chair for Information Systems at the Department of Informatics at Technische Universität München (TUM) since 2002. He is a member of the Department of Informatics and the Faculty of Business Administration as well as a member of the "Carl von Linde-Akademie". Since 2004 he has been a member of the Program Faculty of the Elite Graduate Program „Finance and Information Management (FIM)" within the Elitenetzwerk Bayern. Until May 2007 he was Academic Director of the Executive Training Program ¡communicate!. Since January 2004 he has been a Board Member of the Center for Digital Technology and Management (CDTM) at Technische Universität München. Krcmar is the founder of Informations- und TechnologieManagement Beratungsgesellschaft (ITM) and co-founder of several spin-offs out of the academic environment. His research interests include Information and Knowledge Management, IT-enabled value webs, Service Management, Computer Supported Cooperative Work, Information Systems in Health Care and eGovernment.

Fred Kruse has been head of the Coordination Centre PortalU at the Lower Saxony Ministry of Environment and Climate Protection. In 1982 he received his degree as physicist with focus on theoretical and numerical physics from the University of Bremen. He worked on the subject of elementary particles in astrophysical phenomena and received a doctoral degree in 1987. From 1987 to 1990 Fred Kruse worked as postdoctoral research fellow in the domain of climate modeling at the Alfred Wegener Institute (AWI) for Polar and Marine Research in Bremerhaven. From 1990 to 1995 he worked at the Regional Computing Centre of Lower Saxony in Hanover. Since 1995 he has been working at the Lower Saxony Ministry of Environment and Climate Protection. As project manager for PortalU, Fred Kruse is responsible for the coordination of the PortalU project partners (German federal government and 16 federal states) and the presentation of the project to international partners. H represents the Coordination Centre in the INSPIRE process as a technical expert for metadata.

Silvana Kühtz graduated in Engineering from Politecnico di Bari (Italy). From 1992 onwards, she attended the Imperial College of Science, Technology and Medicine, University of London (UK) to conduct experimental research, completing her studies with a PhD degree and a diploma in Hydrodynamics in 1996. She was appointed Assistant Professor at Università della Basilicata, faculty of Engineering, Department of Environmental Physics and Engineering, Potenza (Italy), where she gave lectures in *Turbomachinery, Applied Energetics, Regional Economic Policy, Economics and Management of Energy Sources, Renewable Energy Sources* and *Energy Use of Water* and leads the course *Language Future and Possibility*. She has been a PhD tutor since 2007. Her research topics include energy resource management, energy-economy-environment interactions, input-output techniques and LCA, environmental certifications, greening behaviours and marketing, carbon footprint, barriers to innovative behaviours. She has published books and papers in international journals and has been invited to contribute to conferences on these topics.

Helmut Lessing has significant experience in the conception and acquisition of interdisciplinary, national and international projects. Among the multitude of projects led by Helmut Lessing, the software design and the conceptual development of the meta-information system 'Environmental Data Catalogue' is especially important. Nowadays, this widely used system is known as "PortalU". Moreover, Helmut Lessing coordinated the development of the 'European Environmental Data Catalogue' and established and led the EU-Topic-Center ETC/CDS located in Hanover for several years. He was substantially involved in the conception, acquisition, and realization of both the IP 'renew' and the interdisciplinary 'Phytoremediation' project supported by the BMBF, which he finished successfully in 2006. The development and empirical evaluation of several fuel cell systems are essentially based on his work. Helmut Lessing has been the chairman of several work groups on both state and federal level. He was a representative of the Federal Council of Germany for the subject area European Environmental Agency, Environmental Information and Observation Network. Thus, he possesses comprehensive knowledge in the field of the coordination of interdisciplinary, industry-oriented developments on both national and international level.

Xueqiang Lu has been deputy director of the Tianjin Academy of Environmental Sciences, China since August 2007. In 2005, he obtained his doctoral degree in environmental studies from Nagoya University, Japan. From 1995 to 2001 he worked at the Tianjin Academy of Environmental Sciences. From 2006 to 2007, he took up a postdoctoral position at the University of Auckland, New Zealand. Dr. Xueqiang Lu has published more than 30 scientific papers and two books in English, Japanese and Chinese. His research interests include environmental geochemistry, environmental engineering and environmental modeling.

Rinaldo C. Michelini, full professor at the school of Engineers of the University of Genova, Italy. ASME Fellow, Member of IFIP WG 5.1 (CIME) and WG 5.5 (COVE), SCS (Senior), Russian Academy of Engineering (Correspondent), etc. Author/co-author of more than 500 technical papers/chapters/books in the areas of integrated design, robotics, expert automation, industrial diagnostics.

Anneke Minke majored in Information Management and Information Technologies. In 2006, she passed with distinction and was awarded the promotion price of the partner companies of the University of Hildesheim. Since then, she has been research assistant with the group "economics and operations research" at the University of Hildesheim. In addition to teaching and lecturing, she is currently working on her doctoral thesis. In her research, she focuses on change mining and dynamic market development. Therefore, she is interested in data mining techniques and how they can be applied to different areas such as market research and environmental monitoring. Her research results have been presented at several international conferences.

Andreas Möller is head of the working group "New Media and Environmental Informatics" and a member of the Institute for Environmental and Sustainability Communication at Leuphana University Lüneburg, Germany. Also, he is head of the Department of Sustainability Sciences at Leuphana

University. Andreas Möller studied Computer Science at the universities of Passau, Kiel and Hamburg (diploma degree in Computer Science 1995, PhD 2000). Since 2002 he has been Professor for New Media and Environmental Informatics at Leuphana University. Since starting with a student research project in 1993, he has been working on new concepts for material flow analysis (Material flow networks (MFNs), MFN-based life-cycle assessment, MFN-based cost accounting, corporate and product-related carbon footprinting etc.). Based on his concepts, he developed the material and energy flow analysis tool 'Umberto' in cooperation with colleagues, which is one of the most important software systems in that field. Recent projects are "Komsa" (Optimization of material and energy flow systems, in particular "Verbund" optimization in chemical industry) and "Kuntikum" (Sustainable destination management in tourism industry). His main research areas are computer-based material and energy flow analysis and systems, application of these instruments in different fields like chemical industry or automotive industry, but also tourism industry and sustainability in higher education. In particular, he is focusing his attention on the relationship between new instruments in the field, communication, organizational learning and new standards.

Marlei Pozzebon is Associate Professor at HEC Montréal. Her research interests are the social, political and cultural aspects of technology transfer (global-local negotiation), local and sustainable development, creative cities/citizenships and inclusive finance. Some keywords of her research are structuration theory, critical discourse analysis, qualitative methods, and the use of theories of practice in information systems and international business research. Professionally, she specializes in training and consultancy in the business intelligence area. Marlei has published her articles at *Organization Studies, Journal of Management Studies, Information Technology and People, Journal of Information Technology, Journal of Strategic Information Systems and Journal of Global Management of Information Technology*, among others.

Sajda Qureshi is an Associate Professor at the Information Systems and Quantitative Analysis Department at the College of Information Science and Technology at the University of Nebraska at Omaha. She holds a PhD in Information Systems from the London School of Economics. She has over 60 publications in journals such as Group Decision and Negotiation, Information Infrastructure and Policy and Communications of the ACM, books published by Prentice Hall, Springer-Verlag, Chapman and Hall and North-Holland and conferences such as the ICIS and HICSS. She is currently the Editor-in-Chief of the Journal of Information and Technology for Development.

Luis Fernando Ramos Molinaro obtained a B.Sc. degree in Electrical Engineering from Universidade de Brasília (UNB) in 1979. In 1981 he received his M.Sc. degree in Electrical Engineering from Universidade Federal de Campinas. In 1991 he gained his PhD in Electrical Engineering from Universidade de São Paulo. He is currently Associate Professor II at the UNB, working on the following areas: telecommunications, video conferencing, education, communication networks, process management and management of IT organizations. He worked in consulting and training for Compaq, HP, Solectron, IBM, Brasil Telecom. His research interests include information technologies, information systems, software engineering, enterprise architecture design, modeling and integration, collaboration and networked and virtual organizations.

Barbara Rapp studied Environmental Informatics and received her Diploma in Computing Science from Carl von Ossietzky University Oldenburg, Germany, in 2006. Her thesis was in the field of agent based simulation of intelligent real-time pricing for decentralized energy production. She has worked at OFFIS Institute for Computer Science and is currently a research assistant to Prof. Dr. Michael Sonnenschein (holder of the chair in Environmental Informatics) and to Prof. Dr.-Ing. Jorge Marx Gómez (holder of the chair in Business Information Systems I) at the University of Oldenburg. Ms. Rapp teaches advanced Java technologies as well as decentralized energy systems at the University of Oldenburg. She has published several papers in leading conferences on environmental management, including the EnviroInfo conference and the R' World Congress. In addition she authored book chapters on e-learning and demand-side management. Her main scientific interests include pattern recognition, machine learning and multi-agent systems in the field of decentralized energy systems.

Roberto P. Razzoli, researcher at the PMAR Lab of the University of Genova, Italy, since 1993. His scientific activity is about eco-sustainable design, mobile and modular robots, industrial automation. He is author/co-author of more than one hundred publications.

Paolo Renna is an Assistant Professor at the Department of Environmental Engineering and Physics at the Engineering Faculty of Basilicata University (Italy). He received a PhD degree in Advanced Production Systems from Polytechnic of Bari. His academic research principally deals with the development of innovative negotiation and production planning in distributed environments and manufacturing scheduling in dynamic environment. Paolo Renna has published several research articles on Multi Agent Architecture design and testing by discrete event simulation in Business-to-Business environments. He is also a co-author of two research books about e-marketplaces and production planning in production networks. Moreover, he has developed coordination approaches in multi-plant production planning environment and innovative scheduling approaches in flexible and reconfigurable manufacturing systems.

Hedda Schattke works as a research assistant on the research project FAEN "Sustainable meat economy in Lower Saxony, Germany" at Carl von Ossietzky University Oldenburg/Germany. The focus of the project lies on developing sustainable communication and marketing strategies for the production of livestock products in Lower Saxony. The project is funded by the German Ministry for Science and Culture of Lower Saxony. As a doctoral candidate her research interests encompass strategic management and communication strategies, sustainable nutrition and intercultural management.

Meike Schmehl holds a diploma in Geoecology from the Technical University of Braunschweig/Germany. She was a research assistant at the department of "Environmental Systems Analysis" at the Institute of Geoecology, Technical University of Braunschweig, from 2003 to 2006 and was also a member of the research group "Sustainable Energy and Material Flow Management" at the Scientific Center for Environmental Research, University of Kassel/Germany. There she worked in research projects on the life cycle assessment of material systems based on renewable resources and on the material flow analysis of the sustainable use of biomass for energy. In June 2007 she joined the University of Göttingen/Germany as a research assistant. Since 2009 she has been working in the sub-project "Development and testing of assessment criteria and methods" of the project "Sustainable use of bioenergy: bridging climate protection, nature conservation and society" (www.bioenergie.uni-goettingen.de). Her PhD thesis (in progress) is on multi-criteria analysis of renewable resources.

Nils-Holger Schmidt was born in Hanau in 1981. He graduated from Georg-Buechner-Gymnasium (high school) in Bad Vilbel in 2000. After a period of civilian service he studied Information Systems at Georg-August-University Göttingen, Germany, where he received his diploma in 2006. During his studies he completed internships at Dresdner Bank and Horváth & Partners and was involved in the international student organization AIESEC. After his graduation from university he worked eight months for a Peruvian travel agency in Lima. Since 2007 Nils-Holger Schmidt has been a research assistant to Prof. Dr. Lutz M. Kolbe at the Chair of Information Management at Georg-August-University Göttingen. His main research interests are Green IT, Eco-oriented Information Management and IT Sustainability.

Maha Shakir has been an Assistant Professor of Information Systems (IS) at Zayed University UAE since 2004. From 1999-2004 she worked as an IS instructor and then as a Lecturer at both Massey University and The University of Auckland, New Zealand. From 1986 to 1997 she practiced the design, coordination, and implementations of many construction projects. Maha Shakir's primary research areas are IS strategy, strategic management of IS, and the implementation of enterprise system applications (e.g., ERP, SCM, and CRM). Her current work involves studies of enterprise systems in the Arab Gulf countries, e-procurement in the petroleum industry in the Middle East, Arab women adoption of IT, and the role of IS in developing business sustainability. Her publications appeared in *MIS Quarterly Executive, University of Auckland Business Review, Journal of Cases on Information Technology, International Journal of Information Systems and Change Management, Journal of Decision Systems*, ERP edited books, Laudon & Laudon MIS textbook, and several international IS conferences. Maha's case study "E-Procurement through Supply Chain Integration: Reaching out to SMBs" won First Prize in the Society for Information Management's 2006 Paper Awards Competition [www.simnet.org]. The case was developed in collaboration with Dr Graham Smith and Erkan Gulec.

Adson Silva Rocha received a B.Sc. degree in Computer Engineering from the Electrical and Computer Engineering School (EEEC) at Universidade Federal do Goiás (UFG)/Brazil in December 2005. In November 2008 he obtained his M.Sc. degree in Computer Engineering from the same institution while holding a scholarship from the National Council of Technological and Scientific Development (CNPQ – www.cnpq.br) and being part of a research team working with Electric Power Feeder Routing Optimization. He is currently a doctoral student of Electrical Engineering at Universidade de Brasília (UNB)/Brazil and works as a researcher in a Digital Television (DTV) project supported by CAPES (www.capes.gov.br), from which he receives a scholarship. From January 2005 to August 2009, Adson Silva Rocha worked as a Systems Analyst with professional experience in software development processes and quality assurance. His main research interests are Artificial Intelligence and Computational Optimization Methods.

Kenn Steger-Jensen gained a PhD in Enterprise Resource Planning (ERP) and Advanced Planning and Scheduling (APS) Information Systems from Aalborg University in 2004 and a M.Sc. degree in Industrial Management from Aalborg University in 2000. He has been Associate Professor of Supply Chain Integration at Aalborg University since 2004. His research interests are within supply chain planning and manufacturing planning and control theory in general. Working areas are within modeling and solving inter-organizational decision and KPI, planning, scheduling and optimization problems; information systems as APS, ERP, SFC, MES and integration. Lecturing across different master programs in areas as manufacturing planning and control theory, scheduling theory, shop floor control theory and systems, ERP systems, APS systems, IT systems development, design of IT systems, Management Sciences and Operational Research.

Paul Turner is an Associate Professor in the School of Computing & Information Systems at the University of Tasmania. He graduated from the University of London in 1992, completed a Masters degree in Information Systems and Technology in 1994 and was awarded his doctoral degree in 1999. Prior to moving to Australia, Paul was a visiting research fellow at the Universitaires Notre-Dame de la Paix in Belgium where he worked on a variety of European Commission contracts in the technology domain. His current research interests are in basic, applied and strategic systems approaches to e-health, forensic computing and e-business. Since 2001, Paul has published more than 100 peer-reviewed papers in academic journals, books and conferences and has been directly involved in raising research grants, consultancies and scholarships to a value of more than $5 million. Paul is currently Director, eHealth Services Research Group at the University of Tasmania.

Michael von Hauff is a full Professor of Economics and Economic Policy at the Technical University of Kaiserslautern. He studied Economics at the University of Augusta/Georgia, USA, and at the Universities of Stuttgart and Constance. He received his PhD (Dr. rer. pol.) in 1977 and received his postdoctoral lecture qualification from the University of Stuttgart in 1987. In 1995, he was a visiting professor to the University of Delhi/India. Since 2003, he has been a frequent guest lecturer at the Nanyang Technological University in Singapur and at the Institute of Economics/Yangon Myanmar. Michael von Hauff is a member of the editorial boards of several international journals, such as *Progress in Industrial Ecology – An International Journal* and *International Quarterly for Asian Studies*. Moreover, he is a member of several national and international organizations, including the European Academy of Sciences and Arts. In 2009 he received the German Environmentalist Award for his scientific contributions and work on behalf of raising the level of awareness with regard to sustainable development.

Juan Wen has been a sectional director at the Tianjin Academy of Environmental Sciences (TAES) since 2006. In 2003, she received her master's degree from Shandong Normal University, China. She has been working at TAES since 2003. Since 2004 she has been studying for a doctorate degree at Hebei University of Technology, China. From 2005 to 2008 she participated in the research project on demonstration of circular economy construction for steel and power industries, which was funded by the Tianjin Municipal Science and Technology Commission. She was a leader of two projects on eco-industrial parks planning for two national industrial parks in Tianjin from Nov 2006 until now. She has published about 10 scientific papers and one book. Her main research interests are eco-industrial parks, circular economy and low-carbon economy.

Peter Wolcott is an Associate Professor of Management Information Systems at the University of Nebraska at Omaha. He has long-standing interests in the international dimensions of information technologies. His current research projects are in the areas of IT for development, municipal e-government, and the global diffusion of the internet. His work has been published in *Communications of the ACM, IEEE Computer, Journal of the AIS, Communications of the AIS, The Information Society, The Journal* *of Data Warehousing, International Journal of E-Business Research, Journal of Enterprise Information Management*, and other journals and proceedings. He earned his PhD at the University of Arizona in Business Administration (Management Information Systems) in 1993.

Petra Wolf has been leading a research group on Public Sector Information Management at the Chair for Information Systems at Technische Universität München since 2007. She received her PhD in Economics from Universität Hohenheim in 2006. She managed two research projects on Business-to-Government processes focusing on the environment area, one of which was funded by the German Federal Ministry of the Interior. Her main research interests include Business-to-Government processes and Information Management issues in the public sector like IT-Governance, IT-Controlling and Enterprise Architecture Management.

Rüdiger Zarnekow holds the Chair for Information and Communication Management at the Berlin Institute of Technology. His research focuses on the areas of IT service management, strategic IT management and business models for the ICT industry. Previously, he worked at the Institute of Information Management at the University of St. Gallen, Switzerland, where he lead the competence center "Industrialization of Information Management". Rüdiger Zarnekow has been working as a consultant in the area of IT management for many years. He is the author of various books and scientific papers.

Index

D

E

H

I

J

T

U

V

W

X